"The publication of many of C. Clifton Black's essays and sermons is highly welcomed. Their range, their insight, and their elegance repeatedly testify not only to the author's erudition but also to his eagerness to find the truth and speak it. Black's contribution to reading the New Testament and grappling with its message in a multiplicity of ways is both profound and timely."

—C. Kavin Rowe
Duke Divinity School

"Clift Black's learned essays and reflections cover a range of topics including interpreting Scripture, the church and its ministry and faith, death and grief, sin, prayer, and much more. But their real subject matter is the Gospel of God—the grace of God manifested in Christ Jesus for the life of the world. Not only does that Gospel reverberate throughout this collection, but it shapes Black's posture as an interpreter of Scripture for the church and its life and faith—a posture marked by humility, receptivity, and gratitude."

—Marianne Meye Thompson
Fuller Seminary

"Clift Black's essays are at turns witty, provocative, surprising, or profound (and sometimes all of these at once), but always intellectually and spiritually stimulating. This volume reveals the mind and heart of a prayerful, Trinitarian scriptural theologian who bears witness to the significance of both history and theology for the practice of exegesis and for the life of the church."

—Michael J. Gorman
St. Mary's Seminary & University, Baltimore

"This new collection combines some of the best anglophone New Testament theology of the past forty years with deep reflection on current biblical scholarship in relation to the church's thinking, preaching, and praying through the study of its scriptures. An engaging style with more than occasional humor makes it accessible well beyond the seminary teachers and clergy who stand to benefit most from these mature fruits of a brilliant and productive career."

—Robert Morgan
Linacre College, Oxford University

"Clifton Black is a master essayist who follows his own mandate: 'At every point I must simplify: space is limited; one must cut to the matter's heart.' The result is a treasure of over 400 pages to be savored one thoughtful, elegantly written essay at a time. But Black is neither a spectator nor a color commentator. He is a combatant, landing one blow after another in defense of the vital importance of biblical theology—the quest to interpret the core message and themes of the Bible for the church—while calling others to join the fray. Biblical scholars who ignore his call will do so at their own peril! The future of our discipline is at stake."

—ALAN CULPEPPER
Mercer University

"Clifton Black's essays demonstrate historical acumen and, above all, theological depth. Central questions of Christian faith are dealt with competently and at the same time in a contemporary manner."

—UDO SCHNELLE
Martin Luther University Halle-Wittenberg

"As 'a churchman first, whose scholarship has been practiced in service of the gospel,' Black presents here a collection of essays that combines exegetical craftsmanship with theological depth in a refreshingly independent manner."

—REINHARD FELDMEIER
University of Göttingen

"Anyone who wonders about the contemporary meaning or status of 'biblical theology' or the very notion of a 'biblical theologian' need wonder no more. Here is biblical scholarship in the service of the church from one of its premier practitioners. Clifton Black's considerable gifts as a scholar, essayist, and churchman are evident on every page. May these treasures, both old and new, stir in others the call to this kind of biblical theology."

—JOEL B. GREEN
Fuller Theological Seminary

"Clifton Black is a Princeton institution, widely admired for his depth of Christian learning, his charm and style, and his disarming sense of humor. He is one of today's leading literary and theological scholars of the Gospel of Mark and the history of biblical interpretation—and also, by his own account, 'a churchman first.' All these qualities come together in this fine anthology of thirty of his best essays, loosely but significantly organized under the contested heading of 'biblical theology'—which is shown here to range from scholarly debates about Paul and the Gospels to their astonishingly wide application in homiletical and pastoral ministry."

—MARKUS BOCKMUEHL
Keble College, University of Oxford

BIBLICAL THEOLOGY

Essays Exegetical, Cultural, and Homiletical

സ

C. Clifton Black

WILLIAM B. EERDMANS PUBLISHING COMPANY
GRAND RAPIDS, MICHIGAN

Wm. B. Eerdmans Publishing Co.
4035 Park East Court SE, Grand Rapids, Michigan 49546
www.eerdmans.com

© 2024 C. Clifton Black
All rights reserved
Published 2024

Book design by Lydia Hall

Printed in the United States of America

30 29 28 27 26 25 24   1 2 3 4 5 6 7

ISBN 978-0-8028-8444-2

Library of Congress Cataloging-in-Publication Data

A catalog record for this book is available from the Library of Congress.

In memory of Leander E. Keck (1928–2024)

Contents

Preface		ix
List of Abbreviations		xii

PART 1: HORIZONS — 1

1. New Testament Theology: An Attempt to Define and Describe Its Dimensions — 3
2. Biblical Theology Revisited: An Internal Debate — 17
3. Remembering Otto Piper — 41
4. Exegesis as Prayer — 61

PART 2: STOPOVERS — 77

5. Short Shrift Made Once More — 79
6. Whose Kingdom? Whose Power? Whose Glory? — 89
7. God's Promise for Humanity in the New Testament — 108
8. Sin in the Synoptic Gospels — 125
9. Shouting at the Legally Deaf — 144
10. Pauline Perspectives on Death in Romans 5–8 — 158
11. The Persistence of the Wounds — 180
12. Ave Maria, Gratia Plena — 193
13. The Church in the Synoptic Gospels and Acts — 210

14.	The Johannine Epistles and the Question of Early Catholicism	230
15.	Christian Ministry in Johannine Perspective	256
16.	For the Life of the World	269
17.	Rightly Dividing the Truth of Word	280
18.	Revisiting the King James Bible	287
19.	Journeying through Scripture with the Lectionary's Map	296
20.	The Kindness of Strangers	313

	PART 3: FEUILLETONS	331
21.	A Tale of Two Pities	333
22.	Three	340
23.	The Man in Black	349
24.	A Laugh in the Dark	359
25.	Elegy for a Border Collie	366

	PART 4: DECLARATIONS	371
26.	Biblical Preaching: Ruminations of a Geezer	373
27.	Return of the Double-Minded	380
28.	A View from the Parapet	385
29.	Where Do You Want to Eat?	388
30.	Jesus Christ Is Lord	396
	Acknowledgments	409
	Bibliography	413
	Index of Authors	457
	Index of Subjects	467
	Index of Scripture	475
	Index of Other Ancient Sources	503

Preface

IN EARLY 2022 DR. AJMAL ZEMMAR and a dozen other neurosurgeons published a paper that for the first time documented the detection of active brain waves of the sort corresponding to meditation, dreaming, and memory retrieval thirty seconds before and after a geriatric patient's heart had stopped beating.[1] "This [phenomenon] could possibly be a last recall of memories that we've experienced in life, and they replay through our brain in the last seconds before we die."[2] What we've always heard could be true: at death we may relive our entire lives, at least its most indelible events, in a lightning flashback.

While at the moment I'm feeling fine and no neurologists were harmed in the making of this book, reviewing the essays that became its chapters did cause my life to flash before my eyes. How could it be otherwise? The earliest chapter was first published when I was twenty-nine; the latest, thirty-nine years later.

Unless the author's name is Elizabeth Hardwick (1916–2007) or Joan Didion (1934–2021)—or, within a narrower compass, C. H. Dodd (1884–1973) or Rudolf Bultmann (1884–1976)—few publishers will assume the financial risk of essay collections. I have been blessed by Wm. B. Eerdmans's gamble on me not once but twice. The first coalesced around one of the New Testament's Gospels.[3] This second anthology is held together by a viewpoint—that of a biblical theologian—in an era when scholars cannot agree on what biblical theology

---

1. Raul Vicente et al., "Enhanced Interplay of Neuronal Coherence and Coupling in the Dying Human Brain," *Frontiers in Aging Neuroscience* 14 (February 22, 2022): 1–11. https://doi.org/10.3389/fnagi.2022.813531.

2. Zemmar, quoted in Holly Honderich, "Life May Actually Flash before Your Death—New Study," *BBC News*, February 23, 2022, https://www.bbc.com/news/world-us-canada-60495730. As do all responsible scientists, this one carefully hedged his assessment with noteworthy variables: this was a single patient, one who had developed epilepsy and had suffered a fall. Still, he opined, "I think there's something mystical and spiritual about this whole near-death experience."

3. C. Clifton Black, *Mark's Gospel: History, Theology, Interpretation* (Grand Rapids: Eerdmans, 2023).

is and, if they could, whether its exercise is legitimate.[4] I should lay my cards on the table. I consider myself a churchman first, whose scholarship has been practiced in service of the gospel. For both good and ill the church has usually operated with some elemental responsibility to Scripture—however firm or flimsy, reasoned or inchoate. If biblical theology has evanesced from many college and seminary campuses, it has never evaporated entirely from Christian congregations. I have understood my vocation to be supporting that enterprise with integrity, using the meager resources at my disposal. You, gentle readers, may be appalled by just how paltry they are, but I have reached an age to appreciate the insight of that peerless essayist, Max Beerbohm (1872–1956): "There is much to be said for failure. It is more interesting than success."[5]

Of this volume's thirty chapters, a third were assigned to me by an editor or were invited for a specific purpose. Four appear here for the first time. The rest were written on spec. I plucked topics from the clear blue, handled them as capably as I could, and then sent them out into an indifferent world. Somehow they caught the attention of someone who judged them potentially interesting to others. What you are holding is a garland of some hearty perennials—human nature, life and death, sin and punishment, grace and responsibility, Scripture and its interpretation, the church and its ministry, the lordship of Christ—speckled with surprises. I hope you may find something instructive and, as the occasion warrants, provocative and amusing. None of these essays declares the last word on any subject. If taken as administered, all should stimulate others' pursuit of knowledge more truthful than my ability to discern. That, I believe, is the duty of scholarship, whether in science or the liberal arts.

Dr. James Ernest, whose friendship I have cherished for three decades, advanced this project with an alacrity that took me by surprise. Laurel Draper and Jenny Hoffman managed the book's production with faultless acuity, efficiency, courtesy, and wisdom. Holly Knowles, who prepared the various indexes, is among the best in the business. If you enjoy the great good fortune of publishing with Eerdmans, you are working not only with top professionals but among members of a family that cares about quality.

Before her death in 2022, my secretary Joan Blyth transcribed several of this book's densest chapters from hard copies into an electronic format. Kaitlynn C. Merckling, candidate for PhD in New Testament at Princeton Seminary, again assisted me in countless ways great and small. And again, my thanks to Harriet Fesperman Black are inexpressible.

---

4. See chapters 1 and 2.
5. "A Small Boy Seeing Giants," in *The Prince of Minor Writers: The Selected Essays of Max Beerbohm*, ed. Phillip Lopate (New York: New York Review of Books, 2015), 372.

Preface

While I was editing studies from years past, there came another flashback: the faces of those at various schools from which my work originated. The earliest essays were born in graduate seminars at Duke University during an era when students' submissions to professional journals in religious studies were the exception, not the rule. In the pages that follow you will find tributes to teachers who prodded me into mailing some papers to editors. (Such audacity was always tempered by inclusion of a stamped, self-addressed envelope for return of rejected manuscripts, of which I've enjoyed my share.) During my dissertation years I also shared with most others the joy of interviewing for scarce teaching jobs, always landed by someone else. Without my *Doktorvater*, D. Moody Smith (1931–2016), and William Scott Green, then chairman of the Department of Religion and Classics at the University of Rochester, my foot would never have gotten across academe's threshold. James E. Kirby, dean of Perkins School of Theology (1981–94) at Southern Methodist University, made possible my first faculty appointment in theological education. A decade later Thomas W. Gillespie (1928–2011), president of Princeton Theological Seminary, offered me the position I held for the next quarter century. As far back as 1980, when I was ordained in The United Methodist Church, one of its Boards of Ministry and Bishop L. Bevel Jones III (1926–2018) sanctioned my aspiration for service beyond the local church as a theological educator. Had not all these benefactors provided me encouragement or employment, this book would not exist. By its contents I hope not to have betrayed those who extended a hand when I most needed it.

This volume is dedicated to the late Leander E. Keck, Winkley Professor Emeritus of Biblical Theology (1979–98) and dean emeritus of Yale Divinity School (1979–89). For embarrassing reasons I cheated myself of an opportunity to study with him during his tenure at Emory University's Candler School of Theology (1972–79). By way of compensation I read everything I could that poured from his pen. Most scholars are smart. Many are knowledgeable. Some are productive. The genuinely insightful are few. For more than six decades Professor Keck defined the highest echelon, mentoring two generations of clergy and academics with a rare blend of intellectual courage and humility. No one has taught me more about the Bible's historical-critical exegesis within a theological framework for the church's edification. In later years he honored me with his friendship. To his memory I tender this book as a token of esteem and gratitude.

C. C. B.
Princeton, New Jersey
May 2024

Abbreviations

Ancient Sources

1 Apol.	Justin Martyr, *Apologia I*
1 En.	1 Enoch
2 En.	2 Enoch
2 Bar.	2 Baruch
2 Esd.	2 Esdras
4 Macc	4 Maccabees
1QS	Manual of Discipline, or Community Rule (Dead Sea Scroll)
1QH	Hodayot, or Thanksgiving Scroll (Dead Sea Scroll)
4Q177	Fragment 177 from Qumran Cave 4 (Dead Sea Scroll)
4Q548	Fragment 548 from Qumran Cave 4 (Dead Sea Scroll)
Acts Thom.	Acts of Thomas
Ad eccl.	Rupert of Deutz, *Ad ecclesiam*
Agr.	Tacitus, *Agricola*
Agric.	Philo, *De agricultura*
Ai. Lok.	Sophocles, *Aias Lokros*
A.J.	Josephus, *Antiquitates judaicae*
Alc.	Euripides, *Alcestis*
Ap. John	Apocryphon of John
Apoc. Abr.	Apocalypse of Abraham
Apoc. Adam	Apocalypse of Adam
Apoc. Mos.	Apocalypse of Moses
Apol.	Plato, *Apologia*
Ascl.	Asclepius
b.	Babylonian Talmud (followed by the title of a tractate)
B.J.	Josephus, *Bellum judaicum*
b. Bek.	Bekhoroth
b. Ber.	Berakot

b. Meg.	Megillah
b. Ned.	Nedarim
b. Pesaḥ.	Pesachim
b. Šabb.	Šabbat
b. Sanh.	Sanhedrin
b. Ta'an.	Ta'anit
BAC	Biblioteca de Autores Cristianos
Bam.Rab.	Bamidbar [Numbers] Rabbah
C.H.	*Corpus Hermeticum*
Conf.	Augustine, *Confessiones*
Conf. Ling.	Philo, *De confusione linguarum*
Crat.	Plato, *Cratylus*
De civ. Dei	Augustine, *De civitate Dei*
De hum. cond.	Basil of Caesarea, *De humana conditione*
De incarn.	Athanasius, *De incarnatione*
De Trin.	Augustine, *De Trinitate*
Did.	Didache
Disc.	Gregory Nazianzen, *Discourses*
Doctr. chr.	Augustine, *De doctrina christiana*
Enn.	Plotinus, *Enneads*
Ep.	Augustine, *Epistles*
Epist.	Jerome, *Epistulae*
Ep. Pet. Phil.	Epistle of Peter to Philip
Exp. Luc.	Ambrose, *Expositio Evangelii secundum Lucam*
Fug.	Philo, *De fuga et inventione*
Gen.Rab.	Genesis Rabbah
Gos. Eg.	The Gospel of the Egyptians (*Holy Book of the Great Invisible Spirit*)
Gos. Phil.	The Gospel of Philip
Gos. Thom.	The Gospel of Thomas
Gos. Truth	The Gospel of Truth
Haer.	Irenaeus, *Adversus haereses*
Hist. eccl.	Eusebius, *Historia ecclesiastica*
Hyp. Arch.	The Hypostasis of the Archons
Ign. *Eph.*	Ignatius, *To the Ephesians*
Ign. *Magn.*	Ignatius, *To the Magnesians*
Ign. *Phld.*	Ignatius, *To the Philadelphians*
Ign. *Pol.*	Ignatius, *To Polycarp*
Ign. *Smyrn.*	Ignatius, *To the Smyrnaeans*

Ign. *Trall.*	Ignatius, *To the Trallians*
Il.	Homer, *Iliad*
Iph. Aul.	Euripides, *Iphigenia in Aulis*
Iph. Taur.	Euripides, *Iphigenia in Tauris*
j. Dem.	Demai (Jerusalem Talmud)
Jub.	Jubilees
Leg. all.	Philo, *Legum allegoriae*
LW	*Luther's Works.* American edition. Edited by Jaroslav Pelikan and Christopher Boyd Brown. 79 vols. St. Louis: Concordia Publishing House, 1955–2021
m.	Mishnah (followed by the title of a tractate)
m. 'Abot	Pirke 'Abot
m. B. Bat.	Baba Batra
m. Ber.	Berakot
m. Kil.	Kil'ayim
m. Pesaḥ.	Pesachim
m. Šabb.	Šabbath
m. Ter.	Terumot
Man.	Prayer of Manasseh
Medit.	Marcus Aurelius Antoninus, *Meditations*
Mem.	Xenophon, *Memorabilia*
Men.	Epicurus, *Letter to Menoeceus*
Noaḥ	*Noaḥ* (haggadic midrash; see *Tanḥum. B.*)
Od.	Homer, *Odysseia*
Paraph. Shem	*The Paraphrase of Shem*
Pesiq. Rab Kah.	Pesiqta de-Rab Kahana
Phaed.	Plato, *Phaedrus*
Pol. Phil.	Polycarp, *To the Philippians*
Pr. Man.	Prayer of Manasseh
Protag.	Plato, *Protagoras*
Pss. Sol.	*Psalms of Solomon*
Rhet.	Aristotle, *Ars rhetorica*
Sed.Ol.Rab.	Seder Olam Rabbah
Serm.	Augustine, *Sermon*[es], *Conversation*[s]
Shir.Ha-Shar.Rab.	Shir Ha-Sharim Rabbah
Sif. Deut.	Sifre Deuteronomy
Som.	Philo, *De somniis*
Spec.	Philo, *De specialibus legibus*
T. Abr.	Testament of Abraham

Tanḥum. B.	Midrash Tanḥuma B. [Yelammedemu]
Theog.	Hesiod, Theogony
Thoms. Cont.	The Book of Thomas the Contender
Treat. Res.	The Treatise on the Resurrection
Tri. Trac.	The Tripartite Tractate
Tro.	Euripides, Trōides
Tusc. Disput.	Cicero, Tusculanae Disputationes
Vit. Mos.	Philo, De vita Mosis

SECONDARY SOURCES

AB	Anchor Bible
ABD	*Anchor Bible Dictionary*. Edited by David Noel Freedman. 6 vols. New York: Doubleday, 1992
ABRL	Anchor Bible Reference Library
ACNT	Augsburg Commentary on the New Testament
ANRW	*Aufstieg und Niedergang der römischen Welt: Geschichte und Kultur Roms im Spiegel der neueren Forschung*. Part 2, *Principat*. Edited by Hildegard Temporini and Wolfgang Haase. Berlin: de Gruyter, 1972–
ANTC	Abingdon New Testament Commentaries
AS	Arden Shakespeare
ATR	*Andover Theological Review*
BETL	Bibliotheca ephemeridum theologicarum Lovaniensium
BEvTh	Beiträge zur evangelischen Theologie
BGAD	*A Greek-English Lexicon of the New Testament and Other Early Christian Literature*. 3rd ed. Edited by Frederick William Danker, Walter Bauer, William Frederick Arndt, and Felix Wilbur Gingrich. Chicago: University of Chicago Press, 2000
Bib	*Biblica*
BibAnn	*The Biblical Annals*
BJRL	*Bulletin of the John Rylands University Library of Manchester*
BNTC	Black's New Testament Commentary
BSNA	Biblical Studies in North America
BZ	*Biblische Zeitschrift*
BZNW	Beihefte zur Zeitschrift für die neutestamentliche Wissenschaft
CB	Cascade Books
CBQ	*The Catholic Biblical Quarterly*

ABBREVIATIONS

CC	Continental Commentaries
CCRBS	Clark Critical Readings in Biblical Studies
CCT	Challenges in Contemporary Theology
CH	Church History
ChrCent	The Christian Century
CIT	Current Issues in Theology
ComViat	Communio viatorum
ConBOT	Coniectanea Biblica: Old Testament Series
CSCD	Cambridge Studies in Christian Doctrine
CSS	Cistercian Studies Series
CTM	Concordia Theological Monthly
CurTM	Currents in Theology and Mission
CWS	Classics of Western Spirituality
DBW	Dietrich Bonhoeffer Works
DDSR	Duke Divinity School Review
Di	Dialog
DMAHA	Dutch Monographs on Ancient History and Archaeology
EL	Everyman's Library
EncJud	Encyclopedia Judaica. 2nd edition. 22 volumes. Chicago: Macmillan Reference, 2006
ESV	English Standard Version
ETL	Ephemerides Theologicae Lovanienses
EvQ	The Evangelical Quarterly
EvT	Evangelische Theologie
ExpTim	The Expository Times
FF	Face to Face
Greg	Gregorianum
HBT	Horizons in Biblical Theology
HK	Hannoverischer Kurier
HNTC	Harper's New Testament Commentary
HT	Harper Torchbooks
HThKNTSup	Herders Theologischer Kommentar zum Neuen Testament Supplementband
HTR	Harvard Theological Review
HTS	Harvard Theological Studies
HTSTS	HTS Theological Studies
IB	The Interpreter's Bible
ICC	International Critical Commentary
ICT	Introducing Catholic Theology

IDB	*The Interpreter's Dictionary of the Bible.* 4 volumes. Edited by George W. Buttrick. Nashville: Abingdon, 1962
IDBSup	*The Interpreter's Dictionary of the Bible: Supplementary Volume.* Edited by Keith Crim. Nashville: Abingdon, 1976
IJST	*International Journal of Systematic Theology*
IlRev	*Iliff* [School of Theology] *Review*
ILR	*Israel Law Review*
Int	*Interpretation*
IRUSC	Interpretation: Resources for the Use of Scripture in the Church
JBL	*Journal of Biblical Literature*
JBR	*Journal of Bible and Religion*
JLR	*Journal of Law and Religion*
JR	*Journal of Religion*
JRH	*Journal of Religious History*
JSNT	*Journal for the Study of the New Testament*
JSNTSup	Journal for the Study of the New Testament Supplement Series
JSOTSup	Journal for the Study of the Old Testament Supplement Series
JSPSup	Journal for the Study of the Pseudepigrapha Supplement Series
JTI	*Journal of Theological Interpretation*
JTISup	Journal of Theological Interpretation Supplement Series
JTS	*Journal of Theological Studies*
JWK	*Jahrbuch für westfälische Kirchengeschichte*
KJV	King James Version
Lattimore	*The New Testament.* Translated by Richmond Lattimore. New York: North Point Press, 1996
LJS	Lives of Jesus Series
LM	*Lutherische Monatshefte*
LOA	Library of America
LSJ	*A Greek-English Lexicon.* Compiled by Henry George Liddell and Robert Scott. Revised and augmented by Henry Stuart Jones. 9th edition. Oxford: Clarendon Press, 1961
LTT	Library of Theological Translations
MAJT	*Mid-America Journal of Theology*
MB	Monde de la Bible
MNTC	Moffatt New Testament Commentary
MNTS	McMaster New Testament Studies
NAB	New American Bible
NCB	New Century Bible
NCBC	New Century Bible Commentary
NEB	New English Bible

Neot	*Neotestamentica*
NHC	Nag Hammadi Codices
NIB	*The New Interpreter's Bible*. Edited by Leander E. Keck. 12 vols. Nashville: Abingdon, 1994–2004
NICNT	New International Commentary on the New Testament
NJPS	*Tanakh: The Holy Scriptures; The New JPS Translation according to the Traditional Hebrew Text*. 2nd ed. 1999
NovT	*Novum Testamentum*
NovTSup	Supplements to *Novum Testamentum*
NRSV	New Revised Standard Version
NTL	New Testament Library
NTOA	Novum Testamentum et Orbis Antiquus
NTS	*New Testament Studies*
NTT	New Testament Theology
OBT	Overtures to Biblical Theology
OED	*The Compact Edition of the Oxford English Dictionary with Supplement*. 2 vols. 2nd ed. Edited by James A. H. Murray et al. Oxford: Oxford University Press, 1986
OTL	Old Testament Library
OTP	*Old Testament Pseudepigrapha*. Edited by James H. Charlesworth. 2 vols. New York: Doubleday, 1983, 1985
OWC	Oxford World's Classics
PBTM	Paternoster Biblical and Theological Monographs
PJ	*Perkins [School of Theology] Journal*
PL	*Patrologia Latina* (=*Patrologiae Cursus Completus*: Series Latina)
ProEcc	Pro Ecclesia
PSB	*The Princeton Seminary Bulletin*
PTR	*Princeton Theological Review*
RB	*Revue biblique*
RBL	*Review of Biblical Literature*
REB	Revised English Bible
RelSRev	*Religious Studies Review*
RelStTh	*Religious Studies and Theology*
RGG	*Religion in Geschichte und Gegenwart*
RL	*Religion in Life*
RSV	Revised Standard Version
SBLDS	Society of Biblical Literature Dissertation Series
SBLMS	Society of Biblical Literature Monograph Series

SBT		Studies in Biblical Theology
SD		Sacra Doctrina
SEÅ		*Svensk exegetisk årsbok*
SIGC		Studien zur interkulturellen Geschichte des Christentums
SJ		Studia Judaica
SJLA		Studies in Judaism in Late Antiquity
SJT		*Scottish Journal of Theology*
SJTOP		Scottish Journal of Theology Occasional Paper(s)
SLB		Spiritual Legacy Books
Smith-Goodspeed		*The Holy Bible: An American Translation.* The Old Testament, translated by J. M. Powis Smith et al.; The New Testament, translated by Edgar J. Goodspeed. Chicago: University of Chicago Press, 1939
SNT		Studien zum Neuen Testament
SNTSMS		Society for New Testament Studies Monograph Series
SNTW		Studies of the New Testament and Its World
SP		Sacra Pagina
SPNT		Studies on Personalities of the New Testament
TBT		Topoi Biblischer Theologie
TDNT		*Theological Dictionary of the New Testament.* Edited by Gerhard Kittel and Gerhard Friedrich. Translated by Geoffrey W. Bromiley. 10 volumes. Grand Rapids: Eerdmans, 1964–76
TDOT		*Theological Dictionary of the Old Testament.* Edited by G. Johannes Botterweck and Helmer Ringgren. Translated by John T. Willis. Revised edition. 17 volumes. Grand Rapids: Eerdmans, 1977–2021
Theol		*Theology*
ThTod		*Theology Today*
TI		Theological Inquiries
TS		*Theological Studies*
TZ		*Theologische Zeitschrift*
UBSGNT		United Bible Societies Greek New Testament
USQR		*The Union Seminary Quarterly Review*
WSA		Works of Saint Augustine: A Translation for the 21st Century
WW		*Word and World*
YPR		Yale Publications in Religion
ZNW		*Zeitschrift für die neutestamentlichen Wissenschaft und die Kunde der älteren Kirche*
ZTK		*Zeitschrift für Theologie und Kirche*

Sigla

alt.	[slightly] altered
Aram.	Aramaic
AT	Author's translation
comp.	compiled by
DSS	Dead Sea Scrolls
et al.	*et alii* (Lat.), "and others"
Gk.	Greek
HB	Hebrew Bible
Heb.	Hebrew
L	Hypothetical source unique to Luke
Lat.	Latin
LXX	Septuagint
M	Hypothetical source unique to Matthew
n(n).	note(s)
N.B.	*nota bene* (Lat.), note carefully
n.s.	new series
Q	*Quelle* (German), hypothetical sayings sources underlying Luke and Matthew
QL	Qumran Literature
ser.	series
//	parallel with

Part 1

HORIZONS

CHAPTER 1

New Testament Theology:
An Attempt to Define and Describe Its Dimensions

> Never follow anyone else's path. Unless you're in the woods and
> you're lost and you see a path. Then by all means follow that path.
>
> —Ellen DeGeneres

IN RECENT SCHOLARSHIP "NT THEOLOGY" has proven notoriously difficult to define.[1] Here, for what it's worth, is my attempt: *NT theology may be characterized as an exegetically executed, theologically sensitive endeavor to describe and to assess the NT's comprehensive interpretations of God's involvement with humanity and the world, especially as that relationship is revealed in Jesus Christ.* Let us now try to unfold that.

THE HISTORICAL TRAJECTORY OF NEW TESTAMENT THEOLOGY

From the Patristic Era through the Reformation

The early and medieval church. Explicit, coherent theologies of the Christian Bible are traceable as early as Irenaeus of Lyons (c. 130–c. 202), whose *regula fidei* (rule of faith) stipulated that the NT's message is properly interpreted as a development of the OT's chronicle of God's interaction with Israel (*Against Heresies* 1.10.1 [c. 180]). For Augustine of Hippo (354–430) the NT's meaning lies hidden in the Old; that of the OT is revealed by the New (*On Christian Doctrine* 2.1–14 [c. 397]). Attention to Scripture's literal sense, amplified by

---

1. See Udo Schnelle, *Theologie des Neuen Testaments* (Stuttgart: Vandenhoeck & Ruprecht, 2007), translated by M. Eugene Boring as *Theology of the New Testament* (Grand Rapids: Baker Academic, 2009), 25–40.

various spiritual senses, characterized theological commentary produced in medieval monastic and cathedral schools, culminating in the *Summa Theologiae* (1485) of Thomas Aquinas (c. 1225–74). The quest for the NT's—indeed, the Bible's—theological coherence was eased by the assumption that Christ is Scripture's central point of reference.

Luther and Reformation orthodoxy. Martin Luther's (1483–1546) quarrel with Pope Leo X turned on the Holy Spirit's unique residence in a single interpreter (*Address to the German Nobility*, 1520). With the important caveat that the interpreter requires inspiration by the same Spirit operative among Scripture's various authors, Luther opened the possibility of a hermeneutical democratization that modern NT theological projects would presuppose. Perception of the NT's theological unity and diversity was sharpened by the Reformers' avowal that all Scripture, though inspired, was neither historically inerrant nor theologically harmonious nor equally profound. (Luther famously disparaged the Epistle of James and the Johannine Apocalypse.)[2] In time Lutheran and Reformed orthodoxy, like its Roman Catholic counterpart, came to associate NT theology with *dicta probantia*: compilations of scriptural prooftexts on which church dogma was based (such as Philipp Melanchthon's [1497–1560] *Loci Communes* [1521]).

From the Enlightenment through the Twentieth Century

Gabler and his successors. Luther distinguished Israel's particular law code (*Sachsenspiegel*) from natural law, inscribed on the human heart and universally binding ("How Christians Should Regard Moses," 1525). By the eighteenth century, rationalism, a secularized version of natural-law theory, accorded the primary basis of human authority to autonomous reason in its search for truth. Rooted in Renaissance humanism, the Enlightenment in Europe and North America produced critical studies of Scripture, questioning its historical and doctrinal reliability: the hallmarks of historical criticism. Thus was set the stage for Johann Philipp Gabler's (1753–1826) inaugural address at Altdorf

---

2. "I almost feel like throwing Jimmy into the stove, as the priest in Kalenberg did" (Martin Luther, *Career of the Reformer* IV, ed. Helmut T. Lehmann and Lewis W. Spitz, *Luther's Works* 34 [St. Louis: Concordia, 1960], 317). Regarding Revelation: "Finally, let everyone think of it as his own spirit leads him. My spirit cannot accommodate itself to this book. For me this is reason enough not to think highly of it: Christ is neither taught nor known in it" ("Preface to the Revelation of St. John," *Luther's Works* 35: *Word and Sacrament* I, ed. E. Theodore Bachmann [Philadelphia: Fortress, 1960], 399).

University in 1787.[3] For Gabler, truth resides in transhistorical "universal ideas" (*dicta classica*) or "the unchanging idea of the doctrine of salvation," clothed in "some particular era or testament" (Sandys-Wunsch and Eldredge, 142), The task of biblical theology is to peel away the contingent husk in which the NT witness has been "accommodated," in order to recover for the benefit of systematic theologians "the unchanging testament of Christian doctrine" (143). That constant message may be recognized as such by its commonality throughout Scripture. Biblical theology, and by inference NT theology, is simple, pure, and unchanging, because it deals with historical expressions of commonplace religion; systematic theology (or dogmatics) is sophisticated, forever being adapted to changing times and different circumstances (137, 143–44). Assuming the compatibility of reason with revelation, Gabler stands with feet planted in both premodern and modern exegesis. Divinely inspired, the Bible, especially the NT, consists of "sacred books" that provide "a firm and certain hope of salvation" (134). Historically conditioned, biblical authors wrote for their own times, often in mythic forms appropriate to their age but unsuitable for our own (142–43).

Gabler synthesized and clearly articulated the views of his Enlightenment precursors. Two contributions may be mentioned as important for subsequent research. First is the distinction between religion ("every-day, transparently clear knowledge") and theology ("subtle, learned knowledge") (136). Second is the procedure of differentiating historical recovery from systematic formulation. The latter anticipated Krister Stendahl's (1922–2008) differentiation of what the text originally meant from what it means in a later context.[4]

Roughly a decade after Gabler's lecture, his colleague Georg Lorenz Bauer (1755–1806) published the first historical-critical OT theology,[5] at once distinguishing that enterprise from NT theology and raising questions for their subsequent reintegration. Emphasizing unconditional obedience to God's law, Bauer offered the first modern treatment of NT ethics,[6] which sharpened

---

3. Translated and presented by John Sandys-Wunsch and Laurence Eldredge. "J. P. Gabler and the Distinction between Biblical and Dogmatic Theology: Translation, Commentary, and Discussion of His Originality," *SJT* 33 (1980): 133–58. Subsequent citations to this work will appear in the text.

4. "Theology, Biblical," *IDB* (1962) 4:418–32.

5. Bauer, *Theologie des Alten Testaments, oder, Abriss der religiösen Begriffe der alten Hebräer* (Leipzig: Waygand, 1796); translated as *The Theology of the Old Testament, or, A Biblical Sketch of the Religious Opinions of the Ancient Hebrews: From the Earliest Times to the Commencement of the Christian Era* (London: Fox, 1838).

6. Bauer, *Biblische Moral des Neuen Testaments*, 3 vols. (Leipzig: Beygandfeschen Buchhandlung, 1804–5).

Gabler's historical perspective by differentiating Jesus's religion from that of the evangelists and discriminating the various NT witnesses. Wilhelm Martin Leberecht de Wette (1780–1849) extended Bauer's differentiation by grouping NT books in their presumed religious provenances: Jewish Christianity (the Synoptics, most of the Catholic Epistles, Revelation), Alexandrian Hellenism (the Gospel and Letters of John, the Epistle to the Hebrews), and Pauline Christianity (letters ascribed to Paul).[7] Structuring their analyses of the NT in accordance with such topics as Christology, theological anthropology, and soteriology, both Bauer and de Wette produced systematic theologies whose source and norm were biblical.

The nature of New Testament theology: Wrede and Schlatter. During much of the nineteenth century, NT theology suffered partial eclipse by historical preoccupations filtered through Hegelian idealism: Ferdinand Christian Baur's (1792–1860) five-volume *History of the Christian Church* and David Friedrich Strauss's (1808–74) *Life of Jesus*.[8] In a theologically liberal era Bernhard Weiss's (1827–1918) conservative essay in NT theology predicated careful examination of God's salvific self-revelation in history. More influential was Heinrich Julius Holtzmann's (1832–1910)[9] liberal presentation of the historical Jesus as a religious genius, Paul as Christology's creator, and John as an Alexandrian consummation of Logos mysticism. All of these works were doctrinally tinged—even Strauss's *Life*, a frontal assault on liberal Christology.

Enter William Wrede (1859–1906), whose lectures for clergy at Breslau on "The Task and Methods of 'New Testament Theology'" (1897)[10] rent asunder the conceptual marriage that Gabler had attempted to broker a century earlier. For Wrede "the method of doctrinal concepts"—grouping thoughts expressed by the NT in alignment with dogmatic topics—betrays scientific criticism and provokes caricature of NT writers as systematicians in the modern sense. That method's acknowledgment of canonical documents is likewise misguided:

7. De Wette, *Biblische Dogmatik: Alten und Neuen Testaments: oder, kritische Darstellung der Religionslehre des Hebraismus, des Judenthums und Urchristenthums: zum Gebrauch akademischer Vorlesungen*, 3rd ed. (Berlin: Reimer, 1831).

8. Baur, *Geschichte der christlichen Kirche* (Tübingen: Fues, 1863–77); Strauss, *Das Leben Jesu*, 4th ed. (Tübingen: Oslander, 1835–36), translated by George Eliot as *The Life of Jesus Critically Examined*, ed. Peter C. Hodgson, LJS (Philadelphia: Fortress, 1972).

9. Weiss, *Biblical Theology of the New Testament*, 3rd rev. ed., trans. David Eaton (Edinburgh: T&T Clark, 1882–83); Holtzmann, *Hand-Commentar zum Neuen Testament* (Freiburg: Mohr, 1892).

10. Wrede in Robert Morgan, ed. and trans., *The Nature of New Testament Theology: The Contribution of William Wrede and Adolf Schlatter*, SBT 2nd ser. (London: SCM, 1973), 68–116.

a document's canonization makes no difference for either the Protestant theologian or historical investigator.[11] New Testament theology is, or should be, the attempt to understand the development of primitive Christian religion in its historical situation: "We at least want to know *what was believed, thought, taught, hoped, required and striven for* in the earliest period of Christianity; not what certain writings say about faith, doctrine, hope, etc."[12] Although it was left for Wilhelm Bousset (1865-1920) to perform such a task,[13] procedurally Wrede believed that NT theology should begin with Jesus as increasingly "dogmatized" by early Christian adherents, then move to the primitive church (of which "we should have to know more than we in fact do know"), Paul ("the creator of a Christian theology"), Gentile Christianity, John (who "made the picture of Jesus' life entirely into a mirror of his own ideas"), and Ignatius (who typifies and embodies "personal Christianity at the beginning of the second century").[14] For Wrede, "NT theology" is a double misnomer: none of its subject matter was born canonical; it is less with theology than with religion that we are concerned, specifically "the history of early Christian religion and theology."[15] Thus Wrede disjoined what Gabler had differentiated: religion and theology. The historian as such is not competent to serve the church. Unlike Gabler, Wrede is indifferent to modern dogmatics: "How the systematic theologian gets on with its results and deals with them—that is his own affair."[16]

The sharpest rebuttal of Wrede's position may be that of his contemporary Adolf Schlatter (1852-1938), whose NT theology[17] approximates Weiss's approach and conclusions. Schlatter does not dismiss the necessity of historical research: "What has happened in the past demands of us, by the very fact that it *has* happened, that we grasp it in its *givenness*" (Morgan, 127). Careful observation of the biblical text and self-surrender to its data are the histori-

---

11. Morgan, *Nature of New Testament Theology*, 70-71, 115.
12. Morgan, *Nature of New Testament Theology*, 84-85.
13. Bousset, *Kyrios Christos: Geschichte des Christusglaubens von den Anfängen des Christentums bis Irenaeus* (Göttingen: Vandenhoeck & Ruprecht, 1913), translated by John E. Steely as *Kyrios Christos: A History of the Belief in Christ from the Beginnings of Christianity to Irenaeus* (Nashville: Abingdon, 1970).
14. Quotations, Bousset, *Kyrios Christos*, 104, 105, 106, 113, 89. Quotations from Bousset taken from the English translation.
15. Bousset, *Kyrios Christos*, 116.
16. Bousset, *Kyrios Christos*, 69.
17. Schlatter, *Die Theologie des Neuen Testaments*, 2 vols. (Calw and Stuttgart: Verlag der Vereinsbuchhandlung, 1909-10). Schlatter's programmatic essay, "The Theology of the New Testament and Dogmatics," is translated and included in Morgan's *Nature of New Testament Theology*, 117-66. Subsequent citations from this source will appear in the text.

an's sine qua non. New Testament theology lies on the boundary of scientific investigation "if by 'science' one means agreement and fixed tradition and successful cooperation by many researchers leading to a unitary result" (155). The fundamental point of difference from Wrede lies in Schlatter's understanding of the historian and the historical task. The historian is no *neutral* observer but, rather, one whose own perception is molded by historically conditioned convictions. An objective, "merely historical purpose" is an illusory self-deception, born of "speculative Kantianism" (123, 124). "Our task [as historians] is to attach our concrete, historically conditioned lives to God," whose revelation in history the NT proclaims (154–55). Thus, religious criteria inevitably reenter through the door Wrede had slammed shut. The historian's own consciousness is wedded to God. Moreover, faith is endemic to the historical task: "As soon as the historian sets aside or brackets the question of faith, he is making his concern with the New Testament and his presentation of it into a radical and total polemic against it" (122). Contrary to Gabler, for whom NT theology merely purges circumstantial coloring from biblical events, for Schlatter the tasks of NT theology and dogmatics are inextricably reciprocal, "permea[ting] the whole course of historical work" (126). Contrary to Wrede, who disallowed canonical distinctions, the mixing of NT and post-canonical materials defies "the historian's own dogmatic judgment" (147). If the historian proceeds beyond the NT, it should be to the contents of the OT "since of all the factors reaching back into the past, none is so important as this" (145).

By somewhat unpredictable routes, twentieth-century scholarship pursued the alternatives that Wrede and Schlatter posed. Concentrating on traditional genres within the Gospels, form critics such as Martin Dibelius (1883–1947)[18] answered Wrede's challenge to reconstruct earliest Christian beliefs, values, and aspirations within their broader religious and cultural setting. Form criticism's legacy continues in NT social-scientific criticism.[19] Wrede's abjuration of canonical distinctions is maintained with illuminating results in Gerhard Kittel (1888–1948) and Gerhard Friedrich's (1917–45) ten-volume *Theological*

---

18. Dibelius, *Die Formgeschichte des Evangeliums* (Tübingen: Mohr, 1919), translated by Bertram Lee Woolf as *From Tradition to Gospel* (New York: Scribner's Sons, 1965).

19. Among many others: Wayne A. Meeks, *The First Urban Christians: The Social World of the Apostle Paul* (New Haven: Yale University Press, 1983); Gerd Theissen, *Lokalkolorit und Zeitgeschichte in den Evangelien: Ein Beitrag zur Geschichte der synoptischen Tradition*, NTOA 8 (Fribourg and Göttingen: Editions universitaires/Vandenhoeck & Ruprecht, 1989), translated by Linda M. Moloney as *The Gospels in Context: Social and Political History in the Synoptic Tradition* (Minneapolis: Fortress, 1991).

Dictionary of the New Testament (dedicated to Schlatter).[20] Lamenting that Wrede's vision remains unrealized, Heikki Räisänen (1941–2015) sketched a program for doing so.[21]

Eschatology seemed an abortive approach to NT theology after the dead end reached by the nineteenth-century quest for the historical Jesus.[22] Yet Schlatter's call for historians' engagement with the God who acts in history is manifest in his progeny, who led the variegated biblical theology movement in Britain and North America during the decades before and after World War II. Their labors are exemplified by E. C. Hoskyns (1884–1937) and Francis Noel Davey (1904–73), Otto A. Piper (1891–1982), Oscar Cullmann (1902–99) and G. Ernest Wright (1909–74) and Reginald Fuller (1915–2007).[23]

Re-proclaiming the kerygma: Barth and Bultmann. Schlatter's truest successor may have been the Swiss theologian Karl Barth (1886–1968), who broke with Enlightenment epistemology by regarding all humans as living nowhere other than within a God-centered history, the sphere of God's self-communicative action. Barth's representation of world history is usually through OT narratives and sagas, which, as in patristic and medieval exegesis, are often typologically related to the NT.[24] The monument to neo-orthodoxy's "theology of the word"—the Reformation's identification of divine revelation in the kerygma, the proclaimed word of God, instead of biblical history—is Barth's commentary on Romans,[25] in whose preface he expresses "feel[ing

---

20. Kittel and Friedrich, *Theologisches Wörterbuch zum Neuen Testament* (Stuttgart: Kohlhammer, 1932–79), translated by Geoffrey W. Bromiley as *Theological Dictionary of the New Testament* (Grand Rapids: Eerdmans, 1964–76).

21. *Beyond New Testament Theology: A Story and a Programme* (London: SCM, 1990).

22. Albert Schweitzer, *Geschichte der Leben-Jesu-Forschung* (Tübingen: Mohr Siebeck, 1913), translated by W. Montgomery, J. R. Coates, Susan Cupitt, and John Bowden as *The Quest of the Historical Jesus* (Minneapolis: Fortress, 2001).

23. Hoskyns and Davey, *The Riddle of the New Testament* (London: Faber and Faber, 1931); Piper, *God in History* (New York: Macmillan, 1939; for further discussion of Piper's contributions, see chapter 3); Cullmann, *Christus und die Zeit: Die urchristliche Zeit- und Geschichtsauffassung* (Zollikon-Zürich: Evangelischer, 1946), translated by Floyd V. Filson as *Christ and Time: The Primitive Christian Conception of Time and History* (Philadelphia: Westminster, 1950); Cullmann, *Heil als Geschichte: Heilsgeschichtliche Existenz im Neuen Testament* (Tübingen: Mohr, 1965), translated by Sidney G. Sowers as *Salvation in History* (New York: Harper & Row, 1967); Wright and Fuller, *The Book of the Acts of God: Christian Scholarship Interprets the Bible* (Garden City, NY: Doubleday, 1957).

24. See Neil B. MacDonald, *Karl Barth and the Strange New World within the Bible: Barth, Wittgenstein, and the Metadilemmas of the Enlightenment*, PBTM (Waynesboro, GA: Paternoster, 2000).

25. Barth, *Römerbrief* (Bern: Baschlin, 1919), translated by E. C. Hoskyns as *The Epistle

him]self most closely related" to Schlatter.²⁶ The avowed aim of Barth's *Church Dogmatics* (1932–70)²⁷ is *Nachdenken*: faithful listening to biblical narratives, "after-pondering" their God as the One who loves in freedom, then thinking through all the implications of God's self-revelation for the church's faith and life.²⁸

Rudolf Bultmann's (1884–1976) *Theology of the New Testament*²⁹ is universally recognized as the twentieth century's most important experiment in NT theology. It is also the most fascinating: an unstable hybrid of Wrede and Schlatter's equally stubborn, seemingly contradictory positions. Bultmann's self-assessment of his *Theology* is telling: "It stands, on the one hand, within the tradition of the historical-critical and the history-of-religion schools and seeks, on the other hand, to avoid their mistake, which consists of the tearing apart of the act of thinking from the act of living and hence of a failure to recognize the intent of theological utterances."³⁰ Theology's "intent"—its *Sache*, or subject-matter—like that of history, is human self-understanding, whose character remains the same across time. In these assumptions lies the structuring principle of Bultmann's work. The backdrop for NT theology is Jesus's message—the call to human decision at the dawning of God's reign— and its reformulation in the earliest church's kerygma: "The proclaimer [Jesus] became the proclaimed" (Bultmann in Grobel, 1:3). Because "Paul's theology is at the same time anthropology," Bultmann can reconstruct from "the founder of Christian theology" a coherent position whose poles are humanity prior to faith's revelation and humanity under faith (1:187, 191). Before faith loses its eschatological tension, deteriorating into "bourgeois piety" in the NT's sub-apostolic writings (2:114), John presents humanity confronted by the crisis of decision for or against Jesus, "both the bringer of the Revelation and ... him-

---

to the Romans, 6th ed. (London: Oxford University Press, 1933). Subsequent quotations taken from the English.

26. Barth, *Epistle to the Romans*, 7.

27. Barth, *Die kirchliche Dogmatik*, 14 vols. (Zollikon: Verlag der Evangelischen Buchhandlung, 1932–70), translated by Geoffrey W. Bromiley and Thomas F. Torrance as *Church Dogmatics*, 14 vols. (Edinburgh: T&T Clark, 1936–77).

28. Consult David F. Ford, *Barth and God's Story: Biblical Narrative and the Theological Method of Karl Barth in the "Church Dogmatics,"* SIGC 27 (Frankfurt am Main: Lang, 1981); repr. Eugene, OR: Wipf & Stock, 2008.

29. Bultmann, *Theologie des Neuen Testaments* (Tübingen: Mohr Siebeck, 1948), translated by Kendrick Grobel as *Theology of the New Testament*, 2 vols. (New York: Scribner's Sons, 1951, 1955).

30. Bultmann, *Theology of the New Testament*, 2:246–51. Subsequent citations from Bultmann taken from Grobel's translation will appear in the text.

self the revelation" (2:43)—an exegesis developed in Bultmann's monumental yet problematic commentary, *The Gospel of John*.[31]

Both Bultmann and Barth systematize NT theology in ways the NT does not. Bultmann generates theology through historical criticism; Barth's theology of history challenges that method's assumptions. Reminiscent of Gabler, Bultmann's "demythologization"[32] is a well-intentioned attempt to retrieve what NT writers meant from what they said; for Barth just what the NT narratives say defines what they mean. Both Bultmann and Barth accord to NT study a potential for radical change in the interpreter's self-understanding. Since NT theology is for Bultmann essentially anthropocentric, that change is of primary importance; for Barth it is secondary, because NT theology is Christocentric.

RECURRING QUESTIONS FOR CONTINUED STUDY

1. **How does one approach NT theology?** The discipline's historical dimension remains as uncontested in our day as Scripture's "plain" or "literal" sense was among premodern exegetes. Yet the question of approach abides, comprising two interrelated parts. One concerns the interpreter's *perspective*. Is NT theology primarily confessional, even denominational (thus, Joseph Bonsirven, SJ [1880–1958]; Theodore G. Stylianopoulos [1937–][33])? Existentialist (Bultmann; Georg Strecker [1929–94][34])? Extra-ecclesial, for the sake of the global village (Räisänen)? Historically descriptive within the "socially constructed framework of communion with the saints" (Philip S. Esler [1952–][35])? *Structuring*

---

31. Bultmann, *Das Evangelium des Johannes* (Göttingen: Vandenhoeck & Ruprecht, 1950), translated by G. R. Beasley-Murray, R. W. N. Hoare, and J. K. Riches as *The Gospel of John: A Commentary*, ed. G. R. Beasley-Murray, R. W. N. Hoare, and J. K. Riches (Philadelphia: Westminster, 1971). This landmark commentary's primary problem lies in Bultmann's exegesis of hypothetical sources underlying John. See D. Moody Smith Jr., *The Composition and Order of the Fourth Gospel*, YPR 10 (New Haven: Yale University Press, 1960).

32. *Jesus Christ and Mythology* (New York: Scribner's Sons, 1958).

33. Bonsirven, *Théologie du Nouveau Testament* (Paris: Aubier, 1951), translated by S. F. L. Tye as *Theology of the New Testament* (London: Burns & Oates, 1963); Stylianopoulos, *The New Testament: An Orthodox Perspective* (Brookline, MA: Holy Cross Orthodox Press, 1997).

34. Strecker, *Theologie des Neuen Testaments*, ed. Friedrich Wilhelm Horn (Berlin and New York: de Gruyter, 1996), translated by M. Eugene Boring as *Theology of the New Testament* (New York and Louisville: de Gruyter/Westminster John Knox, 2000).

35. Esler, *New Testament Theology: Communion and Community* (Minneapolis: Fortress, 2005), quotation, 276.

principles for NT theology have tended to be historical-genetic (Strecker), systematic-conceptual (François Vouga [1948–]), or some conjunction of attitudes diachronic and synchronic (Ferdinand Hahn [1926–2015]; Ulrich Wilckens [1928–2021])[36]. Paul Sevier Minear's [1906–2007] "exposition of the NT gospel"[37]—neither its doctrines nor their alleged development—is the Melchizedek of modern NT theology: without obvious ancestry or offspring. There is no univocally correct answer to the question of approach; the NT authors, themselves theologically invested, adopted a panoply of genres and points of view. The pudding's proof lies in a chef's talent to awaken fresh savoring of the texts being served.

2. **Does the NT exhibit a unifying core?** After historians disqualified dogmatic answers to this question, Ernst Käsemann (1906–98) spoke for many: "The New Testament canon . . . provides the basis for the multiplicity of the [church's] confessions."[38] Some recent studies highlight the NT's theological diversity (Strecker; Joachim Gnilka [1928–2018][39]). I. Howard Marshall (1934–2015) offers a detailed minority report, accenting the NT's harmonious, "essentially missionary theology."[40] Käsemann himself, following Schlatter, regards the apocalyptic lordship of the crucified Christ as "the real clue" amid the NT's pluralism.[41] Similarly, James D. G. Dunn's (1939–2020) synchronic–diachronic inquiry concludes that "the unity between the historical Jesus and the exalted Christ" is the integrative center for earliest Christianity's diverse expressions.[42] Lately, under the influence of Nils Alstrup Dahl (1911–2001), one detects a more deliberately theocentric articulation of the NT's core: the self-revelation of Israel's God in Jesus Christ (Hahn; Wilckens; Peter Stuhlmacher [1932–]), emerging from imaginary, roundtable debates among NT witnesses (Vouga;

---

36. Vouga, *Une théologie du Nouveau Testament*, MB 43 (Geneva: Labor et Fides, 2001); Hahn, *Theologie des Neuen Testaments*, 2 vols. (Tübingen: Mohr Siebeck, 2002); Wilckens, *Theologie des Neuen Testaments*, 3 vols. (Neukirchen-Vluyn: Neukirchener, 2002).

37. Minear, *The Kingdom and the Power: An Exposition of the Gospel* (Philadelphia: Westminster, 1950); repr. Louisville: Westminster John Knox, 2004).

38. Käsemann, "The Canon of the New Testament and the Unity of the Church," in *Essays on New Testament Themes*, trans. W. J. Montague, SBT 41 (London: SCM, 1964), 95–107; quotation, 103.

39. Gnilka, *Theologie des Neuen Testaments*, HThKNTSup 5 (Freiburg im Breisgau and Basel: Herder, 1994).

40. Marshall, *New Testament Theology: Many Witnesses, One Gospel* (Downers Grove, IL: InterVarsity Press, 2004), 34.

41. Käsemann, "The Problem of a New Testament Theology," *NTS* 19 (1972–73): 235–45.

42. Dunn, *Unity and Diversity in the New Testament: An Inquiry into the Character of Earliest Christianity* (London: SCM, 1977).

George Bradford Caird [1917–84]) or from renewed respect for the NT's narrative world (Frank Matera [1942–]).[43] This development is reminiscent of the mid-twentieth-century biblical theology movement,[44] tweaked to take seriously (as does Barth) the Bible's use of stories to communicate its vision of reality.

3. **How is NT theology related to OT theology?** This question is as old as the NT itself, whose constituent witnesses variously interact with Israel's Scripture. The issue exploded in second-century Gnosticism: Marcion of Sinope's (85–160) divorce of the church and its emergent Scriptures from Israel and its Bible. Hans Hübner (1930–93) assesses the NT account of God's self-revelation as adequate in isolation.[45] At the other extreme, Stuhlmacher insists on the entire canon within NT theology's purview, dubiously arguing for historical closure of both Testaments simultaneously.[46] Appreciation of OT citations and allusions in NT texts has long been assumed and refined (thus, Charles Harold Dodd [1884–1973]; Richard B. Hays [1948–][47]). The location of NT theology within the broader Christian canon, advocated by Schlatter, received fresh impetus by Brevard S. Childs (1923–2007)[48] and other proponents of canonical criticism. Before proceeding to NT theology, N. T. Wright (1948–) devotes an entire volume to Israel's faith and other aspects of the church's milieu.[49] As NT theology evolves into biblical theology, maintaining a dialectical balance between the Testaments—honoring their theological interdependence without fusing their contents into some spurious amalgamation[50]—remains a perennial challenge.

---

43. Dahl, "The Neglected Factor in New Testament Theology," *Reflections* 75 (1975): 5–8; repr. in *Jesus the Christ: The Historical Origins of Christological Doctrine*, ed. Donald H. Juel (Minneapolis: Fortress, 1999), 153–63; Stuhlmacher, *Biblische Theologie des Neuen Testaments*, 2 vols. (Göttingen: Vandenhoeck & Ruprecht, 1992–99); translated by Daniel P. Bailey with Jostein Adna as *Biblical Theology of the New Testament*, ed. Bailey with Adna (Grand Rapids: Eerdmans, 2018); G. B. Caird, *New Testament Theology*, comp. and ed. L. D. Hurst (Oxford: Clarendon, 1994); Matera, *New Testament Theology: Exploring Diversity and Unity* (Louisville: Westminster John Knox, 2007).

44. See Brevard S. Childs, *Biblical Theology in Crisis* (Philadelphia: Westminster, 1970).

45. Hübner, *Biblische Theologie des Neuen Testaments*, 3 vols. (Göttingen: Vandenhoeck & Ruprecht, 1990–95).

46. Stuhlmacher, *Biblical Theology of the New Testament*.

47. Dodd, *According to the Scriptures: The Sub-Structure of New Testament Theology* (London: Nisbet, 1952); Hays, *Echoes of Scripture in the Letters of Paul* (New Haven: Yale University Press, 1993); *Echoes of Scripture in the Gospels* (Waco, TX: Baylor University Press, 2016).

48. Childs, *The New Testament as Canon: An Introduction* (Philadelphia: Fortress, 1984).

49. Wright, *The New Testament and the People of God* (London: SPCK, 1992).

50. A specimen of exceptional quality: Reinhard Feldmeier and Hermann Spiecker-

4. **Is Jesus's proclamation intrinsic to NT theology?** From the discipline's inception this question has nagged interpreters. During the second half of the twentieth century, recovering an implied theology from Jesus's own preaching was often reckoned a necessary first stage of NT theology (thus, Werner Georg Kümmel [1905–95]; Joachim Jeremias [1900–1979]; Leonhard Goppelt [1911–73][51]). For many it remains so (Stuhlmacher; Caird; Wright[52]; Marshall). Bultmann evinces ambivalence: the existential force of Jesus's preaching anticipates that of the primitive kerygma even though Jesus's message is a presupposition for NT theology, not one of its constituents.[53] Other recent contributions tend to encompass, not the historically reconstructed Jesus, but rather the proclamation of Jesus as rendered by the NT evangelists (Räisänen; Gnilka; Wilckens; Matera). Different procedures follow in part from an investigator's prior decision whether NT theology is an essentially descriptive (historical) or normative (dogmatic) enterprise.

5. **How does philosophy bear on NT theology?** The brief answer is "heavily and often covertly." To articulate their views NT writers themselves drew, not only from the OT, but also from Hellenism and Greek religion and philosophy. Likewise, every generation of NT interpreters partakes of its era's philosophical milieu. The Reformers were children of Scholasticism and humanism; Wrede and Barth and Bultmann (to mention only three) were informed by Immanuel Kant (1724–1804), Georg Wilhelm Friedrich Hegel (1770–1831), and Martin Heidegger (1889–1976). As a self-reflective discipline, current NT theology is coming to terms with modernity's resources and limitations (A. K. M. Adam

---

mann, *Der lebendige Gott: Eine Einführung in die biblische Gotteslehre* (Tübingen: Mohr Siebeck, 2011), translated by Mark E. Biddle as *God of the Living: A Biblical Theology* (Waco, TX: Baylor University Press, 2011). See also Feldmeier and Spieckermann, *Menschwerdung*, TBT 2 (Tübingen: Mohr Siebeck, 2018), translated by Brian McNeil as *God Becoming Human: Incarnation in the Christian Bible* (Waco, TX: Baylor University Press, 2021).

51. Kümmel, *Die Theologie des Neuen Testaments nach seinen Hauptzeugen: Jesus, Paulus, Johannes* (Göttingen: Vandenhoeck & Ruprecht, 1969), translated by John E. Steely as *The Theology of the New Testament According to Its Major Witnesses: Jesus—Paul—John* (Nashville: Abingdon, 1973); Jeremias, *Neutestamentliche Theologie* (Gütersloh: Mohn, 1971), translated by John Bowden as *New Testament Theology* (New York: Scribner's Sons, 1971); Goppelt, *Theologie des Neuen Testaments*, 2 vols., ed. Jürgen Roloff (Göttingen: Vandenhoeck & Ruprecht, 1975–76), translated by John E. Alsup as *Theology of the New Testament*, 2 vols., ed. J. Roloff (Grand Rapids: Eerdmans, 1981–92).

52. Wright, *Jesus and the Victory of God* (London: SPCK, 1996).

53. Bultmann, *Jesus* (Berlin: Deutsche Bibliothek, 1929), translated by Louise Pettibone Smith and Erminie Huntress as *Jesus and the Word* (New York: Scribner's Sons, 1934); Bultmann, *Theology of the New Testament* (1951), 1:3.

[1957–]).⁵⁴ Whereas a contemporary "hermeneutics of suspicion" drinks from the wells of Ludwig Feuerbach (1804–72), Karl Marx (1818–83), and Friedrich Nietzsche (1844–1900), an ecclesially sympathetic "hermeneutics of conviction" (Kevin Vanhoozer [1957–])⁵⁵ converses with such philosophers as Hans-Georg Gadamer (1900–2002), Paul Ricoeur (1913–2005), and Jacques Derrida (1930–2004). Why NT theology itself has been to date a preponderantly European project, with occasional Anglo-American contributions but few from Asia, Africa, or Latin America, is an unresolved question whose answer may entail the history of philosophy, perhaps also cultural epistemology.

6. **How does NT theology bear on dogmatics, witness, and practice?** "Dialectically and ambiguously," one might reply. As rarefied as academic NT theology often appears, its exponents have typically engaged the church, whether devotedly or not. Renewed efforts to describe and to encourage reciprocity among NT theology and patristics, dogmatics, and praxis characterize late twentieth and early twenty-first century scholarship (so Frances M. Young [1939–]; Francis Watson [1956–]; Joel B. Green [1956–] and Max Turner [1947–]).⁵⁶ Important in this endeavor is Robert Morgan's (1940–) clarification that NT theology does not argue for Christianity's truth but, rather, assists in clarifying its authentic identity—reminiscent of Barth's quip, "The best apologetics is a good dogmatics."⁵⁷

Concluding Reflections

In the early decades of the twenty-first century, NT theology appears alive, well, and vigorous.⁵⁸ Like the NT itself, its ablest contributors are sensitive

---

54. Adam, *Making Sense of New Testament Theology: "Modern" Problems and Prospects* (Macon, GA: Mercer University Press, 1995).

55. Vanhoozer, *Is There a Meaning in This Text? The Bible, the Reader, and the Morality of Literary Knowledge* (Grand Rapids: Zondervan, 1998).

56. Young, *The Art of Performance: Towards a Theology of Holy Scripture* (London: Darton, Longman, and Todd, 1990); Watson, *Text, Church and World: Biblical Interpretation in Theological Perspective* (Edinburgh: T&T Clark, 1994); Green and Turner, eds., *Between Two Horizons: Spanning New Testament Studies and Systematic Theology* (Grand Rapids: Eerdmans, 2000).

57. Morgan, "Can the Critical Study of Scripture Provide a Doctrinal Norm?," *JR* 76 (1996): 206–32; John Godsey, ed., *Karl Barth's Table Talk*, SJTOP 10 (Edinburgh: Oliver and Boyd, 1963), 62.

58. C. Kavin Rowe. "New Testament Theology: The Revival of a Discipline," *JBL* 125 (2006): 393–410.

to text and context, diverse in their aims, procedurally rigorous, and strategically imaginative. If history be a reliable guide, its health and fertility will depend on a continuously calibrated balance of its descriptive and normative aspects: exegetically *understanding* the NT's multifarious claims for God's salvation in Jesus Christ while *standing under* the liberating judgment of that conviction.[59]

So ends my best, albeit stodgy, bird's-eye view of NT theology. What if we open the aperture onto *biblical* theology? That is the exercise posed by the next chapter: more whimsical in format, as serious as a heart attack.

---

59. By my lights, this epitomizes an adequate rebuttal of John Barton's claim that theological interpretation of the Bible is inherently eisegetical (*The Nature of Biblical Criticism* [Louisville: Westminster John Knox, 2007]). Discernment of any text's meaning is sine qua non for intelligent, respectful profession of its truth. It does not follow, however, that affirmation of the truth of a text necessarily follows from a deeper understanding of its meaning. The latter may eventuate in refusal of a text's claims, whether the text be *King Lear* or the Fourth Gospel. In "Biblical Criticism and Religious Belief" (*JTI* 21 [2008]: 71–100), R. W. L. Moberly cogently engages Barton's assessments.

CHAPTER 2

Biblical Theology Revisited: An Internal Debate

> The curtain rises on a vast primitive wasteland, not unlike certain parts of New Jersey.
>
> —Woody Allen, "A Guide to Some of the Lesser Ballets"

Bold-Faced Black

SO IT'S COME TO THIS. You're talking to yourself in public. Even worse: in print.

Bald-Faced Black

Better in print than online. In space no one can hear you meme.

You call this doggerel an essay?
No. That would be an insult to the entire canine world. This I call a "work in progress."

Offering something this cockamamie will render you ridiculous before your readers.
If by now my readers haven't figured me out, what they make of this chapter will neither add to nor subtract from their estimate. Besides, the venerable Q&A / *videtur–sed contra* style served St. Thomas rather well.

In your dreams. If you thought half as lucidly as Aquinas, you'd stick your quill back in your goose. Let's get down to cases. You claim to have "revisited biblical theology." What has your revisit taught you to this point?
I've learned that, in academic scholarship, precious little of it is either "biblical" or "theological." G. L. Bauer (1705–1806) disjoined OT theology from NT the-

ology over two centuries ago.¹ Since then a scant handful—among others, Paul Minear (1906-2007), Brevard Childs (1923-2007), Paul Hanson (1939-2023), Walter Moberly (1952-)²—have encompassed both testaments. They deserve our most sincere thanks.

My most unsettling discovery is that some among even those who have attempted biblical theology—a coherent, comprehensive description and assessment of religious views expressed in both Testaments—are not actually doing theology, at least not in the first instance. Usually they are executing *historical* reconstructions of what, as William Wrede memorably said over a century ago,³ was "believed, thought, taught, hoped, required, and striven for" in ancient Israel, earliest Judaism, and the earliest era of Christianity.

Do you agree with that grouchy old buzzard Wrede?
Not for the most part. Wrede's answer triumphed—and that's part of our problem.

Wrede (1859-1906) rent asunder the conceptual marriage that Johann Philipp Gabler (1753-1826) had attempted to broker in 1787.⁴ For Wrede, German liberal theology's "method of doctrinal concepts"—grouping thoughts expressed by the NT in alignment with dogmatic topics—betrays "scientific criticism" and provokes caricature of NT writers as systematicians in the modern sense. That method's default setting on canonical documents is likewise misguided: a document's canonization makes no difference for either the Protestant theologian or historical investigator. NT theology is, or should be, the

---

1. Woody Allen, "A Guide to Some of the Lesser Ballets," in *Without Feathers* (New York: Random House, 1975), 15-21; quotation, 16.

Bauer, *Theologie des Alten Testaments, oder, Abriss der religiösen Begriffe der alten Hebräer* (Leipzig: Weygand, 1796).

2. Minear, *Eyes of Faith: A Study in the Biblical Point of View* (Philadelphia: Westminster, 1946); Childs, *Biblical Theology of the Old and New Testaments: Theological Reflection on the Christian Bible* (Minneapolis: Fortress, 1993); Hanson, *The People Called: The Growth of Community in the Bible* (San Francisco: Harper & Row, 1986); R. W. L. Moberly, *The Bible, Theology and Faith: A Study of Abraham and Jesus*, CSCD (Cambridge: Cambridge University Press, 2000).

3. Wrede, "The Task and Methods of 'New Testament Theology,'" in Robert Morgan, ed. and trans., *The Nature of New Testament Theology: The Contribution of William Wrede and Adolf Schlatter* (London: SCM, 1973), 84 (italicized in the original).

4. Gabler, "On the Proper Distinction between Biblical and Dogmatic Theology and the Specific Objectives of Each," in John Sandys-Wunsch and Laurence Eldredge, "J. P. Gabler and the Distinction between Biblical and Dogmatic Theology: Translation, Commentary, and Discussion of His Originality," *SJT* 33 (1980): 133-58.

attempt to understand the development of primitive Christian religion in its historical situation: the earliest Christians' beliefs and aspirations, not how their literary artifacts may be plundered for our reconstructions of "faith," "hope," whatever. Wrede believed that the responsible procedure is to begin with Jesus as he was increasingly "dogmatized" by early Christian adherents, then move to the primitive church (of which "we should have to know more than we in fact do know"), Paul ("the creator of a Christian theology"), Gentile Christianity, John (who "made the picture of Jesus' life entirely into a mirror of his own ideas"), and Ignatius (who typifies and embodies "personal Christianity at the beginning of the second century").[5] "New Testament theology" is, for Wrede, a double misnomer. First, none of its subject matter was born canonical. Second, it is less with *theology* than with *religion* that we should be concerned, specifically "the history of early Christian religion and theology."[6] Wrede uncoupled what Gabler had only differentiated: religion and theology.

You conclude, then, that Wrede was altogether wrong?

No. He got some things right. First, hindsight teaches us that there is genuine gain by interpreting loaded terms in both the OT and NT within a conceptual framework larger than the canon. No fair-minded exegete fails to learn important nuances of, say, *tsedeq* or *pistis* by consulting Botterweck and Ringgren's *Theologisches Wörterbuch zum Alten Testament* (1973–95) or Kittel and Friedrich's *Theologisches Wörterbuch zum Neuen Testament* (1933–74), encyclopedias that expand our intellectual horizons into the Ancient Near East and Mediterranean antiquity. Second, Wrede's impulse to differentiate modern dogmatic categories from less systematized, ancient formulations was sound in two respects. First: the prophets and the apostles functioned more as preachers, at most what we would call practical theologians, far less as systematicians. Like Gabler before him, Wrede asserted that theology is *a dimension of* religious experience though *not coterminous with and therefore interchangeable* with it. Second: even if he himself did not frame the matter theologically, Wrede's proposal creates space for biblical authors to stand apart from modern readers, the better to critique, rather than to mirror or otherwise to confirm, their theological assumptions. From its inception that has been a capital contribution of historical criticism for the church.

---

5. Wrede, "Task and Methods," quotations 104, 106, 113, 89.
6. Wrede, "Task and Methods," 116.

Then why do you consider Wrede contributory to the problem, not of its solution?
Because (a) Wrede's understanding of history and, therefore, of historical criticism was naive; (b) his take on constructive theology was at best indifferent, at worst hostile; and (c) his position has prevailed in biblical scholarship to the church's detriment.

Wrede writes as though historical research were neutral, to protect biblical interpretation from its practitioners' "religious commitments." We didn't have to wait for postmodernism to expose the illusion of objectivity. Another great modernist, Adolf Schlatter (1852–1938), spotted this in 1909: "A historical sketch can only take shape in the mind of a historian, and . . . in this process the historian himself, with all his intellectual furniture, is involved. If this fact is lost sight of, then it is no longer science in which we are involved, but crazy illusions."[7] Schlatter put his (historian's!) finger on an even deeper problem with Wrede's position: "As soon as the historian sets aside or brackets the question of faith, he is making his concern with the New Testament and his presentation of it into a radical and total polemic against it."[8] In effect Schlatter turned Wrede's fundamental critique against himself: If the NT's authors had been illegitimately "modernized" into dogmaticians, then neither should they be modernized as Troeltschian historians. All biblical authors, without exception, wrote "from faith for faith"—as no responsible historical critic in 2024 would deny.

Furthermore, for Wrede the historian as such is not competent to serve today's church, whenever "today" might be. Unlike Gabler, Wrede is indifferent to modern dogmatics: "Like every other real science, New Testament theology has its goal simply in itself, and is totally indifferent to all dogma and systematic theology. How the systematic theologian gets on with its results and deals with them—that is his own affair."[9]

And why was Wrede so persuaded?
Because, as a dutiful child of the Enlightenment, he assumed that "historical facts" and "religious values" could and should be cleanly separated. In his own words:

---

7. Schlatter, "The Theology of the New Testament and Dogmatics," in Morgan, *Nature of New Testament Theology*, 125–26.

8. Schlatter, "Theology of the New Testament and Dogmatics," 122.

9. Wrede, "Task and Methods," 69. In the original these two sentences appear in reverse order.

Could dogmatics teach New Testament theology to see the facts correctly? At most it could color them. Could it correct the facts that were found? To correct facts is absurd. Could it legitimize them? Facts need no legitimation.[10]

At best this overreaches what historians, so operating, can retrieve; at worst it's nonsense. Whether we speak of Habakkuk or Paul, "The righteous shall live by faith" is not a "fact," like the mathematical postulate of the Pythagorean theorem. As a matter of fact—or, if you prefer, common sense—dogmatics, *pace* Wrede, might very well help biblical exegetes to understand the *theological* claims made in that literature. While anxious Lutherans might rejoice to sing his chorus, "Facts need no legitimation"—i.e., the truth of the gospel depends on no historical criticism—Wrede's magisterial dictum obscures rather than clarifies the task of NT *theology*.

Hold on. You just said that Wrede, like Gabler, differentiated "religion" from "theology."
He did—then immediately confused the issue by asserting that what NT *theologians* should really be studying is "early Christian *history of religion.*"[11] Those two disciplines are kindred but not identical. Let's put it this way: the historian of ancient Israel or of earliest Christianity may or may not be able to verify that Habakkuk and Paul made the claim, "The righteous shall live by faith." The historian of religious ideas may be able to fill in enough gaps to render terms like "righteousness" and "faith" more intelligible in semantic domains remote from our own. It takes more or other than a historian, however, to explain what that claim intends. To be precise, it takes a theologian—not merely a phenomenologist of religion, of its adherents, and of their ideas.

Then why did Wrede's position, not Schlatter's, carry the day in biblical interpretation?
Schlatter's views conceded too little to the historical-critical Zeitgeist, and his own historical reconstructions were suspect because of their consistent alignment with conservative Christianity. For hard-nosed historical critics, the game was up the moment Schlatter claimed that even historians hold religious values, transmitted through "the large communities in which we live

---

10. Wrede, "Task and Methods," 69–70.
11. Wrede, "Task and Methods," 116 (my emphasis).

and on which we depend."[12] Wrede's project, on the other hand, was immediately appropriable by *religionsgeschichtlich* scholars like Hermann Gunkel (1862–1932) and Wilhelm Bousset (1854–1920) and their form-critical progeny, such as Martin Noth (1902–68) and Rudolf Bultmann (1884–1976), who in turn begat contemporary social-scientific criticism (Gerstenberger, Theissen[13] et al.)—most of whom would rather check all religious claims at the door before getting on with their work.

Well, what's wrong with that?
In itself, nothing. Scholars are free to study whatever they like, however their interests so move them. The best of their work is insightful and incisive; the rest, pedestrian and usually harmless. But not everything scholars want to do, and how they want to do it, is profitable for the church and the world in which it serves. "All things are lawful; but not all things build up" (1 Cor 6:12).[14] Moreover, scholars are *not* free to dictate to biblical theologians what they will do and how they will do it.

Watch it. Your rhetoric is simmering to an unseemly boil.
Is it? Here's what one of the most talented of those social-scientific exegetes, Wayne Meeks (1932–2022), declared almost two decades ago in his presidential address to *Studiorum Novi Testamenti Societas*:

> We should start by erasing from our vocabulary the terms "biblical theology" and, even more urgently, "New Testament theology." Whatever positive contributions these concepts may have made in the conversation since Gabler, we have come to a time when they can only blinker our understanding. First, the notion "biblical theology," despite all the qualifications we have learned to make regarding it, in practice tends always to smuggle in a cognitivist model of religion . . . privileging doctrine at the expense of life. Second, "biblical theology" implicitly claims textual and historical warrants for propositions that in truth arise only out of continuing transactions between text and reader through many times and places, and it invites our complicity as historians in this masking of the source of authority.

---

12. Schlatter, "Theology of the New Testament and Dogmatics," 152.
13. Gerstenberger, *Theologien im Alten Testament: Pluralität und Synkretismus alttestamentlichen Gottesglaubens* (Stuttgart: Kohlhammer, 2001); Theissen, *Die Religion der ersten Christen: eine Theorie des Urchristentums* (Gütersloh: Kaiser/Gütersloher, 2000).
14. Unless otherwise indicated, all translations are the author's own.

Whenever we hear the phrase, "The Bible clearly teaches," in contemporary debates, we may be sure that this covert relocation of the warrant is taking place. Third, "biblical theology" has functioned ideologically in the attempt to secure our own positions in the theological hierarchy, as the teachers of the teachers of the church. We have not done very well in that role, and we should give it up.[15]

Professor Meeks's reasons for denying even an *option* for biblical theology in our day are strained, verging on the bizarre. Agreed: there's a necessarily cognitive dimension in biblical theology, for the simple reason that the Christian religion has a cognitive or theological component embedded *within* its life, not "*at the expense of* life": "Always be prepared to make a defense to anyone who calls you to account for the hope that is in you" (1 Pet 3:15b). Christianity is not thereby *reduced* to cognitivism—an obscurantist reductionism that Meeks himself is smuggling in. (Since few methods of current historical exegesis are more cognitivist than social-scientific criticism, thick with Geertzian description,[16] Meeks, its expert practitioner, should beware the pot's calling the kettle black.) Second, I've no idea who in Meeks's hearing is pompously thumping "the Bible clearly teaches," but it's a safe bet they do not teach at Yale or at Princeton. Third, some biblical scholars indeed recognize as their vocation "teaching the church's teachers"; I can honestly say that none I know makes such a claim to shore up their credibility in some imagined theological hierarchy. In most of the schools represented by the Society for New Testament Studies, that idea is laughably incredible. Finally, "not doing very well" in a historically recognized role—biblical theology has, after all, a longer lineage than historical criticism—is no reason "to give it up." It may well be a reason to do it better.

Studying Scripture in the Ivy League is like learning about women at the Mayo Clinic.

Cheap shots aside, I'm glad you got those small potatoes off your chest.
I feel better for it. *Cogito ergo* spud: I think, therefore I yam.

Spare us, please. May we return to Wrede's triumph over Schlatter?
Well, I never said that it was unmitigated.

---

15. Meeks, "Why Study the New Testament?," *NTS* 51 (2005): 155–70; quotation, 167–68.
16. Clifford Geertz, *The Interpretation of Cultures: Selected Essays* (New York: Basic Books, 1973).

Where's the evidence that Schlatter's confessional approach to biblical theology bore fruit?

Two heavyweights come to mind: Bultmann and Karl Barth (1886–1968).[17]

Bultmann's *Theology of the New Testament* (1951–55)[18] is universally acknowledged as the twentieth century's most important experiment in NT theology. Though remembered for many things, his own self-assessment of that attempt is sometimes forgotten: "The presentation of New Testament theology offered in this book stands, on the one hand, within the tradition of the historical-critical and the history-of-religion schools and seeks, on the other hand, to avoid their mistake, which consists of the tearing apart of the act of thinking from the act of living and hence of a failure to recognize the intent of theological utterances."[19] The one hand takes from Wrede: "a . . . really historical grasp and reflection that is truly history of *religion*."[20] The other hand receives from Schlatter: "There is no need to associate the concept of 'theology' with an artificial separation of thought and existence."[21] In short, Bultmann tried to hybridize Wrede and Schlatter's equally stubborn, seemingly contradictory positions. That's what makes his *Theology* so fascinating and, possibly, influential: no matter which set of modernist assumptions the reader adopted, in Bultmann one might find a home—up to a point.

I know where you're hedging—up to the point that the reader accepts Bultmann's assumption that the "heroes" of NT theology, Paul and John, could be existentially demythologized.

Well, yes. Another problem is Bultmann's less than auspicious view of the OT: "Faith requires the backward glance into Old Testament history as a history of failure, and so of promise, in order to know that the situation of the justified man arises only on the basis of this miscarriage."[22] The OT as an abortion, the NT as faith's pregnancy carried to full term: somewhere Marcion smiles.

---

17. For further comparison of Bultmann and Barth's respective projects, see chapter 1.

18. Bultmann, *Theology of the New Testament*, 2 vols., trans. Kendrick Grobel (New York: Scribner's Sons, 1951, 1955); German original: *Theologie des Neuen Testaments* (Tübingen: Mohr Siebeck, 1953).

19. Bultmann, *Theology of the New Testament*, 2:250–51.

20. Bultmann, *Theology of the New Testament*, 2:251.

21. Bultmann, *Theology of the New Testament*, 2:246.

22. Bultmann, "Prophecy and Fulfillment," in *Essays on Old Testament Hermeneutics*, ed. Claus Westermann, trans. James Luther Mays and James C. G. Greig (Richmond, VA: John Knox, 1964), 50–75; quotation, 75.

Why bring Barth into the picture? He's no biblical specialist.
So what? Who invited Derrida or Levinas to the Mad Hatter's tea party?
  Barth belongs here. In his third *Römerbrief* preface (1922) he acknowledged "feel[ing him]self most closely related to Schlatter."²³ Where Barth really cut loose, however, was in his *Church Dogmatics*.²⁴ There he broke with Enlightenment epistemology by regarding all humans as living nowhere other than within a God-centered history, the sphere of God's self-communicative action.

Are you claiming such a view as basic to the theological perspectives adopted in the OT and NT?
I'd say that it's conceptually closer to the Bible's own witness than Bultmann's call to a decision for authentic human existence. As theories go, that's only marginally better than Mark Russell's (1932–2023) hypothesis that Saturn's rings are composed entirely of lost airline baggage. Remember, too, that Barth's aspiration was nothing but *Nachdenken*: a faithful listening to the biblical narratives in both testaments, "post-pondering" their testimonies to God as "the One who loves in freedom" and then thinking through all the implications of God's self-revelation for the church's faith and life.

Time out. Do you realize you've spent eight pages on a history of biblical interpretation? This essay is as boring as Fred Allen's hamlet in Maine: "The town so dull that when the tide went out it refused to come back."²⁵
Why else study history than to recognize your mistakes when you make them again?

So near, yet so what? Have you a positive point to register?
I think it boils down to this: if biblical theology has a productive future in our day, then biblical scholars are going to have to be trained to think not only historically but theologically, from stem to stern, with all that implies both philosophically and confessionally.

---

  23. Karl Barth, *The Epistle to the Romans*, 6th ed., trans. E. C. Hoskyns (Oxford: Oxford University Press, 1933), 7.
  24. Karl Barth, *Die kirchliche Dogmatik*, 14 vols. (Zollikon: Verlag der Evangelischen Buchhandlung, 1932–70); trans. G. T. Thomson and G. M. Bromiley, ed. G. M. Bromiley and T. F. Torrance, 14 vols. (Edinburgh: T&T Clark, 1936–77).
  25. Fred Allen in Groucho Marx, *The Groucho Letters: Letters from and to Groucho Marx* (New York: Simon & Schuster, 1967), 89.

Wait, wait. Are you suggesting that all biblical scholars must be required to study theology?
No. Only those who care about the church, its faith and its theology. For those with such a vocation, historical and systematic theology will have to be as much a part of their curriculum as Hellenistic Greek and papyrology. Arguably more so, for in every era theology is as informed by its own discipline and philosophical assumptions as is historical investigation and the tools of its trade.[26]

Are you dumping historical criticism?
Absolutely not. Historical thinking is inescapable for the contemporary church, the academy, and the larger world in which they all live. Were it not so, there would be no cable History Channel, and *The Da Vinci Code* moonshine, tricked out as suppressed history, could never have purchased Dan Brown a villa on the Adriatic. First-rate historical investigation, like first-rate philosophical inquiry, still has its place. What I'm saying, at least, is that Lessing was right but needn't have feared his conclusions. To paraphrase: the truth about God and ourselves, to which Scripture bears witness, is not directly accessible by or contingent upon historical inquiry. But unless we are hell-bent to view it as such, there is no "ugly ditch" between the "accidental truths of history" and the "necessary truths of reason"[27]—only different intellectual procedures properly suited to different objectives.

You said that was the least you'd claim about history and its investigation. What's the most?
That Barth—though not he alone—got it right. In the eyes of faith and of theology that attempts to interpret faith, history does not belong to us. We just live there. History is a realm of the created order, and creation belongs to God. And so do we, along with everything that we do. Regarded *sub specie aeternitatis*, "All history is the history of grace."[28]

---

26. Of late it's become fashionable to speak of "contextual theology," sometimes as a substitute for systematics. Having witnessed some of its practice, I regard that as a well-intentioned but serious mistake. By definition, historical theology attends to the social and economic contexts in which Christian faith has been explicated. On account of intellectual laziness, theologians will always need to discipline their thought systematically: logically, with clarity of method, structure, and coherence. Contextual theology had better beware absorption into sociology and politics, lacquered with a religious veneer.

27. G. E. Lessing, "On the Proof of the Spirit and of Power" (1777), in *Lessing's Theological Writings*, ed. and trans. Henry Chadwick (London: Adam & Charles Black, 1956), 18.

28. Nicholas Lash, "How Do We Know Where We Are?," in Lash, *Theology on the Way to Emmaus* (London: SCM, 1986), 67.

That's a theological claim about history that historical inquiry cannot verify.
That's right. Now you're catching on.

I have here a list you've compiled: "Six Suggestions for Remapping Biblical Theology." Our readers would appreciate your commenting on them, beginning with

> Thesis #1: For theologically invested biblical interpreters, let a moratorium be declared on NT theology as generally practiced for the past two centuries. Let us instead reconsider biblical theology of both Testaments as scriptural theology, a discipline both normative and descriptive.

I may be wrong, but my impression is that NT theology as practiced in the modern era may be wheezing to the end of its current usefulness. During the past decade alone we have received massive "NT theologies" from the Continent, structured as historical-genetic reconstructions, systematic-conceptual surveys, or some procedural combination thereof.[29] The historical-genetic accounts plow Wrede's well-worn furrows. The systematic-conceptual analyses carry us not far beyond Bultmann, occasionally flirting with the sort of "method of doctrinal concepts"—historically cast, to be sure—that Wrede excoriated in nineteenth-century liberal Protestantism. If we are to progress, rather than merely to rehearse, a fresh approach is invited.

A second observation: If NT theology is again to nourish the church, it must take the OT more seriously than it lately has.

Don't tell me: We must lay sacrifice at the altar of Intertextualität.
No, the reasons are much deeper than clamoring to be au courant. The NT's authors themselves found it practically impossible to think theologically apart from the Jewish Bible, as C. H. Dodd taught us many decades ago.[30] Their basic concepts were not original with Christianity but derivative from the synagogue's Scripture.

---

29. Georg Strecker, *Theologie des Neuen Testaments*, ed. Friedrich Wilhelm Horn (Berlin: de Gruyter, 1996), translated by M. Eugene Boring as *Theology of the New Testament* (New York: de Gruyter, 2000); François Vouga, *Une Théologie du Nouveau Testament*, MB 43 (Geneva: Labor et Fides, 2001); Ferdinand Hahn, *Theologie des Neuen Testaments*, 2 vols. (Tübingen: Mohr Siebeck, 2002); Ulrich Wilckens, *Theologie des Neuen Testaments* (Neukirchen-Vluyn: Neukirchener, 2002–5).

30. Dodd, *According to the Scriptures: The Sub-Structure of New Testament Theology* (London: Nisbet, 1952).

You are reiterating Brevard Childs's canonical approach. Correct?
There's an obvious overlap. Death may have prevented Childs from going as far as he might have—a possibility that will surprise biblical scholars who think he'd already gone much too far. But that's for another debate.

For an unabashedly theological approach to Scripture Childs deserves our thanks, even though some problems attended his project. Especially in the 1970s and '80s, it proved hard for him to breathe freely under the historical-critical mantle, even when on his own terms its *magisterium* was no longer apt for his endeavor. This, in turn, made him fair if frustrating game for critics who've chastised him for inadequate clarity about the canon itself. Whose canon? The Septuagintal? The Masoretic? Roman Catholic? Eastern Orthodox? The Protestant? All overlap but none is identical with the others. Yet in the last decade of his vast publications, Childs was commendably moving beyond *sola scriptura*: the Bible as the single canonical guide for Christian thought and practice.[31]

Isn't it?
Of course not. An unfortunate hangover of the Reformation is an implied delimitation of "canon" to a body of literature regarded as scriptural.[32] Yet there are many canonical, or regulative, resources and practices that overlap with but are not equivalent to the Christian Bible: the church's liturgy and sacraments, orders of ministry (lay and ordained), art and music, many other traditional distillates.[33] *Sola scriptura* is nowhere claimed *within the Bible*; it is itself a hermeneutical principle arising from a particular construal of *tradition*. A truly "canonical approach to scripture" would invite this entire range of canonical resources and practices to bear on interpretation of the church's Scripture.

You say "biblical theology" should be reconsidered as "Christian scriptural theology." What's the difference?
The Christian "Bible," consisting of Testaments Old and New, is a neutral designation, like TANAK, the Qur'an, or the Upanishads. One can study any of

---

31. See, for instance, Brevard S. Childs, "Toward Recovering Theological Exegesis," *Pro-Ecc* 6 (1997): 16–26. Dennis T. Olson, "Seeking 'The Inexpressible Texture of Thy Word': A Practical Guide to Brevard Childs' Canonical Approach to Theological Exegesis," *PTR* 14 (2008): 53–68, offers a splendid conspectus of Childs's comprehensive process of exegesis.

32. See David Brown, *Trinity and Imagination: Revelation and Change* (Oxford: Oxford University Press, 1999).

33. Thus, William J. Abraham, *Canon and Criterion in Christian Theology: From the Fathers to Feminism* (Oxford and New York: Clarendon/Oxford University Press, 1998).

those books without regarding them as scriptural. In a secular university's Department of Religious Studies it is appropriate for Christians to read the Qur'an, for Muslims to read the Vedas, for Hindus to read the Hebrew Bible, for Jews to read the NT, for agnostics to read any or all of them, without conversion to the religious body for whom each of those works occupies a central place. In today's religiously suspicious and volatile world, it would be a very good thing if more of that happened. Such an experience would be even richer if students were led into those books by, respectively, imams and satgurus and rabbis and priests: well-trained "native speakers" of their religions, who could help sympathetic outsiders to appreciate the nuances and subtleties muffled on the printed page, obscured even more when translated.

For Christians, however, the Bible in two Testaments occupies a place different from the primary writings of other religious bodies. Simply put, for Christians that Bible is scriptural: it reveals to them a particular God, whose life elicits from theirs peculiar responsibilities within and beyond the church. Wrede was wrong: Christians should not be *required* to sacrifice either their confession or their intellect when studying those works that for them are scriptural. And while Gerhard Ebeling (1912–2001) correctly diagnosed the internal contradictions within eighteenth-century biblical theology—its ambivalence toward dogmatics and its predisposition to identify the Bible's internal *Mitte*[34]—I am suggesting responses, if not solutions, to both intellectual contretemps.

> *That seems to lead us to thesis #2: "Scriptural theology" interprets the Christian Bible as Scripture. That is to say, the endeavor acknowledges the sacramental character of the church's charter documents. As with baptism and the Eucharist, Scripture is a homely place where God has promised to meet us, to reveal himself to us, and to sanctify us.*

Concordant with orthodox doctrines related to the incarnation, it is important to recognize both the truly human and truly divine character of Scripture. Water may be subjected to spectroscopic analysis. Bread may be broken down into its chemical elements. Biblical literature may be considered historico-critically. Routine gatherings of religious adherents may themselves be studied socio-scientifically. Provided that the mode of investigation suits the analytical aim, each of these has its proper place. None of them, however, is adequate as a *theological*

---

34. Gerhard Ebeling, *Wort und Glaube* (Tübingen: Mohr Siebeck, 1960); translated by James W. Leitch as *Word and Faith* (London: SCM, 1963).

account of what happens when the worshipping church receives the gifts of Sacrament and of Word. The Triune God, self-communicated to us as Father–Son–Holy Spirit, has pledged regularly to meet and to support the church in special ways through divinely selected, ordinary media: water, bread, wine, texts.

And what of sanctification?
Through God's freely chosen means, humanity matures in its knowledge, reverence, and love of God above all things, to the end that God may better adapt the church to participate in his consummate redemption of the world through Jesus Christ.

Thesis #3: The practice of "scriptural theology" assumes the same subliminal, proto-Trinitarian pattern that sets the agenda for articulation and continued development of all dimensions of the church's life, trust, and practice.

Why stipulate this?
If not then other, less orthodox assumptions will quickly barge in to occupy its place.

Orthodox twenty-first-century Christians stand in the same position as those in the first: for them it is no longer possible to identify Israel's God without reference to Jesus, any more than they can identify Jesus without reference to Israel's God. The theological explanation of that epistemic reality is that the one Spirit through whom God the Father relates to God the Son, and vice-versa, is the same Spirit through whom the Father relates through the Son to the Body of Christ, the church—and the selfsame Spirit through whom the church relates through the Son to the Father. That Trinitarian hermeneutic integrates, silently or expressly, every practice of the church—including scriptural interpretation—that actualizes humanity's created destiny to live in full communion with the God whose will is love.[35]

Do you really intend to foist Nicaea and Chalcedon onto the Book of Psalms?
No, if by your question-begging "foist" you're implying an *equalization* of claims in the Psalms with the resolutions of patristic Trinitarian debate.[36]

---

35. I explore such a Trinitarian hermeneutic in "Trinity and Exegesis," in *Reading Scripture with the Saints*, CB (Eugene, OR: Wipf & Stock, 2014), chapter 1.

36. A temptation to which Craig A. Carter succumbs in *Interpreting Scripture with the Great Tradition: Recovering the Genius of Premodern Exegesis* (Grand Rapids: Baker

I suggest only several simple things. First: without the Psalms a good deal of the NT's theology and its subsequent credal formulations could never have been articulated. In this respect Robert Jenson is surely right: "The Hebrew Scriptures [are] the Root of Trinitarianism."[37] Thus there is consanguinity between the hermeneutic here suggested and the texts being interpreted—a deeper affinity than the Bible's mere historical character, assumed by historical criticism. Second: The Psalms may—for Christians, should—be read *in the light of* God-inspired, scripturally consonant, ecclesially recognized traditional distillates. It happens all the time: every Sunday in most churches and, in a materially different though formally similar way, every Saturday in most synagogues. Within the church catholic it has been so from the start, as David Yeago has persuasively demonstrated.[38] All I ask is that we be clear and honest about what most of the church's teachers and preachers are already and quite properly doing; to do it more acutely, more joyfully, and without embarrassment; and to honor it with privilege over the ephemeral prestige of nonecclesial biblical scholarship and its covert worship of what John Webster (1955–2016) perceptively nails as "the sublimity of reason."[39] To paraphrase Oscar Wilde on Henry James's fiction: Some exegetes produce commentaries as if it were a painful duty.

You sound like a true child of Schlatter.
At heart I am, though ironically closer to Wrede at the point of many *strictly historical* judgments.[40] But Schlatter got one very important thing right: biblical scholars whose vocation entails service within the church cannot be mandated to divest themselves of "the truth of the gospel" for the sake of a specious historical neutrality. That, truly, would amount to "the rending of

---

Academic, 2018). See my assessment of Carter's project in *RBL* (July 22, 2022), https://www.sblcentral.org/API/Reviews/1000331_72132.pdf.

37. Robert W. Jenson, "Second Locus: The Triune God," in *Christian Dogmatics*, ed. Carl E. Braaten and Robert W. Jenson (Philadelphia: Fortress, 1984), 102–5.

38. David S. Yeago, "The New Testament and the Nicene Dogma: A Contribution to the Recovery of Theological Exegesis," *ProEcc* 3 (1994): 152–64.

39. John Webster, *Holy Scripture: A Dogmatic Sketch*, CIT (Cambridge: Cambridge University Press, 2003), 104.

40. William Wrede, *Das Messiasgeheimnis in den Evangelien* (Göttingen: Vandenhoeck & Ruprecht, 1901), translated by J. C. G. Greig as *The Messianic Secret*, LTT (London: James Clarke, 1971). Although Wrede was mistaken to reduce all divine mystery in the Gospels to a narrow "Messianic secret," subsequent redaction criticism has proved correct his more fundamental historical assessment of the theological proclivities of the evangelists.

the act of thinking from the act of living."⁴¹ That's what Bultmann learned from Schlatter, even if much of his own career as NT exegete toed Wrede's *religionsgeschichtlich* line.

Beyond its severance from the OT, the problem with Bultmann's *Theology* is that, in an attempt to render the New Testament accessible to modern thinking, it was beguiled, at points distorted, by Heidegger's existentialism,⁴² which was canonical nowhere except within a few square miles of Marburg.

What philosophical orientation would you substitute in its place?
None, as such. That was David Friedrich Strauss's solution,⁴³ and it won't wash. Mind you: every Christian era has been carried by philosophical winds in its day, whether Stoicism (the NT period), Neoplatonism (Augustine and Maximus Confessor), Aristotelianism (Aquinas and Luther), and today's modernist and postmodernist options. That is an aspect of the Christian interpreter's own historical contingency. Some current philosophical options (those, say, of Gadamer and Ricoeur) seem to me more compatible with the church's gospel than others (Rorty, and in his more rambunctious moments Derrida⁴⁴). But philosophy, like history and even like theology, is finally *ancilla* of the gospel, not a substitute for it (1 Cor 2:1–16). For Strauss orthodoxy was an overbearing monster to be fled, or slain. Perhaps for some, in that context, it had become such. In our very different day Trinitarian dogma may be pure oxygen for a suffocating church. To state the issue contrariwise: if classical resources of Trinitarian and incarnational faith no longer hold epistemic purchase in a world riddled with dangerously misplaced trusts and murderous self-deception, then Christian theologians might as well pack it in and drop what they must concede as a charade.⁴⁵

---

41. Bultmann, *Theology of the New Testament*, 2:246–51.
42. Martin Heidegger, *Sein und Zeit* (Halle: Niemeyer, 1927).
43. David Friedrich Strauss, *Das Leben Jesu*, 2 vols. (Tübingen: Osiander, 1838–39).
44. Hans-Georg Gadamer, *Wahrheit und Methode: Grundzüge einer philosophischen Hermeneutik* (Tübingen: Mohr, 1960), translated by Joel Weinsheimer and Donald G. Marshall as *Truth and Method* (New York: Crossroad, 1989); Paul Ricouer, *Interpretation Theory: Discourse and the Surplus of Meaning* (Fort Worth: Texas Christian University Press, 1976); Richard Rorty, *Objectivity, Relativism, and Truth* (Cambridge: Cambridge University Press, 1991); Jacques Derrida, *De la grammatologie* (Paris: Les Éditions de Minuit, 1967).
45. For a scrupulous examination of the epistemological purchase of Trinitarian thought, consult Bruce D. Marshall, *Trinity and Truth*, CSCD (Cambridge: Cambridge University Press, 2000).

Thesis #4: "Scriptural theology" is not a method. More accurately, it is a penitent, self-critical Christian attitude or approach to biblical exegesis. It is, specifically, a theological context within which interpretation occurs, potentially embracing a variety of methods that collectively endeavor to describe and to assess the Bible's intracanonical interpretations of God's relationship to humanity and the world, especially as that engagement is revealed in Jesus Christ.

Would you care to make all that even more opaque?
Look. I'm no partisan of a particular method or cluster of methods. I've been eclectic, or baffled, all my life. Choose the simplest exegetical tool that, in your judgment, is most responsive to the questions raised by the text in front of you. Only remember that, if you operate as a scriptural theologian, your ultimate responsibility is to reveal Scripture's express or tacit gospel for the church's edification—which is not the same as sanctioning everything the church may say and do.

Say more.
Lenny Bruce (1925–66): "Everyday people are straying away from the church and going back to God."[46]

Say still more, less epigrammatically.
Like sacramental theology, scriptural theology stands in dialectical tension with the real-world worshipping community with whom it is perpetually conversant. When that community—*in sich realiserende Auslösung*—strays from the gospel or rejects its gift and its demand from a God who inspires love and requires obedience, then scriptural theology's task is to call the church to account. Whether it is a church or a bridge being constructed, the engineer and crew have to assess stress factors and discard substandard materials. That is why scriptural interpretation within the church should renounce sin, the devil and all his works, even as do baptisands and communicants.[47] This, moreover, is why scriptural theology must never be neoplatonically reified in isolation

---

46. Precise source unknown. Quoted by Robert Byrne in *The 2,548 Best Things Anybody Ever Said* (New York: Simon & Schuster, 2003), no. 643.

47. "Baptisands": those baptized. "Communicants": those who celebrate Holy Communion, or the Lord's Supper.

from true-to-life injustices to creation's welfare, human being, morality and intellect. If Almighty God deemed it fitting to dwell fully within history in all its social and historical contingencies for the benefit of their redemption, then our interpretive practices can do no less. Thus, we return to the proper role of historical study within biblical and all theological scholarship: to quote Rowan Williams, "[Christian language] grows out of a particular set of communal and individual histories, and its images and idioms are fundamentally shaped by this fact."[48]

What do you mean by "the Bible's intracanonical interpretations"?
Here I use the adjective "canonical" in its customary sense, referring to that literature held by the church as regulative. The compound "intra–" acknowledges the reality that Christian Scripture comprises a choir of voices, harmonious and discordant, in ongoing conversation not just with the church but also among one another. The same conditions obtain within Scripture as within the church, Christ's many-membered body, as with the Triune God: Being is always relational, because relationship is eternally rooted in God's being. Accordingly, scriptural theology regards the Bible's polyphony as a gift to be celebrated and a mystery to confound,[49] not a mess to be pureed.

But how does the church, or the scriptural theologian in the church's service, arbitrate those disparate voices in cases where a practical decision must be reached?
A small but necessary clarification: the scriptural theologian's service is first to God's gospel, which has called the church into being but is never a substitute for it.

Another caveat: Not every disagreement within Scripture is of equal weight, all touching on God's salvation. Premodern interpreters were clearer about that than we often give them credit. St. Thomas: "Nothing is contained under the spiritual sense that is necessary for faith that Scripture does not hand down *openly elsewhere* through the literal sense" (*Summa theologiae* 1a.1.10). The emphasis is mine, because, when used with brilliance, adverbs are important.

Pace Luther and other worthies, by now we should know there's no center within Scripture itself. As Frances Young observes, "Scripture does not offer

---

48. Rowan Williams, "The Discipline of Scripture," in Williams, *On Christian Theology*, CCT (Oxford: Blackwell, 2000), 49.
49. Andrew Louth, *Discerning the Mystery: An Essay on the Nature of Theology* (Oxford: Clarendon, 1983).

its own key to its own interpretation."⁵⁰ If there be a point of concentration, invariably the interpreter brings it to the Bible: the Lutheran "canon within the canon," Eichrodt's "covenant," Bultmann's anthropocentrism, Cullmann's Heilsgeschichte.⁵¹

So which of these is correct?
While each throws some light, none is satisfying; nor is it for a single interpreter to decide *die Mitte*.

Who decides? And by what criteria?
That's what thesis #5 aims to address.

> *Thesis #5: In practical cases of theological dispute within Scripture, the supreme court of interpretive appeal is the* regula fidei *of the church catholic.*

The "rule of faith"—a traditional distillate of Scripture itself, comprising the pith of classical creeds and their sacramental implications—has survived for two millennia and may be the only thing that yet holds together a fractious Christianity. It is the property of neither Christian fundamentalism nor liberalism, those intellectual twins separated at birth. It belongs to no sect or denomination, no individual or party. The canon of faith is a birthright bequeathed to all Christians at their baptism, the fortification of all in the Eucharist. In the face of real doctrinal differences, the rule of faith may be the only comprehensive, delimiting ecclesial consensus on what constitutes the church's true self.⁵²

What constitutes "the rule of faith"?
We might put that question to our ecclesially minded readers, if they're still awake. For now, taking our lead from Irenaeus: The truth of God's gospel, the divine economy revealed and given to the church by God, is that God eternally operates through "two hands," the Son and the Spirit, to relate himself to the

---

50. Frances Young, *The Art of Performance: Towards a Theology of Holy Scripture* (London: Darton, Longman & Todd, 1990), 61.

51. Walter Eichrodt, *Theologie des Alten Testaments*, 3 vols. (Berlin: Evangelische Verlagsanstalt, 1948), translated by J. A. Baker as *Theology of the Old Testament*, 2 vols. (Philadelphia: Westminster, 1961, 1967); Oscar Cullmann, *Heil als Geschichte: heilsgeschichtliche Existenz im Neuen Testament* (Tübingen: Mohr, 1965), translated by Sidney G. Sowers as *Salvation in History* (Philadelphia: Westminster, 1967).

52. Cf. Ebeling, *Word and Faith*, 162–90.

church for the saving redemption of the world (*Haer.* 4.20.1). Please note the consistency: the church's hermeneutical *regula fidei*, like Scripture itself, bears a proto-Trinitarian structure.

Here I detect little sympathy for the Renaissance ideal of an individual genius standing against tradition, lately reclaimed in some postmodern projects.
You're right. The only "genius"—the Enlightenment's shallow term, not mine—who was and remains in position to assail human tradition, religious and otherwise, is Jesus Christ (Mark 7:1–23). If Christ is none other than what the church's creed professes, then in him inheres, to say the least, considerable advantage over the rest of us. Yet the performance of scriptural theology *via regula fidei* does not—Hey, Presto!—banish all historical ambiguities. If anything, it is more likely to reveal faithful interpreters' vulnerability and the gospel's tensile strength.

> *Thesis #6: The genuine aim of scriptural theology—in line with the patristic and monastic tradition, and more recently with such interpreters as Barth and Bonhoeffer—is to assist the church in perceiving and then activating, at the Spirit's behest and with more faithful acuity, God's self-presentation in Scripture through the indispensable lens of the gospel of Christ.*

Here what I'm driving at—rather, find myself being driven to—is akin to what Barth and especially Dietrich Bonhoeffer (1906–45) described as *Vergegenwärtigung*: the gospel's "making itself present" in, before, and in confrontation of what a yet unredeemed world regards as truth.[53] Unlike Barth I am amused but unperturbed by the "almost indefinable odour," as he wrote Bonhoeffer, "of a monastic ethos and pathos . . . [that] disturbs me."[54] To sharpen a point with which I think Bonhoeffer would have agreed: this *Vergegenwärtigung* happens in the OT as well as the NT, because the Triune God underwrites all of Scripture, which the attentive church takes as its doctrinal reference point. In line with the church's *regula fidei*, I disavow, beside Bonhoeffer, the benighted attempt of a would-be autonomous interpreter who, by dint of self-

---

53. Dietrich Bonhoeffer, "Vergegenwärtigung neutestamentlicher Texte" (1935), in Bonhoeffer, *Gesammelte Schriften*, vol. 3: *Theologie–Gemeinde: Vorlesungen, Briefe, Gespräche*, ed. Eberhard Bethge (Munich: Kaiser, 1960), 303–24.

54. Letter of Barth to Bonhoeffer (Bergli, Oberrieden, October 14, 1936) in *The Way to Freedom: Letters, Lectures and Notes 1935–1939 from the Collected Works of Dietrich Bonhoeffer*, vol. 2; ed. and trans. Edwin H. Robertson and John Bowden; London: Collins, 1966), 121.

delusion, would judge Scripture before the tribunal of modernity's reason or postmodernity's solipsism. "That 'making present' of the Christian message, leads directly into paganism."[55] I part with Bonhoeffer at a few points. "Wherever Christ comes to speech in the word of the New Testament," he asserts, "there is 'making present.'"[56] I would prefer to say that genuine *Vergegenwärtigung* occurs when the Triune God expresses himself to the receptive church in word and in sacrament. Whereas Bonhoeffer claims, "God is with us today only as long as we are there, . . . taken back to the holy history of God on earth,"[57] I would rather say that God is *always* with us, whether or not we are there with God. The self-actualization of God's own presence does not depend on our being attentive to God. Through Spirit, sacrament, and word, God has promised never to abandon the church to its own pitiful resources. It is the church that too routinely absents itself from God.

Your counterpoint—"what a yet unredeemed world regards as truth"— sounds like a straw man.
I quote a senior adviser to President Bush, twenty months after the US invasion of Iraq (2003–11):

> [Our critics live] in what we [in the White House] call the reality-based community, . . . those who believe that solutions emerge from your judicious study of discernible reality. That's not the way the world works anymore. We're an empire now, and when we act, we create our own reality. And while you're studying that reality—judiciously, as you will—we'll act again, creating other new realities, which you can study too, and that's how things will sort out. We're history's actors . . . and you, all of you, will be left to just study what we do.[58]

---

55. Bonhoeffer, "Vergegenwärtigung neutestamentlicher Texte," 305 ("Diese Vergegenwärtigung der christlichen Botschaft führt direct ins Heidentum").

56. Bonhoeffer, "Vergegenwärtigung neutestamentlicher Texte," 307 ("Wo Christus im Wort des Neuen Testaments zu Worte kommt, dort ist Vergegenwärtigung").

57. Dietrich Bonhoeffer, *Life Together*, DBW 5, ed. Gerhard Ludwig Müller, Albrecht Schönherr, and Geffrey B. Kelly; trans. Daniel W. Bloesch (Minneapolis: Fortress, 1996), 62. In fairness to Bonhoeffer, we should note that the context of this and kindred claims is often in refutation of the claim that God supported *Nationalsozialism* (see, e.g., "Vergegenwärtigung neutestamentlicher Texte," 313).

58. Ron Suskind, "Without a Doubt: Faith, Certainty, and the Presidency of George W. Bush," *New York Times Magazine* (October 17, 2004): 42–51, 64, 102, 106; quotation, 51.

No. "The earth is *the Lord's* and the fullness thereof" (Ps 24:1). Only a messianic American Calvinist and his equally self-deluded retinue would claim "creation of our own reality" and a laissez-faire imperialism to force it upon the rest of the world. The ones left to study what they have done may be grateful only that they are not among those of all nations who lost their lives to an illusion so bloody.

Thus spake the prophet Adlai Stevenson: "Your public servants serve you right."[59] *Might we test your theses? What might a "scripturally theological" interpretation of John 8:31–59 look like?*
Thanks for the slow-pitched softball.

This text epitomizes what is true for all Scripture: on it we must patiently ruminate. We dare not nibble and spit it out, any more than we receive the Lord's Supper at a salad bar. Scriptural theology depends on an attitude toward exegesis that proceeds from and returns to prayer, expressed in the classical tradition of *lectio divina*.[60]

Second: John 8:31–59 points up in the sharpest possible way what is at stake in scriptural theology as presented here: either Scripture such as John 8 is little more than an embarrassment and travesty for contemporary sensibilities, or it is truly God's salvation *extra nos*, "from outside ourselves." The effective proof of the latter is that not a single author for Eerdmans would have the gall to present her peers a statement as polemical as what we find here—nor, in all likelihood, would her editors allow it.

Third: the Jesus we encounter in John's Gospel is the Christ of the holy catholic church's confession: the one and only Son who was with God from the beginning (1:1–3), who comes down from above (3:31; 8:23), reveals the Father who sent him (14:8–11), saves those born from above who believe in him (3:1–17), sends the *paraklētos*—the Spirit who is one with the Father and the Son (16:12–25)—to counsel those who trust in him (14:14–17, 25–31) and to confront those who don't (16:7–11; cf. 3:18–21). Johannine theology authorizes the great church's ecumenical confession. While John does not articulate the Nicene-Chalcedonian Creed, the deep structure of the Fourth Gospel's theology is proto-Trinitarian. The same could arguably be said of 1 Corinthians 8:6, Philippians 2:5–11, and Colossians 1:15–20—which, in turn, appear to be quasi-

---

59. IMDB, *The Mike Wallace Interview*, season 1, episode 57, Adlai Stevenson, aired June 1, 1958. See https://www.imdb.com/title/tt2123762/.

60. Mariano Magrassi, *Bibbia e preghiera: La* lectio divina (Milan: Editrice Àngora, 1990), translated by Edward Hagman as *Praying the Bible: An Introduction to* Lectio Divina (Collegeville, MN: Liturgical, 1998). See also chapter 4 of the present volume.

credal and hymnic expressions of early Christian rumination on such texts as Deuteronomy 4:35–39; 6:4; Malachi 2:10; and Isaiah 45:21–24.

Fourth: by Jesus's own testimony, "Salvation is of the Jews" (John 4:22). The interpreter who fully recognizes herself as "Abraham's offspring, [an heir] according to [the] promise" embedded in the gospel's divine economy (cf. Gal 3:29)—an interpreter, in short, who embraces the merciful gift of inclusion among God's people Israel (cf. Eph 2:11–22; 1 Pet 2:9–10)—will recognize in John 8 "the Jews" not as an Other to be tormented but *her own race*, in the Spirit if not in the flesh. Within John 8 are authentic children of Abraham (vv. 39b–40), "the Jews who have believed in" Jesus (v. 31), as well as Jews in whom his word finds no place (v. 37), who think Jesus a bastard (v. 41) and mean to kill him (vv. 37, 40). That division within Israel is akin to congregants at Nazareth who aim to murder Jesus when he reminds them of Scripture that offends their sensibilities (Luke 4:23–30). Jerusalem has always done away with its prophets (Matt 23:29–39; cf. 2 Chr 24:20–22). The historical fact that John 8 has been suborned to justify Christian persecution of Jews—siblings' murder of siblings—is *an indictment of such Christians' own parentage*. By their murder they have proved *themselves* to be children of the devil: a murderer and liar through and through (John 8:44). To paraphrase Walt Kelly's Pogo Possum: We have met the Jews, and they is us.[61] And if that seems to some an exegetical sleight of hand, then they might reread 1 John 3:11–18, which reasons similarly about hateful, murderous fraud *within the church*.

How does this interpretation of John 8 differ from that of conventional historical criticism?

Naturally there are intersections, even as premodern exegetes insisted on intersections of readings literal and spiritual. Reasonably sound historical imagination like Lou Martyn's[62] has helped us clarify things we might easily have forgotten, such as Christianity's origin in Judaism and, before those ways parted, the gospel's promise of "a fall and rising for many in Israel" (Luke 2:34). Give Stevie Smith (1902–71) full marks for candor: "If I had been the Virgin Mary, I would have said 'No.'"

Still, many historical critics, apart from Martyn's intention, have by now so deep-frozen the Fourth Gospel in its alleged original setting—a hostile

---

61. Walt Kelly (1913–73), *Pogo: We Have Met the Enemy and He Is Us* (New York: Simon & Schuster, 1972).

62. Martyn, *History and Theology in the Fourth Gospel*, 3rd ed., NTL (Louisville: Westminster John Knox, 2003).

controversy between Jewish Christianity and proto-rabbinic Judaism—that thawing the text for the church's preaching and teaching has proved extraordinarily difficult. Exhibit A is the Revised Common Lectionary (1992), which expurgates everything in John 5, 7–8, save twelve verses (5:1–9, 7:37–39, both designated as "alternative texts"). However well-intentioned, such bowdlerized Bible—protecting Christians from their own Scripture—always misguides, leaving the church a patsy for its own darkest temptations to hubris, triumphalism, and all other "sinful desires of the flesh." Disregard of John 8:31–59 is a case in point—all the more dangerous when consensus results of historical criticism are claimed to sanction that dismissal.

Here is the matter's nub and crux: neither history nor philosophy nor critical theory can suffice to illumine the gospel, released by the Spirit in the church and for the world. As in every generation we must learn afresh the roundelay: to read Scripture theologically and to reason theologically out of Scripture. We listen to the tenor of each scriptural voice, in harmony or discord with its fellow choristers; we locate their tones in the symphony of Christian tradition; we strike the chords evoked by a new audience.

My, all these words you've spent. Reading them is like staring at a cow for an hour.
My readers join with me in thanks for your questions, while waiting for the first shoe to drop.

I'm sure they'll agree this paper fills a much-needed gap.
Every professional exegete has a theological essay in him. That's the best place for it.

CURTAIN

CHAPTER 3

Remembering Otto Piper

> Remember the days of old, consider the years of many generations; ask your father, and he will show you; your elders, and they will tell you.
>
> —Deuteronomy 32:7 (ESV)

A CLAIM TO REMEMBER MY PROFESSORIAL chair's namesake will seem risible, perhaps the height of presumption, to many readers. In the year that Otto Piper retired from the Princeton Seminary faculty, I was matriculating for the second grade in Thomasville, North Carolina. With respect to Piper, presumption is the last sin I would wittingly commit. But remember I must, as must we all. In institutions of higher learning, "the creation of new knowledge" has become commonplace in characterizing their raison d'être. In that there is truth. It is not, however, the whole truth. In the academy, as in the church, a pervasive amnesia must be combated, for which a vital memory is indispensable. It is quite impossible for the people of God to know where they are going, and why, if they cannot recall where they have been both in carriage and miscarriage. Re-member-ing—deliberately reconstituting the members of Christ's body, both the living and the dead—is a sacred obligation, incumbent on all who enjoy the privilege of refreshment at Princeton during their wilderness wanderings. For those who knew him, even more for those who could never have had that privilege, let us now praise Otto Alfred Wilhelm Piper (1891–1982).[1]

---

1. Earlier drafts of this article were read with critical care by Dean of Academic Affairs emeritus James F. Armstrong,† President emeritus Thomas W. Gillespie,† the Reverend Dr. James A. Glasscock,† and Professor Daniel L. Migliore. Their assistance was invaluable. I am also indebted to Messrs. Robert Benedetto, William O. Harris† (emeritus), and Kenneth Henke (emeritus), all of the Seminary Library's Department of Special Collections.

Professor Otto A. Piper in his study at 58 Mercer Street, Princeton, New Jersey. Photograph by Ann Meuer; digitized by Brian Shetler; courtesy of the Seminary's Theodore S. Wright Library's Special Collections

The Personal Piper

Otto Piper (pronounced "peeper") was born on November 29, 1891 in Lichte, Germany, to a middle-class family. His maternal grandfather was a staunch, confessional Lutheran; some of his ancestors were French Huguenots who fled across the Rhine after repeal of the Edict of Nantes (1598). His theological education began in Erfurt's *Gymnasium*, where he studied church history, read in Latin the Augsburg Confession, and translated NT books in Greek. Typical of German students of his day, Piper's advanced theological training was undertaken as a wandering scholar, hearing lectures by the finest Protestant and Catholic scholars at the Universities of Jena, Marburg, Paris, Heidelberg, Munich, and Göttingen. At Marburg, Hans Lietzmann (1875–1942) and Walter Bauer (1866–1946) trained him in historical criticism. World War I interrupted Piper's studies at Heidelberg; he volunteered for service in the infantry, sustained a facial wound in combat, and was almost left for dead on the western front.[2] The war made of Piper a pacifist and redoubled his decision to become a theological teacher, "no longer satisfied with any interpretation of the Christian faith which could not stand the test of the terrors of battle, the heartache over the loss of relatives and dearest friends, the agony of a broken body and the self-destructive fury of warring nations."[3] The war also disabused Piper of his generation's neo-Kantian idealism. As he would later write, "The Bible unmasks both the optimistic utopias and the cynical *Realpolitik* of modern man as wishful thinking.... The belief in progress—this elusive deity of the modern age—is stigmatized as absurd by the revelation of the vanity of civilization."[4]

After receiving his doctorate in theology from Göttingen in 1920,[5] Piper served there for a decade as *Privatdozent* and professor of systematic the-

---

2. The bullet taken by young Piper, exiting the back of his head without penetrating his brain, left him with one useless eye, for which he compensated in reading by use of a magnifying glass. That lens is rendered in the portrait of Piper by Eileen Mary Fabian, which used to hang in classroom #2 of Stuart Hall, on the Princeton Seminary campus. The irreparable injury to his facial muscles made smiling difficult for him. That is a primary reason for so many somber photographs of Piper as an adult.

3. See F. W. Graf, "Lutherischer Neurealismus: Otto Piper, ein früher Pazifist," *LM* 8 (1988): 357–61. Piper insisted that pacifism is no posture of weakness. God calls us to peace, a vocation demanding courage that only the Holy Spirit can provide. Otto A. Piper, "What the Bible Means to Me: Discovering the Bible," *ChrCent* 63 (February 27, 1946): 267.

4. Piper, "What the Bible Means to Me: The Theme of the Bible," *ChrCent* 63 (March 13, 1946): 334–35.

5. His dissertation was published as *Das religiöse Erlebnis: Eine kritische Analyse der Schleiermacherschen Reden über die Religion* (Göttingen: Vandenhoeck & Ruprecht, 1920).

ology, during the same unstable era of the Weimar Republic in which Rudolf Bultmann (1884–1976) and Paul Tillich (1886–1965) began their careers at Marburg. By one account,[6] it was Piper who, having read a commentary on Romans by a young Swiss pastor, recommended Karl Barth (1886–1968) for his first academic post at Göttingen in 1921. In 1930 Piper succeeded his friend Barth in the chair of theology at the University of Münster, beginning three years of open defiance of nascent Nazism.[7] Following imprisonment and dismissal from his chair, in 1933 Hitler expelled from Germany Piper and his wife of Jewish descent, Elizabeth Salinger (d. 1948). Years later Piper remarked, "I had some differences with Hitler and it seemed better for Germany if one of us left. As he seemed indispensable at the time. . . ."[8] The Pipers and their young children—Ruth (b. 1921), Gerhard ("Gero," b. 1922), Manfred (b. 1925)—immigrated to Great Britain, where he taught for a year at Woodbrooke College, Birmingham (1933–34), afterward at the University Colleges of Swansea (1934–36) and Bangor (1936–37). There being no resources for his salary in Wales, Piper's colleagues pooled and shared with him portions of their own earnings. Following a visiting professorship in systematic theology at Princeton Theological Seminary (1937), at the invitation of President John A. Mackay (1889–1983), in 1941 Piper was appointed there as the Helen H. P. Manson Professor of New Testament Literature and Exegesis. With his extraordinary education, he could as easily have been appointed to a post in philosophical theology, the history of Christian thought, or systematics. On October 21, 1949, Wittenberg College (Springfield, Ohio) conferred on Piper an honorary Doctor of Law degree. He held the Manson Chair until his retirement from the seminary on September 1, 1962.

During and after World War II, Piper knew firsthand inexpressible suffering, punctuated by unswerving Christian dedication. Gerhard and Manfred were drafted into the American armed forces. On Christmas Eve, 1944, Gero died by the hand of his German kinsmen at the Battle of the Bulge in Luxembourg. Meanwhile, his father conducted a relentless program in European relief, conscripting Princeton students to help him collect, inventory, package,

---

6. Gerald L. Borchert, "This Man—Otto Piper of Princeton," *The Seminarian* 12 (May 4, 1962): 3–4.
7. See W. M. Heidemann, "'. . . immer Fühlung mit allen Teilen der Kirche': Der münsterische Theologieprofessor Otto A. Piper auf dem Weg in die Emigration 1933–1938," *JWK* 80 (1987): 105–51.
8. Otto A. Piper, "The Professor Was Dispensable, So . . . ," *The Province* (Vancouver, British Columbia: July 9, 1960): 22.

and post clothing for German refugees.⁹ After the war, Piper was founder and president of the nondenominational American Emergency Committee for German Protestantism, a voluntary, unremunerated organization that sought to secure American sponsors for some five thousand German pastors. In recognition of these humanitarian efforts, in 1960 President Heinrich Lübke of the Federal Republic of Germany decorated him with the Officer's Cross of Merit, First Class: Germany's only state decoration.

Piper was naturalized an American citizen in 1942. During a sabbatical leave in Germany, he renewed a thirty-five-year-old acquaintance with another Elisabeth (Rüger), whom he married in 1950. For complicated reasons, approval of her application for an American visa was delayed for eighteen months; she could not join her husband in Princeton until 1952. In addition to his responsibilities at the seminary, Piper was a minister of the United Presbyterian Church, USA, a member of the Society of Biblical Literature, and president of the American Theological Society (1954–55). He held guest lectureships in Edinburgh (1935), Heidelberg (1950), Campinas (1957), and Montpelier (1958). Closer to home he delivered, among others, the Stone Lectures at Princeton (1938), the Smyth Lectures at Columbia Seminary in Decatur (1949), and the Sprunts at Union Theological Seminary in Richmond (1959). Piper died in Princeton, New Jersey, February 13, 1982, not far from the retirement home he and Elisabeth had built at 26 White Pine Lane, in Princeton Township.

THE PUBLISHED PIPER

Piper published twenty-four books and hundreds of essays and articles in German, French, Dutch, Spanish, Slovak, and English, for an audience comprising scholars, clergy, and laity. Reflecting his broad background, his published interests were grounded in biblical studies while ranging into contemporary theological trends, Joan of Arc, Dostoyevsky, spirituality and mysticism, patristics and Gnosticism, ecumenical and political theology.¹⁰

---

9. "We students were asked to help him sort and inventory every box. For years we spent many hours around the large Piper dining room table helping him. When the boxes were packed and sealed with a slip listing the contents, he would load them into his old black Dodge sedan and drive off to the post office to mail them. This went on until the mid 1950s" (Daniel J. Theron, "Remembering Professor Otto Piper," *inSpire* 6 [Summer/Fall, 2001]): 41.

10. Among his many contributions in the area, see Otto A. Piper, *Recent Developments in German Protestantism* (London: SCM, 1934); idem, "The Interpretation of History in Continental Theology," *USQR* 50 (1939): 211–24, 306–21; Piper, "The Church in Soviet Germany,"

Still, much of Piper's scholarship was concentrated in two areas. The first, manifested in such books as *Weltliches Christentum* (*Worldly Christianity*), *Gottes Wahrheit und die Wahrheit der Kirche* (*God's Truth and the Church's Truth*), and *God in History*[11] is the theme of God's action in human history. For Piper, following J. C. K. von Hoffmann (1810–77), the biblical narrative of Heilsgeschichte ("holy history," as he preferred to translate) and all subsequent history influenced by it constitute evidence of God's activity in history, the theater "in which the Holy Spirit of God takes a direct part."[12] Christian hope is founded in God's providential control of history, asserted most clearly in the incarnation and resurrection of Jesus Christ. Christ's ministry, both earthly and glorious, "carries absolute finality . . . and is the decisive event in the whole development of the [human] race."[13] Because sinful humanity is forbidden the privilege of bringing about history's God-intended end, the idea of progress and the attempt to realize even Christian ideals in the social realm apart from the divine Spirit's power are as misguided and evil as they are naive. That, however, sanctions neither fatalism nor quietism, for Christians share the goal of their risen Lord, owe their faith to a divine impetus, and by that faith are "enabled to draw constantly on the energies of a new life that flow from the Resurrected One."[14] "Church and fight against Satan are correlative terms";[15] under the Spirit's aegis, "[Christianity's] choices are tantamount to

---

ChrCent 67 (1950): 1386–88; Piper, "Jeanne d'Arc: Wes Geistes Kind war sie?," *HK* (July 3, 1929, Morgen Ausgabe). Piper, "Der 'Großinquisitor' von Dostojweski," *Die Furche* 17 (1931): 249–73; Piper, "Meister Eckharts Wirklichkeitslehre," *Theologische Blätter* 15 (December, 1936): 294–308; "Praise of God and Thanksgiving: The Biblical Doctrine of Prayer," *Int* 8 (1954b): 3–20; repr. (with Floyd V. Filson) as *The Biblical Doctrine of Prayer* (Atlanta: Presbyterian Church of the United States, c. 1954); Piper, "The Apocalypse of John and the Liturgy of the Ancient Church," *CH* 2 (1951): 10–22; Piper, "The Gospel of Thomas," *PSB* 53 (1959): 18–24. See his contribution to *Die Kirche und das dritte Reich: Fragen und Förderungen Deutscher Theologen*, ed. Leopold Klotz (Gotha: Klotz, 1932), 90–95; Piper, *Protestantism in an Ecumenical Age: Its Root, Its Right, Its Task* (Philadelphia: Fortress, 1965).

11. Otto A. Piper, *Weltliches Christentum: Eine Untersuchung über Wesen und Bedeutung der außerkirchlichen Frömmigkeit der Gegenwart* (Tübingen: Mohr [Siebeck], 1924); Piper, *Gottes Wahrheit und die Wahrheit der Kirche* (Tübingen: Mohr [Siebeck], 1933); Piper, *God in History* (New York: Macmillan, 1939).

12. Piper, *God in History*, 67; see also Otto A. Piper, "Á Interpretacão Cristã da Historia," *Revista* 9 (1954): 17–32, 265–81; *Revista* 10 (1955): 23–36; *Revista* 11 (1955): 23–45; *Revista* 12 (1956): 27–47, 313–40.

13. Piper, "Christian Hope and History," *EvQ* 26 (1954): 158.

14. Piper, "Christian Hope and History," 159.

15. Piper, "Christian Hope and History," 161.

divine verdicts,"[16] and "every realization of our hope can be regarded only as a step towards the ultimate goal, which is the full triumph of Christ."[17] Albeit veiled, "everything in history serves God's glory."[18]

The Bible "is the record of God's dealings with mankind in holy history"; "each of its words is spoken to us personally: it is the offer of salvation to us (*pro nobis*), and thus it is adequately apprehended only when the exegete recognizes the bearing a passage has upon his own life and predicament and that of the group in which he is living."[19] Thus, Piper's *heilsgeschichtlich* emphasis was inseparable from a second preoccupation, Christian ethics, in such works as *Die Grundlagen der evangelischen Ethik* (*The Foundations of Evangelical Ethics*)[20] and *The Biblical View of Sex and Marriage*.[21] Conditioned and guided by the church as the body of the risen Lord, which still seeks God's eschatological kingdom, believers are "not anxious to bring about a new and better world." Paradoxically, however, they find themselves "used by [their] Lord as his agent through whose activity a new world comes into being," a reestablishment of "the cosmic order, in which everybody and everything receives the place for which it is destined."[22] Consistent with this view, Piper's last major synthetic work, *Christian Ethics* (1970), prescinds from inductive analysis of moral particulars, preferring instead "an intuitive apprehension of the whole subject matter," which "starts from the assurance that the Bible proclaims a unified message"—namely, holy history—"in and through the diverse views expressed therein."[23] For Piper, ethics, "the practical implications of the Christian existence," must not be allowed to devolve into casuistic prescriptions or particular problems of social reform; "there can be no true meaning except when human life is directly related to God as its ultimate determinant."[24] Likewise, "the Biblical view of sex is decisively determined by the fact that man is a sinner

---

16. Piper, "What the Bible Means to Me: The Bible as 'Holy History,'" *ChrCent* 63 (March 20, 1946): 363.

17. Piper, "Christian Hope and History," 165.

18. Piper, *God in History*, 176.

19. Piper, "Modern Problems of New Testament Exegesis," *PSB* 36 (1942): 10, 11.

20. Piper, *Die Grundlagen der evangelischen Ethik*, 2 vols. (Gütersloh: Bertelsmann, 1928, 1930).

21. Piper, *The Biblical View of Sex and Marriage* (New York: Scribner's Sons, 1960).

22. Otto A. Piper, "Kerygma and Discipleship: The Basis of New Testament Ethics," *PSB* 56 (1962): 18, 20.

23. Piper, *Christian Ethics* (London: Nelson, 1970), xi, xii.

24. Piper, *Christian Ethics*, 3, 376.

and that therefore in his sex life, as in other spheres of life, he is in need of God's forgiving love."[25]

Piper's Principles

Piper resisted ideological labels. He complained of enduring "the vitriolic attacks by fundamentalists who denounced [him] as a disguised modernist and the haughty demands of liberals who could not understand that a critical scholar should believe that the Bible is the Word of God."[26] He acknowledged the influence on his thought of Wilfred Monod (1867–1943), the French Protestant theologian who initiated him into "the 'realism' of the Bible." By biblical realism Piper meant the apprehension, by faith, of "real things," like God's Spirit and demonic forces, which transcend everyday sensory experience yet govern the universe and human life.[27] The God we meet in the Bible cannot be reduced to "the ground of being," as Tillich's ontology implies. Neither is Christian faith "subjected to the tyranny of an *a priori* anthropology à la Heidegger" that, by human means, discovers a general truth and tags it as "the Word," à la Bultmann.[28] The Bible's reality lies in its variegated yet unified testimony to God's compassionate judgment of humanity in the realm of history.[29] "The contention of all [the biblical] writers is that there is a God who through them commands all men to do *his* will, and who, being concerned with the *eternal* destiny of man, offers a way of life eternal in Jesus Christ."[30]

In his Manson inaugural address at Princeton (February 9, 1942), Piper articulated four hermeneutical axioms of special importance: the clarity of the Bible, the Bible's authority, the purpose of biblical revelation, and the Bible's intelligibility.[31] (1) By clarity, Piper referred to respect for the biblical text's literal sense and the sincerity of its writers. (2) The Bible's authority resides in its divine efficacy as a means of grace that overwhelms, convicts, comforts,

---

25. Piper, *The Christian Interpretation of Sex* (New York: Scribner's Sons, 1941), x.
26. Piper, "Discovering the Bible," 268.
27. Piper, "Principles of New Testament Interpretation," *ThTod* 3 (1946): 192–204.
28. Piper, "The Depth of God," a review of *Honest to God*, by J. A. T. Robinson (Philadelphia: Westminster, 1963), in *PSB* 57 (1963): 45; Piper, "The Authority of the Bible," *ThTod* 6 (1949): 167.
29. Piper, "Discovering the Bible," 267.
30. Piper, "What the Bible Means to Me: How I Study My Bible," *ChrCent* 63 (March 6, 1946): 300, Piper's emphases.
31. Piper, "Modern Problems," 6.

illumines, and calls forth faith in Christ, its ultimate subject matter. "It is out of his free sovereign grace that God speaks through [the Bible], and there is only one subject he wants us to understand from the bottom of our heart, namely the fact that he has come to rescue us from the bondage of sin, death, and the devil, and to make us certain of the fact that in Jesus Christ his purpose is accomplished."[32] Correlatively, (3) the purpose of biblical revelation is Christocentric, which requires insight to discern the Bible's unity amid its varied expressions: "God reveals Himself through the Bible in order to lead people to the recognition of His grace in Jesus Christ"[33] The Bible is not merely a record of God's past revelation; "it is also and above all a divine act by means of which God directly offers salvation in Jesus Christ to every reader."[34] By their intimate relationship to this divine kerygma, the Gospels of the NT occupy a central position within the canon, on which the rest of the Bible depends for its authority.[35] (4) The Bible's intelligibility depends on mediation of the Holy Spirit, which allows the interpreter to "live in real communion with those whose faith he shares," thus "to experience the same spiritual realities the writers had experienced."[36] Such "pneumatic exegesis" is restrained from subjectivism by historical criticism, which honors the dynamism and diversity of the biblical witness; by the doctrinal standards of faith in the church's life and consciousness, by which the interpreter is conditioned and to which one is accountable; and by the exegesis of Christ's whole church, by which one denomination's exegetical teaching is checked by others.[37]

For Piper, biblical interpretation consists of two different though coherent processes: exegesis and appropriation. The task of exegesis is to render the Bible both intelligible and comprehensible. Intelligibility depends on discovery of a text's "life movement" from author to reader.[38] Comprehension consists, first, in specifically locating each biblical idea within the author's comprehensive view of reality and, second, in correlating the ideas of biblical documents with those of our own mind.[39] Appropriation is the interpreter's personal response to the intrinsic challenge mounted by the document, a faith-engendered appreciation of the Bible's claim to convey a divine message of

32. Piper, "Authority of the Bible," 173.
33. Piper, "Modern Problems," 9, italicized in the original.
34. Piper, "Modern Problems," 10.
35. Piper, "Authority of the Bible," 167–73.
36. Piper, "Modern Problems," 12.
37. Piper, "Modern Problems," 13.
38. Piper, "Principles of New Testament Interpretation," 193–97.
39. Piper, "Principles of New Testament Interpretation," 197–200.

supreme and universal importance. "Modern Biblical interpretation has made relatively great progress in the field of exegesis but has often utterly failed in understanding the task of appropriation,"[40] owing to modernism's disdain of biblical supernaturalism and its tendency to remove the sting of the biblical message, lest the complacency of natural systems of thought be disturbed.[41]

Princeton's Piper

Examining only the small outcroppings of a mountain of correspondence, journal extracts, and newspaper clippings in the seminary's archive, one cannot leave them without appreciating the deep impression of Otto Piper's talent and personality on Princeton Seminary and their extensive reach during his tenure on its faculty. In four large areas, his influence was palpable.

A Teacher of Princeton's Seminarians

Compared to the expectations placed on his continental counterparts, typically insulated from workaday pedagogy for their advanced research, Professor Piper must have been jolted by his customary teaching load at Princeton. During academic year 1942–43, immediately after his installation in the Manson Chair, the seminary's catalogue listed his courses for that year:

- Gospel History (a prescribed first-year course);
- The Synoptic Gospels (a prescribed second-year course);
- Apostolic History (a prescribed third-year course);
- Biblical Theology of the New Testament (another prescribed third-year course);
- The Parables of Jesus;
- Sacraments in the New Testament;
- The Gospel of John;
- Exegesis of Paul's Epistle to the Romans;
- The New Testament Interpretation of History;
- The Making of the New Testament; and
- Methodology of New Testament Studies.

40. Piper, "Principles of New Testament Interpretation," 201.
41. Piper, "Modern Problems," 9.

The tote across two semesters: a staggering twenty-two hours of teaching.[42] Piper knew that such a load was ridiculous, as he acknowledged in a letter to his students of the classes of 1938–47. His European colleagues across the pond had far more time to get more of their own work published, to the detriment of American scholarship. Yet Piper realized the compensations:

> However, the constant contact which one has here [in the States] with the life of the church-at-large through sermons, conferences and retreats, has its real advantages. It keeps the Seminary professor from becoming purely academic and makes him aware of the fact that his primordial task is the training of future ministers.[43]

Those future ministers loved him for it. Taken virtually at random, here is a commendation posted by one Bachelor of Divinity matriculant to President Mackay:

> The course here at Seminary which has meant the most to me in terms of my personal spiritual growth and which has helped me to the greatest extent in formulating my theological views has been the course in the Exegesis of First Corinthians under Dr. Piper. In spiritual insight and understanding as well as knowledge, he is to my mind one of the most outstanding men on our faculty. It seems to me, too, that he has a message for our Church and our age—he is not only a teacher, but a prophet as well![44]

When persuaded the occasion justified, Piper did not spare seminarians a jeremiad. Everyone of that era remembers him as deeply pious person, who regularly attended worship in Miller Chapel. Thus it was with humility—"Worship services should not be used as an opportunity to analyze those who officiate"—yet credibility that Professor Piper once took the seminary's students to task for "an excessive emphasis placed upon the confession of sins":

---

42. Anonymous, "Otto Alfred Piper 1891–1982," *PSB* n.s. 4 (1983): 52–55.
43. Letter by Piper, February 10, 1948, 1. I am deeply indebted to the Rev. Mr. Norman A. Robinson, pastor emeritus of Wyalusing Presbyterian Church, Pennsylvania, for making available to me his original copy of this letter. It now is housed in the seminary's archives. All other letters, as well as unpublished manuscripts, that are cited in this chapter are housed in this repository.
44. To John A. Mackay, April 21, 1940.

Firstly, in mourning [our] faults, are we really aware of our sins? . . . Or may it be that as we bring the defects of our seminary life to the attention of those present in chapel, we actually want to make the chapel service a sounding board for our complaints about seminary life. Finding fault with fellow students we pose as the lonely advocates of a long overdue reform. . . . Do we actually worry about our hypocrisy which makes us think we do the right thing merely because we have strict moral standards? . . . Perhaps even more serious than this, however, is the fact that with our egotistic concern for our personal problems and other people's shortcomings we fail to make God the center of our worship. We neglect the element of adoration and thanksgiving that alone makes Christians to worship God in truth. It is only when we remember what great love and compassion Christ has shown for us and how wonderfully God has put at our disposal both the resources and the opportunities for his service that we are able to realize the gravity of our sin. We are bound to overrate ourselves as long as we fail to use what God offers us. It is only when with a grateful heart we put our trust in God's gracious gifts rather than in our own will for goodness that we learn to move in the right direction in our daily life.[45]

An Ambassador of "Theological Pedagogics"

From his earliest years in his new homeland, Piper's impact on the education of laity and clergy, adults and youth, was instantly recognizable and honored. Some of these unsolicited testimonials were directed to President Mackay; others landed on the desk of George Irving, then General Director of the Department of Faith and Life for the Board of Christian Education of The Presbyterian Church, USA. For instance, one pastoral participant in Piper's off-campus seminars wrote this to Mr. Irving:

> One feels that Dr. Piper's thinking has been clarified and chastened by experience. He does not appear to hold opinions so much as to be held by convictions. Therefore he is especially fitted to lead us through many of our modern superficialities back to the underlying fundamentals, in rediscovering which many of us see the hope of a revived church.[46]

---

45. Otto A. Piper, "Piper Discusses Need for Thanksgiving in Worship," *The Seminarian* 11 (April 14, 1961): 3.

46. To George Irving, June 16, 1938.

Yet another acclamation was mailed to Mr. Irving, prior to the Trustees' appointment of Piper to the seminary's regular faculty:

> Every one of us who has had the splendid opportunity to be schooled at Princeton should make it his concern to bring men of consecration, suffering and intellect to Princeton like Dr. Piper. The only regret I have is that I cannot go back and sit at Dr. Piper's feet for three years instead of for three lectures. Let us move heaven and earth to keep him there, for under his teaching many of our future leaders in the Presbyterian Church will be enabled to move earth a little closer to heaven.[47]

One of Piper's many published articles in *Theology Today*—"That Strange Thing Money"—was reprinted in stewardship booklets across the country and subsequently expanded into a book.[48] This was an apt product from the pen of one whose life incarnated responsibility for the neighbor.

A Prime Mover in a Graduate Program for the Training of Doctoral Students

At the inception of Princeton's doctoral program, Piper was a guiding force in its creation, deliberately modeled on the then more rigorous pattern of a European ThD. This dimension of Piper's contribution was multifarious. On the one hand, he was a programmatic architect. As early as 1944—the year in which the first Princeton Seminary doctorate was conferred—Piper articulated what he regarded as sound principles for graduate study in theology.[49] As he surveyed established seats of learning in Oxford and Cambridge, Paris and Tübingen, Basel and Lund—and the disarray they all had suffered during the Second World War—Piper wrote, from firsthand experience, of what would be needed to make Princeton's doctoral program of the first rank:

> Thus the increase of factual knowledge, indispensable as it is, nevertheless is to be treated as a secondary goal. . . . Creative imagination is the talent to discover the implications of a given truth and its application to new

---

47. To George Irving, June 17, 1938.

48. Otto A. Piper, "That Strange Thing Money," *ThTod* 16 (1959): 215–31; Piper, *The Christian Meaning of Money* (Englewood Cliffs, NJ: Prentice-Hall, 1965).

49. The recipient was Donald McKay Davies, whose dissertation, "The Old Ethiopic Version of Second Kings," was supervised by OT Professor Henry Snyder Gehman.

situations; the ability to see facts in their entirety and thus the relation of their parts to one another and to the whole; and the intuitive perception of connections between apparently disparate and unrelated facts and their distinctive integration into . . . an historical process or system.[50]

Only through a professor's close guidance of a student's reading, in conjunction with seminars devoted to critical evaluation of original sources in the light of research by other competent scholars, could such creative imagination be cultivated. Piper was worried by the average student's tendency merely to cram information: "There is little danger, as a rule, that a graduate student should suffer from over-specialization. He is far more in peril of scattering his work too thinly over the whole field, and of nowhere growing roots."[51] Piper was equally convinced, in 1944, that the seminary library was "not at all equipped" with working facilities for graduate students.[52] It is no surprise that he played an important role in the upgrading of what became the Robert Elliott Speer Library (renamed, in 2020, the Theodore Sedgwick Wright Library, in memory of the seminary's first African American alumnus [1828]).

On the other hand, Piper was no minimalist in his perception of theological education at the graduate level. In various letters to President Mackay, he worried that the nearly complete abandonment of Latin—both patristic and modern ecclesiastical—would place Princeton and other American students at a disadvantage in competition with their international peers. In addition, and for the same reasons, he bemoaned the seminary's dearth of sufficient electives in ancient church history, in Greek, Latin, and Oriental (*sic*) patristics.[53] Yet Piper's sympathies were far from a Eurocentric parochialism. While insisting that Princeton's doctoral program required major improvements in order to level the international field on which its graduates would have to play, he was just as quick to defend before his European colleagues "the [peculiar] genius of American theology."[54]

> America is the only country in the world, where Protestantism was absolutely free to grow in accordance with its own principles. Therein lies the historical significance of American theology. . . . Thus in the most general

---

50. Otto A. Piper, "Principles of Graduate Study in Theology," *PSB* 38 (1944): 22, 23.
51. Otto A. Piper, "Principles of Graduate Study," 25.
52. Otto A. Piper, "Principles of Graduate Study," 26.
53. Letters to John A. Mackay, November 15, 1945; February 28, 1948.
54. In two articles published in *British Weekly* (January 14 and 21, 1954).

sense American theology is ecclesiastical theology, i.e., it gives expression to the spiritual life of the church people as a whole, whereas in Europe it is academic. [In Europe] it is the professor who tries to impose his views on the laity, even though he may call his system *Kirchliche Theologie*.⁵⁵

Nor was Piper content to articulate abstract principles while others did the heavy lifting of quotidian graduate instruction. He directed twenty-two from among the eighty-nine doctoral dissertations completed at Princeton Seminary between 1944 and 1960⁵⁶—this from a scholar who steadily maintained his own prolific scholarship and admonished his colleagues, "Under the conditions prevailing at most seminaries it can be said that two candidates per professor constitute a heavy [supervisory] load, and three are the extreme limit."⁵⁷ His torrent of letters to "My dear Mackay" reveals an impassioned, occasionally feisty defender of his doctoral students: nominating one or another of them as teaching fellows for the seminary's basic instruction, sometimes complaining of their paltry remuneration. One of his *Doktorkinder* recalled driving twenty-six hours nonstop from his parish for the oral defense of his dissertation before the biblical department. Piper was furious, vowing never again to allow a student of his to drive twenty-six hours, then face an oral. "The questions to you were *stupid*. And you *answered* them!"⁵⁸

The Gentleman Scholar

A year before his retirement from the seminary faculty, Piper received a grant of $29,500.00 from the Lilly Endowment to oversee the compilation and publication of every published work in the field of NT scholarship since the invention of printing. That project was never completed. Yet, when spring returned to campus each year, the first eruption of floral color, tended by a floppy-hatted horticulturalist, could be reliably enjoyed at 58 Mercer Street. Some claimed to have witnessed Dr. Piper sharing a park bench with Professor Einstein during

---

55. *British Weekly* (January 14, 1954), n. p.
56. James F. Armstrong and James H. Smylie, eds., *Catalogue of Doctoral Dissertations, Princeton Theological Seminary 1944–1960* (Princeton: Princeton Theological Seminary, 1962). As chairman of the faculty committee on publications, Piper oversaw this catalogue's preparation. In supervising two doctoral theses, he collaborated with Professors Paul L. Lehmann (1907–94) and Bruce M. Metzger (1914–2007).
57. Piper, "Principles of Graduate Study," 25.
58. Transcribed from an interview with William O. Harris (October 14, 1997).

torrid Princeton summers.⁵⁹ And all the biblical graduate students of that era remember the regular teas to which they were invited in the Piper home, every Friday afternoon at four o'clock, at which Elisabeth served sweets as the professor presided over conversations ranging across theology, philosophy, politics, economics, and psychology. Sometimes he would read to his guests a letter from a former student, describing life in a church or academic post from some region of the globe. On one occasion, as the professor enjoyed telling the story, the family's big black cat, Heidi, leaped on a visitor's lap and proceeded to stir the man's tea with its tail. Too timid to ask for another cup, the guest drank the tea, with no ill effects. Allegedly, Piper himself was the farthest thing from pompous. Legend has it that a student once tempted him with the question: "Dr. Piper, the followers of Hegel are called Hegelians, and those of Barth are called Barthians. What will your followers be called?" Said Piper to his Satan: "I'd call them damned fools."⁶⁰

Whither Piper's Legacy?

For several reasons Piper's influence on subsequent biblical scholarship is ambiguous. As Dr. Hendrik Niether remarked to me in private conversation (May 2, 2022), Piper had been seated in his professorial chair at Münster only three years before his dismissal by the Third Reich. Although he had previously served for a decade as *Privatdozent* and professor of systematics at Göttingen, his career as a recognized scholar was only beginning when it was arrested: first politically, then academically. Another disadvantage that he suffered may be attributable to his wide-ranging intellect and resistance to specialization. Most of his publications fell between the stools of biblical interpretation and constructive theology. He published no book-length commentaries; while of high quality, his technical exegesis was sparse.⁶¹ Like every scholar, he felt the momentary sting of a paper's rejection for publication—in one case owing to an editor's judgment that Piper's submission was too heavily confessional and in-

---

59. Borchert, "Otto Piper of Princeton," 4.
60. This anecdote and that of Heidi the cat were recounted, and later transcribed, by Piper's student Daniel J. Theron, at the dedication of two portraits of the professor by Eileen Mary Fabian (see nn. 2, 10). The rest of this paragraph's information comes from Anon., "Otto Alfred Piper 1981–1982," 52–55.
61. Thus, Otto A. Piper, "I John and the Didache of the Primitive Church," *JBL* 66 (1947): 437–51; Piper, "Johannesapokalypse," *RGG*, 3rd ed. (1958), cols. 822–34.

adequately analytical.⁶² Most of his scholarship lay in the area of Christian dogmatics; yet his focus on biblical interpretation, his rejection of the prevailing philosophical categories of his day, and his leeriness of conventionally accepted, systematic *loci* made his extensive contributions in that area unpalatable to many of his contemporaries. In his perceptive "Appreciation," which introduces Piper's *Festschrift*, Seminary President James I. McCord (1919–90) observed, "It is not that you cannot pin him down; rather, you cannot pen him in."⁶³

One sympathetic reviewer of *God in History* conceded, "To some it will seem to be gnosis with a vengeance."⁶⁴ Piper was no gnostic. So relentless is his view of revelation, however, that aspects of his historical reconstruction seem naively gnosticizing. "Hence it was the will of God that [the Eastern Church] should be disabled by the impact of the Arabs"; "the religious enthusiasm of the Crusaders succeeded in bringing the European nations together once more."⁶⁵ Piper was aware of the danger: "Thus the authority of the Bible is not based upon the fact that Revelation is a higher type of communication of truth—that is the error underlying all gnostic systems—but rather upon the fact that the Bible confronts us with facts that are more comprehensive and more important than anything else we know."⁶⁶ Substitute "claims" for "facts" in that sentence, and one wonders if Piper's distinction of gnosis from the gospel—"God's word to man [which] is of such a *superior* type of truth"⁶⁷—lacks formal difference. Piper's treatment of Christian ethics evoked similar questions: "One man's faith is another's confusion, for it comes suspiciously near a Biblicism which evades too many moral and theological issues by attributing direct causation to the hand of God, and hoping that the empirical evidence will fit."⁶⁸ On balance, Piper's slippage into corroborative events, historical or ethical, in the external world as guarantors for the experience of faith or the truth of holy history compromises his self-avowed regard of the Christian life as "'*cruca tecta*,' covered by the Cross."⁶⁹

---

62. Letter to Piper, January 9, 1946.

63. James I. McCord, "Otto Piper: An Appreciation," in *Current Issues in New Testament Interpretation: Essays in Honor of Otto A. Piper*, ed. William Klassen and Graydon F. Snyder (London: SCM, 1962), xiii.

64. Horace T. Houf, review of *God in History*, by O. A. Piper, *RL* 8 (1939): 471.a.

65. Piper, *God in History*, 150, 152.

66. Piper, "Authority of the Bible," 163.

67. Piper, "Modern Problems," 10 (my emphasis).

68. Gordon Reginald Dunstan, "Editorial," review article of *Christian Ethics*, by Otto A. Piper (1970), *Theol* 74 (1971): 498.

69. Piper, *God in History*, 178.

As the twenty-first century grapples with religious pluralism, specifically with the terrors wrought by religious adherents, some of Piper's assertions about "the Jewish problem" jar today's sensibilities. Again, Piper was no anti-Semite: "[The church] must love [Israel] as our elder sister with a deep and sincere compassion."[70] Later, in an exegesis of Romans 9–11, Piper argued that the church should challenge Judaism to make the special contribution in history assigned to it by God, without trying to convert Jews to Christian faith in a manner by which they would lose their distinctive identity.[71] Still, Piper's presentation of Judaism and other religions is tainted by a Christian triumphalism that, at worst, rendered one of his peers "nauseous"[72] and, at best, is challenged by Paul's claim that all things—even Christ himself—will eventually be subjected to the God who "may be all in all" (1 Cor 15:28 ESV).

In theological study, as in every human endeavor, fashions change. For that reason, many of Piper's comments on the Bible and its interpretation sound startlingly fresh to postmodern ears. An era seeking theological refreshment in Scripture, which reads the Bible more holistically and recognizes the importance of the reader's social situation—including a confessional location within the church—may appreciate Piper's point of view to a degree greater than did some of his contemporaries. To assert with the Reformation, as did Piper, that the Bible is a divinely appointed means of grace that depends for its appropriation on the activity of God's Holy Spirit, chimes at present with major currents in both Roman Catholic and Protestant theology.[73] Perhaps most attractive to legatees of Piper's scholarship is its equipoise of fortitude and humility. Having refused to be cowed by Hitler and his fascist thugs, Piper was never intimidated by fellow academicians who regarded his reading of the Bible as wrong, even wrongheaded. Yet nothing so rankled him as biblical interpretation that resisted God's self-revelation by only confirming the reader's pet theories or stubborn prejudices.[74] For Piper, the Bible confronts its interpreter with mysteries impenetrable apart from divine self-disclosure. The proper attitude toward the Bible is that of a learner. "Gone is the presumption

---

70. Piper, *God in History*, 110.
71. Otto A. Piper, J. Jocz, and Harold Floreen, *The Church Meets Judaism* (Minneapolis: Augsburg, 1961).
72. Joseph Haroutunian, review of *God in History*, by Otto A. Piper (1939), *JBR* 7 (1939): 207.
73. See Telford Work, *Living and Active: Scripture in the Economy of Salvation*, SD (Grand Rapids: Eerdmans, 2002); John Webster, *Holy Scripture: A Dogmatic Sketch*, CIT (Cambridge: Cambridge University Press, 2003).
74. Piper, "Modern Problems," 7, 14.

that one already knows everything of the nature and purpose of the Father of Jesus Christ. One will rather read it in a state of constant expectancy and, when the light of truth dawns upon one's heart, be prepared to give up any view of God and human life previously held."[75] As a motto, the biblical interpreter of any age can do far worse than that, and scarcely much better.

Otto Piper's training of a generation of the church's ministers and doctors, like his practical relief of a war-riven world, defy calculation. The last words must be his, for they remain as pertinent as they are prescient, decades after their original utterance:

> Today, the predominant outlook of church people and non-Christians is amazingly similar, not because outsiders have been persuaded to adopt the Christian view but rather because the members of the churches, like their spiritual leaders, prefer conformity with the nonbelieving world to the protesting spirit of their ancestors.[76]

> There is real danger that our nation should imitate those whom we fought, that generals should govern our country, that we should pursue imperialistic aims, that our freedom should be threatened by an omnipotent political police, and that as a nation we should trust in the power of the sword.[77]

Finally, from what appears to have been his last lecture in Miller Chapel to his sisters and brothers in Christ at Princeton, whom he so dearly loved:

> If there is a progress of goodness and justice in this world, the reason is not so much to be found in our goodness, but rather in the grace of God: that is to say, his willingness by his power to transform our good intentions into effective energies by the redemptive love of Christ. On our part, that means that we have to shift the center of Christian life and thought from ethics to soteriology, or to use the Pauline phrase, from justification by the law to justification of grace. . . . To do justice to that way, a complete change of our values will be required. . . . We have to learn the Christian virtues of humility and patience, if in our life we are to follow the narrow path that leads to true life.[78]

---

75. Piper, "How I Study My Bible," 301.
76. Piper cited in "Current and Quotable," *These Times* (October, 1960): 9.
77. Piper's letter to students of the classes of 1938–47, 3.
78. Manuscript of a lecture delivered in Miller Chapel, November 21, 1972, 5, 6.

Characteristically, Professor Piper ended that lecture with prayer, which opened with the praise of God and so concluded:

> Teach us, we beseech thee, more adequately to understand the mystery of your grace.... Teach us, we pray, the incredible secret of the resurrection, [namely] that not only when we are in good health or in the possession of ample resources, but also when our strength fails us and when we lack earthly goods, Christ's risen life will supplement what is lacking in our thoughts and actions; so that through the weakness of man your kingdom may become your kingdom, [for] which with all the powers of goodness we praise you.
> Amen.[79]

---

79. Manuscript, 7–8.

CHAPTER 4

Exegesis as Prayer

> Let Thy Scriptures be my pure delight: let me not be deceived in them, nor deceive by them.
>
> —St. Augustine of Hippo (*Confessions*, Book 2)

A Biblical Theologian's Assessment of Prayer

In 1954 Otto Piper published his assessment of "The Biblical Doctrine of Prayer," in an essay entitled "Praise of God and Thanksgiving."[1] Embedded in its first paragraph is the opening announcement of his study's thesis: in contrast with other ancient prayers, as well as with contemporary Christian practice, biblical prayer is not anthropocentric, but rather theocentric:

> In modern Protestantism prayer is often interpreted as a dialogue between father and child, based upon the assumption that man is on a par with God. No wonder that it becomes fully man-centered, that is, a means of acquiring peace of mind, and that adoration is no longer practiced. Things are quite different in the Bible. There the praise of God is the constitutive factor of all prayer.[2]

Piper considers two closely related, complex dimensions of the praise of God. First, there is adoration, which is conveyed in such biblical verbs as *barakh* (bless), *eulogeō* (praise), and *doxazō* (glorify). Operating from exegesis of Gen-

---

This chapter is a revision of the author's inaugural address as Otto A. Piper Professor at Princeton Theological Seminary, delivered in Miller Chapel on March 27, 2002.

1. Otto A. Piper, "Praise of God and Thanksgiving: The Biblical Doctrine of Prayer (1)," *Int* 8 (1954): 3–20.

2. Piper, "Praise of God and Thanksgiving," 3.

esis (1:22; 27:1–41) and Ephesians (1:3, 13), Piper argues that "*barakh* designates an act, by which the evaluation of another being is expressed by transmitting to him a highly precious gift, as a result of which the recipient partakes of the donor's specific power of blessing."[3] The primary agent of all benediction is God: it is God's initiatory blessing of us that evokes from us a reciprocating ability to bless God. Because of the term's dilution in modern usage, Piper steers between the Scylla of magic and the Charybdis of rationalism. On the one side, biblical blessing is not a manipulative act by which human beings confer on earthly objects supernatural qualities.[4] On the other, adoration is not equivalent to an expression of aesthetic admiration, whereby a human standard of evaluation is applied to an object. Rather, in blessing us God transforms us into beings that partake of the divine nature, "the earthly evidence of [God's own] glory . . . as a result of which all the values which we knew previously no less than our former standard of values, have lost their finality."[5] Characteristic of that transformation is its assignment of us as God's chosen people and its all-encompassing engagement of ourselves, in the totality of our lives for as long as we live:

> Bless the LORD, O *my soul*;
> and *all that is within me*, bless his holy name! (Ps 103:1; RSV)

> I bless the LORD *at all times*;
> praise of Him is *ever* in my mouth. (Ps 34:1[2]; NJPS)

To these instances, quoted with emphasis by Piper, one could add Paul's memorable exhortations in 1 Thessalonians 5 (16–18a RSV): "Rejoice always, pray constantly, give thanks in all circumstances." For the Apostle and the Psalmist, all that they do is with permanent awareness that God's gracious approach to them has transformed a relationship with God that empowers the divine gift to be returned to its Giver in the form of human praise.

---

3. Piper, "Praise of God and Thanksgiving," 5. As far as I can tell, recent OT scholarship has not drastically veered from this interpretation of *barakh*, save to pay more explicit attention to its converse, the curse. See Patrick D. Miller, *They Cried to the Lord: The Form and Theology of Biblical Prayer* (Minneapolis: Fortress, 1994), 282–303.

4. *Pace* Piper, subsequent scholarship tends to acknowledge magical features in the early stages of OT blessing: thus, Josef Scharbert, "בָּרַךְ," *TDOT* (1977): 2.304; Miller, *They Cried to the Lord*, 283–90; most emphatically, Claus Westermann, *Blessing in the Bible and the Life of the Church*, OBT (Philadelphia: Fortress, 1978), 53–59.

5. Piper, "Praise of God and Thanksgiving," 5–6.

Acknowledging themselves as beneficiaries of God's activity, notably at creation[6] and in covenant, human beings indicate the object of their adoration and its reasons. "God is worshipped because he has revealed himself as God to the believers, and not because the believer thinks it is good and useful for man to have religion."[7] By these works, God manifests himself as superior in love, "a God who distributes out of an infinite and inexhaustible abundance,"[8] and reliably purposeful (Ps 104:24; Rom 16:25-27; Eph 1:3-14; Col 1:15-20; 1 Tim 3:16). As Second Isaiah anticipates in Israel's restoration (Isa 40:27, 31) and as the Fourth Evangelist makes explicit through Jesus' own passion (John 8:54; 12:23, 28; 13:3; 14:13; 15:8), the divine plan is paradoxically realized through humiliation, suffering, and death.[9] Thus is revealed God's holiness, the essential quality belonging to the LORD alone (Isa 6:3; Rev 4:8): "In the Trisagion . . . [t]he seraphim disclose the secret of created life, that is, that only God's holiness is capable of imparting meaning to all that exists and lives."[10] By that standard, in the opening blessing of 2 Corinthians (1:3-12) Paul is able to measure the true value of a suffering apostleship to a suffering church. Hardship is not thereby trivialized or explained away; it becomes a praiseworthy demonstration of our communion with the suffering Christ who is simultaneously the risen Lord of compassionate consolation. In that connection, interestingly, Piper suggests that "the formula 'Father of our Lord Jesus Christ' does not by itself predicate God as dealing with us in a fatherly way, but rather denotes that through contact with Christ we have experienced God's glory."[11] At stake in the NT's use of paternal language, as Piper regards it, is neither a generic appellation or alias for God, nor a metaphysical statement about Jesus's relationship with God, but rather a claim about believers' revivified relationship with their Creator through Christ: God's self-revelation to us of glory (John 14:9; cf. 2 Cor 4:6) and God's regeneration in us of new life (1 Pet 1:3-9).

---

6. Whether Israelite praise is rooted as firmly in its view of creation as in its interpretation of history remains debatable (Scharbert, "בָּרַךְ," 306-7). Miller points up the fundamentally social location of praise within the family (*They Cried to the Lord*, 281-83).

7. Piper, "Praise of God and Thanksgiving," 9.

8. Piper, "Praise of God and Thanksgiving," 10.

9. For recent studies of Israel's attempt to square its praise of God with human suffering, consult Patrick D. Miller, "'Enthroned on the Praises of Israel': The Praise of God in Old Testament Theology," *Int* 39 (1985): 5-19; Walter Brueggemann, *Israel's Praise: Doxology against Idolatry and Ideology* (Philadelphia: Fortress, 1988); Samuel E. Balentine, *Prayer in the Hebrew Bible: The Drama of Divine-Human Dialogue*, OBT (Minneapolis: Fortress, 1993), 199-224.

10. Piper, "Praise of God and Thanksgiving," 11.

11. Piper, "Praise of God and Thanksgiving," 13.

The second dimension of God's praise is thanksgiving (*yadah* [hiphil]; *homologeō; exomologeō*). Piper grants little material difference in the Bible between praise of God and thanksgiving;[12] *todah* reinforces the theological tendencies already witnessed. The Giver to whom believers are indebted is revealed by those gifts as unstintingly generous: the One whose astonishing graciousness in the past stimulates praise for providence still to come, whose assurance is firm (Pss 85, 111, 118, 136; Matt 11:25; Eph 1:3; Rev 11:17–18). The true estimate of God's gifts of election, redemption, and steadfast love is reckoned in relation to God's saving purposes. Thus, such Psalms as 111 and 138, as well as the Lukan Magnificat (Luke 1:46–55) and Benedictus (1:68–79), model genuine thanksgiving: "When we recall the whole work of God we are able also to appraise correctly the value and function of the things which happen to us,"[13] including both our amenities and misfortunes (Ps 84; Rom 8:28–39; 2 Cor 2:14–16; Phil 3:7–8). Unlike the modern emphasis on our subjective happiness and the value we ascribe to a donation,[14] biblical figures like Mary and Zechariah efface themselves before the gift, extolling God—the sovereign, free, and munificent Lord—with due praise for unbelievable privileges of which they know themselves in no way deserving. Typically, we are blind to countless evidence of God's grace; by nature, we are so dull and rebellious of heart that we take for granted our creation, preservation, and salvation as entitlements (cf. Ps 103:2; Isa 40:21; Rom 1:21). In the biblical tradition it is different: believers "do not look at the universe and its fate from the angle of their personal interests, but rather contemplate it as it appears in the light of God's will."[15] In that light, things of apparent insignificance become good and valuable when dedicated to God's design; conversely, things of highest aesthetic or utilitarian value are not only worthless but dangerous if by our lack of praise we leave them unrelated to God's purposeful love.[16]

The prayer of thanksgiving is the test of our faith. In it we make manifest whether or not we acknowledge God as the giver of all things; by it we show whether or not we place the spiritual benefits which Christ offers to us infinitely high above all earthly things; and in its light it becomes evi-

12. Piper, "Praise of God and Thanksgiving," 15.
13. Piper, "Praise of God and Thanksgiving," 18.
14. Piper's recurring uneasiness with human emotions attending Israel's praise and thanks is not easily sustained by many OT texts: among others, Ps 9:2; Isa 12:6; Jer 33:10–11. See Günter Mayer, "ידה‎," *TDOT* 5 (1986): 427–43, esp. 434–35.
15. Piper, "Praise of God and Thanksgiving," 20.
16. Piper, "Praise of God and Thanksgiving," 17, citing 1 Tim 4:4–5.

dent whether or not we believe that, being one with our Lord, we are able to triumph over all evils.... By combining thanksgiving with the praise of God, the Bible teaches us genuine gratitude.[17]

How well does Otto Piper's treatment of praise and thanksgiving wear some seventy years later? While a comprehensive assessment is impossible here, a few observations are worth registering. One of his primary claims—that blessing is God's gracious preservation of life, which needy humans must constantly receive and ask for—has not, I judge, been overturned.[18] That said, I am struck by the degree of unity Piper finds in the biblical witness.[19] As signaled by his essay's subtitle, "The Biblical *Doctrine* of Prayer" (emphasis added), Piper's inclination—typical of the postwar biblical theology movement of which he was a leader—is to highlight theological unity not only between but also within the Testaments.[20] After seven decades of countervailing encouragement to discern difference and diversity within the canon, such an approach no longer comes as reflexively to me or possibly to many of us. While every instance of correspondence may not be equally persuasive, I am prepared, nevertheless, to confess the blinkered vision of the historical moment that I inhabit, and to acknowledge the contribution to theological reflection of Piper's more synthetic, less analytical, approach.

At the beginning of his essay, Piper makes an interesting yet contestable move. From his initial premise that God distinctively occupies the center of biblical prayer, he draws the conclusion that "the praise of God is the constitutive factor of all prayer." Here, three questions arise at once. First, even if one grants the theocentricity of biblical prayer, it does not therefore follow that "the constitutive factor of all biblical prayer" must be that of *praise*. Theologically, one might prefer it that way; exegetically, there are other possibilities, as we shall see. Second, is it the case that ancient prayers outside the Bible, if not lack-

---

17. Piper, "Praise of God and Thanksgiving," 19, 20.
18. See, for instance, Hans-Joachim Kraus, *Theology of the Psalms*, trans. Keith Crim, CC (Minneapolis: Fortress, 1992), 54–55.
19. Elsewhere Piper wrote, "The history of exegesis has shown that no adequate understanding of the Bible or any of its parts is possible which is not based upon the ... [axiom that] underlying the whole Bible there is one message—the substantial unity of the canon of the Bible" ("How I Study My Bible," *ChrCent* 63 [March 6, 1946]: 299–301; here, 299).
20. Brevard S. Childs, *Biblical Theology in Crisis* (Philadelphia: Westminster, 1970), remains the standard chronicle of the biblical theology movement and its dissolution. Scharbert ("בָּרַךְ," 284–308) offers a temperate consideration of the complex development of blessing within Israelite religion and theology.

ing adoration, are at root anthropocentric? The ancient evidence is mixed but tilts away from Piper's judgment, for reasons that in the early 1950s he could not have known, or at least could not have fully realized. In a recent study, Oxford's Simon Pulleyn upholds a scholarly consensus "that prayers of gratitude are not very frequent in archaic and classical Greece and that when one does find them, they are not particularly effusive."[21] On the other hand, we now know from the Essene psalter and such works as *Words of the Luminaries* (4Q504) and *Songs of the Sabbath Sacrifice* (4Q400–407) that praise is the dominant motif of many prayers at Qumran —so much so that the joining of earthly and angelic praise of God is a recurring theme in that community's *Daily Prayers* (4Q503).[22] Third, taken on their own terms, the OT psalms exhibit an oscillation between lament and praise, petition and thanksgiving.[23] As Patrick Miller observed, "Praise, therefore, does not really stand by itself. . . . There is some sense in which praise is the end of the conversation"[24] between God and humanity—not the beginning of a nondialogical hymn, as Piper would have it. At any rate, biblical prayer embraces many dimensions of human need and desire: praise and thanksgiving to be sure, but also lament, petition, intercession, and confession.[25] Certainly, within the OT Psalter laments and pleas for help outnumber hymns and thanksgivings by a ratio of almost two to one.

Less in critique, more by way of observation, I think it fair to say that what Piper gave us in 1954 was not so much an analysis of any prayer in the

---

21. Simon J. Pulleyn, *Prayer in Greek Religion* (Oxford: Clarendon, 1997), 39–55 (here, 39). In the vast mass of personal inscriptions accompanying votive sacrifices, Pulleyn finds the closest equivalent to Israel's praise of the LORD; nevertheless, "[Greek] Prayer was not of itself an autonomous mode of religious action" (15).

22. Eileen M. Schuller, "Prayer in the Dead Sea Scrolls," in *Into God's Presence: Prayer in the New Testament*, ed. Richard N. Longenecker, MNTS (Grand Rapids: Eerdmans, 2001), 66–88; see also James H. Charlesworth, *Critical Reflections on the Odes of Solomon*, JSPSup 22 (Sheffield: Sheffield Academic Press, 1998), 14–77. Distinguishing the biblical witness from its Near Eastern matrix was peculiarly important to the Biblical Theology movement in America (Childs, *Biblical Theology in Crisis*, 47–50).

23. Claus Westermann, *Praise and Lament in the Psalms* (Atlanta: John Knox, 1981).

24. Miller, *They Cried to the Lord*, 223. Piper's view seems more reminiscent of Abraham Joshua Heschel: "I am not ready to accept the ancient concept of prayer as a dialogue. Who are we to enter a dialogue with God? The better metaphor would be to describe prayer as an act of immersion, . . . drowned in the waters of [God's] mercy" ("Prayer as Discipline," in Heschel, *The Insecurity of Freedom: Essays on Human Existence* [New York: Farrar, Straus & Giroux, 1966], 255).

25. As, in a companion piece to Piper's essay, Floyd V. Filson investigated "Petition and Intercession: The Biblical Doctrine of Prayer (2)," *Int* 8 (1954): 21–34. More recently, consult Miller, *They Cried to the Lord*, 55–134, 244–80.

Bible, as it was, instead, the beginning of a theology of prayer, grounded in the biblical witness and weighted toward the NT. Whether or not he intended it, Piper's essay reads as an erudite meditation on the majestic themes of Ephesians 1:3–14: the eternal reciprocity of creative blessing, initiated by "the God and Father of our Lord Jesus Christ" (RSV), whose magnificently loving plan for us evokes our rapt thanksgiving and places in context "the sufferings of this present time" (Rom 8:18 RSV). From that hub, Piper's thought stretches out toward other biblical testimonies, insightfully drawing them into the orbit of his confession—which, as he repeatedly notes, is "an act of faith" that "fills one with joy."[26] Indeed, throughout this article, the veil between Professor Piper, the learned exegete, and Otto Piper, the believing Christian, becomes so transparent that it is practically impossible to differentiate them, perhaps even reprehensible to try:

> We have not understood God's purpose in revealing himself as long as we are not moved by our insights to praise him.[27]

> Hence an unbelievable privilege has been granted to us. . . . [Through Christ] we have the forgiveness of sins. Thereby we are enabled to live in the Messianic age, and the Holy Spirit is at work in our hearts.[28]

> God takes a personal interest in our lives, and thus indicates the high price he sets on us. Yet we do not therefore live for our own sake. The meaning of our life consists in the fact that we were made sons *eis auton* (Eph 1:5), that is, for God's sake.[29]

The only thing conspicuously lacking from Piper's presentation of the "Praise of God and Thanksgiving" is that motto which Bach affixed to the end of his sacred compositions: *Soli Deo gloria*, "To God alone be glory." If you suppose I say that in ridicule, you could not more grossly mistake my intention. By my lights, this is the enduring merit of Otto Piper's essay, which was but a particle of his comprehensive work and life among us: in the very act of biblical interpretation, Professor Piper was encouraging us to bless and adore the Lord. For him, prayer was not a religious auxiliary, a pietistic nod before

---

26. Piper, "Praise of God and Thanksgiving," 16–17, 18, 20.
27. Piper, "Praise of God and Thanksgiving," 6.
28. Piper, "Praise of God and Thanksgiving," 16, 18.
29. Piper, "Praise of God and Thanksgiving," 19.

getting down to the serious business of biblical exegesis. Of course, scriptural interpretation is serious—more so than we are always aware. It is also more joyful, for in Christ's resurrection God has had the last laugh.[30] When proceeding in alignment with the same Spirit that animated Scripture's creation and canonization within the church, *exegesis is an expression of prayer*. The glorification of God and the sanctification of life constitute the ultimate reason for Scripture's interpretation, as for everything else that Christians are and do.

Biblical Prayer and Biblical Exegesis

On its face, such a claim ought not be controversial. I have heard numerous offenses charged to the apostle Paul's account; never have I heard anyone lambaste his counsel to the Corinthians, "So . . . whatever you do, do all to the glory of God" (1 Cor 10:31 RSV). Who's going to argue with *that*? Well, in my experience a lot of people have, many of whom I regard as friends. Many years ago, at another theological school, a senior colleague drew me into his office to ask if the rumor was true: that I prayed at the beginning of a class. This Dutch uncle gave me to understand that such conduct was inappropriate, as it confused students whether they were in school or in church. Another colleague at a different school would visibly shudder at mere mention of the word "piety," having been scarred from years of classroom encounters with hearts strangely warmed and brains evidently lobotomized. Then there was the memorable lunch with a friend from my graduate-school days, at which—without a shred of malice—he expressed deep concern about the *harm* I did my students by suggesting that I believed the witness of the Bible I was training them to read with a critical eye. In other words, my responsibility was to teach students to analyze Psalm 119:97—"Oh, how I love your law! / all the day long it is in my mind" (AT)—while forestalling the prospect that anyone in my course would ever be caught uttering such a thing. Thus was fulfilled the prophecy of my teacher, the church historian David Steinmetz (1936–2015): "Other generations were afraid of appearing 'loose'; we are fearful of being thought either 'morbid' or 'pious.' As sex was a taboo subject for our grandparents, so death and piety are taboo subjects with us."[31]

---

30. On "Basic Christian Existence as 'a Laugh,'" see Daniel W. Hardy and David F. Ford, *Praising and Knowing God* (Philadelphia: Westminster, 1985), 71–88.
31. David C. Steinmetz, *Memory and Mission: Theological Reflections on the Christian Past* (Nashville: Abingdon, 1988), 169. In the original, these sentences appear in reverse order.

Exegesis as Prayer

Throwing caution to the wind while building on Piper's foundation, I want to suggest some *dispositions* of prayer that I consider essential for the proper exegesis of Scripture, understanding "propriety" as a manner of interpretive attunement that is congenial with Scripture's own character, content, and completion. At the outset let me be clear that I am *not* prescribing a particular form or language of prayer to which all interpreters must subscribe. With prayer, one size does not fit all, nor anyone at all times; as Dom John Chapman (1865-1933) wisely counseled his correspondents, "Pray as you can, and do not try to pray as you can't."[32] Nor am I equating "dispositions" with "moods" (which are sudden and spasmodic), even less with "methodological approaches" (which can prove intellectually vapid or morally vacuous).[33] By dispositions, I borrow a leaf—even as did my denominational father, John Wesley (1703-91)—from Jonathan Edwards (1703-58), who discerned in persons graced by faith profound and enduring motives, "[the] more vigorous and sensible exercises of the inclination and will," that marshal human emotion, intellect, and will toward the moral excellence and supernal beauty of God.[34] Saint Augustine, on whom Edwards was dependent, put the matter more concisely by describing prayer as "the affectionate reaching out of the mind for God."[35] When the biblical interpreter mentally reaches out for God with affection, what capacities will be cultivated in a mind so renewed for exegetical activation? As Edwards himself attempted a *via media* between rationalistic defense of decorous doctrine and revivalist claims for enthusiast experience, so shall I suggest a constant need in our day for better balance among goods

---

32. *The Spiritual Letters of Dom John Chapman*, ed. Roger Hudleston (London: Sheed and Ward, 1935), 109.

33. In "How I Study My Bible" (299), Piper observes, "Like the natural sciences and sociology, theological criticism is at present passing through what is aptly called 'the crisis of methodology'"—vindicating in 1946 the Preacher's lament that under the sun there is nothing new (Qoh 1:9-11).

34. Jonathan Edwards, *A Treatise concerning the Religious Affections*, ed. John E. Smith (New Haven: Yale University Press, 1959), 98. On the significance of Edwards's treatise for hermeneutics, see John E. Smith, "Jonathan Edwards: Piety and Its Fruits," in *The Return to Scripture in Judaism and Christianity: Essays in Postcritical Scriptural Interpretation*, ed. Peter Ochs (New York and Mahwah, NJ: Paulist, 1993), 277-91; for liturgy, Don E. Saliers, *The Soul in Paraphrase: Prayer and the Religious Affections* (New York: Seabury, 1980).

35. Augustine, *Serm.* 9 (*De Passione*) 3 (*Oratio namque est mentis ad Deum affectuosa intentio*); cited by Thomas A. Hand, *Augustine on Prayer* (New York: Catholic Book Publishing, 1986), 19, 20, 35, 53, 78. For a superb presentation of interpretive dispositions in Catholic perspective, see Mariano Magrassi, *Praying the Bible: An Introduction to* Lectio Divina, trans. Edward Hagman (Collegeville, MN: Liturgical, 1998), 57-101.

that have become lopsided. In particular, I would propose three complementary and intersecting aptitudes, three prayerful dispositions, for the exegete in our time: a capacity for holiness, a transfigured affection, and a disposition for thankful praise.

A Disposition for Holiness

"Who is like You, O LORD, majestic in holiness?" (Exod 15:11 adapted).

If Otto Piper was correct that "only God's holiness is capable of imparting meaning to all that exists and lives,"[36] then we should regularly repent of investing exegesis with cheap significance. Christians hold that Jesus of Nazareth is the apex of God's self-revelation; likewise, it has pleased God to "abbreviate" (Bernard of Clairvaux [1090–1153]) or "accommodate" (John Calvin [1509–64]) himself, through the testimony of Scripture, to a measure accessible by mortals. That, like the incarnation, should occasion greater wonder, not its diminution. Wonder, however, has receded into eclipse since the seventeenth century, as many interpreters have inflated their confidence in human abilities while truncating their intellectual tolerance for a reasoned faith.[37] The not-so-pretty pass to which things have come in 2024 is, I fear, perennial conclaves of masters of a page no longer sacred, mesmerized by technique, restless with a God-Idea while fearing real passion for God. The culprit in all this is *not*, as fundamentalists think, the discipline of historical criticism—which, with its attendant flowering of philological and literary inquiry, is only the most recent stage of the venerable quest for the Bible's literal sense.[38] *Scientia* (knowledge) is a noble gift of God, who is not well honored by ignorance and superstition. The problem, in my view, is that we have allowed ourselves to become arrested in "science" of a narrow sort and have forgotten—or dismissed—Augustine's realization that knowledge is but the third rung of a ladder whose first steps are the fear of God and a receptive spirit (*pietas*), as we climb to communion with God by way of fortitude, mercy, love for our enemies, and wisdom (*Doctr. chr.* 2.7.9–11). In Eden, the original sin was of knowledge embezzled (Gen 3); as Paul reminded Corinth (1 Cor 8:1–13), to be stuck in knowledge while lacking love is no sign of Christian hygiene. Few spectacles are more ludicrous or more

---

36. Piper, "Praise of God and Thanksgiving," 11.
37. See William C. Placher, *The Domestication of Transcendence: How Modern Thinking about God Went Wrong* (Louisville: Westminster John Knox, 1996).
38. See Beryl Smalley, *The Study of the Bible in the Middle Ages* (Notre Dame: University of Notre Dame Press, 1964).

pathetic than a scholarly seminar whose members beat the hell out of one another over differing interpretations of the love command in John (13:34).

To interpret Scripture with a disposition for holiness means to release our narcissistic grip on magistry and to reclaim our vocation to its opposite, which is ministry. While some students I teach could use massive infusions of the Spirit's confidence, others of us do well to repent of shallow mastery and to grow in humility. Humility is not self-degradation, which is a sin. To surrender oneself before Scripture is to become like the soil from which we were created (Gen 2:7), *humus* that is fertile and needs mulching. Humble reading is hospitable to another's voice, patient, wholly attentive, still. Listen again to Professor Piper, writing in 1946:

> One who has been struck by the saving message of God will approach the Bible as a learner. Gone is the presumption that one already knows everything of the nature and purpose of the Father of Jesus Christ. One will rather read it in a state of constant expectancy and, when the light of truth dawns upon one's heart, be prepared to give up any view of God and human life previously held.[39]

If Simone Weil could recognize a sacrament in school exercises like geometric proofs,[40] can we not acknowledge the miracle of being penetrated by the love of God and neighbor through the exercise of biblical exegesis?[41] To confess that, however, means we shall have to retire commonplaces like "making the Bible relevant," as though Scripture were inert until we do something with it. If we've gotten the cart before the horse—if the primary question is What, through Scripture, is God making of us?—then our more appropriate response is to kneel mentally before the mystery of divine love that is Scripture's sum and substance. That mystery is holy; it is Other. We risk consumption by Love that is a tiger, not a teddy bear (Heb 4:11–13).

---

39. Piper, "How I Study My Bible," 301. Note Rowan Williams: "Prayer . . . is precisely what *resists* the urge of religious language to claim a total perspective: by articulating its own incompleteness before God, it turns away from any claim to human completeness" (*On Christian Theology* [Oxford: Blackwell, 2000], 13).

40. Simone Weil, "Reflections on the Right Use of School Studies with a View to the Love of God," in Weil, *Waiting for God* (New York: Harper & Row, 1951), 105–16.

41. For historical perspective, consult Jean Leclercq, *The Love of Learning and the Desire for God: A Study of Monastic Culture* (New York: Fordham University Press, 1961); for theological development, see Andrew Louth, *Discerning the Mystery: An Essay on the Nature of Theology* (Oxford: Clarendon, 1983).

A Disposition for Transfigured Affection

"For you have died, and your life has been hidden with Christ in God" (Col 3:3).

Those who have thought deeply on the subject disagree whether the test of our prayer lies in how we live when not praying or whether prayer, stirred and sustained by the Holy Spirit, is as autonomic and all-pervasive as breathing.[42] The first view seems to me more Matthean (see Matt 7:21–23), the second more Pauline (Rom 8:26–27). I find truth in both. However we parse the matter, both claims converge at a common point: prayer and life, authentically practiced, become transparent to each other and interpenetrating. This is surely the case if, at heart, all our prayers are for God's glorification and the sanctification of life. On that basis Otto Piper could say, "The praise of God presupposes that God . . . himself has given us a new standard of values, as a result of which all the values which we knew previously no less than our former standard of values, have lost their finality."[43] In the crucible of debate, Saint Paul articulated this principle with a diamond's density and clarity: "I have been crucified with Christ; it is no longer I who live, but Christ who lives in me; and the life I now live in the flesh I live by faith in the Son of God, who loved me and gave himself for me" (Gal 2:20 RSV). If prayer feeds a life by faith in God's Son, how may we regard our interpretation of Scripture as crucified with Christ?

We begin by acknowledging that exegesis, like prayer, is a spiritual gift with multiple dimensions. Pelagianism forever crouches at the interpreter's door, tempting her to pride in a bank of historical knowledge, an ear for a text's music, a facility with biblical and cognate languages—or driving her to despair of ever attaining such things. (Pride and despair are mirror images of a single, insidious temptation to self-sufficiency.) Only our embrace of God's grace, crystallized in the gospel of Christ crucified, can keep constantly before us the awareness that truly we have nothing that we haven't first received as a gift (1 Cor 4:6–7)—including Scripture and prayer themselves. Even more than the gift, we have received the Giver: exegesis with prayer as its motor enacts in time and space the eternal, reciprocating conversation of love within God as

---

42. The first opinion is characteristic among western theologians such as Martin Luther (1483–1546) for whom prayer is primarily obedience to God's command (introduction to the Lord's Prayer in *The Large Catechism of Martin Luther* [1529], trans. Robert H. Fischer [Philadelphia: Fortress, 1959], 64–65). The second may be more common in Eastern Orthodoxy (thus, Anonymous, *The Pilgrim's Tale* [1884], ed. Aleksei Pentkovsky, CWS [New York and Mahwah, NJ: Paulist, 1999], 49–57).

43. Piper, "Praise of God and Thanksgiving," 5–6.

Father, Son, and Holy Spirit. Viewed in a Trinitarian light, any understanding of biblical exegesis as "conversation with the text" requires an account of the One who calls that conversation into existence, the One who constitutes its subject matter as love, the One who empowers us with a fitting response. Amid all the blood spilled over the doctrine of Scripture's inspiration, I fear we have not always honored the same Spirit that enlivens Scripture's words *from* the page after they were committed to it. Let us do so now: by prayerful exegesis, we glorify the Spirit who is pulling us into God's own primary speech.[44]

Exegesis in the shadow of Golgotha remembers the people of God, from and for whom Scripture was evoked, and the ministry of reconciliation for which that people needs equipment (2 Cor 5:19–21). Only through a community of prayer do we learn to pray—all of the first-person *plural* pronouns of the Lord's Prayer are there for a reason. Likewise, only through a community of interpretation do we learn to interpret. The practices of these two communities, however, do not always overlap. In our time, sad to say, much training in biblical scholarship occurs in settings where prayer has been severed from its task and responsibility, where the nurturance of a faithful church is non sequitur. Visits to the religion aisles of Barnes & Noble or Amazon's websites have become for me chilling summonses before the bar of judgment: much of what I find among the biblical resources are speculative fantasias, whether by Tim LaHaye (1926–2016) or the Jesus Seminar.[45] There is comparatively little that invites the church's laity or even curious passersby into the mysterious world of biblical faith that questions us, little to remind a reader that exegesis, like prayer, is not cold conjecture but relationship with a God so madly in love with us and the world that only the foolishness of the cross makes sense (1 Cor 1:18–31).

Cruciform exegesis resembles petitionary prayer in this respect: if serious, its practitioner is inextricably bound up with its fulfillment (Matt 25:31–46).[46]

---

44. For this lead I am indebted to Ann and Barry Ulanov, *Primary Speech: A Psychology of Prayer* (Atlanta: John Knox, 1982).

45. A self-selected group of approximately 150 scholars and laity, founded by Professor Robert W. Funk (1926–2005), best known for its attempt to establish the historicity of Jesus's words and deeds (see, e.g., Funk, ed., *The Gospel of Jesus: According to the Jesus Seminar* [Santa Rosa, CA: Polebridge Macmillan, 1999]). Highly controversial, this group has been criticized by scholars both conservative and liberal for the competence of many of its members, its limited presuppositions, biases against canonical Gospel in favor of noncanonical materials, and flawed criteria (see, among others, Howard Clark Kee, "A Century of Quests for the Culturally Compatible Jesus," *ThTod* 52 [1995]: 17–28; Raymond E. Brown, *An Introduction to the New Testament*, ABRL [Garden City, NY: Doubleday, 1997], 819–23). For more on LaHaye, see chapter 21 of this volume.

46. See C. Clifton Black, "The Education of Human Wanting," in *Character and Scripture:*

The man who subjects innocents to unspeakable atrocities, while passing the buck instead of repenting his execrable abuse of power, forfeits the privilege of interpreting the book of Judges (11:12–40; 19:1–30; 21:1–25). The theologian confident that she could formulate more elegant explanations for suffering than Elihu and all the friends put together had best tarry before rushing to judgments about Job. Only those who know firsthand the potential for sin to rot the core of a devotional life can begin to appreciate the depth of Paul's withering diagnosis in Romans (7:7–25). What Evelyn Underhill once cautioned about prayer applies with equal gravity to exegesis. In the following quotation substitute "Scripture" and "interpretation" for (or alongside) "soul" and "prayer," and the point should be clear:

> Each time you take a human soul with you into prayer, you accept from God a piece of spiritual work with all its implications and with all its cost—a cost which may mean for you spiritual exhaustion and darkness, and may even include vicarious suffering, the Cross. In offering yourselves on such levels of prayer for the sake of others, you are offering to take your part in the mysterious activities of the spiritual world; to share the saving work of Christ. . . . Real intercession is not merely a petition but a piece of work, involving perfect, costly self-surrender to God for the work he wants done on other souls.[47]

For the Wesleyan interpreter, here is an area of exegesis in chronic need of "perfection in love." Some among my Presbyterian friends may also recognize an enterprise *semper reformanda*, "always in need of reformation."

A Disposition for Grateful Praise

"My soul proclaims the greatness of the Lord" (Luke 1:46).

Eucharist is the carriage of a Christian. Accordingly, exegesis, like prayer, is hard to justify if it does not culminate in gratitude and adoration. Anthony Bloom has said, "All the food of this world is divine love made edible";[48] the same is true for knowledge that feeds mind and soul. Professor Piper was correct: mere

---

Moral Formation, Community, and Biblical Interpretation, ed. William P. Brown (Grand Rapids and Cambridge: Eerdmans, 2002), 248–63, as well as chapter 6 of this volume.

47. Underhill, *Collected Papers of Evelyn Underhill*, ed. Lucy Menzies (London: Longmans, Green and Co., 1946), 57–59.

48. Bloom, *School for Prayer* (London: Darton, Longman & Todd, 1970), 41.

admiration of, say, Jeremiah's poetry or Mark's narrative reflects an engagement only of our aesthetic or mental faculties. Prayerful exegesis happens when Scripture's radiance seizes one's very self, when "My God!" is the only thing worth saying. Across time, a heart cultivated for thanksgiving lets go of envy and resentment; we learn to be grateful for friends, colleagues and students, who enable us to see in Scripture God's beauty where we have been blind. An adoring mind outgrows childish parades of novelty and cleverness among those whom we guide through Scripture; and so we heed C. S. Lewis's weary plea, "I wish they'd remember that the charge to Peter was Feed my sheep; not Try experiments on my rats."[49] The ultimate aim of exegesis, as of prayer, is to know and to love God and to do God's will. We know that purpose has been satisfied when we delight in Scripture, praise its Lord, and realize our lives' meaning in nothing other than our adoption as God's children for God's own sake (Eph 1:5-6).

Gratitude may have come more readily for Otto Piper than for some others. As an officer in the First World War, Piper was shot in the face just beneath his right eye and left for dead on the western front. Only after the Red Cross discovered that a soldier already loaded onto their truck had died was Piper found alive and taken away in that casualty's place. By 1932 he was an outspoken critic of emergent Nazism, for which Hitler imprisoned and eventually expelled him.[50] After five years of hopscotching across the United Kingdom with wife and children for temporary academic appointments, he and they came to rest in Princeton, New Jersey. His sons were drafted for service in the American military; one was killed in action. For years during and after World War II, Piper conscripted his students for assistance in shipping and sending garments for European relief.[51] Piper did not passively endure suffering; he served God in it. Thus, when he declared the Bible a means of grace, through which God imparts and stimulates blessing among us,[52] that declaration carries the ring of lived truth.

Regarded *in conspectu Dei*, "before the face of God," exegesis is intrinsically connected with prayer. Such is the case whatever the vagaries of our life to-

---

49. Lewis, *Letters to Malcolm: Chiefly on Prayer* (New York: Harcourt Brace Jovanovich, 1963), 5.

50. While reason for such opposition seems self-evident ninety years after the fact, revisionist historians like Christopher Hitchens argue that appeasement of the Third Reich characterized both British and American policy until, respectively, 1939 and 1941 ("The Medals of His Defeats: Examining the Revisionist Version of Winston Churchill," *The Atlantic Monthly* 289 [April, 2002]: 118–37).

51. For more information, see chapter 3.

52. Piper, "How I Study My Bible," 300.

gether.⁵³ On occasion we shall find in Scripture unalloyed contentment, and rest as a weaned child with its mother (Ps 131:2). At other times we must wrestle the text at Jabbok's ford (Gen 32:23–32), and understand Abba Agathon's comment that there is no labor greater than that of prayer to God: "Prayer is warfare to the last breath."⁵⁴ No matter. Prayer is shot through biblical interpretation, just as every offering for God's sake tinctures "bright and clean" all facets of the Christian life and makes even our "drudgery divine":

> This is the famous stone
> That turneth all to gold:
> For that which God doth touch and own
> Cannot for less be told.
> In Christ *we* are what God has touched and owns.⁵⁵

How could we help but bless and thank God for that? *Soli Deo gloria.*

---

53. "[I]n its totality it is peculiar and characteristic of theology that it can be performed only in the act of prayer" (Karl Barth, *Evangelical Theology*, trans. Grover Foley [New York: Holt, Rinehart and Winston, 1963], 159–70; quotation, 160).

54. Benedicta Ward, ed. and trans., *The Sayings of the Desert Fathers: The Alphabetical Collection*, CSS 59 (Kalamazoo, MI, and Oxford: Cistercian Publications/Mowbray, 1975), 22.

55. George Herbert, "The Elixir," in *George Herbert and the Seventeenth-Century Religious Poets*, ed. Mario A. Di Cesare (New York and London: Norton, 1978), 65–66.

Part 2

STOPOVERS

CHAPTER 5

Short Shrift Made Once More

> "Help us to find God," said the disciples to the elder.
> "No one can help you to do that," the elder replied.
> Astonished, the disciples asked, "Why not?"
> "For the same reason that no one can help fish find the ocean."
>
> —St. Benedict

GRANT THOSE DISCIPLES THIS MUCH: it was God they were looking for.[1] Within today's church and academy—even the environs of biblical scholarship—that intent is not always so clear. Thus, while writing commentary on the Letters of John,[2] I found myself scudding among learned lobsters seemingly forgetful of Scripture's pervasive milieu. To make my point, I must set back the clock by seventy years and beg the reader's indulgence as I map a fairly late exegetical development. An interpretive debate of marginal interest to those outside the guild's hall of mirrors can splay, on closer inspection, a theological enfilade with important implications for everyone.[3]

FROM *LOGOS* TO *ECCLESIA*

One of the twentieth century's landmark contributions to research in the Johannine epistles is also one of the briefest: an eight-page contribution to the

---

1. The epigraph above is quoted by Joan Chittister, *Wisdom Distilled from the Daily: Living the Rule of Saint Benedict Today* (San Francisco: HarperSanFrancisco, 1990), 28.
2. Published in Leander E. Keck et al., eds., *The New Interpreter's Bible* (Nashville: Abingdon, 1998), 12:363–469.
3. With many commentators I assume that 1 John was written after the Gospel of John; that it was written by someone other than the Fourth Evangelist, probably by the same anonymity who in 2 and 3 John refers to himself as "the elder"; and that 1 John may be conveniently called an epistle, even though it doesn't much resemble one.

second *Festschrift* for Rudolf Bultmann, originally published in 1954. This essay, penned by one of Bultmann's illustrious pupils, Hans Conzelmann, took as its title the opening words of 1 John (in German) "Was von Anfang war,"[4] or (in English) "What was from the beginning,"

> What we have heard, what we have seen with our eyes, what we looked upon and touched with our hands, concerning the word of life—the life was made manifest, and we have seen it, and bear witness to it, and proclaim to you the eternal life that was with the Father and was made manifest to us—what we have seen and have heard we proclaim also to you, so that you too may have fellowship with us. Moreover, our fellowship is with the Father and with his Son Jesus Christ. And these things we are writing so that our joy may be fulfilled. (1 John 1:1–4)[5]

Conzelmann's thesis sprang from his interpretation of this prologue, viewed in the context of 1 John overall. He recognized in this passage the echo of the Fourth Gospel's better-known prologue, while pointing up an important difference between the two: according to John, "that which was in the beginning" is the preexistent *logos*, whereas 1 John apparently refers to the origin of *the tradition of the Johannine church*. In the First Epistle, according to Conzelmann, "The church orients itself to its origin and understands this as an absolute date, against which no other ... is of any interest whatever. Its eschatological self-consciousness is transposed into a reflection on the historical essence of Christian society."[6] In Conzelmann's view, this conceptual shift betokened a critical turn in Johannine Christianity's self-understanding: toward the church's interpretation of its *own* primal history as distinct, complete, and decisive, and of its tradition as foundational, authoritative, and normative for the community's ongoing life.[7] Conzelmann concluded that 1 John

---

4. Conzelmann, "'Was von Anfang war,'" in *Neutestamentliche Studien für Rudolf Bultmann zu seinem siebzigsten Geburtstag am 20. August 1954*, ed. Walther Eltester, BZNW 21 (Berlin: Töpelmann, 1954; 2nd ed., 1957), 194–201; repr. in Hans Conzelmann, *Theologie als Schriftauslegung: Aufsätze zum Neuen Testament*, BEvTh 65 (Munich: Kaiser, 1974), 207–14.

5. Here and elsewhere in this chapter all translations are my own unless otherwise indicated.

6. Conzelmann, "'Was von Anfang war,'" 200.

7. This account was later elaborated in Conzelmann's *An Outline of the Theology of the New Testament* (New York: Harper & Row, 1969), 289–317. Thus: "We see [in 1 John 4:2] the first beginnings of the extension of dogma by the positive development of the confession of faith and a critical defence against false doctrine" (302). For further consideration of the ecclesiology betokened by the Johannine epistles, see chapter 14.

could be properly characterized as "a Johannine pastoral epistle": that is, as an "emergent Catholic" adaptation of the Fourth Gospel's legacy for a new day, much as 1 Timothy appropriated the Pauline heritage in the second or third Christian generation.[8]

The staying power of Conzelmann's assessment of 1 John suggests that it is in touch with some important characteristics of that letter. Alongside C. H. Dodd,[9] Conzelmann encouraged NT interpreters to pay attention, not only to the linguistic and conceptual similarities between John and 1 John, but also to their equally impressive differences in viewpoint. Like the Pastorals, the Johannine epistles are concerned with questions about valid teaching and right conduct: Christian orthodoxy and orthopraxy. Moreover, the Johannine letters imply a related issue on which the Pauline Pastorals offer more explicit counsel: namely, the locus of authority within the church and the relationship of that authority to such ecclesiastical matters as tradition, polity, and appropriate criteria by which the Spirit's authorization might be adjudicated. But Conzelmann's reading of 1 John fully flowered some twenty years later, in scholarship that was increasingly absorbed with the adversarial tenor of the Johannine epistles and the implications of that conflict for construing those letters' life setting.

FROM HETERODOXY TO ORTHODOXY

In Conzelmann's opinion, reflection on the church's tradition had become the means for distinguishing orthodoxy and heresy in a Johannine church that, by the time of 1 John, was schismatically at odds with itself. The evidence within the epistle for an intramural split is not hard to come by. Thus, 1 John 2:19, 22:

> They went out from us, but they did not belong to us; for if they had belonged to us, they would have remained with us. But by going out they made it plain that none of them belongs to us. . . . Who is the liar but the

---

8. Conzelmann, "'Was von Anfang war,'" 201. Georg Strecker (*The Johannine Letters: A Commentary on 1, 2, and 3 John*, trans. Linda M. Moloney, Hermeneia [Minneapolis: Fortress, 1996], 5n13), notes that Conzelmann's famous conclusion had been anticipated in Otto Baumgarten's reference to 1 John as a "pastoral circular letter" (*Die Johannesbriefe*, SNT 4 [Gottingen: Vandenhoeck & Ruprecht, 1918], 185).

9. C. H. Dodd, "The First Epistle of John and the Fourth Gospel," *BJRL* 21 (1937): 129–56; Dodd, *The Johannine Epistles*, MNTC (New York: Harper & Brothers, 1946).

one who denies that Jesus is the Christ? This is the antichrist, the one who denies the Father and the Son.

To those comments may be added these, later in the epistle:

> Many false prophets have gone out into the world. By this you know the Spirit of God: every spirit that confesses Jesus Christ come in the flesh is of God, and every spirit that does not confess Jesus is not of God. Rather, this is the spirit of antichrist, of which you have heard that it was coming—well now, here it is in the world already. (1 John 4:1b–3)

To judge from such remarks, it appears that some within the Johannine community had denied that Jesus Christ has come in the flesh, and had broken off communion with the elder and his audience. On its face, the position rebutted in 1 John appears to have some affinity with docetism, a second-century theological trend that disavowed Jesus as "flesh-bearing," claimed that Christ "merely seemed to suffer," and rejected the saving significance of Christ's death.[10]

Since the Middle Ages most interpreters of 1 John have detected in that document an argumentative edge. While modern commentators disagree on the precise shape of the elder's opposition, most concur on what Fernando Segovia has described as "the deeply polemical character" of 1 John, and of the Johannine letters generally.[11] No interpreter has made a more painstaking attempt to reconstruct the terms of this controversy than Raymond Brown, whose commentary on the Epistles of John is by any estimate a milestone in Johannine study.[12] Where Conzelmann's essay is spare and suggestive, Brown's 840-page commentary is exhaustively meticulous and staggering in scope. Brown's assessment of the epistles' place in the development of Johannine Christianity is complex, fine-grained, and as impossible as it is needless for me to reconstruct fully.[13] In essence, however, Brown hypothesized that 1 John's opponents were

---

10. Thus, Ignatius of Antioch, *Smyrn.* 5.2; 7.1; *Trall.* 9.1; 10; *Magn.* 11.

11. Segovia, "Recent Research in the Johannine Letters," *RelSRev* 13 (1987): 132–39; quotation, 135.

12. Raymond E. Brown, *The Epistles of John: Translated with Introduction, Notes, and Commentary*, AB 30 (Garden City, NY: Doubleday, 1982).

13. For full discussion, see Brown's *The Community of the Beloved Disciple: The Life, Loves, and Hates of an Individual Church in New Testament Times* (New York, Ramsey, NJ, and Toronto: Paulist, 1979), N.B. 93–144. Summaries of Brown's theory as it bears on the epistles' interpretation may be found in *Epistles of John*, 69–115, and Brown, "The Relation-

not external rabble-rousers, outside the Johannine community, but were instead one offshoot of Johannine thought itself. *Both* the author of 1 John *and* his adversaries accepted the Johannine proclamation of Christianity as it has come to us in the Fourth Gospel. In effect, the elder and the secessionists were fighting over the proper interpretation of that Gospel's theology. Taking their bearings from the Johannine kerygma, which highlights the glory of Christ, those who had broken away from the community adopted a Christology so high that it annulled Jesus's humanity and dismissed its importance for salvation. By contrast, and with an emphasis that appears retrograde from the Fourth Gospel, the elder insists on the human ministry of "Jesus Christ come in the flesh," who was revealed to take away sin (1 John 3:5; 4:2). In Brown's view, the perspective adopted by the elder's adversaries was eventually swallowed up by full-blown Gnosticism, in all its proliferative variety. The position advocated by the elder himself was ultimately absorbed by the Great Church of the second century, which, thanks to the Johannine epistles, was given an orthodox way of appropriating the Gospel of John.

From Controversy to Consolidation

The different though kindred theories of Conzelmann and Brown for reading 1 John are fascinating and perceptive. Both make intellectually satisfying sense of particular aspects of that document; both have stimulated a broad range of scholarship. One point at which they converge is worth noting: namely, the seeming centrality of the church in their interpretations of the First Epistle. According to Conzelmann, the elder urges the Johannine community to orient itself to its own origin; "reflection on the historical existence of Christian society" is, in 1 John, the doctrinal order of the day. In Brown's view, the historical rupture of the Johannine church does not merely loom behind 1 John's composition; that schism serves as the hermeneutical key that turns almost every exegetical lock in an often obfuscatory epistle. Construed either positively or polemically, the theology in 1 John emerges as primarily ecclesiocentric.

This result strikes me as rather curious: for, as I read 1 John, its *manifest* content is not so relentlessly concentrated on the church. Conzelmann's theory prepares us for a document that should locate the church near the center of

---

ship to the Fourth Gospel Shared by the Author of 1 John and by His Opponents," in *Text and Interpretation: Studies in the New Testament Presented to Matthew Black*, ed. Ernest Best and Robert McLachlan Wilson (Cambridge: Cambridge University Press, 1979), 57–68.

theological reflection, as does Ephesians, or at least for an epistle that practically regulates its community's ministry in the face of doctrinal crisis, like 1 Timothy. First John does neither of these things, not even remotely. Brown's hypothesis throws considerable light on 1 John's clearly controversial passages, reproduced above. The problem here, however, is that the topic of intramural strife occupies hardly more than fifteen out of 1 John's one hundred and five verses—less than one-seventh of the book. The elder's thought has been seared by schism; that no one would deny. Yet when I read 1 John, I find myself wondering whether that letter is as pervasively polemical as Brown seems to suggest.

Though perhaps in a minority, at this point I am not a solitary wonderer: others have begun to ask if such interpretations of this epistle may not mask as much as they unveil. Judith Lieu, for example, has challenged the approach that regards 1 John as a fundamentally polemical writing. She has suggested, to the contrary, that the elder's primary interest is not adversarial but "is directed within the community to confirm its members in their assurance and to struggle with those aspects of its theology which some could—and indeed did—develop in a way which led to ... schism."[14] Lieu sensibly invites us to pay more attention to what the author of 1 John actually says than to what we can only guess his antagonists behind the letter may have been thinking. And she poses a very astute question: if the elder were *chiefly* engaged in polemicizing against the secessionists, then why doesn't he do so more explicitly and extensively than the evidence of 1 John bears out?[15] Nevertheless, Lieu seems to share with those whom she criticizes a basic presupposition: for her, the thought of the epistle is primarily directed *within the community*. Along with Brown and Conzelmann, Lieu appears to regard the theology of 1 John as church-centered.[16]

Discerning interpreters all, Conzelmann, Brown, and Lieu have clarified demonstrably important dimensions of 1 John's thought. The elder *is* interested in the maintenance of Johannine tradition and the encouragement of

---

14. Lieu, "'Authority to Become Children of God': A Study of 1 John," *NovT* 23 (1981): 210-28; quotation, 212. See also Lieu, *The Theology of the Johannine Epistles*, NTT (Cambridge: Cambridge University Press, 1991), 8-16.

15. The same point is registered even more sharply in a critique of Brown's thesis by Brevard S. Childs, *The New Testament as Canon: An Introduction* (Philadelphia: Fortress, 1984), 482-85.

16. Precisely where Lieu locates the "center" of the elder's thought is hard to determine. On the one hand, "1 John is notable for its theocentricity" (*Theology*, 103); on the other, "whereas in the [Fourth] Gospel it is Jesus who plays the focal role [in the decision for faith], in I John it is the community" (*Theology*, 107n14; see also Lieu, *The Second and Third Epistles of John: History and Background*, SNTW [Edinburgh: T&T Clark, 1986], 206).

Christians left behind after a harrowing divorce within the Johannine church. To deny these conclusions would be exegetical folly. To elevate any of them as the letter's primary concern seems to me, however, exegetically unwarranted. As far as I can see, the elder's thought does not revolve around the church. It centers, instead, on God.

From Ecclesiocentricity to Theocentricity

The topic of God cannot be comfortably nestled into the remaining pages of any brief chapter. Here I cannot fully substantiate my claim that God lies at the heart of the elder's theology in 1 John. The best I can do is to sketch some lines along which, to my mind, an appropriate defense might be made.

One might begin with some observations based on simple arithmetic: no other noun occurs more frequently in the text of 1 John than *ho theos*, "God." The name "Jesus" appears twelve times; "Christ," eight times.[17] "Church" (*hē ekklēsia*) occurs not even once in 1 John.[18] By contrast, *ho theos* appears sixty-three times in the First Epistle, to which could be added twelve occurrences of *ho Patēr*, "the Father," that clearly refer to God.[19] These seventy-five explicit references to God do not include the 105 occurrences of the third-person singular pronoun, some of which in context probably refer to Christ but many of which likely refer to God. It is possible, of course, to notch lots of trees and lose sight of the forest. Nevertheless, the sheer weight of these numbers remains impressive. To me they suggest that, if we attend to God in assessing the thought of 1 John, we shall not stray far from the elder's track.

"That which was from the beginning, . . . what we have seen and have heard we proclaim also to you," is the origin of the Johannine church and its traditional heritage—or so Conzelmann believed. Unfortunately for him, however, that is not what the elder says. Immediately after the letter's prologue, the elder himself tells us what the object of the church's proclamation really is:

---

17. *Ho Iēsous*: 1:3, 7; 2:1, 22; 3:23; 4:2, 3, 15; 5:1, 5, 6, 20; *ho Christos*: 1:3; 2:1, 22; 3:23; 4:2; 5:1, 6, 20.

18. The term does appear three times in 3 John (6, 9, 10). Lieu observes (*Theology*, 93) that 3 John contains a number of "institutional" terms, like "to send forward" and "fellow workers," that are more characteristic of the Pauline tradition but do not appear elsewhere in Johannine literature.

19. *Ho theos*: 1:5; 2:5, 14, 17; 3:1, 2, 8, 9 (2x), 10 (2x), 16, 17, 20, 21; 4:1, 2 (2x), 3, 4, 6 (3x), 7 (3x), 8 (2x), 9 (2x), 10, 11, 12 (3x), 15 (3x), 16 (4x), 20 (2x), 21; 5:1, 2 (2x), 3, 4, 9 (2x), 10 (3x), 11, 12, 13, 18 (2x), 19, 20 (2x); *ho patēr*: 1:2, 3; 2:1, 13, 15, 16, 22, 23 (2x), 24; 3:1; 4:14.

> Now this is the message we have heard from him and proclaim to you: that God is light and in him there is no darkness at all. If we say that we have fellowship with him while we walk in darkness, we lie and do not do the truth. But if we walk in the light as he himself is in the light, we have fellowship with one another. (1 John 1:5–7b)

The wording of this statement is critical, because it orients the reader of 1 John to the way in which its author thinks, here and throughout.[20] According to the elder, the church is not an autonomous society, a club that creates its own charter, a party that patches up its differences by means of a little politic give-and-take. Nor, please note, does the church stand as Thesis One of the Johannine credo. *God* is the confessional starting point, and the church's self-understanding is utterly derivative from the nature of God. The church walks in the light as God is in the light. If the church knows that its sins have been forgiven, it is because the church has experienced God as faithful, just, and forgiving (1:9; 2:12). If one purifies oneself, it is because one's hope rests in God, the touchstone for purity (3:3). What the church knows of truth, it knows only by the self-revelation of God, who is truth (5:20). The church loves, not because love is humanitarian, expedient, "what the world needs now,"[21] much less a self-engendered possibility. Rather, "love is from God, and everyone who loves is begotten of God and knows God. . . . We love, because [God] first loved us" (4:7, 19). Nowhere in 1 John does the elder begin with the church's experience, reasoning from that basis to what it believes to be true of God. The elder's thought consistently moves in the opposite direction: it is the character of God, revealed by God, that norms the church's self-understanding and conduct.

Within this context the emphases of Raymond Brown and Judith Lieu fall squarely into place. At two points within 1 John the elder challenges some kind of denigration of Jesus's incarnation that compromised Jesus's messiahship and was, for that reason, counter to Christ or "anti-Christ." The ratcheting up of the elder's rhetoric tips us off to how much he believed was at stake in this controversy. In essence, the elder anticipated Luther's confession: "I begin with the swaddling clothes and accept the one who came, and seek for the one that is in heaven, but I haven't got a ladder to climb up to heaven!"[22] That ladder, in the elder's Johannine tradition, is none other than Jesus, the Word who

---

20. For some of my phrasing, I am indebted to Dodd, *Johannine Epistles*, 8.
21. Quoting the popular song by Hal David (1921–2012) and Burt Bacharach (1928–2023), recorded in 1965 by Jackie DeShannon (1941–).
22. Cited by Christof Windhorst, "Luther and the 'Enthusiasts': Theological Judgments in His Lecture on the First Epistle of John (1527)," *JRH* 9 (1977): 339–48; quotation, 346.

became flesh and tabernacled among us (John 1:14, 51). In the elder's view, "abiding in [that] word" is inseparable from "obedience to the commandment," orthodoxy indivisible from orthopraxy, for the simple reason that the church does not know what love is, apart from the God whose Son Jesus is: "By *this* we know love, that he laid down his life for us; and so we ought to lay down our lives for one another" (1 John 3:16).[23] In effect the elder claims that if we get Jesus wrong, then we shall surely misconstrue the God who saves us; and if our understanding of God is corrupted, then our conduct as Christians will be inevitably deformed. Thus, while the First Epistle of John may have been triggered by a Christological controversy, the elder's own concern is ultimately *theo*logical, as he makes abundantly clear: "No one who denies the Son has the Father either; the one who confesses the Son has the Father also" (2:23).

Precisely on this theological basis does the church's confidence rest:

> See what love the Father has given us, that we should be called children of God: and that is what we are. . . . Beloved, right now we are God's children, though what we shall be has not yet been revealed. But we do know that at this revelation we shall be like him, for we shall see him as he is. (1 John 3:1a, 2)

Lieu is surely correct: the elder is far more obviously interested in bolstering his readers than in smiting his enemies. But notice that Christian assurance is not grounded in the church's ability under stress, any more than Christians' acts of justice or purity are preconditions for God's favor. To believe that would be to conclude that children give birth to themselves.[24] By contrast, 1 John is diamond-clear, and just as adamantine, that the initiative for creating children of God resides entirely with God. God's children are responsible agents, but they are response-able—enabled to respond—by the prevenient, gratuitous endowment of God's perdurable, self-sacrificial love for them.

Fifty years ago Nils Dahl called attention to "The Neglected Factor in New Testament Theology"—the overlooked element being "any comprehensive or penetrating study of 'God in the New Testament.'"[25] To suggest that Conzel-

---

23. *Ho huios*, "the Son," occurs as an appellation for Jesus twenty-two times in 1 John: 1:3, 7; 2:22, 23 (2x), 24; 3:8, 23; 4:9, 10, 14, 15; 5:5, 9, 10 (2x), 11, 12 (2x), 13, 20 (2x). Of all descriptions of Jesus *ho huios* is the one that most obviously implies God, the Father who sent him (John 5:19–24).

24. As Lieu knows very well: *Theology*, 33–38.

25. Nils A. Dahl, "The Neglected Factor in New Testament Theology," *Reflections* 75 (1975): 5–8; repr. Dahl, *Jesus the Christ: The Historical Origins of Christological Doctrine*, ed. Donald H. Juel (Minneapolis: Fortress, 1991), 153–63; quotation, 154.

mann, Brown, Lieu, and others have ignored the doctrine of God in the First Epistle of John would be both inaccurate and unjust. But Dahl's diagnosis reminds us that what we take for granted is especially susceptible to underestimation and potential disregard. Surely in the study of 1 John's theology it is high time for us to reappraise its view of God. That, manifestly, is the hub from which radiate most of the elder's subsidiary concerns, including the church's identity, fracture, and ultimate hope.[26] Even more: as we ponder the thinking of all the NT writers, starting at some point other than God—failing, at bare minimum, to return regularly to that point—is skating on very thin ice.[27]

Such a proposal may seem blindingly obvious to some, a laboring of what goes without saying. Like every human endeavor, however, NT research is at times stunningly myopic. That which goes for too long without saying must finally be reasserted with some force, if for no reason other than to correct our parlous proclivity to mistake theology's *circle* of concerns for its *center*. Apart from such correction we constantly court biblical knowledge without scriptural wisdom.

> Said a disciple to the elder, "Master, I have gone thoroughly through Scripture. What more do I lack?"
> The elder answered, "Dear friend, the question is not, Have you gone through Scripture? The question is, Has Scripture gone through you?"[28]

---

26. C. K. Barrett's assessment of the Fourth Evangelist may be even more pertinent to the elder: "There could hardly be a more christocentric writer than John, yet his very Christocentricity is theocentric" ("'The Father Is Greater Than I' John 14.28: Subordinationist Christology in the New Testament," in Barrett, *Essays on John* [Philadelphia: Westminster, 1982], 19–36; quotation, 32). See also the nuanced treatment by Paul W. Meyer, "'The Father': The Presentation of God in the Fourth Gospel," in *Exploring the Gospel of John in Honor of D. Moody Smith*, ed. R. Alan Culpepper and C. Clifton Black (Louisville: Westminster John Knox, 1996), 255–73.

27. In what turned out to be his scholarly valediction, George Caird expressed his sense of the matter with typical eloquence: "The question we must ask is not whether these books [of the New Testament] all say the same thing, but whether they all bear witness to the same Jesus and through him to the many splendoured wisdom of the one God" (*New Testament Theology*, compiled and ed. L. D. Hurst [Oxford: Clarendon, 1994], 24).

28. Adapted from Joan Chittister, *The Rule of Benedict: Insights for the Ages*, SLB (New York: Crossroad, 1992), 179–80.

This essay was originally dedicated in memory of Raymond E. Brown, SS (1928–98), and remains so. Fr. Brown was a churchman of exhaustive erudition and even rarer wisdom.

CHAPTER 6

Whose Kingdom? Whose Power? Whose Glory?

> Justice and power must be brought together, so that whatever is just may be powerful, and whatever is powerful may be just.
>
> —Blaise Pascal

SIR FRANK KERMODE (1919–2010) argued that a classic is not simply a piece of literature that acquires permanence, being read long after it was written. For Kermode, a classic is a work of infinite pliability, able to be accommodated in whatever culture it later finds itself; it "subsists in change, prevails, by being patient of interpretation."[1] While Sir Frank did not explore the possibility, I wonder if his definition highlights a difference between the literary classic and scriptural literature: for the really notable feature of any religion's sacred writings is neither their durability, nor their toleration of multiple readings, but rather their perennial capacity to dis-accommodate readers who find in them a home. Scriptures make for those who inhabit them unsettled domiciles; in them a religion's adherents may feel at home though never entirely at ease. This article's case in point: thirty-eight simple words from the Gospel of Luke, which translate from the Greek thirty-eight of comparable simplicity.

> Father, may your name be hallowed; may your kingdom come.
> Keep giving us each day our daily bread.

This essay was originally delivered as the Nadine Beacham and Charlton F. Hall Sr. Lecture in New Testament and Early Christianity at the University of South Carolina on April 11, 2013. I dedicate this chapter to Mr. Charlton F. Hall Jr., of Columbia, South Carolina, with thanks for his benevolence in sponsoring this lectureship in his parents' memory and for so graciously receiving me during my visit to the USC campus. Since then I have expanded this chapter's exegesis into a book-length commentary, *The Lord's Prayer*, IRUSC (Louisville: Westminster John Knox, 2018).

1. Frank Kermode, *The Classic: Literary Images of Permanence and Change* (Cambridge, MA, and London: Harvard University Press, 1983), 134.

And forgive us our sins,
for we ourselves forgive everyone indebted to us.
And let us not fall victim to temptation. (Luke 11:2b–4)[2]

No words from the Bible are more often repeated by Christians than these. Somewhere, every minute of every day, someone is reciting what has become known as the Lord's Prayer or the Pater Noster ("Our Father"). From its earliest utterance the Lord's Prayer has taught Jesus's followers not only how to pray but also what is essential in prayer. For most Christians these words set the standard of all prayer. Thus were they regarded by Augustine of Hippo (354–430): "If we pray rightly and as becomes our needs, we can say nothing but what is already contained in this prayer of our Lord" (*Ep.* 130.22). Likewise, in the last century, Simone Weil (1909–43): "The Our Father contains all possible petitions; we cannot conceive of any prayer not already contained in it. It is to prayer what Christ is to humanity."[3]

How may one speak of prayer in a secular society? In our workaday world we may ponder prayer as we would consider any human practice that is basic and consequential. "Prayers have this diagnostic value," suggest Philip and Carol Zaleski: "They present in microcosm the longings, beliefs, ideals, and assumptions that drive the inner life of individuals and the corporate life of human cultures. In prayer, the dreams of a civilization take lucid and articulate form."[4] Prayer is primary speech: a form of human discourse that acts, coordinating the head with the heart and the gut.[5] Some anthropologists reckon prayer as old as any known cultural artifact, perhaps as universal as language itself. Prayer has a place, not only in the church or the synagogue, the mosque or the temple, but in the university as well. No expression of human experience is barred from the academy. Religious devotion is among the oldest, most pervasive of human activities.

My aim in this study is to meditate on a particular prayer: the one with which I am most familiar as both an observant Christian and a professional theologian. Familiarity need not breed contempt, but it can lull into complacency. Like Poe's purloined letter, the things nearest us are the hardest to perceive. One must pause to reflect. The way I shall travel has three stations.

2. Unless otherwise indicated, all translations in this chapter are my own.
3. Simone Weil, *Waiting for God* (New York: Putnam's, 1951), 226–27.
4. Philip Zaleski and Carol Zaleski, *Prayer: A History* (Boston and New York: Houghton Mifflin, 2005), 15.
5. Ann and Barry Ulanov, *Primary Speech: A Psychology of Prayer* (Atlanta: John Knox, 1982).

First, I shall consider some exegetical aspects of the Lord's Prayer critical for its understanding.[6] Second, I am interested in exploring how that prayer pulls some threads of the civil religion that weaves the contemporary American ethos. Third, I shall close with thoughts on how this prototypical Christian prayer may offer bridges for conversation with other religious traditions. My aim, then, is to offer a description, a critique, and a hope. At every point I must simplify: space is limited; one must cut to the matter's heart. None of what follows is the last word. It is a place to begin.

Some Essential Features of the Pater Noster

In the context of Jesus's original teaching, the Pater Noster appears to have been thoroughly eschatological, angled toward the final age (see, e.g., Luke 17:20–21). Raymond Brown argued this over sixty years ago, and his argument still holds up.[7] That does not make of Jesus's words a flea-market relic. Instead, it helps those who would understand Christianity to appreciate the end-time coloring that permeates its claims, its liturgy, and its view of everyday circumstances. Contrary to the beliefs of innocents and crackpots, eschatology is not a clock by which one sets the alarm of "a rapture." Eschatology is a way of leaning forward now into God's in-breaking dominion, which is already beginning to put things right before their consumption.

Father

Ancient Israel used many metaphors to address God. The Psalter abounds in them: "governor" (Ps 8:1[2], 9[10]); "shepherd" (Pss 23:1; 80:1); "king" (Pss 93:1; 99:1; 145:1); "my stronghold, my crag, and my haven" (Ps 18:1[2]); "my rock, . . . my shield, the horn of my salvation, and my refuge" (Ps 18:2[3]). Most often the Psalmist simply cries, "O LORD" or "O God." Reference to God as "father" is rare in the HB: it occurs fourteen times, never in direct address.[8] As we shall see, paternal imagery for God is better attested in later synagogue liturgy. In

---

6. To extend my thoughts in fresh directions, this essay reasserts some claims made in an earlier study, "The Education of Human Wanting: Formation by *Pater Noster*," in *Character and Scripture: Moral Formation, Community, and Biblical Interpretation*, ed. William P. Brown (Grand Rapids and Cambridge: Eerdmans, 2002), 248–63. This chapter also encapsulates some commentary in *Lord's Prayer*, ICUSC.

7. Raymond E. Brown, "The Pater Noster as Eschatological Prayer," *TS* 22 (1961): 175–208.

8. For instance: Isa 9:6; Pss 68:5; 89:26; 103:13; Mal 1:6; cf. Wisdom 14:3; Sirach 23:1, 4.

this context, Jesus's address to God as "Father" is not unprecedented, though it is distinctive. The NT refers to God as "Father" about 170 times, 109 of which occur in sayings of Jesus in the Fourth Gospel (among others, John 5:17; 6:32; 10:15–38; 14:2–17:25; 20:17–21).

The NT's appeals to God as *patēr*, "father," embrace various connotations. One is *comprehensive authority*. Like "kingship," attributing to God fatherhood acknowledges God as the one who creates a people, and the one to whom those elect are ultimately accountable (Matt 7:21–23; 18:23–35; Acts 17:26–28; 1 Pet 1:17). The Synoptic Gospels portray Jesus as the "beloved Son" on whom God has conferred faithful execution of divine authority.[9] In John (14:8–9) Philip asks Jesus to show him and other disciples the Father; Jesus replies, "The one who has seen me has seen the Father."

Another nuance, present in address to God as "father," is often neglected yet obvious: its *familial* character. "Father" does what no other metaphor can: it identifies the one who prays as a sister or brother of Jesus, who appealed to his Father as the Son who does nothing of his own accord but only what he sees the Father doing (John 5:19; 11:41–42; cf. Matt 11:27; Luke 10:22). A Jewish child's right of inheritance passed through the father, not the mother (b. B. Bat. 115a; cf. Gen 21:10; Ruth 1:2–14; Gal 4:6–7). To address God as Father has nothing to do with gender as such, but everything to do with a child's gracious adoption as heir to God's covenant with Israel.[10] Moreover, all the Gospels whisper an estrangement of Christians from their blood-kin and religious homes for the sake of the gospel (Matt 8:21–22; Mark 13:9–13; Luke 18:28; John 9:18–23). Jesus assures his followers of their embrace in a family, over which presides "my Father and your Father" (Mark 10:29–31; John 20:17). That's probably why NT writers portrayed local Christian congregations as "household[s] of God" (Gal 6:10; Eph 2:19; 1 Tim 3:15; 1 Pet 4:17). The upshot of this for understanding the Pater Noster: the prayer is personal though never private. To address God as Father is to confess mutual accountability within a family that in every time and place appeals for "*our* daily bread," release from "*our* debts," and *our* direction out of temptation (Matt 6:11–13; Luke 11:3–4). These plural pronouns are crucial: they pull the Prayer's pray-ers out of selfish individualism into a relationship of ever-expanding generosity.

---

9. Matt 3:17; 9:6, 8; 12:18; 17:5; 28:18; Mark 1:22; 2:10; 9:7; 12:6; Luke 20:13; note also John 5:26–27, 30.

10. See Marianne Meye Thompson, *The Promise of the Father: Jesus and God in the New Testament* (Louisville: Westminster John Knox, 2000).

Resonant in the prayer's address to God as Father is a third note: *the cry for help in time of need.* Thrice in the NT—Mark 14:36, Romans 8:15, and Galatians 4:6—God is summoned as "*Abba*! Father!" Embedded in each of these texts is an obedient child's spontaneous cry, in desperate straits, to a beloved parent of compassionate providence. That rhymes with John's Gospel, in which Jesus increasingly prays to the Father as suffering suffuses the story (11:41–42; 12:27–33; 17:1–26), and with the Epistle to the Hebrews: "In the days of his flesh, [Jesus] offered up prayers and supplications, with loud cries and tears, to the one who was able to save him from death, and he was heard because of his reverent submission. Although he was a Son, he learned obedience through what he suffered" (5:7–8). In none of these cases is God the tormentor. To the contrary: God is the Father to whom tormented children flee for help. Yet the Father no more spares them suffering than he spared his own Son, giving up Jesus for all so that all may also receive everything with Jesus (Rom 8:32).

To summarize: in biblical context, to pray to God as Father is to unite oneself with Christ and the church, submitting oneself to God's merciful authority. Nowhere in the NT is an ascription of fatherhood to God used to justify male authority. Insecure, stupid Christians have sometimes perverted that metaphor into an abusive patriarchy. That can be neither denied nor justified. It is a sin of which the church should repent. Such perversion has stimulated others to tar Christianity as a pathological religion with "an abusive theology that glorifies suffering," predicated on "divine child abuse."[11] That charge is no less foolish or faithless. Of that, too, the church should repent. Common to both distortions is an unacknowledged anthropocentrism: the projection onto God of humanity's own puerility, injustice, and selfishness. The Gospels are clear that Jesus's disciples are in no way to judge their "heavenly Father" (Matt 6:9b) by the conduct of earthly fathers, who are, in spite of all they may give their children, evil (*ponēroi*: Matt 7:9–12 // Luke 11:11–13). "Call no one your father on earth," Jesus warns, "for you have one Father—the one in heaven" (Matt 23:9; see also 8:21–22). Prayer to the heavenly Father enables Jesus's disciples to grow into the likeness and life of God (Eph 6:1–4, 18). The rest of the prayer is its own commentary on what it means to pray, with wisdom and love, to God as Father.

---

11. Joanne Carlson Browne and Rebecca Parker, "For God So Loved the World?" in *Christianity, Patriarchy, and Abuse: A Feminist Critique*, ed. Joanne Carlson Browne and Carole R. Bohn (New York: Pilgrim, 1989), 1–30, N.B. 26.

May Your Name Be Hallowed, May Your Kingdom Come

The first and second petitions mark the clearest intersection between the Pater Noster and the great Jewish Kaddish[12] which is also eschatologically tinctured:

> *Exalted and hallowed be His great Name*
>   in the world which He created
>   according to His will.
> *May He establish His kingdom*
>   in your lifetime and in your days,
>   and in the lifetime of the whole household of Israel,
>   speedily and at a near time.
>   And say: Amen.[13]

When praying the Lord's Prayer, it is crucial that Christians remember that their Lord was a devout Jew. When his followers pray as Jesus taught them, they sing an antiphon of praise with the synagogue. The prayer perpetually reminds a predominantly Gentile church that Jesus is their one and only point of entrée to the gracious covenants, law, and promises of God to Israel.[14]

What is the "name" of God? What does it mean to "hallow" it? Who does the hallowing? In the Bible one's name is no mere label; in one's name lies one's peculiar essence (Gen 2:19; 32:28). When God causes his name to inhabit a place, it is a way of saying that God himself dwells there (Deut 12:5-11). In Ezekiel, God promises to restore Israel from exile for his own name's sake: "Thus said the LORD God: Not for your sake will I act, O House of Israel, but for My holy name, . . . I will sanctify My great name. . . . And the nations shall know that I am the LORD" (36:22-23 NJPS).

In the first instance, therefore, it is not Israel that hallows God's name. Rather, *God* hallows the divine name: sets it apart, consecrates it, sanctifies it. God demonstrates singular, supreme divinity over all other gods and authorities by redeeming Israel. The purpose of its redemption is that the nations may

---

12. The earliest version of this venerable Jewish prayer, typically used in mourning rituals, may be traced to 900 CE, though its constituents may be much older.

13. The "Half *Kaddish*" of the rabbinic period, as presented in *The Lord's Prayer and Jewish Liturgy*, ed. Jakob J. Petuchowski and Michael Brocke (New York: Seabury, 1978), 37.

14. Romans 9:1-5; Eph 2:1-22. See Asher Finkel, "The Prayer of Jesus in Matthew," in *Standing Before God: Studies on Prayer in Scriptures and in Tradition*, ed. Asher Finkel and Lawrence Frizzell (New York: KTAV, 1981), 131-69.

acknowledge God as God, the true Sovereign over all. In Ezekiel (36:25–27), God's hallowing of the divine name purifies a profane Israel.

Thus, in the Pater Noster, we may reasonably surmise that it is God who hallows his name, even as the Father is finally responsible for establishing God's kingdom and for the universal execution of divine will.[15] The triple petitions in Matthew's more elaborate version of the prayer—hallow your name; let your kingdom come; may what you will, happen (Matt 6:10bc)—boil down to the introductory petitions in Luke (Luke 11:2bc; cf. Matt 6:9c–10a): May you, God, act in such a way that you may be truly acknowledged as God. As Paul puts it with his characteristic bite, "Though everyone is a liar, let God be proved true!" (Rom 3:4).

Keep Giving Us Each Day Our Daily Bread

The initial petitions of the Lord's Prayer concentrate on the character of God's authority: parental, royal, and holy. The petition for bread opens a complementary series of requests for divine provision of nourishment, release, and protection.[16] What to this point in the prayer has been latent becomes patent: humanity's intrinsic neediness. Broadway's Little Orphan Annie is too self-assured: "The sun'll come up tomorrow"—but we may not. Human beings are contingent creatures, lacking within themselves the resources necessary for their sustenance. The Pater Noster expresses those needs, draws to the surface primary human desires, and trains one's gaze upon the only One capable of fulfilling them.

For the earliest Christians "bread" bundled multiple connotations. In addition to simple food (Matt 7:9; Mark 6:8; Acts 20:11), it summoned up memories of manna, which the LORD rained from heaven upon Israel in the wilderness every day for forty years (Exod 16:4–25). Looking forward, Christians expected bread to be served at the Messiah's end-time banquet (Luke 14:15; cf. Matt 8:11; Luke 22:29–30; Rev 7:13–17). Looking backward, in remembrance of Jesus's Last Supper with the Twelve, bread became a fundamental element in Christians' observance of the Lord's Supper (Mark 14:22–25; 1 Cor 11:23–26).[17] Manna, messianic feast, and Eucharist converge in the claims of the Johannine Jesus:

---

15. See Matthew's longer form of the prayer (6:10bc; cf. Ps 135:6), where we find examples of "divine passives": Greek verbs conjugated in the passive voice as reverential circumlocutions for describing activities whose agent is God.

16. I translate *didou* as an iterative imperative: "Give, and keep giving to us."

17. Its celebration molded the ways they retold stories of Jesus's feeding of multitudes (Matt 14:13–21 // Mark 6:30–44 // Luke 9:10–17; Matt 15:32–39 // Mark 8:1–10).

"I am the living bread that came down from heaven. If anyone eats of this bread, he will live forever; and the bread that I shall give for the life of the world is my flesh" (John 6:51).

When praying the Pater Noster it is impossible to filter out all but one of these connotations—not only impossible, but also undesirable and theologically dubious. From Israel's days in the Sinai until now, the people of God have experienced manifold hunger. Heavenly manna filled famished stomachs; loaves from the oven have been taken, broken, and thankfully offered as Christ's body to sustain the body of Christ. When Christians pray for bread, they ask for nourishment in all forms.[18] Petitioning every day and all of time for "the sacrament of the present moment,"[19] they beseech God, who is the Giver and, in Christ, the Gift (John 6:53-58).

And Forgive Us Our Sins, For We Ourselves Forgive Everyone Indebted to Us

Did ever a passage better exemplify the worry attributed to Mark Twain: "It ain't those parts of the Bible that I can't understand that bother me; it is the parts that I do understand"? Forgiveness, its petition and pledge, is the Lord's Prayer at its toughest.

The incurring of debt and its forgiveness are as old as culture; its association with sin and salvation runs deep in Israelite soil (e.g., Isa 40:2; 55:6-7; Jer 31:34). Yet we stumble by confusing forgiveness with things not implied by that metaphor. As the saying goes, "Forgive and forget." That's not only false; it's impossible. One cannot forgive what has been forgotten. Some meanness or malice we have suffered—or inflicted—may be unforgettable. In extreme cases it should be. Forgiveness is neither the denial of injury nor a pretense that no harm's been done. Injury denied is injury magnified. The efficacy of forgiveness depends on no-nonsense recognition of debt. Concocting excuses for sin is no substitute for forgiveness: we may cut an offender slack by the yard without covering the offending inch that remains. Another error is to twist forgiveness into the placement of someone "on probation": postponing indignation until a later offense, or until our unresolved fury over its prede-

---

18. Etymologically, the extremely rare word *epiousios* may refer (at minimum) to bread (1) for the "existing day" (= daily), (2) "necessary for existence" (both derivative of *epi* and *einai* ["to be"]), or (3) "for the coming day" (*epi* and *ienai* ["to go/come"]). Brown notes ("Pater Noster as Eschatological Prayer," 195): "In the third century the word puzzled Origen (*De oratione* 27, 7), who could find no example of it in other Greek writers. Seventeen centuries later we are not much better off." For further discussion, see Black, *Lord's Prayer*, 150-57.

19. The phrase is Jean Pierre de Caussade's: *Abandonment: or, Absolute Surrender to Divine Providence* (New York: Benziger Brothers, [1887] 1952), 92-94.

cessor can no longer be contained. All such strategies fail. In spirituality as in economics, forgiveness is a deliberate decision to release someone indebted to us from compensation, however just that restitution may be. Forgiveness is finally a matter of mercy, and it costs dearly.

So many are the lies in which humans wrap themselves: a presumption of entitlement; an egotism so woolly that we'd settle for the puny indifference of "getting a break." Apart from the Pater Noster's injunction, we might go frightening stretches of our lives oblivious to the fact that all of us are forgiven debtors. The prayer mandates repentance: its petitioners appeal to the Father in a family whose members are, by the same prayer, learning to forgive us the abuse we have heaped on them. There's the rub. In asking God for forgiveness, do we assume, following Pudd'nhead Wilson's Calendar, "Nothing so needs reforming as other people's habits"?[20] Or can one recognize what C. S. Lewis discerned: "To be a Christian means to forgive the inexcusable, because God has forgiven the inexcusable in you"?[21] Debt-forgiveness is, at bottom, self-renunciation. Who wants that? Only those who relinquish themselves to God in a prayer like this.

And Let Us Not Fall Victim to Temptation

The prayer's final petition completes the eschatological arc described by previous appeals for God's hallowing of his name, the kingdom's coming, and providential bread.[22] Many early Christians expected a retaliatory outburst, a "great tribulation," overlapping with the present age before God completely reclaims this world for benevolent wholeness (*shalom*).[23] From this vantage point, severe attacks upon the faithful are neither divine punishments nor dumb luck. Jesus's Prayer locates such trials along the horizon of his own battle with "powers and principalities," before God's righteous peace can reassemble us among all things in everything (1 Cor 15:20–28; Eph 6:10–20; Col 2:13–15).

The prayer's Greek text may be translated in the way it is often uttered: "And lead us not into temptation." Did Jesus regard God as the agent of temptation? Possibly, though not likely. In none of the Gospels is temptation an

---

20. Mark Twain, *Mississippi Writings: The Adventures of Tom Sawyer, Life on the Mississippi, Adventures of Huckleberry Finn, Pudd'nhead Wilson*, ed. Guy Cardwell, LOA (New York: Library of America, 1982), 1005.

21. C. S. Lewis, "On Forgiveness," in Lewis, *The Weight of Glory and Other Essays* (New York: Simon & Schuster, 1996), 135; so, too, Matt 18:21–35; Luke 17:3–4.

22. That end-time hue is deepened by Matthew's addition of the prayer for deliverance from the Evil One (6:13b; also Did. 8.2) and by the doxology that scribes added to Matt 6:13 ("for yours is the kingdom, and the power, and the glory, forever; amen").

23. Matt 10:34–36 // Luke 12:49–53; Mark 13:5–13; 2 Thess 2:7; Rev 3:10; 7:9–17.

instrument of "character-building": Jesus counsels his disciples to pray that they may not enter trials (Matt 26:41; Mark 14:38; Luke 22:40, 46). Throughout the NT, temptation is not divine, but diabolical.[24] The Epistle of James denies that God tempts anyone (1:13). All this echoes ancient Jewish prayers offered at morning and evening, some form of which Jesus himself may have prayed:

> Bring me not into the power of sin,
> And not into the power of guilt,
> And not into the power of temptation,
> And not into the power of anything shameful. (b. Ber. 60b.)

For his disciples, as for Jesus himself, tribulations precede the Ultimate Trial. Jesus's followers are not exempt. They pray that they may not be victimized, so overwhelmed by temptation that they lose faith and fall away (Luke 8:13; cf. Matt 13:21; Mark 4:17). In that season God understands and stands ready to succor: as Paul wrote to the Corinthians, "God can be depended on not to let you be tried beyond your strength but, when temptation comes, to give you a way out of it so that you can withstand it" (1 Cor 10:13b Smith-Goodspeed).

To judge from the Gospels, Jesus embodied what he taught: a life turned Godward, daring to live in a present he believed was being rectified by God's future sovereignty. The prayer he taught his followers to pray articulates that faith. To address God as beneficent authority, to pray that God's governance will come and restore a fractured world, is to place oneself entirely at God's disposal and, by so doing, to ask that God will transform the pray-er into one who wants nothing other than the fulfillment of God's will. To pray the Pater Noster is to live off God's future right now.[25] That is what makes it eschatological. That is what makes it disruptive. And therein lies its promise.

Positive Prayer as Tacit Critique

Risking reductionism, we have concentrated on a pair of entwined claims in this prayer: (1) God's transcendent providence; (2) humanity's quintessential neediness. Jesus taught his disciples to pray to God as a beneficent parent and judge of final appeal: the God whose Name—whose essential charac-

---

24. Matt 4:1 // Mark 1:13 // Luke 4:2; Luke 4:13; 1 Cor 7:5; 1 Thess 3:5.
25. Consult the acute analysis in Leander E. Keck, *Who Is Jesus? History in Perfect Tense*, SPNT (Columbia: University of South Carolina Press, 2000; repr. Minneapolis: Fortress, 2001), 64–112.

ter, ways, and thoughts—are different from our own (cf. Isa 55:8–9), whose authority is unlike any this world has ever known. The difference is one of kind, not of degree. The kingdom, which this prayer beseeches, is one you'll find nowhere in Rand McNally. Neither is it the highest, finest government we could possibly imagine. Jesus never defined "the kingdom," and for good reason neither should we: any such attempt finally runs aground on human presumption—our projection to some nth degree of what human beings consider powerful and glorious. With our first step in that direction we are already lost: we are only foisting ourselves, our aspirations and programs, onto God, instead of opening ourselves to the One who desires relationship with us on terms other than those we would set. Like the ten words Moses received on Sinai (Exod 20:2–17 // Deut 5:6–21), the Lord's Prayer acknowledges human need but doesn't start there. It opens with divine holiness on God's own terms, God's sovereignty over every human desire or design. The Lord's Prayer, like the Torah, begins and ends with God.

The Pater Noster's *theo*centricity—its concentration on a living, loving, sovereign God—calls into question pervasive incursions on God's holiness in our day. These assaults have "soft" and "hard" expressions. A fluffing of God's transcendence can warp divine authority into a delusion of God's patronage over the presumed excellences of the United States and a dangerously manic nationalism. In this soft version "God Bless America" can be trumpeted with a hubris that discounts the Lord's blessed commitment to *all* peoples. (With Irving Berlin's [1888–1989] unwitting assistance, "God Bless America" has become the American president's equivalent of "Have a nice day.") The hard form of the Almighty's diminution is active in radically postmodern secularism. A generation that swallows its Nietzsche [1844–1900] whole—"the will to power" that regards God as author of evil or the dead name for a loathsome norm of goodness—will choke on the petitions of the Lord's Prayer all the way to its nihilist bankruptcy.[26]

If that's not sufficiently offensive, the prayer makes things worse: it is a frontal assault on our belief in the sovereign self. So deeply is this conviction embedded in American culture, and so alien is it to the prayer Jesus taught his disciples, that its examination is mandatory.

Ancient Israelites and Hellenistic Jews enjoyed a well-developed sensitivity to their frailty, vulnerability, and the reality of death.[27] In Job's words:

---

26. Friedrich Nietzsche, *The Will to Power* ([1901/1906]; trans. and ed. Walter Kaufmann [New York: Vintage, 1968]); Nietzsche, *On the Genealogy of Morals* ([1887]; trans. and ed. Walter Kaufmann [New York: Vintage, 1989]).

27. Consult Hans Walter Wolff, *Anthropology of the Old Testament* (Philadelphia: Fortress, 1974), 33–35.

> If [God] but intends it, He can call back His spirit and breath;
> All flesh would at once expire, And mankind return to dust.
> (34:14–15)

The Pater Noster presupposes such radical dependence of creatures on their Creator. If God does not provide the one who prays with bread every day, she will starve. If the Father does not strengthen his children when tempted, they shall fall. As a whole, the prayer assumes of humanity an irreducible contingency. To pray this prayer is, in effect, a vote of no confidence in our natural competence.

To put it bluntly, most Americans, most of the time, do not act as though they believe that. The autonomy of the sovereign self has been a keystone of our shared European creed for nearly a half-millennium. I'm no political theorist[28]—those who are must correct me where I err—but my hunch is that our reflexive self-esteem as "masters of our fate and captains of our souls"[29] runs as deep as Machiavelli's obsession with the magistrate's seizure and consolidation of power[30] and with "the mortal God"—the earthly potentate as Leviathan—who, for Thomas Hobbes (1588–1679), socializes human beings by protecting them from lives and appetites that are "solitary, poore, nasty, brutish, and short."[31] Though John Locke (1632–1704) was more sanguine about *The Reasonableness of Christianity* for the "Body Politick,"[32] he did us no favor by privatizing the religious conscience, absolutely isolating it from the commonwealth. With that, the lid flew off Pandora's box: Rousseau's worship of civil religion, Hegel's divinization of human history, Kant's autonomous moralist, Mill's sovereign individual, and Emerson's hymn to "Man Thinking."[33]

---

28. The summary that follows is indebted to Jean Bethke Elshtain, *Sovereignty: God, State, and Self (The Gifford Lectures)* (New York: Basic Books, 2008).

29. Thus, William Ernest Henley (1849–1903), "Invictus" (1875), in *The New Oxford Book of English Verse, 1250–1950*, ed. Helen Gardner (New York: Oxford University Press, 1972), 792.

30. Niccolo Machiavelli (1469–1527), *The Prince* [1532] (New York: Norton, 1977).

31. Thomas Hobbes, *Leviathan, or The Matter, Forme and Power of a Common Wealth Ecclesiastical and Civil* (New York: Penguin, 1983), esp. 186.

32. Volume 6 in *The Works of John Locke in Nine Volumes*, 12th ed. (London: Rivington, 1824).

33. Jean-Jacques Rousseau (1712–78), *On the Social Contract [or, Principles of Political Right] with Geneva Manuscript and Political Economy*, ed. Roger D. Masters, trans. Judith R. Masters (New York: St. Martin's, 1978); Georg Wilhelm Friedrich Hegel (1770–1831), *Elements of the Philosophy of Right* [1820], trans. T. M. Knox (London: Oxford University Press, 1976), esp. 210; Immanuel Kant (1724–1804), *Critique of Pure Reason*, trans. Norman Kemp Smith

Whose Kingdom? Whose Power? Whose Glory?

Our sacrifice on the altar of self-sovereignty also has "soft" and "hard" manifestations. Brief and brittle is its expression by television's representative theologian, Bart Simpson, who, when asked to return thanks at supper, said, "God, we paid for all this ourselves. So thanks for nothing." At its most dangerous, when a self-styled Christian nation in 2003 apes first-century imperial Rome, it can sound like this:

> [Our critics live] in what we call the reality-based community . . . those who believe that solutions emerge from your judicious study of discernible reality. That's not the way the world works anymore. We're an empire now, and when we act, we create our own reality. And while you're studying that reality—judiciously, as you will—we'll act again, creating other new realities, which you can study too, and that's how things will sort out. We're history's actors . . . and you, all of you, will be left to just study what we do.

So spake a senior adviser to the president of the United States in 2004, twenty months after the US invasion of Iraq (2003–11).[34] By the end of 2012, an estimated 4,804 military personnel had died.[35] Estimates of total fatalities as a result of the conflict, including civilians, range from 174,000 to 1.2 million.[36]

Adlai Stevenson (1900–1965), who twice ran for the presidency and was twice defeated, spoke for himself and his follow politicos: "A lie is an abomination unto the Lord, and a very present help in time of trouble."[37] The big lie is not some cherry picking of evidence for a bogus casus belli. The deeper, uglier lie—about ourselves and those whom we elect—is that we can say, with unflappable self-delusion and a poker-straight face, "We create our own reality": a laissez-faire imperialism forced down the rest of the world's throat. Sartre quipped, "Hell is other people."[38] Sartre was wrong. Hell is ourselves in self-imposed, solitary confinement: unaccountable to others, enslaved to do

---

(New York: Modern Library, 1958), esp. 257, 259; John Stuart Mill (1806–73), *On Liberty* [1859] (New York: Penguin, 1983); Ralph Waldo Emerson (1803–82), "The American Scholar: An Oration Delivered before the Phi Beta Kappa Society at Cambridge, August 31, 1837," in *Essays & Lectures*, ed. Joel Porte, LOA (New York: Library of America, 1983), 54, 63–71.

34. Ron Suskind, "Without a Doubt: Faith, Certainty, and the Presidency of George W. Bush," *New York Times Magazine* (October 17, 2004): 51.

35. Iraq Coalition Casualty Count (https://www.iraqbodycount.org).

36. The Iraq Body Count Project (https://www.iraqbodycount.org/database/); Opinion Research Business Survey (https://orb-international.com).

37. Jonathan Green, ed., *The Book of Political Quotes* (New York: McGraw Hill, 1982), 212.

38. Jean-Paul Sartre, *No Exit and Three Other Plays* (New York: Vintage, 1955), 47.

our damnedest. Viewed from the perspective of Jesus's Prayer, hell is a refusal of relationship to God and neighbor—to both of whom we are always in debt. The one who prays that God's kingdom may come yearns to be free but realizes, with Dietrich Bonhoeffer, that freedom is neither an inherent human quality, nor a possession, nor a mode of existence. "Being free means 'being free for the other,' because the other has bound me to him. Only in relationship with the other am I free."[39] Until we can accept that as true and risk living into that truth, we'll continue to lock ourselves into a post-9/11 socio-pathology in which we are *forever* at war, *never* at peace.[40] We have now so habituated ourselves to violence that we have normalized derangement. Beside the NRA's Wayne LaPierre, we point the finger of mental illness at others[41]—but never at ourselves.

The Prayer of Jesus as Invitation to Interreligious Communion

To end on a note so disconsolate would betray the intent of Jesus's Prayer. Those who pray to God as Sovereign Father have no reason for despair without hope (1 Thess 4:13). As I reflect on the Pater Noster, I am struck by the degree to which a prayer so definitive of Christian piety and practice intersects with the aspirations of other religions. To be clear: I am not advocating that the prayer Jesus taught his disciples be reduced merely to an instrument of interreligious dialogue. However desirable such would be, that is a penultimate, human enterprise. Communion with God for God's own sake is the Pater Noster's genuine purpose. Yet in this prayer lies a paradox: the more intense its focus on God, the greater its capacity to construct the one who prays it into

---

39. Bonhoeffer, *Creation and Fall: A Theological Interpretation of Genesis 1–3; Temptation*, trans. John C. Fletcher (London and New York: SCM/Macmillan, 1959), 37.

40. See chapter 24.

41. A week after the mass murder of twenty children and six adults at Sandy Hook Elementary School in Newtown, Connecticut (December 14, 2012), LaPierre (1948–), executive vice president of the National Rifle Association of America, issued a formal statement (December 21, 2012; italics in the original): "The truth is that our society is populated by an unknown number of genuine monsters—people so deranged, so evil, so possessed by voices and driven by demons that no sane person can possibly *ever* comprehend them.... How can we possibly even *guess* how many, given our nation's refusal to create an active national database of the mentally ill?" (press conference transcript: 2, 3). LaPierre's solution: "We need to have *every single school in America* deploy a protection program proven to work—and by that I mean *armed security*" (8). His reason: "The *only* thing that stops a *bad* guy with a gun is a *good* guy with a gun" (5).

a being more fully human, a creature more sympathetic with fellow creatures of disparate beliefs. We are all indebted to one another.[42]

Already we have noted the similarity of Jesus's petitions with prayers of the synagogue. "Father, may your kingdom come" rhymes with the opening of the *Abhinu Malkenu* ("Our Father, Our King"), the great litany of the Jewish High Holidays whose germinal form can be traced to Rabbi Akiba (ca. 40–137):

> Our Father, our King, we have no King but You.
> Our Father, our King, for Your sake have mercy upon us.
> (b. Ta'an. 25b)

The Kaddish, a mainstay of synagogue liturgy, "exalt[s] and hallow[s] [the LORD's] great Name," praying that "He may establish His kingdom." An ancient form of the third among the Eighteen Benedictions acclaims, "Holy are You / and awe-inspiring is Your Name."[43] Among "The Substance [or Abstract] of the Eighteen" (b. Ber. 29a) are petitions reminiscent of Jesus's prayer:

Forgive us, so that we may be redeemed.
  Keep us far from sorrow, and feed us from the pastures of Your land.
(m. Ber. 4.3)

In every time of crisis let [the] needs [of Your people] come before You.
(m. Ber. 4.4)

Some elements pervasive in synagogue liturgy are conspicuously absent from the Pater Noster: imprecations against the unrighteous; thanksgiving for the Torah; prayers for Zion, Jerusalem, and the temple.[44] It is curious that

---

42. The following comments are restricted to the Abrahamic religious traditions. For comparisons of Jesus's teaching in the Gospels with Hinduism and Buddhism, see George M. Soares-Prabhu, *The Dharma of Jesus*, ed. Francis X. D'Sa (Maryknoll, NY: Orbis, 2003), esp. 50–74, 175–228.

43. Petuchowski and Brocke, *Lord's Prayer and Jewish Liturgy*, 28.

44. Notably, the Twelfth of the Eighteen Benedictions (*birkath ha-minim*): "For the apostates let there be no hope, / and uproot the kingdom of arrogance speedily in our days. / May the Nazarenes and the sectarians perish as in a moment. / Let them be blotted out of the book of life, / and not be written together with the righteous. / You are praised, O Lord, who subdues the arrogant" (b. Ber. 28b); "Open my heart to Thy Torah" (b. Ber. 17a); "May it be Thy will, O Lord our God, to grant us long life, . . . a life in which we may be filled with the love of Torah and the fear of heaven" (b. Ber. 16b); The Seventeenth Benediction: "Be pleased, O Lord our God, to dwell in Zion; / and may Thy servants worship You in

these ingredients, highlighting Israel's distinctiveness, are muted in a Jewish prayer that was rapidly adopted by a religious movement chiefly populated by Gentiles. Even more striking is the lack of any direct petition for the people and land of Israel: a stable fixture in Jewish liturgical texts of the rabbinic era.[45] Be that as it may, many Jewish scholars[46] recognize in Jesus's Prayer characteristics of Jewish private prayer: an address to God in the second person, brevity, and a simple style. Moreover, the Pater Noster exhibits what Abraham Heschel wrote of Jewish prayer: "In prayer we shift the center of living from self-consciousness to self-surrender. God is the center toward which all forces tend. Prayer . . . enables us to see the world in the mirror of the holy."[47] For that reason this poignant memoir of the *Shoah* by Baruch Graubard may be less surprising than one might expect:

> I was at that time an outlaw escaped abroad to Slovakia after many difficult experiences. I had surrendered and forgotten my identity. In 1944 I slid into an identity borrowed from a Franciscan monastery in Prescov. It hardly fitted me but fitted more than any other. Then I discovered a token of this identity in the Lord's Prayer. That was like a Jewish prayer, like an abbreviation of the Eighteen Benedictions. A calm prayer, only I missed the petition for peace. The Father was addressed only indirectly as King, and it seemed to me at that time that the Father, too, was in need of help just like me.

Jerusalem" (b. Ber. 29b); "May the righteous rejoice in the rebuilding of Thy city, / in the establishment of Thy temple" (b. Šabb. 24a).

45. Among a host of examples: "O cause a new light to shine upon Zion"; "O Rock of Israel, / arise to the help of Israel. / Deliver, as you have promised, Judah and Israel"; "Have compassion, O Lord, in Your abundant mercies, / upon Israel, Your People, / upon Jerusalem Your city, / upon Zion, Your glorious dwelling-place"; "Grant Your peace / upon Israel, Your people, / upon Your city, / and upon Your inheritance"; "May the service of Your people Israel ever be pleasing to You. / And may our eyes see Your return to Zion in mercy. / You are praised, O Lord, who restores His divine Providence to Zion" (Petuchowski and Brocke, *Lord's Prayer and Jewish Liturgy*, 21, 26, 29, 30, 34). In this light it is all the more blasphemous of modern Christians to conscript Jesus's allegiance to America or any other nation. If he distinguished God's dominion from the particular piety for Israel customary of his day, on what grounds may his followers now conflate *hē basileia tou theou* with their favorite brand of nationalism?

46. See, e.g., C. G. Montefiore, *Rabbinic Literature and Gospel Teachings* (New York: KTAV, 1970), 125–35; Joseph Heinemann, *Prayer in the Talmud: Forms and Patterns*, SJ 9 (Berlin and New York: de Gruyter, 1977), 191–92.

47. Abraham J. Heschel, *Between God and Man: An Interpretation of Judaism*, ed. Fritz A. Rothschild (New York: Free Press, 1959), 198.

Perhaps he was calmer, more certain of his goal and knew the future. The prayer opened an inner relationship to hope for me, and conquered fear.[48]

What of Abraham's other children, those who honor the Prophet (570–632)? I can no more speak with authority about Islam than I can of Judaism; my attempt in either case would be the height of presumption. I ask only that Jews and Muslims reach out to me in the goodness of their faith, and help me better understand it, as I would try within my own tradition while reaching out to them. As a non-Muslim I am sensitive to the place of prayer, *tsalāt*, as one of five pillars on which Islam rests. Especially impressive is *Surat al-fāti'a*, the Opening of the Qur'an's first chapter:

> In the name of Allah, most merciful, most compassionate.
> Praise to Allah, Lord of the universe, most merciful,
>   most compassionate.
> Master of the day of judgment.
> You alone do we worship, and from You do we seek help.
> Guide us along the straight path:
> The path of those whom You have blessed,
> Not the path of those on whom is Your anger,
> Nor the path of those who are astray.[49]

Though these words of *al-fāti'a* and of the Pater Noster are not interchangeable, in some respects they are mutually resonant.[50] Both are exquisitely terse yet comprehensive. Structurally, both are bipartite: the pray-er begins with direct address

---

48. Baruch Graubard, "The *Kaddish* Prayer," in Petuchowski and Brocke, *Lord's Prayer and Jewish Liturgy*, 39–72; quotation, 61.

49. Sura 1.1–7 in *The Holy Qur'an: Text, Translation and Commentary*, ed. Abdullah Yasuf Ali (Elmhurst, NY: Tahrike Tarsile Qur'an, 2011), 14–15. For Seyyed Hossein Nasr this prayer is "the heart of the Quran and contains the message pertaining to the dimensions of the ultimate relation between human beings and God" (*The Heart of Islam: Enduring Values for Humanity* [New York: HarperOne, 2002], 131).

50. Cf. Ahmad ibn Hanbal (d. 855), *al-Zuhd* 302: "Christ said, 'Make frequent mention of God the Exalted, also of His praise and glorification, and obey Him. It suffices for one of you when praying, and if God is truly pleased with him, to say: "O God, forgive my sins, reform my way of life, and keep me safe from hateful things, O my God."'" Also Ibn Hanbal, *al-Zuhd* 312: "Jesus said, 'Why do I not observe in you the best of worship?' They said, 'What is the best of worship, Spirit of God?' He said, 'Humility before God'" (cf. Sura 5.82). Both quotations are from the translation of Jarif Khalidi, *The Muslim Jesus: Sayings and Stories in Islamic Literature* (Cambridge: Harvard University Press, 2001), 69, 71.

to God before petitioning God's help. That would be expected of Islam, whose very meaning is "perfect submission." The adjectives *rachmān* and *rachīm*, "peerlessly merciful, incomparably compassionate," dovetail with Jesus's teaching about God in the Gospels. "Lord and Master [of all worlds]" acknowledges what Jesus implies with reference to God's "kingship" or "dominion," which in the Gospels embraces both nurturance and judgment. "Praise . . . in the name of Allah" is akin to the expression of hope, "Let your name be hallowed."[51] The Pater Noster's register of "give," "forgive," and "prevent [from temptation]" is without precise equivalent in the Qur'an's "Opening," though *Sūrat al-fāti'a* sums up humanity's inherent want and satisfaction in God alone: "You alone do we ask for help. / Show us the straight way." Elsewhere the Qur'an encourages Muslims to pray to God for sustenance and forgiveness; indeed, a Muslim colleague informs me, "The virtue of human forgiveness of others [is extolled] as the highest moral response to having been wronged in any way."[52] Both the Lord's Prayer and the Qur'an's "Opening" use first-plural pronouns: to pray either prayer is to locate oneself among all who praise God and are strengthened by a fellowship of faith.[53]

The Pater Noster reveals both the limits and the prospects for interreligious conversation. Though "Father" is an unexceptional metaphor for God in Juda-

---

51. In *Understanding the Qur'an: Themes and Style* (London and New York: Tauris, 1999), Muhammad Abdel Haleem argues, "In English ['Hallowed be thy name, thy kingdom come, thy will be done' are] all placed in the subjunctive mood which is rather tentative and sounds to a Muslim as if you are praying *for* God, not *to* Him. The description of God in the *Fāti'a*, in Arabic and English, is more affirmative: praise *belongs* to God, He is the Sustaining Lord of All, Master of the Day of Judgement" (25–26). On this point Haleem's analysis creates problems where none exists. However misleading an English translation of Matt 6:9c–10ab // Luke 11:2bc may be, none of its verbs in Greek is cast in the subjunctive mood. All are aorist imperatives: *hagiasthētō, elthetō, genēthētō*. There's nothing tentative in those constructions, nor is there anything in this prayer or elsewhere in Jesus's teaching that denies God as sustaining Lord of all and master of judgment, to whom mortal praise is uniquely due.

52. Professor Maria Massi Dakake, George Mason University (private correspondence, April 5, 2013). Note also the Buddhist *Mahāvagga* 10.2.320: "Hatred is not appeased by hatred; hatred is appeased by non-hatred alone" (cited by Soares-Prabhu, *Dharma of Jesus*, 220).

53. Haleem (*Understanding the Qur'an*, 25) suggests, "'Our [Father'] limits God to a particular community and to a particular relationship of fatherhood, compared to 'The Sustaining Lord of All Creation' not the Lord of the Muslims, or the Arabs." Again, Haleem's restrictive exegesis of the Pater Noster lacks textual basis: nothing in this prayer or in Jesus's teaching confines God's association with Israel alone, much less with Jesus's particular followers (cf. Matt 8:10 // Luke 7:9). As I note immediately below, genuine theological disagreements separate Christians and Muslims; nothing is gained, and much is lost, by generating needless difficulties. Haleem's conclusion, however, is accurate: "Both [the *Fāti'a* and the Lord's Prayer] have in common the earnest desire to glorify God and eagerness to please Him" (27).

ism, it is objectionable to Muslims, whose Qur'an repeatedly asserts that Allah has no offspring (e.g., Sura 112.1–4). However sympathetic in general character the Lord's Prayer may be with those of either Islam or Judaism, Muslims and Jews do not recognize Jesus as Lord: the final "Seal of the Prophets,"[54] the Messiah greater than whom none may be expected (b. Sanh. 98a–99a; Maimonides, *Mishneh Torah: Hilchot Melachim* 11–12). The divinity, as well as humanity, that classical Christianity accords to Jesus is deeply problematic, indeed offensive, to most Jews and Muslims,[55] who understandably cannot accept such a claim as anything other than a violation of the radical monotheism that Christians also affirm. Precisely because Jesus occupies a place of nonnegotiable importance for orthodox Christians, the prayer he taught his disciples is, for them, the bedrock of all other prayers. The Pater Noster is Christianity's "default setting" in prayer because the one whom they revere as Lord and Christ taught them to pray like this.

Yet Christians do well to bear in mind something important: nowhere in their Lord's Prayer does Jesus point to himself or his own significance. Instead, Jesus concentrates his disciples' attention on the God of Abraham, Isaac, and Jacob: the one God[56] to whom Jews and Muslims pray also and with no less devotion. The Pater Noster's Christological significance is implicit and contextual, neither explicit in nor constituent of the prayer itself. The prayer of Jesus underlines the limits of human ability—including the contingent finitude of all religious understanding—and beseeches a merciful, just God to restore, in perfect peace, a diseased and tormented world. That is an essential hope in which Jews, Christians, Muslims and all human beings of goodwill share alike. The day may yet come when, in praying most fervently the prayers native to their traditions, religious peoples may recognize more clearly the face of God in those other than themselves. And as that day dawns—as the shadows of fear are burned away by love's light—God's name may be more truly sanctified and God's kingdom may more quickly come.

---

54. Sura 33.40: the position occupied by Muhammad.
55. John 5:18; 8:58–59; Sura 5.17: "They have disbelieved who say, 'Truly, Allah is the Messiah, the son of Mary'"; also Sura 5.175.116.
56. Sura 37.4: "Truly your God is one [*tawchīd*]"; cf. Deut 6:4–5; Matt 22:37 // Mark 12:29–30 // Luke 10:27.

CHAPTER 7

God's Promise for Humanity in the New Testament

> Two things are infinite: the universe and human stupidity; and I'm not sure about the universe.
>
> —Albert Einstein

The Bible as Broom

Scripture can be used for many purposes. For much of Christian history, it has been raised as "a lamp unto my feet, and a light unto my path" (Ps. 119:105 KJV). Lamentably, still too many Christians seize it as a claymore for laying waste to their antagonists. A gentler and important use is that of a broom, which sweeps away the mind's cobwebs. Scripture performs that necessary function when the contemporary church considers what it means to be human. Thus, one learns that "human dignity," strictly speaking, is not a biblical topic.[1] With James Luther Mays[2] I concur that the nearest biblical parallel to such a claim may be the psalmist's wonderment that our LORD has made mortals "little less than the angels" and "adorned [them] with glory and majesty" by reason of the sacred trust over God's creatures that is placed into human hands (Ps. 8:5–9).[3] Notwithstanding its importance in subsequent theological anthropology, humankind's creation "in the image" (*tselem*) and "likeness" (*demut*) of God is, in the biblical tradition, a claim that is comparatively rare (found only in Gen 1:26-27; 5:1-3; 9:6) and conceptually obscure. Such ambiguity surprises

---

1. For an alternative view, which may exaggerate Christianity's hierarchical character, see Robert P. Kraynak, "'Made in the Image of God': The Christian View of Human Dignity and the Political Orders," in *In Defense of Human Dignity: Essays for Our Times*, ed. Robert P. Kraynak and Glenn Tinder (Notre Dame: University of Notre Dame Press, 2003), 81–118.

2. See Mays, "The Self in the Psalms and the Image of God," in *God and Human Dignity*, ed. R. Kendall Soulen and Linda Woodhead (Grand Rapids: Eerdmans, 2006), 27–43.

3. Translations in this chapter are my own, unless otherwise indicated.

when Genesis is read against the backdrop of ancient Chinese, Egyptian, and Mesopotamian creation myths, where creation of humanity in God's image is frequently narrated and remarkably graphic.[4] Given the Bible's reticence to address anthropological questions in terms to which its twenty-first-century readers may gravitate, Edward Curtis aptly observes, "the interpretation of the image of God has often reflected the *Zeitgeist* and has followed whatever emphasis happened to be current in psychology, or philosophy, or sociology, or theology"[5]— to which one is tempted to add the biological sciences.

The first thing to be said, therefore, is that throughout Christian scripture humanity's worth is not intrinsic but, instead, derivative of creation *after God's likeness*. In the Bible, human dignity depends entirely on humanity's possession by God and on God's decision to esteem and redeem it.[6] To grasp that point is critically important. Immediately, it challenges the language of "human dignity" in a postmodern situation, which is occasionally mesmerized by mushy respect for a variable "Other"[7] and a not infrequent, anthropocentric pursuit of self-esteem. To speak with candor about the promise of God and God's perdurable achievements throws down a gauntlet to Western societies that are functionally if not avowedly atheistic.

A second point needs registering. Christian Scripture bespeaks numerous antinomies in its varied interpretations of humanity, its predicament and promise. At first glance, that may appear cause for disappointment, if not complaint. On reflection, however, one may celebrate the Bible's internal tensions as a precious gift. From the start, Christian visions of the human being have been as multidimensional as human creatures themselves. My task in this chapter is to invite its reader to begin coming to terms with this aspect of the NT's multidimensionality. I aim to map and to correlate three discrete, significant streams within the NT that take seriously what it means to be human, in the sight of God in whose image we are created. Of necessity, such an essay must be selective, representative, and suggestive. Even so, it should suffice to

---

4. See Claus Westermann, *Genesis: An Introduction* (Minneapolis: Fortress, 1992), 36–38.

5. Curtis, "Image of God (OT)," *ABD* 3 (1992): 389–91; quotation, 389–90.

6. For a systematic investigation of this claim, see Christoph Schwöbel, "Recovering Human Dignity," in Soulen and Woodhead, *God and Human Dignity*, 44–58.

7. For Emmanuel Levinas, the "other" refers primarily to another human self, to whose integrity attention should be paid at the point of one's encounter with it (*Ethics and Infinity* [Pittsburgh: Duquesne University Press, 1985]). Although subsequent deconstructionist theory has sometimes celebrated "difference" *tout court*, Gillian Rose replies, "'The Other' is misrepresented as sheer alterity" (*Judaism and Modernité: Philosophical Essays* [Oxford: Blackwell, 1993], 8).

allow Matthew, John, and Paul each to have his say, while demonstrating large areas—eschatological, christological, and theological—where their different voices overlap.

The Matthean Vision

No other Gospel addresses more studiously than Matthew the vocation and destiny of those subject to "the kingdom of heaven" (see, e.g., 5:1–7:29; 13:1–52). So extensive is this consideration that Matthew has long been regarded, with good reason, as a manual of discipline for that *ekklēsia* (church) built by Jesus (Matt 16:18). The First Gospel is not, however, simply a compendium of regulations. In form, of course, it is a story of Jesus; as the evangelist tells it, that story illuminates in the first instance Jesus's own character and conduct, then by implication that of his disciples and of the world they are commissioned to evangelize (28:16–20). That story's presiding theme is righteousness (*hē dikaiosynē*): pure and perfect obedience to God's will that marries thought, deed, and word in the manner evinced by Jesus, "God-with-us" (1:23; 5:48). A basic premise of Matthew's theological approach is that God's Torah, or instruction, is the healthy ordering principle for human, not merely Christian, life. Because Jesus's life was in deepest accordance with that teaching, perfectly rectified to its shape and substance, Christ is Torah's *norma normans* ("normative norm": thus, 5:17–20). In castigating Israel's leaders for their failure to uphold the law, Jesus stands in the venerable line of prophetic critique exemplified by such figures as Jeremiah (5:1–9:26) and Ezekiel (12:21–14:23). It is, therefore, fundamental that Jesus characterizes the moral ecology of God's kingdom neither as the highest good nor as the realm in which human virtue is validated, but as righteousness. Leander Keck aptly paraphrases Matthew's metaphor: "Where God's kingship is fully effective, there all things are right . . . and rightly related to everything else."[8] In other words, created humanity's *summum bonum* is an obedience rectified to the Creator's sovereign will, proleptically active in Jesus.

The fundamental threat to humanity, to which Jesus himself was exposed yet did not succumb, is the fragmentation of righteousness into a diabolical dis-integrity (Matt 4:1–11): the severance of deed from word, the divorce of inner intention from outward appearance, the masking of interior corruption

---

8. Keck, "Ethics in the Gospel according to Matthew," *IlRev* (Winter, 1984): 39–56. The quoted clauses are reversed in the original (47–48).

by a pious veneer (cf. 6:14-24). Matthew's customary term for this internal division is "hypocrisy" (23:28), about which at least three things should be registered. First, the First Gospel's "typical hypocrites" are those scribes and Pharisees (23:13, 23) whose emergent leadership in the evangelist's own day threatened the self-identity and existence of his fledgling, Christian Jewish-Gentile community (23:1-2).[9] Second, hypocrisy for Matthew is not merely a matter of pretense but, rather and more fundamentally, the condition of those who are radically self-deceived, both about their inner selves and about humanity's relationship to God and the world (23:25-28).[10] Such persons delude themselves by acting as though ostentatious religiosity could secure God's approval, or human approbation were the proper end of life (6:2, 5, 16; 23:5-7). Third, hypocrisy in the First Gospel afflicts not only the adversaries of Jesus and his disciples but also the church itself. Were that not so, Jesus in Matthew would have no reason to lament the inadequacies of Pharisaic Judaism before the crowds and his disciples (23:1-39), to castigate a brother who is deluded in his judgments (7:1-5), or to warn followers that their entry into the heavenly kingdom could be forever barred (5:17-20). As John Meier has noted, "The cleavage between good and bad thus runs through the whole of humanity; it does not run neatly between the church and unbelievers."[11] Matthew's Gospel describes the quest for integrity among disciples in the Matthean church, metaphorically captured in Jesus's aphorism, "The body's lamp is the eye: If your eye be clear-sighted, whole and luminescent will your body be" (6:21).[12]

The linchpin in Matthew's theology is christological: all lines converge upon Jesus, his identity, conduct, and significance. Jesus is more than a mere herald of the kingdom's dawning (4:17). The sum of his life, from birth to death and resurrection, "fills to the full" the law and the prophets (among others, 1:22-23; 2:15, 17) by recapitulating the story of Israel, this time obediently tracing the arc of God's will (3:13-17). To Jesus may be correctly applied every christological title: teacher (8:19), healer (8:1-9:3), Son of God (8:29), Son of David (9:27), Son

---

9. Thus, among others, Graham Stanton, *A Gospel for a New People: Studies in Matthew* (Edinburgh: T&T Clark, 1992), 113-68.

10. Dan O. Via Jr., *Self-Deception and Wholeness in Paul and Matthew* (Minneapolis: Fortress, 1990), 92-98.

11. Meier, *The Vision of Matthew: Christ, Church and Morality in the First Gospel*, TI (New York: Paulist, 1979), 177.

12. Compare Abba Bessarion's miniature midrash on this text: "The monk ought to be as the Cherubim and the Seraphim: all eye" (Benedicta Ward, ed. and trans., *Sayings of the Desert Fathers: The Alphabetical Collection*, rev. ed., CCS 59 [Kalamazoo, MI: Cistercian, 1984], 42).

of Man (8:20), Lord (14:28, 30), Wisdom incarnate (11:19). It is hard to discern any of these titles as central; Matthew interweaves them all into his Gospel's tapestry. To mix the metaphor, Jesus in Matthew is truly "the man who fits no formula";[13] instead, he gathers up all formulations—anthropological and ecclesiological—then explodes them. Moreover, in the First Gospel, Jesus cannot be understood in isolation from either everyday society or eschatological commonwealth. In Jesus God's kingdom and community meet:

> Now when John while in prison heard about the works of the Christ, he sent word by way of his disciples and said to him, "Are you the one who is coming or are we to expect another?" And Jesus answered them, "Go, announce to John what you hear and see: the blind see anew and the lame walk, lepers are cleansed and the deaf hear, and the dead are raised up and the poor are evangelized. And blessed is the one who does not stumble because of me." (Matt 11:2–6)

In no sense is Christ extrinsic to the morality he teaches. Mature obedience is not simply commanded (5:48); it inheres in Jesus himself, who models its realization.

This invites some nettlesome exegetical questions. Does Matthew regard the human self *in se* as fractured, or only human deeds as needing correction? Put differently, is the anthropological problem one of essence or of action, a flaw in the doer or in the deed; and what difference does Christ's intervention make in resolving that problem? The answers are not blindingly obvious. Matthew is not clear; his theological tendency is to blend a variety of views at the expense of systematic coherence. From cursory inspection of this Gospel, one could leave it convinced that the self is quite competent to do what is expected of it—as dilated in the Sermon on the Mount—and that, if only Moses had said it more adequately (5:21–48), Jesus needn't have bothered. John's query is not stupid: "Are you the one who is to come or are we to expect another?" Jesus's ultimate reply, however, suggests that matters may not be so simple: "Blessed is the one who does not stumble because of me." In fact, the First Gospel is littered with those who stumble over Jesus, often with murderous effect (2:13–17; 21:33–44). Seventy-five percent of those who hear word of the kingdom are unable to grasp it (13:18–22). Weeds and wheat are intermixed, because both the sower and his enemy are at work (13:24–30). Something within the tenant farmers is so wretched that they would kill for an inheritance

---

13. Eduard Schweizer, *Jesus* (London: SCM, 1971), 13–51.

not theirs (21:33-41). Rachel's grief is inconsolable, for her infants are no more (2:18). Even at their best—as parents who know how to give their children good gifts—human beings are evil (7:9-11). The context of these passages is unmistakably eschatological, suggesting that the righteous and wicked things we do occur on a cosmic battlefield bigger than the individual conscience (N.B. 13:37-38). In that regard, the wording of Jesus's spontaneous thanksgiving to God in Matthew 11:25-27 is crucial, for it makes clear (first) that receipt of "all things" from the Lord of heaven and earth depends entirely upon revelation to nursing infants, not upon ratiocinations by "the wise and discerning," and (second) that such revelation comes only through the Father's Son, to whom "all things have been delivered." The last clause, echoed in the Great Commission of the risen Christ at the Gospel's end (28:18), suggests, without fully articulating, that Jesus for Matthew is more than the moral exemplar par excellence, the pattern for what those who can do should do. It is because the Christ of the church is "God-with-us" (1:23), right now (18:20) and unto the consummation of the age (28:20), that his disciples can do what he commands of them. In Matthew, Christology effectively absorbs pneumatology: in place of the Spirit's empowering presence is Immanuel, who has eschatologically burst into human history and promises never to abandon his church.

The Johannine Vision

John's view of humanity before God is harsher than Matthew's, in part because it stems from a more vitriolic separation of Christians from Jews near the end of the first century.[14] While the matter remains vigorously debated, Matthew, the most overtly Jewish of all the Gospels, seems to me reflective of a community in transition: firmly embedded in Judaism, the First Gospel appears to be peeling away from an increasingly dominant Pharisaism toward a Christian sect still recognizably Jewish (e.g., Matt 23:1-23). In the Fourth Gospel, however, the divorce between Jews and Jewish Christians appears complete, and almost completely ugly: "For already the Jews had decided that if anyone confessed [Jesus] as Christ, such a one was to be expelled from the synagogue" (John 9:22; see also 12:42; 16:2). "The Jews"—at times identified with the Pharisees, though not consistently so (7:3-8:59; 9:13-41; 18:33-38)—are rendered as antagonists almost to the point of anachronism: one could read

---

14. The now classic articulation of this proposal is J. Louis Martyn, *History and Theology in the Fourth Gospel*, 3rd ed., NTL (Louisville: Westminster John Knox, 2003).

John and nearly forget that Jesus and his disciples were Jewish, as Matthew and the other Synoptics take for granted and as John himself does not deny (4:22). In Matthew, Jesus's controversy with his coreligionists more obviously pivots upon Torah and its proper interpretation: "For I tell you that unless your righteousness far surpasses that of the scribes and Pharisees, by no means can you enter the kingdom of heaven" (5:20). In John, the sticking point has more obviously become the Messiah himself, the claims made for Jesus's dignity and divinity: "The Jews answered [Jesus], 'Not for a noble work do we intend to stone you, but for blasphemy—for you, though a human, make yourself out to be God'" (10:33; see also 5:16–18, 30–47; 7:14–44; 8:21–59). No wonder they think so. Jesus of the Fourth Gospel is more than merely Israel's Messiah (1:43–51), although that would be quite something. He is, as C. H. Dodd put it, "the final concentration of the whole creative and revealing thought of God, which is also the meaning of the universe, in an *individual* who is what humanity was designed to be in the divine purpose."[15] It is as though John has carried Matthew's christological premise of Christ as Immanuel to its radical conclusion: Jesus more than simply testifies to God's glory; he actually radiates it (1:14; 17:22, 24).

Although John does not use the terms as exact synonyms (see, e.g., 14:19, 27, 30), "the Jews" of the Fourth Gospel to some degree represent "the world," this evangelist's multivalent shorthand for the human condition. John 1:10 conveniently bundles this term's various connotations: the true light was in the world (a neutral comment about the created order), "and the world came to be through him" (a positive affirmation, restated in 3:16–17; 12:46), "yet the world knew him not" (a negative assertion of religious humanity's general rejection of God's self-revelation in Jesus). The world's dissentient view assumes precedence in John, defining the pole of all things antithetical to God: sin (15:22, 24), lies (8:44), enslavement (8:34–36), death (5:24), and especially darkness (1:5). Jesus's coming into the world exposes its perversity: "This is the judgment, that the light has come into the world, and people loved darkness rather than light, for their deeds were wicked" (3:19). Accordingly, in Jesus's declaration to the crowd, John comments with deceptive simplicity on the parlous condition of humanity without faith in Jesus:

> "Now is the judgment of this world, now will the ruler of this world be cast out: . . . Yet for a short time the light is among you. Walk while you have

---

15. Dodd, *The Interpretation of the Fourth Gospel* (Cambridge: Cambridge University Press, 1953), 282 (emphasis added).

the light, that the darkness may not overtake you; for the one who walks in darkness does not know where he is going. While you have the light, entrust yourself to the light, that you may be sons of light." These things Jesus said, and, having gone away, he hid himself from them; for though he had done so many signs before them, they did not trust in him. (John 12:31, 35–37)

Apart from believing in and confessing Jesus as the Son of Man in whom God is decisively glorified, humanity is "in the dark." For those like Nicodemus, "a ruler of the Jews [who] came to him by night" (3:1–2), attracted to Jesus yet unable to make a commitment to him, darkness registers as befuddlement, a seriocomic misunderstanding of what Jesus is driving at (3:3–15). For other religious authorities, stumbling in the dark turns homicidal: "They will excommunicate you from the synagogues; indeed, the hour is coming when all who kill you will think they are offering sacrifice to God" (16:2).

By contrast, "doing the truth" means entering the light (3:21), which for John is tantamount to believing in God = believing in Jesus = accepting by faith that Jesus uniquely reveals God (1:18; 12:44; 14:10–11; 17:8). Those who believe in Jesus are drawn into a new and indestructible sphere of life (3:14–16; 6:40, 47), characterized by public testimony to Christ in the teeth of persecution (15:18–27), assurance in the face of mortal danger (10:1–18), joy and peace amid the world's tribulations (16:21–33), and—most emphatically—obedience to Jesus's commands, epitomized as self-giving love for one another (13:34–35; 15:12–17). Here the Fourth Evangelist's point of contact with the First is at once both obvious and obscure. In John's Gospel there is none of the exquisitely detailed moral instruction that Matthew unrolls by the yard. Nevertheless, the love command in John arguably distills Matthew's mass of paraenesis, much as Jesus himself in Matthew identifies unreserved love for God and love of neighbor as one loves self as the two commandments on which depend the law and the prophets in their entirety (Matt 22:37–40). Matthew is more explicit than John that one's enemies are to be loved (Matt 5:44), but John does not contradict that injunction. Indeed, by refusing to endorse violence or reciprocity of that hatred to which Jesus's disciples are inevitably subjected (John 15:18–25; 17:14), the teaching of Jesus in John resonates with that of the Matthean Jesus, who insists that loving as God loves is utterly gratuitous, never a matter of tit for tat (Matt 5:43–48).

John's moral discourse matches Matthew's in at least four other respects. First, in both cases self-renunciation for others' benefit is a moral norm (John 12:25; Matt 5:38–42). Second, the commandment is not restricted to members of the community; its scope is universal (Matt 28:19–20; John 12:32–

33). Third, love is learned within the context of the church, which subverts this world's political and cultural mores (John 10:21; Matt 12:34–39). Fourth, love expresses the disciple's obedience to Jesus, which cannot be reduced to mere confession, no matter how orthodox (Matt 7:21–23; John 13:34–35).[16]

If, for all their points of contact, Matthew is richer than John in moral teaching, John is more direct than Matthew in articulating the decisively new situation into which Jesus's incarnation, crucifixion, and glorification have thrust human life, as well as the means by which Christ's continuing presence is realized among the company of disciples. Release from the world's darkness and delusion is ultimately God's doing: in Johannine terms, one is "begotten of God" (John 1:13), "begotten from above" or "begotten of the Spirit" (3:3, 8). Because the Son does nothing of his own accord but only what he sees done by the Father who sent him (5:19–24), then it is equally true to say that Christ is the proximate cause of human liberation: "If you abide in my word, truly you are my disciples; and you will know the truth, and the truth will set you free" (8:31–32). That is the real reason behind John's seemingly odd insistence that Jesus is "not of this world" (8:23; 17:14; 18:36–37). Only one whose origin is from God and whose activity transcends this world's blighted warrants can liberate the human self for God's radical reconstitution.[17] Likewise, the Holy Spirit, characterized as "another advocate" (14:16), is sent from beyond this world by the Father, to abide with Jesus's disciples, to remind them of all that he has said, and to judge this world's sin (14:17; 15:25–26; 16:7–11). The baptismal formula in Matthew's Great Commission ("in the name of the Father and of the Son and of the Holy Ghost" [28:19]) may be proto-Trinitarian in form, but John actually nudges us in the direction of what later Christian theology unfolded as the economic Trinity.[18]

Finally, however, Matthew concurs with John that the entrusting self can take no credit for its faith but has only God to thank for its election. While neither evangelist offers a reasoned account for unbelief, both of them point to the same human culpability—the desire to be recognized and praised by other mortals, rather than by God (Matt 6:1–4; John 12:42–43)—and both interpret

---

16. In this paragraph's formulation, I have been aided by D. Moody Smith, "Ethics and the Interpretation of the Fourth Gospel," in *Word, Theology, and Community in John*, ed. John Painter, R. Alan Culpepper, and Fernando Segovia (St. Louis: Chalice, 2002), 109–22.

17. See Leander E. Keck, "Derivation as Destiny: 'Of-Ness' in Johannine Christology, Anthropology and Soteriology," in *Exploring the Gospel of John in Honor of D. Moody Smith*, ed. R. Alan Culpepper and C. Clifton Black (Louisville: Westminster John Knox, 1996), 274–88.

18. See, for instance, Claude Welch, *In This Name: The Doctrine of the Trinity in Contemporary Theology* (New York: Scribner's Sons, 1952), 293–94.

resistance to Jesus by appealing to Isaiah's oracle of Israel's blinding by God (Isa 6:9–10; Matt 13:14–15; John 12:40). Contrary to later gnostic schemes, the self does not awaken to knowledge of its "incomparable self" and "god-like nature."[19] To the contrary, "You did not choose me, but I chose you" (John 15:16); "No one can come to me unless drawn by the Father who sent me" (6:44; cf. Matt 16:17, which ascribes Peter's confession to divine revelation, not to flesh and blood). Both Matthew and John construe as a supernatural event, not as a mortal achievement, Christian faith that Jesus is definitively the Christ, "the Son of the living God" (Matt 16:16), who by his crucifixion reveals, while radically redefining, God's essential glory (John 7:39; 13:31; 17:5).

THE PAULINE VISION

Paul's view of the human condition and its divine redemption bears some resemblance to John's. In both cases, our predicament is one of radical bondage to the tyranny of sin, from which Christ liberates those who entrust themselves to him and transfers them into a new relationship with him and with God (thus, among others, John 8:31–36; Rom 6:17–23; Gal 4:4–7). Alongside Romans 7:7–25, Romans 1:18–3:20 is Paul's key statement of religious humanity's plight viewed with hindsight, from the vantage point of the cross; in that sense, we may observe Paul's soteriology unfolding in reverse, from solution to plight. In John, Jesus explicates that retrospectively Christian point of view: "If I had not come and had spoken to them, they would not have sin; but now they have no pretext for their sin" (John 15:22).

The differences in Paul's formulation are of both degree and kind. Nowhere in John or Matthew is the pathology of sin probed with the intensity of Romans 1:18–3:20. In John, sin is characteristic of "the world" that refuses to believe in Jesus, choosing instead to hate him and those who confess him (15:18–16:11). For Matthew, sin is less christologically focused, bearing instead the conventionally Jewish connotations of "missing the mark" (18:15, 21), failure (3:6), or guilt (12:31; 27:4). While such nuances are certainly present in his letters (e.g., Rom 2:12; 1 Cor 8:12; Gal 1:4), Paul markedly personifies sin as a tyrant, a domain of enslaving force, to which humanity—even religious

---

19. "God created men, and men created God. It would be fitting that the gods should worship men" (*Gos. Phil.* [NHC II.3.71–72]). Consult Kurt Rudolph, *Gnosis: The Nature and History of Gnosticism*, trans. and ed. Robert McLachlan Wilson (San Francisco: Harper & Row, 1987), 88–113.

humanity at its best—is inexorably subjected unless liberated by a superior power: "For we have already accused all, both Jews and Greeks, as being under the power of sin" (Rom 3:9b). Within this context, we may distinguish Paul's radical consideration of the law. Beyond the Fourth Gospel, which in a general way regards Scripture as bearing witness to Christ (John 5:39–40; cf. 1 Cor 15:3–4), and contrary to Matthew, who describes righteousness as fulfillment of Torah's every jot and tittle (Matt 5:17–20), Paul denies that humans, by dint of satisfying the law, can be rectified with God (Rom 3:20; Gal 2:16).

Paul's reasons for this denial are many and unsystematically coordinated, but at least two may be mentioned here. First, while the law subordinately points to Christ (Rom 3:21, 31; Gal 3:1–29), it cannot supplant Christ's lordship: "For if justification [*hē dikaiosynē*] is by legal means, then Christ died for nothing" (Gal 2:21). That is to say, in cases where Torah is regarded as a rival to Christ for human salvation, legal righteousness must yield to "the word of the cross" (1 Cor 1:18; so also Matt 12:1–14). Second, while the law exposes sin (Rom 7:7, 13) and serves a temporarily custodial function (Gal 3:23–26), the law itself has been commandeered by sin's power; consequently, justification by Torah is constitutive of that deathward, ancien régime from which Christians, by faith, are set free (Rom 7:1–8:8). Sin has twisted God's own commandment, which is "holy and just and good" (Rom 7:12), eliciting the very opposite of that for which the religious self aspires: the service of sin precisely in the service of God.[20] Here, Paul offers a theological reason for Matthew's compatible though unexplained claim: even in nurturing parenthood, the very point where humanity functions at its selfless best, humans remain evil (Matt 7:11). Paul also explores in greater detail the circumstances by which God makes possible genuine integrity. Those who have been baptized into Christ Jesus, buried with him by baptism into his death (Rom 6:1–23; see also Gal 2:10), are transferred from wretchedness into a fundamentally new creation that partakes of a new life restructured by the Spirit (Rom 8:1–39), reconciliation with God (2 Cor 5:16–21), and conduct controlled by Christ's love (Rom 12:1–13:14). As in John and Matthew, Paul is explicit that the signature of life in the Spirit is self-renunciation inspired by Christ's own *kenosis*: "And for all Christ died, that those who live may live no longer for themselves but for him who for them

---

20. For acute analysis of this aspect of Pauline thought, see Paul W. Meyer, "The Worm at the Core of the Apple: Exegetical Reflections on Romans 7," in Meyer, *The Word in This World: Essays in New Testament Exegesis and Theology*, ed. John T. Carroll, NTL (Louisville: Westminster John Knox, 2004), 57–77.

died and was raised" (2 Cor 5:15). The moral implications derive from a deeper theological shift: "It is only under the lordship of Christ that the devout man ceases to make his worship a means of self-justification and self-praise."[21]

Even a cursory treatment of Pauline anthropology and soteriology must reckon with "Adam, a type of the one to come" (Rom 5:14). Here the exegetical waters are deep and treacherous, though a few buoys may be marked with some confidence. To begin at the least controversial point: by drawing the contrast between Adam and Christ in both Romans 5:20-21 and 1 Corinthians 15:20-28, Paul is making an *eschatological* statement about the complete break from humanity as it has labored under sin, disobedience, and death, and the radically new creation bound up in Christ's obedience on the cross and its vindication by God's having raised him from the dead. Paul is reasonably clear about this. For him, Christ does not represent, as Irenaeus seems to suggest (*Adv. haer.* 4.38.1), the pinnacle of humankind, advancing from childish immaturity to a consummation of latent potential. Contrary to Irenaeus (3.18.1; 4.38.1-3; 5:19-21), Ambrose (*Exp. Luc.* 7.142), Augustine (*De civ. Dei* 14.10-11, 26), and a host of interpreters afterward, it is not indisputably evident that Paul presupposes a theological scheme that progresses from original blessedness, through a fall from righteousness, to the restoration of humanity's fractured image of God. Paul, in fact, never discusses humanity's "original state." Notwithstanding a subtle reference to lost glory in 1:23, Paul's real focus in Romans 1-3 is on the plight of humanity as it is: thoroughly estranged from God. Paul speaks, not of the restoration of Adam's lost blessedness, but of Christ as humanity created eschatologically afresh, alive in the Spirit and apart from the dust of the old (1 Cor 15:20-28). To understand human beings as Paul does, one does not start with Adam, whose creation in "the image and glory of God" Paul of course knows from Genesis (certainly, 1 Cor 11:7; Rom 1:23, possibly) but never develops soteriologically. Instead, one begins with Christ's crucifixion and resurrection. From that vantage point, one may look backward, upon our shared mortality with Adam, as well as forward to humanity's conformation *in Christ*, who is the image of God (Rom 8:29; 1 Cor 15:49). Similarly, "our hope of sharing God's glory" lies exclusively "through our Lord Jesus Christ" (Rom 5:1-2; Phil 4:19). Significantly, Paul does not refer to a restoration in us of the glory Adam knew. Rather, "glory [is] of the Lord, [and we] are being

---

21. Ernst Käsemann, "On Paul's Anthropology," in Käsemann, *Perspectives on Paul*, trans. Margaret Kohl (London: SCM, 1971), 16; see also Victor Paul Furnish, *Theology and Ethics in Paul*, 2nd ed., NTL (Louisville: Westminster John Knox, 2009), 164-206, 224-27.

changed into his likeness from one degree of glory to another; for this comes from the Lord who is the Spirit" (2 Cor 3:18 [RSV]).[22]

Closely related with this Adamic imagery are Paul's references to humanity's restoration in accordance with the divine image (*hē eikōn*). While Paul does not synthesize his comments in this matter, his extant letters offer us enough clues to discern a rough shape for his thought. An *eikōn* was a representation of something or someone: a portrait or likeness, such as the image on a coin (Matt 22:19–20 // Mark 12:15–16 // Luke 20:24) or embossed medallions (*signa*) of the emperor's head on military banners (*B.J.* 2.169; *A.J.* 18.55).[23] Paul applies the language of "image" in two directions, to the redeemer and to the redeemed. In 2 Corinthians 4:4. Christ is the *eikōn* of God: if one could hold a mirror to the invisible God, the reflection would be that of Christ. While Paul assumes the claim, in Genesis 1:26–28, that creation in God's image is a property of man (and woman: 1 Cor 11:7),[24] as living beings humans have worn "the image of [Adam,] the dusty one" (1 Cor 15:49). In a different context, Paul speaks of primordial sin as idolatry, humanity's foolish exchange of the incorruptible God's glory for derivative images of corruptible creatures (Rom 1:23). In effect, Christ's coming reverses that polarity: those whom God has called are predestined to conformity with the Son's image (8:29). Those who have worn the image of the earthly one will wear the image of the heavenly one (1 Cor 15:49). Those who behold in Christ God's radiance are undergoing metamorphosis, from splendor to splendor, into God's own image, which Christ reflects (2 Cor 3:18). In ways that have cast doubt on its Pauline authorship, the Epistle to the Colossians develops such claims, with respect both to the redeemer and to the redeemed. More explicitly than in 1 Corinthians 1:18–2:16

---

22. In thinking through this paragraph's issues, I have been helped by John A. Ziesler, "Anthropology of Hope," *ExpTim* 90 (1979): 4–9, and John Muddiman, "'Adam, the Type of the One to Come,'" *Theol* 87 (1984): 101–10.

23. Irenaeus's differentiation of "image" from "likeness"—Jesus being the *imago Dei*, humans created "after" his likeness (*Haer.* 5.16.2)—subsequently developed in medieval theology, presses a distinction that cannot be scripturally sustained.

24. Paul's allusion, in 1 Cor 11:2–16, to the creation accounts of Genesis occurs within his convoluted argument about appropriate attire for men and women at worship—an exegetical knot that cannot and need not be unraveled here. For our purposes, we need only observe that, in 11:7, the narratives in Gen 1 (the Priestly account) and 2 (the Yahwist legend) have been harmonized, allowing Paul to assume simultaneously human creation in the image of God (Gen 1:27) and woman's fabrication out of man (Gen 2:21–23). Such an assumption permits Paul in this case to reason out a sequence of reflected glory (woman mirrors man's glory, which mirrors God's) while preventing him from claiming that woman is the image of man. By implication, in 1 Cor 11:7, both woman and man are *God's* image.

or Philippians 2:5–11, Colossians "christologizes" Hellenistic Judaism's view of primordial Wisdom as God's agent in creation and redemption (Sir. 24; cf. Prov 8:22–31), reassigning those majestic achievements to the crucified and exalted Christ (Col 1:15–20). While Colossians 3:3–4 maintains Paul's restraint in speaking of the eschatological consummation as lying in the future (Rom 6:4–5; 1 Cor 15:42–57), at other points Colossians speaks of believers' resurrection as an accomplished fact (2:12–13; 3:1). Nevertheless, individual and corporate morality is the product of a divinely driven human destiny, "ongoing renewal in [obedient] knowledge, in the likeness of its creator" (3:10; cf. Gen 1:27; Rom 12:2). Like Romans (6:1–14), Colossians (2:11–12; 3:15–17) ties God's burial of the old person and resurrection of the new with baptism into Christ and life within Christ's body.

Converging Visions

It is time to summarize our Cook's tour of some anthropological views within the NT. I have expended enough effort in distinguishing the approaches adopted by Paul, John, and Matthew that sharpening our focus on their areas of agreement seems a fit conclusion.

First, *each of these views is radically eschatological.* In the NT humanity's glory lies not in the best calibrated balance of aspirations against achievements—personal vis-à-vis corporate, enlightened or otherwise—but only through the invasive disclosure of God's integrity through Jesus Christ incarnate, crucified, and raised from death. "From that time Jesus began to proclaim, saying, 'Repent—for the kingdom of heaven has drawn near'" (Matt 4:17). "For God's righteousness is being unveiled in [the gospel] through faith for faith, as it is written: 'The righteous will live by faith'" (Rom 1:17; cf. Hab 2:4). "This is the judgment: the light has come into the world, and people loved the darkness more than the light, for their deeds were evil" (John 3:19). For these witnesses, human destiny is one piece of a larger mystery being revealed to the eyes of faith (Matt 13:11; 1 Cor 2:1, 7; John 9:35–41). Humanity's encounter with God—and thus with itself—through Jesus Christ is, in Joachim Jeremias's felicitous expression, "an eschatology in process of realization" (*sich realisierende Eschatologie*).[25] In the NT world, at least among some Hellenistic Jews, the eschatological dimension of this claim was probably not as disturbing

---

25. Jeremias, *The Parables of Jesus*, 2nd rev. ed., trans. S. H. Hooke (London: SCM, 1972), 230. Jeremias credits Ernst Haenchen (1894–1975) for coining this phrase.

as the predicate of its unfolding in Jesus of Nazareth. In our own world, the problem is more often the reverse. We can tolerate various affirmations of a progressive revelation into which Jesus can be incorporated. It's the claim that, in Jesus Christ, God has abrasively, with finality, exploded this world for its (and our) transformation that sets liberal and postmodern teeth on edge.

That assertion leads directly to the second area of appreciable overlap among the anthropological claims of Paul, Matthew, and John: their *christological concentration*. As excursions into the renewed "quest for the Jesus of history" have amply demonstrated, the ghost of the liberal Jesus—the sage raconteur of proto-Kantian ideals—stubbornly resists exorcism. For contemporary sensibilities, one of the most baffling features of Jesus Christ, as presented in the NT, is a scandalous particularity that in no way compromises his critical, universal personhood. Put bluntly, in the Fourth Gospel and in Paul's Letters—even in Matthew, to a surprising degree (see 11:25-30)—Jesus is not important because he is a wise teacher. He *is* God's Wisdom, and therein lies his importance. To draw from a different metaphorical range, Jesus is not Everyman but, rather, the Son of Man—the apocalyptic measure against which human fidelity to God's will is or shall be measured (e.g., Matt 24:26-44; John 1:43-5:29; 1 Thess 5:1-11). Christ is not the purveyor of tips for social amelioration or better self-adjustment; he is Adam's antitype, the corporate person into whom believers are consolidated, nothing less than God's new initiative for a creation reconciled to himself (Rom 5:12-21; 2 Cor 5:16-19). Whatever their modes of expression, these representative views concur in regarding Jesus Christ as intrinsic to God's renewal of the human being, along with everything else.[26]

Thus we come to a final point of commonality: *Like the NT in general, Paul, Matthew, and John regard the human being as inextricably related to God.* As the doctrine of the incarnation assumes and maximizes, the God of Scripture is inherently relational: God-with-us, with Israel and the nations, from ages unto ages (Matt 1:23; 28:18-20). In essence, the human plight is the refusal of that relationship: the overweening decision to go it alone, the inflating of our precariously contingent claims to an ultimate importance they cannot bear, our regarding God—if at all—as a convenient ally of our dependent self in-

---

26. A profound outworking of this insight is expressed by Maximus the Confessor (c. 580-662): "[Christ's] relationship with man . . . is something much wider than redemption; it coincides with deification. The real anthropological meaning of deification is Christification" (quoted by Panayiotis Nellas, *Deification in Christ: Orthodox Perspectives on the Nature of the Human Person* [Crestwood, NY: St. Vladimir's Seminary Press, 1987], 39).

stead of as Creator, Judge, and Redeemer.[27] The only dignity the NT envisions for human beings is their Christ-driven realignment with God (Matt 5:48; John 1:1-13), their liberating transformation into that splendor God has always intended for them (John 17:20-26; 2 Cor 3:12-4:6; Phil 3:20-21).

Of all pills this may seem the nastiest to swallow, for the simple reason that Western secularism since the Enlightenment usually operates with something more akin to Hellenistic Stoicism than classical Christianity. Cicero concisely captured this point of view:

> There is, I assure you, a medical art for the soul. It is philosophy, whose aid need not be sought, as in bodily diseases, from outside ourselves. We must endeavor with all our resources and all our strength to become capable of doctoring ourselves. (*Tusc. Disput.* 3.6)

Doctoring ourselves—whether by philosophy, business, politics, science, even theology—seems the standing order of our day. And so we recklessly demean those humans whom we call "the disabled" who cannot act as their own physicians (cf. Matt 9:12-13). For the Stoics, one *can* be one's own physician, because humans are essentially reasonable creatures; one *must* be one's own physician, because human dignity is realized by becoming precisely as self-sufficient and indifferent to human turmoil as the gods are believed to be. Just there is Martha Nussbaum, by her own admission sympathetic to Stoicism's particular "therapy of desire," brought up short by the limits of its treatment:

> [The Stoic] is to trust nothing and nobody but herself. But how deeply, then, can she trust and care for others? . . . She is to value her own reason as *the* source of her humanity and her integrity, the one thing of real intrinsic worth in her life. So long as that is with her, she can go through life fulfilled. So long as that is free, she has her dignity, whatever the world may do to her. But what, then, can she consistently think of her deepest ties to other people? Of the prospect of losing them or being betrayed by them? . . . Can

---

27. In *God and Human Dignity* (ed. Soulen and Woodhead; see n. 2 in this chapter), the contributions by Elaine L. Graham ("The 'End' of the Human or the End of the 'Human'? Human Dignity in Technological Perspective," 263-81) and M. Douglas Meeks ("The Economy of Grace: Human Dignity in the Market System," 196-214) demonstrate the devastating consequences of this error with reference, respectively, to contemporary technology and the market system.

one live in reason's kingdom, understood in the way the Stoics understand it, and still be a creature of wonder, grief, and love?[28]

By rejecting what Nussbaum calls "reason's zealous hegemony" as adamantly as it embraces God's passionate involvement with the world and its creatures, the NT remains one of our culture's most annoying gadflies. Permeating its various views, the central theological issue in human dignity is the merciful sovereignty of God.[29]

---

28. Martha C. Nussbaum, *The Therapy of Desire: Theory and Practice in Hellenistic Ethics* (Princeton: Princeton University Press, 1994), 358. To Nussbaum I am obliged for the quotation from Cicero, immediately preceding (*Therapy of Desire*, 316). For a perceptive analysis of "Nussbaum's enriched liberalism," consult Eric O. Springsted, *The Act of Faith: Christian Faith and the Moral Self* (Grand Rapids: Eerdmans, 2002), 193–214.

29. I thank Professors Dale C. Allison Jr., Beverly R. Gaventa, and Marianne Meye Thompson for their gracious critiques of an earlier draft of this essay.

CHAPTER 8

Sin in the Synoptic Gospels

> When Satan tells me I am a sinner he comforts me immeasurably, since Christ died for sinners.
>
> —Martin Luther

The Vocabulary of Sin in the Synoptics

We begin our study with those terms in Matthew, Mark, and Luke that most frequently connote sinful conduct. Seven such words, plus cognates, are commonplace.[1]

Missing the Mark

By far the most common verbal root is *hamart-*, whose fundamental meanings in classical and Koine Greek are to "err," "be at fault," "miss the mark," or "fail."[2] Some declension of this term appears sixty times in the first three Gospels (Matthew [15x]; Mark [13x]; Luke [32x]):

- *hamartanō*, "to commit a wrong" (7x): "Take heed to yourselves; if your brother *sins*, rebuke him, and if he repents, forgive him." (Luke 17:3 RSV)[3]
- *hamartēma*, a "transgression," whether slight or serious (2x): "Truly I tell you, people will be forgiven for their *sins* and whatever blasphemies they utter." (Mark 3:28)

---

1. Unless otherwise indicated, all biblical translations adopt the NRSV. "AT" designates this author's translation.
2. See Gottfried Quell, Georg Betram, Gustav Stählin, and Walter Grundmann, "ἁμαρτάνω, ἁμάρτημα, ἁμαρτία," *TDNT* 1:267–316. This semantic cluster usually translates the Hebrew terms *hatta't* (miss the mark) and *'aven* (iniquity) in the LXX.
3. See also Matt 18:15, 21b; 27:4; Luke 15:18, 21; 17:4.

- *hamartia*, "deviation from a right standard" (24x): "And [the Jerusalemites and Judeans] were baptized by [John] in the river Jordan, confessing their *sins*." (Matt 3:6)[4]
- *hamartōlos*, "one exhibiting conduct in disaccord with standard moral expectations," "the irreligious" (27x): "I have come to call not the righteous but *sinners*." (Mark 2:17b)[5]

Substandard, Bad

The second most common expression for sin in the Synoptics derives from the root *ponēr-*: "a condition bad or grievous," "useless," "worthless," "base," or "knavish."[6] Some form of *ponēr-* occurs forty times (Matthew [25x]; Mark [3x]; Luke [12x]):

- *ponēria*, something "wicked," "base," or "malicious" (3x): "Now you Pharisees clean the outside of the cup and of the dish, but inside you are full of greed and *wickedness*." (Luke 11:39; cf. Matt 22:18; Mark 7:22)
- *ponēros*, that which is "wicked," "evil," "worthless," "degenerate," or "vicious" (36x): "For [God] makes his sun rise on the *evil* and on the good, and sends rain on the righteous and on the unrighteous." (Matt 5:45b)[7]

Liability

Seventeen times Matthew and Luke refer or allude to sin with some form of the root *opheil-*: that which is "owed," "due," or "indebted":

- *opheiletēs*, a "debtor": "As we also have forgiven our *debtors*." (Matt 6:12; cf. 18:24; Luke 7:41[2x]; 13:4; 16:5[2x])
- *opheilē*, an obligation or duty: "I forgave you all that *debt* because you pleaded with me." (Matt 18:32)

---

4. In addition: Matt 1:21; 9:2, 5, 6; 12:31; 26:28; Mark 1:4, 5; 2:5, 7, 9, 10; Luke 1:77; 3:3; 5:20, 21, 23, 24; 7:47, 48, 49; 11:4; 24:47.

5. Also Matt 9:10, 11, 13; 11:19; 26:45; Mark 2:15, 16; 8:38; 14:41; Luke 5:8, 30, 32; 6:32, 33, 34; 7:34, 37, 39; 13:2; 15:1, 7, 10; 18:13; 19:7; 24:7.

6. The LXX uses these terms to translate forms of the Hebrew *rasha'* (bad, evil). See Günther Harder, "πονηρός, πονηρία," *TDNT* 6:546–66.

7. So, too, Matt 5:11, 37, 39; 6:13, 23; 7:11, 17, 18; 9:4; 12:34, 35, 39, 45; 13:19, 38, 49; 15:19; 16:4; 18:32; 20:15; 22:10; 25:26; Mark 7:22, 23; Luke 3:19; 6:22, 35, 45; 7:21; 8:1b–2a; 11:13, 26, 29, 34; 19:22.

- *opheilō*, "to be in debt": "For we ourselves forgive everyone *indebted* to us." (Luke 11:4b; cf. 16:7; 17:10; Matt 18:28[2x], 30, 34; 23:16, 18)

Aberrant

Ten times Matthew and Luke present one of three forms of the root *adik-*, that which is "unruled," "disordered," or "wrong":

- *adikeō*, "to wrong," "cheat," "mistreat," or "injure": "Friend, I am *doing* you no *wrong*." (Matt 20:13; cf. Luke 10:19)
- *adikia*, that which "violates a right standard of conduct," "injustice," "wrongdoing," "unrighteousness," "wickedness": "Depart from me, all you workers of *iniquity*." (Luke 13:27 RSV; cf. 16:8, 9; 18:6)
- *adikos*, "contrary to what is right," "unjust," "crooked": "The Pharisee . . . was praying thus, 'God, I thank you that I am not like other people: thieves, rogues [*adikoi*], adulterers, or even like this tax collector.'" (Luke 18:11; cf. 16:10, 11; Matt 5:45)

Miscellaneous

Fewer than ten times the Synoptics employ each of these correlative terms:

- *anomia*, a lawless disposition: "So you also on the outside look righteous to others, but inside you are full of hypocrisy and *lawlessness*." (Matt 23:28; cf. 7:23; 13:41; 24:12; Luke 22:37)
- *kakia*, "wickedness," "vice," "depravity": "Sufficient unto the day is the *evil* thereof." (Matt 6:34 KJV);
- *paraptōma*, a "violation of moral standards," "offense," or "wrongdoing" (from a Greek root whose etymology is a "false step" or "blunder"): "For if you forgive others their *trespasses*, your heavenly Father will also forgive you." (Matt 6:14; cf. 6:15; Mark 11:25)

Some preliminary observations:

1. While forms of *hamartia* are the terms for sin most often adopted in all three Synoptics, Luke uses them more than twice as much as either Matthew or Mark.
2. Conversely, Matthew favors *ponēros* and *ponēria*, which appear therein twice as often than in Luke and over twelve times more often than in Mark.

3. Even though "righteousness" or "uprightness" (*dikaikosynē*) is a key Matthean term (3:15; 5:6, 10, 20, 6:33; 21:32), its verbal negation (*adik-*) occurs four times more often in Luke. Matthew is more partial to *anomia*, that which transgresses law or commandment (cf. 5:17–19).
4. Sin's description as "indebtedness" is comparatively rare in the Synoptics— surprisingly so in Luke, whose dominant metaphor for salvation is forgiveness (*aphiēmi* and its cognates: 1:77; 3:3; 5:20, 21, 23, 24; 6:37; 7:47, 48; 11:4; 12:10; 17:3, 4; 23:34; 24:47).
5. Of all the Synoptics Mark speaks least about sin: explicitly, only seventeen times.
6. It is surprising how little the Synoptic Gospels, taken altogether, refer to sin by one or another of these terms: from this inventory, only 136 times. To be sure, the seven semantic fields considered here do not exhaust all possibilities (cf. *skandalizō*, "to stumble": Matt 18:6–9 // Mark 9:42–47 // Luke 17:1–2). Moreover, the evangelists can advert to disobedience (Matt 3:7–10 // Luke 3:7–9; Matt 4:1–11 // Luke 4:1–13) without using any of these terms. Nevertheless, the Synoptics comprise about 36 percent of the NT; that they should explicitly address the subject of sin so infrequently is interesting. When one remembers the high degree of material overlapping the Synoptics (e.g., Matt 3:1–6 // Mark 1:1–6 // Luke 3:1–6; Matt 9:1–8 // Mark 2:1–12 // Luke 5:17–26), the percentage of fresh, focused attention to sin is further reduced. The Synoptic Gospels neither neglect nor belabor the topic.
7. The sample quotations, presented above, demonstrate that "sin" is relegated to no single group or class. Sin is a universal human condition, besetting Jesus's disciples, antagonists, and the populace at large.

Patterns of Thought about Sin in the Synoptics

In many ways Jesus's teaching about sin in the Synoptics deviates from or deemphasizes important aspects of its presentation in the OT. He never castigates idolatry, Israel's worship of false gods (cf. 1 Sam 15:23; 2 Chron 33:7; Isa 40:19; Jer 18:15; Ezek 23:49; Hos 10:6). Unlike the prophets Jesus never accuses Israel of violating its covenant with the LORD God (Isa 24:5; Jer 11:10; 22:9; Ezek 17:18–19; Hos 8:1; Mal 2:5–10 cf. Ps 78:10, 37). Luke (3:38) notes Adam among Jesus's ancestry, but Adam's primordial sin (Gen 3:1–21) is never mentioned (cf. Rom 5:14; 1 Cor 15:22). No differentiation is suggested between inadvertent and willful sins (cf. Lev 4–5; Num 15). Jesus does not accuse his listeners of forsaking God (Deut 31:16; 2 Chr 7:19; Ps 119:53; Isa 1:28; Jonah 2:8) or warn them away from defiant rebellion against the Almighty (cf. Exod 23:21; Josh 22:18–19; 1 Sam 12:14–15; Isa 1:20; Jer 28:16; 48:8; Hos 7:14). Nowhere in Jesus's teaching is there anything like the harrowing diagnosis of Israel's recurring sin in Psalm 106:6–47. The closest intersections between Jesus's allusions and OT metaphors lie in his address of his generation as "adulterous" or unfaithful (Matt 12:39; 16:4; Mark 8:38; cf. Exod 34:15–16; Isa 1:21; Ezek 16:32; Hos 4:10–15), and his cautions against causing others to "stumble" (Matt 18:1–10; Mark 9:42–50 // Luke 17:1–4; cf. Prov 4:19; Jer 18:15; Mal 2:8). As Elijah redivivus (Mark 6:14–29; cf. 1 Kgs 18–21), blasting Israel's arrogance and summoning its repentance (Matt 3:1–10; Luke 3:3–14), John the Baptist is more obviously reminiscent of the OT prophets than is Jesus (Matt 16:13–16 // Mark 8:27–29 // Luke 9:18–20).[8]

In all strata of the Synoptic tradition—Mark, Q (the sayings-source hypothetically underlying Matthew and Luke), sources unique to Matthew (M) and to Luke (L)—the center of Jesus's proclamation is *hē basileia tou theou*: "God's kingdom, reign, sovereign governance." Intertestamental Judaism offers glimmers of this metaphor, associated with the coming of a messiah ("anointed delegate") who would annihilate lawless Gentiles and unite Israel in righteousness (Pss. Sol. 17.1–32). In Jesus's preaching the kingdom is not coterminous with Israel or any geopolitical entity; neither is it styled as inner spirituality or a utopian dream. Instead, the kingdom is a metaphor for God's dynamic sovereignty throughout eternity (Matt 13:36–43), already yet secretly erupting in human history (Matt 13:18–23; Mark 4:22): on the verge (Mark 1:15; 9:1), already present (Luke 6:20; 17:20–21), and yet to be consummated (Matt 13:24–30; Luke 13:29). A gift from God, not a human achievement (Mark 10:23–27; Luke 12:32), the kingdom overturns conventional expectations (Matt 20:1–16; Luke 6:20; 9:59–60). It requires radical acceptance (Matt 18:23–35; Luke 9:60) and infant dependence (Mark 10:14–15; Luke 18:16–17). Those with faith anticipate its surprising future with joy and wonder (Luke 14:7–24); the faithless are hardened in their rejection (Mark 4:11–12, 25). The kingdom's coming is entwined with Jesus's routing of satanic powers: "But if it is by the finger of God that I cast out the demons, then the kingdom of God has come to you" (Luke 11:20; cf. Matt 12:28). In the Synoptics where Jesus is, there is God's kingdom. Still, Jesus resists the center of attention: he points away from himself, toward the gospel's concrete manifestations in the reclamation of Israel's victimized, poor, and hopeless (Matt 11:2–6; Luke 7:18–23).

The kingdom of God is the architecture within which the Synoptics understand sin and its defeat. At the Lord God's bequest, "[Jesus] will reign over the

---

8. To this rule there is the occasional exception: thus, the Elisha tradition in 2 Kgs 4:42–44 has colored Matt 14:15–21 // Mark 6:40–44 // Luke 9:12–17.

house of Jacob forever, and of his kingdom there will be no end" (Luke 1:33). "[Mary] will bear a son, and you are to name him Jesus, for he will save his people from their sins" (Matt 1:21; cf. Luke 1:76–77).[9] Broadly construed, God's kingdom, instantiated by Jesus, is God's merciful power to rectify a corrupted creation, to put in right relationship with God all that has been fractured and divorced from its Creator. Although Torah is synchronous with the kingdom's demands (Matt 22:35–40; Luke 16:17), the kingdom, as interpreted by Jesus, also explodes some commandments (Matt 5:38–39, 43–44) or drives more deeply to the heart of their intent (Mark 10:2–12). In the Synoptics "the kingdom of God" occupies the centrality of "covenant" in the OT's prophetic and Deuteronomic traditions. For that reason the dynamic of human response is reoriented: instead of looking backward toward Mount Horeb, repenting of failure or refusal to maintain covenant fidelity, the believer is called by Jesus to live forward into God's new, invasive claim upon a creation whose divine reclamation is in progress. "The law and the prophets were in effect until John came; since then the good news of the kingdom of God is proclaimed, and everyone is pressed to enter it" (Luke 16:16 AT).[10] In simple terms: the prophets and John preached, "Repent of your sins, and God will save you." Jesus affirmed God's preexisting mercy, *prior to* repentance, as the motivating power for living in accordance with God's righteous kingdom: "Neither do I condemn thee: go, and sin no more" (John 8:11 KJV).[11]

Luke 19:1–10 presents of the dynamics of sin and salvation present in all the Synoptics.

> He entered Jericho and was passing through it. A man was there named Zacchaeus; he was a chief tax collector and was rich. He was trying to see who Jesus was, but on account of the crowd he could not, because he was short in stature. So he ran ahead and climbed a sycamore tree to see him,

---

9. The name "Jesus" (*Iēsous*) renders the Hebrew name "Joshua" (*yeshua'*), cognate with the verb "to save" (*yasha'*) and the noun "salvation" (*yeshu'ah*).

10. The final verb in this clause, *biazetai*, may be translated in the middle or passive voice: respectively, "everyone is pressing into it" or "everyone is strongly urged into it." The latter may be preferable; neither need connote violence (cf. Matt 11:12). See Joseph A. Fitzmyer, *The Gospel According to Luke (x–xxiv): Introduction, Translation, and Notes*, AB 28A (Garden City, NY: Doubleday, 1985), 2.1117–18.

11. Although this is the punch line of a story found in John (7:53–8:11), that pericope appears to have been interpolated into the Fourth Gospel. In any case it is more like the Synoptic controversy narratives than anything else in John (cf. Matt 22:15–40 // Mark 12:13–34 // Luke 10:25–28; 20:20–40).

because he was going to pass that way. When Jesus came to the place, he looked up and said to him, "Zacchaeus, hurry and come down; for I must stay at your house today." So he hurried down and was happy to welcome him. All who saw it began to grumble and said, "He has gone to be the guest of one who is a sinner." Zacchaeus stood there and said to the Lord, "Look, half of my possessions, Lord, I will give to the poor; and if I have defrauded anyone of anything, I will pay back four times as much." Then Jesus said to him, "Today salvation has come to this house, because he too is a son of Abraham. For the Son of Man came to seek out and to save the lost." (AT)

Luke's slender descriptions of Zacchaeus are significant. First: he is a "chief tax [or "toll"] collector" (*architelōnēs*). Characteristically—and uniquely—in the Synoptics, "tax collectors" are coupled with "sinners" (*am ha'arets*: the unrepentant wicked: Mark 2:14–17 // Matt 9:10–13 // Luke 5:29–32; Matt 11:17 // Luke 7:34; Luke 15:1–2). Alternatively, "tax collectors" are conjoined with "Gentiles" (Matt 5:46–47 // Luke 6:32–34; Matt 18:17), "Gentile sinner" being a commonplace slur for the nations disobedient to Torah (Pr. Man. 8; Jub. 23:24; Gal 2:15). Yet another variation: *telōnai kai pornai*, "tax collectors and prostitutes" (Matt 21:31–32). In Luke 3:12 and 7:29 tax collectors are fit subjects for John's baptism; in Luke 18:9–14 a miserable tax collector is contrasted with a smug Pharisee. Exactly why *telōnai* are singled out for invective is not clear from the primary sources. According to Josephus, roughly contemporaneous with the Gospels, it may be because Jews hired by Roman overlords to collect oppressive taxes from their fellows were regarded as traitors: "Jews who made themselves Gentiles" (*A.J.* 17.204, 307). Centuries later, in the Babylonian Talmud, "tax collectors" are generally suspect of thievery and extortion (b. Sanh. 25b; b. Bek. 31a).[12] Whatever Luke's precise intent, he concurs with Matthew and Mark in presenting tax collectors as despicable types. Zacchaeus appears even worse: he is a chief or managerial (*archi-*) tax collector (cf. the *archisynagōgoi*, "synagogue rulers," in Luke 8:49; 13:14).

There's another strike against Zacchaeus: he is "rich" (*plousios*). In the Synoptics wealth in itself is not indicative of sinful practice (cf. Matt 27:57; Mark 12:41 // Luke 21:1). The primary difficulty posed by possessions is the temptation to rely on them instead of God's gracious provision (Matt 19:16–30 // Mark 10:17–31 // Luke 18:18–30; cf. Matt 6:25–34 // Luke 12:22–31). Among the Synoptics Luke is especially sensitive to the dangers of wealth, a transient good

---

12. John R. Donahue, "Tax Collectors and Sinners: An Attempt at Identification," *CBQ* 33 (1971): 39–61.

that competes with God for human affection and utter reliance: "No slave can serve two masters; for a slave will either hate the one and love the other, or be devoted to the one and despise the other. You cannot serve God and wealth" (AT; Luke 16:13 // Matt 6:24; cf. Luke 12:16–21). As temptations to covetousness, riches also corrupt human relationships: the wealthy can become indifferent to their needy neighbors (Luke 14:12–24; 16:19–31), oblivious to the Lord who "has filled the hungry with good things, and sent the rich away empty" (1:53; cf. 6:24). Zacchaeus acts contrary to expectation: like the blind beggar of the tale immediately preceding (18:35–43), he exerts extraordinary effort to see Jesus (19:3–4).

Zacchaeus's aggressive action and downward gaze are matched by Jesus's progress and upward acknowledgment: "Hurry and come down; for I must stay at your house today" (19:5). The honor of Jesus's presence is bestowed *today* (*sēmeron*; cf. 4:21; 5:26; 13:32–33; 23:43) in response to genuine outreach but *in advance of* any good work (cf. 4:18, 38–39, 42–44; 5:1–11, 12–16, 17–26; 6:6–11; 18:15–17, 35–43). In Jesus, the hospitality of God *must be* (*dei*) freely extended to the unsavory without expectation of reciprocity (cf. Luke 5:27–32; 14:1–24; 15:1–2; Matt 5:43–48 // Luke 6:32–36; Matt 8:5–13 // Luke 7:1–10).[13]

Zacchaeus, however, does reciprocate, triggering a series of swift, revealing exchanges. (a) Having shinnied down from his sycamore perch, he welcomes Jesus "joyfully" (*chairōn*, Luke 19:6): precisely the response to Jesus's coming that Luke's Gospel repeatedly stresses (1:14, 44; 2:10; 10:17; 15:10; 24:41; see also Matt 2:10; 13:44; 25:21, 23; 28:8). (b) The tax collector's joy evokes a joyless reaction: "All who saw it began to grumble and said, 'He has gone to be the guest of one who is a sinner'" (Luke 19:7). Already that criticism has been leveled against Jesus: "And the Pharisees and the scribes were grumbling and saying, 'This fellow welcomes sinners and eats with them'" (15:2; see also Matt 9:10–11 // Mark 2:15–17 // Luke 5:29–30). In the biblical tradition "grumbling" (Heb., *ragan*; Gk., *diagongyzō, gongyzō* [adjective, *gongysmos*]) is associated with those who err (Isa 29:24), those spiteful of divine grace (Deut 1:27; Ps 106:24–25; Matt 20:11), the jealous, the slanderous, and the wicked (Wis 1:10–11; Sir 46:7; James 5:9 [*stenazō*]). In Luke 19:7 this conduct is generalized beyond Pharisees and scribes: here it is the response of *all* witnesses—suggesting the degree of infamy in which this chief tax collector was held. (c) Disregarding their

---

13. Halvor Moxnes, *The Economy of the Kingdom: Social Conflict and Economic Relations in Luke's Gospel*, OBT (Philadelphia: Fortress, 1988), 127–38. Jesus's offer to stay with Zacchaeus resembles promises of Israel's future vindication at a banquet hosted by the LORD (Isa 25:6; Ezek 39:17–20; 1 En. 62:14; Matt 22:1–10 // Luke 14:12–24).

insult, Zacchaeus volunteers an astonishing donation to the poor[14]—in Luke, the peculiar recipients of Jesus's good news (1:52–53; 4:18; 6:20; 7:22; 14:13, 21; 16:20; 18:22)—and promises fourfold restitution of anything he has embezzled (19:8). Only the widow in the temple treasury gives up more than Zacchaeus: "For all of them have contributed out of their abundance, but she out of her poverty has put in all she had to live on" (21:4). (d) Replying to Zacchaeus, Jesus is given the last word: not congratulations on a job well done; instead, assurance of salvation to a wayward son of Abraham, the "patron saint" of Israelite hospitality (19:9; cf. 15:24, 32; Gen 18:1–8; Heb 13:2). The story ends on a christological point: the reason for the Son of Man's coming is not to destroy but rather to fulfill a mission of search-and-save (Luke 19:10).[15]

The legend of Zacchaeus exemplifies Jesus's climactic beatitude and woe in his Sermon on the Plain (Luke 6:22–24):

> Blessed are you when people hate you, and when they exclude you, revile you, and defame you on account of the Son of Man. Rejoice in that day and leap for joy, for surely your reward is great in heaven; for that is what their ancestors did to the prophets. But woe to you who are rich, for you have received your consolation. (AT)

Zacchaeus eludes catastrophe: in gratitude for Jesus's favor, he's a camel who can release the drag of wealth into the hands of the needy who cannot reciprocate, thereby squeezing through the needle's eye and securing "eternal life," the only reward that matters (Luke 18:18–30; cf. 12:33–34). His and Jesus's defamation by others ("a sinner" and "a sinner's guest") carries no significance whatever; they are transmogrified by the countercultural mores of God's kingdom: "Just so, I tell you, there will be more joy [*chara*] in heaven over one

---

14. Conjugated in the simple present tense, the verb *didōmi* may be interpreted as a customary practice or as a statement of intent "from this time forward" (Fitzmyer, *Luke (x–xxiv)*, 2.1225).

15. Among the many actions associated with "the Son of Man" in Jewish apocalypticism is heavenly judgment of the wicked (1 En. 38.2; 46.1; 47.3; 48.10; 52.4; 69.27–29; 4 Ezra 7.28–29; 11.1–12.32). That nuance persists in the Synoptic traditions, especially Q, M, and L (Matt 13:41–42; 24:37–44 // Luke 17:26–27; Matt 16:27; Matt 25:31–33; Luke 9:26; 11:30; 12:8–9; 17:28–30). More pervasive, however, are sayings about the Son of Man's (= Jesus's) own condemnation and suffering (Matt 8:20 // Luke 9:58; Matt 12:40; Matt 16:13, 21 // Mark 8:31; Luke 9:22; Matt 17:12 // Mark 9:12; Matt 17:22; Mark 9:31 // Luke 9:44; Matt 20:18 // Mark 10:33–34 // Luke 18:31–33; Matt 26:2, 45 // Mark 14:41; Luke 24:7) for the sake of saving others, within and beyond Israel (Matt 9:6 // Mark 2:10 // Luke 5:24; Matt 20:28 // Mark 10:45). In Mark the Son of Man's redemptive suffering and death are most pronounced.

sinner who repents than over ninety-nine righteous persons who need no repentance" (15:7). Accordingly, Jesus refuses to measure repentance by predictable religious norms: he never restricts righteousness to his own disciples (Mark 12:28–34 // Luke 10:25–28), nor does he accuse of sin those who refuse to follow him (Matt 19:16–22 // Mark 10:17–22 // Luke 18:18–25).[16]

In the Synoptics sin's deepest infestation is among the self-righteous. They do not avail themselves of God's mercy because they cannot recognize in themselves the failure (*hamartia*) and indebtedness (*opheilēma*), the malice (*ponēria*) and transgression (*paraptōma*), which they readily ascribe to others. "You are those who justify yourselves in the sight of others; but God knows your hearts; for what is prized by human beings is an abomination in the sight of God" (Luke 16:15). Exemplary of this conduct is the merciless slave in Matthew 18:23–35: forgiven by his king of an impossibly unpayable debt, he jails a peer who owes him 00.0001 percent less.[17] The Synoptics teem with "blind guides" (Matt 15:14; 23:16, 24; cf. Luke 6:39) of many different kinds:

- Pharisees and Sadducees—the popularly pious and the priestly aristocracy[18]—who presume on their ethnic privilege (Matt 3:7–10 // Luke 3:7–9; Matt 8:10–12; Luke 4:25–30; 16:22–31)[19] or scriptural insight (Matt 12:1–15 // Mark 2:23–3:6 // Luke 6:1–11; Matt 22:23–33 // Mark 12:18–27 // Luke 20:27–40; Matt 23:1–36 // Mark 12:38–40 // Luke 11:37–44; 20:45–47), or are simply threatened by the Messiah they refuse to recognize (Matt 21:33–46 // Mark 12:1–12 // Luke 20:9–19; Matt 26:59–68 // Mark 14:55–65 // Luke 22:66–71);
- scribes or "teachers of the law"[20] who see in Jesus's healing only blasphemy (Matt 9:1–8 // Mark 2:12 // Luke 5:1–26);

---

16. Contrast the preaching of Peter and Paul in Acts 2:38; 3:19; 5:31; 10:43; 13:38; 22:16; 26:18.

17. Similarly, Matt 24:45–51 warns against abuse of power among fellow slaves in the household of God.

18. For a clear historical overview, consult E. P. Sanders, *Judaism: Practice and Belief, 63 BCE–66 CE* (London: SCM, 1992), 315–40, 380–451.

19. In view of Luke 3:8, Jesus's reassertion of Zacchaeus as "a son of Abraham" (19:9) acquires another dimension: God is able to raise up even a quisling—Caesar's collaborator—to the status of Abraham's child. The attitudes described here are by no means confined to Jesus's adversaries. In Luke 9:51–56 the disciples James and John are upbraided for furious prejudice against Samaritans; in 17:7–10 they are warned away from presuming upon apostolic entitlement.

20. On the *sofer* or *grammateus* in ancient Jewish society, see Anthony J. Saldarini, *Phar-*

- hypocrites who parade their religiosity or superior discernment of sin (Matt 6:16–18; 7:1–5 // Luke 6:41–42; Matt 23:27–36);
- "false prophets" in sheep's clothing (Matt 7:15; cf. 24:11, 24 // Mark 13:22; Luke 6:26);
- miracle-mongers who flout or despise God's will (Matt 7:21–23 // Luke 6:46; Matt 27:40–44 // Mark 15:29—32 // Luke 23:35–38);
- the faithless who demand of Jesus miraculous credentials (Matt 12:38–42 // Mark 8:11–13 // Luke 11:29–32; Matt 16:1–4);
- persecutory potentates and traitorous kindred (Matt 10:16–23 // Mark 13:9–13 // Luke 21:12–19; Matt 27:3–26 // Mark 15:1–15 // Luke 23:1–25);
- Jewish cities less repentant than their pagan neighbors (Matt 11:20–24 // Luke 10:13–15);
- craven disciples who are irresponsible stewards (Matt 25:14–30 // Luke 19:11–27; cf. Mark 4:24–25; Luke 16:1–8) or outright cowards (Matt 26:69–75 // Mark 14:66–72 // Luke 22:54b–62); and
- heartless disciples, blind to Jesus in their needy neighbors (Matt 25:31–36).

God's hospitality is extended to all, pious Simon (Luke 7:36–50) and sinful Zacchaeus alike (19:1–10). Yet sinners who recognize themselves as such possess a curious advantage: *the Christ of the Synoptics fraternizes with sinners and welcomes them into the kingdom*:

Simon Peter ... fell down at Jesus's knees, saying, "Get away from me, Lord, for I am a sinful man!" ... Then Jesus said to Simon, "Do not be afraid; from now on you will be catching people." (Luke 5:8, 10 AT)

When the scribes of the Pharisees saw that he was eating with sinners and tax collectors, they said to his disciples, "Why does he eat with tax collectors and sinners?" When Jesus heard this, he said to them, "Those who are well have no need of a physician, but those who are sick; I have come to call not the righteous but sinners." (Matt 9:11–13 // Mark 2:16–17 // Luke 5:29–32 AT)

But the tax collector, standing far off [from the Pharisee in the temple] would not even look up to heaven, but was beating his breast and saying, "God, be merciful to me, a sinner!" I tell you, this man went down to his

---

isees, Scribes and Sadducees in Palestinian Society: A Sociological Approach (Wilmington, DE: Glazier, 1988), 241–76.

home justified rather than the other; for all who exalt themselves will be humbled, but all who humble themselves will be exalted. (Luke 18:13-14 AT)

Jesus said to [the chief priests and the elders of the people], "Truly I tell you, the tax collectors and the prostitutes are going into the kingdom of God ahead of you." (Matt 21:31b AT)

No pattern pertaining to sin and salvation is more recurrent in the Synoptics than this, discernible in every stratum of their constitutive traditions. Very likely this welcome of those considered flagrantly wicked is traceable to Jesus himself; it is intelligible as a genuine bone of contention between himself and his more conventionally pious Jewish contemporaries.[21] For those in the first or twenty-first century, conditioned by Scripture to separate themselves from contamination by the wicked until they have mended their ways (Num 16:26; 1 Sam 2:9; 2 Chr 7:14; Ps 119:155; Prov 15:29; Isa 26:10; Ezek 33:8; 1 Cor 5:13; 2 Tim 3:13, among hundreds of examples), Jesus's attitude and actions remain scandalous.

Some Perennial Issues

While a complete investigation is impossible here, a number of interpretive problems bearing on sin and salvation in the Synoptics invite notation.

Is Sin a Power in the Synoptics?

Although sin's personification as an insidious tyrant is commonly associated with Paul (Rom 3:9; 5:12-21; 6:1-23; 7:7-25; Gal 3:22), it is arguably as old as Genesis (4:7): "And if you do not do well, sin is lurking at the door; its desire is for you, but you must master it" (cf. Wis 1:4; 10:13; Sir 21:2; 27:10; 1QH 1.27; 4.29-30). The Synoptics tend not to personify sin's power in this manner. Some references are made to the evil that corrupts humanity's moral compass without specifying its origin: "For it is from within, from the human heart, that evil intentions come" (Mark 7:21 // Matt 15:19); "If you then, who are evil, know how to give good gifts to your children, how much more will your Father in heaven give good things to those who ask him!" (AT; Matt 7:11

---

21. For well-reasoned analysis, see E. P. Sanders, *Jesus and Judaism* (Philadelphia: Fortress, 1985), 174-211.

// Luke 11:13; see also Matt 5:45; 9:4; 12:34–35 // Luke 6:45; Matt 13:49). More commonly, sin's nefarious power in the Synoptics is attributed to the devil, "the evil one" (Matt 5:37; 6:13; 13:19, 38–39), or to his minions (Matt 12:45 // Luke 11:26: Matt 25:41; Luke 7:21; 8:2), who tempt the righteous, including Jesus himself (Matt 4:1–11 // Luke 4:1–13), or pervert God's good intentions for the world (Matt 13:19 // Luke 8:12). Especially in traditions available to Matthew (M), a contest between "the children of the kingdom" of the Son of Man and "the children of the evil one" is imagined (Matt 13:24–30, 36–43) but left undeveloped in the Synoptics.[22] Therein Jesus does not "cast out sin"; rather, he casts out demons or unclean spirits that, in Jewish apocalypticism, traffic in sin (Mark 1:21–28 // Luke 4:31–37; Mark 5:1–20 // Matt 8:28–9:1 // Luke 8:26–39; Mark 7:24–30 // Matt 15:22–28; Mark 9:14–29 // Matt 17:14–18 // Luke 9:37–43a; Matt 9:32–33 // Luke 11:14).

Sin, Sickness, and Calamity

Especially in Deuteronomic theology, the suffering of particular diseases is attributed to the LORD God as retribution for Israel's disobedience of the covenant (Deut 28:15–68; cf. 1 Sam 16:14–23; 1 Kgs 8:3–53; 14:1–16; 2 Chr 21:11–15; Ps 107:17–18; Amos 1:3–3:2). Focusing that point of view upon the individual sufferer (2:1–8; 22:5–11; 34:5–9), the book of Job challenges its theological adequacy. Although apocalyptically inflected books like Daniel (3:1–30; 6:1–28; 11:1–12:13) and Tobit (Tob 2:1–14; 3:8; 6:1–17) associate the suffering of the righteous with demonic forces, it is fair to say that the linkage of healing with repentance from sin pulses throughout much of the Jewish Bible:

> [At Marah] the LORD made for [Israel] a statute and an ordinance and there he put them to the test. He said, "If you will listen carefully to the voice of the LORD your God, and do what is right in his sight, and give heed to his commandments and keep all his statutes, I will not bring upon you any of the diseases that I brought upon the Egyptians; for I am the LORD who heals you." (Exod 15:25b–26)

> My child, when you are ill, do not delay,
> but pray to the Lord, and he will heal you.
> Give up your faults and direct your hands rightly,
> and cleanse your heart from all sin. (Sir 38:9–10)

22. Cf. the DSS: 1QS 1.9–10; 4Q177 13.7–11; 4Q548 2.9–16.

In the Synoptic Gospels catastrophic effects are attenuated from the cause of sin:

> At that very time there were some present who told him about the Galileans whose blood Pilate had mingled with their sacrifices. [Jesus] asked them, "Do you think that because these Galileans suffered in this way they were worse sinners than all other Galileans? No, I tell you; but unless you repent, you will all perish as they did. Or those eighteen who were killed when the tower of Siloam fell on them—do you think that they were worse offenders than all the others living in Jerusalem? No, I tell you; but unless you repent, you will all perish just as they did." (Luke 13:1–5 AT)

Extraordinary suffering no longer signifies inordinate sinfulness. Jesus's teaching in this passage turns such reasoning upside-down: in response to God's kingdom, repentance is incumbent upon *everyone*, lest all suffer consequences conventionally presumed only of "consummate sinners" (cf. Matt 5:21–48). Also worth noting in Luke 13:1–5 is the emphasis on *repentance*, twice mentioned, not on sins, which are never mentioned. Repentance is not a matter of feeling sorry for one's wickedness or insufficient religiosity; to repent is to turn and hold steady one's life Godward (cf. Luke 13:6–9; Matt 3:2 // Mark 1:15; Matt 4:17; Mark 6:12). As a matter of course, a life Godward oriented will give up sinning, instead bearing toward righteousness (Luke 13:6–9; cf. Matt 3:8 // Luke 3:8; 17:3–4).

Mark 2:1–12 // Matt 9:1–8 // Luke 5:17–26 seem an exception to this rule: "When Jesus saw their faith, he said to the paralytic, 'Son, your sins are forgiven'" (Mark 2:5 // Matt 9:2 // Luke 5:20).[23] On close inspection, however, neither here nor in any of the Synoptics' healing stories does Jesus stipulate a sufferer's repentance from sins, demonstrated or assumed, as prerequisite for healing. Not sin's abandonment, but rather *faith*—trust that Jesus wields God's gracious power to cure—creates the climate for salvation (Matt 9:22 // Mark 5:34 // Luke 8:48; Mark 10:52 // Luke 18:48; Matt 9:29; 15:28; Luke 7:50; 17:19). Forgiveness of sins is broached, not as a step in the paralytic's cure, but rather to establish the truly controversial point in Mark 2:6–12: "Why

---

23. Thus, Joel Marcus: "[A] rabbinic tradition, *b. Ned.* 41a, offers a striking parallel to [Mark 2:5] when it says that 'a sick person does not arise from his sickness until all his sins are forgiven him.' Here, as in Mark, we find a linkage between sin and sickness, the phrase 'sins are forgiven,' and a reference to the healed person 'rising' from his bed" (*Mark 1–8*, AB 27 [New York: Doubleday, 2000], 1.221).

does this fellow speak in this way? It is blasphemy! Who can forgive sins but God alone?" (2:7; cf. Matt 9:3 // Luke 5:21). Throughout the Synoptics variations of this challenge recur: "Why do John's disciples and the disciples of the Pharisees fast, but your disciples do not fast?" (Mark 2:18; cf. Matt 9:14 // Luke 5:33). "They watched him to see whether he would cure him on the sabbath, so that they might accuse him" (Mark 3:2; cf. Matt 12:10 // Luke 6:7). "By what authority are you doing these things? Who gave you this authority to do them?" (Mark 11:28; cf. Matt 21:23 // Luke 20:1–2). Ironically, it is Jesus's *cure* of disease that provokes sin among the faithless: "The Pharisees went out and immediately conspired with the Herodians against him, how to destroy him" (Mark 3:6; cf. Matt 12:14 // Luke 6:11; see also Matt 9:34; Matt 12:24 // Mark 3:22 // Luke 11:15; Luke 4:23–30; 11:53–54). Conversely, "Blessed is anyone who takes no offense at me" (Matt 11:6 // Luke 7:23 AT).

Forgiveness in the Lord's Prayer

Two petitions in the prayer Jesus teaches his disciples raise an interesting theological question.

> And forgive us our sins,
> for we ourselves forgive all who are indebted to us. (Luke 11:4 AT)

> And forgive us our debts,
> as [*hōs*] we also [*kai*] have forgiven those indebted to us.
> (Matt 6:12 AT)

Does God's forgiveness of our sins depend on, or extend no farther than, our own forgiveness of those sins committed by others against us? Another ancient Jewish prayer (ca. 180 BCE) suggests such a conclusion:

> Forgive your neighbor the wrong he has done,
>   and then your sins will be pardoned when you pray.
> Does anyone harbor anger against another,
>   and expect healing from the Lord?
> If one has no mercy toward another like himself,
>   can he then seek pardon for his own sins?
> If a mere mortal harbors wrath,
>   who will make an atoning sacrifice for his sins?
> Remember the end of your life, and set enmity aside;

> remember corruption and death, and be true to the commandments. (Sir 28:2-6)

The petition for forgiveness in Matthew and Luke is both like and unlike the instruction offered in Sirach. Overarching all three is what might be called a channel of mercy, through which divine and human release of sin flows bidirectionally. This idea is clearly expressed in Matt 6:14-15: "For if you forgive others their trespasses, your heavenly Father will also forgive you; but if you do not forgive others, neither will your Father forgive your trespasses" (cf. Matt 7:2 // Mark 4:24 // Luke 6:38). One unable to offer forgiveness is incapable of receiving it.

The point at which the Lord's Prayer veers away from Sirach is an apocalyptic theocentricity. The context of Sirach 28:2-6 is the social fabric of an upright life anchored in wisdom (24:1-29:28). The prayer Jesus taught his disciples emerges from the good news of God's in-breaking kingdom, for whose coming they are first instructed to pray, that the Heavenly Father's holy sovereignty may rectify everything on earth (Matt 6:9-10 // Luke 11:2). Within that framework there can be no quid pro quo (Luke 7:40-43; 17:7-10): the disciple, also in need of rectification, depends entirely on God for sustenance (Matt 6:11 // Luke 11:3), forgiveness (Matt 6:12a // Luke 11:4a), and rescue from temptations to evil (Matt 6:13 // Luke 11:4b). The forgiveness rendered by Jesus's disciples is an illustration of life healed by God's power,[24] in line with their empowerment to "cure the sick, raise the dead, cleanse the lepers, cast out demons": all received without payment and given without payment (Matt 10:8; cf. Mark 6:7 // Luke 9:1-2). The evangelists are well aware that the ability of Jesus's disciples to forgive debts owed them by others depends upon and pales beside the forgiveness they have first received from God (Matt 18:21-35; Mark 11:20-25; Luke 15:11-32).[25]

The Unforgiveable Sin

In Mark 3:28-29 Jesus issues a solemn pronouncement:

---

24. The *hōs kai* (as also) construction in Matt 6:12 suggests an exemplary case (BAGD 1104b). The prophets expected pardon of Israel's iniquity on the day of salvation (Isa 55:6-9; Jer 31:31-34; Ezek 36:22-32).

25. The interplay of God's forgiveness of mortals and their forgiveness of one another is examined by Jeongsoo Park, "Sündenvergebung im Matthäusevangelium: Ihre theologische und soziale Dimension," *EvT* 66 (2006): 210-27.

> Truly I tell you, people will be forgiven for their sins and whatever blasphemies they utter; but whoever blasphemes against the Holy Spirit can never have forgiveness, but is guilty of an eternal sin. (Mark 3:28–29; cf. Matt 12:31–32 // Luke 12:8–10)

The setting for the warning in Mark (3:22, 30) and Matthew (12:24) is his adversaries' accusation that his ability to cast out demons derives from his allegiance to their ruler, Beelzebul (cf. John 7:20; 8:48). Aligning Jesus with demonic forces is tantamount to committing a sin that cannot be released, though all other sins are forgivable. Why is this so? Mark does not explain; such parables (3:23) are left for Jesus's audience to unravel. Throughout history the church has worried over this question—understandably so, since the stakes for salvation are so high.[26]

Previously in Mark, scribes have attributed blasphemy to Jesus for releasing a paralytic's sins, on the ground that only God may remit them (2:5–10). In that case Jesus challenged "such questions in [their] hearts" but did not reproach them as unpardonable. Though bewildered, the scribes appear to have attempted the protection of God's sovereignty. The circumstances in Mark 3:22–30 have shifted. By ascribing demonism to Jesus, scribal misapprehension devolves into a fatal abuse: it is blasphemy, which, in Hellenistic Greek as in modern English, connotes the desecration of God. In both the LXX and the NT blasphemy is ultimately a violation of God's majesty (2 Kgs 19:4, 6, 22; Isa 52:5; Rev 13:6; 16:11, 21); penultimately it comprises derision of godly persons or things (Isa 66:3; Ezek 35:12; 2 Macc 8:4; 12:14; 15:24; Acts 6:11; Titus 2:5). So also in Mark 3:28: identifying as diabolical the one who conveys God's Holy Spirit (1:8, 10) is a peculiar blasphemy, beyond the pale of normal remission, because one thereby drives oneself away from the true agent of forgiveness (cf. "the deathward sin" in 1 John 5:16–17). To stretch the metaphor in Mark 2:17: one will never surrender to therapeutic surgery if one is so deluded that she thinks her physician is a homicidal monster. To put Jesus in league with Satan is so utterly perverse that its proponents put themselves under conditions in which forgiveness is a practical impossibility. In their parallels to this Markan passage, Matthew (12:22–32) and Luke (12:8–12) move the focus away from Christology to pneumatology: "every sin and blasphemy" (Matt 12:31), even that uttered against the Son of Man (Matt 12:32; Luke 12:10a), can be forgiven,

---

26. Nicholas Lammé, "Blasphemy Against the Holy Spirit: The Unpardonable Sin in Matthew 12:22–32," *MAJT* 23 (2012): 19–51, surveys exegetical opinion from the patristic era to the present.

but no desecration of the Holy Spirit so vile that it identifies its origin in Satan himself. This notion seems an apocalyptic variant of "sin with a high hand" (*beyad ramah*: Num 15:30–31; cf. Deut 17:12): defiant, relentless repudiation of the salvation offered by God's Spirit.²⁷

Purity and Sacrifice, the Temple and Jesus

Israel's ritual sacrifice—articulated in Leviticus (1–7), developed across the centuries after the Babylonian exile, and observed at the time of Jesus and his earliest followers—was practiced to repair the breach, constantly opened by sin, between the nation and God. Given those assumptions, it is striking that the Synoptics never present Jesus as urging anyone to offer sacrifice through priestly mediation.²⁸ Although Jesus's hostile activity in the temple (Matt 21:12–13 // Mark 11:15–19 // Luke 19:45–48; cf. John 2:13–22) has been typed as its "cleansing," evidence for its pollution is hard to come by.²⁹ Whatever Jesus's intent may have been, the Synoptics point to a different explanation. By his disruption of standard cultic procedure, Jesus gestured toward the temple's *destruction*: thus, the fig tree's cursing, the Temple Mount's toppling (Matt 21:18–22 // Mark 11:12–14 and Mark 11:20–25), and the prediction of the temple's doom (Matt 24:1–51 // Mark 13:1–37 // Luke 21:5–36). Commandeering the temple for his final public teaching (Matt 21:23–23:29 // Mark 11:27–12:44 // Luke 20:1–21:4), Jesus redirects attention away from "all whole burnt offerings and sacrifices" toward unreserved love of God and neighbor (Mark 12:28–35; cf. Deut 6:4–5; Lev 19:18; 1 Sam 15:22). Likewise—and astonishingly—Jesus abrogates the laws of kashrut (Lev 11; Deut 14), relocating defilement in the human heart (Matt 15:1–20 // Mark 7:1–23).³⁰

---

27. Among other ancient Jewish groups, profanation of the sabbath (Jub. 2:27), disavowal of circumcision (Jub. 15:33–34), and disrespect of a community's members and special teachings (1QS 7.16–17) were considered unpardonable offenses.

28. The directives in Mark 1:44 // Matt 8:4 // Luke 5:14 and Luke 17:14 concern, not sin, but reintegration into society of those whose disease had previously isolated them. References to worship at the temple (Matt 5:23–24; Luke 1:8–23; 2:22–40; 18:9–14; 24:52) are not dominical dictates; they simply assume its practice.

29. Admittedly, interpretation of Jesus's disturbance in the temple remains controversial. See Craig A. Evans, "Jesus' Action in the Temple: Cleansing or Portent of Destruction?" *CBQ* 51 (1989): 237–70.

30. Drawing on Gen 6:5; 8:21, later rabbis tended to locate the *yetser hara'*, "evil inclination," in the human heart (e.g., b. Ber. 5a.2; Pesiq. Rab Kah. 124a–b). The remedy, however, was to fortify one's adherence to Torah (Prov 3:5–8), not to annul its commandments.

The concept of Jesus's self-sacrifice for sin is embryonic in two sayings in the Synoptics: "For the Son of man came not to be served but to serve, and to give his life a ransom for many" (Mark 10:45 // Matt 20:28); "This is my blood of the covenant, which is poured out for many for the forgiveness of sins" (Matt 26:28 // Mark 14:24 // Luke 22:20; cf. Exod 24:8; Zech 9:11).[31] The general idea is clear enough: Jesus donates his life for others' salvation (thus, Luke 23:13–43). The effective means of that redemption is left unexplained, evoking a mélange of metaphors in Israel's history: Passover (Num 9:1–14), the Day of Atonement (Lev 16), the suffering servant (Isa 42:1–4; 52:13–53:12), the faithful Maccabean martyrs (2 Macc 6:18–7:42; 4 Macc 6:1–7:10). Except for the Epistle to the Hebrews, the particulars of Jesus's atonement for sin are similarly inchoate elsewhere in the NT. That sets the agenda for soteriological reflection in subsequent Christian thought.

Conclusions

Although sin is a genuine concern of the evangelists, in none of the Synoptics does Jesus analyze the subject. Nor, as a rule, does he harangue his listeners for their iniquity.[32] By word and deed—often oblique, at times painfully direct—Jesus testifies to God's sovereignty already at work in his ministry, straightening the crooked in alignment with a holy, rectifying power. Embodying the future of salvation, Jesus embraces the wicked and enables their turning to the merciful and forgiving God, who redirects them toward forgiveness of others and formation of a loving community. The sin of those who reject this good news is exposed: whether as grace or as judgment, an encounter with God's kingdom leaves no one unchanged. After Good Friday, when evil had done its worst, God vindicated Jesus's selfless obedience, transformed the wicked, and sanctified the unholy. That, for Christians, is the import of Christ's resurrection.

---

31. "For the forgiveness of sins" is absent from the Markan and Lukan parallels, as well as from 1 Cor 11:25.

32. Matthew 23:1–36 is a rare exception, motivated by that Gospel's peculiar circumstances: see Ulrich Luz, *Matthew 21–28: A Commentary*, trans. James E. Crouch, Hermeneia (Minneapolis: Fortress, 2005), 92–94. Even there, however, the targets are "blind hypocrites" whose teaching should be followed though they themselves fail to practice it (vv. 2–3).

CHAPTER 9

Shouting at the Legally Deaf

> Most of us spend the first six days of each week sowing our wild oats—then we go to church on Sunday and pray for a crop failure.
>
> —Fred Allen

SEVEN DECADES LATER, does Allen's quip still ring true?[1] If so, many of today's churchgoers receive little help from the pulpit. Sociologist Marsha Witten analyzed the texts of forty-seven sermons preached on Luke 15:11–32 between 1986 and 1988 by pastors in the Presbyterian Church (USA) and the Southern Baptist Convention. Among her findings, 32 percent of the preachers characterized God as daddy; 39 percent, God the sufferer; 28 percent, God the extravagant lover (all Presbyterian, save one); the hair's-breadth remainder, God the judge (all Southern Baptist).[2] The shades of John Calvin and Roger Williams are not smiling.

Our ancestors didn't pussyfoot around divine judgment; the Gospels gave them no cause.

> The men of Nineveh will stand up at the judgment with this generation and condemn it. (Matt 12:41a // Luke 11:32a NIV)

> Whoever slanders the Holy Spirit can never be forgiven; he is guilty of an eternal sin. (Mark 3:29 // Matt 12:32 // Luke 12:10 REB)

---

1. Allen, *"All the Sincerity in Hollywood . . .": Selections from the Writings of Radio's Legendary Comedian*, ed. Stuart Hample (Golden, CO: Fulcrum, 2001), 107.
2. Witten, *All Is Forgiven: The Secular Message in American Protestantism* (Princeton: Princeton University Press, 1993), 31–54.

It is better to enter your life a cripple than to keep both your feet and be thrown into hell. (Mark 9:46 // Matt 18:8 NEB)

Fear him who, after killing you, has power to hurl you into the pit. Yes, fear him, I tell you. (Luke 12:5 // Matt 10:28 Smith-Goodspeed)

But those enemies of mine, who did not want me to be king over them, bring them here and slaughter them in my presence. (Luke 19:27 Lattimore)

For an hour is coming in which all those in the tombs will hear his voice and will come forth. Those who have done what is right will rise to live; those who have practiced what is wicked will rise to be damned. (John 5:28–29)[3]

Such assertions are attested in all the Gospels, in every traditional stratum. That Jesus never spoke in such terms, that all the evangelical traditions got him wrong in this respect, strains credibility until it snaps.

Vignettes of Judgment

Detached dicta invite misapprehension and faulty conclusions. To understand the dynamics of divine justice in the Gospels, selected passages should be considered in a specific context. Here I shall concentrate on Matthew, in which the repeated fall of God's hammer evokes "weeping and gnashing of teeth" (8:12; 13:42, 50; 22:13; 24:51; 25:30; cf. Luke 13:28). Three instances of Jesus's parabolic teaching are representative of this Gospel: the weeds among the wheat (13:24–30) and its allegorical interpretation (13:36–43); the unforgiving servant (18:23–35); the separation of the sheep from the goats (25:31–46). Uniquely Matthean, these anecdotes of destiny are distributed throughout this Gospel (13:1–52; 18:1–35; 24:1–25:46).

"And They Will Throw Them into the Furnace of Fire": *Matthew 13:24–30, 36–43*

This parable likens the kingdom of heaven to everyday farming (cf. Matt 13:3–23, 31–32). Its eschatological disposition is clear in the telling—deferred judg-

---

3. Translated by Raymond Brown, *The Gospel according to John: Introduction, Translation and Notes*, AB 29 (Garden City, NY: Doubleday, 1966), 213.

ment until a final harvest and separation (v. 30; cf. Dan 12:1-3)—clearer still in the allegorical correlations: the Son of Man as sower (Matt 13:37); the devil as adversary (vv. 38-39a); reaping angels (vv. 39c, 41); the kingdom's children ("good seed") versus diabolical progeny ("the weeds," v. 38); "the harvest" at "the end of the age" (v. 39b), culminating in a fiery purge of wickedness and its perpetrators (v. 42). The righteous, by contrast, shine in the presence of their heavenly Father (v. 43).

This parable also whispers Christology, mission, and the church. Initiating all is the Son of Man who sows (cf. 13:3b, 31, 33, 44, 45, 47-48, whose various agents are not identified). His seed, which is superb (*kalon*), is sown in *his* (*autou*) field (v. 24), identified as the world (*ho kosmos*: v. 38; cf. 5:14; 18:7): the theater of the gospel's proclamation (24:14; 26:13; 28:18-20). Presumably "the kingdom's children" manifest the same qualities of the rich soil in 13:8—hearing with discernment and bearing bountiful fruit (v. 23). Such traits are typical of Jesus's true disciples in Matthew (5:16; 7:24-25; 13:51-52).

There's a hitch, however. Several, in fact, all clustered in 13:27-29. Toxic weeds, or darnel (*ta zizania*),[4] proliferate among the Son's fine grain (*to siton*), in his own field (vv. 25-26). Where did they come from? Why shouldn't they be immediately uprooted? The latter question seems easier to answer: they were discovered, not by the housemaster, but by his slaves (v. 27). He accepts their findings but not their competence to unearth the bad without destroying the good (vv. 28b-29). Temporarily the noxious grows among the nourishing; at harvest, angels of the Lord (*kyrios*: v. 27) will do the sorting, burn the darnel, and gather good grain for safe storage (v. 30).

The harder question: Whence came the toxic plants in the Lord's own field? Without inspection he knows the answer: his hated enemy (*echthros*)—the devil (13:39a; cf. Luke 10:19)—sowed the poison (Matt 13:25, 28a). While the world sleeps a diabolical power infects what is healthy, then steals away. Tares and wheat can be differentiated (v. 27b) but not separated without courting catastrophe (v. 29). It is no business of the servants to attempt fine discrimination now; at the close of the age, the Lord's angels are charged with destroying the destructive and securing the righteous (vv. 40-43; cf. 24:30-31). Haunting intertestamental apocalyptic,[5] "the fiery furnace" is a NT rarity: it appears only

---

4. Rabbis considered *ziv* (Heb.) or *ziva'* (Aram.) a degenerative kind of grain (m. Kil. 1.1), precluded from offering to the priests from the harvest's produce: "[Tares] are not edible" (m. Ter. 2.6).

5. Those whose "names shall be blotted out of the Book of Life . . . shall wail and make lamentations in a chaotic wilderness, and in the fire they shall burn" (1 En. 108.35). Fourth

here, at the end of the twin parable of the dragnet (Matt 13:47–50), and twice in Revelation (1:15; 9:2; cf. Ezek 22:17–22; Dan 3:1–30). Matthew's customary depiction of final judgment's horror, "weeping and gnashing of teeth" (13:42), is juxtaposed with "the righteous [who] will shine like the sun in their Father's kingdom" (v. 43; cf. the face of Jesus transfigured in 17:2).[6]

Judgment falls not merely as the final curtain; the entire parable is draped in divine decisions. First: the Lord judges this world, which belongs to him, as a place of dangerous ambiguity. A cadaverous power operates in the good he has sown. Apparently pure, the baby's bottle has been laced with strychnine. Second: even humans who know this are judged incompetent to dispose of such evil (cf. Luke 9:51–56). If we are incapable of uprooting the weeds without spoiling genuine fruit, then our sharpest discernment suffers macular degeneration (Matt 7:22–23; 16:2–4)—just as our discipleship may go flat (5:13; 25:14–30), our speech risks condemnatory carelessness (12:36; 23:16–22), and our morals are candidates for radical surgery (5:28–30; 18:8–9). Third: this parable ends with no pat on the disciple's back for a job well done. Both the wicked and the righteous are assured of their just deserts, but the exact identities of those in either category are never fixed. Anyone with ears had better pay attention (13:43b; 11:15; 13:9; cf. Ezek 3:27). We may suppose we can distinguish wheat from tares, confident that we are Wheaties, but the parable pulses in the opposite direction.

"Should You Not Have Had Mercy?": Matthew 18:23–35

Jesus's parable of the unforgiving servant is a text of terror Phyllis Trible never got around to.[7] Its very premise is frightening. I paraphrase: "You want to know what the kingdom of heaven is like? How's this: a king wanted to settle his account with his slaves" (Matt 18:23). Forget golden harps at the pearly gates; it's time to balance the books. The first debtor summoned to court owes "ten thousand talents" (v. 24). Let's run the numbers. A talent amounted to a laborer's wages across fifteen years. If a Roman child, born among the ur-

---

Ezra 7.31 contrasts "the pit of torment" and "the furnace of *gehenna*' (Heb. = *Gehenna* [Lat.]) with "the place of refreshment" and "the paradise of delight."

6. Harking back to Exod 34:30, the beaming faces of the righteous is a Jewish commonplace, reflective of *hashekinah zu*, God's glorious splendor (2 Bar. 51.3; 1 En. 39.13; 4 Ezra 7.97; Bam.Rab. 12.4; 13.2; *Sed.Ol.Rab.* 7.2; *Shir.Ha-Shar.Rab.* 1.2.1; 3.10.1–4; 4.12.2. For drawing my attention to these representative rabbinic texts, I am grateful to Kaitlynn C. Merckling.

7. Trible, *Texts of Terror: Literary-Feminist Readings of Biblical Narratives*, OBT (Philadelphia: Fortress, 1984).

ban poor, could expect to live not much longer than twenty years,[8] then a ten-thousand-talent debt could not be paid off in less than fifteen thousand lifetimes. This slave's default reaches to Andromeda Galaxy. To pay it off is *impossible*; there's at least a hint of embezzlement. Such is this parable's first terror: the frisson that curdles an empty stomach when one has been caught red-handed, with no means of escape.

Another terror: the judge's sentence. "The Lord" (*ho kyrios*) commands that the debtor, his wife, his children, and all his assets be sold into slavery until restitution is made (v. 25). Scholars quibble whether such disposition of insolvency, attested in the OT (2 Kgs 4:1; Neh 5:5; Isa 50:1), was enforced in the time of Jesus. That misses the point. The payback is as outsized as the debt.

Matthew 18:26 interrupts the horrors with the slave's prostrate plea for his sovereign's forbearance, predicated on a ludicrous promise of full recompense. Astonishingly, the sovereign is moved by compassionate bowels (*splanchnistheis*), cancels the debt outright, and releases the slave (v. 27). A happy ending, enough to explain Jesus's reply to Peter in Matthew 18:21–22.

This being a text of terror, the story continues. While exiting the king's chambers, that very slave finds a peer who owes him a hundred denarii: 00.0001 percent of the slave's own debt. Throttling the poor schnook,[9] he demands, "Pay what you owe" (v. 28). Verse 29 replicates the action (prostrate, begging for patience) in v. 26; the second slave repeats, nearly word-for-word, the plea of the first. The sole deviation is noteworthy: the first slave promised to repay everything (v. 26), a manifest impossibility; the second promises recompense of a microscopically smaller loan (in today's dollars, about $154). The slave throws *his* debtor into jail until *his* bill is paid in full (v. 30). Appalled by these proceedings, fellow slaves report them to their Lord (v. 31).

The final act returns to the parable's original setting. The first slave is recalled. The king minces no words: "You bastard.[10] I forgave you every cent of debt you owed me, since you begged me to. Shouldn't you have been merciful to your fellow slave, just as I was merciful to you?" (vv. 32–33). Enraged, the king hands the slave over to torturing jailers (*tois basanistais*) until he can pay the debt in full (v. 34). Good luck with that. In case his disciples—themselves fellow slaves of their Lord—have missed the point, Jesus underscores it: "So,

---

8. So Richard L. Rohrbagh estimates in *The New Testament in Cross-Cultural Perspective*, CB (Eugene, OR: Wipf & Stock, 2006), 25.

9. Under Roman law (*manus iniectio*) a private citizen could coerce another in default before the magistrate (cf. m. B. Bat. 10.8). Matthew notes that physical abuse. The king never laid a finger on his own debtor.

10. Literally, "You wicked slave" (*doule ponēre*), whose tone, in this context, is too delicate.

too, shall my heavenly Father do to you, unless each of you forgives his brother from your heart" (v. 35).

Whereas Matthew 13:36–43 grapples with a mysterious corruption at work in the world, the parable of servants forgiven and unforgiven is focused on the Matthean community, framed by references to Christian siblings in 18:15–22 and 35, and concentrated on the painful issue of forgiveness. Every effort should be made to reconcile offending parties within the *ekklēsia* (18:17a) to that household of faith (18:10–22). The basis for this conduct lies in the character of God, who with incredible mercy has forgiven us greater offense against himself than can ever be calculated, much less repaid. Forgiveness, however, is not a static declaration but a reciprocating force: the power by which we learn to forgive others, in realization of our own conviction and release from indebtedness (thus, the Lord's Prayer's fifth petition: 6:12). Clearly Matthew was concerned about this issue, because he returns to it: "For if you forgive others their trespasses, your heavenly Father will also forgive you; but if you do not forgive others, neither will your Father forgive your trespasses" (6:14–15; cf. Mark 11:25). Matthew also reiterates that God's forgiveness precedes our own, anticipating even our contrition and petition for release (9:2, 6). Yet humans can short-circuit the current of divine forgiveness by refusing to repent (12:38–42) or attributing diabolism to the Holy Spirit (12:31–32).[11] Equal to God's mercy and justice in Matthew 18:23–35 is the mystery of the slave's deportment: accepting the king's just retribution, he instantly forgets his own forgiveness and abuses one better than he for the meanest reasons. This text's greatest terror lies deep in a human heart, void of the mercy with which God has filled it.

"Depart from Me into the Eternal Fire": Matthew 25:31–46

No essay on divine recompense in the Gospels could bypass this text, recognizable even among those ignorant of Scripture. Resisting strict allegorization, Matthew's tableau of the Great Assize crowns Jesus's end-time address to his disciples (24:1–25:30) on Passover eve (26:1–5).

A detour into ancient back-alleys grants us perspective on Matthew's famous thoroughfare.

---

11. "The way of escape has been provided by God. Those individuals who face destruction do so by their own choosing, not because God's retributive justice demands their demise" (Christopher D. Marshall, *Beyond Retribution: A New Testament Vision for Justice, Crime, and Punishment* [Grand Rapids: Eerdmans, 2001], 199). See also Stephen H. Travis, *Christ and the Judgement of God: The Limits of Divine Retribution in New Testament Thought*, 2nd ed. (Peabody, MA: Hendrickson, 2008), 220–42.

> [The unrighteous] will come like cowards at the reckoning-up of
> their sins. . . .
> Then the upright man will stand with great boldness
> Face to face . . . with those who set his labors at naught. . . .
> They will talk to themselves in repentance,
> And in their distress of mind they will groan. . . .
> But the upright live forever, . . .
> And the Most High takes care of them. (Wis 4:20a, 5:1–2, 15 [AT])

And I watched until a throne was erected in the pleasant land [of Israel], and the Lord of the sheep sat upon it. . . . And I saw at the same time that an abyss like it, full of fire, was opened in the middle of the earth. And they brought those blinded sheep, and they were all judged and found to be sinners. And they were thrown into the fiery abyss, and they burned. . . . And I saw those sheep burning, and their bones burning. (1 En. 90.20a, 26–27)[12]

And the visitation of those who walk in [all the paths of justice and truth] will be for . . . fruitful offspring with all everlasting blessings, . . . and a crown of glory with majestic raiment in eternal life. However, . . . the visitation of those who walk in [all the paths of darkness and evil cunning] will be for . . . eternal damnation for the scorching wrath of the God of revenge, . . . with the humiliation of destruction by the fire of the dark regions, . . . without there being a remnant or a survivor among them. (1QS 4.6b–8, 11b–14)[13]

All these texts, most about a century older than Matthew 25:31–46, are superficially similar to it: a cleavage between the upright and the unrighteous; face-to-face vindication and condemnation; consequences blissful or hideous. Matthew has raided his era's treasury of apocalyptic images: the Judge seated on a glorious throne (25:31), conviction of sheep and shepherds (vv. 32–33), threats of punishment and blessings of eternal life (25:34, 46). At a deeper level, Matthew chimes with many of these texts' beliefs in a life well lived before God: trust in God's mercy (5:7; cf. Wis 3:9; 1 En. 1.8; 39.5; 1QS 4.3–4), meekness (Matt 5:5; cf. 1 En. 108.7; 1QS 3.8), compassion (Matt 9:36; cf. Wis 10:5; 1 En. 50.3; 1QS 4.3–5), wisdom (Matt 12:42; cf. Wis 7:22b–10:21; 1 En. 5.8; 1QS 4.3),

---

12. Translated by George W. E. Nickelsburg in *1 Enoch: A Commentary on the Book of 1 Enoch, Chapters 1–36, 81–108*, ed. Klaus Baltzer, Hermeneia (Minneapolis: Fortress, 2012), 402.

13. Florentino García Martínez, ed., *The Dead Sea Scrolls Translated: The Qumran Texts in English*, 2nd ed., trans. Wilfred G. E. Watson (Leiden: Brill; Grand Rapids: Eerdmans, 1996), 6–7.

obedience to Torah (Matt 7:12; cf. Wis 6:12–20; 1 En. 108.1; 1QS 4.2–3); most important, righteousness (Matt 6:33; cf. Wis 12:12–22; 1 En. 10.16–18; 1QS 2.24).

Yet the difference between these texts and Matthew 25:31–46 is vast—deeper than the goats' consignment to "eternal punishment," tepid by comparison to 1 Enoch's grisly barbecue or the annihilation of evildoers in Qumran's Community Rule. Those vindicated there and in the milder Wisdom of Solomon are on the side of the angels. "The upright" know who they are. The books to whom they are addressed alleviate their affliction and consolidate their confidence. In Wisdom the ungodly acknowledge their reprehensible stupidity in two dozen eloquent metaphors—"fools that we were!" (5:4). In Matthew, *all* are shocked by their judgment—sheep no less than goats. *Nobody* knew exactly what she was doing or to whom she was doing it. The conduct on which all are judged are *gĕmîlût ḥăsādîm*, "the giving of loving-kindness": feeding the hungry, giving drink to the thirsty, hospitality to strangers, clothing the naked, visiting the sick and imprisoned (25:35–39, 42–43; cf. Isa 58:7; Sir 7:35). None of this constitutes Ethics 920: Advanced Problems in Moral Reasoning. Equally revealing is the sheep and goats' identical question (Matt 25:37–39, 44): "Lord, when was it that we saw you?" The implication is obvious: had they known it was Jesus in need, they would have been on their best behavior. They never knew it. No one recognized the Lord in "the least of these." The "consummate integrity" (*teleios*) demanded of Jesus's disciples is precisely such uncalculating mercy, without expectation of reward (5:43–48).[14] The goats bumble into eternal punishment; the sheep, into eternal life (25:46). Matthew projects no Technicolor slides of either hell or heaven. His stress lies on hordes of bewildered livestock.

Gathering Threads

With shifting accents Matt 13:24–30, 36–43, 18:23–35, and 25:31–46 develop common themes that intersect with concerns expressed by the other evangelists.

1. *Divine judgment is just that: justice rendered by God, not by humanity.* Not every decision can be delayed until the final reckoning; mortals are responsible for maintaining discipline here and now (Matt 18:15–18). Nevertheless,

---

14. Midrash on Ps 118:19 (243b §17): "In the future world man will be asked, 'What was your occupation?' If he replies, 'I fed the hungry,' then they reply, 'This is the gate of the Lord. He who feeds the hungry, let him enter.' So with giving drink to the thirsty, clothing the naked, with those who look after orphans, and with those, generally, who do deeds of lovingkindness. All these are gates of the Lord, and those who do such deeds shall enter within them" (Claude G. Montefiore and H. Loewe, eds. and trans., *A Rabbinic Anthology* [New York: Schocken, 1974], 433).

all mortal judgments are contingent, derivative of the authority of "my Father in heaven" (18:19) and verified by the Christ who stands among "two or three gathered in [his] name" (18:20). "Judge not, that you be not judged" (7:1 RSV), is no prescription for paralysis. It is a warning that our judgments are judged by God's righteous standard (18:32–33), a reminder that the sins we count against others may pale in magnitude beside our own, when viewed with an unbiased eye (7:2–5; Luke 6:37–42). Other Gospels recall that Jesus himself expressed reluctance to judge others (Luke 12:14; John 12:47). Persistently in John, Jesus's judgments do not derive from his own authority; they are valid only because they accord with "the will of him who sent me" (5:30–38; 8:12–30; 12:44–50).

2. *Divine judgment proceeds from divine grace.* In all of these parables, God's mercy is either expressed or clearly implied *before* a conviction, *as* its basis. Good seed is first sown in a field belonging to the Son of Man (Matt 13:24, 37–38). Before being forced to pay compensatory damages, a loveless servant tramples the king's forgiveness of his own staggering debt (18:27). Benevolent service to those in need, demonstrated by Jesus himself throughout this Gospel (8:1–9:34; 14:13–26; 15:21–39), is the criterion by which both sheep and goats are judged (25:35–36, 42–43). The structure of Jesus's great discourses in Matthew bears the same characteristic: all open with declarations of God's beatitude upon the impoverished (5:1–12), Israel's lost sheep (10:5–14), great crowds on whom word of the kingdom is sown (13:1–3), and humble children (18:1–4). Even the last discourse, Jesus's extended meditation on Jerusalem's judgment (24:1–25:46), is prefaced by a mother hen's lament for her wayward brood (23:37–39). Condemnation in Matthew is never the heavenly Father's first act; in every case reproach is aroused by human refusal of divine grace: "Blessed is anyone who takes no offense at me" (11:6; cf. 11:20–24). Judgment's location within grace is captured in Matthew's unique description of Jesus's yoke as gentle and easily borne (11:29–30). Other Gospels get at this issue in different ways. In every episode of Mark 2:1–3:6, an act of grace—forgiveness of sins (2:5), consorting with sinners (v. 15), eating while others fast (v. 18), plucking grain on the Sabbath (v. 23), healing a man's withered hand on the Sabbath (3:1–3, 5)—elicits religious antagonism, which Jesus refutes (2:6–10, 16–17, 19–22, 25–28; 3:4). Cradling the infant Jesus in his arms, Simeon praises God for the salvation he has lived to see (Luke 2:28–32), then warns Mary that her child is destined for the fall and rise of many in Israel—"and a sword shall pierce your own soul too" (vv. 34–35). So also John: "And this is the judgment, that the light has come into the world, and people loved darkness rather than light because their deeds were evil" (3:19; 11:9–10; 12:45–46).

3. A corollary follows: *in Matthew neither grace nor judgment is an inert abstraction; both are dynamic actions among parties in relationship.* Wheat and tares are known by the agents, noble or diabolical, who sow them (13:24, 25, 37–39). The unforgiving slave's deportment is outrageous, because he himself was released from so much (18:27–30, 32–33). Final judgment is based on how we treat Jesus, unrecognized in our needy siblings (25:40, 45). Justice, reward, and punishment are not cold calculations punched out of a mechanical world. Although Matthew offers abundant moral direction, its primary question is not "What should I do?" but "To whom am I accountable?" (cf. Mark 8:34–9:1; 10:42–45; Luke 10:25–42; John 8:31–47).[15]

4. *The context in which responsibility is taken is the community of Christ's disciples.* Matthew's Jesus focuses his teaching on conduct becoming his followers. Accordingly, the parables we have examined are conspicuously intramural in their references to "the slaves of the householder" (13:27), "fellow slaves ... who reported to their lord" (18:31), and "members of my family" (25:40). The particulars of God's conviction of those outside the church are none of our business; certainly we are not deputized as the Almighty's agents in these affairs. Within the church we infants (11:25) have enough problems of our own, grappling with the mystery of sin among ourselves (13:26–27; 18:28–30) and our blindness to Jesus (25:37–39, 44). Matthew is guarded about the disciples' capacity to exercise proper discipleship (13:28b–30)—an excellent reason for locating final judgment exclusively in the Lord's jurisdiction (13:30b, 40–42a; 18:23–25, 32–34; 25:31–33), with solemn assurances that the scales of justice will finally be balanced (13:42b–43; 18:34–35; 25:45–46). Mark's view of the disciples is even more jaundiced (6:52; 8:17). "Whoever serves me must follow me, and where I am, there will my servant be also" (John 12:26a). "So you also, when you have done all that you were ordered to do, say, 'We are worthless slaves; we have done only what we ought to have done!'" (Luke 17:10).

5. *The Gospels depict a fearful symmetry of beatific reward and horrible punishment.* Compared with the Dead Sea Scrolls and other specimens of Jewish apocalypticism, Matthew does not trowel thick layers of heavenly delights or hellish torments. Mention of both, however, does land as a punch in the gut (13:42–43; 18:34–35; 25:46; cf. 5:25–30; 10:28–33; 18:7–10). Like Jesus himself (4:1–11), disciples are tempted by diabolical forces with a stubborn vitality (5:37; 6:13b; 12:33–37). Unlike Jesus, his followers are wicked yet capable of good (7:11), "little ones [whose] angels continually see the face of my Father in heaven" (18:10).

---

15. See Leander E. Keck's discussion, "Rethinking 'New Testament Ethics,'" *JBL* 115 (1996): 3–16.

Wheat and tares grow within the church (cf. Luke 22:3, 31–32; John 6:70; 13:2); whether Matthew believes both bloom in a single heart is less certain: some injunctions suggest the disciple's power to choose to bear good fruit (7:17–18) or watch with a sound eye (5:22–23) or enslave oneself to God, not wealth (5:24). What no disciple can afford is cocksureness: mistaking God's mercy for patronage (20:1–16) or trading on Jesus's good name without integrity (7:21–23). So, too, Luke: an unbridgeable gulf prevents the once poor Lazarus, now nestled in Abraham's bosom, from relieving the once rich man's flaming agony in Hades (16:19–31). "Whoever believes in the Son has eternal life; whoever disobeys the Son will not see life, but must endure God's wrath" (John 3:36).[16]

6. *All of Matthew's vignettes share another quality: surprise.* In a moral universe reliable consequences follow from entering a gate either narrow or wide (7:13–14). Still, all does not unfold in ways disciples can predict. Evil erupts where only goodness was expected; now is not the time, nor are we the ones, to sort things out (13:27–30). The magnificently forgiven turns ruthless on a dime; daybreak plummets into midnight (18:23–25). We know the Son of Man will return, just as he has promised (16:27; 24:36–44). When he does, we may be sure that we shall never recognize our Lord or know what we were doing for or to him (25:31–46). Luke's parable of the prodigals—an incredibly merciful father of two wayward sons—heaps surprises on its listeners until their hearts explode (15:11–32). Mark ends at 16:8 with the biggest surprise of all.

Torturous Questions

When reading the Gospels do we assume that their audiences always shared the evangelists' beliefs or, rather, that they needed help to see and hear? Though perhaps wishful thinking on my part, I have long believed that Matthew's parables exemplify Flannery O'Connor's working principle:

---

16. Logically, C. F. D. Moule was correct: "If God has willed the dire consequences that ensue on sin, it does not necessarily follow that he has willed them retributively, punitively. It may be that he has willed them as the only way of doing justice to the freedom and responsibility of the human personality, as he has created it" ("Punishment and Retribution: An Attempt to Delimit Their Scope in New Testament Thought," in Moule, *Essays in New Testament Interpretation* [Cambridge: Cambridge University Press, 1982], 235–49; quotation, 237). Exegetically, it is difficult for me to visit passages like Matt 18:34–35 and 25:41–46a and believe that Moule's view accurately conveys the Evangelist's own. David J. Neville's "Toward a Teleology of Peace: Contesting Matthew's Violent Eschatology," *JSNT* 30.2 (2007): 131–61, offers a properly gritty account.

> I use the grotesque the way I do because people are deaf and dumb and need help to see and hear. . . . When you can assume that your audience holds the same beliefs you do, you can relax a little and use more normal ways of talking to it; when you have to assume that it does not, then you have to make your vision apparent by shock—to the hard of hearing you shout, and for the almost blind you draw large and startling figures.[17]

If not the Evangelist's intent, whose intricacy is beyond recovery, his grotesqueries create that effect. If first- or twenty-first-century Christians need reminding of "the yawning abyss of quality in the difference between God and man"[18] then a sovereign's hacking of a craven steward (Luke 19:11–27) or his torture of a heartless slave (Matt 18:23–35) is one way of doing the job. None of the evangelists uses this technique to stimulate despair:[19] otherwise, their reassurance that God can save those incapable of saving themselves makes no sense (Matt 19:26; Mark 10:27; Luke 18:26–27). But Matthew seems especially concerned that the church feel the touch of God's left hand (25:41): "So my heavenly Father will also do to every one of you, if you do not forgive your brother or sister from your heart" (18:35). Had his listeners not been partially deaf, would Matthew have jogged their responsibilities to the needy, not once, but four times (25:35–39, 42–44)?

As far back as Genesis' primeval history, ascribing human traits to God has been a jig danced on a minefield. Responsible historians read Matthew in the light of Jewish apocalypticism in fairness to the world of that Gospel's composition; responsible theologians interpret his images with respect to changed religious sensibilities. Inchoate principles of selection bedevil our policy. If we convince ourselves that the Gospels' visualizations of a God of frightening judgment must be discarded because they are outmoded, ridiculous, and dangerous anthropomorphisms, on what basis can we retain the Gospels' pictures of a God of startling mercy: anthropomorphisms no less antiquated, over-the-top, and scandalous? If we discard the grotesque, the glorious will have to go with it, unless we verbalize, then validate, the tacit and

---

17. Flannery O'Connor, *Mystery and Manners: Occasional Prose*, ed. Sally and Robert Fitzgerald (New York: Farrar, Straus & Giroux, 1961), 33–34.

18. Søren Kierkegaard, *The Journals of Søren Kierkegaard*, November 20, 1847, trans. Alexander Dru (London: Oxford University Press, 1938), 222.

19. Because such freaks are used to *differentiate* God from humanity, none of these parables should be warped into justifications for human activity. The obvious may be necessary to state in an era blotted by "extraordinary rendition," a.k.a. torture, sanctioned by self-proclaimed "God-fearing souls." See chapter 22.

untenable notion that Scripture reveals to us only the God that underwrites our prejudices. "God is love" (1 John 4:16b), but it is a love "hard as death" (Song 8:6) with an inbuilt passion for justice enraged by human wickedness (Rom 1:18–2:1).[20] Both testaments are unflinching in this comprehensive view. Picking only those cherries to our taste is as theologically spurious as it is exegetically dishonest: it puts us in the delusional position of judging the Judge, while esteeming ourselves sophisticated, free, and righteous. Thus we flirt with pastoral malpractice: no-fault sermons, robed in quack therapy, which refuse calling to account Christians who "have offended against [God's] holy laws, [who] have left undone those things which we ought to have done, and . . . have done those things which we ought not to have done."[21] Every generation a new herd of rough beasts slouches toward Bethlehem to be born; a truthful preacher owes the congregation periodic reports on their progress. If that lies beyond our capacity, at least let us cultivate a godly fear. If Jesus needed such to be heard (Heb 5:7 RSV), why, in the days of our flesh, shouldn't we?

Even so, more must be said. If adamant declaration of a just God's judgment were all we needed to hear, then the prophets (Isa 28:1–29; Amos 5:14–25; Mic 6:6–8) or John the Baptist (Matt 3:7–12; Luke 3:7–18) would have sufficed. A crucified and vindicated Messiah is intrinsic to that mandate: true north, to which the Gospels' moral compass points. If Jesus is God with us (Matt 1:23), if this Son of Man befriends sinners (11:19) and came to sacrifice his life to ransom theirs (20:28), if tortured Emmanuel died crying the lament of God's abandonment (27:26–50), if this Christ was raised to newness of life with cosmic authority, promising adherence to us until the age's end (28:5–7, 16–20)—if all this is true, if the Judge has been judged in our place,[22] then Matthew has superimposed reconciliation's tonic chord on sin's minor key. Parabolic penalty is not erased—but the tortured yet triumphant Son of God continues to accompany all weeping evildoers hurled into the fiery furnace (13:41–42), every tormented debtor (18:34), both sheep and goats, gathered or scattered (25:46; 26:31–32). None of the evangelists connects all these dots as tightly as we might wish; all of them, however, present Jesus in ways that

---

20. Following Luther, Emil Brunner: "[God's] wrath is simply the result of the infinitely serious love of God" (*The Christian Doctrine of God* [Philadelphia: Westminster, 1950], 170). On God's anger, see Miroslav Volf, *Exclusion and Embrace: A Theological Exploration of Identity, Otherness, and Reconciliation* (Nashville: Abingdon, 1996), 295–301.

21. *The Book of Common Prayer According to the Use of The Episcopal Church* (New York: Church Publishing, 2007), 41–42.

22. Karl Barth, *The Doctrine of Reconciliation: Church Dogmatics* 4.1, trans. Geoffrey W. Bromiley (Edinburgh: T&T Clark, 1956), 211–83.

make sense of the connections made by other NT witnesses (Rom 5:6–21; Eph 2:1–10; Col 2:9–15; 1 Pet 2:21–25). The theological correlate: God is not *either* the heavenly Father *or* the rigorous Judge *or* the sympathetic Sufferer. God is *all* of these and more, without separation or confusion.

So it seems to me. My fellow slaves may be vexed by this argument. In that event reapers with sharper scythes must sort things out. Divine justice is unfathomable. Finally I am sure only that a pure flame will reveal what I have done, that my tested occupation will smell more of the soup kitchen than of printer's ink, and that, whatever the final outcome, God's judgment shall land as—

—a surprise.

CHAPTER 10

Pauline Perspectives on Death in Romans 5–8

> I am ready to meet my maker, but whether my maker is prepared for the great ordeal of meeting me is another matter.
>
> —Sir Winston Churchill

IT HAS BEEN SAID THAT there is no such thing as "the New Testament doctrine of death."[1] This chapter's proposal is that neither is there such thing as "the Pauline doctrine of death." On the contrary, I suggest that Paul was the inheritor of numerous perspectives on death bequeathed to him by the variegated culture in which he lived, and the tensions detectable in his own outlook on the subject are commensurate with those in his milieu. My procedure in testing this proposition will be, first, to scout the terrain of Paul's Jewish and Hellenic *Umwelt*, to identify some conceptual landmarks; second, to explore a portion of the apostle's own literary landscape from these points of reference. Owing to limitations of space, only a fraction of Paul's output may be subjected to scrutiny: Romans 5–8.[2] Although attention will be concentrated on these four chapters, occasional side glances will be cast when necessary upon other

---

1. Leander E. Keck, "New Testament Views of Death," in *Perspectives on Death*, ed. Liston O. Mills (Nashville: Abingdon, 1969), 33. While Keck's article is superb, its title is somewhat misleading: as much, if not more, attention is devoted to life after death as to death itself.

2. The decision to admit only these chapters as the principal field of investigation is not arbitrary. Of the ninety-five occurrences of *thanatos* (death) and its cognate forms in the undisputed Pauline letters, forty-nine, or 52 percent, appear in Romans. Of that number all but seven of the occurrences are in chaps. 5–8 (1:32; 14:7, 8 [3x], 9, 15). The present essay, however, is not a rigorous word study. It is, rather, an organized collection of observations on the concepts of death in Romans 5–8, gravitating toward those verses containing *thanatos* and its cognates. James Barr's caveats regarding the confusion of "word" and "concept" in examinations of biblical theology remain well worth heeding (*The Semantics of Biblical Language* [Oxford: Oxford University Press, 1961], 206–62).

passages elsewhere in that letter and in the undisputed Pauline epistles.[3] Our study will conclude with a synthesis of results, accompanied by a few critical questions of the outcome and some observations on the significance of Paul's perspectives on death for contemporary theological reflection.

SOME JEWISH AND GRECO-ROMAN VIEWS OF DEATH

The titles of this section and its subdivisions are not intended to suggest rigid distinctions between Semitic and Greek perspectives on the subject. Among others, W. D. Davies and Martin Hengel have convincingly demonstrated that, at least as early as the fourth century BCE, these cultural spheres blended with each other.[4] However, it is fair to say that certain views may be identified as *predominantly* Jewish or Greek, and that these may be distinguished for the sake of convenience in the cursory examination that follows.

Death in Semitic Thought.[5] As expected of documents spanning many centuries, the OT preserves a number of different views on death. Broadly considered, death is understood in at least three different ways: *biologically*, as life's cessation (Gen 35:18; Ps 90:3; Job 34:14-15); *mythologically*, as a demonic agent or power (Isa 25:6-8; Job 18:13); and *metaphorically*, as the loss of that

---

3. These I take to be 1 Thessalonians, Galatians, 1 and 2 Corinthians, Romans, Philippians, and Philemon. Within the Deutero-Pauline corpus, representatives of the pertinent word group appear only in Colossians (1:22 [*thanatos*]; 2:20, 3:3 [*apothnēskō*, "die"]), 1 Timothy (5:6 [*thnēskō*, "be dead"], 6:16 [*athanasia*, "immortality"]), and 2 Timothy (1:10 [*thanatos*]; 2:11 [*synapothnēskō*, "die with"]).

4. Davies, *Paul and Rabbinic Judaism: Some Rabbinic Elements in Pauline Theology*, 4th ed. (Philadelphia: Fortress, 1980); Hengel, *Judaism and Hellenism: Studies in Their Encounter in Palestine during the Early Hellenistic Period*, 2 vols., trans. John Bowden (Philadelphia: Fortress, 1974); Robert A. Kraft, "The Multiform Jewish Heritage of Early Christianity," in *Christianity, Judaism and Other Greco-Roman Cults: Studies for Morton Smith at Sixty*, Part 3: *Judaism before 70*, ed. Jacob Neusner, SJLA 12 (Leiden: Brill, 1975), 174-99. More recently, see Anders Klostergaard Petersen, "Paul the Jew Was Also Paul the Hellenist," in *Paul the Jew: Rereading the Apostle as a Figure of Second Temple Judaism*, ed. Gabriele Boccaccini and Carlos A. Segovia (Minneapolis: Augsburg Fortress, 2016), 273-99.

5. Gerhard von Rad, *Old Testament Theology*, vol. 1, trans. D. M. G. Stalker (New York and Evanston: Harper & Row, 1962), esp. 383-418, offers an excellent secondary treatment of the OT perspectives. Surveying the OT but moving beyond it into later Jewish and early Christian literature are Lloyd R. Bailey Sr., *Biblical Perspectives on Death*, OBT (Philadelphia: Fortress, 1979), and George W. E. Nickelsburg Jr., *Resurrection, Immortality, and Eternal Life in Intertestamental Judaism*, HTS 26 (Cambridge: Harvard University Press, 1972). To the work of von Rad and Bailey I am especially indebted in the survey that follows.

rich existence intended by the LORD for his creatures (Deut 30:15, 19; Ps 13:3-4; Ezek 37:3-12). The ancient Israelites did not view death as an absurd, inimical intruder; it was accepted as a constituent of an orderly, supervised creation (1 Kgs 19:4; 2 Kgs 2:3; Job 1:21). Mortality appears to have been relativized and the fear of death tempered by Israel's communal rather than individualistic consciousness (Gen 48:21; Deut 31:2-3), its appreciation of other values besides life (Prov 10:7; Isa 56:3-5; cf. Sir 44:1-2, 12-13), and its historically grounded confidence in God (Ps 90:12-14). Nevertheless, even in the OT there are intimations of the idea that death is an intrusion into the Creator's design (Isa 25:8), that without sin (manifested in the hubris of *'adam*, "humankind") there would have been no death (Gen 2-3). As is well known, the notion of resurrection from the dead, and the reversal of mortality which that implies, makes its first, flickering appearances in Isaiah (26:19) and Daniel (12:2-3).

This adumbrated shift in the valuation of death is plainer in the intertestamental literature. For example, the connection between sin and death is strengthened: death is not humanity's normal lot but the result of violating God's rule (Wis 1:13; 2:23-24; 1 En. 5.9; 4 Ezra 7:62-131). A particular interest becomes manifest in depicting death as a curse, ascribed to the transgression of Adam or Eve or both (Sir 25:24; 2 En. 30.17; Apoc. Mos. 14; 2 Bar. 54.15; 2 Esd 3:7; cf. Josephus, *A.J.* 1.49, 51; Philo, *Vit. Mos.* 2.147); however, it is significant that hereditary *sin* is never clearly attributed to the primordial duo.[6] Nor is there complete relief from individual responsibility and guilt for the commission of sins that lead to death (4 Ezra 7:116-19; 2 Bar. 48; 54; Apoc. Mos. 30; 40; Apoc. Abr. 23; 1 En. 84.4-6). The fear of death becomes explicit: "But . . . we grow up with the power of thought and are tortured by it; we are doomed to die and we know it" (2 Esd. 7:[64]; cf. T. Abr. 14 [recension B]). Yet the literature of this period is no more univocal in its estimation of mortality than is the OT. Death, therefore, can be considered more neutrally as a paying of one's account with God (Sir 1:13; 11:21-28), by which only the wicked need feel threatened (Wis 2:1-10, 21-22; 3:10a; 4:20), or as a positive occasion for faithful witness (2 Macc 6:23-28), hope (2 Macc 7:10-11, 23) and even a blessed release from suffering (Wis 3:4-5; 4:7-14; T. Abr. 14).

With its heavily realized eschatology, the Qumran community appears to have been little concerned with biological death. Yet one finds reference to

---

6. Cf. Apoc. Mos. 32: "All sin has come through me [i.e., Eve] into creation." However, as Joseph A. Fitzmyer points out, this statement asserts only that Eve was the first sinner, not that her sin has since been inherited by humanity (*Pauline Theology: A Brief Sketch* [Englewood Cliffs, NJ: Prentice-Hall, 1967], 55). Here and elsewhere in this chapter, translations are my own unless otherwise indicated.

death in the scrolls in senses mythological (1QS 3:17-22; 1QH 6:29-34) and metaphorical (1QH 11:3, 10-13). A similar balance between universal determinism and individual responsibility with respect to sin and death is also achieved in the QL (1QH 15:18-29).[7]

Since Paul antedates the tannaitic literature, that evidence must be handled with circumspection. Still, it is worth noting that the rabbis exhibit a similar variety of perspectives on death. The prevalent view seems to have been that death is a part of the natural order; however, it is suggested that good deeds prolong a person's life (b. Šabb. 55a-b). The idea continued to be propounded that the sin of Adam and Eve entailed the death of their posterity (Gen. Rab. 16.6); indeed, without sin there is no death (b. Šabb. 55a-b). Yet it is well known that the rabbis attributed atoning significance to the death of a martyr or repentant person (Sif. Deut. 333; m. Yoma 8:8). Death settles an account with God (b. Šabb. 151b).[8]

My compass is brief, and more may not be said. However, it should be evident that in no historical stage or community of ancient Judaism was there a single, uniform definition of death or attitude toward it.[9] Against such a varied constellation of beliefs one begins to understand Romans 5-8.

Death in Ancient Greek and Hellenistic Thought.[10] A comparable variety of views on death is evident among the Greeks. One of the earliest, attested during the period extending from ca. 1000 to 300 BCE, is that, inasmuch as life is the supreme good (*Theog.* 758) and death is the termination of that life, death is something horrible (*Od.* 2.487-88; *Rhet.* 2.23 [citing Sappho]). And so, no one wishes to die (*Alc.* 669; *Iph. Aul.* 1252-53; cf. *Crat.* 403b). Mitigat-

---

7. For further discussion of the perceptions of death and afterlife at Qumran, see particularly Nickelsburg, *Resurrection*, 144-66. Note also Walter Grundmann, "The Teacher of Righteousness at Qumran and the Question of Justification by Faith in the Theology of the Apostle Paul," *Paul and Qumran: Studies in New Testament Exegesis*, ed. Jerome Murphy-O'Connor (Chicago: Priory, 1968), 85-114.

8. E. P. Sanders observes that the logic behind atoning death is an extension of the view that sufferings atone (*Paul and Palestinian Judaism: A Comparison of Patterns of Religion* [Philadelphia: Fortress, 1977], 157-82, esp. 172-74). See also George Foot Moore, *Judaism in the First Centuries of the Christian Era* (New York: Schocken Books, 1971), 1:474-78.

9. One-sided generalizations should therefore be avoided: "Thus death is only intelligible to [the Hebrew mind] in the light of the wickedness and sinfulness of humanity" (D. T. Holden, *Death Shall Have No Dominion* [St. Louis: Bethany, 1971], 107). Such a statement not only outruns the evidence but obscures more than it clarifies.

10. Two extensive probes of the subject, to which I am indebted in what follows, are Franz Cumont, *After Life in Roman Paganism* (New Haven: Yale University Press, 1923), and Rudolf Bultmann, "θάνατος," *TDNT* 3:7-25. On the social setting of death in imperial Rome, consult Donald G. Kyle, *Spectacles of Death in Ancient Rome* (London: Routledge, 2000).

ing positions also occur: death, at least, brings rest or release from suffering (*Tro.* 606–7; 634); at best, it evokes glory or confers heroism (*Il.* 18.115–17; 19.420–21).[11] A far more positive evaluation was ventured by Plato, for whom a just life can find its fulfillment in death (*Phaed.* 64a; 67e; 80e). Adopting the old Orphic and Pythagorean terminology of *sōma* (body) and *psychē* (soul), Plato also posited the conception of death as a friend: death releases the preexistent, eternal soul from the circuit of birth, death, and rebirth into an alien, temporal, and mortal body (cf. *Phaed.* 114–15). Death, for Plato, was not so much the enemy as was this cycle of life.[12]

Other Greek philosophical traditions responded differently. In both Stoicism and Epicureanism death was conceived as a natural phenomenon. In neither school is death to be feared, although for quite different reasons. For Epicurus, death is nothing to the human self, because at its occurrence that self is annihilated (*Men.* 19–30). For the Stoic Marcus Aurelius Antoninus, the movement toward one's demise entails ethical consequences, such that death incites one to fearless dignity and a positive purposefulness in life (*Medit.* 2.5, 11; 5.29; 7.56). A Neoplatonist such as Plotinus could suggest that physical death is an *agathon* (good) in that its object is the release of the *psychē* for its true life apart from *sōma* (*Enn.* 1.6.6; 1.7.3; 4.8.3). In Philo, the Stoic and Neoplatonic streams of thought intersect: from an ethical standpoint, death is the result of *hēdonē*, "pleasure" (*Agric.* 98), such that the unrighteous are "the dead who are yet alive" (*Som.* 2.66; cf. *Conf. ling.* 36–37; *Fug.* 59); yet physical death is also the separation of the soul from the body (*Leg. all.* 1.105) and is, therefore, an *agathon*.[13]

Finally, despite the slipperiness of the source materials in documenting one's observations, a word must be said about the Gnostic perspectives on

---

11. The notion of a "good" death is evident in both Greek and Semitic thought. More interesting, however, is the difference between them in what this idea connotes. Whereas ancient Israelites understood a "good" death as the capstone of a long life (Gen 15:15; 25:8; 46:30; Job 5:26; cf. the "bad" death implicit in 2 Sam 18:32–33; Isa 38:1–3, 10–12; Job 36:13–14), "to die well" (*kalōs apothnēskein*) in classical Greek thought was so to die that one's fame redounded to his or her city (Sophocles, *Ai. Lok.* 473; Euripides, *Iph. Taur.* 321–22).

12. For further discussion, see Francis Ryan Montgomery Hitchcock, "St. Paul's Views of the Body and Death Contrasted with Plato's," *Churchman* 30 (1916): 558–65.

13. A perceptive comparison of "Philo of Alexandria and Romans 5:12–21: Adam, Death, and Grace" is executed by Jonathan Worthington in *Reading Romans in Context: Paul and Second Temple Judaism*, ed. Ben C. Blackwell, John K. Goodrich, and Jason Matson (Grand Rapids: Zondervan, 2015), 80–86.

death.¹⁴ Fundamentally based upon an Orphic view of humankind,¹⁵ Gnosticism presupposes a divine spark, or seed, buried within human beings and tyrannized by the material body (*Ap. John* 2.31.4-23; *Paraph. Shem* 7.7.18-31; *Ep. Pet. Phil.* 8.137.5-10; cf. *Tri. Trac.* 1.106.15-26; *Haer.* 1.14.1). Thus, for the one who has received the revelatory *gnōsis* of salvation as escape from the material world, metaphorical understandings of life and death stand their biological counterparts on their head: physical life is actually death, and physical death is the release of that divine essence which is truly life (*C.H.* 1.28; *Thoms. Cont.* 2.143.11-27; *Hyp. Arch.* 2.96.20-97.10; cf. *Treat. Res.* 1.48.14-34). A radical shift occurs as well with the gnostic relationship of sin and death: unlike the understanding evident in Jewish intertestamental literature, sin and mortality are derived not from the event of human disobedience to the divine will but from a flaw in created existence itself, perpetrated by this world's creator (*Gos. Phil.* 2.75.2-15; cf. *Ep. Pet. Phil.* 8.135.10-136.16; *Ap. John* 2.20.29-21.14; *C.H.* 1.15). Escape from this ontic tragedy is anticipated through the gaining of esoteric knowledge and is consummated, for the gnostic, at death: only then may one's genuine self return home to the divinity whence it originated (*Acts*

---

14. At least two problems arise at this point. First, as with the rabbinic literature, our extant gnostic documents do not date from pre-Christian times; hence we can only infer possible gnostic influences in the NT. Second, the debate remains unresolved about whether the Hermetic literature is properly to be categorized as "gnostic." C. H. Dodd, for example, distinguished Hermetism and Gnosticism in his reconstruction of the background of the Gospel of John (*The Interpretation of the Fourth Gospel* [Cambridge: Cambridge University Press, 1953], esp. 10-53, 97-114). This distinction may no longer hold, in light of the discovery of tractates within the Nag Hammadi corpus that manifest similarities in both form and content to the Hermetic material (*The Discourse on the Eighth and Ninth, The Prayer of Thanksgiving, Asclepius* 21-29). Without suggesting a premature resolution of this problem, in the following discussion I shall nevertheless regard the *Corpus Hermeticum* as reflective of a type of gnosis. Even if one were finally to decide against such an identification, I doubt that it would materially affect my suggestions here concerning Gnosticism or its possible import for the exegesis of Romans 5-8.

15. Since the focus of this essay is Pauline and antecedent perspectives on death, I shall not tarry over the mystery cults. Their concern, as I understand it, was not so much to interpret physical death as to furnish, through ritual, an avenue of escape for the eternal soul imprisoned in a mortal body. Yet there seems to be some kinship between Gnosticism and the mysteries. Bultmann, for instance, perceives in the former the philosophical explication of rites celebrated in the latter (*Primitive Christianity in Its Contemporary Setting* [New York: World, 1956], 162-71). It should also be noted that, as in the mystery cults, *athanasia* could also be secured for the gnostic through the sacraments (see *C.H.* 1.15; *Tri. Trac.* 1.129.7-15; *Gos. Eg.* 3.66.1-9).

Thom. 9.108–13; cf. *Gos. Truth* 1.22.2–16). For this reason, in much gnostic speculation death is not the feared enemy. For the one with knowledge, it is the welcomed liberator (*Ascl.* 6.76.7–20; *Ap. John* 2.27.5–12; but cf. Apoc. Adam 5.76.9–28).

Summary. The preceding consideration of death in Greek and Semitic thought is no derailment from our intention to examine Paul's perspective; rather, it lays a straight track toward our ultimate destination. For conceptual clarity the varied interpretations educed from the Pauline milieu may be summarized like this:

I. Death as Completion
   A. A part of the natural order
   B. Payment of an account owed to God, or payment made through atoning sacrifice (principally Semitic)
   C. Release from suffering
   D. An occasion for hope or witness (Semitic) or heroism and glory (Hellenic)
   E. An incentive for ethical behavior and the fulfillment of a righteous life

II. Death as Depletion
   A. A terror to be feared
   B. The loss of life's richness
   C. An intrusion into the Creator's design (Semitic) or an ontic flaw in creation (Hellenistic)
   D. A tyrannous, cosmological power
   E. Something associated with sin: either derived from or punishing transgression

As we have witnessed, the substance of most of these interpretations can be formally expressed in one or more of three senses: the biological or physical, the mythological, or the metaphorical. Obviously, some of the nuances lend themselves more naturally to one form of expression: hence, I. A., biological; II. D., mythological; II. B., metaphorical.

The references to death in Romans 5–8 become far more intelligible, with respect both to the apostle's own theology and to its antecedents, when viewed through the conceptual lens such an outline provides.[16] One burden of the ensuing investigation is to test this suggestion.

---

16. This procedure seems more logical, as well as more respectful of historical devel-

Pauline Perspectives on Death in Romans 5–8

In this section we shall proceed by dividing these four chapters of Romans into eight thematic units and noting the nuance(s) of Paul's language about death in each, with an eye in particular to the Semitic and Greco-Roman perspectives that have been elicited. The eight units to be probed are Romans 5:1–11, 5:12–21, 6:1–14, 6:15–7:6, 7:7–25, 8:1–11, 8:12–30, and 8:31–39.[17] Insufficient space precludes detailed exegesis of any of these segments. That which follows makes no claim to be a thorough exploration of the text. This is only a reconnaissance maneuver, upon which a more detailed analysis might later be extrapolated.

Romans 5:1–11. The overriding theme of this passage is the believer's salvation and the peace with God that is the result of justification (i.e., reconciliation; see 5:1–5, 11). The principal subject of death in this passage is Christ, the Son of God, and the primary nuance of death is that of sacrificial atonement for sin: "But God demonstrates his own love for us in that while we were yet sinners Christ died for our sake" (5:8). For Paul it is this death that effects reconciliation between God and humanity, making possible the salvation of humankind. Here we witness the principally Semitic conception of death as a payment owed to God for sin, given a decisively christological reinterpretation.[18] Yet another nuance of death is evident in this passage, which is juxtaposed with the motif of Christ's atoning death: the hypothetical sacrifice of oneself on behalf of a righteous or good person, a sacrifice whose accomplishment is, for Paul, highly unlikely given the human instinct for self-preservation (5:7). Here we may detect the classical Greek motif of the heroic death, so familiar in the Homeric literature. Notice that Paul is able to establish

---

opment, than that employed by Thomas Barrosse, "Death and Sin in Saint Paul's Epistle to the Romans," *CBQ* 15 (1953): 438–59. Barrosse's method seems inappropriate in at least two respects. First, it assumes at the outset, on the basis of inference from the Pauline literature, the senses in which the apostle utilizes the language of death and then goes hunting for (and, to no one's surprise, discovers) their exemplification in Romans. Second, it identifies those senses in anachronistic terms (i.e., "eternal" death and the putatively Thomistic categories of "physical" and "spiritual" death). By deriving my conceptual framework from the literature of Paul's *Umwelt*, antecedent to and contemporaneous with his own writings, I hope that the method adopted here sidesteps both of these procedural pitfalls.

17. This chapter division follows that of C. K. Barrett, *A Commentary on the Epistle to the Romans*, HNTC (New York: Harper & Row, 1957), 100–174, with some minor modifications.

18. The same confession, "Christ died for our sins," underlies 1 Cor 15:3, which appears to stem from pre-Pauline tradition (see also 1 Cor 11:24). Hence it is questionable that Paul himself was responsible for this christological definition of atonement. See also A. M. Hunter, *Paul and His Predecessors*, new rev. ed. (Philadelphia: Westminster, 1961), 18, 31–32.

this contrast between human and messianic sacrifice and to highlight the truly magisterial and operative quality of the latter over against the former precisely by playing off one popular conception of death against another.

Romans 5:12–21. This unit develops the well-known contrast between Adam and Christ, adumbrated by Paul in 1 Corinthians 15:21–22. What the apostle does here but did not attempt in the Corinthian letter is to explain the connection of death with Adam as the result of the latter's primal transgression (Rom 5:12). Against this backdrop Paul can bring into focus the corporate and grace-full effects of Christ's obedience for the believer (5:15, 17–19). At this juncture we should simply note several items. (1) Especially when viewed in the context of his discussion of new life in Christ (chapters 6 and 8), Paul's main interest in this section is not the origin of sin but the origin of death.[19] (2) This having been granted, we further recognize that Paul, in accord with one conceptual strain in intertestamental Judaism, does link death with sin: for Paul, death is the result and the accompaniment of sin in the world, even in the period before the giving of the law (5:14). Thus there is a kind of sin-oriented or deathward determinism in Paul (N.B. 5:16b–19), counterbalanced with reference to individual responsibility and guilt in 5:12c ("and thus death spread to all human beings, inasmuch as all sinned"; see also 5:19; 6:12–13).[20] (3) Romans 5:18–19 implies that mortality, properly understood as the consequence of sin, was not part of the Creator's design; it is an intrusion that could be rectified only through Christ's self-sacrifice. In this claim we discern two other Semitic perspectives on death: the motif of sacrificial atonement (continued from 5:1–11) and the image of death as stemming from human disobedience to God's order (i.e., an "ethical rupture" rather than the Hellenistic "ontic flaw"). (4) Yet death for Paul is not just an intrusion; in some sense it is also an intruder, a personal and cosmic power who demonically reigns in this age (5:14, 17; cf. 1 Cor 15:25–26). In this respect it is like sin; indeed, death is the manifestation of sin's reign (5:21). Here we see Paul employing the myth-

---

19. Thus, André Feuillet, "Le règne de la mort et le règne de la vie (*Rom.*, v. 12–21): Quelques observations sur la structure de l'Epître aux Romans," *RB* 77 (1970): 481–521. Recall that intertestamental Judaism likewise ascribed to Adam and Eve hereditary death, not hereditary sin.

20. A. J. M. Wedderburn ("The Theological Structure of Romans v. 12," *NTS* 19 [1973]: 339–54) correctly identifies this tension between apparent determinism and individual responsibility as derived from Jewish apocalyptic thought. More recently, see Joseph Longarino, "Apocalyptic and the Passions: Overcoming a False Dichotomy in Pauline Studies," *NTS* 67 (2021): 582–97.

ological language of apocalypticism to characterize a biological and ethical phenomenon as a cosmological tyrant.

To summarize: in the space of a relatively brief passage, Paul's understanding of death displays the melding of not fewer than four different shades of meaning: death as the consequence and concomitant of sin, as a means of sacrificial atonement, as an intrusion into the order designed by God, and as an intruder that tyrannizes the present age.

Romans 6:1-14. This unit represents perhaps one of the most complex treatments of the relationship between sin and death in the entire Pauline corpus, and—whatever Paul's intention may have been—most scholars would agree that the exegetical task has been rendered even more difficult by the presiding metaphor of baptism.[21] We can but scratch this text's surface in an attempt to discern the differentiae in its construals of death.

Even the most cursory reading of Romans 6:1-14 reveals the prominent interplay between sin and death[22] and, in that respect, builds upon one of the primary motifs we perceived in Romans 5:12-21. Yet in the present passage we may notice a slight shift in the nature of their association: whereas death in the preceding unit was considered both derivative of and the punishment for sin, here the emphasis is upon the believer's death *in relation to* sin, accomplished through baptism (6:2, 10-11; cf. 6:6b).[23] This new subtlety is quite understand-

---

21. Günther Wagner, *Pauline Baptism and the Pagan Mysteries* (Edinburgh and London: Oliver and Boyd, 1967), remains a standard monograph on the subject. Along a different tack, the work of Franz Gerhard Cremer ("Der 'Heilstod' Jesu im paulinischen Verständnis von Taufe und Eucharistie: Eine Zusammenschau von Röm 6,3f und 1 Kor 11,26," *BZ* 14 [1970]: 227-39) may be open to dispute insofar as its description of Paul's "sacramental theology" is far more lucid and theologically explicit than the apostle's own treatment is. More recently, Teresa Kuo-Yu Tsui has emphasized the apocalyptic tenor of Rom 6:3 and Gal 3:27: "'Baptized into His Death' (Rom 6,3) and 'Clothed with Christ' (Gal 3,27): The Soteriological Meaning of Baptism in Light of Pauline Apocalyptic," *ETL* 88 (2012): 395-417. On the twin motifs of "dying and rising" with Christ, Robert C. Tannehill, *Dying and Rising with Christ: A Study in Pauline Theology* (BZNW 32; Berlin: Töpelmann, 1967), and Eduard Schweizer, "Dying and Rising with Christ," *NTS* 14 (1967): 1-14, remain well worth consulting.

22. A thorough exegesis of Rom 6:1-14 undertaken from this standpoint constitutes the bulk of Ivan Thomas Blazen, "Death and Sin According to Romans 6:1-14 and Related Texts: An Exegetical-Theological Study with a Critique of Views" (PhD diss., Princeton Theological Seminary, 1979).

23. Although *apothnēskein tē hamartia* can be construed as a *dativus commodi* or even as a dative of possession, C. F. D. Moule had made a convincing case for its interpretation as a dative of relation (see Rom 7:4, 6; 14:7-8; 2 Cor 5:14b, 15; Gal 2:19; 6:14; 1 Pet 2:24; 4:1). See "Death 'to Sin,' 'to Law,' and 'to the World': A Note on Certain Datives," in *Mélanges*

able, inasmuch as Paul wishes, at 6:1–3, to sharpen the focus upon the moral implications of the Christian life.

Certainly this is not the only nuance of "dying" and "death" displayed in this passage. There is also repeated reference to the death of Christ in 6:3, 5, 9, 10: here the stress appears to lie upon Christ's real biological loss of life, although it is clear that Paul cannot regard that physical death as anything other than part of a larger, eschatological event (6:4, 5, 9, 10). Indeed, it is precisely because it does possess the character of an eschatological occurrence that Paul can assert the believer's own existential death with Christ in baptism, a dying that frees the Christian from death for the future hope of resurrection (6:5, 8; contrast Eph 2:5–6; Col 2:12).[24] With succinct accuracy Robert Tannehill reformulates Paul's thought: "Through dying with Christ the Christian has been released from the old world and has entered the new."[25] Yet Paul is careful to qualify his expression of eschatological hope in Romans 6:5, wherein *symphytoi . . . tō homoiōmati tou thanatou autou* ("united . . . in the likeness of his death") implies a hedge, either against interpreting baptism as a repeated or mystical event (see n. 15) or against misunderstanding believers' resurrection as a present reality.[26]

Still another layer in the meaning of death lies in the ambiguous observation in 6:7: "For the one who has died [*ho apothanōn*] has been acquitted from

---

bibliques en hommage au R. P. Béda Rigaux, ed. Albert Descamps and André de Halleux (Gembloux: Duculot, 1970), 367–75.

24. For more detailed treatments, see André Feuillet, "Mort du Christ et mort du Chrétien d'après les épîtres pauliniennes," *RB* 66 (1959): 481–513; and L. Faskekaš, "Taufe als Tod in Röm. 6,3ff.," *TZ* 22 (1966): 305–18. A problem common to both of these studies is the anachronism implicit in their discussions of "sacrament" in Pauline theology. More plausibly, Walter Diezinger suggests that Romans 6:1–4 betrays possible indebtedness to a familiar type of rabbinic exegesis, applied here to Ps 87:5–6 (LXX) ("Unter Toten freigeworden: Eine Untersuchung zu Röm. iii–viii," *NovT* 5 [1962]: 268–98). On the apocalyptic connotation of *syn-* and *sym-* compounds with reference to Christ in the Pauline letters, see Schweizer, "Dying and Rising with Christ," 1–6. With regard to Holden's comment that "Paul usually thinks of death as a part of the hereafter" (*Death Shall Have No Dominion*, 102), we needn't belabor the obvious: as stated, this appraisal seriously misunderstands Pauline theology.

25. Tannehill, *Dying and Rising with Christ*, 127.

26. See the suggestions of Tannehill, *Dying and Rising with Christ*, 32, and Hans Conzelmann, *An Outline of the Theology of the New Testament* (New York and Evanston: Harper & Row, 1969), 271. Florence A. Morgan draws an exhaustive exegesis of Rom 6:5a to this conclusion: "If we have died to sin as Christ died and remain so, with the result that death to sin has become inherent in us, we shall certainly also rise as Christ rose, with the result that resurrection will also inhere in us" ("Romans 6:5a: United to a Death like Christ's," *ETL* 59 [1983]: 267–302; quotation, 301).

sin." This seemingly innocent statement has been read in a variety of ways: as based upon a rabbinic legal maxim ("Death pays all debts"; see b. Šabb. 151b),[27] as an expression of expiatory theology,[28] and in a martyrological sense.[29] In my view Romans 6:7 is quite comprehensible when taken juridically: having died, the old self has been destroyed (6:6) and thus is acquitted, because the once-deserved guilty verdict cannot now be rendered.[30] Whether or not this interpretation finally be the most persuasive is less important for my present thesis than the very range of interpretations inferable from *ho apothanōn*.

The mythic language of death as a cosmological tyrant, apparent in Romans 5:12–21, returns in 6:9b: death is depicted as a power that was lord over Christ until the latter was raised (see 6:10–11, 15–23). Finally, we witness in this text an interesting twist in the traditional Semitic notion that death can provide an incentive for righteous behavior: underneath the exhortation in 6:12–14 (cf. 6:1–2) is the idea that having died to sin, one is now fully at God's disposal for the doing of righteousness. That is to say, the believer forsakes sin not out of any ulterior motive "to put her house in order" while looking ahead to eventual death but, rather, out of the knowledge that she *has already died* to sin through the action of God in Christ to reconcile the world to himself (cf. 2 Cor 5:19). Therefore, in Romans, death as a motive force for moral conduct is no longer, predominantly, a future event of which we are prudentially mindful. Instead, death is an antecedent, existential experience from which we have been liberated, in order that we might now yield our members as instruments of righteousness (6:13).

Thus far, in the first fourteen verses of Romans 6 we may detect not fewer than seven related though subtly different conceptions of death: as a physiological event, as an associate of sin, as liberation, as a settlement of debt or an atoning sacrifice (according to some exegeses of 6:7), as an occasion for tempered hope, as the impetus for righteous living, and as a tyrannical power. This passage alone would suffice to validate my thesis. The argument can only be strengthened by reading further in Romans.

Romans 6:15–7:6. This unit develops some themes already introduced. First, there's the continued association of death with sin. Sin is one of two

---

27. William Sanday and Arthur C. Headlam, *A Critical and Exegetical Commentary on the Epistle to the Romans*, 5th ed., ICC (Edinburgh: T&T Clark, 1902), 159.

28. Gottlob Schrenk, "δικαιόω, κ.τ.λ.," *TDNT* 2:174–225, esp. 218–19.

29. Robin Scroggs, "Romans vi.7: Ο ΓΑΡ ΑΠΟΘΑΝΩΝ ΔΕΔΙΚΑΙΩΤΑΙ ΑΠΟ ΤΗΣ ΑΜΑΡΤΙΑΣ," *NTS* 10 (1963): 104–8.

30. Thus also John A. Ziesler, *The Meaning of Righteousness in Paul: A Linguistic and Theological Enquiry*, SNTSMS 20 (Cambridge: Cambridge University Press, 1972), 200–201.

masters to whom one may become enslaved, and the result (*eis*, 6:16),[31] fruit (*karpos*, 6:21), end (*telos*, 6:21), or payoff (*opsōnia*, 6:23) of that enslavement is *thanatos*. In short, death as punishment is the natural consequence of sin, even as the only other eschatological possibility, eternal life, is the upshot of slavery to obedience or to righteousness (6:16, 18, 22).[32]

A number of motifs converge in the analogy from marriage in 7:1-6. (1) The similitude itself hypothesizes the case of a woman released from her obligations to her husband by her spouse's *physical* death (7:2-3). (2) This comparison affords Paul the opportunity to speak of the *release* of the Christian from the law by that death, accomplished through participation in the body of Christ (7:1, 4). (3) For Paul such freedom is fundamental, because the law has been commandeered by *sin*: that is to say, by the power of sin the law has become an instrument whereby human beings strive to live to themselves and not to God (cf. 7:5), with the result that the law actually increases the trespass and activates death (see 5:20-21; 1 Cor 15:56; 2 Cor 3:6). (4) Implicitly, therefore, death is also a *power* commensurate with sin, from under whose lordship believers have been transferred to the lordship of Christ (see 7:6). Paradoxically, therefore, death is both the oppressor and the medium by which believers in Christ are released from their oppression. Clearly, Paul's argument at this point significantly differs from later rabbinic conceptions. The latter, as we have observed, can depict death as atonement for transgression, even as does Paul. But the idea of a transference of lordships, culminating in the law's abrogation, is as foreign to rabbinic theology as it is fundamental to Pauline thought.[33]

Romans 7:7-25. This unit's main function is to clarify the relationship between the law and sin, foreshadowed in 5:20 and 7:1-6.[34] In this context it's no surprise

---

31. I cautiously accept *eis thanaton* as part of the original text at 6:16. However, even if this phrase were deleted on text-critical grounds, the present argument would remain supported by the other, undisputed references to death in this pericope.

32. Notice here that, because ethical and eschatological motifs are interwoven, the language employed by Paul is at once juristic (i.e., metaphorical) and cosmological (i.e., mythological).

33. Thus, Sanders (*Paul and Palestinian Judaism*, 547): "The difference is between saying that one dies on account of transgression and that one dies to an enslaving power as a means of gaining liberty."

34. I shall not engage the vexed question of the identity of *egō* (I) in 7:14-25. The alternatives and their supporting arguments have been adequately summarized by C. Leslie Mitton ("Romans—vii. Reconsidered," *ExpTim* 65 [1953/54]: 78-81, 99-103, 132-35) and C. E. B. Cranfield (*A Critical and Exegetical Commentary on the Epistle to the Romans*, ICC [Edinburgh: T&T Clark, 1975], 1:342-47); there is no need to rehearse them here. I am of the opinion that, in so speaking, Paul is referring retrospectively to himself as well as to his

that the principal nuance of death is that of its relation to sin: death is derived from and is the inevitable, punitive consequence of transgression (see 7:9).

In what precise sense does Paul mean that, when once-dormant sin came back to life, he died (*apethanen*, v. 10; N.B. the aorist tense)? To answer this, we must recover the background against which the apostle probably intended his statements to be read. When Paul refers to his once being alive apart from the law, I take this to reflect, not some autobiographical ruminations on his youthful innocence before becoming a bar mitzvah, but rather his identification with *'adam* in Genesis 2:17 (cf. Rom 5:12-21). That old folktale appears chiefly concerned with death as a biological fact, and the point the Yahwist wished to score may have been that mortality is the Creator's intention for human beings.[35] However, this is not the story's only implication, for it appears as well to be an etiology on the enmity that has pervaded creation since that primordial act of disobedience to the Creator: hostility between serpent and woman, woman and child, woman and man, man and nature, and—most fundamentally—humanity and God (Gen 3:14-19). It is this latter exegetical route, I think, that Paul chooses to follow in Romans 7:7-25. The point he wishes to drive home here is similar to that witnessed in 7:5: through sin's deceitful use of the law to arouse human desires for life through legal fulfillment, humanity prior to Christ had become increasingly, unbridgeably estranged from God (7:7-8). The ultimate degree of that alienation between humanity and God is, for Paul, best characterized as death (7:9-11, 13). That Paul is not chiefly concerned here with physiological *thanatos* is suggested, not only by the aforementioned use of the aorist tense in 7:10, but also by the dynamic or progressive character of death: "But it was sin . . . having brought about death in me through the good" (7:13).

This is not to suggest that all other possible nuances of "death" are excluded in this passage. On the contrary, one very plausible interpretation of *tou sōmatos tou thanatou toutou* in 7:24 invokes the image of sin and death as powers that dominate humanity (cf. 6:15-23): that is, "this body which is tyrannized by death."[36] However, in my estimation, the primary sense in which death is to be understood

---

readers (i.e., Christians who "know the law," 7:1). Even if this interpretation were proved untenable, it would not substantially alter my observations in what follows.

35. So Bailey, *Biblical Perspectives on Death*, 38-39. Note also Gerhard von Rad's comment: "One cannot say that man lost a 'germ of immortality' any more than one can say that a material modification occurred in him, as a consequence of which he must now fall prey to death; the narrator already said in ch. 2.7 [sic] that man was created of dust" (*Genesis: A Commentary*, rev. ed., OTL [Philadelphia: Westminster, 1972], 95).

36. Ernst Käsemann, *Commentary on Romans*, trans. Geoffrey W. Bromiley (Grand Rapids: Eerdmans, 1980), 210-11.

in this textual unit is that of existential estrangement from God, which derives from sin.[37] Consequently, death as alienation through sin in 7:7–25 is the antithetical complement to life as reconciliation through Christ in 6:1–7:6.

Romans 8:1–11. In this pericope Paul develops the theme of the Christian's new life in the Spirit, to which reference was made at the conclusion of 6:15–7:6. As one would expect, this passage contains several references to death, all of which function as a counterpoint to the apostle's central argument.

Once more we may move expeditiously by simply highlighting the different connotations the concept bears. (1) Again, death is intimately connected with sin (and law) in 8:2. This is to say that, for Paul, death is largely, if not basically, an *ethical* problem, a matter of setting one's mind on the things of the flesh so as to walk (i.e., "live," *peripatousin*) *kata sarka*, "according to the flesh" (8:4, 6). Romans 8:7 appears to confirm my exegesis of the previous passage: to walk in this deathward way, to set the mind on the flesh, is sin insofar as it is enmity toward God (*echthra eis theon*, 8:7). (2) In 8:2 there is also the recurrence of death as a power, the executor of that domineering sin which has suborned even the God-given law for its nefarious purposes. With the apocalyptic shift of the eons, connoted by the giving of the law of the spirit of life in Christ Jesus, these powers of sin and death have been decisively usurped.[38] (3) With *to sōma nekron* (the body [is] dead) and *ta thnēta sōmata hymōn* (your mortal bodies) at 8:10–11, Paul may have at least partly in mind death as a biological reality, parallel with the very real physical death from which God raised Christ Jesus (v. 11). Consequently, death's days as a tyrannical power may be numbered, but it still constitutes those wages of sin which must yet be paid by the Christian sinner (cf. 6:23). However, since Paul suggests that this bodily death is *already* a reality and that the Spirit is *already* at work in giving life,[39] the death to which

---

37. By using the adjective "existential" instead of "spiritual," I do not intend to suggest that Paul is the more "Heideggerian" and the less "Thomistic." Obviously, both characterizations are anachronistic. "Existential" may capture more fully in modern parlance the death, in life, of the whole person than does "spiritual death" (contra, e.g., C. H. Dodd, *The Epistle of Paul to the Romans*, MNTC [New York: Harper & Brothers, 1932], 80–81). As for Paul's own language, the only thing that is expressly *pneumatikos* ("spiritual") in this passage is the law (7:14).

38. Following Käsemann, *Commentary on Romans*, 215–16.

39. Since the focus of this chapter is death, I have refrained from digressive consideration of its converse. At this juncture, however, perhaps I should state my views on the Pauline doctrine of "immortality," implicit in Rom 8:11 and explicit only at 1 Cor 15:53–54 (*athanasia*). To begin with, Nickelsburg's careful study (see n. 5 above; esp. 177–80) decisively refutes the unitary Jewish perceptions of death and life presupposed in the work of Oscar Cullmann (*Immortality of the Soul or Resurrection of the Dead? The Witness of the New Testament* [London:

the apostle refers may also be that existential death effected in baptism (cf. 6:6). These two nuances needn't be mutually exclusive; the language may well be at once literal and metaphorical. In any case it is important to note that Paul's thought returns to the moral implications of his statements: even as death manifests itself in walking in the flesh, in ways of transgression (cf. 8:3-6), so, too, does life manifest itself in righteousness (8:10).

Romans 8:12-30. The significantly ethical component in Paul's understanding of death persists in 8:13: for those who live according to the flesh, death is the inevitable, inescapable outcome (cf. 1:32) and, as such, is sufficient ground for fear (*phobos*, 8:15). Yet, in 8:13, the apostle shifts almost immediately to a felicitous use of the verb *thanatoō* (to put to death) with a positive connotation: the Spirit has a perpetually eradicable function in putting to death the deeds of the body, even as believers have been put to death through the body of Christ (7:4; cf. 6:11). So it is, paradoxically, that through a kind of death the Spirit cancels our fear of death and bears witness to the believer's adoption as a child of God (8:14-17).

Though not explicitly mentioned in 8:18-25, the images of death are implicit throughout and amplify the richness of Paul's conception. (1) As much as any other text, this passage attests to the broad, cosmic sweep of Paul's thinking about death. It is not merely the case that individual human beings die; the whole creation has been subjected to futility and has been groaning in travail together (vv. 20, 22). In such statements as these we are again reminded of the curse on the ground in Genesis 3 (see my comments above on 7:7-25) as well as the cosmic vision of intertestamental apocalypticism and even OT proto-apocalypticism (see Isa 66:22). The images of subjection and bondage in Romans 8:20-21 are reminiscent, moreover, of Paul's mythological depic-

---

Epworth, 1958]): Paul's Semitic background would not necessarily have precluded any belief in immortality on his part. Nevertheless, I know of nowhere that Paul explicitly construes Gen 2-3 as referring to humanity's "original immortality"; insofar as he does not so interpret the text, I believe that his exegesis was true to its intention (N.B. Gen 2:7; see also n. 35 above). If "immortality" be implied in Rom 8:11, we must be clear that Paul is not speaking of a "natural" immortality, which had been recovered after "the fall," but of a gratuitous imperishability, the result of God's free gift through Christ (so also 1 Cor 15:53, 54; 2 Cor 5:1-5). For further consideration of these issues, see Robert T. Fortna, "Romans 8:10 and Paul's Doctrine of the Spirit," *ATR* 41 (1959): 77-84; F. F. Bruce, "Paul on Immortality," *SJT* 24 (1971): 457-72; Benedict Englezakis, "Rom. 5,12-15 and the Pauline Teaching on the Lord's Death: Some Observations," *Bib* 58 (1977): 231-36. Ben C. Blackwell has helpfully revisited the correlation of God's bestowal of incorruptibility upon redeemed humanity with the reclamation of its intended glory: "Immortal Glory and the Problem of Death in Romans 3.23," *JSNT* 32 (2010): 285-308; Blackwell, "The *Greek Life of Adam and Eve* and Romans 8:14-39: (Re-)creation and Glory," in Blackwell, Goodrich, and Matson, *Reading Romans in Context*, 108-14.

tion of death as a personal and destructive cosmic force (see esp. 6:15–23). (2) Moreover, in Paul's view the creation has been subjected in hope (8:20) even as we groan inwardly while awaiting the redemption of our bodies (8:23). From this belief two important points must be drawn. First, as Leander Keck has underscored,[40] in the context of Hellenistic views of death it is critical that Paul says that Christians await, not *release from* their bodies, but their bodies' *redemption*. Second, that redemption is not confined to a singular *sōma* but is operative with respect to *the whole* of the Creator's work.[41] The lordship of Christ, sealed by his resurrection from the dead, functions as nothing less than the universal reclamation of God's sovereignty over everything that has been created, with the result that "all Israel will be saved" (Rom 11:26), that "in Christ all shall be made alive" (1 Cor 15:22).[42]

Romans 8:31–39. In this passage Paul lyrically sums up his convictions on the assurance of the believer's salvation. Death is mentioned with reference to Christ Jesus (*ho apothanōn*, 8:34b) and to those who trust him (*thanatoumetha* [we are put to death], 8:36, borrowing from Ps 44:22; cf. 2 Cor 4:11). In the first instance death refers patently to the physical death of Christ; in the second, patently to the sufferings, or loss of life's richness, among disciples. In both instances the latent reference is to death as an eschatological event: Christians share in suffering the messianic affliction (8:35; cf. 8:17) that Christ experienced but from which he has since arisen victorious, having conquered death.[43] In Paul's final reference to death in this pericope (8:38), many of the subtleties we have discerned converge in the single word *thanatos*: (literally) mortality, (metaphorically) suffering during this life (see 8:36), (mythologically) the cosmological power that is ranged with "angels," "principalities," and "powers" (8:38). However, its basic nuance is suggested by 8:39: death is that which essentially alienates humanity from God. How striking it is, therefore, that for Paul nothing, not even the supreme separator, can finally separate those in Christ from the love of God.

40. Keck, "New Testament Views of Death," 76.
41. A matter carefully examined by Susan Groves Eastman, "Christian Experience and Paul's Logic of Solidarity: The Spiral Structure of Romans 5–8," *BibAnn* 12 (2022): 233–53. Kyle B. Wells, "The Liberation of the Body of Creation: Towards a Pauline Environmental Ethic," *JTS* 73 (2022): 92–103, offers a different angle of vision.
42. Thus Keck ("New Testament Views of Death," 76): "What is at stake in the resurrection, then, is the Creator's relationship to what he has made. Paul can think of nothing that is ultimately to be classed as unredeemable, as nothing but disposable slag. For Paul, what God created, he will redeem—all of it." See also Beverly Roberts Gaventa, "Neither Height nor Depth: Discerning the Cosmology of Romans," *SJT* 64 (2011): 265–78.
43. So Käsemann (*Commentary on Romans*, 249), who notes that this psalm was used by the rabbis with reference to the martyrdom of the pious.

Pauline Perspectives on Death in Romans 5–8

SOME CONCLUSIONS AND FURTHER QUESTIONS

Surely the first of the two theses proposed at this chapter's beginning has by now been substantiated. Only through a cavalier reductionism could one argue for some monolithic understanding of death in Pauline thought. Using Romans 5–8 as a test case, we have witnessed the multiple dimensions of the apostle's perspectives on death, at several points lying in tension with one another. It remains for me to synthesize the results of our inquiry to verify my second, complementary thesis: that the connotations of death for Paul were not totally new inventions, like Melchizedek sans progenitors. Rather, the apostle's comprehensive conception was indebted to, and is best understood against, the backdrop of the diverse perspectives of his own checkered world of thought. A return to the rubrics suggested by our survey of the Semitic and Greco-Roman views of death should most clearly demonstrate this.

As with his Jewish and Greek antecedents, Paul recognizes death to be a biological reality (Rom 6:6; 7:2-3; cf. 8:10, 38; 14:7, 8); yet nowhere in Romans 5–8 do we receive the impression that he thinks of it simply as part of the created, *natural order* (I. A.).[44] It's just the reverse: death is *an intrusive warp in the Creator's design* (II. C.), an aberration not just of an individual's life but of all humanity (5:18-19), even of the entire cosmos (8:20-22). It is hardly surprising that Paul's references to the physical death of Jesus Christ invariably convey suprapersonal, eschatological implications (6:3, 4, 5, 10, 11; 8:34b; cf. 14:9). This is most clearly portrayed in Rom 6:9a: "We know that Christ, having been raised from the dead, will never again die."

Whence, then, did death originate? For Paul, the gnostic response is wrongheaded: death is no defect built into the ontological makeup of things (cf. *Gos. Phil.* 2.75.2-15; *C.H.* 1.15). In line with his Semitic heritage, he *associates death with sin* (II. E.): death is either derivative (5:12, 14, 18, 19; 7:9; 8:4, 6) or the punitive consequence (6:16, 21, 23; 7:5; 8:13; cf. 1:32) of sin.[45] Death, for Paul, is a uniquely apt metaphor for humanity's pre-Christian existence, because it captures that estrangement from God which is the essence of sin (7:9-11, 13; 8:7; cf. 8:39).[46] But

---

44. Here and throughout this section, the italicized phrases refer to the descriptions of death as "completion" and "depletion" in the outline on p. 164 above. The Roman numerals and alphabetical letters, parenthetically indicated, refer to the items so designated in that outline.

45. As far as I can tell, Paul never completely reconciles the tension between death as both arising from sin and the punishment for it, nor does he appear to indicate any interest in doing so. See also R. W. Thomas, "The Meaning of the Terms 'Life' and 'Death' in the Fourth Gospel and in Paul," *SJT* 21 (1968): 199-212, esp. 208-12.

46. Here I generally agree with Günther Bornkamm (*Paul*, trans. D. M. G. Stalker [Lon-

this death has been decisively counteracted by the death of another, even Jesus Christ, whose *atoning sacrifice* on our behalf (I. B.) has been accepted by God (5:8, 18–19; cf. 14:15). The ratification of that acceptance is God's raising of Jesus from the dead (cf. 4:17).[47] Accordingly, there is only one truly *heroic death*—paradoxically, that of the crucified Christ (contrast 5:7)—and it is in the death and resurrection of that one that our *hope* resides (I. D.: 6:1–14; cf. 8:20).

Meanwhile, in this hope believers and all creation remain subject to death, which is experienced as *a tyrannous, cosmological power* (II. D.: 5:14, 17; 6:9b, 16, 21, 23; 7:6, 24; 8:2; cf. 8:20–21, 38; 1 Cor 15:25–26). Death has been dethroned as lord over creation by the Lord Jesus; yet death persists as a pretender to the throne, assuring our mortality and *robbing this life of its fullness* (II. B.: Rom 8:36; cf. 8:38; 1 Cor 15:31; 2 Cor 4:11). Although these are prospects that could easily *evoke fear* (II. A.: cf. Rom 8:15; 2 Cor 7:10), believers yearn in faith for the redemption of their bodies (Rom 8:23) and in the confident hope that death's destruction is ultimately sure and has already begun to be realized, through the power of God in Christ to subject all things to himself (thus, 1 Cor 15:26–28).

The major components of Paul's understanding of death in Romans 5–8 have been isolated; something of their cultural lineage has been traced; and an attempt has been made to sketch out the manner in which Paul integrates them in the course of his argument in those chapters. Some general questions based on this exercise might yet be raised.

First: Is it possible to identify Paul's overall perception of death in Romans 5–8 as principally Semitic or Hellenic? I think not. To be sure, it is possible to correlate a given Pauline theme with a chiefly Hebraic outlook (e.g., atonement) or to tag a certain stream of Hellenistic thought as antagonistic with Paul's perspective (e.g., the Gnostic notion of death as an ontic flaw). In these two cases the apostle's point of view would emerge as the more Semitic. In general, however, the reservoir of ideas from which Paul draws already reveals a thorough commingling of Greek and Jewish motifs. The most

---

don: Hodder and Stoughton, 1971], 124): "Death is not something appointed and natural, but the power which makes its victim prisoner and sets the seal on his lost state." However, notice the manner in which Bornkamm has swept together in this brief sentence at least three different images of death: as an expression of the natural order, as a cosmological power, and as a testimony to human separation from God. My point, here and throughout, is not that Bornkamm and others are wrong but that such undifferentiated formulations lack precision. There is a gain in conceptual clarity when we separate out the elements in Paul's understanding of death and examine their ancestry.

47. By no means, though, is "atonement" the only image used by the apostle with regard to Christ's death. See the thoughtful analysis by Morna D. Hooker, "'Who Died for Our Sins, and Was Raised for Our Acquittal': Paul's Understanding of the Death of Christ," *SEÅ* 68 (2003): 59–71.

one can say is that the perception of death in Romans 5–8 is heavily dependent upon Hellenistic Judaism, with all of the ambiguous variety that term encompasses.

Second: May the Pauline perspective in these chapters be characterized as either predominantly "death as completion" or preponderantly "death as depletion"? The foregoing analysis suggests that both categories are appropriate in the description of certain complexes of Pauline thought in Romans; yet the two rubrics seem best correlated with two different subjects. Specifically, the imagery of depletion tends to characterize the death of creation and humankind, whereas the imagery of completion tends to characterize the death of Christ. This is not to suggest that, for Paul, depletive nuances are never implicit in Christ's death: kenosis is, after all, a significant feature of the Christ-hymn in Philippians 2:6-11 (see also Rom 6:3). Nor would I claim that human death is never perceived by Paul as in some sense completive: in that same imprisonment epistle he can boldly assert that, for him, "to die is gain" (Phil 1:21; cf. also Rom 7:4). My suggestion is more narrowly circumscribed, arising as it does from the exegesis of Romans 5–8. When, in these four chapters, Paul refers to death in negative terms of lack, oppression, or estrangement, more often than not he is speaking anthropologically. When in those same chapters the flow of his argument leads him to depict death as a positive fulfillment (e.g., as an occasion for hope or as atonement for sin), more often than not he is speaking christologically. Ultimately the two perspectives merge in the apostle's understanding of the church's corporate fellowship in Christ: it is precisely because believers have died in Christ, participating in Christ's completive death, that their own demise has been radically transmuted from loss to gain (cf. Rom 6:1-11).

Third: Having acknowledged the cultural horizon against which Romans 5–8 should be read, can we locate any points at which Paul's observations on death part company with, or proceed beyond, those of his Jewish and Greek forbears or contemporaries? Indeed we can: at three points at least, the traditional views on death have been given a unique, perhaps even original, Pauline twist. These might well represent Paul's distinctive contributions to modern theological reflection on death.

- Unlike that of his Hellenic and Jewish milieux, Paul's point of view is predictably, uncompromisingly christological. The monumental shift of the eons, that which has once and for all redefined death and its power over creation, is the cross of Christ Jesus.[48]

---

48. The phraseology here is not reductionistic. Paul so closely links cross and resur-

- Unlike most of the Greco-Roman perspectives (contrast I. C.) and many in contemporary culture, Paul's thinking about death is not limited to the sphere of anthropology. In his view, everyone and everything longs, not for release or escape from bodily existence, but for bodily redemption or transformation.[49] To be sure, this lies in continuity with Paul's Jewish predecessors, particularly in intertestamental and apocalyptic Judaism. However, that which differentiates Paul and the Hebraic perspective on this point is, once again, the centrality of the cross: for the apostle, the enfranchisement of creation from the power of death *has already begun* through the power of Christ.[50]
- Fundamental to Paul's understanding of death is his linkage of mortality to morality. Unlike some Hellenistic views, death is not primarily an ontological imperfection with unfortunate physiological consequences from which release is sought. Nor is it a neutral process that entails no adjustment of values beyond the grave (the Epicurean view, to which many moderns are unknowingly indebted).[51] For the apostle, death is basically a moral fact, the tragic result of Adam's transgression. When believers die with Christ, that to which they die—that is, that from which they are redeemed—is sin (Rom 6:2, 10–11; 8:13; cf. 6:6b, 7, 8; 7:1, 4, 6; 8:10–11).[52] This in turn marks an important transvaluation of certain traditional Jewish perspectives, to which many Christians today still cling. It is no longer a matter of behaving ethically in this life so that God will remember us at our death (which, after all, would be but another hubristic and futile exercise in justification by works of the law). Precisely the reverse is asserted by Paul: those who are members of the body of Christ ought to walk in ways of righteousness because *already* they have been brought from death to new life (see 6:13, 19).[53]

---

rection that he can refer alone to either the crucifixion (1 Cor 2:2) or the resurrection (1 Thess 1:10; Rom 8:11) as a symbol of the entire soteriological complex. See Rudolf Bultmann, *Theology of the New Testament*, 2 vols. (New York: Scribner, 1951), 1:292–93.

49. By contrast, the pervasive anthropocentricity of much modern theology is only beginning to be recognized and eschewed. A standard-bearer in this movement was ethicist James M. Gustafson: *Ethics from a Theocentric Perspective: Theology and Ethics*, vol. 1 (Chicago: University of Chicago Press, 1982).

50. See Charles B. Cousar, "Paul and the Death of Jesus," *Int* 52 (1998): 38–52.

51. As pointed out by Keck, "New Testament Views of Death," 54.

52. See William Horst, *Morality, Not Mortality: Moral Psychology and the Language of Death in Romans 5–8* (Lanham: Lexington Books, 2022).

53. See Felipe de Jesus Legarreta-Castillo, *The Figure of Adam in Romans 5 and 1 Corinthians 15: The New Creation and Its Ethical and Social Reconfigurations* (Minneapolis: Augsburg Fortress, 2014). Patristic exegesis did not hesitate to develop this Pauline insight.

There is much more to be said about Paul's perspectives on death than has been presented here. A thorough treatment of the topic would necessitate both an investigation of a far wider range of Pauline literature (e.g., 1 Cor 15:12–58; 2 Cor 4:7–12; 5:1–10; Phil 1:19–26) and reflection on a number of significant questions that would surface in the course of further exploration.[54] For instance, to what extent is Paul's fear of death shaped by the prospect of his own imminent demise and by his yearning to complete his own special missionary task? To what degree is the expectation of radical change from this life to the next an occasion for both dread and hope in Paul's conception of *thanatos*? To such queries as these no response has been hazarded here.[55] However, the preceding consideration of the images of death in Romans 5–8 has surely sufficed to indicate the breadth of the apostle's indebtedness to the pluriform cultural forces of his day, as well as the depth of his own creative capacity to transform those influences into distinctively Pauline insights. The rich lode that is Romans has not been exhausted. It never will be. If carefully mined, Paul's weightiest letter has yet more treasures to yield for theological reflection on Christian life and death.[56]

See Chris L. De Wet, "The Practice of Everyday Death: Thanatology and Self-Fashioning in John Chrysostom's Thirteenth Homily on Romans," *HTSTS* 71 (2015): 1–6.

54. See František Ábel, "'Death as the Last Enemy': Interpretation of Death in the Context of Paul's Theology," *ComViat* 58 (2016): 19–54.

55. Such issues are raised by a number of older studies: e.g., C. Leslie Mitton, "Paul's Certainties: V. The Gift of the Spirit and Life beyond Death in 2 Corinthians v. 1–5," *ExpTim* 69 (1958): 260–63; Lucien Cerfaux, *The Christian in the Theology of St. Paul* (London: Chapman, 1967), 195–98; Chalmer E. Faw, "Death and Resurrection in Paul's Letters," *JBL* 27 (1959): 291–98; Edmond Jacob, "Death," *IDB* 1 (1962): 802–4; C. F. D. Moule, "St. Paul and Dualism: The Pauline Conception of Resurrection," *NTS* 13 (1966): 106–23; Tannehill, *Dying and Rising with Christ*; Ronald Cassidy, "Paul's Attitude to Death in II Corinthians 5:1–10," *EvQ* 43 (1971): 210–17. More recently, see the provocative study by James L. Jaquette, "Life and Death, Adiaphora, and Paul's Rhetorical Strategies," *NovT* 38 (1996): 30–54. By its nature death presents a perennial problem for biblical and pastoral theology (Charles E. Brown, "'The Last Enemy Is Death': Paul and the Pastoral Task," *Int* 43 [1989]: 380–92). A systematic review of the pertinent primary texts and revision of their exegesis in the secondary literature are ever to be welcomed.

56. I am deeply indebted to the late Professor James L. Price, whose Romans seminar at Duke (spring 1982) provided the impetus for this article. He was the first to encourage me to revise a seminar paper for publication, when it would otherwise have been buried in a horsehair trunk.

CHAPTER 11

The Persistence of the Wounds

> O God, what am I going to do?
> He's gone—and I'm left
> with an empty pit in my life. . . .
> How could you have allowed this to happen?
> I thought you protected your own!
>
> —Ann Weems

OF ALL OCCASIONS FOR LAMENT, the death of a child must rank as the parent's most searing. When Ann Weems penned those words after the death of her twenty-one-year-old son Todd, they had to have surfaced from the depths of an anguish that only parents like her could possibly plumb.[1]

THE HOWL AND THE VOW

Rachel knew. So claimed the prophet Jeremiah in a lengthy poetic oracle that surveys the comprehensive slaughter of her grandson Ephraim's children—the Northern Kingdom, Israel, in 721 BCE—and the exile of her stepson Judah's children—the Southern Kingdom, in 587 BCE—from Ramah to Babylon (Jer 30:4–31:22). According to one tradition (1 Sam 10:2; cf. Gen 35:20), Rachel had been buried five miles north of Jerusalem, near Ramah. Jeremiah imagines ghostly wailing: Mother Rachel, howling with inconsolable lamentation, for the murder and deportation of all her sons who were no more (Jer 31:15):

> Thus declared the LORD:
> A cry is heard in Ramah—

---

1. Weems, *Psalms of Lament* (Louisville: Westminster John Knox, 1995), 20.

The Persistence of the Wounds

> Wailing, bitter weeping—
> Rachel, weeping for her children.
> She refuses to be comforted
> For her children, who are not.[2]

Who would dare restrain a mother from weeping for children who have ceased to be?

In fact, according to the prophet, the Lord does just that:

> Thus declared the Lord:
> Restrain your voice from weeping,
> Your eyes from shedding tears;
> For your labor has its reward,
>   Declares the Lord:
> They shall return from the enemy's land.
> There is hope for your future,
>   Declares the Lord:
> And your children shall come back to their country. (Jer 31:16–17)

Such restraint of a mother's tears lies only in the province of God, who alone can restore that which was not. Jeremiah promises Rachel that her pangs, at her children's death as at their birth, will not prove in vain. That assurance matches the profusion of comforting metaphors that spill out of this oracle: Jacob will be delivered from crushing tribulation (Jer 30:7); Maiden Israel shall again learn the rhythm of the dance (31:4); Israel's remnant shall be gathered from the earth's farthest reaches (31:8); Jacob shall be redeemed (31:11); Ephraim, punished and moaning, shall be dandled by the constant Parent whose heart never stopped yearning for him (31:18–20). In brief (Jer 30:3): "Behold, days are coming—declares the Lord—when I shall restore the fortunes of my people, Israel and Judah, said the Lord; and I shall bring them back to the land that I gave to their fathers, and they shall possess it."

An Agonized Reprise

Turn the scriptural page. It is some four centuries later. The Evangelist Matthew recounts the events surrounding Jesus's birth (1:18–2:23). Unlike Luke's version,

---

2. All translations in this chapter are my own.

in which the sword that will pierce Mary's soul (2:35) is all but submerged by blessings and joy (1:28, 42–48, 68; 2:10, 28), Matthew's infancy narrative bears ineradicable stains of intrigue and murder. The birth of Jesus, David's son and God's truly anointed (Matt 1:1), is hurled in the teeth of Herod the Great, Israel's nominal and ruthless sovereign (2:1–3). When tricked by the Magi, whom he lured to direct him to Israel's genuine savior (1:21; 2:7–8), in fury Herod mandates infanticide, slaying all of Bethlehem's boys two years old or under (2:16). Gazing upon unspeakable slaughter, Matthew (2:18) hears afresh the voice of Jeremiah:

> A voice was heard in Ramah,
> Loud wailing and grieving—
> Rachel, weeping for her children,
> And she would not be consoled, for they were not.

The listener should pause to let the full weight of this lament sink in. Many are the distractions that would divert what must arrest us. Churchgoers may go for years without hearing a sermon that struggles with this passage. Matthew 2:13–23 appears only once in the Revised Common Lectionary: for use on the First Sunday after Christmas Day in Year A, "unless the readings for the Epiphany of the Lord"—which include Matthew 2:1–12—"are preferred."[3] I'd wager that they almost always are. And so, if they hear any Scripture at all, worshipers in the pew celebrate Christmas with Luke's far happier story ringing in their weary ears. Professional exegetes, without excuse for ignoring Matthew's very different account, may fall into traps of other kinds. For them, Matthew 2:18 has a most convenient pigeonhole: the First Evangelist's well-known "formula quotations," five of which are clustered in his infancy narrative.[4] The scholar will also detect in Matthew 2 echoes of Exodus 1:15–2:10, 11:1–10, and 12:29–32. The commentator may note the resemblances of Matthew's scriptural interpretation to that in the DSS, murmur something critical or apologetic of its transgression of contemporary exegetical norms, then proceed to another topic. Meanwhile, Bethlehem's mothers join with Rachel in wailing for their children, disconsolate, for they had ceased to be.

A most noteworthy aspect of Matthew's remembrance of Jeremiah at this terrible point is what the Evangelist chooses *not* to quote: namely, the prophet's

---

3. *The Revised Common Lectionary: Consultation on Common Texts* (Nashville: Abingdon, 1992), 26.

4. Matthew 1:23 (citing LXX Isa 7:14 and 8:8, 10); 2:6 (Mic 5:2); 2:15 (Hos 11:1); 2:17–18 (Jer 31:15); 2:23 (whose referent may be Isa 11:1 or 53:2 but remains ambiguous).

immediately subsequent promise that Rachel's tears are dabbed away, because she will get her children back (Jer 31:16-17).[5] One cannot explain this conspicuous gap as Matthew's inclination to keep things dark, since, as a matter of fact, his formula quotations incline toward sunny assurances:

> "His name shall be called Emmanuel," which is interpreted, "God with us." (Matt 1:23bc)

> From you [O Bethlehem] shall come a ruler,
> Who will shepherd my people Israel. (2:6b)

> The people who sat in darkness have seen great light,
> And for those who sat in Death's region and shadow
>   light has arisen on them. (4:16 [Isa 9:2])

> He took our infirmities,
> And he bore our diseases. (Matt 8:17 [Isa 53:4])

The Evangelist's decision in 2:18 to leave Rachel weeping demands a better explanation.

A more satisfying answer lies embedded in the complex material surrounding Matthew's citation of Jeremiah. Before Herod enacts his pogrom, an angel of the Lord appears in a dream to Joseph, informing him of the plot against the child and instructing him to take the child and his mother to Egypt (Matt 2:13-14). Joseph complies (2:15). After Herod's own death, the Lord's messenger returns in a dream to Joseph, redirecting the child to the safety of Galilee, beyond the clutches of Herod's son Archelaus (2:19-23). To be sure, Matthew is strumming an unusually dense theological chord, which interlaces God's particular providence for the infant Jesus's welfare (narrated with the Elohist trappings of divine intervention via dreams and angelic intermediaries), Jesus as Israel *redivivus* (exiled into, then called out of, Egypt), and a rationale for relocating Bethlehem's newborn to Nazareth. If we listen

---

5. For a perceptive analysis of Matthew's use of Jeremiah at this and other points, consult Michael Knowles, *Jeremiah in Matthew's Gospel: The Rejected Prophet Motif in Matthean Redaction*, JSNTSup 68 (Sheffield: Sheffield Academic Press, 1993). Matthew's interpretation of Jeremiah 31:15-17 also deviates from subsequent rabbinic readings of that text, whose outlook is preponderantly positive (Knowles, 33-52).

carefully, however, a dissonant note still penetrates: though Jesus narrowly escapes death by the hand of the political establishment, he isn't delivered to Egypt to hide out forever. The Lord calls his Son out of Egypt, not merely to connect the dots with Hosea's oracle, but in order *to send him back* into death's shadow,[6] where weeping mothers bury their infants for no reason other than a tyrant felt threatened, into the region where the Messiah's people remain in acute need for salvation.[7] Matthew realizes that a dry-eyed Rachel would be grossly premature. Not only are her children still no more; before long, Mary's child will join them in the nothingness of death.

Emmanuel Abandoned

The truth about Jesus's own end is harder than "nothingness," which could suggest human quietus as an Epicurean's painless, blissful insentience.[8] In Matthew, as in Mark (15:34), the crucified Jesus's final articulate cry is the Psalmist's ultimate lament: "My God, my God, why have you left me in the lurch?" (Matt 27:46; Ps 22:1). As bitter a pill as nonexistence is for humans to swallow, it goes down more smoothly than the experience of death as God-forsakenness. Again, we must beware evasive maneuvers that would dull the knife-edged offense: for instance, the suggestion that a quotation from Psalm 22:1 is overwhelmed by that lament's confident conclusion (vv. 22–31). I confess that such an interpretation has never persuaded me, for the simple reason that, if anything in Psalm 22:22–31 lay nearer the heart of these

---

6. So Richard J. Erickson: "The one who escaped at Bethlehem comes back to endure it all himself, *and to reverse it!*" ("Divine Injustice? Matthew's Narrative Strategy and the Slaughter of the Innocents (Matthew 2.13–23)," *JSNT* 64 [1996]: 5–27; quotation, with Erickson's emphasis, 26).

7. Transcribing the comments of his parishioners in the global south, Ernesto Cardenal offers bracing points of view on Matthew's narrative in *The Gospel in Solentiname* (Maryknoll, NY: Orbis, 1976), esp. 70–86. "It's very rough," says one woman, "but what happened then has gone on in every age. . . . And more Herods will come along, because whenever there's someone struggling for liberation there's someone who wants to kill him, and if they can kill him they will" (71–72).

8. As Epicurus (c. 342–270 BCE) wrote to Menoeceus: "For all good and evil consists in sensation, but death is deprivation of sensation. . . . So death, the most terrifying of ills, is nothing to us, since so long as we exist, death is not with us; but when death comes, then we do not exist" (quoted in *The New Testament Background: Writings from Ancient Greece and the Roman Empire That Illuminate Christian Origins*, ed. C. K. Barrett, rev. ed. [San Francisco: HarperCollins, 1989], 79–80).

evangelists' theologies, why, then, did they not apply *those* words of hope on the dying Jesus's lips (as, in different ways, Luke and John have opted to do: Luke 23:34, 43, 46; John 19:28, 30)? It seems to me equally suspect to rush to the Almighty's defense in Matthew and in Mark, protesting that the apocalyptic ambience of their crucifixion accounts demonstrates, to the contrary, that God's beloved Son was truly not abandoned at three o'clock that afternoon (Matt 27:45, 47–49, 51–54; Mark 15:33, 35–38). *Sub specie aeternitatis*, under the appearance of eternity (Spinoza), that is true. *Sub specie cruciatus*, under the aspect of torturous execution, it is no less true—from the evangelists' points of view—that Jesus ultimately, faithfully prayed to a God whose presence he could no longer perceive. That, surely, is the point of Matthew's nightmare at Golgotha. "All of you will desert me this night" (26:31). All, without exception, did just that: Judas (26:14–16, 25, 46–50; 27:3–10); Peter (26:40, 69–75); Zebedee's sons (26:37, 40–45); the tatters of the Twelve (26:56); sinful dullards, into whose hands the Son of Man was delivered (26:45; 27:47–49); Caiaphas and the Sanhedrin (26:57–68); Pilate and his wife (27:15–26); Jewish rabble and Roman guard (27:15, 21–23, 25, 27–31); elite and hoi polloi (27:39–43); crucified bandits, Jesus's fellow victims (27:38, 44); and finally, from the cross: "*Eli, Eli, lama sabbachthani?* . . . My God, my God, why have you deserted me?" (27:46). Attuned to the undertone of that searing question, one still can hear Rachel's continuous lament for her other lost children: wailing unrelieved, devoid of palliative, lacking immediate answer or solace. At Golgotha, at the unfathomable convergence of human sin and divine intent, the last of Bethlehem's children was slain. The true heir to the throne whom Herod was really after (27:37), Pilate managed to destroy.

And that would have been the end of that, had Albert Schweitzer been correct that Jesus's immeasurable greatness lay in his deluded yet heroic martyrdom for a lost cause that could only crush him.[9] Matthew, however, has no truck with such chilled Romanticism. For the First Evangelist, Jesus's greatness lies not in a freedom fighter's ultimate self-sacrifice. Jesus was and is the Christ, son of David, son of Abraham, Son of God: the one on whom God's Spirit incomparably rests; whose righteousness causes heavens to split and a supernal voice to announce to those with hearing ears, "*This* is my beloved Son, with whom I am well pleased" (Matt 3:13–17). Moses and Elijah appear in the disciples' vision, but only Jesus is transfigured; to him alone must attention be paid, an injunction that collapses weak knees and throws faces to the

---

9. Albert Schweitzer, *The Quest of the Historical Jesus: A Critical Study of Its Progress from Reimarus to Wrede*, trans. W. Montgomery (New York: Macmillan, 1968), esp. 370–71.

ground (17:1–8). "All things have been delivered to me by my Father; and no one knows the Son except the Father, and no one knows the Father except the Son and any one to whom the Son chooses to reveal him" (11:27). Whatever else the Evangelist may mean by identifying Jesus as Emmanuel, "God with us" (1:23), surely it means, for Matthew, that Jesus is the solitary hinge on which pivot both heaven and earth, the unique link between God and the church. In Jesus the Christ, theology and ecclesiology are irrevocably joined. Only when we begin to comprehend the extraordinary dimensions of such a claim can we begin to appreciate how devastating the crucified Jesus's cry of dereliction really is. *God-with-us wails in God-forsakenness.* For such a paradox there is no resolution. There can be only gross human misunderstanding (27:47–49), a dying outcry (27:50), and upheaval the like of which the world has never seen (27:51–53).

". . . And, Live We How We Can, Yet Die We Must"

Modern readers tend toward embarrassment by Matthew's Technicolor apocalypticism at Golgotha: the rip of the temple's curtain, the earthquake, the splitting of rocks, the graves' disgorgement of dead saints who appear in Jerusalem. Compared with contemporary sensibilities, compared even with the other Gospels, all this seems over the top.[10] Perhaps, however, there is proportion in Matthew's vision. When, crucified and derelict, God-with-us suffers death at its most accursed (Deut 21:22–23), a single teardrop from heaven will not suffice. The scope of lament implied in Matthew 27:51–54—God's cry of grief over a tortured creation—corresponds to the magnitude of God's own loss. As André LaCocque observes, the Messiah's death throws the cosmos into convulsions.[11] And if, by chance, one of the saints raised in Jerusalem that day had been an infant's body butchered by Herod—a tiny, surrogate victim for the true King who had to die so that others would live (Matt 20:28; 26:26–29)—that little one's resurrection would never have stilled Rachel's weeping. It would only have validated the reason that she, too, continued to

---

10. True to Matthean form, however, these circumstances echo apocalyptic images in the OT: Joel 2:10; Ezek 37:12; Isa 26:19; Nah 1:5–6; Dan 12:2. They also provide a bookend for the astronomical aberrations in his infancy narrative: Matt 2:1–2 (cf. Num 22–24).

11. André LaCocque, "The Great Cry of Jesus in Matthew 27:50," in *Putting Body & Soul Together: Essays in Honor of Robin Scroggs*, ed. Virginia Wiles, Alexandra Brown, and Graydon F. Snyder (Valley Forge, PA: Trinity Press International, 1997), 138–64.

cry. Were Todd Weems returned to the arms of his mother, Ann, her lament—even joy-crazed—would persist, precisely because there was neither justice nor mercy, neither power nor glory, in her son's death to start with. So it was with the Father's own beloved Son. And yet, God's actions in Matthew 27:51-53 bespeak no flailing incoherence. There is sense in it, and purpose. The righteousness of Jesus, denied by his hecklers—for surely God would rescue the righteous (Wis 2:17-24)—finds vindication in the raising of the saints. No longer does God sit in his holy temple (Ps 11:4), whose destruction the ripped curtain epitomizes. God remains with us, crucified with us and for us.[12]

Eventually, however, all exegetical fillips fail and every theological commonplace is burnt away, for lament leads human creatures into the inmost heart of God, in whose image we are indelibly crafted. As long as we live with God in a world destined for glory yet still unredeemed, at times unspeakably blasphemed, we shall lament even as we rejoice. Well-intentioned but mistaken counselors have confused grief with lament, implying that lamentation expresses a definable stage in a predictable grieving process. A person or family proceeds through "stages of grief," which, if executed successfully—that is to say, in accordance with psychotherapeutic protocols—eventuates in a mentally reconstituted individual or group. Others must speak to the cogency of that model.[13] This I know, by faith and from experience: grief may wane or become numbed, but lament is not a "stage" from which children destined for the glory of God evolve, then leave behind (Col 1:24-29). As long, for Christians, as every Friday recollects Good Friday, just as each Sunday instantiates the Day of Resurrection, our life in God telescopes time beyond discrete stages in sequence. Because that is so, the only life we know is entwined with death; the only joy, interlaminated with lament. Until the consummation of the ages, God and Rachel and all the company of saints will weep for their children, because they were not.

There is no explaining such mystery. There can be only testimonies to it.

---

12. For further discussion, see Paul S. Minear, "The Messiah Forsaken . . . Why?," *HBT* 17 (1995): 62-83. Shakespeare: "Why, what is pomp, rule, reign, but earth and dust? / And, live we how we can, yet die we must" (*Henry VI*, Part II, 5.2.27).

13. Nicholas Wolterstorff: "I skimmed some books on grief. They offered ways of not looking at death and pain in the face, ways of turning away from death out there to one's own inner 'grief process' and then, on that, laying the heavy hand of rationality. I will not have it so. I will not look away. I will indeed remind myself that there's more to life than pain. I will accept joy. But I will not look away from Eric dead. Its demonic awfulness I will not ignore. I owe that—to him and to God" (*Lament for a Son* [Grand Rapids: Eerdmans, 1987], 54).

The Godforsaken God

Poet and apostle bear witness to lament's corporate dimension.

> Alas—
> Lonely sits the city
> Once so crowded with people.
> She that was great among nations
> Has become like a widow.
> The princess among cities
> Has become a slave.
> . . .
> My teeth he has broken on gravel;
> He has ground me into the dust.
> My life is bereft of peace;
> I forgot what happiness is.
> . . .
> But this do I call to mind,
> And so I have hope:
> The Lord's steadfast love has not ended,
> His compassion is not spent. (Lam 1:1; 3:16–17, 21–22)

I reckon the sufferings of the present season incomparable to the coming glory to be revealed to us. For creation waits with intense yearning for God's adoptees to be disclosed. . . . For we know that all creation moans as one and until now collectively suffers labor pains—and not only that: but we ourselves, who have the Spirit's first-fruits, we too moan inwardly while awaiting our adoption, the redemption of our bodies. For in hope we were saved. (Rom 8:18–19, 22–24a)

A metropolis is laid waste. A survivor stumbles through smoldering rubble, offering an elegy for Jerusalem. Centuries later, on this side of Easter, Paul invites the church in Rome to wait with him in a birthing room. It is the cosmos, God's creation in its entirety, that writhes in travail, beginning to give birth to a glory only glimpsed and to this day not yet fully delivered. Like the poet and the apostle, we are not detached spectators. We, too, are seized by besetting, universal pangs: the ache—subsiding only long enough to redouble its inexpressible intensity—that empties all memory of happiness. Yet the spine of lament is hope: not the vacuous optimism that "things will get better," which in the short run is usually a lie,[14] but the deep and irrepressible conviction, in the teeth of present evidence, that God has not severed the umbilical cord that has always bound us to the LORD. Anguish concealed God from both psalmist (Ps 22:1) and the Crucified One (Matt 27:46), but neither could finally let go of his adoption. The God who forsakes was and remains "*My* God, *my* God." And somehow our God suffers our own God-forsakenness.[15]

DYING, WE LIVE

Reenter poet and apostle:

> How long, O LORD? Will you forever ignore me?
> How long will you hide your face from me?
> How long shall my mind be troubled,
> And grief in my deepest self the day long?
> How long shall my enemy have the upper hand?
> Look at me—answer me, O LORD, my God.
> . . .
> But in your fidelity I trust;
> In your deliverance my inmost self shall rejoice. (Ps 13:1–3a, 5)

. . . in all ways pressed but not crushed, at a loss but not despairing, hounded but not forsaken, thrown down but not destroyed, always carrying about in the body the killing of Jesus, so that also the life of Jesus may be manifested in our body. For we the living are constantly handed over to death for Jesus's sake, so that Jesus's life may also be manifested in our mortal body. So death is operative in us, but life in you. (2 Cor 4:8–12)

In late December some years ago, I returned to the town where I had grown up, to the cemetery where my family is buried. Not far from my parents' graves, the sunlight caught something that twinkled. Walking over for a better look, I discovered a Christmas tree: a foot tall, painstakingly ornamented. Beside

---

14. "I hoped for happiness, but evil came; / I looked for light, but there was darkness" (Job 30:26).
15. See James L. Mays, "Prayer and Christology: Psalm 22 as Perspective on the Passion," *ThTod* 42 (1985): 322–31; Terence E. Fretheim, *The Suffering of God: An Old Testament Perspective*, OBT (Philadelphia: Fortress, 1984).

that miniature sat an immaculately dressed, tiny bear. Though I saw no one else nearby, both decorations looked fresh enough to have been placed at the grave only five minutes earlier. I peered at the epitaph, wondering if I would recognize the child's name. I didn't—but was thunderstruck by the inscribed dates: "1957–1959." In an eternal moment, the gravestone shuddered beneath my feet. Tree and bear wept for a full forty years of unending loss.

So it is with lament. Its very nature is constant and durative. An impatient, death-denying society demands that sufferers "get over it." Across millennia, by contrast, the psalmist asks over and again, "How long, O Lord? How long?" In this life are things for which there's no getting over; such belong to the land of lament. With maturity, by God's grace, the scales of woe and trust become balanced. In the meanwhile, we pray that we shall rejoice over deliverance yet to come, as we adorn the graves of those dead and loved and remembered.

Psalmist and apostle also remind us that lamentation, though rarely private, is intensely personal. Indeed, in a startling reversal of expectation, St. Paul transposes the whole of his ministry into the key of lament. In his view, life is no dirge; rather, it has been transfigured, root and branch, by Jesus's cross and resurrection. For the sake of the Crucified, "we the living are forever handed over to death," so that our besieged and corruptible bodies may reveal the indestructible life that Christ now lives. For the Christian who believes, "You have died, and your life is hid with Christ in God" (Col 3:3), lament is not an occasional tune, hummed by others. It has become the signature theme of every life in Christ.

The Touch That Knows

"Mortals, join the mighty chorus."[16]

> Since Jews demand signs and Greeks search for wisdom, we proclaim Christ who is crucified, a snare for Jews and folly for Gentiles—but to those called, both Jews and Greeks—Christ: God's power and God's wisdom. For God's foolishness is wiser than people, and God's weakness mightier than people. (1 Cor 1:22–25)

> Then one of the elders said to me, "Don't cry. Look—the lion of the tribe of Judah, the root of David, has conquered, to open the book and its seven seals." And I saw, between the throne and the four living creatures and the

---

16. Quoted from the hymn, "Joyful, Joyful, We Adore Thee," by Henry van Dyke (1852–1933).

elders, a lamb, standing as if slaughtered, with seven horns and seven eyes which are the spirits of God that have been dispatched into all the earth. And he came and took the book from the right hand of the one seated on the throne. And when he took it, the four living creatures and the four-and-twenty elders fell down before the lamb, each with a harp and golden bowls full of incense, which are the prayers of the saints. And they sang a new song, saying:

> Worthy are you to take the book
>   And to open its seals:
> For you were slaughtered, and you bought for God with
>   your blood,
> From every tribe and tongue and people and nation,
> And made them for our God a dominion and priests,
>   And they shall reign on earth.
> . . .
> Worthy is the slaughtered lamb to receive
> The power and wealth and wisdom and might
> and honor and glory and blessing. (Rev 5:5–10, 12)

And the eleven disciples went to Galilee, to the mountain where [the risen] Jesus had directed them. And when they saw him, they bowed down, though some had doubts about it. (Matt 28:16–17)

I don't know that a name was ever coined for it, but the avoidance of Good Friday among many Christians is a heresy of long standing. Its tacit justification seems to be that Easter Sunday signals a victory so complete that God effectively annihilated Golgotha. Such confusion makes for a theology that is not merely bad but heartless and even dangerous. In place of the Christian gospel of God's triumph, it substitutes the bad news of human triumphalism. It stills the voice of lament—often throwing the additional burden of guilt on the plaintive—and dares to attempt what even God refused: obliterating the wounds of Christ Crucified.

Christians should occasionally pause to marvel that God raised Jesus from death itself but did not wipe away his lacerations. "Look at my hands and my feet—it's really me. Touch me and see—a spirit doesn't have flesh and bones, as you see me have" (Luke 24:39). To Thomas: "Put your finger here and look at my hands, and bring your hand and thrust it into my side; and stop being faithless, but believe it" (John 20:27; cf. 19:31–37). Ending only with the promise that Jesus has been raised and will reunite with his disciples, Mark's Gospel has no need for a story so told: the last of Jesus we see in that Gospel is the one hanging, then buried. Matthew's disciples regard the Risen Crucified with mixed feelings: they worshiped, yes, but had their doubts. In the Seer's vision, the lamb worthy to unseal the book, to purchase a people, and to receive all reverence in heaven and on earth resembles in some respects the militant horned ram of 1 Enoch 90 but is altogether unlike that bellwether in one crucial aspect: Christ, *Agnus Dei*, remains slaughtered. Revelation insists upon that lamb—victorious yet butchered—with unmistakable repetition. Paul makes the same point more subtly in 1 Corinthians 1–2: "For I determined to know among you nothing save Jesus Christ, *who indeed continues to be the one crucified*" (2:2, whose appositive emphasizes a perfect passive participle). The NT is remarkably consistent on this point: by raising Jesus from the dead, God did not eradicate the scars of his death but, instead, vindicated this Crucified One, and no other, as the Messiah.

Just there lies the most important reason for the practice of lament. Without it, whether they know it or not, Christians again deny the One whom God has both vindicated and forever verified as Christ on the cross. The wounds of the Messiah's crucifixion are the inexpungible identification by which God has embodied himself for us, for our healing, for the salvation of all. Until that day when every tear has been wiped away and death shall be no more (Rev 21:4), all of God's people—Rachel and Ann, Jesus and Paul, all of us without exception—unite their voices in lament, hopeful but without closure. Among them is yet another parent who lost a child: philosopher Nicholas Wolterstorff, whose twenty-five-year-old son Eric died in a mountaineering accident:

> So I shall struggle to live the reality of Christ's rising and death's dying. In my living, my son's dying will not be the last word. But as I rise up, I bear the wounds of his death. My rising does not remove them. They mark me. If you want to know who I am, put your hand in.[17]

---

17. Wolterstorff, *Lament for a Son*, 92–93.

CHAPTER 12

Ave Maria, Gratia Plena

Ave Maria, gratia plena,
Dominus tecum;
benedicta tu in mulieribus,
et benedictus fructus ventris tui Jesus.
Sancta Maria, Mater Dei,
ora pro nobis peccatoribus nunc,
et in hora mortis nostræ.
Amen.[1]

Εὐεργέτην τεκοῦσα,
τὸν τῶν καλῶν αἴτιον,
τῆς εὐεργεσίας τὸν πλοῦτον,
πᾶσιν ἀνάβλυσον
πάντα γὰρ δύνασαι,
ὡς δυνατὸν ἐν ἰσχύϊ,
τὸν Χριστὸν κυήσασα,
θεομακάριστε.[2]

NO TOPIC IS MORE DEFINITIVE of Protestant theology than grace. No figure in Roman Catholic and Eastern Orthodox piety is more venerated than Mary, the mother of Jesus. Here I wish to conjoin topic and figure, to ponder the biblical cameos of Mary as a paradigm of grace in early Christian thought.[3] My aim is to reflect exegetically and constructively on seven NT pericopes,

---

1. *Saint Benedict's Prayer Book for Beginners* (York: Ampleforth Abbey, 1993), 108. A translation of this epigram and that which follows appears at the end of this chapter.
2. *The Service of the Small Paraklesis (Intercessory Prayer) to the Most Holy Theotokos* (Brookline, MA: Holy Cross Orthodox Press, 1984), 8.
3. This approach is hardly ragged from overuse. James Moffatt's classic study, *Grace in the New Testament* (New York: Long & Smith, 1932), mentions Mary only twice, in passing, with references to *hē charis* (grace) in Luke 1:30 (31) and *kecharitōmenē* (she who is highly favored) in Luke 1:28 (100), and with a suggestion that she may be the one speaking in *Odes of Solomon* 11.1–2 (100–101). *Ekarpophorēsen* (brought forth fruit) in *Ode* 11.1 refers to grace in the speaker's heart (i.e., "Grace . . . brought forth fruit"; cf. the Syriac version, in which the heart is the subject of the verb). See Michael Lattke, *The Odes of Solomon: A Commentary*, ed. Marianne Ehrhardt, Hermeneia (Minneapolis: Augsburg Fortress, 2016), 153–57. I thank Kaitlynn Merckling for her help in teasing out both Moffatt's intent and that of the Syriac *Odes*.

with attention to their theological nuances both differing and convergent.[4] To engage in depth the tradition of Mariological doctrine beyond its biblical roots[5] would trespass the bounds of a brief chapter and my own competence. I shall suggest, nevertheless, that even a cursory review of the NT's depictions of Mary affords us much in our contemplation of God's grace.[6]

A New Testament Conspectus of "The Mother of My Lord"

The Virgin Who Will Conceive God's Messiah (Luke 1:26–56)

Though not the earliest, canonically or chronologically, Luke 1:26–56 is the biblical presentation of Mary whose stamp on subsequent doctrine and piety has been most profound. For our purposes there is no passage more fruitful from which our own reflections may blossom. Examined exegetically, this text may be considered a balanced set of mirroring pairs: (a) the angel Gabriel's visitation to Mary of Nazareth (vv. 26–31); (b) Gabriel's canticle in praise of Jesus (the Annunciation, vv. 32–38); (a') Mary's visitation to her kinswoman, Elizabeth of Judah (vv. 39–45, 56); (b') Mary's canticle in praise of God (the Magnificat, vv. 46–55). Such careful composition underscores Luke's primary themes.

Gabriel's visitation to Mary (1:26–31). The keynote of this pericope, as of the entire passage, is sounded by Gabriel's salutation of Mary (1:28): *Chaire, kecharitōmenē, ho kyrios meta sou* ("Joyous greetings, she on whom great favor has been freely bestowed! The Lord [is] with you"[7]). No English translation can do justice to Gabriel's concise felicitations, which emphasize how Mary

---

4. Not included is Rev 12:1–17, whose unnamed woman is now generally recognized as referring at best secondarily—but even then, uncertainly—to Mary. See Richard P. McBrien, *Catholicism: New Edition* (San Francisco: HarperCollins, 1994), 1080–81.

5. Hilda C. Graef, *Mary: A History of Doctrine and Devotion* (London: Sheed & Ward, 1985 [originally published in two parts, 1963 and 1965]), remains an indispensable sounding of this practically bottomless river of research.

6. This chapter was originally written in honor of Thomas A. Langford (1930–2000), William Kellon Quick Professor of Theology, Dean of the Divinity School (1971–81), and Provost (1991–97) of Duke University: a masterly teacher and incomparable statesman for both the academy and the church. I rededicate this essay in his memory.

7. Here and throughout, all translations are my own unless otherwise indicated.

is viewed in God's eyes: *Chaire*,[8] *kecharitōmenē*,[9] "Glad tidings, she who has been regarded with high privilege!" In both classical Greek and Jewish Greek of the diaspora, *hē charis* (grace or esteem) refers basically to what delights, bestirring in its beholder joy and, among the gods, the power to beautify that which evokes such favor.[10] The closest cognate in Hebrew embraces the same cluster of nuances: the essence of *khen* is at once beauty and a positive disposition to it (Ps 84:11; Prov 22:11; Sir 40:17, 22). Within the same verbal family *khen* characteristically refers to a human's deeply affectionate favor (Ruth 2:2, 10, 13; 1 Sam 16:22; 20:3; Esth 2:15, 17; 5:2); *hannun*, to Yahweh as "gracious" (Exod 34:6; 2 Chr 30:9; Neh 9:17, 31; Pss 86:15; 103:8; 111:4; 116:5; 145:8; Joel 2:13; Jonah 4:2).[11] In both the OT (Gen 39:21; Exod 3:21; 11:3; 12:36) and classical Greek (Aristotle, *Rhet.* 2.7.1385a), *khen* and *hē chara* stress the favor of a superior that is utterly gratuitous and bestowed upon an inferior, apart from any merit of the beneficiary or expectation of reward.

The angel's greeting of Mary in 1:28, *Chaire, kecharitōmenē*, ("Hail, O favored one" [RSV]), includes Luke's first adoption of a term in the *chari-* (grace-) family.[12] Another follows almost immediately, in 1:30: "Fear not, Mary, for you

---

8. How *chaire* should be rendered is debatable: as forcefully as "Rejoice" (cf. Zeph 3:14 [LXX]; thus the NAB and Joel B. Green, *The Gospel of Luke*, NICNT [Grand Rapids: Eerdmans, 1997], 86–87), or as insipid as "Hello" (cf. Acts 15:23; 23:26; Phil 3:1; 4:4; Jas 1:1; so Raymond E. Brown, Karl Paul Donfried, Joseph A. Fitzmyer, and John Reumann, eds., *Mary in the New Testament* [Philadelphia: Fortress, 1978], 130–32). Given the immediate context of Luke 1:28, within the light of that Evangelist's pervasive association of Jesus's advent with *chara* (joy; see 1:14; 2:10; 8:13; 10:17; 15:7, 10; 24:41, 52), I favor a translation inclined toward the first alternative, without pressing that sense to excess.

9. Some strains of medieval Mariology evolved to interpret *kecharitōmenē* as implying Mary's possession of every secular and spiritual gift, an *already realized* perfection that acquitted her fit to conceive the Christ (see Graef, *Mary*, 1.170–73). By contrast, as Raymond E. Brown observes, in my view correctly, "for Luke Mary's special state is to be constituted by the divine favor involved in the conception of Jesus" (*The Birth of the Messiah: A Commentary on the Infancy Narratives in the Gospels of Matthew and Luke*, new updated ed., ABRL [New York and London: Doubleday, 1993], 326).

10. For documentation in relevant ancient sources, see Hans Conzelmann, "χάρις, κ.τ.λ.," *TDNT* 9:373–76, as amended by John Nolland, "Grace as Power," *NovT* 28 (1986): 26–31.

11. For further information, consult David Noel Freedman, Jack R. Lundbom, and Heinz-Josef Fabry, "חָנָה," *TDOT* 5:22–36.

12. Alone among the Synoptic evangelists, Luke uses words from this group: thirteen occurrences in the Gospel (1:28, 30; 2:40, 52; 4:22; 6:32, 33, 34; 7:21, 42, 43, 47; 17:9), twenty-one in Acts (2:47; 3:14; 4:33; 6:8; 7:10, 46; 11:23; 13:43; 14:3, 26; 15:11, 40; 18:27; 20:24, 32; 24:27; 25:3, 9; 25:11, 16; 27:24).

have found favor [*charin*] with God." Underpinning Gabriel's pronouncements are those Hebrew and Greek assumptions we have just noted. First, grace in Luke 1:26–31 is essentially God's delighted esteem (1:28, 30). Second, through direct intervention by a divine emissary (1:26, 28), that favor is bestowed at God's munificent initiative upon a "nobody": one Mary, from the Galilean backwater village of Nazareth (1:26–27; cf. John 1:46). Mary's fullness of grace is by no means a prerequisite of her visitation by the Holy Spirit; rather, her miraculous conception will confirm that remarkable favor from God that she *already* enjoys (thus the aorist tense of the verb *heuriskō*: "for you *have found* favor"). Third, far from presuming on a privilege so wonderful, Mary responds with unspoken questions and visible terror (Luke 1:29–30a). Fourth, while uncoerced and uninvited, Gabriel's dispatch by God is right on time: six months into Elizabeth's pregnancy (1:24, 26, 36)—when her fetus has developed sufficient capability to leap for joy at Mary's forthcoming voice (1:44)—yet during Mary's betrothal, before its consummation (1:27, 34). The latter point signifies a fifth dimension of God's grace: its manifestation as powerful love, which will culminate in the conception and birth of a son to Mary, astonishingly independent of human impregnation.[13] Sixth, the name to be given that child, Jesus (1:31; a common form of the Hebrew name Joshua, "Yahweh saves"), like Joseph's membership in the house of David and the appearance of a divine envoy named Gabriel, implies an aspect of grace that for Luke is vitally important: though unique in its expression, God's affectionate esteem for Mary is consistent with the saving conduct of the Lord, who has always been with Israel as he is now with Mary (1:28; cf. Luke 1:7 with Gen 18:11; Luke 1:17 with Mal 4:5–6; Luke 1:19, 26 with Dan 8:16; 9:21; Luke 1:27 with 2 Sam 7:12–17; the narrative style of Luke 1:5–2:52 with 1–2 Sam and 1–2 Kgs). As a virgin—a young woman capable of childbearing—Mary of Nazareth also takes an unprecedented place amid a venerable succession of barren women who surprisingly gave birth to many of Israel's leaders: Sarah, to Isaac (Gen 18:9–15; 21:1–7); Rebekah, to Jacob (Gen 25:21–26); Rachel, to Joseph (Gen 30:1, 22–24); Manoah's wife, to Samson (Judg 13:2–25); Hannah, to Samuel (1 Sam 1:1–28); Elizabeth, to John the Baptist (Luke 1:5–25, 57–80).

The Annunciation (1:32–38). The Annunciation articulates the sheer magnitude of God's favor toward Mary, the astounding means of its accomplish-

---

13. Patrick J. Bearsley's comment strikes the bull's-eye: "Mary's virginal conception attests to the omnipotence and transcendence of God, who does not need to work through human agency or in human ways to achieve His effects" ("Mary the Perfect Disciple: A Paradigm for Mariology," *TS* 41 [1980]: 461–504 [here, 496]).

ment, and its varied corroboration. This peasant girl will beget more than merely a son. Jesus is destined for incomparable greatness, to be acclaimed "the son of the highest" (1:32a; see also 8:28; 9:35), to reign without end over the house of Jacob, in fulfillment of God's promise to David (1:33; see 2 Sam 7:16; Isa 9:7; Dan 7:14). When Mary replies that she has not been sexually intimate (Luke 1:34), Gabriel explains that she will conceive by dint of the Holy Spirit; precisely for that reason, "the child begotten will be called holy—Son of God" (1:35). The warrants for this promise are three, couched in reverberant language. (1) "Behold" (*idou*)—Elizabeth, once called sterile, is now in her second trimester: evidence that "not anything said" (*ouk . . . pan rhēma*) will be impossible with God (1:36–37). (2) "Behold" (*idou*)—Mary consents to her station as the Lord's obedient slave (*hē doulē kyriou*; see also 1:48): "May it be for me in accordance with what you have said" (*to rhēma sou*), expressing hope that lingers after Gabriel's departure (and with him, his assurance; 1:38).[14] (3) The angelic confidence espoused by Mary—that with God anything is possible (1:37)—echoes an OT affirmation repeatedly hurled in the teeth of apparent impossibility (Gen 18:14; Job 42:2; Zech 8:6).

Though *hē charis* and its cognates do not appear in Luke 1:32–38, by implication this pericope teaches or reminds us of important characteristics of grace. Grace is God's radical, safeguarding, astonishing creation of new life where none existed.[15] The analogue for the Spirit's promised coming upon (*epeleusetai*) and overshadowing (*episkiasei*) the virgin (1:35) is not Zeus's rape of Leda—an episode justly arousing terror at violation, in stark contrast with the joy of healing (or salvation) of which Mary will sing (1:47). The proper biblical analogues include the cloud that protects mortals from the Almighty's dazzling presence (Exod 24:15–18; Luke 9:34) and the hovering of God's transformative *ruach* (wind, breath, spirit) over the waters of chaos (Gen 1:2; Ps 33:6; Jdt 16:14; 2 Bar. 21.4) and Israel's faithful (1 Sam 16:13; Isa 32:15; Acts 1:8; 2:17). Correlatively, grace elicits trust from the Lord's slaves, both women (Luke 1:38;

---

14. In Acts (2:18; 4:29; 16:17) "slave" refers to any believer who serves under God's rightful authority. Accordingly, the term's application to Mary in Luke 1 by no means sanctions any general subjection of women to men (cf. Luke 7:10) The exegetical issues here are finely discerned by Beverly Roberts Gaventa, *Mary: Glimpses of the Mother of Jesus*, SPNT (Columbia: University of South Carolina Press, 1995), 54.

15. As early as Ps 136:1–9 and continuing through the rabbinic, medieval, and mystical traditions of Judaism, creation itself was regarded as an act of grace. See David R. Blumenthal, "The Place of Faith and Grace in Judaism," in *A Time to Speak: The Evangelical-Jewish Encounter*, ed. A. James Rudin and Marvin R. Wilson (Grand Rapids: Eerdmans, 1987), 104–14, esp. 104–5.

Acts 2:18) and men (2:18). Among those chosen servants in Luke's Gospel is Jesus himself (Luke 22:27), whose receipt of David's throne from the Lord God is no less a gift (1:32; 22:29) than the grace of Mary's pregnancy. Jesus, like his mother, points us to God as the delighted, generous Giver (12:32).

Mary's visitation to Elizabeth (1:39-45, 56). By subtly echoing the elements of Gabriel's visitation to Mary, Mary's visitation to Elizabeth reinforces Luke's presentation of grace. An aura of breathless joy envelops the scene: Mary hastens (1:39); with delight the fetus jumps (1:41, 44); Elizabeth pours out a canticle of praise (*anephōnēsen kraugē megalē*, 1:42; cf. 1 Chr 15:28; 16:4, 5, 42 [LXX]). Confronted with the wonder of divine incursion, Elizabeth concedes her human inadequacy (Luke 1:43) while her unborn child leaps with gladness (1:44; see also Acts 2:26).[16] The strength and percipience of Elizabeth's prophetic song (Luke 1:43-45) derive, not from her own power or discernment, but from her being filled with the Holy Spirit (Luke 1:41; see also 1:67).[17] The formulation of 1:43-45 is significant: tied by phraseology to Israel's past, Elizabeth's blessings of her Lord and his trusting mother proclaim that consummate, end-time joy has *now* broken into their human history (see also 4:21).[18] Such grace explodes the ordinary calendar, creating its own season. In that eschatological light Luke's comment that Mary stayed with Elizabeth for another three months (1:56) is arguably more than a throwaway tag line: Mary remains with her kinswoman, far advanced in pregnancy, until Elizabeth's own time of deliverance is fulfilled (1:57). In Luke's hands pregnancy and childbearing have become allusive signposts for the God-given preparation and completion of Israel's righteousness before God (see Luke 1:6, 14-17, 68-80).

The Magnificat (1:46-55). One of the loveliest specimens of biblical poetry, the Magnificat braids the many threads of grace in Luke 1:26-45. The form of

---

16. "And it came to pass that as Elizabeth heard, . . . the baby jumped" (Luke 1:41: a familiar Semitic construction, especially prevalent in Luke 1–2); "Richly blessed are you among women" (1:42; see also Judg 5:24; Jdt 13:18).

17. Alongside Matt 1:23, the implicit Christology of Luke 1:43 inches toward what would later become the personification of Mary as Theotokos, "the one who gave birth to the one who is God" (not simply *Mater Dei*, "Mother of God"). Neither Luke nor Matthew employs that Greek term, however. The earliest uses of Theotokos cannot be securely traced earlier than the fourth century, when its conceptuality assumed importance amid the Arian controversy (Athanasius, *Orations against the Arians* 3.29). Against the Nestorians, the Council of Ephesus (431) made it binding on all Christian faithful to acclaim Mary as Theotokos. For relevant primary documents, see James Stevenson, ed., *Creeds, Councils and Controversies: Documents Illustrating the History of the Church AD 337–461*, rev. W. H. C. Frend (London: SPCK, 1989), 287–321.

18. For explicit analogies of end-time consummation with a birthing mother, see John 16:21-22; Rom 8:18-25.

its rendition could not be more appropriate to its subject matter: before grace, in all its matchless beauty, prose will not suffice. Mary's affirmation is not an algebraic formula to be solved. It is, it must be, *an aria* to be sung, and the same could be said of the other canticles in Luke 1–2.[19] Moreover, Mary's response is irreducibly one of *faith*.[20] This canticle contains a single verb conjugated in the future tense ("[all] will call [me] fortunate" [*makariousin*], v. 48). Every other verb is conjugated in the present or, more frequently, the aorist (past) tense, referring to what God is doing or has already begun to do. The specific activities for which Mary praises the Lord—the scattering of the haughty (v. 51b), the overthrow of sovereigns and exaltation of the lowly (v. 52), the filling of the hungry with good things and the sending of the rich away empty (v. 53)—are considered *faits accomplis*. Such is the language, not only of faithful hope (see Rom 8:24–25; Heb 11:1), but of a renewed confidence that God *already* is transforming the values by which society conventionally operates (see Rom 12:2). In that connection there is no mistaking the *theocentric* character of the Magnificat: from first to last, this is a song about what God has done and may be trusted to continue. Correlative with his portrait of Jesus, Luke's presentation of Mary is deliberately crafted to point his reader to God.

That God, this hymn tells us, is the One who has "looked upon" (*epeblepsen*) a particular Nazarene girl, which harks back to the ancient sense of *hē charis* as an affectionate, favorable regard of someone. What God has done for Mary falls consistently, albeit unexpectedly, in line with the help God has always promised and supplied Israel, from Abraham (Gen 17:6–8; 18:18; 22:17) through David (2 Sam 7:11–16) and beyond (Luke 1:54–55). Expressly acknowledged, God's constancy is even more subtly suggested in Mary's song by its saturation with OT expressions ("the Mighty One" [Luke 1:49], see Zeph 3:17; "great things" [Luke 1:49], see Deut 11:7; Judg 2:7; God's "strong arm" [Luke 1:51], see Exod 6:6; Deut 26:8; Ps 89:10, 13) and motifs ("God my Savior" [Luke 1:47], see Ps 24:5; Isa 12:2; God's "mercy" [Luke 1:50, 54], see Exod 34:6; 2 Sam 7:15; Israel as God's "servant" [Luke 1:54], see Isa 41:8). Like Hannah, whose canticle over Samuel's birth (1 Sam 2:1–10) is echoed by the Magnificat, Mary openly locates herself among the humble and hungry (Luke 1:48, 52–53) who cannot rely on their own strength but surrender their lives entirely to God's blessings. And like Hannah, the pregnant virgin rhapsodizes her praise of God's holy name

---

19. Theology and musicology embrace in the remarkable study of Samuel Terrien, *The Magnificat: Musicians as Biblical Interpreters* (New York: Paulist, 1995).

20. This point receives thoughtful exploration in Gail R. O'Day, "Singing Woman's Song: A Hermeneutic of Liberation," *CurTM* 12 (1985): 203–10.

(Luke 1:49; see also Ps 111:9). Mary's spirit (*to pneuma*) finds gladness in God; her inmost self (*hē psychē*) magnifies the Lord (Luke 1:46; see also Ps 69:30; Sir 43:31).[21]

The Concerned Yet Mistaken Parent (Luke 2:41–52; Mark 3:31–35; John 2:1–12)

The next three pericopes stem from different, probably independent traditions about Jesus: his youth, his mature ministry, and his passion. An intriguingly common denominator among them all, however, is the sketch of Mary by Luke, Mark, and John.[22]

Luke 2:41–52. The conclusion of Luke's infancy narrative recounts the legend of young Jesus's discovery in the temple by his distraught parents. So familiar is that story, so memorable its punchline ("Did you not know that I must be in my Father's house?"), that we might overlook Luke's interesting details about Jesus's parents, especially his mother.

That picture is complex, its brevity notwithstanding. Consistent with his earlier portrayals of Mary and Joseph (2:21–25, 39) and of Zechariah and Elizabeth (1:6, 59–64), Luke emphasizes that Jesus's parents were religiously observant and obedient to God's commands: thus, their visit to Jerusalem at Passover during Jesus's twelfth year is one of many that they customarily made every year (2:41–42). Understandably, upon realizing that their child was not among them during their return home, they search for him: first, among the entourage to Nazareth (2:39, 44); eventually, back in Jerusalem (2:45). Thus far, Jesus's parents appear as dutiful as we have grown to appreciate them in Luke 1:26–2:40. But what kind of parents, we may justifiably wonder, would travel a full day before confirming that their (miraculously) firstborn and—so far as we can tell from Luke 2—only son was *not* among their caravan (2:44)? And, when they get back to Jerusalem, why does it take Jesus's parents *three days* of searching before they find him in the temple (2:46)—whose environs, after all, child and parents would have visited, if their excursion's original purpose was celebration of the Passover? Upon recovering the lost

---

21. Brown, *Birth of the Messiah*, 358–60, thoroughly tabulates the OT background of Luke 1:46–55. The fulfillment of God's promises and Israel's restoration are primary themes in the Magnificat and other canticles in Luke 1–2, as demonstrated by Stephen Farris, *The Hymns of Luke's Infancy Narratives: Their Origin, Meaning and Significance*, JSNTSup 9 (Sheffield: JSOT, 1985), esp. 151–60.

22. Mark 3:31–35 is probably the source of Luke 8:19–21. The traditions preserved in Luke 2:41–52 and John 2:1–12 are without parallel in the other Gospels.

child, they—Mary, in particular—express astonishment and torment by his conduct (2:47–48). By that time, however, Luke's readers may be forgiven for feeling somewhat the same about the parents.

Surprisingly, our doubts about their alacrity are corroborated by young Jesus himself. To translate 2:49 literally unto woodenness: "How is it that you sought me? You didn't know—did you—that in the [matters] of my Father I must be [involved]?" Contrary to conventional renderings of this verse, Jesus's question is framed by Luke in a way implying that he didn't expect his parents to be any more discerning than they turned out to be—nor, for that matter, more discerning than the temple-teachers, amazed by Jesus's perspicacity and his answers (2:47). The parents' ignorance of their child's ultimate allegiance to God is in no measure dissipated by Jesus's questions of them: "Yet they did not understand the utterance [*to rhēma*; see also 1:37–38] that he spoke to them" (2:50). That the evangelist means not to suggest sheer cockiness of a precocious youngster is immediately confirmed by Luke's affirmations of Jesus's obedience to his parents, and his progressive wisdom, maturity, favor—grace (*chariti*)—among God and people (2:51a, 52; see also 1 Sam 2:26; Isa 11:12; Luke 1:80). That grace, however, does not depend on Mary's being an extraordinarily responsible, pious, or perceptive mother, without need of pondering "these things" (again, *ta rhēmata*, 2:51b; see also 2:19). Indeed, one of the points made by Luke's narration of this remarkable story is that, through Jesus, God's grace is truly bestowed, from the beginning and consistently, on those who, like Mary, misunderstand or reproach it—who, in fact, tend to look for grace everywhere but where it must be found.[23]

Mark 3:31–35. This is another pericope about the family in search of Jesus (here, an adult). This story, like Luke 2:41–52, has been rubbed smooth by its familiarity. Standing outside his home, impeded by a great crowd, Jesus's mother and brothers send for him.[24] On being informed that they are seeking him, Jesus redefines his brother, sister, and mother as anyone who does the will of God.

What to us may ring as a charming religious platitude would have landed with a thud on first-century Jewish and Roman ears. No social unit of antiquity was more basic than the family, no ties more binding than those of kinship.

---

23. Luke's last reference to Mary strikes the same chord: Jesus's mother and brothers remained in devoted company with the Eleven in Jerusalem, after Jesus's ascension (Acts 1:14).

24. In spite of tortured attempts by some commentators to translate *hoi adelphoi autou* as "his cousins" rather than "his brothers," Mark is obviously ignorant of the later doctrine of Mary's perpetual virginity.

Jesus's rebuff of his mother and brothers, instead esteeming strangers obedient to God's will, is reminiscent of young Jesus's reply to his mother that both she and his earthly father ought to expect finding Jesus involved in his (Heavenly) Father's business (Luke 2:48, 49b).[25] In 3:31–35 Mark seems to go out of his way to distance Jesus from his family. The latter are said to be standing outside (*exō*, 3:32)—the space occupied, as Mark's readers soon will learn, by those who see but do not see, who hear but do not understand (4:11–12). In 3:32 his mother and brothers are also reportedly "searching for" (*zētousin*) Jesus. Those who do that in Mark usually have hostile intentions (see 8:11, 12; 11:18; 12:12; 14:1, 11, 55)—as sinister as "those close to him" (*hoi par' autou*), "his family" (NRSV), who in 3:21 set out to seize Jesus because they think him mad. If the family members in 3:31 are not identical with the posse in 3:20, Mark closely associates both groups, not only with each other, but also with the scribes from Jerusalem who consider Jesus demonically possessed (3:22, 30). For those opponents Jesus spins a web of parables, one of which envisions the collapse of a house divided against itself (3:23–26).[26] Although they probably used Mark as one of their sources, Matthew and Luke appear to have been troubled by this division of Jesus and his family: both the First and the Third evangelists soften the wording of Mark 3:31–35 (cf. Matt 12:46–50; Luke 8:19–21) and separate that story from the Beelzebul controversy (cf. Matt 12:22–32; Luke 11:14–23; 12:10).

Mark's intention is not scrupulously clear; Jesus is, after all, speaking parabolically (3:23). Read in the light of 6:1–6a, the only other passage in Mark referring to Jesus's mother and brothers (and sisters), 3:31–35 uncomfortably suggests that those seemingly closest to Jesus—hometown acquaintances, religious leaders, even his mother, siblings, and finally the Twelve (8:31-33; 9:32–41; 10:35–45)—are not thereby assured of understanding him. Prophets enjoy some honor, except among their relatives and in their own homes (6:4).

John 2:1–12. The miracle of the wine at the wedding in Cana is another episode in which the mother of Jesus (never named in John) plays a minor but complex role. Although the story begins as though Jesus's mother is going to be its principal antagonist, even by 2:1 the reader of the Fourth Gospel knows

---

25. More blatant and equally countercultural is Jesus's astonishing elevation of preaching God's sovereignty over a survivor's responsibility to bury his father (Matt 8:21–22 // Luke 7:59–60).

26. Many commentators interpret Mark 3:19b–35 as one of that Evangelist's characteristic "intercalations" or "sandwiches" of traditions. See, for example, the discussions by Morna D. Hooker, *The Gospel according to Saint Mark*, BNTC (Peabody: Hendrickson, 1991), 114; and C. Clifton Black, *Mark*, ANTC (Nashville: Abingdon, 2011), 108–9.

that characters like John the Baptist, priests and Levites, and the disciples are introduced for the purpose of pointing up Jesus's significance (see John 1:6–8, 15, 19–28, 29–34, 35–39, 40–42, 45–49). So, too, does Jesus's mother function in 2:1–12.[27]

Perhaps the most intriguing feature of Mary's conversations with others in this passage is the repeated, odd disjunction between what she says and what is said to her. When the wine for the wedding guests is depleted, Jesus's mother does not explicitly request that he do anything about it; hers is the simpler observation, "They haven't got wine" (2:3). As is characteristic of Jesus in this Gospel (see, e.g., 4:10–14, 47–50; 16:16–19), his reply seems aloof, even irrelevant to his mother's statement: "What [is that] to me and you, woman? My hour has not yet come" (2:4). By different means, John creates a wedge of incomprehension between son and mother: Jesus's sovereign resistance to human, even maternal, claims on him, which we have also observed in Luke and in Mark. Instead of replying to her son, Mary says to the waiters, "Whatever he tells you, do [it]" (John 2:5): a command equally lacking clear justification. Jesus's instructions to the stewards are to fill some ritual jars with water, then to draw out some of that water for the headwaiter (2:6–8). The story ends, riddled with as many disjunctions as opened it. The servants knew where the water came from, but it's not clear that *they* know of its transformation into wine (2:9). The headwaiter knows that he is tasting the best wine in the house, though *he* does not know where it came from (2:9–10a). The bridegroom's response to his wine-steward's compliment (2:9b–10) is left unreported, but from John's narration there is no reason to suppose that the groom knows what the headwaiter is talking about, or *anything* of what has transpired. The Evangelist's penultimate explanation—that Jesus's activity at Cana was the first of his signs (*ta sēmeia*) that revealed his glory (*hē doxa autou*, the property of divinity [2:11a; see 1:14; 12:41])—seems odd on its face: what should we make of a revelation that virtually no one has recognized? This tale's real conclusion, 2:11b–12, fits the jagged pieces into place. Jesus's ambiguous signs have profoundly revelatory value *for his disciples*: those who believed in him and abided (*emeinan*) with him (see also 1:12; 15:4–10). For those in John without faith in Jesus, his signs are not convincing (2:23–25; 11:47–48); for those who

---

27. For extended defense of this proposal, see Barnabas Lindars, *The Gospel of John*, NCB (Grand Rapids: Eerdmans, 1972), 579–80; Rudolf Schnackenburg, *The Gospel according to St. John* (New York: Crossroad, 1985), 3:274–79; Raymond E. Brown, *The Death of the Messiah: From Gethsemane to the Grave*, ABRL (New York: Doubleday, 1994), 2:1019–26; Francis J. Moloney, *The Gospel of John*, SP 4 (Collegeville, MN: Liturgical, 1998), 503–4.

already believe—including John's readers—those signs evoke and corroborate their faith (4:50–54; 20:30–31).

In which camp does Mary stand? After 2:5 she disappears from the wedding gala. In 2:12 she reappears among Jesus's brothers and disciples who stay (or abide) with him in Capernaum. Her presence there is not unimpeachable testimony to her own faith in Jesus, since by 7:1–10 even his brothers do not believe in him. Yet John hints that Jesus's mother will fare better as a believer. Although it is not clear that she understands her son's reference to "his hour" (of crucifixion: 7:30; 8:20; 12:23, 27; 13:1; 17:1), that comment mysteriously prompts her to spur others to do whatever Jesus tells them. Since in John's Gospel the Son does nothing other than what he sees the Father doing (5:19), to do what Jesus commands is critically important for his disciples (15:10–17). Mary may no more comprehend Jesus as "the gift of God" (*hē dōrea*) than does the Samaritan woman at Jacob's well (4:10), but the subsequent reactions of both women to Jesus suggest an incipient faith in him capable of amplification (see 4:15, 19, 29; 19:25). And while John leaves unexplained the symbolism of so much wine ("twenty or thirty gallons," 2:6), Frank Kermode's suggestion is intriguing: "Perhaps it is the grace beyond grace [1:16], the messianic wine of being that replaces the inferior wine of the Torah, which [for John] is appropriate only to becoming."[28]

A Vulnerable Woman and Mother (Galatians 4:1–7; Matthew 1–2; John 19:25b–27)

Galatians 4:1–7. The NT's remaining references to Mary are comparatively slender. In Galatians 4:1–7 Paul contrasts the human condition of bondage to the world's enslaving forces (*ta stoicheia tou kosmou*), including the law, with that of liberation from it. At a time of divine selection, God broke into this disarrayed, oppressive cosmos through the agency of his own Son, to snap the shackles of our enslavement (4:4; see also Rom 8:3). God completed this invasion by sending his Son's own Spirit, to achieve our adoption as sons (*hē huiothesia*): our transfer from this world's enslavement into a new life of incorporation into the Son (*ho huios*). God's Son was himself "born of woman, born under law" (Gal 4:4): Jesus was fully human and utterly vulnerable (see also

---

28. Kermode, "John," in *The Literary Guide to the Bible*, ed. Robert Alter and Frank Kermode (Cambridge: Harvard University Press, 1987), 449. In support of Kermode's reading, see John 1:45 (Jesus as the fulfillment of Jewish tradition) and Jeremiah 31:12; Amos 9:13–14 (abundance in the age to come).

Phil 2:7), subject to all the tyrannies of this life—including death—experienced by every human "born of woman" (Job 14:1; 15:14; 25:4; Matt 11:11 // Luke 7:28). To draw from these metaphors an implication neither central nor foreign to Paul's argument: the woman by whom God's Son was born was herself "born of woman," equally enslaved as every human after the fall and equally emancipated from that slavery by the grace of Christ in which redeemed humanity now lives (Gal 2:20–21).[29]

Matthew 1–2. In the Lukan infancy narrative Mary is a primary actor and Joseph, her mute partner; in Matthew's birth narrative those roles are precisely reversed. Mary's function in Matthew 1–2 is twofold. First, in the genealogy of Jesus (Matt 1:1–17), she is identified as one among five women (vv. 3, 5a, 5b, 6b, 16a) in an otherwise conventional patrilineage.[30] Second, under the circumstances attending Jesus's conception and birth, Mary and her infant son constitute the silent center around which whirls a cyclone of legal obligations (1:18–20), angelic guidance in dreams (1:20–25; 2:12–15, 19–23), foreign homage (2:1–2, 9–12), celestial portents (2:2b, 9–10), political intrigue (2:3–4, 7–8, 13, 16, 22), and mass infanticide (2:16), all held together by scriptural fulfillment (1:22–23; 2:5b–6, 15b–18, 23b).[31]

As regards Mary, at least three themes recur throughout these joyous yet terrifying pericopes. First, by her appearance in Jesus's genealogy and her virginal conception of Christ through the Holy Spirit, Mary exemplifies the *astonishing, personal novelty* with which God breaks into human history, along Israel's familiar paths in particular. Second, because of those irregularities, Mary is presented by Matthew as the last in a series of Hebraic-Jewish women who have been *threatening* to the conventional order of marriages and politics and have been *threatened* by it. The second part of that theme is most vividly dramatized by the upright (*dikaios*) Joseph and the murderous Herod, both of whom intend without success to dispose of Mary and her offspring in very different ways (1:19–20; 2:13, 16). Third, while Mary and her child are repeatedly protected by God's agents, *divine providence comes at high cost*. The gifts lavished on the newborn Jesus by jubilant Gentile Magi (2:10–11) are mirrored by

---

29. For an incisive exegesis of Galatians 4:1–7, which discovers therein "nothing less than the theological center of the entire letter . . . , the good news of Paul's letter to the Galatians," consult J. Louis Martyn, *Galatians: A New Translation with Introduction and Commentary* AB 33A (New York and London: Doubleday, 1997), 384–408; quotation, 388.

30. The heavily controverted reasons for the inclusion of women in the Matthean genealogy are thoroughly explained and assessed by Brown, *Birth of the Messiah*, 71–74.

31. M. Eugene Boring, "The Gospel of Matthew: Introduction, Commentary, and Reflections," *NIB* 8 (1995): 151–54, offers a superb analysis of Matthew's use of scripture.

disconsolate Jewish mothers whose hands drip with the blood of their infant sons (2:16–17). Both these tableaux receive strikingly apt commentary in the two stanzas of Luke's Nunc Dimittis: in the child Jesus devout Simeon sees the Lord's salvation of all peoples (2:25–32) and a sword that will slice through Israel, not excepting Mary's own soul (2:33–35).

John 19:25b–27. Here we cannot review the history of exegesis of John 19:25b–27, much less resolve the perennial question of whom or what may be symbolized therein by Jesus's mother.[32] Since throughout the Fourth Gospel his mother (2:1–12) and the disciple whom he loved (13:21–30; 20:1–10; 21:7, 20–24) have neither name nor identity apart from their particular relation to Jesus, those figures at the foot of the cross are probably important for John's understanding of a new relationship created by the now crucified/glorified Christ. In 2:1–12, Jesus's association with his mother was attenuated because his hour had not yet come (2:4). From that it seems to follow that, in 19:25b–27, Jesus, "the one who comes from above" (3:31), whose hour of exaltation has arrived (3:13–15; 12:23; 13:1; 17:1), is revealing (*ide*, behold; see also 1:29; 3:26; 19:14) his creation of a new family, transcending this world's kindred, whose essence is loving discipleship that abides in the Son and in the Father (12:32–33; 13:34–35; 14:20–21; 15:12–17). The Fourth Evangelist is not in the least interested to trace the development of faith within Jesus's natural mother. John is profoundly concerned with the one-of-a-kind Son who graciously reveals the loving Father who sent him, the God by whose will believers in Christ are begotten (1:12, 16–18; 3:5–8, 16; 5:19–24; 6:60–65; 10:11–18; 14:6–14; 17:20–26). Accordingly, in this Gospel Mary does not beget Jesus, who is "from above, not of this world" (8:23; see also 1:1–5, 9–14). The mother of Jesus, like all disciples, is herself begotten "not of blood, neither of fleshly will nor of man's will, but of God" (1:13).

Grace Viewed through a Marian Prism

Across the history of Christian doctrine, the mother of Jesus has played many roles: immaculately conceived Daughter of Zion, ever-virginal Second Eve, Theotokos and Queen of Heaven, Paragon of Chastity, *Mater Dolorosa* ("Mother

---

32. The favorite proposals: New Eve, Lady Zion who begets a new people, Mother Church whose baptism begets Christians, Spiritual Mother of heavenly nurturance. For survey and assessment, consult Schnackenburg, *Gospel according to St. John*, 3:279–82; Brown, *Death of the Messiah*, 2:1021–25.

of Sorrows") and Mediatrix, among others.[33] More recently, Mary has been viewed as the disciple par excellence, the feminine essence of the Holy Spirit enfleshed as a woman, and a bridge-figure within the ecumenical movement.[34] Without intending to imply its superiority over all other estimates, how might we limn Mary's figure in the NT as an exemplar of grace? For convenience our conclusions may be categorized theologically and anthropologically.

The Truth about God

First, like other biblical personalities, Mary's experience reveals that *grace is the intrinsic nature of God:* God's utterly gratuitous disposition of merciful favor upon his creatures (Luke 1:28, 30; 12:32). For this reason, every passage examined in this chapter has been *theocentrically* oriented, concentrated on God's will (Mark 3:35), business (Luke 2:49), and magnificent works (Luke 1:46-55)— especially the sending of his Son for human redemption (Gal 4:4). Not Mary, not even Jesus, has been the focal figure in these vignettes: both the Son and his mother direct attention away from themselves toward God, who is supernally gracious (Matt 1:23; Luke 1:32, 45, 47; Gal 4:6).

Second, grace is *an eschatological reality*, transcendently invading this world in God's own appointed time (Luke 1:26, 36, 43-45; John 2:4; 19:25b-27; Gal 4:4-7). Thus, it is radically free from all human instigation (Luke 1:34-35), unfettered by the bounds of human possibility (Matt 1:11; Luke 1:37), and hostile to this world's enslaving powers (Gal 4:3) and wicked principalities (Matt 2:3-4, 13, 16, 22).[35]

Third, all of these stories attest to *the coherence of God's favor toward Mary with that divine mercy that Israel's children have always known*. This, I think, holds even in pericopes suggesting that the law has been commandeered by nefarious forces (Gal 4:1-9; see also Rom 8:1-8) or surpassed by Christ's coming (John 2:1-12). Nestled in the temple (Luke 2:46-49) as the fulfillment of God's promises to Abraham's posterity (Luke 1:32-33, 43-45, 54-55), Mary's son is the saving climax to which Israel's history has always been unfolding (Matt 1:1-17, 22-23; 2:5, 15, 17-18, 23).[36]

---

33. See Jaroslav Pelikan, *Mary through the Centuries: Her Place in the History of Culture* (New Haven and London: Yale University Press, 1996).

34. Bearsley, "Mary the Perfect Disciple"; Bertrand Ruby, *Mary, the Faithful Disciple* (New York and Mahwah, NJ: Paulist, 1985).

35. Tina Beattie, *Rediscovering Mary: Insights from the Gospels* (Ligouri, MO: Triumph Books, 1995).

36. David Flusser, "Mary and Israel," in David Flusser, Jaroslav Pelikan, and Justin Lang,

Fourth, *God's grace is radically creative and magnanimously loving.* It preserves the Davidic dynasty from all threats to its continuance (Matt 1:11, 19; 2:13, 22), generating extraordinary life, holy and loving, in Mary's womb (Luke 1:32-38) and at Jesus's cross (John 19:25b-27). Grace has already subverted the norms by which this world lives (Luke 1:46-53; Gal 4:1-7). In an evil world that prefers a corrupted status quo, grace comes not without cost to Israel's children (Matt 2:16-18; Luke 2:34-35), including God's own Son (John 3:16).

The Truth about Ourselves

Mary's encounters with God's grace exemplify its incursion into human life. First, standing before God's unmitigated generosity toward us, we realize our basic frailty (Gal 4:4), poverty (Luke 1:49), and constant dependence on God for protection (Matt 1:20; 2:12-14, 20-22). That is how grace is recognized for what it truly is: no favor we can curry, notwithstanding our delusions to the contrary, but God's unstinting care for us whose lives are as *radically dependent on divine mercy* as that grace is radically characteristic of God.[37]

Second, *God's grace restructures human relationships and redefines our fundamental loyalties.* No longer are we enslaved to sin, death, and the powers of this age; we have been adopted by God and incorporated into his Son (Gal 4:1-7). This ontological shift means that the claims of our human families are subordinate to God's will and Christ's command of love among that new family of disciples created by his glorious death (Matt 1:18-19; Mark 3:31-35; Luke 2:41-52; John 2:1-4, 19:25b-27).[38]

Third, like Mary, *our response to grace is inevitably ambivalent*: a tumultuous confusion of shock and acquiescence (Luke 1:29; 1:38), gladness and consternation (Luke 1:47; 2:48), remarkable faith and equally glaring presumptuousness (Luke 1:46-55; Mark 3:21, 31-32), unexpected insight (John 2:5, 11) and baffled rumination (Luke 2:19, 50-51). By its very nature God's grace does not depend on the resolution of our blessed perplexities. Through the Spirit

---

Mary: Images of the Mother of Jesus in Jewish and Christian Perspective (Philadelphia: Fortress, 1986), 7-16; John Macquarrie, *Mary for All Christians* (Grand Rapids: Eerdmans, 1990).

37. In this estimate at least, some Roman Catholic and Protestant theologians appear to be converging in agreement: cf. McBrien, *Catholicism*, 1106-7, with Schubert M. Ogden, *The Point of Christology* (San Francisco: Harper & Row, 1982).

38. None of the Marian texts we have examined offers aid and comfort to modern Marcionites. The unity of grace and law in the OT is probed in Jacob M. Myers, *Grace and Torah* (Philadelphia: Fortress, 1975), and Ronald M. Hals, *Grace and Faith in the Old Testament* (Minneapolis: Augsburg, 1980).

God even unties our tongues to articulate our gratitude and ongoing need for grace (Luke 1:41–42, 64–67; 2:27; Gal 4:6).

Fourth, and most essentially, grace means that *God esteems us*, as he regarded Mary, *with delight and deep affection* (1:28, 30). As God's creatures, each of us is as particularly remembered by the Creator as every ordinary male and extraordinary female in Matthew's genealogy (1:1–17). In God's eyes we are beautiful in our capacity to magnify the Lord (Luke 1:46); from the cross Jesus knows that our loving discipleship completes everything intended by God's own love for us (John 19:27–28).[39]

By Mary we are reminded that our inherent neediness is answered by God's intrinsic mercy; that our allegiance, like Israel's, belongs ultimately to God; that our bewilderment is a by-product of the new thing God is doing; that our loveliness never fades in the eyes of our Creator, who is creative love. In honor of Mary, who beside us reaches for God, the prayers of later piety may not, after all, be so far removed from her graceful image in scripture.

Hail Mary, full of grace, the Lord is with thee. Blessed art thou amongst women, and blessed is the fruit of thy womb, Jesus. Holy Mary, Mother of God, pray for us sinners, now, and at the hour of our death. Amen.	Having brought forth unto us the cause and giver of good, From your great abundance of kindness, Pour forth upon us all; For all is possible, For you who carried the Christ, Who is mighty in power: You, who are blessed of God.

---

39. See John Navone's *Toward a Theology of Beauty* (Collegeville, MN: Liturgical, 1996) for a thoughtful attempt to reclaim God's primary delight in creation's beauty as a basis for Christian theology.

CHAPTER 13

The Church in the Synoptic Gospels and Acts

> Jesus announced the kingdom, and it was the church that came.
>
> —Alfred Loisy

ALTHOUGH LOISY'S OBSERVATION HAS BEEN REMEMBERED with rueful irony, he intended to state a sociological principle to which the church, like every institution, is subject: perpetual adaptation to conditions that are ever changing.[1] Thus, he continued: "[The church] came, enlarging the form of the gospel."[2] This chapter investigates the ways in which such inevitable acclimatization is documented in some of Christianity's earliest, most influential writings.

THE BASIC BACKGROUND

By the sixth century BCE we can document the existence of associations comprising members with shared interests who had joined with others and had regularized their organization, leadership and procedures. Such groups were made up of craftsmen, adherents of mystery religions, and students attached to such philosophers as Pythagoras or Epicurus.[3] Second Temple Jews, most of whom were members by birth who gathered in synagogues (Aram. *knst'*) throughout the Diaspora, constitute another fraternal organization; within

---

1. Alfred Loisy, *The Gospel and the Church*, ed. Bernard B. Scott, LJS (Philadelphia: Fortress, 1970), 166.
2. Loisy, *Gospel and the Church*, 166.
3. R. Alan Culpepper, *The Johannine School: An Evaluation of the Johannine-School Hypothesis Based on an Investigation of the Nature of Ancient Schools*, SBLDS 26 (Missoula, MT: Scholars Press, 1975); Walter Burkert, *Ancient Mystery Cults* (Cambridge: Harvard University Press, 1987); Onno M. van Nijf, *The Civic World of Professional Associations in the Roman East*, DMAHA 17 (Amsterdam: Gieben, 1997).

their circle, subgroups such as trade guilds and burial societies were also formed.[4] For everyday Romans or Hellenistic Jews, the earliest churches of the first century CE would have resembled such voluntary associations. For information on how these groups were beginning to regard themselves, our best sources are the NT's Pauline Letters, the Johannine literature, and the Synoptic Gospels and Acts. It is on the latter that this chapter concentrates.

Mark (c. 70 CE)

The briefest and probably earliest of the Synoptics, Mark offers a picture of Jesus's followers, their conduct and responsibilities, only four decades removed from Jesus himself. That portrait is foundational for those of Matthew and Luke, both of which drew upon Mark as a primary source.

As in all the Gospels, abstract reflection on the church is absent from Mark, but its presentation of Jesus's disciples and the character of discipleship stands near its front and center. Understanding Jesus Christ is this evangelist's preoccupation; grasping what commitment to this Messiah entails is ancillary to and informative of Mark's Christology. Early in the Gospel (1:16–20)—instantly after Jesus's baptism, temptation and introductory announcement of good news (1:9–15)—Jesus calls four fishermen (the brothers Simon and Andrew; the brothers James and John), who immediately drop their equipment and follow him. In 1:30 we learn that Simon has a mother-in-law. Unless he was widowed, which Paul implicitly contradicts (1 Cor 9:5), Simon left behind both business and family to follow this unknown Galilean prophet. In 2:14 Levi, a toll collector, a Jew employed by Roman overlords, answers the same summons—"Follow me" (cf. 1:17)—and joins the other five. In the following chapter (3:13–19a) Jesus rounds out his entourage to twelve, "summon[ing] those whom he wanted, [who] came to him . . . to be with him, and to be sent out to preach and have power to cast out demons"[5] (vv. 13–14). (Curiously, Levi is not mentioned among them; Matthew 9:9 and 10:3 refer to the tax collector as "Matthew.") Apart from Andrew and Simon, nicknamed "Peter" (Gk: *Petros*; Aram: *kefa'*, "Cephas"; see Gal 2:7–11), and the sons of Zebedee, the only other member of this dozen who reappears in Mark and about whom we learn anything is Judas Iscariot, "the one

---

4. Shaye J. D. Cohen, *The Beginnings of Jewishness: Boundaries, Varieties, Uncertainties* (Berkeley: University of California Press, 1999); Lee I. Levine, *The Ancient Synagogue: The First Thousand Years* (New Haven: Yale University Press, 2000).

5. AT, here and throughout.

who betrayed him" (Mark 3:19a). Elsewhere in Mark "the Twelve" are mentioned only nine times (4:10; 6:7; 9:35; 10:32; 11:1; 14:10, 17, 20, 43), usually in the setup or recounting of the passion narrative. More often than not, Mark refers to them as "[Jesus's] disciples" (*mathētai*):[6] 2:15–16, 18, 23; 3:7; 4:34; 5:31; 6:1, 35, 41, 45; 7:2, 5, 17; 8:1, 4, 6, 10, 27, 33–34; 9:14, 18, 28, 31; 10:10, 13, 23, 46; 11:1, 14; 12:43; 13:1; 14:12–14, 16, 32; 16:7)—although, as we shall see, "the Twelve" and "his disciples" are overlapping though not coterminous companies.

From these details one may tease out Mark's fundamental attitude toward the disciples and discipleship.

The circuit of discipleship. Discipleship is, primarily, a loop of "calling" and "following," both geographically and figuratively. Jesus is a figure so compelling that addressees accept their vocation on the strength of his sheer utterance. Unlike later rabbis, who accepted applicant pupils as apprentices (cf. m. 'Abot 1), Jesus takes complete initiative in forming his followers, acting more like Elijah, who cast his mantle on Elisha (1 Kgs 19:19). Others in Mark who want to accompany Jesus or to inherit eternal life are either sent home to proclaim the Lord's goodness (5:18–20) or are disqualified by their refusal of stringent discipleship (10:17–22).

The costs of discipleship. Already in Mark's earliest chapters we see that following Jesus carries significant social, financial and political sacrifices: Simon's separation from his family, Levi's relinquishment of imperial retainer, James and John's quitting a small business organization. (Their father's "hired hands" [*tōn misthōtōn*] suggest that the brothers have resigned from The Zebedee & Sons Fishing Company.)

Association with Jesus. The basic responsibilities of Jesus's adherents are "that they be with him," serving as his emissaries in preaching repentance and in exorcism (3:14–15), to which is later added therapeutic anointing of the sick (6:12–13). In other words, Jesus's disciples are expected to do just what their teacher does (cf. 1:21–2:12; 3:1–12; 5:1–43; 6:5), just as he did it: itinerantly, altogether dependent on others' hospitality (6:7–11). Likewise, Jesus's disciples are no more scrupulously observant of some religious conventions than he is (2:1–3:6).

The selection of the Twelve. No reason is offered for Jesus's selection of a dozen among his closest cohort. To infer from a saying preserved in Matthew

---

6. Hellenistic influence on the Gospels is suggested by this familiar nomenclature. While some philosophers styled their adherents as "students" (Plato, *Protag.* 315a–316b, 349a; Xenophon, *Mem.* 1.6.3), the Hebrew equivalent, *talmid*, is very rare in Hebrew scripture (1 Chr. 25:8) and the DSS. After 200 CE (m. 'Abot 1.1), *talmidim* becomes a more common denotation for a rabbi's pupils.

(19:28) and in Luke (22:30), it likely harks back to Israel's original twelve tribes (Gen 49:28; Exod 24:4; 28:21; 39:14; Josh 4:4; Ezek 47:13).

The constituency of the Twelve. This was a motley group. Although we know from Mark and the other Synoptics little or nothing about most of the Twelve, we do learn that, beyond Levi (in cahoots with the Roman Empire), Jesus also called "Simon the Cananaean" (3:18): a description possibly deriving from an Aramaic term for "zeal," either religious (cf. Rom 12:8, 11; Phil 3:6) or revolutionary (cf. Luke 6:15; Acts 1:15). Those associates of Jesus of whom we learn most in Mark are Peter, James, and John—who, though they appear to make up Jesus's inner circle (5:37; 9:2; 13:3; 14:33), repeatedly fumble (8:32; 10:35–41; 14:29, 33, 37; 14:54, 66–72)—and Judas Iscariot, the traitor (3:19a; cf. 14:10, 43). These Twelve were not selected for their like-mindedness, ability, or heroism.

Quite the opposite. A supreme irony in this extraordinarily ironic Gospel is that Jesus's closest companions are "cowards" (the most straightforward translation of *deiloi* in 4:40), lacking in insight, compassion (6:34–35; 8:2–4) or understanding (6:52; 7:18; 8:16–17, 21). They are incompetent because they fail to pray (9:17–18, 28–29), are clannish (9:38), supercilious (10:13–14), fearful (4:38; 6:50) and faithless (4:40; 9:19). They shamelessly jockey for power (9:33–34) and are stupidly self-aggrandizing (10:35–42), blustering (14:29), and yet baffled (14:40). Were it not so serious, their ineptitude would be comical. Having been plainly instructed three times in cross-bearing service for others (8:31, 34–9:1; 9:30–31, 35–37; 10:33–34, 43–45), immediately the Twelve repudiate Jesus's teachings (8:32–33; 9:33–34; 10:35–41). Repeatedly Jesus warns them to "stay awake" (13:33, 37; 14:34); within days, even minutes, of their master's moment of crisis, they are snoring away (14:37–41a). The only person in Mark whom Jesus addresses as "Satan" is Peter, because Simon tempts him away from the path he must take (*dei*: 8:31), luring the one he believes to be the Messiah away from God, toward humans' disposition to save themselves (8:29, 33; cf. 10:45; 14:24). "Get behind me" (8:33) is a double entendre: Jesus disavows Peter's reproach while reminding all disciples (8:33) of their proper place: *following* Jesus. At the very moment that Jesus, on trial for his life, owns his messianic identity and is sentenced to die (14:61–64), Peter, accosted by a servant-girl, forfeits his inmost self (*psychē*) by renouncing his discipleship: "I don't know this fellow you're talking about" (14:71); "I neither know nor understand what you're saying" (14:68; cf. 8:35–37). That's another double entendre. Peter simultaneously lies through his teeth while telling more truth than he realizes: throughout Mark neither he nor his confreres have understood Jesus. Judas triggers his teacher's arrest (14:18b–21), but every one of them at table for their last supper falls away, just as

Jesus predicted and Scripture ratified (14:27; cf. Zech 13:7). While Peter rightly asserts that they have left everything and followed him (10:28), not once in this Gospel does Jesus acclaim of them a faith they never express.

Mark coats this irony with another layer: mostly nameless nobodies recognize in Jesus the power of God's kingdom to relieve them and their loved ones of virtually hopeless affliction. These exhibit faith (*hē pistis*, which may also be translated as "belief," even "trust"): a paralytic and his friends (2:5), a woman who for twelve years has suffered chronic menstruation (5:34), once-blind Bartimaeus (10:52; cf. 5:36; 7:29). The latter acts as a disciple should: ignoring others' rebukes (10:48) and "throwing off his cloak, he sprang up, came to Jesus ... [,] immediately regained sight, and followed him on the way" (10:50, 52b). After Jesus's death, we learn that Mary Magdalene, Mary the mother of James the younger and Joses, Salome and many other women had followed Jesus from Galilee to Jerusalem and ministered to him en route (15:40–41). Like their unnamed "sister" in Bethany (14:3–9), the two Marys and Salome intend to anoint Jesus's body for burial (16:1), honoring him as the disciples of John the Baptist did after his death but the Twelve did not (6:29; 14:50–51).

Mark's evident intent is not to snub the Twelve but to extend the circle of Jesus's disciples to others (9:38–39) and to demonstrate just how hard it is to deny oneself, take up the cross, and follow him. This community's boundaries are unusually fluid—"Whoever is not against us is for us" (9:40)—but the responsibilities of faith can be terrifying: "I believe; help my unbelief!" (9:24; cf. 16:7–8). Both of these challenges converge in Jesus's discourse to four of the Twelve on the Mount of Olives: the good news must be preached to all the nations (Gentiles) under circumstances of harassment for Jesus's sake (13:9–13). As intimated by the repeated injunctions for the Son of Man's suffering and his disciples' self-sacrifice (8:31–9:1; 9:31–50; 10:32–45), Mark's Gospel was written for a community of Jesus's followers undergoing persecution.[7] Some may have held fast, paying the ultimate price (13:12b–13); others, exemplified by Peter, may have broken down under pressure (14:72). Hope for rescue is not futile (13:26–27); Jesus delivers on his promise of fidelity to Peter and others who have defected (14:28; 16:7). From beginning to end, Jesus came to call the sick and the sinners, not those healthy and righteous (2:17), and things that are humanly impossible are not beyond God's capability (10:27). But the way of the cross, which ends in abundant life beyond imagining (10:29–30), is fraught with constant perils (cf. 4:13–20; 16:6).

The doing of God's will. Between Easter and the Son of Man's return, this congregation is encouraged to do "the will of God" (Mark 3:35). What that entails

---

7. C. Clifton Black, *Mark*, ANTC (Nashville: Abingdon, 2011), 36–38, 195–97, 219–20, 229, 234–35, 266–75.

this evangelist does not define, but indicates: do not hesitate to relieve those in need, even if it means bending the law and incurring pious wrath (3:1–6). Continue to undermine Satan's depredations, even if others misconstrue your motives (3:21–27), dishonor you (6:1–6a) or drive you away (5:1–17). Feed the hungry with whatever resources you have (6:30–44; 8:1–10). Recognize and resist the evil that comes from within, instead of senselessly fearing contamination from without (7:1–23). Safeguard the vulnerable (9:42–50; 10:2–16). Uphold the Decalogue (10:18–19; cf. Exod 20:12–16; Deut 5:16–20). Beware temptations to trust in wealth (Mark 10:23–25). Serve others; don't lord it over them (10:42–45). Pray that what accords with faith in God is yours, and you will have it; forgive whatever you hold against another (11:22–26). Respect Caesar, but not at God's expense (12:13–17). Love the LORD your God with everything that is in you; love your neighbor as yourself (12:29–31; cf. Deut 6:4–5; Lev 19:18). Beware of frauds, withstand persecution, trust in God's deliverance and keep alert (Mark 13:3–37). In brief: follow the way of the crucified Messiah. Act as you remember Jesus acted.

The promise of recompence. For those who "have given up everything and followed him" (Mark 10:28), having suffered the rupture of their families (3:19b–20, 31–32; 6:4; 10:29)—even worse, having suffered by the hands of their own siblings, parents, or children (13:12–13a)—Jesus promises his followers their integration into a new, spiritually munificent home with brothers and sisters and mothers in faith (3:35; 10:29–30). This assurance is more than mere metaphor: the extended family was antiquity's basic social unit.[8] Amid his travels, Jesus is depicted "at home," whether his own or another's (1:29; 2:1, 15; 3:19; 7:17, 24; 9:33; 14:3), making sure others find their way home (2:11; 5:19, 35–43; 6:10; 7:30; 8:26; 11:17). The house of the LORD, the temple, will collapse as it had before (13:1–2; cf. Jer 52:12–13; Hos 9:4; Joel 1:9), but Mark's tormented audience is assured "a home for the homeless."[9]

MATTHEW (C. 85 CE)

In Matthew's Gospel families are breaking apart for reasons both similar and different. Local households are coming unglued, violently so, because of Jesus; as in Mark, new families in faith are reconstituted around the traveling Teacher (Matt 10:21–22; 12:46–50), typically gathering in homes (8:14; 9:10, 28;

---

8. Carolyn Osiek and David L. Balch, *Families in the New Testament World: Households and House Churches* (Louisville: Westminster John Knox, 1997).

9. John H. Elliott, *A Home for the Homeless: A Social-Scientific Criticism of 1 Peter, Its Situation and Strategy, with a New Introduction* (Minneapolis: Fortress, 1990).

10:12–14; 13:1, 36; 26:6, 18). On a broader scale, however, Jesus has now become a major point of division among Jews of the late first century. Exactly where, in Matthew, Jews and Gentiles stand in relation to each other is impossible to identify with confidence, because that Gospel's evidence is incoherent. On the one hand, Jesus defames Gentiles' conduct (5:47; 6:7, 32; 10:18; 18:17; 20:19, 25; cf. Rom 1:18–32; 1 Thess 4:5; Titus 1:12; 1 Pet 4:3–4) and commissions the Twelve to avoid Gentiles and Samaritans, going "rather to the lost sheep of the house of Israel" (Matt 10:1–6). On the other hand, Gentiles are named among Jesus's lineage (1:3, 5, 6) and display a degree of reverence for and faith in Jesus exceeding that of Israel's rulers (1:3, 5, 6; 2:1, 9–12; 8:5–13). The risen Jesus commissions his followers to proceed "discipling all the nations" (28:19; cf. 24:14). As suggested in Jesus's exchange with the Canaanite woman (15:21–28; cf. Mark 7:24–30), Israel is offered right of first refusal—or acceptance—of the good news Jesus proclaims, which is then extended to "many [who] will come from East and West to recline with Abraham, Isaac, and Jacob in the kingdom of heaven" (Matt 8:11). Woe betide any who reject that invitation (8:12; cf. 22:1–14).

Equally obscure in this Gospel is where its Jewish Christian readers stand with respect to their coreligionists. Were Jesus's followers in Matthew's day still wrangling with their Jewish siblings within the walls of a common synagogue, or has an extramural split already erupted: two groups, both dedicated to Jewish tradition, each defining itself against the other over Jesus's significance? This question remains controversial, since the Gospel can be read to support either interpretation. "Upon Moses's seat sit the scribes and Pharisees. Therefore, whatever they say to you, do and hold fast to it; but do not do as they do, for they do not 'walk the talk'" (Matt 23:2–3). Matthew tends to refer to "their [i.e., others'] synagogue[s]" (4:23; 9:35; 10:17; 12:9; 13:54); only in his version of the parable of the wicked tenants does Jesus conclude, "I tell you that the kingdom of God will be taken away from you [chief priests and Pharisees] and given to a nation [*ethnei*] producing its fruits" (21:43). Whether the evangelist believes that "nation" to be Gentile (cf. 24:14; Gen 17:4–6; 1 Chr 17:21; Pss 78:55; 106:41; Isa 2:4; Acts 7:45; Rom 16:26) or a more faithful Israel (cf. Amos 9:9; Zeph 2:9) remains an open question. Clearer, overall, is the impression that Matthew writes for a Jewish congregation that accepts Jesus as God's Messiah (Matt 1:1, 17–18; 2:4; 11:2; 16:16, 20), is in rancorous dispute with other Jews who deny that claim (23:4–32; 26:47–68; 27:41–43; 28:11–15), and has begun turning its evangelization toward a wider, more receptive Gentile audience (28:19–20).

Adopting Mark's framework, Matthew fleshes out in greater detail the responsibilities of Jesus's disciples, fusing with Mark traditions distinctively his own (M) or shared with Luke (Q). Most of these additions are located in Matthew's five great discourses: the Sermon on the Mount (5:1–7:28), a missionary address (10:5–42) to the newly formed Twelve (10:1–4), a collection of parables (13:1–52, expanding Mark 4:1–34), instructions on discipline within the community (Matt 18:1–35), and warnings about the last days (24:1–25:46, elaborating Mark 13:1–37). From these lectures by Christ, the sole Master (Matt 23:10), emerge recurrent motifs crucial for this evangelist's view of discipleship.

The cosmic context: the kingdom of God. As in Mark (1:15; 4:26, 30; 9:1, 47; 10:14, 23; 12:34), so, too, in Matthew: the heart of Jesus's preaching is "the kingdom of heaven," God's mysterious reign, now irrupting into human history (Matt 3:2; 4:17; 10:7; 13:11, 33) and to be consummated at a time of the heavenly Father's choosing (24:36). The express subject of most of Jesus's parables (13:24, 31, 33, 44, 45, 47; 18:23; 19:12, 24; 20:1; 21:31, 43; 22:2; 25:1), the kingdom is the frame of reference in which Jesus's exorcisms of demons—triumphant skirmishes with diabolical powers—are properly understood (12:28; so also Luke 11:20). Disciples are called to free themselves from worldly encumbrances to the kingdom's entry (Matt 18:3; 19:23–24): in a word, to "repent" (3:2; 4:17; 21:32) or to turn one's perception of reality Godward, and live as did Jesus: freely obedient to God's will (7:21). Jesus's ministry encounters devilish temptation (4:1–11), resistance from "an evil and adulterous generation" (12:39; 16:4). "An enemy" sows toxic weeds amid good wheat (13:25, 28). Switching the metaphor, a dragnet lands fish of all kinds, good and bad (13:47–48). Only the householder (13:24, 27–30) and his slaves (13:27–28; alternatively, "messengers" or "angels": 13:49–50; 24:31) are competent to distinguish the one to be taken, the other to be left (24:40–41).

The kingdom's prime constituent: righteousness. No other term in Matthew carries a more positive or pervasive weight than *hē dikaiosynē*, which may be variously translated: "righteousness," "uprightness," "justice," "putting right [what is wrong]," "being in right relationship," or "integrity." Among the Synoptics, apart from Luke 1:75, this term appears only in Matthew. In speaking of divine-human interactions, neither Jesus nor Matthew invented these ideas: they dipped from a deep well of OT conviction. God's righteousness comprises his holiness, majesty, honor, fidelity, compassion, and justice (Pss 7:17; 9:8–9; 31:1; 71:2; 111:3; Isa 1:27; 5:16; 42:21; Jer 9:24). Israel's election as God's covenant people was based on divine mercy, not their inherently good conduct (Deut 9:4–6; Isa 59:14); however, by obeying the LORD's commands, Israelites could learn to act justly (Deut 6:25; Job 27:6; 29:14; Pss 23:3; 106:3; Prov 1:3; 2:9; 8:20; Hos 2:19). Especially of Israel's anointed kings (Ps 2:2–7) is justice expected (1 Kgs 3:6; 10:9; 2 Chr 9:8; Prov 16:12; 20:28; Isa 9:7; 32:1; Jer 23:5).

When injustice scorches Israel, the prophet prays, "Let justice roll down like waters, and righteousness like an ever-flowing stream" (Amos 5:24).

Nothing is more mandatory for Jesus's disciples than *dikaiosynē*, as Matthew never tires of telling. Before Jesus was born, Joseph proved himself just (*dikaios*) toward innocent Mary (Matt 1:19). On the eve of his ministry, Jesus fulfilled all righteousness by allowing John to baptize him (3:13–15). Before Pilate capitulated, his wife warned him that Jesus was so righteous that he had given her nightmares (27:19). As a whole, the Sermon on the Mount elucidates the righteousness in which Jesus's followers are being trained. Avoid showboating piety; pray simply and modestly (6:1–18). Beware of idolizing wealth; entrust yourself entirely to God's wise and merciful providence (6:19–34; 7:7–12). Don't be gulled by the seemingly religious—including yourself: a hypocritical skin may conceal rotten fruit (7:15–23). Even God's commandments may be perverted; drive beneath the letter of Torah and live into the core of its intent (5:21–48). Rage and insults are as subject to judgment as murder (5:21–22); dehumanization of a woman is tantamount to adulterous abuse (5:27–32); love, not merely your neighbor, but your enemies, "pray[ing] for your persecutors" (5:43–44; cf. Exod 20:13–14; Deut 5:17–18). Matthew's riposte to fellow Jews who have disclaimed Jesus as Christ is to present the Messiah's maximum intensification of Jewish fidelity. Jesus's constant complaint against "scribes and Pharisees," recognized by their peers as among the most devout (*A.J.* 12–15), is that (at best) their righteousness falls short (Matt 5:19–20) and (at worst) is hypocritical (23:5–36). Jesus has come not to drain but to fill to fullness the Torah and the prophets to the tiniest letter and curlicue (5:17–18). Only so can his followers attain such a *teleiōsis*—mature benevolence—as God enacts by bestowing sunshine and rainfall on just and unjust alike (5:45–48).

A countercultural mercy. To suppose that this Gospel's exhortations were nothing more than defensive maneuvers would be a mistake. Matthew is serious that such righteousness molds Jesus's followers into greater conformity with their sole leader (23:10), who, as God's uniquely beloved Son (3:16–17; 17:1–8), is privileged to reveal to his infant followers, "little ones" (10:42; 18:6, 10, 14), all that the Father has revealed to him but has concealed from the supposedly wise and discerning (11:25–27). Even now "the poor in spirit" and "those persecuted for the sake of righteousness" are recipients of the heavenly kingdom (5:3, 10). Those least esteemed by this world stand at the head of the kingdom's queue (11:11; 18:1–4; 19:13; 21:21). Jesus is training his disciples as the kingdom's "secretaries" ("scribes": *hoi grammateis*), who draw the best of both old and new from Israel's treasury (13:52). Those who recognize its inestimable value are overjoyed by their discovery, giving up for it everything they have (13:44–46). The yoke upon them is bearable (cf. m. 'Abot 3.5), laid upon them by one as gentle and humble as they (Matt 5:5; 11:28–30). But a yoke it certainly is, and Matthew does not soften Mark's warnings: wolves lurk among the lambs (10:16–23); a cross remains for all disciples to grasp (10:26–39). "A student is not above the teacher, nor a slave above his lord" (10:24; cf. John 15:20).

Sawing against the grain of this world's laws of tit-for-tat is Matthew's persistent concern for forgiveness within the community (5:23–26, 38–42, 44–47; 6:12–15; 7:1–5; 9:1–6; 12:31–37; 18:15–35; 26:28). So ubiquitous is the subject that one wonders if this evangelist's readers were susceptible to backbiting or grudge-holding. Two of Matthew's unique and most vivid parables address the matter. The most obvious is that of the forgiven-yet-unforgiving servant: released by his merciful lord from repayment of an astronomical debt, the bastard instantly, mercilessly imprisons a peer who owes him a comparative pittance (18:23–25). The parable of the laborers in the vineyard (20:1–16) gets at a want of clemency from a different angle: even though they haven't been cheated, eleven-hour laborers resent their employer's paying the same wage to one-hour workers. Matthew prescribes an uncommonly detailed procedure for dealing with forgiveness within "the church" (*hē ekklēsia*: twice mentioned in 18:17, two of only three occurrences of the word in the Synoptics). Its overarching principles are safeguarding the offender while trying the offense (cf. Lev 19:15–18; Deut 19:15; cf. 1QS 5:24–6:1). Absent repentance, the wrongdoer is to be regarded "as a Gentile and a tax collector": a curious decision, since both were avoided by scrupulous Jews yet receive Jesus's mercy elsewhere in Matthew (9:10; 10:3; 11:19; 15:21–28; 21:31–32; 28:19). For all its rigor, this Gospel leans toward reconciliation: defendants and plaintiffs should settle out of court (5:25–26); a fellow disciple should repair estrangement before offering anything at the altar of God, who demands mercy, not sacrifice (5:23–34; 9:13; 12:7; cf. Hos 6:6); offenses should be forgiven infinitely (18:21–22).

The enduring presence of the hidden Christ. The church trial prescribed by Matthew 18:15–20 concludes with Jesus's promise, "For where two or three have come together in my name, there am I in their midst" (v. 20). This assurance strikes a complex chord. According to rabbinic teaching from the Mishnah's Pirke 'Abot (3.2): "If two sit together and the words of the law [are uttered] between them, the Divine Presence rests between them" (an aphorism recorded in the third century but probably much older). Jews who aspired to Torah-fidelity were regarded as wearing its yoke: another correspondence with Jesus's teaching (Matt 11:29–30). Moreover, at crucial points in Matthew, Jesus's presence with a renewed Israel is underscored. Explaining to Joseph Mary's virginal conception, an angel directs him to call the newborn

Jesus, for he will save his people from their sins. Now all this happened in order to fulfill the thing said by the Lord through the prophet:
> Behold, a virgin will conceive and will bear a son,
> And they will call his name "Emmanuel,"
>
> which is to be interpreted, "God is with us." (Matt 1:21–23; cf. Isa 7:14)

This prenatal prophecy is echoed in the risen Jesus's last words: "And behold I am with you every day until the consummation of the age" (28:20b). The post-Easter congregation, which may be in for a long wait until the Son of Man returns (24:36–25:30), is not abandoned. In Jesus, the Savior, God is with humankind, and that same Jesus abides with the church in its activity now and forever.

In that affirmation lie confidence and caution. Both are captured in the uniquely Matthean tableau of the judgment of nations, which concludes Jesus's final major discourse (25:31–46). This parable is redolent of Jewish apocalypticism of Matthew's day, envisioning a cleavage between the upright and the unrighteous, face-to-face vindication and condemnation, and consequences either blissful or hideous (cf. Wis 4:20a; 5:1–2, 15; 1 En. 90.20a, 26–27; 1QS 4.6b–8, 11b–14). Between these texts and Matthew 25 lies a crucial difference. In the apocryphal and Qumran texts, those vindicated are on the side of the angels, and they know it. But in Matthew all are shocked by their judgment, sheep no less than goats, because neither group recognized their Lord in the hungry, the thirsty, the stranger, the naked, the sick, or the prisoner (Matt 25:35–39, 42–43). Both herds ask the same question: "Lord, when was it that we saw you?" (25:37–39, 44). The obvious implication: had they known it was Jesus in need, they would have been on their best behavior—but no one recognized their Lord in "the least of these" (v. 20, 45). The consummate integrity expected of Jesus's disciples is revealed in just such uncalculating mercy, what later rabbis styled as *gĕmîlût ḥăsādîm*, "the giving of loving-kindness" (cf. Isa 58:7; Sir 7:35; midrash on Ps. 118:19) without expectation of reward (5:43–48). Jesus remains with the church. Stay hopeful. Pay attention. Act mercifully.

The disciples in Matthew are hardly paragons of righteousness (26:14–16, 25, 31, 36–45, 51–52, 69–75; 27:3–10); neither, however, are they as pathetic as Mark depicts them. Matthew airbrushes many of their blemishes. The storm-battered seamen do not scold their teacher (Mark 4:38) but beg their Lord to save them (Matt 8:25). Unlike the disciples in Mark (8:18), those in Matthew are blessed with seeing eyes and hearing ears (13:16). In Matthew they understand Jesus's parables (13:51; 16:12; 17:13); in Mark they understand nothing (4:12; 6:52; 8:17, 21; 9:32; 14:68). On the mount of transfiguration they do not speak from ignorance and fear (Mark 9:5–6) but prostrate themselves in reverence (Matt 17:6–7; cf. 14:33). In Matthew, Zebedee's sons do not request glorious thrones; their mother importunes on their behalf (20:20–21; cf. Mark 10:35–37). Mark's curtain falls on speechless, terrified women (16:7–8); in Matthew the women depart the empty tomb with fear and great joy, worship the risen Jesus, and deliver the Easter message to the Eleven (28:8–10, 16). These disciples' principal hindrance is not (as in Mark) a lack of faith but a *little* faith (*oligopistos*: Matt 6:30; 8:26; 16:8; 17:20), typified by Peter in Matthew 14:28–33: he bids Jesus to empower his walking on water, and does so until his fearful doubt overcomes his "little faith" (v. 31). Even at Matthew's end, after following Jesus's directions to reunite in Galilee, the Eleven worship him "though some doubted" (28:16–17). Such indecision cannot prevail. "All authority in heaven and on earth has been given" to Jesus (28:18). In turn, his disciples are given their marching orders: "Go, then, and make disciples of all nations, baptizing them in the name of the Father and of the Son and of the Holy Spirit, teaching them to obey everything I have commanded you" (28:19–20a).

Ecclesiologically considered, Matthew's most challenging passage is 16:17–19. After Peter has acclaimed Jesus "the Christ, the Son of the living God" (v. 16), Jesus extols his confessor:

> "Blessed are you, Simon son of Jonah, for flesh and blood have not revealed this to you but, rather, my Father who is in heaven. And I tell you: You are Peter [*Petros*: cf. Isa 51:1–2], and upon this rock I shall build my church and the gates of Hades will not overpower it. I shall give you the keys of the kingdom of heaven, and whatever you bind on earth will be bound in heaven, and whatever you release on earth will be released in heaven."

Most NT scholars doubt that these words, recorded only in Matthew, are traceable to the Jesus of history. Were it otherwise, one would expect something like it to reappear elsewhere in the primitive tradition (especially in Q or L, Luke's special source: as we shall see, Luke also highlights Peter's prominence). Writing some three decades before Matthew, Paul acknowledges Peter's (Cephas's) leadership among early Christians (1 Cor 1:12; 3:22; 9:5; Gal 1:18; 2:9) but claims not to have been intimidated by his stature (Gal 2:11–14). As in the Synoptics generally, Simon Peter is prominent in John's Gospel (1:42; 6:68; 13:6–8, 24, 26; 18:10, 15–25; 20:2; 21:2–11, 15–21) but overshadowed by the unnamed "disciple whom Jesus loved" (13:23, 25; 19:26–27; 20:1–10; 21:7, 20–24; possibly also 18:15–16; 19:35). Although Peter is accorded extraordinary status in Matthew 16:17–19, elsewhere in this Gospel, with few exceptions (14:28; 17:24–27), his conduct exactly matches that in Mark and in Luke (Matt 4:18; 10:2; 17:1; 18:21; 19:7; 26:33–35; 26:58). Granting his notable role as spokesman for the Twelve (15:15; 16:16; 18:21; 19:27; 26:35), Matthew does not conceal Peter's equally prominent deficiencies (16:22-23; 26:36-46, 69-75). Perhaps for that reason Jesus forbids the community to ascribe to any member the traditional titles of rabbi, father, or teacher (23:8-12).

Matthew himself provides the pertinent context for his view of Simon's significance. Jesus does not compliment Peter's human insight; instead, his confession of the Christ is a God-given gift of revelation (16:17b; cf. 11:27). Apocalyptic eschatology controls all that follows, with the church confronting the instruments of Hades. In the short term Peter does not demonstrate exceptional ability. After Easter Jesus *shall* build his community on this stubborn disciple and *shall* give him "the keys" by which future disciples may understand Jesus's teaching and thereby enter the kingdom (cf. 23:13: scribes and Pharisees who lock the kingdom's doors to would-be entrants). Peter *shall* faithfully adjudicate within the congregation what is admissible and prohibited (a derivative authority conferrable on other disciples: cf. 18:18-29). In effect Jesus elects Peter as the Messiah's prime minister in the royal household to come,[10] compatible with epistolary references to the laying of domiciliary foundations whose keystone is Christ (1 Cor 3:10-14; Eph 2:19b-21; cf. 2 Tim 2:19).[11] The Greek term for "church" in Matthew 16:18 (*tēn ekklēsian*) is the same as that which appears twice in 18:17. In the latter verse it implies a local community, akin to a synagogue or *kenesset*. In 16:18 *hē ekklēsia* suggests a comprehensive, idealized institution comparable to the Hebrew *qahal yisra'el* (Lev 16:17; Deut 9:10; 1 Kgs 12:3, 20; 1 Chr 13:2; 2 Chr 6:3, 12; cf. Zeph 2:1) and *hē ekklēsia* in Ephesians (1:22; 3:10, 23; 5:27, 29, 32) and Colossians (1:18, 24). (The etymologies of both *qahal* and *ekklēsia* connote something that is "called out.") Matthew 16:17-19 manifests a conceptual expansion of "the church" from a particular assembly with variable overseers to a universal entity subservient to God's kingdom, governed by Christ with apostolic administration.

Luke-Acts (c. 85-95 CE)

In many ways Mark and Matthew are centripetal documents, composed to hold together different groups of early Christians undergoing pressures of

---

10. John P. Meier, *The Vision of Matthew: Christ, Church and Morality in the First Gospel*, TI (New York: Paulist, 1979), 113.

11. On the complex interpretation of Petrine primacy in church history, see Ulrich Luz, *Matthew 8-20: A Commentary*, trans. James E. Crouch, Hermeneia (Minneapolis: Fortress, 2001), 370-77.

persecution, crises of identity, and germinal needs for organization. Both are beginning to make turns toward the gospel's proclamation to the nations beyond Israel (Mark 11:17; 13:10; Matt 24:14; 25:32; 28:19). If, as some think, Mark was written for a largely Gentile audience, its turn had already been completed. In Luke's two-volume Gospel and Acts, that change of direction is vibrantly executed, lending to both books greater centrifugal force.

A centrifuge requires a fixed axis. In Luke-Acts that center is Jerusalem and the venerable tradition of Jewish piety it represents (see, e.g., 1 Kgs 3:15; 2 Chr 30:13–27; Pss 116:17–19; 122:3–9; 128:5; 135:21; 137:5–6; Isa 2:1–4; Zech 8:1–8). Unlike Mark and Matthew, Luke begins and ends in Jerusalem, specifically in its temple, where devout Jews like Zechariah (father of John the Baptist), Mary and Joseph, and Simeon and Anna bless "the Lord God of Israel" (2:68; cf. 1:8–23; 2:22–24, 27, 37–51), praying for Israel's redemption (2:25, 38), for "knowledge of salvation to his people by forgiveness of their sins through the heartfelt mercy of our God" (1:77–78a). The Third Gospel concludes with the risen Jesus's command that his disciples remain in Jerusalem (24:47) "until [they] are clothed with power from on high" (24:49b). So they do, "with great joy, ... continually in the temple, blessing God" (24:52–53). (In both his Gospel [e.g., 11:1–13; 18:1–14] and Acts [e.g., 1:14; 2:42; 4:24–30; 10:1–16; 20:36], Luke emphasizes prayer more than any other evangelist.) At the beginning of Acts, the risen Lord dispatches his disciples from Jerusalem, throughout Judea and Samaria, to the end of the earth (1:4, 8b). In Luke the good news proceeds toward Jerusalem, to which Jesus sets his face as early as 9:51–53 (cf. 13:22, 33; 17:11; 18:31). In Acts the Holy City (Neh 11:1, 18; Isa 52:1) is the theater of the apostles' early ministry (Acts 2:1–42; 3:1–6:7) as well as the hub to and from which their expanded missions are conducted (8:14–27; 9:26–30; 11:2–22; 12:25; 13:13; 15:1–35; 16:1–5; 20:13–22; 21:15–23:11). In his sermon at Pisidian Antioch, Paul sums up the crux: "Brothers, sons of the descendants of Abraham and those [Gentiles] among you who fear God, ... God raised from the dead [Jesus], who for many days was seen by those who came up with him from Galilee to Jerusalem [and] are now his witnesses to the people" (13:26a, 30–31). Mark assumes Jesus's Jewishness. Matthew intensifies its character. Luke constantly reminds Theophilus (1:1–4; Acts 1:1–5) and probably other Gentile readers that "the Way," prepared by John (Luke 1:76; 3:3; 7:27), promulgated by Jesus (13:33; 20), and extended by his followers (Acts 9:2; 19:9, 23) originated and remained connected with ancient Israel.

Most commentators on Luke deem 4:16–30 a programmatic statement. I would go further: Jesus's inaugural sermon in Nazareth, which Mark (6:1–6a) and Matthew (13:53–58) situate later and only sketch, set the agenda for much of Acts as well as the Third Gospel, revealing much of this Evangelist's view of "the church" (*hē ekklēsia*): a term Luke uses to denote a local assembly (Acts 8:1b; 11:22, 26; 13:1; 14:23, 27; 15:3, 22; 18:22; 20:17, 28), a trans-geographical movement (9:31; 12:1), or both (5:11; 8:3; 12:5). "For the first time, in Antioch, the disciples were called 'Christians'" (11:26c; cf. 26:28; 1 Pet 4:16).

A contentious gospel, grounded in Jewish Scripture and observance. Luke introduces 4:16–30 by stressing that Nazareth is Jesus's home, where he customarily attended synagogue on the Sabbath and now bases his proclamation in Scripture (4:16–20a). He is as devoutly Jewish as those figures Luke portrays (chs. 1–2) before and just after Jesus's birth. Throughout this Gospel Jesus's teaching and healing are associated with Sabbath (4:31; 6:1–9; 13:10–17; 14:1–5) and synagogue (4:33–38; 6:6; 7:5; 8:41; 13:10, 14; 23:54–56). So, too, in Acts: Paul and his colleagues customarily attend and preach in synagogues, often on the Sabbath (13:14, 44; 15:21; 16:13; 18:4). As in Jesus's case, sometimes their message is received enthusiastically (Luke 4:31, 36–37; Acts 13:42–43; 17:10; 18:19–20), sometimes vehemently rejected (Luke 6:6–11; 13:10, 14; Acts 6:9–14; 18:5; 19:8–9). Simeon had warned Mary that her child was "destined for the rise and fall of many in Israel, as a controversial sign" (Luke 2:34). Jesus's beneficent ministry provokes breakup, particularly within families (12:49–53). After his resurrection, Israel remains internally divided over Jesus. In Beroea many Jews and not a few reputable Greeks receive Paul and Silas's preaching with unqualified eagerness; but unbelieving Jewish interlopers from Thessalonica soon arrive, stirring up such trouble that Paul must vamoose (Acts 17:10–16; see also 14:1–7, 19–20; 23:6–10). Scripture cannot reconcile opposing factions (17:2–4, 11; 18:28). Back in Nazareth (Luke 4:16–30), its interpretation ignites a riot.

"The Spirit of the Lord is upon me" (Luke 4:18a). For Luke's understanding both of Christ and of the church, Jesus's opening words from Isaiah 61:1 could not be more consequential. While present in Mark (1:8, 10, 12; 3:29; 12:36; 13:11; 14:38) and Matthew (1:18, 20; 3:11, 16; 4:1; 5:3; 10:20; 12:18, 28, 31–32; 22:43; 26:51; 28:19), the Holy Spirit is, indisputably, the prime mover in Luke-Acts. The same Spirit that authorized Elijah (Luke 1:17) and bears witness to God through Scripture (Acts 1:16; 4:25; 28:25–27) creates Jesus's very existence (Luke 1:35), then empowers his preaching and healing (3:16–22; 4:14, 18; Acts 10:38). So also his envoys must receive the Spirit to perpetuate their Lord's ministry after Easter (Acts 1:2, 5, 8) An outpouring of the Spirit fills righteous Jews (Luke 1:15, 41, 67; 2:27; 4:1; Acts 2:17–18, 33; 4:8, 31; 6:3, 5; 7:55; 9:17; 11:24; 13:9, 52) and, at climactic moments in the church's outreach, God-fearing Gentiles (Acts 2:1–11, 33; 8:14–17; 10:44–48; 11:11–17; 15:6–8; 19:1–7). Combating unclean or malicious spirits (Luke 4:31–37; 8:26–33; 9:37–43a; 11:24–26; 13:10–17; Acts 16:16–18), the Holy Spirit may be resisted, but never without negative results (Luke 12:10;

Acts 5:1-9; 7:51–8:1; 19:11–20). For Luke, the Spirit's communion with receptive human spirits (Acts 15:28; 19:21) is intimate yet universalizing: the Spirit reveals God's will (Luke 2:26), strengthens (1:80), consoles (2:25; Acts 9:31; 10:31), generates joy (Luke 10:21; Acts 13:52) and boldness (Acts 4:31), leads (Luke 4:1; Acts 8:29; 13:4) and binds (Acts 20:22), speaks (2:4; 10:19; 11:12; 13:2; 21:4, 11) and translates (2:8–11), preaches (2:18; 4:8; 19:6) and teaches (Luke 12:12; Acts 18:25), bears witness (Acts 5:32; 20:23) and predicts (11:28), endows recipients with wisdom (6:10), faith (6:3, 5; 11:24) and oversight (20:28), even transports travelers (8:39) and bars their way (16:6). The Spirit can be neither wangled nor bartered (8:9–24); for the repentant, it is God's pure gift (Luke 11:13; Acts 2:38). After Jesus's heavenly exaltation (Acts 2:33; 5:31), the Spirit is Jesus's proxy: "the Spirit of Jesus" (16:7) guards the church of God obtained by his own blood (20:28).

"Good news to the poor" (Luke 4:18b). Another hallmark of Luke-Acts, expressed mainly in materials without Synoptic parallel, is special attention to the impoverished.[12] Unique to Luke are Mary's declaration in the Magnificat—"The hungry [God] has filled with good things, / and the rich he has sent away empty" (1:53)—a blessing of the indigent paired with the wretchedness of the rich (6:20, 24; cf. Matt 5:3), a puzzling characterization of Pharisees as "money-lovers" (16:14), three mandates to invite the poor to banquets (14:12–13, 21), three parables about the heartless avaricious who receive their comeuppance (12:13–21; 16:1–9, 19–31), and the legend of rich Zacchaeus, who gives half his wages to the poor and restores fourfold all that he has swindled (19:1–8). The latter evokes Jesus's cry, "Today salvation has come to this house, since even this one is a son of Abraham" (19:9). In a culture where, at best, about 70 percent scraped by, day by day, at worst hobbled in grinding poverty, Luke's message surely attracted notice.[13] While his vignettes of congregations sharing all things in common seem idealized (Acts 2:44–47; 4:32–37), they may carry a grain of truth;[14] certainly they express Luke's vision of the faithful

---

12. The exceptions: Luke 7:22 // Matt 11:5; Luke 18:22 // Mark 10:21 // Matt 19:21; Luke 18:24–25 // Matt 19:23–24 // Mark 10:23–25; Luke 21:1–4 // Mark 12:41–44.

13. Ekkehard D. Stegemann and Wolfgang Stegemann, *The Jesus Movement: A First Century of Its Social History*, trans. O. C. Dean Jr. (Minneapolis: Fortress, 2001), 88–95.

14. Local gatherings' "breaking of bread" (Acts 2:42, 46; 20:7; 27:35; cf. Luke 5:27–29; 7:36–50 et al.) is reminiscent of 1 Cor 11:4–18. Like the Corinthians' practice, that which Luke describes was likely melded with observance of the Lord's Supper (Luke 22:7–27; 1 Cor 11:23–26), "how [the risen Christ] was made known to them by the breaking of the bread" (Luke 24:35). Apart from the Great Commission in Matt 28:19, baptism for washing away the sins of Christian believers occurs in Acts: 2:38–41; 8:12–16, 36–38; 9:18; 10:48; 16:15, 33; 18:8; 19:3; 22:16; cf. 1:5; 11:16.

church in action (cf. Luke 12:41–48; Acts 7:9–16).[15] Only Luke identifies various women who financially supported Jesus and the Twelve (8:1–3). Wealthy benefactors like Thyatira's Lydia (Acts 16:14–15, 40) probably opened their homes to Christian missionaries (5:42; 8:3; 9:36–43; 10:24–48; 16:14–15; 18:7–10; 21:3–7; 28:7), as did Paul's jailer in Philippi (16:25–34). Beyond sensitivity to economic inequities and the virtue of unreciprocated hospitality, Luke believes that God and wealth compete for human adoration. Between them disciples must choose (Luke 14:33; 16:13).

Release for captives, the blind, and the oppressed (Luke 4:18c). This paraphrase of Isaiah 61:1 summarizes Jesus's ministry of the kingdom in Mark and Matthew; it is not for that reason to be belittled in Luke-Acts. In one episode after another, Jesus satisfies this promise (Luke 4:31–41; 5:12–32; 6:6–11, 17–19, 20–23; 7:1–23, 36–50; 8:22–56; 9:10–17, 37–43; 11:14; 13:10–17; 14:1–6; 17:1–4; 18:15–30, 35–43; 22:49–51; 23:13–25). This is the year of jubilee (4:19; Lev 25:8–12). *Today* God's salvation breaks through (Luke 4:21; cf. 2:11; 4:21; 5:6; 13:32–33; 19:5, 9; 23:24; Acts 13:33; 26:29). Jesus's prodigious authority is conferred on the Twelve (Luke 9:1–6, 10) and on seventy others (10:1–12, 17–20). From them his delegates in Acts receive the baton, deploying the Spirit's power for the healing and liberation of others (2:37–41; 3:1–10; 4:5–22, 29–31; 5:12–16; 6:8; 8:4–13; 9:10–19a, 32–43; 13:33–43; 14:3–4, 8–18; 15:10; 16:16–18; 19:11–20; 27:33–44; 28:8–9). Sometimes the Spirit releases the apostles themselves from their own captivity (Acts 5:17–32; 12:4–17; 16:22–40). In no case does honor redound to the wonder-workers: praise of Jesus (Luke 4:41b, 43; 5:25; 7:16; 8:39; 9:20; 9:43; 10:16; 11:20, 27–28; 17:15, 18; 18:43; 19:37) and of his apostles (Acts 2:47; 3:8–9, 11–16; 14:11–18; 17:16–31) is redirected to God's glory, that the word of the Lord may mightily prevail (Acts 19:20). "We are unworthy slaves who have only done what we ought to do" (Luke 17:10).

The outrage of universal salvation (Luke 4:22–29). Nazarene plaudits sour when Jesus stresses the detestable: according to scripture, the prophets Elijah and Elisha invoked judgment on Israel by extending God's benevolence to Gentiles (a Sidonite widow [1 Kgs 17:1–16]; a Syrian commander [2 Kgs 5:1–15]). This is precisely where Luke-Acts is headed (Luke 24:27; Acts 1:8; 14:16). Without rejecting Israel (Luke 1:16, 64, 68; Acts 2:22; 5:31; 10:36; 13:16, 23; 28:20), God's mercy extends to Samaritans (half-breeds in pious Jewish eyes: 10:30–37; 17:11–19; Acts 1:8; 8:2–25; cf. 2 Kgs 17:24–29). It embraces even those whom Israel once dispossessed (Acts 7:45; 13:19–20a), who had since taken Israel cap-

---

15. Halvor Moxnes, *The Economy of the Kingdom: Social Conflict and Economic Relations in Luke's Gospel*, OBT (Philadelphia: Fortress, 1988).

tive (Luke 21:24; 22:25), and who had killed the Christ (Luke 18:32; Acts 4:24–27) in collusion with Israel's leaders (Luke 9:22; 22:63–23:48; Acts 2:36; 4:10, 27; 7:52). By an unmistakable initiative (Acts 15:7), "God had opened a door of faith to the Gentiles" (14:27; cf. 11:1; 15:7), pouring out upon them as well the gift of the Spirit (10:45), signs and wonders (15:12), and "repentance unto life" (11:18; 15:19; 26:20). No longer has Israel alone been called by God as a people for his holy name (Num 6:27; 1 Chr 17:21); so also has he elected the Gentiles (Acts 15:14, 17; 26:23), just as Simeon prophesied at Jesus's birth (Luke 2:29–32). For this, some Jews and many Gentiles rejoice and glorify God (Acts 11:18; 13:48; 15:3; 21:18–20a; cf. Luke 15:6–10). At a council in Jerusalem, Jewish Christians debate this turn of events at great length (Acts 15:1–7a) but ultimately are persuaded to address Gentile Christians as "brothers" (15:23): in Acts, the typical mode of address among Jews for one another (e.g., 1:15–16; 2:29; 7:2; 11:29; 13:15, 26, 38; 23:6). Other Jews, "zealous for the law" (21:20) and affronted by this boundary-breaking, stir up trouble (14:2), misrepresent Paul's intent, and incite mobs (14:1–7; 17:1–9; 21:17–36). Paul decides that there is no convincing the implacable who thrust from themselves the word of God first preached to them (13:46). Ultimately God sends Paul, "his chosen instrument . . . to carry his name before the Gentiles and kings and sons of Israel" (9:15), to more amenable Gentiles (22:21; 26:17). To the Roman imperium and its discerning officials, Luke repeatedly insists that the church is no threat (10:1–8, 30–33; 13:7; 18:12–17; 23:26–30; 25:13–18, 33–37; 26:30–32; 28:17–18). To the Jewish leaders in Rome, Paul absolves himself: "Let it then be known to you that this salvation of God was sent out to the Gentiles; they will listen" (28:28; cf. 13:46; 18:6). Lest we leave Acts believing that obduracy is peculiar to unbelieving Jews, we should recall the conflicts in Acts 6:1–6 between Hellenists (probably Diaspora Jews with minimal Aramaic background) and Hebrews (Aramaic-speaking Jews), as well as the disputatious Jerusalem Council in Acts 15. Both ethnically volatile, either could have rent the church.

An unimpeachable testimony to God's invincible will (Luke 4:30). After bearing witness that threatens his life, Jesus escapes lynching because a prophet cannot perish away from Jerusalem (13:33–34; 18:31). The vacancy created by Judas's death (Acts 1:15–20) can be filled only by one who accompanied Jesus throughout his ministry and, therefore, can testify to his resurrection (1:21–22; 10:31). (Only in Luke [6:13] does Jesus "name" the Twelve "apostles.") After their reconstitution, Jerusalem remains a place of peril for these envoys (Acts 4:1–18; 5:17–42; 7:54–8:3; 9:2, 13, 21; 10:39; 13:27; 20:22; 21:11–12, 27–36; 22:5, 17–20; 25:1–7, 24; 26:10). Paul's rejoinder to Caesarean Christians frightened for his safety is, for Luke, spot-on: "I am ready, not only to be jailed, but even to die in Jerusalem for the name of the Lord Jesus" (21:13; cf. Jesus's prayer for Simon's fortification in Luke 22:31–32). God's plan (*hē boulē*) has predestined salvation for all, in spite of obstructions (Acts 8:2, 4; 11:19–21; 12:20–24; 16:6–10; 27:13–44) and whatever the cost (4:25b–30; cf. 2:23–24; 5:38–39). God has borne witness (or "testified": *emartyrēsen*) of his compassion for Gentiles (15:8; cf. 14:16–17). All the prophets bear witness that "all who believe in [Jesus] receive forgiveness of sins through his name" (10:43). "The Lord bore witness to the word of his grace, granting signs and wonders to be done by their hands" (14:3). Jesus's testimony was sufficient to seal his execution (Luke 22:70–71). Stephen sacrificed himself for witness to "the Righteous One" (Acts 7:51–60; 22:20): the same testimony of a Roman centurion at Jesus's death (Luke 23:47).[16] So it follows for all disciples: sinners though they be (Luke 5:8; 7:37, 39), their commission is to offer testimony, whether accepted or not, to "what you have seen and heard" (Acts 22:15; cf. 4:33; 22:18; 23:11; 26:16; Luke 9:5; 21:13). The church's mission is to testify, to all, God's ordination of Jesus as judge of the living and the dead (Acts 10:42). As Paul insists at Miletus, "I reckon my own life of no account or value unless I finish the course and the service that I received from the Lord Jesus: to testify fully to the gospel of God's grace" (20:24).

Braiding the Strands

According to the Synoptics, God has called unto himself a people to do his will. The church does not supersede Israel; it extends that people to include all the nations. Merit remains out of the question (Deut 7:7): the least, the ignorant, the vile, even murderers (Moses: Exod 2:12) or their accessories (Saul: Acts 8:1; 22:20) are qualified if they accept the summons to turn Godward. In Jesus of Nazareth, the Son uniquely empowered by the Holy Spirit, the heavenly Father's startling monarchy has begun its reclamation of the earth. While none of the evangelists formulates a Trinitarian doctrine, their different descriptions of a "functional Trinity," epitomized in the baptismal formula in Matthew 28:19, offer important bricks for the building of the Nicene-Chalcedonian Creed, which also affirms "one holy catholic and apostolic church."

The church's basic responsibility is to follow Jesus and, by his commission, to do as he did: feed the hungry, cure disease, shelter the homeless, undermine

---

16. For a plethora of structural parallels between and within Luke and Acts, see Charles H. Talbert, *Literary Patterns, Theological Themes, and the Genre of Luke-Acts*, SBLMS 20 (Missoula, MT: Scholars, 1974).

cruelty with mercy, dignify the despicable, rescue the lost. These are not self-generated, humanitarian projects; they are the essence of the kingdom and expressive witnesses to its Messiah. For those in desperate need, that is good news. For those affronted by such indiscriminate compassion or fearful of the loss of this world's comfort or prestige, it is received as bad news. To oppose a world under siege by diabolic forces, the gospel must have a cutting edge. That sword is not for the church to wield. But to remain faithful, it may be required to suffer amputation (Mark 9:32-48), even death itself (10:39). In one form or another, crucifixion awaits this Christ's disciples. They do not suffer solitarily: they are supported by mothers, sisters, and brothers in faith who bear their own crosses. Of all the images of the church in the NT the family or household of God is predominant.[17]

To some degree all of the Synoptics grapple with the relationship between the church and Israel. Mark skims the subject (12:9). Matthew and Luke virtually throw up their hands in frustration, confounded by the stubbornness of those who doubtless regarded them as equally obtuse. None of the evangelists articulates a well-reasoned explanation, such as Paul attempts in Romans 9-11, for the acceptance of the Nazarene's gospel by a Jewish minority and a Gentile majority. The critical point of division is Jesus himself: whether he is, in fact, the divinely endowed Messiah of Israel and all the nations. On both sides of the divide, it was a mystery then and so it remains. Man supposes; God disposes.

Incomprehension, finally, is irrelevant. In Mark, Matthew, and Luke-Acts alike, the disciples' duty is to follow, in faith, their only Lord. To borrow Eduard Schweizer's apt analogy: after a heavy snowfall, children follow, step by faltering step, their parent's footsteps until they safely make their way home.[18] As well as any metaphor, that captures the depiction of the church in the Synoptic Gospels and Acts.

---

17. Paul S. Minear, *Images of the Church in the New Testament*, NTL (Louisville: Westminster John Knox, 2004), 165-72.

18. Eduard Schweizer, *Lordship and Discipleship* (London: SCM, 1960), 11.

CHAPTER 14

The Johannine Epistles and the Question of Early Catholicism

> The great majority of people will go on observing forms that cannot be explained; they will keep Christmas Day with Christmas gifts and Christmas benedictions; they will continue to do it; and some day suddenly wake up and discover why.
>
> —Gilbert Keith Chesterton

THE DECEPTIVELY SLIGHT LETTERS OF JOHN continue to stimulate a good deal of scholarly conversation.[1] The vexed question of the presence or absence of "early Catholic" elements in the Christian canon's later documents remains unresolved.[2] Sparse, however, are investigations that conjoin the two subjects, *Frühkatholizismus* and the Johannine epistles; to my knowledge a systematic consideration of their conjunction does not exist.[3] The objectives of this

---

1. Germane to the present discussion are John Bogart, *Orthodox and Heretical Perfectionism in the Johannine Community as Evident in the First Epistle of John*, SBLDS 33 (Missoula, MT: Scholars, 1977), and the masterly and provocative commentary by Raymond E. Brown, *The Epistles of John: Translated with Introduction, Notes, and Commentary*, AB 30 (Garden City, NY: Doubleday, 1982).

2. Recent contributions include Siegfried Schultz, *Die Mitte der Schrift: Der Frühkatholizismus im Neuen Testament als Herausforderung an den Protestantismus* (Stuttgart and Berlin: Kreuz, 1976), and James D. G. Dunn, *Unity and Diversity in the New Testament: An Inquiry into the Character of Earliest Christianity* (London: SCM, 1977), 341–66. The origin of the term *Frühkatholizismus* is uncertain; in *The Interpretation of the New Testament, 1861–1961* (Oxford: Oxford University, 1964), 160n1, Stephen Neill credits its invention to Wilhelm Heitmüller (1869–1926). The genealogy of the idea may be traced back at least as far as F. C. Baur's pioneering reconstruction of Christian antiquity, *Die Epochen der kirchlichen Geschichtsschreibung* (1852; repr. Hildesheim: Olms, 1962).

3. In the past decade somewhat more attention has been directed toward locating these letters within a reassessment of the Catholic Epistles as a discrete corpus. See Darian R.

chapter are thus threefold: to focus the question of early Catholicism in the Johannine letters,[4] to draw some preliminary conclusions, and to suggest some directions along which the conversation might continue.[5]

ARE THE JOHANNINE EPISTLES "EARLY CATHOLIC" DOCUMENTS?

One outgrowth of scholarly discourse on the topic of *Frühkatholizismus* has been the identification of certain characteristics, arguably evident in Christian literature antedating the emergence of the "Great Church" (c. 200 CE), which indicate tendencies in the direction of Catholicism. Those to which reference is usually made include the following:[6] a concern for the sources, transmission, and interpretation of tradition; an interest in collecting apostolic literature; a distinction between laity and clergy; an ecclesial organization that is fundamentally hierarchical rather than charismatic; the development of a monarchical episcopate; an emerging principle of transmitted authority or apostolic succession; the conception of faith in terms that are static and

---

Lockett, ed., *Letters from the Pillar Apostles: The Formation of the Catholic Epistles as a Canonical Collection* (Cambridge: Clarke & Co., 2017); Lockett, ed., *The Catholic Epistles: Critical Readings*, CCRBS (London; New York: T&T Clark, 2021).

4. To summarize my working hypotheses concerning the letters' authorship, relation to the Fourth Gospel, and time of composition: (1) All three epistles were written by one person (referred to, interchangeably, as "the writer," "the author," and "the presbyter"; cf. 2 John 1; 3 John 1) who was neither the Fourth Evangelist, the Beloved Disciple, nor the putative redactor of the Fourth Gospel. (2) The author and the communities to which he writes are in historical and traditional continuity with the community behind our Gospel of John. (3) The epistles were written ca. 100–110 CE, after the composition of the Gospel, quite possibly but not necessarily in the chronological sequence in which they have been canonically preserved. For further discussion see C. Clifton Black, "1, 2, and 3 John: Introduction, Commentary, and Reflections," in *The New Interpreter's Bible*, vol. 12 (1998): 366–80; "The First, Second, and Third Letters of John," *The New Interpreter's Bible: New Testament Survey* (Nashville: Abingdon, 2006), 321–31.

5. I affectionately dedicate this chapter to the memory of Professor Franklin W. Young, from whose seminar at Duke University (Spring, 1982) it originated.

6. The principal sources from which these criteria have been culled are John H. Elliott, "A Catholic Gospel: Reflections on 'Early Catholicism' in the New Testament," *CBQ* 31 (1969): 213–23, esp. 214; Ernst Käsemann, "Ministry and Community in the New Testament," in Käsemann, *Essays on New Testament Themes*, trans. W. J. Montague (London: SCM, 1964), 63–94; Käsemann, "Amt und Gemeinde im Neuen Testament," in Käsemann, *Exegetische Versuche und Besinnungen* (Göttingen: Vandenhoeck & Ruprecht, 1960), 1:109–34; Käsemann, "Paul and Early Catholicism," *New Testament Questions of Today*, trans. W. J. Montague (Philadelphia: Fortress, 1969), 236–51.

objective, rather than dynamic and subjective, eventuating in an objectified proclamation and a strict rule of faith; an emphasis upon sound doctrine, or "orthodoxy," as opposed to false teaching, or "heresy"; a moralization of faith, tending toward legalism; a concern for ecclesiastical consolidation and unity; a trend toward "sacramentalism," entailing an image of the church as the purveyor of salvation, and the waning of apocalyptic eschatology in general, and of expectation of the parousia in particular.

For now let us assume that these twelve criteria are sound and that, when a preponderance of such characteristics can be identified in an early Christian document, that literature may be justifiably regarded as "early Catholic." Operating on these assumptions, let us now test for the presence of each of these elements in the Johannine epistles. To streamline our analysis, these criteria may be grouped under four main headings: the issue of authority (embracing traits 1 through 7, listed above), the understanding of faith (traits 8 through 9), the image of the church (10 through 11), and the question of eschatology (12).

The Issue of Authority

The "authority" implied in the aforementioned tendencies is really of two different kinds: traditional and official. Let us consider each in turn.

The Role of Tradition

> Probe #1: What is the author's understanding of the role of tradition relative to the role of the Spirit?

Despite the dearth of OT allusions (only Gen 4:8 in 1 John 3:12), a reliance upon tradition is manifest in these letters, especially in 1 John. Twice the recipients of the letter are reminded of the message (*angelia*) that has been heard from the beginning, and on both occasions the definition of that message appears derivative of traditions that have been preserved in the Fourth Gospel: the association of God with light and evil with darkness (1:5–7; cf. John 1:9; 3:19) and the appeal to the Johannine love commandment (1 John 3:11; 2 John 5; cf. John 15:12–13).[7] The interpretation of Jesus's death as an expiatory sacrifice

---

7. The word *euangelion* does not appear in the Gospel or epistles of John (contrast Rev 14:6); *angelia* appears to be the technical, Johannine equivalent (thus Julius Schniewind, "ἀγγελία," *TDNT* 1:58–59).

(*hilasmos*, 1 John 2:2; 4:10; cf. 1:7) reflects a traditional soteriology that was active, not only in Johannine Christianity (cf. John 1:29; 6:51b; 12:24), but in the traditions available to Paul (Rom 3:25) and the writer of Hebrews (2:17). Moreover, through comparative analyses of other early Christian literature, Otto Piper advanced a persuasive *formgeschichtlich* argument for the existence in 1 John of early, authoritative oral tradition that was preserved in a number of characteristic forms: credal statements (e.g., 1 John 3:5; 5:1, 20), theological axioms (1:5; 3:20; 4:20), eschatological prophecies and convictions (2:18; 4:1), moral commandments (2:27, 28), and ecclesiastical rules (4:2-3).[8] Such indebtedness to primitive church traditions comes sharply into focus in the context of the author's apparent campaign against false doctrine, reflected throughout 1 John. For the presbyter, it is no longer a matter of his readers' abiding merely in the Spirit; with the onset of false doctrine, it has now become necessary to abide in the Spirit's *teaching*, as conveyed through the original tradition that his audience heard (N.B. 3:11, 24).[9]

On the other hand, the tradition implicit in the Johannine epistles is scarcely hard and fast, or transmitted by rote. One inference to be drawn from Piper's analysis is that the author felt free to appropriate traditional material and to incorporate it creatively in his letters, in response to changed conditions in the communities addressed. Arguably he does even more than that: apparently the writer feels at liberty to initiate or to sustain a shift away from the perspective of his traditions and to reinterpret them from a similar but different point of view. Thus, while the prooemium of 1 John is patterned on the prologue of the Fourth Gospel, the referent of *archē* in each is different: in the Gospel it pertains to the preexistent *logos*; in the epistle, it probably refers to the beginning of Jesus's ministry, as traditionally handed down.[10] Whereas the Fourth Evangelist envisions light and darkness as coexistent powers that are existentially characteristic of world history (John 1:5), the presbyter depicts them in a chronological continuum, with the light demarcating a new epoch

---

8. Otto A. Piper, "1 John and the Didache of the Primitive Church," *JBL* 66 (1947): 437-51, esp. 438-40. Along a different tack, but with complementary results, Rudolf Bultmann discerns a source, stylistically related to the alleged *Offenbarungsreden* of the Fourth Gospel, that was employed by the author of 1 John 1:6-2:17 (Bultmann, *The Johannine Epistles*, Hermeneia [Philadelphia: Fortress, 1973], 17-18).

9. Thus Eduard Schweizer, "The Concept of the Church in the Gospel and Epistles of St. John," *New Testament Essays: Studies in Memory of Thomas Walter Manson*, ed. A. J. B. Higgins (Manchester: Manchester University Press, 1959), 239.

10. Hans Conzelmann, "'Was von Anfang war," *Neutestamentliche Studien für Rudolf Bultmann*, BZNW 21 (Berlin: Töpelmann, 1954), 194-201.

as the darkness fades (1 John 2:8).[11] The formulas in 1 John with which the writer's opponents are denounced (4:1-3; 5:5-8) have the appearance, not so much of an original tradition (such as one might find in the Fourth Gospel), but of that tradition's reformulation in the face of a new challenge.[12]

If, while maintaining the stability of the tradition, the author felt free in the Spirit to reinterpret that tradition in appropriate ways, did he deem such freedom a prerogative that was his alone? This question leads us directly into the next probe.

Probe #2: What is the author's understanding of the role of tradition relative to his own authority? Is there an interpretation that is implicitly or explicitly authoritative?

The answer to the first question hinges on one's interpretation of 1 John 1:1-4. The writer manifestly understands himself to be, in some sense, an eyewitness to the historical ministry of Jesus; presumably, it is on this basis that he refutes the claims of those who indiscriminately appeal to the Spirit (4:1). Precisely in *what* sense was he an eyewitness? I think it unlikely that the author of this letter actually touched Jesus with his own hands (see above, n. 4); however, I think it probable that the presbyter, a man of a later generation who believed himself to be in traditional continuity with Jesus, vicariously participated in the experience of the disciples from the beginning and spoke of those earlier events as though he himself had experienced them.[13] It is because he regards himself in continuity with the eyewitness tradition in which the community is rooted that the writer believes that he has the right, acknowledged by his audience, to make theological discriminations and ethical judgments. However—and this must be lodged immediately alongside the foregoing observation—the presbyter does not arrogate this right as uniquely or exclusively his own: in 1 John 2:20, 27, it is clear that the *chrisma*, which every Johannine believer has from Christ, is nothing less than a Spirit-directed ability to interpret the tradition.

As to the second question lodged in this probe, we must reckon with the same tension. On the one side, there can be no human interpretation of tradi-

---

11. Günter Klein, "'Das wahre Licht scheint schon': Beobachtungen zur Zeit- und Geschichtserfahrung einer urchristlichen Schule," *ZTK* 68 (1971): 261-326.

12. See the discussion in Dunn, *Unity and Diversity*, 359-60; note also Tibor Horváth, "3 Jn 11b: An Early Ecumenical Creed?," *ExpTim* 85 (1974): 339-40.

13. There is evidence for such communal consciousness in the OT (Josh 24:7; Amos 2:10), in the Talmud (b. Pesaḥ. 116b), and in Greco-Roman literature (e.g., *Agr.* 45).

tion that the readers must accept as authoritative, since they need no teacher other than the Spirit of the Holy One. On the other side, this in itself is a principle for the interpretation of tradition, a principle that the presbyter would surely desire his readers to accept *as authoritative*. Strange, indeed, is such an "authoritative principle": it undercuts not only the persuasiveness of certain false prophets (which would surely be the author's intended effect: 1 John 4:1), but ultimately his own authority as well (which he surely would not intend). Beyond this conundrum there is a particular approach to the interpretation of tradition that, for the elder, is manifestly authoritative and bears constant repetition: the appeal to tradition as perceived *ap' archēs*, from the perspective of its beginnings (1 John 1:1; 2:7, 13, 14, 24; 3:11; 2 John 5–6). Already in the Fourth Gospel this orientation is adumbrated (John 15:27), but nowhere in John does it attain the level of explicit importance that it carries in the epistles. In this connection it is significant that one of the traits of the presbyter's opponents, with which he takes issue, is their progressivism: "Anyone who goes ahead and does not abide in the doctrine of Christ does not possess God" (2 John 9). It is precisely in this light that his readers are assured of his writing them no new commandment but only that which they have heard from the beginning (2 John 5; cf. 1 John 2:7). From all this we may infer that the interpretation of Johannine tradition has become an urgent problem in some quarters, and that a hermeneutic based on "the beginnings" has become, for the presbyter, a critical norm.[14]

Probe #3: Is there an express concern for the collection of apostolic writings?

To this a simple answer can be given: No. The reason for this lack of explicit concern for authoritative literature can only be surmised. It is possible that we are encountering the recipient communities at a stage so early that such writings could not have been collected in abundance or widely disseminated. There's another, more likely possibility: any community that considered its life so directly and thoroughly under the guidance of the Spirit may have seen little reason, at that point in its history, to amass the literature produced by its human leaders.[15] One might suppose that only when the pressure of false

---

14. Nonetheless, for the presbyter, the Spirit continues to motivate this interpretation. J. Leslie Houlden's comment that there is in 1 John "far too much reliance on mere tradition—on alleged continuity with the early days" (*A Commentary on the Johannine Epistles*, BNTC [London: Adam & Charles Black, 1973], 15) thus seems overstated and—to the extent that it renders a normative judgment instead of descriptive analysis—beside the point.

15. In support of this possibility is the fact that, for these churches, the reading of au-

teaching became more intense, and the leading of the Spirit harder to discern, would such "apostolic literature" as the Johannine epistolary corpus have been assembled. To judge from the presbyter's own perception of Johannine community life, that time is not yet.

The Question of Offices

Probe #4: Are clergy and laity distinguished?

If a clerical office be implied by these letters, their author, the presbyter, would be its most obvious representative. Unfortunately, given the obscurity of the evidence, it is impossible to identify the specific role of the *presbyteros*[16] in the Johannine epistles. The writer appears little concerned to identify his own function with regard to the communities he addresses; in 1 John he identifies himself not at all. Nevertheless, some inferences about him may be drawn.

a. As previously noted, the author of these letters speaks as one possessing self-aware, perhaps even special, authority. Eight times in 1 John he addresses the readers as his *teknia* or *paidia* (2:1, 12, 14, 18, 28; 3:7, 18; 4:4; 2 John 13; 3 John 4; cf. Jesus's address to his disciples in John 13:33; 21:5). The elder is affronted when someone in the church refuses to recognize or is disparaging of him (3 John 9–10). Presumably, his authority was acknowledged by many, perhaps most, of his addressees; otherwise it is improbable that these letters would ever have been preserved so as finally to assume a place in the canon. If, as I reckon likely, the letters of John were addressed to different audiences, the geographical scope of the presbyter's authority may have exceeded the boundaries of one community. Assuming that his sense of responsibility and authority was not limited to the moment of the

---

thoritative documents is curiously downplayed: the presbyter constantly refers to what has been proclaimed and *heard* by him and by them (1 John 1:1–3, 5; 2:7, 24; 3:11; 2 John 6), never to what he or they have *read*.

16. The richness—and ambiguity—of the term *presbyteros* (= *zaqan*), is well-known. Depending on its context, in both Hellenism and Judaism, it can refer either to one who is of greater age than another or to one who wields juridical or administrative power, irrespective of age. It is in the Ignatian corpus that *presbyteros* becomes commonly conjoined with *episkopos* and *diakonoi* to denote what appears to be a college of elders in Christian congregations (Ign. *Eph.* 2.2; 4.1; *Magn.* 2; *Trall.* 2.2; 13.2; *Smyrn.* 8.1) or an episcopal council (*Phld.* 8.1). For an excellent discussion with copious documentation, see Günther Bornkamm, "πρέσβυς," *TDNT* 6:651–83.

letters' composition, surely he must have been a leader of some sort. That he was *the head* of a community or communities cannot be deduced with certainty from the texts. Indeed, as we shall consider presently, it is possible that those congregations, even the presbyter himself, would have had real reservations concerning a leadership so exalted.

b. The presbyter's authority is connected to the tradition to which he testifies. That he can urge, time and again, that his readers adhere to a particular interpretation of that tradition—a hermeneutic "according to the beginnings"—suggests that he understands himself as a guarantor of that heritage, in a manner anticipatory of Papias's later description of presbyters as bearers and transmitters of authoritative tradition (*Hist. eccl.* 3.39.3-4).[17]

c. Nevertheless, the limits of the presbyter's authority should not be underestimated. Allusion to this has already been made with respect to 1 John 2:20, 27: the teaching of any church authority, the presbyter included, would be relativized in a Johannine congregation by the position of the Paraclete as the one authoritative teacher (cf. John 14:26; 16:13) and by the gift of that Spirit to every believer. Compatible with this perspective is the writer's response to "false prophecy": he reminds his readers of the criterion for determining the true Spirit of God yet leaves it for *them* to perform the actual "test of the spirits" (1 John 4:1-3). It seems improbable, therefore, that any clear-cut distinction between clergy and laity *could* exist in a community wherein all have been anointed by the Holy One and, as a result, all have knowledge (*kai oidate pantes*, 1 John 2:20; cf. 2:27).[18]

d. Although the presbyter possesses a special authority to interpret Johannine tradition, that influence appears to reside principally in his own person rather than in any ecclesiastical institution. Certainly no significance is attributed to an "episcopal" or "presbyterial" office—nor could it and remain, in the presbyter's eyes, true to Johannine Christianity at that stage in its development. This may explain his eloquent silence precisely at those points where one might expect an authoritative pronouncement: nowhere in these letters are issued either specific ethical directives or doctrinal decrees. The

---

17. On the role of presbyters in the writings of Irenaeus and Papias, see Willem C. van Unnik, "The Authority of the Presbyters in Irenaeus' Works," in *God's Christ and His People: Festschrift for N. A. Dahl*, ed. Jacob Jervell and Wayne A. Meeks (Oslo: Universitetsforlaget, 1977), 248-60; and Johannes Munck, "Presbyters and Disciples of the Lord in Papias," *HTR* 52 (1959): 223-43.

18. I concur with the decision of the editors of the UBSGNT (3rd ed.) to accept, in the original reading of 1 John 2:20, the nominative masculine plural noun, *pantes* (ℵ B P Ψ cop^sa Jerome Hesychius).

author no more corrects the false prophets in 1 John by virtue of his status as presbyter (cf. 2:19) than he disciplines Diotrephes in 3 John (v. 10 conveying threat, not punishment).[19] Though perhaps not suggestive of nascent Catholicism, this is precisely what one would expect in communities whose tradition derives from the Fourth Gospel, where the authoritative *egō eimi* falls from the lips of Jesus alone.[20]

Probe #5: Is authority transmitted through an "apostolic succession"?

This question must be reformulated: the term *apostolos* never occurs in the Johannine epistles and appears in the Fourth Gospel only once—and then only in a nontechnical reference to one who is lawfully commissioned to represent the person and cause of another (John 13:16).[21] Nevertheless, "apostolic succession" implies, at minimum, the transmission of authority at the behest of the Spirit but in a manner that the community recognizes as trustworthy. Is *this* evident in the letters of John?

Stated so baldly, the answer is No: this simply does not appear to have been a concern germane to the writer's purposes, argumentation, or overall theological outlook (cf. 1 John 2:20, 27). Yet this issue has another side, announced in 1 John's prooemium (1:1–5): throughout these verses the implied first person plural pronouns do not suggest (as they do, for example, in 1 John 3:1–2) a commonality between writer and readers, for the latter are identified in the *second* person in 1:3a ("What we have seen and have heard we proclaim also *to you*, so that *you* also may have fellowship with us"). On the contrary, it may be inferred that "we" in these verses refers to the writer, along with the other interpreters and tradition-bearers, who—doubtless owing to their historical

---

19. This poses a critical problem for Karl Paul Donfried's thesis that the presbyter was, in fact, a bishop ("Ecclesiastical Authority in 2–3 John," in *L'Évangile de Jean: Sources, redaction, théologie*, ed. Marinus de Jonge, BETL 44 [Leuven: Leuven University Press, 1977], 325-33).

20. Rightly pointed out by Raymond E. Brown, *The Community of the Beloved Disciple* (New York: Paulist, 1979), 142n274.

21. Although the case could be made that John 20:19–23 contains the rudiments of what came to be thought of as an "apostolic succession"—a distinctive commissioning with the conferral of special authority—I concur with Bultmann that the evangelist more likely intends to depict, through the inspiration of the disciples, the spiritual equipping of the entire community (Bultmann, *The Gospel of John: A Commentary* [Philadelphia: Westminster, 1971], 693). On the other hand, it is possible that the appendix to the Gospel, chapter 21, reflects a different, or "Petrine," structure of authority, as Pheme Perkins has suggested ("*Koinōnia* in 1 John 1:3–7: The Social Context of Division in the Johannine Letters," *CBQ* 45 [1983]: 631–41, esp. 640).

proximity to the Johannine community's founders—received the *angelia* and then passed it on to others, among whom numbered the author's addressees. If this reasoning be sound, then a corollary inference would be that there existed, in the writer's estimation, a continuum of authority: from Jesus, who had seen God; to the disciples (in general) and the Beloved Disciple (in particular), who had seen Jesus; to the Johannine school of interpreters, who had partaken of this tradition. Here we may not have a full-fledged apostolic succession along the lines of later Catholicism (with designated orders, the conferral of the Spirit by the laying on of hands, and so forth). However, if this appraisal of the author's position be valid, then there indeed appears to be a succession of transmitted authority implied by the Johannine epistles, one that surely would have been highly esteemed in the authentication of tradition.[22]

Probe #6: Are there orders of ministry? Is the organization basically charismatic or hierarchical?

Although the presbyter does not appear to derive his authority from any clerical office, certain references in these letters are patient of the interpretation that there indeed were different sorts of ministers among the recipients. Let us test this interpretation.

a. *Teknia, pateres, neaniskoi, paidia* (1 John 2:12–14): To none of these are attributed particular ministerial functions, nor are such duties assumed of

---

[22]. If the author indeed understood himself as standing in this succession, why would he not explicitly appeal to the authority of the Twelve or of the Beloved Disciple, particularly to undergird his case against the *polloi planoi* of the community? In *The Johannine School: An Evaluation of the Johannine-School Hypothesis Based on an Investigation of the Nature of Ancient Schools*, SBLDS 26 (Missoula, MT: Scholars, 1975), 284n75, R. Alan Culpepper has suggested one possibility to which I am inclined: as the liars appear to have arisen from within the community (1 John 2:19), both they and the presbyter would probably have appealed to the Beloved Disciple for substantiation of their differing christological and ethical claims. Therefore, an explicit appeal by the presbyter to the community's founder would not have been persuasive, and the writer was well aware of this. The most effective stratagem in such a situation would have been for the presbyter to shift the appeal to authority away from the Beloved Disciple to the tradition derived from him (1 John 1:1–4), maintaining that this tradition was complete and exclusive of his opponents' claims (cf. 2 John 7–9). An interesting variation on this theory, redirected to the community behind the Fourth Gospel, has been presented by D. Bruce Woll in his attempt to understand the tension between charismatic and hierarchical authority in John 14 (Woll, *Johannine Christianity in Conflict: Authority, Rank, and Succession in the First Farewell Discourse*, SBLDS 60 [Chico, CA: Scholars, 1981], esp. 127–28).

them; rather, the point in 1 John 2 is to commend these personages for the faith displayed by them in various ways. Moreover, in the context of a letter that constantly refers to its readers as *teknia* (1 John 2:1, 12, 28; 3:7, 18; 4:4; 5:21), *agapētoi* (2:7; 3:2, 21; 4:1, 7, 11), and *adelphoi* (2:9, 10, 11; 3:13, 14, 16, 17; 4:20, 21; 5:16), the main point underscored by these names is the communal relationship that exists between the writer and his readers. Beyond that, these terms of affectionate address serve a rhetorical function in verses whose structure is manifestly characterized by recurring parallelism and almost lyrical repetition (*graphō hymin / egrapsa hymin . . . / hoti . . .*). Neither the context nor the specific content of 1 John 2:12–14 suggests that these figures represent technical, institutional offices.[23]

b. (*Pseudo*)*prophētai* (1 John 4:1): By coupling 1 John 4:1–6 and 2:18–27 (a legitimate move, inasmuch as the christological error attributed to those in the one passage corresponds to that in the other), the picture that emerges of prophecy among the secessionists is suggestive, not of ecstasy, but of word and deed. However, simple association of a particular function with the prophet does not require designation of the *prophētēs* as a specific ministerial order. (i) The term "orders" implies the attribution of specific, varied functions to different groups; here, however, the line of demarcation between *prophētai* and *didaskaloi* is so slender as to be virtually imperceptible.[24] (ii) Although there were, according to the presbyter, *prophētai* in the secessionist camp, there is good reason to infer that such was not the norm among those who had not "gone out into the world" (cf. 1 John 2:15–19). The writer never designates himself or anyone other than the secessionists as "prophets."

c. "The Diotrephes affair" of 3 John will be considered at some length in the next probe. Here it need only be said that the friction between the presbyter and Diotrephes suggests a power struggle, the bone of contention perhaps concerning church structure or polity and almost certainly involving a greater supervisory power claimed by Diotrephes.[25] However we construe

---

23. Ceslas Spicq ("La place ou le rôle des jeunes dans certaines communautés néotestamentaires," *RB* 76 [1969]: 508–27) contends that *neaniskoi* denotes a distinct group, not merely those of a certain age, in the churches of Palestine and Asia Minor. However, he does not consider 1 John 2:12–14 a constitution or list of church officers.

24. The distinctions between apostles, prophets, and teachers are equally blurred in the Didache: the apostle who stays three days is a false prophet (11:3–6), and the prophet is conceived as a teacher (11:10–11; 13:1–2; 15:2). To judge from Did. 10:7–13:1, the basic difference between prophets and teachers appears to be that of residency: the *prophētēs* is a teacher who itinerates.

25. Thus, among others, Raymond E. Brown, "*Episkopē* and *Episkopos*: The New Testa-

3 John 9 ("Diotrephes does not accept me"), the most natural implication is that Diotrephes is not falling into line behind the presbyter as the latter expects of him. If one wished to make a case for a Johannine ministerial hierarchy, this would be the place to start.

Already, however, we have witnessed much that dilutes the strength of such an argument. The presbyter himself never buttresses his position by appealing to a figure whose rank is above his on the ecclesial ladder (e.g., the Beloved Disciple). Moreover, no church offices or ranks are indicated in 1 or 2 John; one suspects that the very concept of order and hierarchy might have been short-circuited by the belief that the one and sufficient *paraklētos* is Jesus Christ (1 John 2:1). Furthermore, may we not reasonably deduce that any community so severely disrupted by unbridled prophetic speech, the suggested solution for which is a communal testing of the spirits, is principally charismatic rather than hierarchical in organization?

Probe #7: Is there evidence of a trend toward a monarchical episcopacy?

If a monarchical episcopacy exists in germinal form in the letters of John, its most likely representatives are the presbyter and his rival in 3 John, Diotrephes. Let us weigh, in turn, the evidence regarding each.

The most frequently rehearsed argument for the presbyter's status as an *episkopos*, thus as a precursory monarchical bishop, is that he writes these letters for apparently different churches, presumably located in a geographical area greater than that bounded by a single community. Thus, the author would emerge as "*the* most important presbyter in a regional network of churches,"[26] whose wide-ranging supervision was challenged by Diotrephes.

The problems with this reconstruction are several. First, as Raymond Brown has observed,[27] the evidence for this "single bishop" model of church structure is lacking elsewhere in the NT and in early Christian literature up to the second century. It seems precipitous to postulate its earliest attestation in a collection of documents that seem so little concerned with any clearly defined organizational structure. Second, it is conceivable that what truly bothers the presbyter

---

ment Evidence," *TS* 41 (1980): 322-38; contra A. J. Malherbe, "The Inhospitality of Diotrephes," in Jervell and Meeks, *God's Christ and His People*, 222-32, who delimits the controversy to Diotrephes's unwillingness to welcome the brethren.

26. Donfried, "Ecclesiastical Authority," 328; cf. Amos N. Wilder, "The First, Second, and Third Epistles of John: Introduction and Exegesis," *IB* 12 (1957): 12.311.

27. Brown, *Community of the Beloved Disciple*, 100.

about Diotrephes is not the latter's refusal to accept his episcopal rank, but the notion of an episcopacy to start with: the author, adopting a basically anti-hierarchical orientation to church polity, may be disturbed that Diotrephes, or anyone else, would want to be bishop. Third, if one recalls Ignatius's primary defense against heresy—the summons to gather obediently around the *episkopos* and to celebrate the Eucharist (*Magn.* 7.1; *Trall.* 2.1–2; *Pol.* 4.1; 5.2; *Eph.* 5.3; *Smyrn.* 8.1; 9.1)—one may question that the presbyter, in his own attack against false teaching, behaves in the manner expected of a primitive bishop.[28]

Could Diotrephes be the prototype of a monarchical bishop? Reviewing 3 John 9–10, exegetes have noted several matters. First, unless we impute doctrinal significance to the *logois ponērois* of v. 10, Diotrephes's theology as such does not seem to be at issue;[29] the presbyter's quarrel with him focuses on his *conduct*. Second, Diotrephes's behavior betrays not only a desire for stricter, more monarchical authority but in fact its very exercise: thus, he is "the one who likes to take the lead over them," who feels free to ignore and even to slander the presbyter. In addition, he is in a position to refuse hospitality to itinerant brothers, to forbid those who would offer such hospitality from doing so, and even to expel from the church those who are hospitable. Indeed, if it is *tous boulomenous* who are being cast out of the church, then *ek tēs ekklēsias ekballei* sounds rather like excommunication, a nuance of *ekballō* that is elsewhere defensible (cf. John 9:34–35) and squares nicely with the argument for Diotrephes as a proto-monarchical bishop.

This argument elicits a variety of responses. Although the presbyter is obviously distressed by Diotrephes's conduct, he is no less rankled by his antagonist's "love of first place" and refusal to recognize the presbyter's authority. In conjunction with the rest of Diotrephes's actions, this might suggest a movement toward an Ignatian episcopacy;[30] then again, it might indicate nothing more than that Diotrephes is a self-appointed demagogue: the sort of local,

---

28. For this reason, Leonhard Goppelt classifies 1 John as "apostolic," the Ignatian epistles as "early Catholic" ("The Existence of the Church in History according to Apostolic and Early Catholic Thought," in *Current Issues in New Testament Interpretation: Essays in Honor of Otto Piper*, ed. William Klassen and Graydon F. Snyder [New York: Harper & Brothers, 1962], 193–209, esp. 202–4).

29. Contra Ernst Käsemann, "Ketzer und Zeuge: Zum johanneischen Verfasser-problem," *ZTK* 48 (1951): 292–311, repr. in *Exegetische Versuche und Besinnungen* (see n. 6), 168–87.

30. Thus George Bradford Caird, "John, Letters of," *IDB* 2:950. However, Hans von Campenhausen contends that the right of excommunication goes beyond even what we find in Ignatius (*Ecclesiastical Authority and Spiritual Power in the Church of the First Three Centuries* [Stanford: Stanford University Press, 1969], 123).

egoistic mischief-maker that the monarchical episcopacy later arose to suppress.[31] At the risk of reductionism, the case for Diotrephes's proto-episcopal authority may finally have to be decided on the basis of one's exegesis of *ek tēs ekklēsias ekballei*: if those being ejected are community members, and if Diotrephes alone is responsible for their ejection, and if (as there is every reason to assume from 3 John 10) this power of expulsion is conceded to Diotrephes by that community, then the irresistible conclusion is that the power wielded by Diotrephes is extraordinary and similar to that which later came to be assumed by monarchical bishops. By comparison, it is by no means clear that the author of the letters has removed anyone from the church or has the power to do so: his authority seems to extend no farther than threatening to lay the matter of Diotrephes's conduct before the congregation (3 John 10a). Nor do the false prophets of 1 John appear to have been drummed out by executive fiat: they walked out by their own volition (2:19). To judge from these letters, the extent of the presbyter's power to root out what he perceives to be unsavory influences among his addressees is to exhort them not to accept anyone who would try to import pernicious doctrine into the community (2 John 10-11). Although the respective roles of the presbyter and Diotrephes resist precise delineation, we must ultimately remain open to the prospects that (a) authority in the Johannine communities of this early period could have fluctuated widely in both kind and degree, and (b) there is at least a slight possibility that, in Diotrephes, we see the emergence of what would become a monarchical episcopacy.[32]

The Understanding of Faith

Probe #8: Is the conception of faith primarily objective and static or subjective and fluid? Has the proclamation become objectified as a strict rule of faith, such that "orthodoxy" and "heresy" are distinguished?

---

31. Thus, C. H. Dodd, *The Johannine Epistles*, MNTC (New York/London: Harper & Row, 1946), 163.

32. In a highly suggestive reconstruction, Brown (*Community of the Beloved Disciple*, 160-61; *Epistles of John*, 738-39) posits that, in the presbyter and Diotrephes, we observe two different styles of authority, both of which were concerned with the suppression of false teaching in their respective communities. Having encountered the practical difficulty of distinguishing true from false itinerant teachers (cf. Did. 11), Diotrephes may have made the prudential decision to exclude all such missionary teachers and to discipline those who received them. Thus he, not the presbyter, would emerge as the transitional figure in the movement toward a "Catholic" ecclesial polity.

Again the question must be transposed into a Johannine key: *pistis* appears only once in our documents, and *pisteuein* occurs but nine times (against which contrast ninety-eight occurrences in the Fourth Gospel). In addition to *pistis*, we must direct our attention to two words whose presence in the Johannine letters impinges upon the present inquiry: *homologein* and *alētheia*.

a. *Pistis* and *pisteuein*: In the Johannine epistles the term *pistis* occurs only in an ethical exposition in 1 John. The author repudiates those who would claim to love God while hating their brothers (4:20–5:2) by proclaiming that to keep the love commandment (as well as the other commandments) *is* to love God (5:3). The power so to obey the commandments and to triumph over the world is assured for those born of God, "and this is the victory that overcomes the world, our faith" (5:4b). Since the context is thus one of ethical commitment and of victory over the world, *pistis* in this verse more likely conveys the subjective, dynamic sense of personal acknowledgment of Jesus's divine sonship and power (see also 5:5) rather than the passive acceptance of some block of "sound doctrine."[33] Similarly, to believe (*pisteuein*) is not merely to give intellectual assent to a slate of propositions or to subscribe to a body of dogma; rather, it is to acknowledge that Jesus is the Christ and the Son of God (3:23; 5:1, 5, 10 [3x], 13), affirming God's love (4:16) and no other spirit (4.1), so as to live in love with one's brother (cf. the overall context).[34]

b. If a shift toward *fides quae creditur* occurs in these epistles, it may be in the use of *homologein*, which appears proportionately more frequently here (6x) than in the Fourth Gospel (4x). For example, in 1 John 4:2, 3 and 2 John 7, the confession of Christ's having come in the flesh appears to function, not merely as the believer's subjective response, but also as an objective test of true and false spirits in the community (see also 1 John 2:23; 4:15).[35] First

---

33. Contra Rudolf Bultmann, *Theology of the New Testament* (New York: Scribner's Sons, 1955), 2:77–78; Bultmann, *Johannine Epistles*, 59.

34. To suggest that "faith" in the letters of John is primarily subjective is not to contend that it is utterly so. It is plausible that a public profession of that belief would also be entailed (Brown, *Epistles of John*, 535, 571–72; cf. also Rom 10:9–10).

35. Leonhard Goppelt (*Apostolic and Post-Apostolic Times*, HT [New York: Harper & Row, 1970], 161–62) suggests that 1 John, along with Hebrews and the Pastorals, understood *homologia* to mean a "confessional formula" but continued to interpret that confession kerygmatically. However, by the time of the fathers, 1 John 4:2 "was reported literally in Polycarp, *Phil.* 7, 1 and in substance by Ignatius (*Smyrn.* 5.2; cf. 7.1). It had become, as 1 John intended, a confessional formula in the liturgy."

John 1:9, which may concern the personal confession of one's sins, presents an exception to this tendency, but then again it may not: it falls within a passage (1:5–10) whose intention is the rebuttal of false teachers who assert their sinlessness. Thus, the confession of one's sins might function as yet another means of distinguishing those who do and do not walk in darkness.

c. Does the term *alētheia* (20x) betray an early Catholic understanding of faith as a *regula fidei* or a more fluid conception?[36] To this question there is no simple answer: *alētheia* in the Johannine epistles conveys different nuances in different contexts. For instance, it can be used to suggest nothing more than "genuinely" or "in reality" (1 John 3:18; 2 John 1 [first occurrence]; 3 John 1) or to describe an upright way of life (1 John 1:6; 2 John 4). In the context presented by 1 John 2:18–27 (warnings against false teachers), the two occurrences of *alētheia* in 2:21 may be construed as references to "right doctrine": a possible tendency toward nascent Catholicism. Yet the majority of references to "truth" in these epistles refer to that distinctively Johannine understanding of revealed, divine reality (1 John 1:8; 3:19; 4:6; 5:6; 2 John 1 [second occurrence], 3; 3 John 8, 12; cf. John 8:44; 18:37). It could be argued that this characteristically Johannine conception has undergone a shift in meaning, not unlike that of *archē* (thus, Conzelmann) and *phōs* (so, Klein), and that *alētheia* in these passages has now come to connote "the correct teaching."[37] Yet the writer displays no reserve in referring to *hē didachē tou Christou* when it more adequately serves his purpose (2 John 9). And though a relationship between "teaching" and "truth" surely exists in these letters, they can hardly be said to be identical and therefore interchangeable: would it have occurred to the presbyter to speak of "walking in the *doctrine*" in 3 John 3–4? It is better, I think, to accept the variety of nuances of *alētheia* in these texts rather than to impose on that word any single meaning (such as that found in 1 John 2:21) in all of its occurrences.

To summarize: although one may discern, in *homologein* and in some instances of *alētheia*, a movement toward *fides quae creditur*, it is subtle and overshadowed by an understanding of "faith" and "truth" as *fides qua creditur*. It may have been precisely because faith in these communities was so dynamic,

---

36. Regarding *regula fidei*, see Houlden, *Commentary*, 3; Willem S. Vorster, "Heterodoxy in 1 John," *Neot* 9 (1975): 87–97. See also Rudolf Schnackenburg, "Zum Begriff der 'Wahrheit' in den beiden kleinen Johannesbriefen," *BZ* 11 (1967): 253–58; B. H. Jackayya, "Ἀλήθεια in the Johannine Corpus," *CurTM* 41 (1970): 171–75.

37. Roland Bergmeier, "Zum Verfasserproblem des II. und III. Johannesbriefs," *ZNW* 57 (1966): 93–100. Cf. also literature cited above, nn. 10 and 11.

so fluid, that it had shaded into beliefs unacceptable to the presbyter—at which point, to stem that tide, he insisted upon the objective status of beliefs regarded by him as nonnegotiable: the command for love of the brother (1 John 2:9-11; 4:20-21) and the confession of Jesus as the Christ who has come in the flesh (1 John 2:22-23; 4:2-3). Insofar as these are the criteria by which truth and error are distinguished, and the separation of the community from "the false prophets" is effected (1 John 4:1-12, 20-21),[38] some rudimentary notion of "orthodoxy" may be operative.[39] On the other hand, the presbyter himself does not implement these criteria, nor is there any evidence that he enforces the decision once the tests for doctrinal or behavioral error have been conducted. The responsibility for both resides with the local congregation (1 John 4:1; cf. 2 John 10). When added to the fact that the term *hairesis* (Acts 5:17) is never employed by the presbyter,[40] all of this suggests that proper and improper teachings are clearly differentiated[41] but not yet regarded as "orthodox" or "heretical."[42]

Probe #9: Does the relationship between faith and works suggest a new legalism?

I think not. Despite the repeated admonition "to keep the commandments" (1 John 2:3-4; 3:22, 24; 5:2-3; cf. John 14:15, 21; 15:10), neither *Haustafeln*, nor

---

38. It should be noted that the opponents of 1 John are "insiders" who have gone out from the community into the world (2:19; 4:1b). In 2 John the reverse is intimated: the threat of deceitful doctrine comes from without (v. 10).

39. Cf. Hans Conzelmann, *An Outline of the Theology of the New Testament* (New York and Evanston: Harper & Row, 1969), 302: "1 John . . . considers the nature of heresy by defining the nature of faith as orthodox faith. . . . We see here the first beginnings of the extension of dogma by the positive development of the confession of faith and a critical defense against false doctrine."

40. Nor does the term occur in the NT in the developed, technical sense (with the possible exceptions of Acts 24:5; 28:22; 2 Pet 2:1).

41. The focus of the community's *Auseinandersetzung* appears to be the proper understanding, or significance, of the incarnation (1 John 2:22; 4:2-3), and Brown's exegesis is persuasive: "The secessionists believed that *the human existence of Jesus, while real, was not salvifically significant*" (*Community of the Beloved Disciple*, 113; Brown's emphasis).

42. While she may underestimate the polemical cast of 1 John, Judith M. Lieu is correct in her judgment that the categories "orthodoxy" and "heresy" are anachronistic, as well as far too rigid to be applied to the NT ("'Authority to Become Children of God': A Study of 1 John," *NovT* 23 [1981]: 210-28). Thus we shall oversimplify the situation of 1 and 2 John, and doubtless mislead ourselves, if we attempt to identify the errors presupposed therein with later, full-blown heresies, such as Docetism or Cerinthian Gnosticism. For a thorough and cogent analysis of this problem, see Brown, *Epistles of John*, 57-68, 766-71.

lists of virtues and vices, nor even specific moral directives are quoted in the Johannine epistles. Beyond that, the paraenesis to be found therein is almost always at the service of *theological* points that the writer wants to score. Thus "keeping the commandments" in 1 John 2:3 (cf. also 1:7) is not the condition to be met for knowledge of God but its unmistakable, behavioral corollary: knowledge manifests itself in one's ethical "walking," in obedience to the commandments and thus in one's love of God and the brother (4:8, 21). Even the reference to "brotherly love," with its obvious allusion to Johannine tradition (cf. 1 John 2:7–11; 4:7–5:5 with John 13:34–35; 15:12–17), is not so much handed down to the readers as a moral *depositum* but is presented as a manifestation of divine love, which is to be extended and perfected by them, as children of God, in community life.[43]

It is the rupture between belief and commandment among the Johannine schismatics that the presbyter finds especially frustrating. Evidently his opponents are proclaiming a spurious Christology that has accorded no salvific significance to moral conduct in the community (cf. 2 John 9; 1 John 4:20–21). They have taken the basic ideal expressed in 1 John 3:6, 9, which the author certainly knows to be violated in real life (1:8; 2:1; 3:4), and have trumpeted their sinless perfection as a realized truth, not as a moral obligation.[44] Thus the resulting ethical problems are, in the author's opinion, natural consequences of doctrinal error (cf. 1 John 2:3–6, 10–11; 3:4–10). His mode of response, significantly, is not to bludgeon with casuistic legalism those who have remained in the community, but to remind them of the imperative (obedience) that has been implied in the indicative (belief) from the beginning (1 John 3:6, 11). Indeed, in both exhortation and refutation, the presbyter's deep and consistent concern for ethical behavior (*ho poiōn tēn dikaiosynēn*: 1 John 2:29; 3:7, 10) is not so much some *frühkatholisch* "ideal of moralistic piety,"[45] a legalistic urging of what one should *do*, as it is an ontological statement of whose child one *is*, if one behaves rightly.

---

43. Likewise, "to abide" (*menein*) in God, in the light, or in the teaching, refers to that immanence of God's presence in the believer's life that issues in the faithfulness of the believer to God (1 John 2:6, 28; 3:6) and the reciprocal fidelity of God to the believer (1 John 2:24, 27; 3:24; 4:13–15).

44. Thus Bogart, *Orthodox and Heretical Perfectionism*, 143. Admittedly, no attempt to explain the seeming contradiction between 1 John 1:8–10 and 3:6, 9 is totally satisfying; see Brown, *Epistles of John*, 411–16.

45. As Bultmann intimates (*Theology of the New Testament*, 2, 212–13); cf. also Conzelmann, *Outline of the Theology*, 310–11.

The Image of the Church

Probe #10: Is there a manifest concern for church unity and consolidation?

One hasn't far to read in 1 John before recognizing that the presbyter's desire for *koinōnia* in 1:3 is no bland gesture of amity but presupposes a schism between true believers and false prophets, which threatens to deteriorate (N.B. 1:6–7; 2:19, 26). Likewise, in 2 John, the same or a similar split is conceded by the author (v. 7), a rift that has reached a point of such exacerbation that the reunion of *planoi* and *teknia* is no longer an issue; there's hope only for thoroughgoing unity of the latter against any encroachments by the former (vv. 10–11). Similarly, a signal concern in 3 John is that itinerant *adelphoi* who have the presbyter's blessing, such as Demetrius (vv. 10b, 12), be received by other communities, "that we may become collaborators with the truth" (v. 8; cf. v. 5).[46] If anything is clear in the Johannine epistles, it is that disunity in and among these communities has become a severe problem. At the time of these letters' composition, the rancor has become so intense that some of the presbyter's most eloquent pleas are for the steadfast union of *one wing* of an already seriously divided church against the other wing(s).

To the question whether or not these documents betray evidence of consolidation into a "Great Church," there are both simple and complex answers. The sectarian consciousness of the Johannine community, its acute sense of exclusiveness from a wicked world (1 John 2:15–17; 3:1b, 13; 4:3, 5; 5:4–5, 19; 2 John 7), would surely have inhibited any outlook that was genuinely "catholic."[47] That is the simple answer. The more intricate one is suggested by several facts. First, whereas *hē ekklēsia* in 3 John 6, 9, 10 refers to particular and independent fellowships, these neighboring congregations are visited by members of other communities, with whom (in the presbyter's view) they have a fraternal or collegial relationship (v. 5, *adelphous*; v. 8, *synergoi*). Second, in 2 John the presbyter writes to what appears to be an independent congregation ("the elect lady," v. 1); yet it is a community so intimately connected with his own

---

46. Such a reception appears to be contrary to the wishes of Diotrephes, who, as Brown astutely suggests, "treats the emissaries of the presbyter in exactly the same way that the presbyter urges the church of 2 John to treat the emissaries of the secessionists; and, of course, the presbyter does not like that one bit" (*Community of the Beloved Disciple*, 133n260).

47. On the sectarian character of Johannine Christianity, see especially Wayne A. Meeks, "The Man from Heaven in Johannine Sectarianism," *JBL* 91 (1972): 44–72, and D. Moody Smith Jr., "Johannine Christianity: Some Reflections on Its Character and Delineation," *NTS* 21 (1974–75): 222–48.

fellowship that he can address "her" as "an elect sister" (v. 13), the members of her church being "her children" (vv. 1, 13).⁴⁸ The implication of all this is that we find in the letters of John neither completely detached conventicles nor a "Great Church," such as would become manifest in the third or fourth century. Instead we witness a church that exists in the Greco-Roman world as a discrete entity, in which individual and independent fellowships are coming to be perceived as units integral to that entity. Therefore, if there be in these letters no movement toward "the Great Church," there is a tendency to view the elect children of God as siblings who participate in an *ecclesia* that is greater than any one of the smaller *ecclesiolae* of which they are members.

Probe #11: Is there a tendency toward sacramentalism? Has pneumatology been subsumed under ecclesiology, with the result that the church is recognized as the purveyor of salvation?

Generally speaking, there are two appraisals of ritual observance in the epistles of John. The first is summed up by Norman Perrin: "The author of [1 John] has . . . a great interest in the sacraments of the church."⁴⁹ The second is captured, with equal concision, by Brooke Foss Westcott: "[In 1 John] nothing is said on any detail of ritual or organization."⁵⁰ These appraisals are mutually exclusive. Which is the more accurate?

Perrin's position deserves the benefit of doubt. He substantiates his claim on the basis of five references in 1 John: 2:12, 20, 27; 3:9; 5:6. Let us briefly attend to each and ask whether or not his sacramentarian interpretation is persuasive.

    a. 1 John 2:12: "I write to you, children, because your sins are forgiven because of Christ's name." An allusion to baptism may be present here; however, it is neither explicit nor necessary for understanding the verse. "Forgiveness of sins" has already been broached in 2:1-2 with the non-baptismal reference

---

48. One might also recall the plethora of intimate or familial appellations applied in 1 and 3 John to their addressees (1 John 2:1, 9, 12-14, 18, 28; 3:7, 15, 18; 4:20; 5:21; 3 John 1, 2, 3, 4, 5, 10b, 11).

49. Perrin, *The New Testament: An Introduction* (New York: Harcourt Brace Jovanovich, 1974), 223. Cf. also Rudolf Schnackenburg (*The Church in the New Testament* [New York: Herder and Herder, 1965], 105), who wishes to interpret the letters of John from a thoroughgoing baptismal perspective.

50. B. F. Westcott, *The Epistles of St. John: The Greek Text with Notes* (London: Macmillan & Co., 1905), xxxviii.

to Christ, the *hilasmos*. "Because of Christ's name" most naturally suggests that the readers' sins have been forgiven, not so much because of their baptism, but because they believe in (and bear?) the name of Jesus Christ, the Son of God (cf. 3:23; 5:13).[51]

b. 1 John 2:20, 27: "But you have been anointed by the Holy One, . . . and the anointing that you received from him abides in you. . . ." The term *chrisma* ("anointing oil") came to mean "anointing," an action very likely associated with baptism in the early church. Thus the allusion in these verses is probably to baptism; this, plus the high evaluation of charismatic teaching in 1 John 2:27, supports Perrin's case. On the other hand, it is dubious that the writer's emphasis here is upon baptism per se, for the false teachers undoubtedly received baptism as well (cf. 2:19).

c. 1 John 3:9: "Everyone who has been begotten of God does not commit sin, because [God's] seed abides in him; and he cannot sin, because he has been begotten of God" (cf. John 1:12-13). I see nothing intrinsic to this verse or to its context that would compel its construal as a reference to ritual. Baptism *might* be in the background, but the allusion is probably an illusion. For the same reasons I harbor similar reservations about a putative baptismal reference in 1 John 5:1a.

d. 1 John 5:6: "This is he who came by water and blood, Jesus Christ, not in water only, but in water and in blood." Unless the context (5:1-5) be deemed to refer to Christian baptism, an argument I find strained, the most plausible interpretation of this obscure verse is that the Son of God (cf. 5:5) is the historical Jesus, from whose side flowed blood and water at the time of his death (cf. John 19:34-35).[52] If a displacement in the author's thought from Christ's humanity to Christian ritual is anywhere present, it is more obvious in the move from v. 6 to v. 8, with a reference to baptism and the Eucharist implied in the latter. The sense of 5:8 might then be that baptism and the Supper are witnesses to Christ out of the power of the Spirit.[53] What is not said, however, is that these two rituals are extraordinarily significant for salvation or exceed in importance the believing of testimony to Jesus (cf. 5:1, 5, 10).

---

51. Thus Bultmann, *Johannine Epistles*, 31; contrast Brown, *Epistles of John*, 303.

52. No exegesis of 1 John 5:6 is wholly satisfying, but this alternative raises fewer problems than any and arguably resolves more than most. Still, if "water" in this verse refers to someone's baptism, surely it would be to that of Jesus, not of the believer. For the other exegetical options, see Brown, *Epistles of John*, 573-78.

53. Of course, the sacramental interpretation is completely undercut if one thinks (following Brown, *Epistles of John*, 584-85) that 1 John 5:7-8, like 5:6, refers simply to the death of Jesus (cf. John 19:34).

Indeed, the same holds for 1 John 2:20, 27. There, as elsewhere, allusiveness characterizes all of these putatively sacramental references. I am not suggesting that the communities addressed by the presbyter were devoid of all ritual; it is quite possible that baptism lies in the background of 1 John 1:5–2:2 (N.B. the implied passage from darkness to light, the role of confession, and the imagery of cleansing). At issue is not the presence of what came to be called sacrament, but of sacrament*alism*. And nowhere in the Johannine letters do we find anything even roughly approximating the high sacramental doctrine of Ignatius, even though he seems to echo certain Johannine traditions of which the writer of the epistles would surely have been aware (cf. Ign. *Phld.* 4.1; Ign. *Eph.* 20.2 / John 6:51–58). Nor in the passages just examined is there any indication whatever that the church qua church has become the dispensary of salvation; on the contrary, the Spirit remains the autonomous, motivating force of the Christian life. Perrin's assessment lands wide of the mark; Westcott's hits the bull's-eye. It is difficult to imagine a higher pneumatology, or a slower movement in the direction of sacramentalism, than that revealed in the Johannine epistles.

The Question of Eschatology

Probe #12: Is apocalyptic eschatology waxing or waning in the community?

Indubitably, the writer of these letters is a beneficiary of the highly realized eschatology that distinguishes the Fourth Gospel. First John closes with the confidence, not that the Son will come, but that he *has* come (*hēkei*) and *has* given (*dedōken*) understanding to believers, that they might recognize the One who is true (5:20; cf. John 1:14; 20:29–31). Already anointed by the Spirit (1 John 3:24b; cf. John 20:22), the true believer has passed out of death into life (1 John 1:2; 3:14; cf. John 6:54; 8:12; 17:3) and even now walks in the light (1 John 1:7; 2:8b–10; cf. John 3:21; 5:35; 8:12; 9:5; 11:9–10; 12:35–36, 46, among others), abiding in Christ (1 John 3:24; cf. 4:16; John 15:10; 17:3). So also in 2 John 9 the church already has attained its goal. The difficulties arise when one "proceeds farther" (*ho proagōn*).

One might think that the edge of eschatological expectation would be irreparably blunted by such a perspective. Nevertheless, the Johannine epistles are remarkable for their future-oriented, even apocalyptic, eschatological imagery.[54] Thus the Johannine congregation is an "elect lady" (2 John 1; cf. v. 13),

---

54. It is principally because of his source- and redaction-critical presuppositions—namely, that the apocalyptic eschatology in 1 John is to be pared away and attributed to the supposed "ecclesiastical redactor"—that Bultmann can suggest, "In [Johannine theology]

a *Heilsgemeinschaft* not unlike that manifested at Qumran (cf. 1 John 4:7–12 // 1 QS 1:9–10; 2:2–3; N.B. also 1 QS 2:24; 5:4, 25; 7:18–19).[55] Reminiscent of Jewish and Christian apocalypticism is the language employed by the presbyter to characterize his opponents: they are *pseudoprophētai* (4:1) and *antichristoi* (2:18, 22; cf. 2 John 7), those stereotypical harbingers of the end time (cf. Mark 13:22), whose sin is that heinous lawlessness (*anomia*; 1 John 3:4) which characterizes the devil (*ho diabolos*; 3:8, 10; cf. 2 Thess 2:3, 7, 9). Because the world is in thrall of the evil one (*ho ponēros*; 5:19; cf. 2:13–14), the beloved children of God are pitted against "this world," with its transitory seductions (2:15–17) and its proclivity for the lies of antichrists (4:5). In light of both its realized eschatological experience and those things yet to come, the community is exhorted to act with rectitude (1:7; 2:5, 10; 3:10), to prepare for the day of judgment and the Messiah's return (2:28; 4:17), and to rest assured that it is the last hour (*eschatē hōra*; 2:18),[56] that even now "the darkness is passing away and the true light already is shining" (2:8).

On balance, the Johannine letters do not exhibit the sort of eschatology that is usually considered compatible with nascent Catholicism: apocalyptic eschatology seems to have intensified rather than receded; gestation rather than abortion appears to have been the fortune of hope for the parousia. Yet it is not impossible that, by the time of these epistles, such apocalyptic language had come to be domesticated and absorbed into a developing, conventional church doctrine that the presbyter, with his keen interest in proclaiming only those things that were heard "from the beginning," felt constrained to reiterate.[57] Therefore, were one inclined to argue for *Frühkatholizismus* in the letters of John, ironically one could do so, not in spite of, but *on the strength of* the apocalyptic eschatology that they display.

---

the idea of the eschatological People of God plays no role. . . . John also lacks the traditional Jewish-Christian eschatology" (*Theology of the New Testament*, 2, 113; cf. *Johannine Epistles*).

55. On the parallels between the QL and the Johannine epistles, see especially Raymond E. Brown, "The Qumran Scrolls and the Johannine Gospel and Epistles," *CBQ* 17 (1955): 403–19, 559–74; Marie-Emile Boismard, "The First Epistle of John and the Writings of Qumran," in *John and Qumran*, ed. James H. Charlesworth (London: Chapman, 1972), 156–65; James L. Price, "Light from Qumran upon Some Aspects of Johannine Theology," in Charlesworth, *John and Qumran*, 9–37.

56. Brown (*Community of the Beloved Disciple*, 143–44) suggests that the presbyter may have interpreted the success of the deceivers "in the world" (1 John 4:5; 2 John 7) as yet another sign that "the last hour" was at hand (1 John 2:18). On the shift in 1 John toward futuristic eschatology, see also C. F. D. Moule, "A Neglected Factor in the Interpretation of Johannine Eschatology," in *Studies in John Presented to Professor Dr. J. N. Sevenster*, ed. W. C. van Unnik, NovTSup 24 (Leiden: E. J. Brill, 1970), 155–60.

57. Cf. D. Moody Smith, "John, Letters of," *IDBSup* (1976): 486–87.

Some Conclusions and Implications

Every reader must weigh for herself the evidence that has been presented. I am not persuaded that the Johannine epistles are *fundamentally* documents of "early Catholicism," as that term has been herein defined. Explicitly in these letters, and implicitly in the churches to which they are addressed, tradition is important, but it is also flexible and dynamic: the presbyter chooses some traditional elements, ignores others, displays freedom to reformulate those retained and to allow his readers the freedom to interpret them in the Spirit. There is no evident interest in the collection of apostolic writings; there are shadowy indications that such an undertaking would not be viewed as especially desirable. No distinction between clergy and laity is discernible; the congregations presupposed by these letters exhibit an ecclesial organization that is primarily charismatic rather than hierarchical. The presbyter's authority is personal, not official; he looks nothing at all like a later monarchical bishop; given the bias and paucity of our evidence, the attribution of such episcopal powers to Diotrephes seems injudicious. "Faith" is conceived primarily as *fides qua creditur*, as subjective commitment rather than static subscription to a body of dogma; the differentiation of teaching that is true and false is established, not by official decree, but through a communal testing of the spirits. A clear definition of "orthodoxy," in contradistinction to "heresy," has not yet been formulated, much less applied. Faith is inextricably united with ethics, but legalistic orthopraxy is scarcely at issue in these documents. Sacramentarian thinking is as foreign to this literature as any trend toward a united, all-encompassing "Great Church": the sectarian stance of the churches with respect to "the world" is exclusive rather than inclusive. The expectation of the parousia has not withered; an apocalyptic consciousness has not waned. Admittedly there are tensions within this material. Nevertheless, its most implicit statements on authority, faith, the church, and eschatology cut against the grain of what is purported to be *frühkatholisch* and could arguably be taken as a reaction against just such a movement.

Depending on one's preconceptions of the Johannine letters before commencing a study like this, such a conclusion may hold little surprise. What should be surprising is the facility with which one could build, on the foundation of our analysis, a plausible case for the *refutation* of this conclusion: an argument for the presence of *frühkatholisch* tendencies in the Johannine letters. To this end, one might recall the presbyter's self-conscious reliance upon various *urchristliche* traditions, as well as his assumption of the right to make judgments about those traditions and to set forth an authoritative principle for their proper interpretation. The Spirit continues to move in the churches to which he writes, but that movement is consistent with the primitive teaching that has previously been heard. As an authoritative guarantor of that teaching, the presbyter addresses his audiences; his authority is implicitly derived from his association with, and historical proximity to, the original creators and interpreters of the Johannine tradition. Implicit also is a qualified hierarchical organization in the Johannine communities. Although the presbyter has apparently not been conceded the authority that Diotrephes displays in his expulsion of persons from the congregation, the author does expect both that his own lead be followed by his addressees and that Diotrephes cease to put himself first (i.e., over the presbyter). Regarding the *fides* of the church, there is a discernible movement toward the acceptance of certain *homologiai* ("Jesus is the Christ, the Son of God, who has come in the flesh") as doctrinally sound tests for the refutation of false teaching (or "heresy," as it later came to be styled). Ecclesiologically speaking, the Johannine congregations do not stand entirely apart from one another but share a common sectarian consciousness. The predominantly realized eschatology of these letters describes a church that has already reached its goal and has no further to go; the persisting apocalyptic imagery bears eloquent witness to that conservation of tradition which is quintessential to *Frühkatholizismus*.

I do not find this second reconstruction as convincing as the first. Taken together, both suggest a variety of unresolved theological tensions in these texts, doubtless commensurate with the sociological tensions that occasioned their composition. The Johannine epistles are not monochromatic but polychromatic. Still, it is unsettling that two such highly divergent reconstructions as those just presented could have emerged from the application of the *same* analytical criteria. If these dozen canons have been fairly implemented, then the criteria themselves must be flawed. Therefore, if anything be clear at this study's conclusion, it is that *the very model of "early Catholicism," as customarily defined, ultimately obscures rather than clarifies*. This is true, not only because the model is too anachronistic[58] and too heavily value-laden[59] to be helpful, but also—indeed, primarily—because the criteria of *Frühkatholizismus* are

---

58. Even to employ such rubrics as "sacrament," "orthodoxy," and "heresy" in the discussion of the Johannine letters is to beg the fundamental question that one is attempting to answer. The correlation of this literature to the theology of the later church is needful, but we must beware of reading those later ecclesiological issues and sensibilities back into the Johannine epistles.

59. Cf., e.g., Hans Küng ("'Early Catholicism' in the New Testament as a Problem in Controversial Theology," in *The Council in Action: Theological Reflections on the Second Vatican Council* [New York: Sheed and Ward, 1963], 159–95), who rightly scores Protestant exegetical

intrinsically ill-defined.⁶⁰ In fact, if one were to leave intact the sociological concepts essential to the criteria (i.e., tradition, shared beliefs, hierarchical organization, rites, and so forth), divesting them only of their superficially Catholic *theologoumena*, one could probably discover "nascent Catholic" tendencies, not only in the letters of John, but also at Qumran, among the rabbis, in Islam, and in one's local Rotary Club. For the standards that have customarily been employed for defining and eliciting "early Catholicism" basically constitute a set of *sociological* tendencies displayed by most complex organizations of human beings, especially religious organizations. They are not, for the most part, essentially or even distinctively *Catholic* characteristics at all.

The quest of the sociological and theological *Sitze* of the Johannine epistles, as well as of other early Christian literature, will and should continue. The fundamental question raised by this essay is whether the category of "early Catholicism" is any longer adequate to advance that pursuit. If so, its definitional criteria, which are now exceptionally fuzzy, will have to be clarified and sharpened if they are to prove serviceable. If not, "early Catholicism" will have to be consigned to those "basic categories of the scholarly discipline" that require "dismantling and reassembling."⁶¹

---

prejudices against "early Catholicism in the N.T.," only to substitute a larger prejudice in its favor: "Only a Catholic can do justice to the Catholicism of the New Testament" (181).

60. Using many of the criteria just applied to the letters of John, an ostensibly plausible case could be made that 1 Corinthians is an "early Catholic" document. Locating himself within an "apostolic succession" (15:1–11), Paul unabashedly asserts his apostolic authority by exhorting, commanding, and threatening the Corinthians to a degree never witnessed in the Johannine letters (1 Cor 4:1–21; 6:1–6; 9:1–14). He orders the excommunication of a malefactor (5:1–13), expunges "heresy" when his own teaching becomes distorted (4:8–13; 8:7–13; 15:35–58), and, at the behest of the congregation, veers more sharply in the direction of legalistic casuistry than the Johannine presbyter ever dares (7:1–40). Also in evidence in 1 Corinthians is a more global understanding of the church (1:2; 10:32; 11:22; 15:9), a seemingly hierarchical ordering of the community's functionaries (12:27–30), a pronounced concern for the sources, transmission, and interpretation of tradition (11:23; 12:3), and an interest in "sacraments" that far exceeds that of 1 John (1 Cor 1:13b–17a; 10:16–17; 11:23–24). By no means am I here suggesting that we should seriously regard Paul as representative of "nascent Catholicism." My point is how little surprised we should be to find *Frühkatholizismus* in John's letters if we can "discover" it in 1 Corinthians.

61. James M. Robinson and Helmut Koester, *Trajectories through Early Christianity* (Philadelphia: Fortress, 1971), 1–8.

CHAPTER 15

Christian Ministry in Johannine Perspective

> Strange things happen. Again and again Christ is present not where, as priests, you would be apt to look for him but precisely where you wouldn't have thought to look for him in a thousand years.
>
> —Frederick Buechner

Light on Ministry in the Fourth Gospel

The Gospel of John is a rich resource for contemporary reflection on ministry, not least because that subject is addressed squarely but rarely. One of our recurrent temptations in reading the NT for insight into ministry, or anything else, is to forage for precepts and prescriptions that are instantly applicable to our own situation. We have our agendas, conscious or subconscious, that channel what we shall read and how we shall listen; and if the Fourth Gospel does not respond to our program, then so much the worse for John. Yet what if we were less anxious to dictate the terms of the conversation and more patiently attentive as John gives voice to his concerns? Our assured answers might be shaken, and unasked questions might be leveled at us. The interrogation of the Johannine literature[1] for its ministerial implications ends in its interrogation of us and our assumptions about ministry.

This essay was originally offered in honor of D. Moody Smith (1931–2016), George Washington Ivey Professor of New Testament, The Divinity School, Duke University. It is now offered in his memory.

1. Excluded from the following discussion is the book of Revelation, whose relationship to the Gospel and epistles of John remains perplexing. See Elisabeth Schüssler Fiorenza, "The Quest of the Johannine School: The Apocalypse and the Fourth Gospel," NTS 23 (1976–77): 402–27.

Some Accents of the Johannine Proclamation

1. Perhaps the most striking feature of the Fourth Gospel is its *relentless Christocentricity*. From the first sonorous verses of the prologue (1:1-18), through the complex controversies that occupy the first twelve chapters, through the farewell supper and its ensuing discourses (13:1-17:26), to the climactic hour of glorification through death and resurrection (18:1-20:31), the figure of Jesus is the prism through which this evangelist would have us view everything else—including, and especially, God. As C. H. Dodd observed, "In Christ therefore we have, realized, the archetype of that true relation of man to God which is henceforth made possible in [Christ]."[2] If this interpretation be faithful to the Johannine witness, then Christ in that Gospel may be fairly regarded as the archetypal minister, the one whose service constitutes the pattern that all of our ministries approximate, to a greater or lesser degree.

The Fourth Gospel suggests that the ministry of Jesus embraces both vertical and horizontal dimensions, as well as a characteristic manner in which these coordinates are held together. The vertical axis is *the witness borne by Christ to the Father who has sent him*. "Truly, truly, I say to you, the Son can do nothing of his own accord, but only what he sees the Father doing; for whatever he does, that the Son does likewise" (John 5:19).[3] In essence, word, and deed, Jesus directs others to God, with whom he shares utmost intimacy. It is this that lends Jesus's miracles in the Fourth Gospel their distinctive property as signs (*sēmeia*), through which the glory of God is made manifest (2:11; 4:54; 20:30-31; cf. 9:3; 11:4, 40-42). This ministry of witness also accounts, in large measure, for the paradoxical juxtaposition of Christ's elevation and subordination in the Fourth Gospel. For John, Jesus is virtually transparent to the intention and character of the Almighty: "He who has seen me has seen the Father; . . . I am in the Father and the Father in me" (14:9-10). Yet the Son is sent by, and dependent on, the Father whom he reveals: "I can do nothing on my own authority; . . . I go to the Father, for the Father is greater than I" (5:30; 14:28).[4]

---

2. Dodd, *The Interpretation of the Fourth Gospel* (Cambridge: Cambridge University Press, 1953), 166.

3. Scripture translations in this chapter are from the RSV unless otherwise indicated.

4. As C. K. Barrett carefully formulates it, "[For] John the historical figure of Jesus was central for his understanding of God; central, but not final" ("Christocentric or Theocentric? Observations on the Theological Method of the Fourth Gospel," in Barrett, *Essays on John* [Philadelphia: Westminster, 1982], 1-18); Barrett, "'The Father Is Greater Than I,' John 14.28: Subordinationist Christology in the New Testament," in Barrett, *Essays on John*, 19-36.

Witness is the vertical component of Jesus's ministry. Its horizontal complement is likened to *shepherding*, "I am the good shepherd. The good shepherd lays down his life for the sheep" (10:11; cf. Ezek 34:1–31). The royal shepherd's responsibility—to safeguard and unify one's entrusted flock—is promised (John 12:32), prayerfully asserted (17:11–12), and dramatically confirmed at Jesus's throne, the cross (19:17–42). This intimates the manner in which Jesus's ministry is exercised: *humbly*. Admittedly, the Johannine Jesus is neither gentle, meek, nor mild. He may be no freedom fighter, for his kingship is not of this world (18:36); still, he is consumed by zeal for his Father's house, ejecting the temple vendors with a cat-o'-nine-tails (2:13–17); he slams his opponents as children of the devil (8:44), and triumphantly hoists his own cross to Golgotha (19:17). It is precisely in this context that John's account of the Last Supper packs such an unexpected wallop: *this* Jesus, who is soon to lay down his life of his own accord, with magisterial power to take it again (10:18), now lays aside his garments and takes the basin with which to wash his disciples' feet (13:3–5). As portrayed by the Fourth Evangelist, the self-effacing humility of the glorious Son of God becomes a kind of parable: an enacted testimony to the projection of divine love, in all of its radiance, onto the shadows of human history (1:9; cf. 1 John 1:5–7).

2. The magnetic needle of the Johannine compass points to the Son, who in turn points to the Father who has sent him (John 17:3). Only from that primary orientation can Christian life take its proper bearings. To shift metaphors, Christian existence is defined by John as *a personal bonding to Christ*: "I am the vine, you are the branches. He who abides in me, and I in him, he it is that bears much fruit, for apart from me you can do nothing" (15:5). Nurturance for fruit-bearing branches is provided by the Holy Spirit, sent by the Son after his return to the Father (16:7; cf. 20:22). In John the emphasis falls heavily upon the one essential gift of the Spirit, which reveals the Father, brings to remembrance all that Jesus has said and done, and enlivens and unites individuals called by Christ (14:16–17, 26; 15:26–27; 16:13–14).[5] Unlike Paul (cf. 1 Cor 12:4–31), the Fourth Evangelist evinces little interest in the diverse charisms and different ministries that distinguish members of the body of Christ.

Developed within John's narrative are some important implications of this personal adhesion to Jesus. First, the union comes by invitation of Christ (John 6:70; 13:18; 15:16; 20:21) and is neither dependent on nor abrogated by the

---

5. With the dispersion of witnesses over time and space, the unification of Christians with Christ assumes particular importance in Johannine thought. For further discussion, see Paul S. Minear, "The Audience of the Fourth Evangelist," *Int* 31 (1977): 339–54.

disciples, whose understanding and conduct remain in some measure imperfect and inept (6:60, 66; 11:13; 12:16; 18:15–27). Second, the election of believers reveals a holistic thrust, as suggested by Jesus's claim to have other sheep, not of the original fold of the disciples and their successors: "I must bring them also, . . . so there shall be one flock, one shepherd" (10:16; cf. 4:39–42; 7:35b; 11:52; 12:20–22). Third, the call of the good shepherd is egalitarian in its sweep, as evidenced by the remarkable roles played by women throughout the Fourth Gospel: the Samaritan woman as missionary witness (4:28–30, 39–42), Martha as christological confessor (11:27; cf. 6:69; 20:31), Mary and others as attendants at Jesus's cruciform coronation (19:25b–27; cf. 12:2–8), and Mary Magdalene as first witness and joyful evangelist of the risen Christ (20:11–18).[6]

3. The keynote of discipleship is *loving service, expressed in faith*. In the Fourth Gospel love is no detached virtue among others; far less is it romanticized. It is the distinguishing feature of Christian existence, because its source and possibility, as well as its standard and measure, is Jesus's own love for the disciples, which in turn mirrors the Father's love for him. "As the Father has loved me, so have I loved you; . . . This is my commandment, that you love one another as I have loved you" (15:9, 12; cf. 13:34–35; 1 John 4:7–12). Raymond Brown pinpointed an obvious but profound characteristic of Johannine Christianity: John's community remembered Jesus as one who loved and was himself loved deeply; as a consequence, that community was shaped by the sine qua non of a person's loving contact with Christ.[7]

Certain aspects of a life lived in abidance with Christ are suggested by the Fourth Gospel. First, unlike second-century Gnosticism or twenty-first-century New Age spirituality, it is love, not self-enlightenment or divinization, that characterizes the believer's union with Christ and with God. Second, it is love, not hate, that is incumbent upon Christ's disciples. The world will likely hate those who bear witness to Jesus (15:18–19); that, however, constitutes no mandate for their reciprocation of hatred (cf. 1 John 4:13–21).[8] Third, it is

---

6. On "The Roles of Women in the Fourth Gospel," see the excellent treatment by Raymond E. Brown in *TS* 36 (1975): 688–99. On the democratic organization of the Johannine community, consult Ernst Käsemann, *The Testament of Jesus: A Study of the Gospel of John in the Light of Chapter 17*, trans. Gerhard Krodel (Philadelphia: Fortress, 1968), 27–55. More recently, see Ruth B. Edwards, "Ministry and Church Leadership in the Gospel of John," in *The Call to Serve: Biblical and Theological Perspectives on Ministry in Honour of Bishop Penny Jamieson*, ed. Douglas A. Campbell (Sheffield: Sheffield Academic Press, 1996), 117–41.

7. Brown, *The Churches the Apostles Left Behind* (New York: Paulist, 1984), 95–98.

8. On this point a comparison with the ethos of the Qumran community is instructive: "[The Master of the Community] shall admit into the Covenant of Grace all those who have

faithful obedience, not mystic communion, that makes love real: "If you love me, you will keep my commandments" (John 14:15; cf. 8:31; 14:24; 15:1–10, 16a; 1 John 2:4–5).

4. To abide in faithful love is to live even now in *the presence of eternity*: "Truly, truly, I say to you, he who hears my word and believes him who sent me, has eternal life; he does not come into judgment, but has passed from death to life" (John 5:24; cf. 3:18, 36; 6:47, 54–58; 17:3). This realized eschatology is variously portrayed by the Johannine Jesus: as a transfer in status from enslavement to friendship (15:15); as the imperishable security of sheep that are known by their shepherd (10:27–28; cf. 17:20); as the assurance of peace and joy amid the evanescence and grief of this world (14:27–28; 15:11; 16:22–33).

5. Although Christ has overcome the world, his followers are not removed from its perils (17:14–18). In Johannine perspective "the world" (*ho kosmos*) is the realm of unbelief, shrouded in darkness (8:12; cf. 11:9–10; 12:46) and governed by Satan (12:31), repudiating God's truth as revealed in Jesus (1:10; 8:23; 14:17; 16:8–11). Insofar as it attempts to define itself as the center of meaning, the world is self-deceived and sinful—even when such delusion and unrighteousness are cloaked in the trappings of religiosity (as symbolized throughout the Fourth Gospel by "the Jews": cf. 5:16, 30–47; 10:31–39; 11:45–53; 16:2).

On the other hand, *the world* is both the object and the arena of God's ultimate demonstration of love: the giving of his only Son (3:16). Thus, for John, the distinctive service rendered to the world by Christ and his followers is to expose and to challenge its pretensions to ultimate truth (15:19). The judgment (*krisis*) of this world, entailed by Jesus's coming and perpetuated by his disciples, is not the by-product of their principal mission but its inevitable outcome. Precisely by bearing witness to him and keeping his commandments, Jesus's followers lay bare, with penetrating light, the turbid unreality and irrelevance of the world's standards (15:18–27; 16:1–11; 17:14–19).[9]

The Fourth Gospel and Ministerial Reflection

From the rich tapestry of Johannine theology, we have drawn five salient threads: the centrality of Jesus, the Christian's bonding to Christ, the call-

---

freely devoted themselves to the observance of God's precepts, that ... they may love all the sons of light, each according to his lot in God's design, and hate all the sons of darkness, each according to his guilt in God's vengeance" (1QS 1.7.9–11; *The Dead Sea Scrolls in English*, trans. Géza Vermes [Harmondsworth, Middlesex: Penguin, 1962], 72).

9. Rudolf Bultmann, *Theology of the New Testament* (New York: Scribner's Sons, 1955). 2:15–69.

ing to love and remembrance, the presence of eternity, and witness within the world. Each of these can be securely tied to some of the challenges of today's ministry.

1. John's focus on *Jesus* wholesomely *relativizes the importance of the church and its ministry*. A goodly portion of contemporary theology proceeds by describing the human situation and then extrapolating from that description what must be true of God and of God's activity in the world. As I read the Fourth Gospel, this gets the matter exactly backward. For John, Jesus Christ stands at the center of Christian theological reflection, and from that center radiates the meaning of everything else. As Robert Kysar sums it up, "Christian existence is defined by Christology."[10]

If we reverse this process—if we begin with our ministries and the church's responsibility—then we risk arrogating primacy of place to *ourselves*, thus distorting both the gospel and the ministry of witness entrusted to us. The minister's task is neither to entice people into accepting the gospel nor to consummate God's new creation. The church and its ministers are not Jesus Christ. Our vocation is to point, in innumerable ways and manifold contexts, to Christ and to the God of limitless love who sent his Son to save this world (John 3:16; 12:44).[11] We are not the light: rather, like John the Baptist, we come to bear witness to the light (1:7-8). Indeed, given our self-preoccupations, the Baptist's testimony stands as a healthy ministerial motto: "I am not the Christ, but I have been sent before him. . . . He must increase, but I must decrease" (3:28, 30; cf. 13:16).

Ironically, this precept is exemplified by none more vividly than the Johannine Jesus. Amid the current welter of assertions of our rights and privileges as ministers, Christ returns, still carrying the towel and basin with which to wash our feet. "What I am doing you do not know now, but afterward you will understand" (13:7). Perhaps, someday, truly we shall understand that, whatever their contributions, all of our ministries are transient, provisional, and penultimate, that "The only *essential* 'ministry' in the Body [of Christ] is the ministry of the Living Christ Himself."[12]

---

10. Kysar, *John*, ACNT (Minneapolis: Augsburg, 1986), 265.

11. Along similar lines, recall the eloquent presentation of "The Ministry of the Community" in Karl Barth, *Church Dogmatics*, vol. 4: *The Doctrine of Reconciliation*, 3/2, ed. Geoffrey W. Bromiley and Thomas F. Torrance (Edinburgh: T&T Clark, 1962), 830-901.

12. W. D. Davies, "Light on the Ministry from the New Testament," in *Christian Origins and Judaism* (London: Darton, Longman & Todd, 1962), 237; cf. 231-45. In formulating this paragraph I am indebted to the insightful treatment of C. K. Barrett, *Church, Ministry, and Sacraments in the New Testament* (Grand Rapids: Eerdmans, 1985), 9-27.

2. Through the Spirit, *the call to ministry is issued to each and all*. Unlike the Synoptics (Mark 3:13–19a par.), John never details the formation of the Twelve, nor does he designate them as "apostles."[13] The Fourth Gospel implies no distinction between the ministries of "laity" and "clergy," between women and men. Neither geography, gender, ethnicity, nor proximity to Jesus, authorizes discriminations among Christians: "The hour is coming when neither on [Gerizim] nor in Jerusalem will you worship the Father. . . . But the hour is coming, and now is, when the true worshipers will worship the Father in spirit and truth" (John 4:21, 23). This holds, not only for Jesus's first followers, "but also for those who believe in me through their word" (17:20). Ministry, for John, is no official status but the elect vocation of all Christians, whose witness is coordinated by the Holy Spirit (14:15–17; 17:23).[14]

Moreover, this calling is intensely personal. Beginning with chapter 1, in which a particular witness to Christ enlists, in turn, another witness (from the Baptist, to Andrew, to Simon Peter [vv. 35–42]; from Jesus, to Philip, to Nathaniel [vv. 43–51]), so the pattern unfolds throughout the Fourth Gospel: *individuals* are typically confronted by Christ (cf. 3:1–21; 4:1–42; 4:46–54; 5:1–9; 9:1–41). While recent ecclesiological reflection has justifiably stressed the corporate dimensions of the church's witness, John's Gospel reminds us that the fruition of the vine depends nonetheless on the intimate abidance of its various branches in Christ (15:1–11).

3. The hallmark of *ministry is self-giving love*, in remembrance of Christ. James Denny, the Scots theologian and preacher (1856–1917), said that he wished he could walk into every church, hold up the cross, and say, "God loves like that."[15] That captures a fundamental Johannine insight: in word and deed, the minister's role is to remind the world of how God loves.

This comes to clearest expression near the end of the Fourth Gospel, with the risen Christ's appearance by the Sea of Tiberias. In addition to Jesus, two figures take center stage in chapter 21. First, Simon Peter is entrusted with the feeding and tending of Jesus's lambs, thus being confirmed as the community's representative pastor. The sole but utterly indispensable qualification for church leadership is Peter's *love* for Jesus (21:15–19). For Simon and his successors, both the power and pattern for serving Christ's flock derive from

---

13. In the Johannine maxim at 13:16, *ho apostolos* denotes an "envoy" or "delegate" and pertains as much to Jesus as to the Twelve. Among the Synoptics, Luke gravitates toward this designation of the Lord's earliest followers (6:13; 9:10; 11:49; 17:5; 22:14; 24:10), which the evangelist sustains in the Acts of the Apostles.

14. For a sensitive elaboration of this Johannine insight, see Edward Schillebeeckx, *Ministry: Leadership in the Community of Jesus Christ* (New York: Crossroad, 1986), N.B. 37.

15. Cited by Thomas A. Langford, "The Minister as Scholar," *DDSR* 39 (1974): 135–41.

the good shepherd, who subordinated himself to the One who sent him, who knows his charges intimately, and who gave himself in love for them, even unto death (10:1–18; cf. 12:24–26; 15:13; 1 John 3:16, 18).

Second, immediately after Peter's commissioning, there appears the anonymous guarantor of the Johannine tradition (John 21:24), who was regarded preeminently by that community as the disciple beloved by Jesus (21:20, 24; cf. 13:23; 19:26). If, in some sense, Peter represents pastoral service, then the Beloved Disciple symbolizes the ministry of remembering and proclaiming the revelation of God's love in Jesus Christ.[16] The two operations go hand in glove: to render pastoral care is to recall the work of the good shepherd; to bear witness to Christ is to participate in love that is responsive to God and responsible to one's sisters and brothers in faith. Love and evangelism are finally one and the same. "By this everyone will know that you are my disciples, if you have love for one another" (13:35 NRSV).[17]

4. *Ministry is offered within the sphere of eternity.* Whether it be committee reports or building maintenance, power brokerage or dangling conversations, sermons unheard or sermons unpreached, much that constitutes modern ministry may seem hollow and without purpose. Our quotidian works of love and remembrance are situated by John's Gospel on a bold and consoling canvas as wide as eternity, as near as the human heart. We labor, not aimlessly but by special appointment (15:16); not as nameless slaves but as friends of Jesus, who knows his own (15:15: cf. 10:14); not in despair but in the anguished joy of a mother giving birth (16:20–21); not in tragedy but in the triumph of him who has overcome this world (16:33); not alone but in concert with Christ, who is working and whose Father is working still (5:17).

5. *Witness to the truth, revealed in Christ, conflicts with a world that feeds on the phony.* John carries the keen edge of the Christian gospel, which cuts across this world's wisdom, conventional and otherwise. If this Evangelist's witness is true, then our culture, if not inherently wicked, is profoundly deluded and systemically diseased, exploiting every available political and religious stratagem to sustain the sin that infects it (cf. 5:37–47; 8:21–59; 11:45–53; 18:28–19:16). "And this is the judgment, that the light has come into the world, and [people] loved darkness rather than light because their deeds were evil" (3:19).

---

16. So also C. K. Barrett, "John 21.15–25," in Barrett, *Essays on John*, 159–67.

17. Moreover, love and evangelism must be coupled, lest the distinctively Christian witness be diluted. As Wolfgang Schrage observes, "Love cannot be separated from Jesus and made an ethical principle or program, to be practiced apart from him" (*The Ethics of the New Testament*, trans. David E. Green [Philadelphia: Fortress, 1988], 301).

Many may find the Fourth Gospel's pessimism too bitter to force down. Still, embedded in John's proclamation is a bracing candor that we ignore at our peril. H. Richard Niebuhr (1884–1962) lamented in our time a Christianity so anemic that it imagined "A God without wrath [who] brought men without sin into a kingdom without judgment through the ministrations of a Christ without a cross."[18] Ministers who accept the challenge of John are called for testimony, to bear witness to the light (1:7). When our voice becomes so muted as to be indistinguishable from the brazenly pagan babel of a secular world, we can be sure that our proclamation is neither Christian nor gospel.

The Dark Side of Ministry in the Gospel and Epistles of John

Theology is never spun from thin air. Reflection on faith is conducted always in conversation, and sometimes in heated debate, with an environing culture and a given set of historical circumstances. Though true of modern theology, this is no less apropos of the Fourth Gospel, notwithstanding its rather rarefied presentation of Jesus.

Some Theological Liabilities in Historical Context

Although the background and origins of Johannine Christianity remain controversial, some measure of scholarly consensus appears to have been reached.[19] The Fourth Gospel probably emerged during a painful period in which Pharisaic Judaism and Jewish Christianity were engaged in self-definition and retrenchment, each against the other. Such a setting would account, on the one hand, for John's portrayal of Jesus in terms that are latently, and in some cases patently, Christian (4:25-26; 5:19-46; 6:35-55; 17:1-26) as well as that Gospel's presentation of Jesus and "the Jews" in perpetual, acrimonious contention (e.g., 7:1-52; 8:12-59; 11:45-53). On the other hand, by the end of the first century CE, some Pharisees may have devised certain liturgical formulations, intended to smoke out Christ-confessing Jews and expel them from the synagogue, an expulsion that seems mirrored in John

---

18. Niebuhr, *The Kingdom of God in America* (New York: Harper & Row, 1937), 193.

19. Robert Kysar, *The Fourth Evangelist and His Gospel: An Examination of Contemporary Scholarship* (Minneapolis: Augsburg, 1975), esp. 83–172, supplemented by Kysar, "The Fourth Gospel: A Report on Recent Research," *ANRW* 3/2 (1985): 2380–480 (N.B. 2425–435), remain convenient, even-handed assessments. My brief presentation of the Johannine community's origins relies heavily on the landmark study by J. Louis Martyn, *History and Theology in the Fourth Gospel*, 3rd ed., NTL (Louisville: Westminster John Knox, 2003).

(9:22; 12:42; 16:2).²⁰ Though anachronistic during the ministry of Jesus, all of these features likely betoken the wrenching divorce of John's own community from its native Judaism.

Against this backdrop, several problematic aspects of Johannine theology become perceptible. First, *John's portrayal of Jesus is high but narrow*. In response to Pharisaic accusations of their incipient unorthodoxy, Johannine Christians intensified, rather than tempered, the offensiveness of their claims about Jesus. Consequently, and to a degree unsurpassed elsewhere in the NT, the Fourth Gospel culminates a tendency to invest Jesus with divine prerogatives (5:19-47; 8:51-58; 11:25-26). Understandably, the Jewish interlocutors in John regard such assertions as blasphemous (5:18; 10:33, 36); in effect, though not without qualification (5:19, 30; 6:38; 7:16-18), Jesus is equated with God: "I and the Father are one" (10:30; cf. 10:38; 20:28). John's excessive emphasis on the exalted Christ nearly overpowers the presumed humanity of Jesus.[21] Such theological decisions harbor pastoral import, as we shall witness momentarily.

Second, left unchecked, *Johannine Christianity tends toward an exaggerated individualism* that truncates the role of the church. From a Gospel so fervently supportive of a congregation under fire, the community of faith could never be utterly absent. Still, in a text reverberating with the dire consequences of personal decisions to confess Christ, the Johannine accent on the individual's response is not surprising. When plucked from that setting, or unrestrained by the broader concerns of a believing community, John's point of view risks sliding into solipsism, in which Christian belief and behavior are considered answerable only to the Spirit's personal testimony. Throughout history, it is no coincidence that the Fourth Gospel has been favored by mystics and individualists, whose credo might be epitomized by an old hymn's stanza:

> And He walks with me, and He talks with me,
> And He tells me I am His own.
> And the joy we share as we tarry there,
> *None other has ever known.*[22]

---

20. Although recent research has nuanced Martyn's hypothesis, now almost six decades old (e.g., Joel Marcus, "Birkat Ha-Minim Revisited," *NTS* 55 [2009]: 523-51), it still seems to be wearing well enough to make sense of Johannine theology and its presentation of "the Jews."

21. Notwithstanding Käsemann's outright denial of Jesus's humanity in John's Gospel (*Testament of Jesus*, 4-26), a more carefully nuanced consideration of this problem is offered by Marianne Meye Thompson, *The Humanity of Jesus in the Fourth Gospel* (Philadelphia: Fortress, 1988).

22. C. Austin Miles (1868-1946), "In the Garden," *The Cokesbury Worship Hymnal*, ed. C. A. Bowen (Baltimore: Methodist Publishing House, 1938), no. 62 (emphasis added).

Third, *Johannine moral teaching is substantively slender and tightly circumscribed.* The crisis provoked by this community's allegiance to Jesus may account for another remarkable characteristic of their Gospel: its slender ethical instruction. Jesus speaks almost entirely of himself, and with striking infrequency about the lived implications of that revelation for those who believe in him. Like the Christology with which it is absorbed, the teaching of Jesus in the Fourth Gospel is rich but unusually narrow in scope.[23]

To be sure, the Farewell Discourses are punctuated by injunctions to love (13:34-35; 15:12-17); however, such exhortations betray a distinctively Johannine tenor. Whereas Jesus in the Synoptics advocates love for enemies and prayer for persecutors (Matt 5:43-48; Luke 6:27-28, 32-36), the love command in John is conspicuously delimited to one's fellow believers: "Greater love has no [one] than this, that [one] lay down his life for his *friends*" (John 15:13, emphasis added). The Fourth Gospel exhibits ambivalence toward Christian responsibility to "the world": while Jesus's disciples are sent into it (17:14-19), for them the world remains alien and unreal, a realm less to be missionized than to be overcome (15:19; 16:33; 17:16). Born of a profound sense of hostile estrangement from its environment, the orientation of Johannine Christianity was decidedly centripetal. Under conditions of stress, that tendency could be aggravated and evolve into sectarianism.[24]

The Epistles of John as a Case Study in Johannine Ministry

Preserved within the canon are three brief documents that afford us insight into some applications, and implications, of a Johannine perspective on ministry.[25] The principal problem underlying the letters of John is a schism among Johannine Christians (1 John 2:19; 2 John 7; 3 John 10), evidently triggered by a depreciation of Christ's having come in the flesh (1 John 2:22; 4:3). Consistent with the Johannine

---

23. If the Synoptics were unavailable to the Fourth Evangelist, then his community's appreciation of their more developed ethical statements may have been unavoidably diminished.

24. The sectarian disposition of the Johannine community has been persuasively contended by Wayne A. Meeks, "The Man from Heaven in Johannine Sectarianism," *JBL* 91 (1972): 44-72, and D. Moody Smith Jr., "Johannine Christianity: Some Reflections on Its Character and Delineation," *NTS* 21 (1974-75): 222-48. A forceful argument against Johannine esotericism is lodged by Rudolf Schnackenburg, *The Gospel According to St. John* (New York: Crossroads, 1982), 3:213-17.

25. The cursory analysis that follows is indebted to the conjectural but not unreasonable reconstruction by Raymond E. Brown, *The Community of the Beloved Disciple* (New York: Paulist, 1979), 93-144. This monograph is the basis for the same author's benchmark commentary, *The Epistles of John: Translated, with Introduction, Notes, and Commentary*, AB 30 (Garden City, NY: Doubleday, 1982).

witness, the elder's rebuttal asserts the centrality of Jesus, the Christ (1 John 2:22; 4:3; 2 John 9), the practice of intramural love (1 John 2:3-6; 3:16-18; 4:7-21), and every believer's exercise of theological discernment (1 John 2:20, 27; 4:1).

Nevertheless, the vulnerabilities of a Johannine orientation also surface from the epistles with stark clarity. To begin with, the controversy that lacerated these communities may have been spawned, at least in part, by the internal dynamics of Johannine theology. From the Fourth Gospel, which spotlights the glorious divinity of Christ, certain Christians may have inferred—much to the Elder's horror—that *Jesus's humanity was soteriologically irrelevant* (cf. 1 John 2:18-22).

Second, the letters of John demonstrate how a community molded by *a dualistic, disaffected temperament* could perpetuate within its own walls a variant of the alienation that conditioned its birth. How cruel the irony that the vitriol spewed by the Johannine Jesus against "the Jews" is redirected, in the epistles, against other Christians (1 John 2:4; 3:4-15; 4:20; cf. John 8:24, 44). So polarized are truth and error, good and evil, that between the contending factions no compromise is possible, no quarter can be given (1 John 4:5-6). Indeed, no portion of scripture speaks more eloquently of love and with greater rancor of its adversaries than First John. Though we can grasp its causes, this aspect of the Johannine attitude seems tragically shallow and profoundly disturbing.

Finally, to counter the schismatics' distortions, *the elder noticeably departs from, or at least moderates, the excessive tendencies of Johannine Christianity*. Whereas John presupposes Jesus's humanity but elaborates his divinity, First John inverts the emphasis (1:1-3; 2:2; 4:2, 10; cf. Rom 3:24-25). Whereas the Fourth Gospel highlights salvation as a present reality, the first epistle underscores the ethical imperatives of eternal life and the future consummation of the elect (2:28; 3:2; 4:17). Although the elder never impeaches the authority of Spirit-filled individuals, his letters presage the general trends of catholic Christianity toward normative creeds (1 John 4:9-10; cf. 1 Tim 2:5-6) and ministerial leadership (Diotrephes [3 John 9]; the Elder himself [cf. 1 John 2:7-8; 2 John 4-5]).[26] While preserving the virtues of Johannine theology for ministry, the epistles thus disclose the ultimate inadequacy of an unmitigated Johannine attitude.

CONCLUSION

In a comprehensive survey conducted some years ago by the Association of Theological Schools, some five thousand Americans and Canadians were asked to name those traits of a minister that they considered most important. Re-

---

26. The nascent structures of Johannine ecclesiology are probed in ch. 14.

ceiving unanimous agreement among men and women, old and young, laity and clergy, Protestants and Catholics, was "an open and affirming style." The second and third areas of ministry regarded as most significant were "caring for persons under stress" and "congregational leadership."[27] It is undeniably laudable that laity would expect of clergy, and clergy would demand of themselves, such qualities as these. Even so, these respondents' *highest* expectations seem disappointingly jejune. As we ponder Christian ministry, are we not in danger of confusing style with substance, then offering the mess to a world already gorged with the one and starved of the other?

Within this context the Gospel and letters of John unfold a vision of discipleship that is original, bold, and indispensable. Their portrayal of Jesus as God's Word incarnate lies at the center of Christianity's distinctive confession. Their testimony to love, as the power unifying God with the world and each of us with the other, penetrates to the core of Christian service.

Though essential, John's declaration is also excessive. The bittersweet fruit of a beleaguered community, the Johannine perspective is lopsided and needs balancing out.[28] As regards theology and ethics, the church catholic has always known this: accordingly, John was yoked with the Synoptics. In matters of ministry, the epistles acknowledge and attempt to offset the hazardous extremes of their Johannine inheritance: for this reason they chasten the Fourth Gospel's proclamation by introducing divergent traditions and germinal structures of doctrine and discipline. The checkered experience of Johannine Christianity reminds contemporary ministers of their intrinsic responsibilities: theological acumen, pastoral perspicacity, and the constant calibration of both to the standard of God's love.[29]

---

27. David S. Schuller, Merton P. Strommen, and Milo L. Breecke, eds., *Ministry in America: A Report and Analysis, Based on an In-Depth Survey of 47 Denominations in the United States and Canada, with Interpretation by 18 Experts* (San Francisco: Harper & Row, 1980), N.B. 30–50.

28. In this connection, see the thoughtful analysis by D. Moody Smith, "Theology and Ministry in John," in *A Biblical Basis for Ministry*, ed. Earl E. Shelp and Ronald Sunderland (Philadelphia: Westminster, 1981), 186–228, esp. 213–14.

29. The substance of this essay was originally presented in lectures to The Conference on Ministry, sponsored in January 1989 by the Western New York Annual Conference of The United Methodist Church. I am grateful for the participants' comments and suggestions, as well as those of the Rev. Susan Pendleton Jones, Professor L. Gregory Jones, and Professor Marianne Meye Thompson.

CHAPTER 16

For the Life of the World

> I am the living bread which came down from heaven; if any one eats of this bread, he will live forever; and the bread which I shall give for the life of the world is my flesh.
>
> —John 6:51

ACROSS A LIFETIME OF STUDY, essays enjoy a great variety of geneses. This chapter came into being when some friends of mine, priests of the Greek Orthodox Church, asked if I would offer a precursory appraisal of scripture's use in *For the Life of the World: Toward a Social Ethos of the Orthodox Church* (2019; hereafter, *FLW*).[1] More on this document will be said momentarily. I'll begin with the stimulus, beyond amity, that prompted my accepting this invitation: the question of scripture's use in ecclesiastical formulations, a topic with which I had never seriously grappled. I begin by trying to ascertain an Orthodox framework for scripture's utilization for theological reflection. Then I'll shift to consideration of that document's general use of scripture. Finally, I'll slice off a significant segment to examine its adoption of scriptural warrants for ethical claims, some of which are fraught in twenty-first-century doctrine among all Christian denominations.

APPROPRIATING SCRIPTURE FOR THEOLOGICAL REFLECTION

Though now five decades old, the most helpful exposition of the range of theologians' possible appropriations of scripture, by my lights, remains David H. Kelsey's *The Uses of Scripture in Recent Theology*.[2] Kelsey's study is framed as

---

1. https://www.goarch.org/social-ethos.
2. Kelsey, *The Uses of Scripture in Recent Theology* (Philadelphia: Fortress, 1975); reissued

a descriptive analysis of the *de facto structure* of doctrinal positions based on the Bible—"what theologians are actually doing [with the Bible] as they pursue their craft" (7)—irrespective of their denominational affiliations, theoretical construals of scriptural authority, or theological proposals.

Kelsey begins by posing several "diagnostic questions." Among them: "What aspect(s) of scripture is (are) taken to be authoritative?" "What is it about this aspect of scripture that makes it authoritative?" "How is the scripture that is cited brought to bear on theological programs so as to authorize them?" (15, 26). For Benjamin Breckenridge Warfield (1851–1921) and Hans-Werner Bartsch (1915–83), scriptural authority depends on a property intrinsic to the text: for Warfield, the *doctrine* of inerrant inspiration; for Bartsch, such quasi-technical *concepts* as the eschatological gifts of "peace" and "life." Alternatively, scriptural authority may inhere, not in conceptual properties, but in its *heilsgeschichtlich recital* of God's redemptive acts (G. Ernest Wright, 1909–74) or in *narrative patterns* by which God makes himself known (Karl Barth, 1886–1968). Finally there's the "muffin-full-of-berries" model. Pick your fruit. For Lionel Spencer Thornton (1884–1961), biblical authority resides in a network of literary *images* that evoke God's self-revelatory restoration of creation; for Paul Tillich (1886–1965), in religious *symbols* conveying the original revelation of Jesus as the Christ and contingent revelatory events; for Rudolf Bultmann (1884–1976), in kerygmatic *myths* expressing God's address to human beings and in theological statements demonstrative of one's existence in faith (14–88).

In each case, Kelsey deduces, the theologian has decided on some pattern in scripture to which an appeal is made (103). In every case scripture's authority is functional: it *does* something. Biblical texts "shape persons' identities so decisively as to transform them . . . when used in certain ways in the common life of the church" (90). "'Scripture' is used to name, not something the church is, but something she must *use*, according to some concepts of 'church,' to preserve her identity. 'Tradition' is used to name, not something the church uses, but something the church *is*, insofar as her reality lies in a set of events and practices that can be construed as a single activity" (96).[3]

Accordingly, there is no single norm that is "Scripture," but, rather, related but different concepts of scripture (14–15). Kelsey identifies three "families" or *modes* of scriptural appeal by which God is imagined as present. One, represented by Warfield, Bartsch, and Wright, is *ideational*, "like having personally appropriated

---

in 1999 by Trinity Press International under the title *Proving Doctrine: The Uses of Scripture in Modern Theology*. Subsequent citations to this source will appear as in-text citations.

3. In the original these two sentences occur in reverse order.

a set of concepts [from scripture] with such seriousness that they decisively shape one's emotions, passions, and feelings." A second mode is that of *concrete actuality*, "when God is taken to be present in and through an agent rendered present by scripture (Barth) or in and through a cosmic process of re-creation (Thornton)." A third family clusters around *ideal possibility*: "God is taken to be present in and through existential events occasioned by scripture's kerygmatic statements, which announce the possibility of authentic human existence (Bultmann), or occasioned by the biblical picture of Jesus as the Christ which mediates the power which makes new being possible (Tillich)" (161). Each mode presupposes a configuration of criteria that constructs or criticizes the church's current forms of speech and activity (92–95, 160, 163). Presupposed by any theologian's appeal to scriptural warrant is a *discrimen*: an imaginative judgment that attempts to "catch up" the mode in which God is present in the church to which that principle of judgment is accountable (167, 170–75). No *discrimen*, no doctrine of scriptural authority, no theological position of any kind guarantees congruence with divine knowledge and will. "Theological proposals are concerned with what *God* is now using scripture to do, and no degree of sophistication in theological methodology can hope to anticipate that!" (215–16 [emphasis added]).

The Intent, Structure, and Use of Scripture in *For the Life of the World*

The Statement's Purpose

As noted by His Eminence Archbishop Elpidophorous of America (1967–), *FLW* intends to offer the Orthodox Christian Faithful "practical and pastoral" reflections on today's social issues, "general guidelines to difficult questions." Its audience is ecumenical: "all people of good will" who respond to "the better angels of our nature, and to richer and deeper communion with God and with one another."[4]

The Statement's Structure

Bracketed by an introduction (1) and conclusion (IX), *FLW* is subdivided into eighty-two sections, arranged in seven chapters: "The Church in the Public

---

4. In a letter (2020) issued from the Greek Orthodox Archdiocese of America, www.goarch.org.

Sphere" (II), "The Course of Human Life" (III), "Poverty, Wealth, and Civil Justice" (IV), "War, Peace, and Violence" (V), "Ecumenical Relations and Relations with Other Faiths" (VI), "Orthodoxy and Human Rights" (VII), "Science, Technology, the Natural World" (VIII).

The Use of Scripture in For the Life of the World

The Discrimen

Kelsey proceeds from diagnoses of theologians' uses of scripture, through construals of the mode in which they perceive God's activity in scripture, to an imaginative *discrimen* "against which the theology criticizes the church's current forms of speech and life" (Kelsey, 163). For our purposes it may be helpful to reverse that procedure. Let us ask: (1) What, for the *FLW*'s framers, is Christianity "basically all about in a single, synoptic, imaginative judgment"? (159). (2) In conceiving the mode of God's presence in scripture, to which of Kelsey's "families" do this statement's authors belong? (3) What specific aspects of scripture are authoritative in *FLW*, and how are they invoked as warrants for this text's proposals? My hunch is that we may better understand *FLW*'s use of scripture by first identifying its a priori assumptions about the character of Christian faith. What, for this document's authors, is the point of doing theology? How do their appeals to scripture serve in clarifying theology's subject matter?

For Kelsey, the theologian's *discrimen*, or concentrated imaginative judgment, comprises two reciprocating coefficients: (1) the mode in which the theologian understands God as present among the faithful and (2) Scripture's use in the community's life (160, 167–69, 212–13). *FLW* does not define its *discrimen* as such. One must intuit that from its authors' most insistent, habitual claims.

FLW's introduction coordinates theology, Christology, pneumatology, anthropology, ecclesiology, soteriology, and missiology.

1. "The Orthodox Church understands the human person as having been created in the image and likeness of God . . . for free and conscious communion and union with God in Jesus Christ, inasmuch as we are formed in, through, and for him" (I.1).[5]

2. "[W]e are made for loving communion . . . with the Kingdom of the Father and of the Son and of the Holy Spirit; and through communion with God as Trinity, human beings are also called into loving communion with their neighbors and the whole cosmos" (I.2).[6]

---

5. See also II.12; III.24, 30; VII.61–62, 65, 67.
6. See also I.1; II.13; III.27; V.47; VI.50–60; VII.62; VIII.68, 70, 80.

3. "The ultimate destiny, moreover, to which we are summoned, is nothing less than our *theōsis*: our deification and transformation by the Holy Spirit into members of the body of Christ, joined in the Son to the Father, whereby we become true partakers of the divine nature (I.3). . . . On the path to communion with God, it is humanity's vocation . . . to bless, elevate, and transfigure . . . this world, so that its intrinsic goodness may be revealed even amidst its fallenness" (I.4).[7]

4. "Our service to God is fundamentally doxological in nature and essentially Eucharistic in character" (I.1). "In giving himself always anew in the Eucharistic mystery, Christ draws us forever to himself, and thereby draws us to one another" (I.5).[8]

Here is my own attempt to articulate the *discrimen* of *FLW*: *Created in the divine image and likeness for communion with the Triune God, fortified by the Eucharistic mystery in which Christ forever draws to himself all creation, human beings are destined for deification by the Spirit's transformative power, which entails their calling to cooperate with God in this world's transfiguration by giving themselves unreservedly to God and to neighbor, in whose face they see Christ*. As witnessed in footnotes 5–8, elements of this complex compound recur throughout the entire document as theological touchstones. As we shall see, this *discrimen* exerts a magnetic attraction of particular scriptural texts—some, repeatedly—to the effective obviation of others. In this *discrimen* one may also discern the classical traits of Orthodox hermeneutics: the assumption of scriptural authority, harmonized with patristic tradition; fidelity to the mystery of Christ, primarily in the Eucharist; the coherence of piety with ethos; pastoral benefit for the faithful, summoned by scripture, tradition, and liturgy "to the sanctifying labor of justice and mercy" (I.7).[9]

The Mode of Scriptural Appeal

Kelsey's taxonomy of modes of scriptural appeal attempts to map various theological settings in which a *discrimen* is applied in the selection of biblical warrants. The hermeneutical family with which *FLW* demonstrates least resemblance is the ideational, represented by Warfield and Bartsch, both of whom

---

7. See also III.15, 18, 20–21, 27; IV.39–40; V.44–47; VI.50, 58, 60; VII.62–69; VIII.68, 70–76, 81–82; IX.79.

8. See also II.8, 12; III.16, 20, 24, 29; V.44; VII.65; VIII.73–75, 78; IX.79.

9. See Georges Florovsky, *Bible, Church, Tradition: An Eastern Orthodox View* (Belmont, MA: Nordland, 1972); Theodore G. Stylianopoulos, "Scripture and Tradition in the Church," in *The Cambridge Companion to Orthodox Christian Theology*, ed. Mary B. Cunningham and Elizabeth Theokritoff (Cambridge: Cambridge University Press, 2008), 21–34.

locate scriptural authority in some intrinsic property of the text. Occasionally *FLW* adverts to biblical "ideals" and "symbols" in characterizing revelatory or salvific events. "The ideal of the Apostolic Church" is upheld "as the purest expression of Christian charity as a social logic and communal practice" (I.6). "Parenthood is a distinctively privileged symbol of love's transfiguring power, as well as of God's love for his creatures" (III.23). Such references to "ideal possibility" are rare in *FLW*; none aligns with Tillich, whose use of "symbols" flirts with christological vacuity,[10] or with Bultmann, whose demythologization of eschatology ends up privatizing human "existence in faith."[11] "There is above all an ultimate *spiritual and ontological identity*, the same faith, the same spirit, the same ethos. And this constitutes the distinctive mark of Orthodoxy" (VI.50, emphasis original).

FLW bears closest family resemblance to the concrete actuality propounded by Lionel Thornton. For him the Bible's unifying theme is "restoration," "a return of our nature to that wholeness of being for which we were designed."[12] Scriptural authority resides in its revelatory linkage of the church to God's own creativity, manifested in "mysteries." A mystery is "like a bright lamp . . . [whose] rays are the medium by which we can see all things clearly."[13] The central mystery is Jesus Christ, the incarnation of divine creativity and the unique connection between history, the "human foreground," and the "cosmic background" of God's victorious restoration of harmony out of chaos. That process is organic, binding both cosmic and personal redemption. "[Christ] is the mould and archetype of creation's order. . . . He manifests what deity is . . . in terms of what every child of Adam should be and may yet become."[14]

The resonance of Spencer's attitude with that of *FLW* is obvious. Its social ethos affirms "the goodness of creation in its first and final forms" (IV.44) and "the love, mercy, and justice of God as revealed in Christ" (IV.39): the divine Logos (I.7; VI.54, 58) through whom all creation was fashioned and is pervaded (VI.55). A constant refrain is God's intent to restore all things to himself (IV.37, 39; V.44; VII.65; VIII.68, 74, 77; IX.80); *theōsis* is humanity's perfect restoration in God's image (I.3; III.15, 20, 31). The marriage of personal and cosmic, temporal and eternal, is realized in mystery: the Eucharist of the self-donative Logos (I.5; III.27; VI.55; VIII.71, 75).

---

10. Kelsey, *Uses*, 71–74.
11. Kelsey, *Uses*, 74–85.
12. Thornton, *The Dominion of Christ* (London: Dacre, 1952), 5, 9, 11, 58.
13. Thornton, *Dominion of Christ*, 2.
14. Thornton, *Dominion of Christ*, 113, 189.

The Application and Warrants of Particular Texts

By my reckoning, *FLW* explicitly appeals to scriptural texts as theological warrants 136 times, with at least seven clear allusions not expressly cited.[15] The distribution of scriptural citation is uneven, with respect to the document's sections and in its appeal to the OT and NT. Most scriptural appeals (42) occur in chapter 4 ("Poverty, Wealth, and Civil Justice"); the fewest (6), in chapter 9 ("Conclusion"). Scriptural warrants from the NT (101) outnumber those from the Old (35) by a ratio of almost three to one. In a church whose liturgy privileges the NT, that is predictable.[16] The largest clusters of OT appeals touch considerations of indebtedness and poverty (16 references in IV.39) and the extension of "hospitality and protection for strangers in need" (9 citations in VII.66). Sixty of 101 NT references are to the Gospels: unsurprising in the light of their importance in Orthodox worship and *FLW*'s recurrent, blanket appeal to "the teachings [or instruction] of Christ" (I.6; III.16; IV.39, 41) or an analogous phrase (e.g., III.15: "the Kingdom of God and its justice"). Almost half of all its Gospel citations (29) are from Matthew,

---

15. Explicit citations: Gen 1:24–31, 26, 31; 2:24; 9:9–11; 12:3; Exod 12:49; 22:21–22, 25; 23:9; Lev 19:9–10, 34; 23:22; 25:35–38, 36–37; Deut 10:17–19; 15:1–11; 23:19–20; 27:19; Judg 6:24; Job 31:32; Pss 15:5; 133:1; 146:3, 9; Isa 3:13–15; 5:8; 10:1–2; 58:6–7; Jer 5:27–28; Ezek 18:17; Amos 4:1; Mal 3:5; Matt 5:4, 9, 42, 43–48; 6:3, 9–13, 19–20, 33; 8:20; 10:29 (2x); 11:28; 18:4, 6 (2x); 19:5–6, 14, 16–30; 22:21, 37–39, 41; 25:31–46 (2x), 34–36, 40 (2x), 41–45, 44–45, 46; Mark 9:42; 10:7–8, 14–16, 17–31; Luke 2:32, 52; 4:18–19, 18–21, 29; 6:24–25; 9:58; 12:7, 33, 58–59; 14:13, 33; 16:9, 25; 17:2; 18:6–17, 18–30; 20:46–47; John 3:17; 9:3; 13:35; 14:27; 15:13; 17:11, 14–15, 21; 18:36; Acts 2:32–35, 42–46, 44–45; 4:32–37; 5:29; 15:5–29; 17:23; Rom 2:15, 8:19, 21, 22, 28; 11:16–24; 13:1–7 (2x); 1 Cor 6:19; 7:14; 9:24–27; 13:5, 12; 2 Cor 4:4, 6; 3:18; 5:17; Gal 3:28 (2x); Eph 4:12; 5:21; Phil 2:6–7; 4:8; Col 1:16; Jas 2:6; 1 Tim 2:4; 5:18; Phlm 15–16; Heb 11:13; 13:2, 14; 13:14; 1 John 3:2; 2 Pet 3:9; Rev 7:11. Seven allusions: Gen 1–2 (V.42: "the opening chapters of Genesis"); Gen 2:24 (III.24: "one flesh"); Ps 128:6 (III.23: "[your] children's children"); Matt 21:12 (II.9: "[Christ's] cleansing the Jerusalem Temple"); Luke 1:41, 44 (III.25: the exuberant leaping of Elizabeth's fetus); John 2:1–11 (III.20: "the wedding feast at Cana"); John 18:36 (III.27: the "kingdom . . . not of this world"). The document explicitly warrants its claims from traditions of the church's fathers and mothers 91 times. Thus, Scripture is cited 1.50 percent more often than traditional sources: near equilibrium in their service as theological warrants.

16. During the liturgical year the Gospels are read almost in their entirety, as are much of Acts and the Epistles. Outside of Lent little of the OT is read: mainly Genesis, Exodus, Isaiah, Ezekiel, Proverbs, Job; sometimes Numbers, Daniel, Baruch, Judges, 1 and 2 Kings; Joel, Zechariah, Malachi. It is strange that *FLW* draws so little from the Psalms (four citations) since, as Archimandrite Ephrem Lash observes, the Psalter is "the backbone of the daily round of offices" ("Biblical Interpretation in Worship," in Cunningham and Theokritoff, *Cambridge Companion*, 35–48; quotation, 37).

which is extraordinarily attentive to the moral implications of Christian faith. The scriptural text most frequently cited throughout *FLW* is Matthew 25:31-46 or some portion thereof (8x). This pericope elicits an unusually emphatic statement: "It is impossible for the Church truly to follow Christ or to make him present to the world if it fails to place *this absolute concern* for the poor and disadvantaged *at the very center of its moral, religious, and spiritual life*" (IV.33, emphasis added). To read this in a treatise that opens, "Our service to God is *fundamentally doxological in nature and essentially Eucharistic* in character" (I.1, emphasis added), is surprising. One may justifiably posit "the seamless coherence of theology, spirituality and daily life,"[17] even as *FLW* contends that service to God and to neighbor is inseparable (Matt 22:37-39). It is the absolutist, seemingly self-contradictory phrasing that startles: the Eucharist as the church's essential fundament, cheek by jowl with service to the destitute as utterly central in the church's religious and spiritual life. *Per definitionem* one must be dominant; the other, derivative. It is difficult to see how *both* can be irreducibly ultimate.

Scriptural Warrants for "The Course of Human Life"

Let us examine one chapter of *FLW* as a test case. Following an introduction that espouses "diverse vocations for Christian living" within *theōsis* (§15), "The Course of Human Life" considers children (§§16-17), adolescence (§18), sexual orientation (§19), marriage (§§20-22) and parenthood (§23), contraception (§24), abortion (§25) and neonatal death (§26), monastic and other expressions of unmarried life (§§27-28), the equal dignity of men and women (§29), the aged (§30), and death (§31). Ten of twenty-three scriptural references occur in §§16, 18, 26; seven, in §§20-21, 23. Thus, 82 percent of this chapter's scriptural appeals refer to marriage and children.[18]

By passing through infancy and childhood, Christ sanctified children. Accordingly, they signify "the life of the Kingdom graciously present in our midst, and must be the object of the Church's ceaseless concern and diligence" (III.16; citing Matt 18:4; 19:14 parr.). Christ mandates their protection from abuse

---

17. Stylianopoulos, "Scripture and Tradition," 30.
18. As for the remaining 18 percent (four verses): 1 Cor 13:12 ("seeing God face to face"); 1 John 3:2 ("we shall be like [God]": III.15); 2 Cor 3:18 ("being changed into [the Lord's] likeness from one degree of glory to another": RSV §31). Alongside Gen 1:26 (I.1), John 17:21, 23, and 2 Pet 1:4, these are the strongest biblical supports for Athanasius's belief in humanity's future deification (*De incarn.* 54.3). Hebrews 13:14 is presented as grounds for the life of monastics, who "remind us that 'we look to the city which is to come'" (III.27).

and violation in all forms (Matt 18:6 parr.). God's love for all children and the church's gratitude for their "exceptional charisms" is one of *FLW*'s most powerful declarations. A quibble may be raised of its characterization of children in the Gospels: the persistent emphasis on their "innocence" or "guilelessness" (III.16, 17). Immediately compared with those whose entry into eternal life is blocked by wealth (Matt 19:16–22 parr.), the advantage enjoyed by children is their lack of authority and utter vulnerability, their "fragility and dependency," as *FLW* puts it (III.16): the helplessness to do what only God can do for them (Matt 19:26 parr.).[19]

"The Church took the institution of marriage—which had previously been a relationship understood largely in proprietary and legal terms, concerned principally with domestic and familial economy—and transfigured it into an indissoluble bond between persons that mystically signifies the love of Christ for his Church . . . [and] a shared effort toward the transfiguration of the world with God" (III.20–21). For these claims, five scriptural warrants are adduced: Genesis 2:24; Matthew 19:5–6 // Mark 10:7–8; John 2:1–10; 1 Corinthians 7:14. Oddly, except for the first three's conceptual association with "an indissoluble bond," none of these texts constitutes best evidence for *FLW*'s argument. Marriage as significatory of Christ's mystical love for his church as a bride is mentioned in Paul (2 Cor 11:2). It is most thoroughly developed in Ephesians 5:21–33, which expresses, in microcosm, the macrocosm of 1:1–5:20: God's use of the church for the purpose of cosmic redemption.[20] In fact, the transmogrification of marriage from an economic buttress to an audacious religious metaphor began with Hosea 2–3 (8th c. BCE), was dilated by subsequent prophets (Jer 2:20–25; 3:1–3; Ezek 16; Trito-Isa 61:10; 62:5; Mal 2:14), and consummated in Revelation (19:6–10; 21:2–14; cf. Isa 65:17).[21]

Most curious of all: eight of the seventeen sections in *FLW* IIII appeal to no scripture at all. And these address some of the most contentious topics in twenty-first-century Christian ethics.[22]

1. In §19 a spectrum of human sexuality is accepted "as a simple physiolog-

---

19. C. Clifton Black, *Mark*, ANTC (Nashville: Abingdon, 2011), 224–29.

20. *FLW* III.20 notes mutual subservience in Eph 5:21 but disregards that epistle's pertinence for its overriding claim.

21. Other conspicuous omissions from the document's presentation of marriage are its delight, happiness, imagination, and trust (Prov 5:18–20; 18:22; 19:14; 31:10–31; Eccl 5:9–12; 9:9; Cant 4:10–11; 5:1): the very charisms attributed to childhood (§16).

22. Less controversial are §17 (on parental guidance), §22 (divorce and remarriage), and §23 (dignified care for the elderly), all of which invite scriptural warrants (respectively, Prov 1:8–7:27; 1 Cor 7:1–40; Lev 19:32; Isa 46:3–4; Sir 3:1–16).

ical and psychological fact, . . . not simply a consequence of private choice." Human identity resides principally in the *imago Dei*, "not in one's sexuality or any other private quality." Absent from III.19 is any reference to, much less contextualization of, biblical prohibitions of same-sex relations (Lev 18:1–30; Rom 1:16–27; 1 Cor 6:9).[23] Is not this a "difficult question" for which most Christians are seeking "general guidelines"?

2. In §§24–25 the destruction of fertilized ova and the practice of abortion are forbidden. Indirect scriptural warrant, drawn from the Feast of the Visitation, is John the Baptist's joyous acclamation, in utero, of Mary's pregnancy (Luke 1:41, 44). Here, as in the Feast of the Annunciation, an unstated premise is declared: "Life begins at the moment of conception." At this point medical science goes mute (cf. VIII.71), doubtless because of its doctrinal irrelevance. The only scriptural text that refers to abortion, as a consequence of a woman's abuse—Exodus 21:22–25—goes unmentioned. That is exegetically prudent: scholars dispute whether the "harm" (Heb. *'ason*) to be remedied is that done to the mother or to the fetus.[24] Associated with infanticide owing to a neonate's exposure (Philo, *Spec.* 111.108–17), the oldest explicit Christian proscriptions of abortion (Gk. *phthora*) occur in the Didache (2.2 [*FLW* III.25]; 5.1–2) and the Epistle of Barnabas (19.5; both c. 100).

3. Based on Basil of Caesarea (*De hum. cond.* 1.18) and Gregory Nazianzen (*Disc.* 37.6), *FLW* asserts without reservation "the full equality and dignity" of women vis-à-vis men (III.29). Dearth of scriptural warrant for this claim is puzzling. Twice (I.6; VII.65) Galatians 3:28 is cited to substantiate points other than this. No pastoral counsel is offered in the exegesis of such texts as 1 Corinthians 14:33b–36, Ephesians 5:22–24, 1 Timothy 2:11–15, or 2 Timothy 3:6–7, seized throughout church history to justify female subordination. "Superstitious prejudices about purity and impurity in regard to women's bodies" (III.29) are dismissed as though defilement by menstruation (Lev 15:19–24; 18:19; 20:18), lochial discharge after childbirth (Lev 12:1–8), or abnormal menstrual flow (Lev 15:25–30) were nonexistent in the OT. My intent is not to reinstate the Priestly Holiness Code but to wonder why its exegesis is never considered "practically and pastorally." Attention to the Spirit's promptings is paid to such women's ministries as theologians and canonists. Nothing is said

---

23. See Jacob Milgrom, *Leviticus 17–22: A New Translation with Introduction and Commentary*, AB 3A (New York: Doubleday, 2000), 1514–93; Robert Jewett, *Romans: A Commentary*, Hermeneia (Minneapolis: Fortress, 2006), 148–92.

24. See Daniel Sinclair, "The Legal Basis for the Prohibition of Abortion in Jewish Law," *ILR* 15 (1980): 109–30; Yihiel Michael Bar-Alin, "Her Pain Prevails and Her Judgment Respected—Abortion in Judaism," *JLR* 25 (2009): 97–186.

of inducements to female clergy, presumably due to a precedent set by the earliest Christian *presbyteroi* and *episkopoi* (1 Tim 3:1–7; 5:17–21; Titus 1:5–9): elder males whose leadership was analogous to that of synagogal counterparts (Luke 8:40–42) and local councils (Luke 7:3). Nevertheless, Scripture presents strong female protagonists: Deborah and Jael (Judg 4–5), Ruth, Esther, Judith, Elizabeth, Mary Magdalene and other female ministers to Jesus (Luke 8:2–3) entrusted with news of his resurrection (Matt 28:1–10 parr.; John 20:1–18), female leaders in Paul's churches (Rom 16:1, 3, 6, 12–13, 15; 1 Cor 11:5–6; Phil 4:2–3), and, *prima inter pares*, Mary the *Theotokos* (Luke 1–2). No one expects Eastern Orthodoxy to tailor its priests to Protestant measurements. One simply wonders why *FLW* offers no biblical warrant even for the female diaconate (III.29; see 1 Tim 3:8–11; cf. 5:3–16).

4. Long regarded by Eastern Orthodoxy "as a tragedy and as a profound assault upon the dignity of the human person," suicide is revisited as the outcome of "mental illness and emotional fragility . . . that significantly compromise a person's rationality and freedom" (III.31). Basis for this conclusion is an episcopal *Pastoral Letter on Suicide* (2007); no appeal to Scripture is made. The Bible details a half-dozen suicides (Judg 9:50–54; 1 Sam 31:4–5 // 1 Chron 10:4–5; 2 Sam 17:23; 1 Kgs 16:18; Matt 27:3–10). In none of these cases is the act censured.

Preliminary Findings

As introduced, this investigation is nothing more than an early assessment. *FLW* is an intricate, 32,419-word treatise, whose scriptural deployment invites analysis more comprehensive than can be presented here. I have tried to capture the statement's primary theological presuppositions about and practical application of Scripture as faithfully as possible. In sum: *FLW* exhibits fine coherence of its hermeneutical premises and mode of scriptural appeals. Its manifest employment of Scripture suggests an uneven *ressourcement*, which, if redressed, would strengthen its laudable endeavor to assist in true reorientation of the moral compass of Christians "immersed in the fire of the Holy Spirit" (IX.79).

CHAPTER 17

Rightly Dividing the Truth of Word

> We live in a fantasy world, a world of illusion. The great task in life is to find reality.
>
> —Dame Iris Murdoch

QUESTION: "HOW DOES THE AREA of the canon with which you most often work contribute to our understanding of what it means to claim that the Scriptures are true?"

Answer: Though straying into other pockets of Scripture, I usually roam the Gospels. Neither Matthew, Mark, nor Luke evinces the slightest interest in the question of Scripture's truthfulness.

Here are the lexical data:

- *alētheia* (truth), seven occurrences: Matthew 22:16 // Mark 12:14 // Luke 20:21; Mark 5:33; 12:32; Luke 4:25; 22:59;
- *alēthēs* (true), two occurrences: Matthew 22:16 // Mark 12:14;
- *alēthinos* (genuine): Luke 16:11;
- *alēthōs* (truly), eight occurrences: Matthew 14:33; 26:73 // Mark 14:70; Matthew 27:54 // Mark 15:39; Luke 9:27; 12:44; 21:3.

Most of these occurrences could be Anglicized, "the fact is" (Mark 12:32; Luke 4:25; 9:27; 12:44; 21:3; Matt 26:73 // Mark 14:70 // Luke 22:59).[1] The highest concentration is in the pericope of Caesar's coin (Matt 22:15–22 // Mark 12:13–17 // Luke 20–26), in which cognates are hypocritically slathered by Jesus's adversaries. Jesus's identity as "truly God's Son" is acknowledged reverentially by his

---

1. These are akin to Jesus's solemn affirmations, *amēn legō hymin*, "Certainly I say to you": thirty-one times in Matthew, thirteen in Mark, six in Luke. The Johannine Jesus doubles the emphasis, *amēn*, fifty times.

disciples and the centurion at the cross in Matthew (14:33; 27:54), ambiguously in Mark (15:39).[2] In none of these instances is scriptural truth at issue. Its veracity is presupposed in exegesis (e.g., Matt 12:3–7 // Mark 2:25–26 // Luke 6:3–4) or midrashic debate (Matt 22:23–33 // Mark 12:18–27 // Luke 20:27–40).

The Fourth Gospel is another kettle of cod. Although it uses *alēthēs* with an ordinary connotation (4:18; 10:41), while Jesus and others respond *alēthōs* (1:47; 8:31; 17:8; 19:35), in John 1:17 and 14:6 Jesus himself *is hē alētheia*: "eternal reality as revealed to men—either the reality itself or the revelation of it."[3] The truth that Jesus is and reveals[4] is beyond cognition; it is inherently relational. Jesus's teaching is not his own but that of "the only true God" (*ton monon alēthinon*, 17:3): "The one who seeks the glory of the one who sent him, this one is truthful [*alēthēn*] and in him there is no wickedness"[5] (7:18; see also 5:19; 7:28; 8:42; 10:18). As for humanity, Jesus is the genuine fulfillment of its basic needs: "the true [*to alēthinon*] light, which enlightens every person" (1:9); "the real [*alēthinon*] bread from heaven," "the bread of life" given by the Father that all who come to Jesus may not hunger (6:32, 35); "the authentic [*alēthinē*] vine," which the Father cultivates for Jesus's disciples, "the fruit-bearing branches" (15:1, 5); the eternal envoy who testifies to the truth and whose judgment is valid (*alēthinē*: 8:16), because the Father testifies to him (8:18; 18:37) and concurs with his decisions (8:16, 26, 50).[6]

It is no surprise, therefore, that the Johannine Jesus throws more light on the Jewish Bible than it sheds on him. "You examine the scriptures in which you consider you have eternal life; yet they also testify to me" (8:39). By con-

---

2. See C. Clifton Black, *Mark*, ANTC (Nashville: Abingdon, 2011), 332–33.

3. C. H. Dodd, *The Interpretation of the Fourth Gospel* (Cambridge: Cambridge University Press, 1953), 177.

4. *alētheia*: John 1:14, 17; 3:21; 4:23, 24; 5:33; 8:32 (2x), 40, 44 (2x), 45, 46; 14:6, 17; 15:26; 16:7, 13 (2x); 17:17 (2x), 19; 18:37 (2x), 38; *alēthēn*: 3:33; 4:18; 5:31, 32; 6:55 (2x); 7:18; 8:13, 14, 17, 26; 10:41; 19:35; 21:24; *alēthinos*: 1:9; 4:23, 37; 6:32; 7:28; 8:16; 15:1; 17:3; 19:35; *alēthōs*: 1:47; 4:42; 6:14; 7:26, 40; 8:31; 17:8.

5. All translations are my own.

6. Rudolf Bultmann's well-known aphorisms, "In the end Jesus as the Revealer of God *reveals nothing but that he is the Revealer*.... [John's] Gospel presents only *das Daß* of the Revelation without describing *ihr Was*," misread the Fourth Gospel and should be laid to rest (*Theology of the New Testament*, trans. Kendrick Grobel [New York: Scribner's Sons, 1955], 2:66). Yet his exegesis of John 8:32—a verse too often bowdlerized by omission of its audience ("the Jews who believed in [Jesus]") and prerequisites ("if you abide in my word, you are truly my disciples") in 8:31—hits the bullseye. "What is meant is not knowledge generally, but the knowledge of revelation [of *hē alētheia*], just as *eleutheria* does not mean freedom of the human mind but freedom from sin (cf. 8:34)" (*TDNT* 1:246).

trast, in the Mishnah's *Sayings of the Fathers*, "The one who has gotten the words of Torah has gotten for himself life in the world to come" (b. 'Abot 2:8). Paul flatly denies this claim (Rom 7:10; Gal 3:21); John nuances his own reservations. "Scripture cannot be annulled" (John 10:35), but Scripture, rightly apprehended, directs its reader to Christ. Moses and the prophets wrote of Jesus as fulfillment of messianic expectation (John 1:41, 45; 5:45–47). In D. Moody Smith's apt formulation, "The intelligibility of the Christian revelation then depends on scripture, but at the same time the intelligibility of scripture depends on the revelation of God in Jesus Christ."[7] For John, the confession of Jesus as Israel's Messiah entails a radical rethinking of Scripture, and that reassessment organically restructures how God is understood.

Returning to the Synoptics, one finds operative the same hermeneutical principle. "Do not suppose," warns Jesus, "that I have come to abrogate the law or the prophets; I have come not to invalidate but to bring to full completion" (Matt 5:17). This consummate righteousness (5:20) is illustrated by six examples (5:21, 27, 31, 33, 38, 43), drawn from scripture ([1] Exod 20:13 // Deut 5:17; [2] Exod 20:14 // Deut 5:18; [3] Deut 24:1–4; [4] Lev 19:12 // Num 30:2 // Deut 23:21; [5] Exod 21:24 // Lev 24:20 // Deut 19:21; [6] Lev 19:18), which substantiate Jesus's superlative explications of Torah, mandated for his disciples (Matt 5:21–48). Likewise, though less extensively, Mark presents Jesus as ultimate arbiter of scriptural intent, either defying Jewish dietary laws (7:14–15, 19b; cf. Lev 17:1–16; Deut 14:3–21) or disallowing divorce on a broader biblical canvas (Mark 10:2–9; cf. Deut 24:1–4; Gen 1:27; 2:24). On the road to Emmaus, the risen Jesus in Luke sounds Johannine: "And beginning with Moses and all the prophets he explained to them all that was in the scriptures concerning himself" (Luke 24:27). All the evangelists consider Jesus Christ the indispensable lens through which Scripture's ultimate aim, and therefore God's purpose, become comprehensible.

That assumption bears on the issue of "scriptural truth." Etymologically *alētheia* connotes that which is disclosed or unconcealed (*a*-privative + the root *lēth*-, "forgotten," "oblivious," "obscured," "hidden"): positively reworded, "genuine," "corresponding to reality," "dependable," "trustworthy."[8] There's no reason to suppose that any of the evangelists, remembering Jesus in Easter's light, would have disputed Paul's assertion that a veil lies over the minds of those who read a passage from "the old covenant" (*tēs palaias diathēkēs*), "be-

---

7. D. Moody Smith, *The Theology of the Gospel of John*, NTT (Cambridge: Cambridge University Press, 1995), 76.

8. LSJ 63b–64a, 1044a; BDAG 42a–44a.

cause only in Christ is it taken away" (2 Cor 3:14).[9] The apostle confirms his position by citing Scripture: "But whenever one turns to the Lord, the veil is removed" (*hēnika de ean epistrepsē pros kyrion, periaireitai to kalymma*; 2 Cor 3:16, paraphrasing Exod 34:34 LXX). Probably Paul construes *kyrion* as referring to Christ (1 Cor 6:14; 12:3), but only divine agency—whether that of God or of the Lord Jesus—can reveal how Moses and the prophets come into focus when viewed from the standpoint of God's gracious glory, unveiled in Christ (Rom 8:18; 1 Cor 2:10). All of scripture—everything in totality—is subjected to Christ, who eventually will be subjected to God (1 Cor 15:28). "The Lord is the Spirit, and where the Spirit of the Lord is, is freedom" (2 Cor 3:17). Such liberty applies also to scriptural discernment, on condition that it is captured and constrained by the mind of Christ (1 Cor 2:16).

Inevitably we have crossed the threshold into revelation: a topic too vast to be covered, too integral to be skirted. Like philosophical theories of truth, like historical criticism itself, "revelation" occupies a different mode of discourse. Explaining matters philosophically or historically, one may appeal to belief in revelation as a philosophical concept or a historical cause, but not to revelation itself.

Even when located within its proper frame of reference—theology—revelation requires special treatment, because its agency and object are irreducibly a priori: God. The world described by scripture is this world, whose creation and intervention from beyond lie entirely at God's initiative (Gen 1:1–2:4a; Exod 20:1–20). The dynamic of divine involvement with human history is that of judgment and restoration (Ps 9:1–20; Isa 11:1–9), which demands of human beings a response: optimally, compliance (Deut 10:12–11:32); adversely, insubordination (Jer 5:1–6:30). The peculiar testimony of the NT witnesses—most of whom, Jewish; all, imbued with Judaism—is that Jesus, by his obedient self-donation at Golgotha, is the definitive index of God's character and will for the world's redemption. His ultimacy lies not in his death for a righteous cause; were that so, any of the Maccabean martyrs would have sufficed (2 Macc 6:18–7:42; 4 Macc 5:1–18:23). Rather, by raising from death this crucified Jew, God uniquely ratified Jesus's expression of divine sovereignty (*hē basileia tou theou*) and, in Paul's words, rectified the ungodly (Rom 4:5). An act so destabilizing for both Jewish and Christian religiosity, an encounter so subversive of hu-

---

9. That perspective illumines Acts 8:26–40. Under the Spirit's direction Philip asks Ethiopia's chancellor of the exchequer, who has come to Jerusalem to worship, if he understands what he is reading in Isaiah (vv. 27–30). "How can I, unless someone guides me?" (v. 31). "Beginning with this scripture [Isa 53:7–8 LXX], [Philip] told him the good news about Jesus" (v. 35). The outcome is the eunuch's immediate baptism and joyous evangelism (vv. 36–39).

manity's self-estimation, is revelatory because of its radical Otherness (1 Cor 1:18–2:16). "Christianity did not emerge when someone arrived with a sacred book. Rather, it emerged in response to preaching the news of Jesus, which included a new way of reading the Scripture of the synagogue."[10]

Accordingly, the God revealed by Jesus in the NT is multiply relational.

> At that time Jesus declared, "I praise you, Father, Lord of heaven and of earth, that you have hidden these things from the wise and insightful, and you have revealed [*apekalypsas*] them to infants. Indeed, Father, so it has been your great delight. All things have been handed over to me by my Father; and no one recognizes the Son except the Father, nor does anyone recognize the Father except the Son and to whomever the Son may choose to reveal [*apokalypsai*] it. Come to me, all who toil and are burdened, and I shall give you relief. Take my yoke upon you and learn from me, for I am gentle and humble at heart, and you will discover rest for your very selves; for my yoke is comfortable and my burden, light. (Matt 11:25–27 // Luke 10:21–22)

Key to understanding this passage is its re-envisioned cascade of Jewish Scripture. Jesus's opening doxology (Matt 11:25–26) constitutes a *Todah*, thanksgiving praise (Ps 138:1–6). "The Lord of heaven and earth," of creation and history, is the God who joyously blesses (Tob 7:17). "The wise and insightful" will be disappointed (Isa 29:14; cf. 4 Ezra 12.36–38). Unlike Jeremiah 31:34 and 1 Enoch 42, God's apocalypse is *now*, not a future expectation. "The precepts of the LORD . . . make wise the simple" (Ps 19:7). Discipleship to Jesus promises eschatological rest (4 Ezra 7.36–38; cf. Heb 4:1–13). Jesus more than dispenses Wisdom and exposits Torah; by offering to all his "yoke," he *is* both Wisdom and Torah (cf. Jer 5:5; Acts 15:10; Sir 6:30; 51:26). Reciprocal recognition of the Father and the Son recalls Exodus 33:12–13 while raising the ante: Jesus, not Moses, is the supreme revealer of divinity (cf. Deut 34:10–12; John 1:18). "*This* unrecognized Son is the *only* one who knows *this* Father. . . . Here and now *this* Son is authorized to disclose *this* Father to whom he chooses."[11] Because God has transferred the predicates of Torah and Wisdom[12] to Jesus, John

---

10. Leander E. Keck, *The Bible in the Pulpit: The Renewal of Biblical Preaching* (Nashville: Abingdon, 1978), 71.

11. Paul S. Minear, "Two Secrets, Two Disclosures," *HBT* 29 (2007): 75–85 (quotations, 78–79).

12. Torah (Ps 119:1) or Wisdom (Prov 4:11) as way; as truth (Pss 119:142; 51:6); as life (Deut 32:46–47; Prov 16:22).

concludes that "no one comes to Father except through [the Son]" (14:6). By unveiling scriptural truth, the crucified/risen Messiah discloses the meaning of a disciple's life: "I no longer live, but Christ lives in me. The life I now live in the flesh, I live in faith, that of the Son of God, the one who loved me and gave himself up for me. I do not invalidate the grace of God: for if rectitude were through the law, then Christ died for nothing" (Gal 2:20–21).[13]

Paul's declaration leads us to a final facet of NT convictions of biblical truth. Interpreted theocentrically and christomorphically, underwritten by the Holy Spirit, Scripture is proven true by its reliable testimony "through faith for faith" (*ek pisteōs eis pistin*: Rom 1:17; cf. Luke 1:1–4; John 19:35; 20:31; 21:24; Titus 1:13; 2:10).

Retrieving an archaic expression might clarify this point. As late as 1928, the solemnization of matrimony in the Anglican *Book of Common Prayer* included this vow:

> I N. take thee N. to my wedded Wife [/Husband], to have and to hold from this day forward, for better for worse, for richer for poorer, in sickness and in health, to love and to cherish, till death us do part, according to God's holy ordinance; and thereto I plight thee my troth.[14]

"To plight one's troth" meant "to pledge one's faith; to make a solemn promise of engagement; *spec.* to engage oneself to marry."[15] One person binds oneself to another in lifelong commitment before God and a worshipping congregation. Long before it acquired the connotations of "conformity with fact" or "concordance with reality," "troth" in Middle English conveyed "faithfulness," "good faith," "steadfast loyalty," and "honesty." These senses align perfectly with apposite paraphrases of *he'emin*: "to gain stability, to rely on someone, to give credence to [another], to trust in someone."[16]

I see no evidence whatever that the writers of what became the NT doubted that their scripture, the synagogue Bible, directed them toward the LORD of their redemption: a faithful God (*'el 'emet*), into whose hands they were as pre-

---

13. "Revelation means the moment in which we are surprised by the knowledge of someone there in the darkness and the void of human life; it means the self-disclosure of light in our darkness" (H. Richard Niebuhr, *The Meaning of Revelation* [New York: Macmillan, 1941], 111).

14. *The Book of Common Prayer and Administration of the Sacraments and Other Rites and Ceremonies of the Church* (New York: Seabury, 1953), 301–2.

15. *OED* 2.402, col. 2.

16. Alfred Jepsen, "אָמַן," *TDOT* 1:292–333; quotation, 308.

pared to entrust their lives as they believed Jesus had, to the bitter end (Ps 31:6; Luke 23:46). So, too, had Abraham (Gen 15:6), Jacob (32:11), David (2 Sam 7:28; Ps 132:11), Isaiah (38:19), Jeremiah (32:41), and the Psalmists (40:12; 86:15; 89:15; 119:43, 142, 151, 160; 132:11; 146:6). All plighted their troth in Israel's God, trusting that the LORD had made to them a promise of loyal commitment. Their fidelity was strained by pressures to conform to *vox populi* (1 Kgs 22:13–18), contesting prophecies (Jer 28:1–17), and practical doubt (Exod 4:1; Isa 53:1; Job 9:16–18). Jonah's dedication was compromised by the LORD's forgiveness of repentant evildoers after the prophet's effective testimony (Jonah 3:1–4:11). Scriptural reliability *makes possible* the reader's encounter with God but neither guarantees it nor proves its authenticity, let alone corroborates one's prejudices, "conservative" or "liberal." The dynamics of human-divine trust prohibit self-confirming outcomes. The living God is holy, free, and unconditionally sovereign; human nature is contingent, historically finite, and susceptible to sin. The name "Israel" (*yisra'el*) connotes the wrestling of beings divine and human (Gen 32:28). In this life it will always be so (1 Cor 13:12).

New Testament faith is vested, not in a book, but in Israel's God, whose selected self-disclosure to the world is Jesus Christ. At bottom that is what Paul means by "the truth of the gospel" (Gal 2:5, 14). Scripture, therefore, is not the Truth: the fallacy on which the sin of bibliolatry wobbles. Like Christ, Scripture *orients* us *toward* Truth: God's self-revelation as the Holy One who meets human creatures in "a solemn promise of engagement," inviting them to risk ultimate trust in their Creator, not in any of the multitudinous idols—religious, political, academic—they perpetually manufacture. The criteria for judging a life based on that invitation's acceptance are well summarized by Martin Luther: "Without constraint a person is willing and desires to do good to everyone and to serve everyone, to suffer all manner of things out of love and praise for God, who has revealed this grace."[17]

---

17. Luther, "Preface to the Epistle to the Romans," in *Luther's Spirituality*, ed. and trans. Philip D. W. Krey and Peter D. Krey, CWS (New York and Mahwah, NJ: Paulist, 2007), 109.

CHAPTER 18

Revisiting the King James Bible

> The translation was extraordinarily well done because to the translators what they were translating was not merely a curious collection of ancient books written by different authors in different stages of culture, but the word of God divinely revealed through His chosen and expressly inspired scribes. In this conviction they carried out their work with boundless reverence and care and achieved a beautifully artistic result.
>
> —George Bernard Shaw

IN CASE IT ESCAPED YOUR NOTICE, the King James Version has made a comeback: not necessarily on church pulpits—from some, it never departed—but in the religion section of a Barnes & Noble near you.[1] Why at least five learned, well-wrought books on the KJV, its predecessors, and successors would have appeared in only two years' time[2] is an intriguing question to which we may presently return. First, some bibliographical reconnaissance is in order.

    1. The quotation above is found in Gustavus Swift Paine, *The Men Behind the King James Version* (Grand Rapids: Baker, 1977), 182. This version's quadricentennial is celebrated in David G. Burke, John F. Kutsko, and Philip H. Towner, eds., *The King James Version at 400: Assessing Its Genius as Bible Translation and Its Literary Influence*, BSNA (Atlanta: Society of Biblical Literature, 2013).
    2. Alister McGrath, *In the Beginning: The Story of the King James Bible and How It Changed a Nation, a Language, and a Culture* (New York: Anchor Books, 2002); Brian Moynahan, *God's Bestseller: William Tyndale, Thomas More, and the Writing of the English Bible—A Story of Martyrdom and Betrayal* (New York: St. Martin's, 2002); David Daniell, *The Bible in English: Its History and Influence* (New Haven and London: Yale University Press, 2003); Adam Nicholson, *God's Secretaries: The Making of the King James Bible* (New York: HarperCollins, 2003); David S. Katz, *God's Last Words: Reading the English Bible from the Reformation to Fundamentalism* (New Haven: Yale University Press, 2004). Altogether these amount to 2,357 pages (Daniell's alone, 900). And you thought *this* book was too long.

The place to begin is with David Daniell's (1929–2016) *The Bible in English*. If there is a better treatment of its subject in one volume, I know it not. To write intelligently on the English Bible one must be a polymath, with dexterity in linguistics (all biblical languages, Latin, and the evolution of the English tongue), British political intrigue, early Protestant religious and theological developments, plus a working knowledge of a half-dozen other related matters—Europe's great universities, medieval shipping (and its piracy), early printing (and its piracy), to name but three. Daniell, who was emeritus professor of English at University College London and honorary fellow at Oxford, demonstrates this formidable competence and another aptitude, just as important: a sense of poetry. Best known in theological circles as Tyndale's editor and biographer,[3] Daniell enjoyed a doubled scholarly life as a Shakespearean scholar (preparing, for instance, the Arden edition of *Julius Caesar* [1998][4]). He loved the English language and had a keen ear for its music. It is that peculiar grace, coupled with wit as irrepressible as erudition, that gives *The Bible in English* a quality that I seldom attribute to a volume: brilliance.

Daniell divides his Herculean labor into two unequal parts: "Before Printing" and "After Printing." Part 1 sets the stage for the English Reformation, tracing the beginnings of the English Bible through its Anglo-Saxon (850–1066) and Middle-English versions (1066–1350), up to the Bible of John Wyclif (1324–84) and the Lollard preachers in the fourteenth and fifteenth centuries. Characteristic of Daniell is this appraisal of the language of the great mystery plays in York, Chester, and Coventry:

> With its long paragraphs of lightly rhyming verse, the English can sound stilted, ponderous (and even, dare one say, boring: heard on a cold wet evening in a dripping garden in front of an ancient damp wall, God can be felt to drone on, somewhat). It can also rise to heart-stopping moments of feeling, as when the cruel soldiers in the York Passion play leave Jesus on the cross with the words: "Let him hang there still, / And make faces at the moon."[5]

Part 2, with thirty-four chapters, leads the reader from Erasmus's (1466–1536) Greek NT (1516) through the many English versions leading to the King James

---

3. William Tyndale, *Tyndale's New Testament*, ed. David Daniell (London: Yale University Press, 1996); Daniell, *William Tyndale: A Biography* (London: Yale University Press, 2001).

4. William Shakespeare, *Julius Caesar*, ed. David Daniell, AS 3rd ser. (New Delhi: Bloomsbury India, 2013).

5. Daniell, *Bible in English*, 103–4. Subsequent citations of this source will appear in the text.

(1611) and its subsequent consolidation (1660–1710). From there, the narrative splits along two parallel tracks: the English Bible in America and in Britain, concluding (roughly) with Today's English Version (1976) and the Revised English Bible (1989). Over twelve hundred new translations into English of the Bible, in whole or in part, were made from the original Hebrew and Greek during the interval between 1945 and 1990. Altogether new translations, observes Daniell, are like city buses: "Nothing comes for a long time, and then several arrive together" (Daniell, 504). Despite its initial suppression, "the number of English Bibles printed since 1526 is incalculable—one thinks of a number, and goes on adding noughts" (767).

One might suppose that nine hundred pages of dense, well-documented history would drone on like God in a cold wet garden, but Daniell holds the reader's interest by retelling his story in all its human foible and fascination. Henry VIII (1491–1547) and his son Edward VI (1537–53) approach us in the guise of Israel's rulers, as some English contemporaries probably regarded their Tudor monarchs: the former as David, greatly beloved, "felling the Philistine giant pope with one simple stone, the Word of God" (207); the latter as Josiah, boy-king with zeal for the Lord. We meet the all-but-forgotten Henry Ainsworth, whose *Book of Psalms* (1612) struggled to wrest obscure, tough-minded Hebrew poetry into a meter that his Separatist congregation in Amsterdam could actually sing altogether. Cleansed of unwarranted aspersions on its annotations' "objectionable Calvinism" (528), the Geneva Bible (1560)— illustrated and handsomely typeset, touchstone for Shakespeare and Milton— commands respect: when only fifty years old, it had gone through three versions and 120 different editions (not reprintings). Sadly, *The Bay Psalm Book* (1640) offers such flapdoodle as "us waste who laid, / Sing us among a Sions song / unto us then they said" (Ps 137:3, purportedly). Three centuries later, on the New English Bible panel, we overhear Sir Godfrey Driver's explanation that the bird in Psalm 102:6 is neither the KJV's allusive "pelican of the wilderness" nor the NEB's eventual selection, "a desert-owl." Rather, Sir Godfrey insisted, "I am a Yellow-Bellied Bulbul," which, as Daniell dryly notes, "may be thought to have lost something, particularly when sung by choristers at Evensong" (747).

It is no surprise that William Tyndale (1494[?]–1536) emerges as the hero of *The Bible in English*. Daniell is the author of that figure's now definitive biography.[6] Such a claim, however, has merit on its face, as Oxford's Alister McGrath (1953–) concurs in his lively Cook's tour of the expanse that Daniell compre-

---

6. Daniell, *William Tyndale: A Biography*.

hends. With Tyndale, for the first time, a translator used as his base, not Jerome's (c. 345–420) Vulgate (late fourth century), but the finest Greek and Hebrew texts then available. Tyndale's genius goes far beyond coining words and expressions that have found a lasting place in everyday speech: "scapegoat," "Passover," "the patience of Job," "O ye of little faith." He did more even than stick to his own criteria of accuracy and clarity in translation, putting the Bible within reach of every English-speaking man, woman, and child—as though that were not aplenty. As Daniell persuasively argues, Tyndale gave us, not only our biblical language, but the English language that to this day most of us speak. Based on a plain Saxon vocabulary, Tyndale's sentences are short and clear, with the simple syntax of subject-verb-object. To Anglicize the Bible, he kicked this speech one notch above the normal idiom, setting it to a nearly flawless cadence. The scope of this achievement is beyond question: Tyndale's version was the unacknowledged template, not only for the popular Geneva Bible (1557–60), but also for the enduring King James Version, about 76 percent of whose OT and 84 percent of whose NT depend on Tyndale. Given the linguistic proximity to the KJV of the Revised Standard (1952) and New Revised Standard (1990) Versions, the New International Version (1978), and the New Jerusalem Bible (1985), few English-speaking Christians read Scripture without Tyndale beside them—just as his are the words with which most of us pray the Lord's Prayer.

Not a bad life's work for an impoverished exile and treasonous heretic, whose heroic scholarship was done on the run across the Continent, eluding his pursuers until betrayed in Antwerp by a villainous countryman, Henry Phillips. That is the story recounted, with novelistic verve, by historian and foreign correspondent Brian Moynahan (1941–2018). *God's Bestseller* reads somewhat like an episode of *The Fugitive* (ABC, 1963–67), with Tyndale as Dr. Richard Kimble and, in the role of relentless Lt. Gerard, Sir Thomas More (1477–1535). That Moynahan produced over four hundred pages on the subject is impressive, not least for the fact that Sir Thomas did not enter Tyndale's world until mid-1529, weeks away from More's appointment as Lord Chancellor and only seven years before Tyndale's execution. During that septennial much of Tyndale's movements was left deliberately fuzzy, to throw his hounds off the scent. What has survived, however—and whose digest makes for eye-opening if sometimes tedious reading—is the war of words that More and Tyndale waged on each other. The first blast was More's (1529), widening the scope of his earlier attacks against Luther ("[whose mouth carries] nothing but bilge-water, sewers, privies, filth, and dung")[7] to draw Tyndale into his gunsights.

---

7. Moynahan, *God's Bestseller*, 29.

In 1531 Tyndale published his reply, in turn provoking More's *Confutation of Tyndale's Answer* (1532) and *Apology* (1533). The final tally: Tyndale's defense, eighty thousand words; More's aggregate polemics against Tyndale, two thousand pages or about three-quarters of a million words. One wishes that Tyndale had conserved precious time and energy to make better progress through the OT, whose translation—including the Psalms—he never lived to finish.[8]

In a special prologue to Genesis, Tyndale claimed that the Bible was "written for [the Christian's] learning and comfort," so that "we may apply the medicine of the Scripture, every man to his own sores." The Bible serves "to strengthen thy faith," salvation coming from the "inward spirit received by faith and the consent of the heart unto the law of God."[9] Just there, Tyndale's "Lutheran evangelicalism" shines through—or, as More would insist, there gushes "a filthy foam of blasphemies" from "a hell-hound in the kennel of the devil."[10] Tyndale gave as good (or as bad) as he got: More, "O natural son of the father of all lies," was "a gleering fox"[11] blinded by greed (the latter a bogus charge). As Moynahan shows, the life-and-death vitriol between these two penultimately rested on Tyndale's sound though antiestablishment translation of four dogmatically loaded terms: *presbyteros* as "senior" (not "priest"), *ekklēsia* as "congregation" (not "Church"), *agapē* as "love" (not "charity"), and *metanoia* as "repentance" (not "doing penance").[12] At bottom—and what one wishes Moynahan made clearer for his reader—were two irreconcilable views of the church and its role in salvation. For Tyndale, the church's living voice resides in the community of believers, endowed by the Holy Spirit in every generation to release Scripture's power for salvation. For More, the Roman Catholic Church was incapable of error, even though he was bound to know that its practices had been corrupted; salvation, therefore, was possible only through papal and clerical ministrations.

The story's end is well-known and irony-riddled. Neither hound nor fox would buy his life with his conscience. Unable to take Henry's Oath of Succes-

---

8. *Tyndale's Old Testament*, ed. (of course) David Daniell (London: Yale University Press, 1992). Tyndale lived to translate the Pentateuch, the historical books (Joshua–2 Chronicles), and Jonah.
9. Tyndale, quoted by Moynahan, *God's Bestseller*, 193.
10. More, quoted by Moynahan, *God's Bestseller*, 104.
11. More, quoted by Moynahan, *God's Bestseller*, 248.
12. By the late medieval era, the latter terms had become entwined with abuse of the Roman Catholic practice of indulgence, which sparked off Martin Luther's (1483–1546) Ninety-Five Theses (1517). Thesis 28 repudiated a saying attributed to Johann Tetzel (c. 1465–1519): "As soon as a coin in the coffer rings, a soul from purgatory springs."

sion (1534), annulling papal jurisdiction over England, Sir Thomas was jailed in the Tower. There he assuaged his dread by spewing more venom on heretics, whom "the demons [long] to plunge into gulfs of ever-burning flames."[13] In 1535, he was beheaded—by royal clemency, commuting More's sentence from hanging, castration, and burning while still alive, then beheading. In 1536 Tyndale, too, received a more lenient execution: strangulation, with the corpse burned at the stake, instead of being drawn and quartered, disemboweled, and burned alive. One year later, Henry VIII licensed fifteen hundred copies of "Matthew's Bible" (1537), the first English Bible sold legally in England. It was, of course, none other than Tyndale's, of which his friend John Rogers (c. 1505–55) became custodian in Antwerp. In 1935 Pius XI (1857–1939) canonized Thomas More, as did, in his own fashion, playwright Robert Bolt (1924–95) on Broadway (1961) and in Hollywood (1966). Moynahan is plain that Bolt picked the wrong protagonist as *A Man for All Seasons*; in truth, actor Paul Scofield (1922–2008) epitomizes serene nobility, uttering nary a word of More's unhinged malice. The latter reminds one of Evelyn Waugh's perceptive Cara, in *Brideshead Revisited*: "When people hate with all that energy, it is something in themselves they are hating."[14]

Has Tyndale's influence on the English Bible been overestimated? Historian Adam Nicholson (1957–), passionate advocate of the King James Version, thinks so. Not for him are Daniell's raptures of Tyndalian felicity: "Jacobean words are clarified, where Tyndale's are clotted; they are memorable where Tyndale stumbles over his grammar."[15] The different assessment stems in part from differences in taste: Nicholson loves operatic rococo; Daniell detests it. More to the point, Nicholson discerns and rejoices in the KJV's expression something two registers above seventeenth-century idiom—"a form [of English] no one had ever spoken":

> The King James Bible, gradually replacing the Geneva Bible, was in the vanguard of [the first great surge in England's literacy levels] and it gave the English, more than any other book, a sense of the possibilities of language, an extraordinary range of richness, more approachable than Shakespeare, more populist than Milton, a common text against which life itself could be read.... The sense of the many threads by which the real physical world is bound to a magnificence which goes beyond the physical; the simple world

---

13. More, quoted by Moynahan, *God's Bestseller*, 324.
14. Waugh, *Brideshead Revisited*, EL 172 (New York: Knopf, 1993), 91.
15. Nicholson, *God's Secretaries*, 223.

held in a musical rhythm; a poetic rather than a philosophical approach to reality, an openness to the reality of dreams and visions: all of these treasured qualities of Englishness can be seen to stem from the habits of mind which the Jacobean translators bequeathed to their country.[16]

Proceeding from different premises McGrath's *In the Beginning* arrives at a similar conclusion: "Paradoxically, the king's translators achieved literary distinction precisely because they were not deliberately pursuing it. Aiming at truth, they achieved what later generations recognized as beauty and elegance."[17]

That a committee could produce such a work of genius seems risible today. Not in 1604, Nicholson argues, when the suppression of individual ego and a sense of "jointness," in everything from politics to furniture, were acknowledged virtues of the age. In a culture drenched in words, not images, the King James Bible was "England's equivalent of the great baroque cathedral it never built, an enormous and magnificent verbal artifice, its huge structures embracing all four million Englishmen, its orderliness and richness a kind of national shrine built only of words."[18]

No less than in Tyndale's time, aesthetics were wedded to religion and politics. In many ways, however, Nicholson's story (and, in the main, McGrath's) is the mirror image of Moynahan's, because so many realities had been turned inside out by 1603, when Scotland's James VI (1566–1625) ascended to the English throne as James I. Whereas Henry's reign had been fraught with strife, much owing to his breach with Rome, James Stuart adopted as his motto *Beati Pacifici*, "Blessed are the Peacemakers." While never "authorizing" an English version of the Bible, by the time he had firmly put both bishops and Puritans in their places at Hampton Court in 1604, he was willing to accept a last-minute suggestion from (Puritan) John Reynolds (1549–1607) that a single vernacular Bible be read in all of England's churches. But it would be on James's terms: the Bible as *irenicon*, "an organism that absorbed and integrated difference."[19] It would be a uniform translation, with the weight of Oxbridge behind it, subject to his Privy Council's oversight (and, if need be, censorship), untainted by antiroyalist radicalism. In short, the time was now ripe for England's sovereign to endorse an English Bible that, as Nicholson aptly puts it, "elide[ed] the kingliness of God with the godliness of kings, to make royal power and divine glory

---

16. Nicholson, *God's Secretaries*, 237.
17. McGrath, *In the Beginning*, 254.
18. Nicholson, *God's Secretaries*, 70.
19. Nicholson, *God's Secretaries*, 77.

into one indivisible garment which could be wrapped around the nation as a whole."[20] The base text was not the annotated (and Calvinist) Geneva Bible, but the Elizabethan Bishops' Bible (1568)—which of course guaranteed that Tyndale's version sailed into the KJV under the political radar.

Six carefully selected translation "companies"—two at Westminster, Cambridge, and Oxford—each with its own director, set to work with detailed instructions and a four-stage winnowing process devised by London's Bishop (later, Archbishop) Richard Bancroft (1544–1610), that assured both self-abnegation for God and King and (in Nicholson's words) "a particularly bureaucratic kind of holiness."[21] Nicholson's work renders, insofar as extant evidence permits, cameos of "God's secretaries." Their product, seven years later, was a Bible with "a torque towards grandeur"[22] that, while slow to catch on, came into its own after the monarchy's Restoration in 1660. In Nicholson's view, it still leaves modern collaborative efforts like the New English Bible (1961–70) panting in banality's dust. Readers may judge for themselves by consulting McGrath's appendix, which arrays the first four verses of Psalm 23 in nine important English versions, from the Wycliffite Bible (c. 1384) through the Revised Standard Version (1952).[23]

Unlike his colleagues, Tel Aviv University's David Katz (1953–) focuses not on the English Bible's creation but, instead, on its reception among different, culturally significant communities across the past four centuries. He conducts the reader on an erudite, breathless adventure through the Bible's appropriation in the English Civil Wars (1642–51), a biblical basis for Sir Isaac Newton's (1642–1727) scientific synthesis, the Bible's demystification by David Hume (1711–76), the persistence of supernaturalism in John Hutchinson (1674–1737) and Emanuel Swedenborg (1688–1772), the influence of modern notions of authorship and copyright in the scholarship of Richard Bentley (1662–1740), Matthew Arnold's (1822–88) response to German higher criticism, the challenge of Darwin (1809–82), and the backlash of fundamentalism. Katz's forte is history of ideas, on a grand canvas with bold strokes of broad brushes. He subscribes to the dictum that "everything connects" without excess fear that such a slogan can be wrong in practice or, if correct, susceptible to forcing connections. His grasp of church history and Christian theology is shaky: He refers to the KJV as "the Authorized Version of 1611"[24] (it wasn't) and holds *The*

---

20. Nicholson, *God's Secretaries*, xiv.
21. Nicholson, *God's Secretaries*, 149.
22. Nicholson, *God's Secretaries*, 159.
23. McGrath, *In the Beginning*, 311–13.
24. Katz, *God's Last Words*, 44–49, 88–93, and elsewhere.

Scofield Reference Bible's (first edition, 1909) assumptions as interchangeable with the Protestant doctrine of *sola scriptura* (they're not). Read *God's Last Words* for a full day's intellectual stimulation, but with caution and a wink that Katz's words aren't the last.

Most of these books close in forlorn sunset. McGrath: "Sadly, we shall never see [the King James Bible's] equal—or even its like—again."[25] Nicholson: "Modern religious rhetoric is dilute and ineffectual, and where it isn't, it seems mad and aberrational."[26] Daniell: "Paul wrote of the horror of sin, of separation from God. . . . English Bibles now must speak the language of the *New York Times*."[27] These are not nostalgic longings; no sane person would regard Tudor England as The Good Old Days. They bespeak, I think, melancholy that ours is a world that seems tone-deaf to a "faith [that] cometh by hearing, and hearing [that] cometh by the word of God" (Rom 10:17, Tyndale/KJV). Perhaps, too, they lament ugly trends toward the Bible's trivialization in the church and its abomination in the academy. "The word is nigh thee," affirmed Paul, "even in thy mouth and in thy heart"; but Scripture offers countless instances of hearts grown cold and wisdom spat out. Writing in *The New Yorker*, Anthony Lane wondered, quite sensibly, about recent attempts to render Scripture politically correct: "You wonder why they bother to read the Bible at all. Tyndale was killed for trying to spread the Word; these guys make a living out of deconstructing it to death."[28] To which, in his jeweled preface to the reader of the 1611 KJV, Miles Smith (1554–1624), member of the First Oxford Company, may return the last word:

> Happie is the man that delighteth in the Scripture, and thrise happie that meditateth in it day and night.
> But how shall men meditate in that, which they cannot understand?[29]

---

25. McGrath, *In the Beginning*, 310.
26. Nicholson, *God's Secretaries*, 239.
27. Daniell, *Bible in English*, 772.
28. Lane, "Scripture Rescripted," *The New Yorker* (October 2, 1995), 98.
29. Smith, quoted in Daniell, *Bible in English*, 779.

CHAPTER 19

Journeying through Scripture with the Lectionary's Map

> Two important characteristics of maps should be noticed. A map *is not* the territory it represents, but, if correct, it has a *similar structure* to the territory, which accounts for its usefulness.
>
> —Alfred Korzybski

A REVIEW OF SCHOLARSHIP across the last five decades, augmented with anecdotal evidence drawn from my own and others' experience of biblical interpretation and preaching, has persuaded me of two things: (1) the Revised Common Lectionary[1] (henceforth, RCL) will not soon disappear from North American churches; (2) few pastors or scholars seem enraptured by that prospect. For as far as the eye can scan the Roman and Protestant horizons, lectionary preaching seems here to stay. While nods toward its history are unavoidable, this essay will not trace the evolution of lectionaries from antiquity to modernity.[2] In the interest of a balanced presentation, I shall refer and respond to some recurrent, even

---

1. Derived from *Ordo Lectionum Missae* (Rome: Vatican Polyglot Press, 1969), *The Common Lectionary* (New York: Church Hymnal Corporation, 1983) and *The Revised Common Lectionary: Consultation on Common Texts* (Nashville: Abingdon, 1992) have proved the most popular products of the Consultation on Common Texts, whose participants include (among others) The Anglican Church of Canada, Christian Church (Disciples of Christ), Episcopal Church, Evangelical Lutheran Church in America, Presbyterian Church (USA), Reformed Church in America, Roman Catholic Church in the United States and in Canada, Unitarian Universalist Christian Fellowship, and The United Methodist Church.

2. Much of that history was helpfully summarized in the April 1977 issue of *Int* (31), devoted to "Lectionaries and Interpretation." See especially John Reumann, "A History of Lectionaries: From the Synagogue at Nazareth to Post–Vatican II" (116–30). Though inevitably dated, Eric Werner, *The Sacred Bridge: The Interdependence of Liturgy and Music in Synagogue and Church during the First Millennium* (London and New York: Dobson/Columbia University Press, 1959), carefully assembles a wealth of information.

damning, criticisms of the lectionary; yet I come neither to bury nor to praise, even less to offer another suggestion for its improvement. My principal aim is to reflect on the composition and use of the lectionary that most mainline preachers now share, exploring some theological paths that have been but lightly trod. While the RCL may, and perhaps should, undergo another revision, I wish to suggest ways in which pastors and people might consider, even enjoy, the lectionary currently at our disposal or any that may someday supersede it.

The Perils of Lectionary Preaching

For readers unfamiliar with its structure, a brief description of the common lectionary is warranted. A lectionary is an ordered arrangement of scriptural selections intended for reading aloud, singing, and preaching during the course of Christian public worship. The most widely used lectionary, for Sundays and major festivals of the church, follows a triennial cycle, each year of which is linked with one of the Synoptic Gospels: Year A with Matthew, Year B, Mark, Year C, Luke. Each gospel is read semi-continuously throughout its designated year. Excerpts from John are read every year during the seasons of Christmas, Lent, and Easter, and to fill gaps in Year B left vacant by Mark, the shortest Synoptic. Coordinated with Gospel selections are two other readings: the first from the OT (or Acts, during the Great Fifty Days from Easter to Pentecost), and the second from an epistle (or from Revelation, during Easter in Year C). A psalm, in whole or in part, is stipulated as a congregational response to the first reading. Notably during Advent, Christmas, Epiphany, and Lent, a principle of complementarity with the story of Jesus has been adopted in pairing OT and Gospel lections. The former provide context, contrast, or "antitype" for the latter. This thematic pattern pervades the season after Pentecost; for these Sundays in Ordinary Time, however, the RCL has introduced an alternative second system, proposing a selective sequence of OT readings. Variously distributed across all three years, representative epistles are not thematically coordinated with either the OT or Gospel readings, but instead are read semi-continuously in particular seasons.

From its inception, this twentieth-century Roman lectionary and its Protestant legatees have suffered heavy attack. To its credit, the Consultation on Common Texts (CCT) has invited correction of its work, revising its 1983 lectionary in the light of thoughtful critique.[3] Objections remain, neverthe-

---

3. For details, consult *The Revised Common Lectionary*, 77–79. A Jesuit supplement to

less, many though not all of which are leveled at the very notion of using a standardized lectionary. Most of these concerns can be categorized under two headings, beginning with practical objections.

First, regular utilization of a lectionary risks a poor match of biblical text and congregational context on any given Sunday. "We face, then, dangers at either extreme: a textual 'bolt from the blue' which may miss the target, or pastoral subjectivity which fails to let the proper textual missile be launched."[4] Of course, all biblical preaching, not merely lectionary homiletics, must navigate a course between that devil and the deep blue sea.

Second, textually speaking, two may be company but three seems a crowd. The rationale for the Roman *Order of Readings for Mass* was irreproachable: "Serious attention must be given to the content and unity of the whole of Scripture, if the meaning of the sacred texts is to be correctly worked out."[5] "The treasures of the Bible are to be opened up more lavishly, so that richer fare may be provided for the faithful at the table of God's Word."[6] In practice, at least in the view of some, "Three lessons are simply too many to try to listen to or preach on with any real success."[7] Weekly frustration has been charged to the lectionary's account, "confus[ing] us as a congregation by placing disparate passages of the Bible in juxtaposition."[8] Yet generalizations of the listening experience are impossible to verify. Multiple readings that bewilder one congregant may stimulate the thinking of another. As for the preacher, I know of no stricture, Protestant or Catholic, that compels a sermon to thread together

---

the Roman Catholic Lectionary was issued in 2002 (https://catholic-resources.org/Lectionary/Supplement-Jesuit.htm); a more general Lectionary Mass Supplement was published by Liturgical Press in 2017 (https://catholic-resources.org/Lectionary/Supplement-Jesuit.htm). As far as I am aware, neither of these updated versions has introduced substantive alterations to the 1983 edition.

4. Lloyd R. Bailey, "The Lectionary in Critical Perspective," *Int* 31 (1977): 139–53; quotation, 145.

5. Pope Paul VI, *Dogmatic Constitution on Divine Revelation* 12 (Rome: Vatican Archives, 1965), https://www.vatican.va/archive/hist_councils/ii_vatican_council/documents/vat-ii_const_19651118_dei-verbum_en.html.

6. *Constitution on the Sacred for Liturgy* 51 in *The Documents of Vatican II*, ed. Walter M. Abbott and Joseph Gallagher (Chicago: Association/Follett, 1966), 120, 155. Also, https://www.vatican.va/archive/hist_councils/ii_vatican_council/documents/vat-ii_const_19631204_sacrosanctum-concilium_en.html.

7. Christopher Seitz, "The Lectionary as Theological Construction," in *Inhabiting Unity: Theological Perspectives on the Proposed Lutheran-Episcopal Concordat*, ed. Ephraim Radner and R. R. Reno (Grand Rapids: Eerdmans, 1995), 173–91; quotation, 176.

8. Walter Sundberg, "Limitations of the Lectionary," *WW* 10 (1990): 14–20; quotation, 15.

more than one lection on any Sunday. On the contrary, ecclesiastical supplements to the lectionary characteristically speak of it as "a guide and resource,"[9] to be implemented with "prudence," "balance," and "pastoral considerations" for "the needs of the people," in order to arouse "among the faithful a greater hunger for the word of God."[10]

Third, exhaustion may be generated by cyclical repetitions, which in turn may tempt the interpreter to abandon a text's central theme in favor of incidental novelty.[11] Again, this is a criticism of the lectionary's abuse, not of the instrument itself. Interpreters are advised to climb off any cycle that is exhausting their resources and to submit themselves to some discipline that will prevent fascination with new trivialities.

Principled objections to the lectionary are more numerous and more biting. Here I cannot answer but can only catalogue some questions.

1. Does sustained preaching in accordance with the lectionary harden homiletical arteries? Are the traditions of doctrinal exposition, denominational emphasis, or prophetic social witness now closed to preachers of the twenty-first century?[12]

2. Does the search for congruence among lections arouse in preachers bad exegetical habits, best "left to Origen or the author of the *Fairie Queene*"?[13] "The world in which generalized type and antitype were the common coin of religious interpretation is not one in which modern worshipers live."[14] Maybe so; yet contemporary Christians still flirt with different kinds of typology, all of which are problematic, and some disastrous.[15] Even after typology's heavy hand has been removed, is thematic arrangement of selected lections inherently problematic? "The major problem with these more incidental thematic connections is that they encourage the preacher to reach beyond the [OT and gospel] texts to some sort of 'eternal truth' outside them both, and to dismiss

---

9. *Revised Common Lectionary*, 10.

10. *Documents on the Liturgy 1963–1979: Conciliar, Papal, and Curial Texts* (Collegeville, MN: Liturgical, 1982), 566, 576, 577, 579.

11. Bailey, "Lectionary in Critical Perspective," 145.

12. Horace T. Allen Jr., *A Handbook for the Lectionary* (Philadelphia: Geneva, 1980), 38; though see Dieter T. Hessel, ed., *Social Themes of the Christian Year: A Commentary on the Lectionary* (Philadelphia: Geneva, 1983).

13. Roy A. Harrisville, "God's Mercy—Tested, Promised, Done! (An Exposition of Genesis 18:20–32; Luke 11:1–13; Colossians 2:6–15)," *Int* 31 (1977): 165–78, quotation, 166.

14. Gerard S. Sloyan, "The Lectionary as a Context for Interpretation," *Int* 31 (1977): 131–38; here, 132.

15. Lawrence H. Stookey, "Marcion, Typology, and Lectionary Preaching," *Worship* 66 (1992): 251–62.

all those questions of particularity and historical conditioning that are the lifeblood of exegesis itself."[16]

3. Another hermeneutical complaint: has the common lectionary put the venerable practice of *lectio continua*—orderly preaching through a biblical book, from beginning to end—at the mercy of "the snippet principle of the Bible"?[17] "The Bible's greatness can come through only when large portions are read regularly and uninterruptedly."[18] Walk into a Presbyterian or Methodist or Catholic church on any Sunday morning, Gerard Sloyan laments: "One does not hear enough about [the Bible] because one does not hear enough of it."[19] For Christopher Seitz, *lectio continua* is indispensable for construing specific scriptural passages in their literary context. Accordingly, the lectionary should be reduced to simpler Old and NT pairings that point up and heighten the dialectic created by "the Bible's own canonical organization . . . , [which] has deferred to a larger conceptual statement about what constitutes the essential episodes in the Christian story, primarily brokered in the Gospel lessons through the course of one year."[20]

4. For other critics, preaching "brokered in the Gospel lessons" is no solution but a major ingredient of the problem. Thanks to the common lectionary, Walter Sundberg protests, pulpits now gush "a surfeit of sermons grounded in gospel texts" that leads to "a 'unitarianism of the Son,' . . . a red-letter mentality in the church that ends up advocating a desiccated form of pietism."[21] Were that not bad enough, the OT, now shrunk into "grace-notes to the gospel,"[22] can scarcely "be heard on its own terms; rather, an external 'promise' and fulfillment scheme will be imposed upon it."[23] Although the RCL contains a broader sample of OT texts than ever before, by a considerable margin Isaiah remains (outside the Psalter) the most frequently cited OT book, with

---

16. Richard Nelson, "Reading Lectionary Texts in Pairs," *Di* 2 (1982): 95-101; quotation, 99-100; similarly, Harrisville, "God's Mercy," 169.

17. Gerard S. Sloyan, "Some Suggestions for a Biblical Three-Year Lectionary," *Worship* 63 (1989): 521-35; here, 531; cf. Hughes Oliphant Old, *The Patristic Roots of Reformed Worship* (Zurich: Theologischer, 1975), 194-95.

18. Sloyan, "Lectionary as a Context for Interpretation," 136.

19. Sloyan, "Some Suggestions," 530.

20. Seitz, "Lectionary as Theological Construction," 178.

21. Sundberg, "Limitations of the Lectionary," 19, developing a suggestion made by H. Richard Niebuhr, "The Doctrine of the Trinity and the Unity of the Church," *ThTod* (1946): 371-84.

22. Sloyan, "Some Suggestions," 530.

23. Lloyd R. Bailey, "Lectionary Preaching," *DDSR* 41 (1976): 25-35; quotation, 27-28.

two-thirds of its lections drawn from chapters 40–66.[24] Such intracanonical imbalance, it is frequently alleged, has radically truncated Israel's abundant and variegated religious themes, thus shortchanging the church of theological diversity in its own heritage while foreshortening Christians' perspective to preoccupation with "an anointed figure for the last age."[25]

5. Then there is the matter of bowdlerization. More than five decades ago, the Roman Council frankly acknowledged the problems.

> On pastoral grounds, biblical texts that *are truly difficult* are not used in the readings for Sundays and solemnities. The difficulty may be objective, based on the serious literary, critical, or exegetical problems the texts raise or the difficulty may lie in the faithful's power to grasp the meaning of some texts. [The omission of] certain verses from biblical readings . . . is not something to be done lightly, lest the meaning of the text or the intent and, so to speak, style of the Scriptures be distorted. But, for pastoral reasons, it seemed best to continue this tradition, taking care that the essential meaning of the text remain unchanged . . . [when omitting] the one or two verses unsuitable pastorally or involving truly difficult questions.[26]

No one doubts the pastoral sincerity behind this explanation. Questions inevitably arise, however, over what is "essential [to the] meaning of the text" and what "lie[s] in the faithful's power to grasp." Is David's love for his son essential and comprehensible, but not three darts slammed into Absalom's chest (Proper 14, Year B, omitting 2 Sam 18:14)? Elijah's victory over Baal's prophets, but not his slaughter of them (Proper 4, Year C, omitting 1 Kgs 18:40)? As Richard Nelson marveled, "One would hardly guess that Israel had ever raised a sword in anger,"[27] and the RCL does little to correct that impression. Nor does the NT escape pastoral emendation: from the lectionary one would never know that an ancient church once branded its schismatics as antichrists (1 John 2:18–29; cf. Easter 2 and 3, Year B).

---

24. Comparable statistics, based on the Roman *Ordo* (1969), are cited by Nelson, "Reading Lectionary Texts in Pairs," 95.

25. Sloyan, "Lectionary as a Context for Interpretation," 135–36; similarly, Bailey, "Lectionary in Critical Perspective," 149–50; Nelson, "Reading Lectionary Texts in Pairs," 95.

26. *Documents on the Liturgy*, 576 (quoting from the introduction to the *Lectionary for Mass* [1969]), emphasis original.

27. Nelson, "Reading Lectionary Texts in Pairs," 95. Similarly, Sloyan ("Lectionary as a Context for Interpretation," 138): "There is a delicacy bordering on squeamishness in certain of the Roman Lectionary's omitted verses."

The Psalter presents a special case of abridgment and expurgation. The RCL contains an impressive 105 psalms and ten canticles. By comparison with its 1983 antecedent, the current CCT product seeks "to respect the breadth and diversity of the psalter" and "the integrity of the content of the psalm itself," judiciously abbreviating "where length precluded the use of the whole."[28] Questions remain, however. Laments constitute over one-third of the Psalter; hymns of trust, about one-eighth. Why does the lectionary disproportionately represent the latter over the former? Is it purely coincidental that curses have been lifted from many laments that still survive (e.g., Pss 5:10; 40:15–16; 63:9–11; 69:22–28; 139:19–22)?[29] Are users of the lectionary tempted to deny anger and weeping, even when promised that gladness will return and reconciliation will prevail?[30]

6. On the other hand, in the view of many, biblical censorship has not gone far enough. The chief causes for concern are misogyny and anti-Judaism. Thus, the lectionary sins by commission: "The two most frequently cited texts in the justification of violence against women—Genesis 1–2 and the household codes—are part of the three-year Sunday cycle."[31] Ephesians 5:21–33 has since been deleted from the RCL, though excerpts from Genesis 1–2 appear as lections on four Sundays across Years A and B. (Genesis 1:1–2:4a remains in the Easter Vigil for all three years.) And there are sins of omission, notably John 7:53–8:11, "the text with which many abused women find the most identification" because Jesus defends a woman about to be physically battered.[32]

Even with the elimination of John 5:7–8 (save 5:1–9 and 7:37–39),[33] some see anti-Jewish mischief built into the lectionary's framework or reception as "realized eschatology with a vengeance": "the triumphal understanding that all that has been realized in the Christ of glory has been realized in Christians,"

---

28. *Revised Common Lectionary*, 7.

29. A characteristic example occurs in Lent 3, Year C: verses 1–8 of Psalm 63 (a song of trust mixed with an individual lament) are directed for use, but not vv. 9–11 (imprecations that one's enemies be gutted by sword and made prey for jackals).

30. See William L. Holladay, *The Psalms through Three Thousand Years: Prayerbook of a Cloud of Witnesses* (Minneapolis: Fortress, 1993), 287–315.

31. Marjorie Procter-Smith, "'Reorganizing Victimization': The Intersection between Liturgy and Domestic Violence," *PJ* 40 (1987): 17–27; quotation, 19.

32. Susan Brooks Thistlethwaite, "Every Two Minutes: Battered Women and Feminist Interpretation," in *Feminist Interpretation of the Bible*, ed. Letty M. Russell (Philadelphia: Fortress, 1985), 96–107; here, 101–2.

33. Matthew 27:24–25 remains embedded within 26:14–27:66 (alternatively, 27:11–54) in the liturgy for Passion (Palm) Sunday of Year A.

most of whom have no countervailing exposure to contemporary Judaism as a living religion.[34] Gerard Sloyan concludes:

> It would seem that no amount of critical scholarship is going to meet the pastoral problem caused by the fact that the sacred books of the Christians contain a polemic against a people who, subsequent to their writing, became almost totally other than the community of the writers. A better plan would seem to be to remove celebrants, lectors, preachers, and people from harm's way by a judicious editing of the readings. The practice is already current. It must be extended—without, however, destroying Jesus as the person believed in by Christians as sent by God in history to work just judgment.[35]

After so lengthy a recital of woe, some may wonder if a more excellent way were not the ultimate extension of "current practice": to purge liturgy of the lectionary without remainder. With all its pitfalls, can anything good come of it?

ACQUIRING "A TASTE FOR HOLY CONVERSATION"

This essay will disappoint the reader who expects some scholarly deus ex machina to swoop down and wipe clean every taint from the common lectionary. The Roman *Ordo* and its ecumenical offspring are products of the best scholarship available for the past half-century. If the features of this lectionary are troubling—its attention to each gospel's distinctive vision within a salvation-historical framework, its scissoring and sandpapering of biblical pericopes—then the fault lies not in deviance from but in adherence to the critical trends of its time.[36] Should the day dawn that a *lectio* be made even

---

34. Sloyan, "Lectionary as a Context for Interpretation," 135; see also James E. Parkes, "The Bible in Public Worship: A Source of Antisemitism," *FF* 2 (1976): 3–6; Bailey, "Lectionary Preaching," 30–31; Nelson, "Reading Lectionary Texts in Pairs," 100.

35. Gerard S. Sloyan, "The Jews and the New Roman Lectionary," *FF* 2 (1976): 5–8; here, 7. The "current practice" to which Sloyan refers includes expurgation of "Jesus' bitterer encounters with 'the Jews' in the Fourth Gospel" ("Lectionary as a Context for Interpretation," 138).

36. Presuppositions, for instance, of Heilsgeschichte and redaction criticism are explicit in Allen, *Handbook for the Lectionary*, 14–17; and Reginald H. Fuller, *Preaching the Lectionary: The Word of God for the Church Today*, rev. ed. (Collegeville, MN: Liturgical, 1984), xviii–xxv.

more *continua*, with greater narrative flow, we can safely bet that someone in another fifty years will scorn that amplification. As the product of fallible human beings, there has never been a perfectly realized lectionary, flawlessly interpreted, and there never will be. Let us refrain from heaping abuse on the current lectionary and those congregations using it. Consider this: in an age that has raised a tombstone for biblical theology—when consensus eludes scholars on how, even whether, that project should be revived[37]—the ecumenical church has refused to be crippled and, instead, has continued to attempt a theological rendering of its scripture with the lectionary as guide. This project has been spearheaded weekly by overextended priests and pastors, whose training, commendably augmented by sympathetic scholars,[38] remains conditioned by historical and literary criticism that is often theologically attenuated. That is no small feat. It is high time for us to applaud it.

More important than identifying the next steps in lectionary revision is a question usually unasked: What fundamental good does a lectionary serve? In itself, a lectionary is not a necessary good (or evil, for that matter). Nor are the benefits commonly associated with the lectionary—discipline for a preacher, a parish's exposure to biblical breadth—their own highest goods. The only real justification of a lectionary is its capacity to draw us more deeply into the mystery of God's love for us, that our hearts may be enlarged to love God more

---

37. A fine appraisal, with extensive bibliography, is presented by Mark G. Brett, "Canonical Criticism and Old Testament Theology," in *Text in Context: Essays by Members of the Society for Old Testament Study*, ed. A. D. H. Mayes (Oxford: Oxford University Press, 2000), 63–85. See also chapter 2 of the present volume.

38. Fuller, *Preaching the Lectionary*; Sherman E. Johnson, *The Year of the Lord's Favor: Preaching the Three-Year Lectionary* (New York: Seabury, 1983); Fred B. Craddock, John H. Hayes, Carl R. Holladay, and Gene M. Tucker, eds., *Preaching the New Common Lectionary* (Nashville: Abingdon, 1984–87); Walter Brueggemann, Charles B. Cousar, Beverly R. Gaventa, and James D. Newsome, *Texts for Preaching: A Lectionary Commentary Based on the NRSV* (Louisville: Westminster John Knox, 1993–95); Roger E. Van Harn, ed., *The Lectionary Commentary: Theological Exegesis for Sunday's Texts*, 3 vols. (Grand Rapids: Eerdmans, 2001); Joel B. Green et al., eds., *Connections: A Lectionary Commentary for Preaching and Worship; Year B, Volume 1: Advent through Epiphany* (Louisville: Westminster John Knox, 2018); Green et al., *Connections: Year B, Volume 3: Season after Pentecost* (Louisville: Westminster John Knox, 2020); Green et al., *Connections: Year C, Volume 1: Advent through Epiphany* (Louisville: Westminster John Knox, 2020); Green et al., *Connections: Year B, Volume 2: Lent through Pentecost* (Louisville: Westminster John Knox, 2020); the many contributors to the series Proclamation, 1–6 (Philadelphia and Minneapolis: Fortress, 1970–95); the journals *Word and Witness* (Lake Worth, FL: 1976–99), *Biblical Preaching Journal* (Lexington, KY: 1988–), and *Lectionary Homiletics* (Midlothian, VA: 1989/90–); and the online resource *Working Preacher* (https://www.workingpreacher.org).

fully, ourselves properly, and our neighbors more selflessly. Such is the acid test for all liturgical instruments. Hymnody should be beautiful, but not for art's sake. Prayer cultivates religious affections, but not for piety's parade. Preaching feeds faith, not cleverness. A lectionary exists to steer us into Scripture; Scripture exists to cultivate in us a life crucified with Christ, a life in flesh now lived by faith in God's Son who loved us and gave himself for us (Gal 2:20).

Is there anything peculiar to a common lectionary that enhances the journey into Scripture for the healing of our lives? Allow me to flag four possibilities.

First: *The interrelationships among lections remind us of the intrarelational character of Scripture itself and the God whom Christians worship.* Obviously, the common lectionary takes as its programmatic cue Scripture's inherent intertextuality, exemplified, from among many NT instances, by the coordination of Genesis 2:18–24 with Mark 10:2–16 (Proper 22, Year B). The Old and New Testaments mirror, interrogate, and illuminate each other.

Second: *Such intracanonical dynamism offers us purchase on the vexing issue of salvation history.* There is no question that a "promise-fulfillment" motif is biblically discernible—but whether it governs either Scripture or lectionary in the ham-fisted manner occasionally suggested is, I think, highly disputable.[39] I do not find in Scripture a unidirectional, static relationship between Testaments Old ("the promise") and New ("the fulfillment")—and I doubt that most biblical authors did either. After all, "promise and fulfillment" is a major theme *within* some OT books. In Deuteronomy (4:26, 30–31) that theme oscillates back and forth:

I call heaven and earth to witness against you today
   [Promise] that you will soon utterly perish from the land [Fulfillment] that you are crossing the Jordan to occupy.
   [Promise] In your distress, when all these things have happened to you in time to come,
   [Fulfillment] you will return to the LORD your God and heed him.
   [Promise] Because the LORD your God is a merciful God, [Fulfillment] he will neither abandon you nor destroy you; nor will he forget the covenant with your ancestors
   [Promise] that he swore to them. (NRSV)

---

39. Nor am I the first to dispute it. See also Terrence E. Fretheim, "The Old Testament in Christian Proclamation," *WW* 3 (1983): 223–30; Joseph Jensen, "Prediction-Fulfillment in Bible and Liturgy," *CBQ* 50 (1988): 646–62; Roland E. Murphy, "Forum: A Note on the Biblical Character of the Lectionary," *Worship* 74 (2000): 547–50.

Even a gospel like Matthew's, studded with "formula quotations" (1:22–23; 2:5–6, 14–15, 17–18; 4:13–16, among others), exhibits this oscillation: in Jesus, the Christ has come, circuitously descended from Abraham's line (1:1–17); Jesus promises his execution and vindication (16:21–28; 17:22–23; 20:17–19), whose accomplishment resonates oddly with Israel's laments (27:32–56; cf. Pss 22:1, 7, 8, 18; 69:21; 109:25; Wis 2:18–20); the risen Jesus assures the disciples of his authority's realization and promises eternal communion with them (Matt 28:16–20). Clearly, if today's sermons trumpet "realized eschatology with a vengeance," the blame for that rests not on the lectionary but on a Christian triumphalism that has oversimplified the theological complexity embracing both Testaments.[40]

Third: *In Christian Scripture there is a "dynamic coinherence" effectively mirrored by the lectionary's juxtaposition of texts.* More important: the lectionary reflects the doctrine of the Trinity as a uniquely Christian articulation of the church's experience of God. By this comment I do not intend any artificial correlation between God and the OT lesson, Jesus and the Gospel, the Spirit and the epistle. Such a "generic modalism" would be utterly bizarre and no less heterodox than old-fashioned Sabellianism. My point is simpler, though perhaps more enigmatic. In its common life, viewed through the prism of Scripture, the church has known God as One-in-Three. Put differently, Christians experience God relationally, on multiple planes: not only as a God self-revealed to humanity as just and merciful but also as a God whose love is intrinsically, indivisibly, and eternally self-reciprocating as that of Father, Son, and Holy Spirit. The lectionary's maintenance of a perpetual conversation within Scripture, among its constituents, does not capture the God of the Nicene-Chalcedonian affirmation. No human formulation captures God. That intracanonical conversation can be considered a muffled echo of the mighty conversation of love within the Godhead that continues throughout eternity and is drawing all of creation into its orbit. Viewed in that light, the preacher need not regard the lections on a given Sunday as a maze to be threaded, a triple-decker puzzle to be solved. Rather, their composite audition is an invitation, extended to the church, to enter afresh the mystery of the God it has gathered again to adore, who cultivates in worshipers "a taste for holy conversation" (Jerome, *Epist.* 130.16 (*PL* 22 [1845] 1119 [AT])).

Fourth: *The lectionary's axial construction conforms to the church's liturgical experience of the God of Israel and of Jesus Christ.* From its inception as the

---

40. By contrast, consult the wiser investigations of Elizabeth Achtemeier, *The Old Testament and the Proclamation of the Gospel* (Philadelphia: Westminster, 1973); and Thomas M. Raitt, "Jeremiah in the Lectionary," *Int* 37 (1983): 160–73.

Roman *Ordo*, the common lectionary has been rebuked for its inordinate complexity. Why combine *lectio selecta*, plucked readings coordinated with major seasons of the church year, with *lectio continua*, sequential coverage of books, notably during Ordinary Time (and in the weekday cycle)?[41] While explicit justification for either pattern is not hard to find,[42] I have yet to discover a rationale for their entwinement.

Let me suggest one. However deep or shallow its historical basis—which is lost beyond our ability to reconstruct—the lectionary's configuration recalls and extends, formally and theologically, the pattern of scriptural liturgy inherited by the church from Judaism. To this day, the Torah is read during the course of a year in synagogue: every word, from Genesis to Deuteronomy, in Orthodox congregations; abbreviated, sequential passages, among the Reform; in a triennial cycle, one-third read each year, by many Conservative congregations. Thematically yoked with these readings from Torah have been, for many centuries, excerpts from the prophets (the haftarah or "conclusion" of the scripture readings).[43] Sabbath by Sabbath, year upon year, the story of Israel's creation, enslavement, idolatry, and redemption has provided the framework into which Jews have integrated and sung the story of their life as a people before the LORD. At Passover, in the recital of the Exodus narrative at the seder (literally, the "order" of service), time is telescoped into the critical moment of liberation: "In every generation, let each man look on himself as if he came forth out of Egypt" (m. Pesaḥ. 10.5; cf. Exod 13:8). Observance of Passover and Sabbath converge at the point of memory, remembrance of God's creation of the world (Exod 20:11; 31:17), remembrance of the LORD's creation of Israel (Deut 5:15).[44]

The parallel with the church could not be plainer. "We hold our common assembly on the Sun's Day because it is the first day, on which God put to flight darkness and chaos and made the world; and on the same day Jesus Christ our

---

41. In the common lectionary no biblical book is covered in its entirety, a fact that has prompted Eileen Schuller's sensible observation that it is more accurate to speak of a *lectio semicontinua* ("The Bible in the Lectionary," in *The Catholic Study Bible: The New American Bible*, ed. Donald Senior et al. [New York and Oxford: Oxford University Press, 1990], 440–51 [N.B. 444]). For an example of the Weekday or Daily Office Lectionary, which is arranged in a two-year cycle, consult *The Book of Common Prayer and Administration of the Sacraments and Other Rites and Ceremonies of the Church* (n.p.: Seabury, 1979), 933–1001.

42. See, for instance, *Documents on the Liturgy*, 574–75.

43. Werner, *Sacred Bridge*, 52–58; anon., "Triennial Cycle," *EncJud* 15 (1972): 1386–89.

44. Consult Hiyam Halevy Donin, *To Be a Jew: A Guide to Jewish Observance in Contemporary Life* (New York: Basic Books, 1972), 61–96.

Saviour rose from the dead" (*1 Apol.* 67).[45] Every Christian Sabbath is a recollection and re-presentation of Easter, when "Christ our Passover has been sacrificed" for us (1 Cor 5:7b), for the renewal of God's creation and redemption of all the nations (2 Cor 5:17; Eph 2:11-22). That is why the lectionary accords to the Gospels a place of privilege: as Israel venerates Torah as its foundational narrative, so the church honors the story of Jesus as that of Christian life under his lordship. In that respect, the liturgical observance of Sabbath, whether by Jews or by Christians, has not been externally imposed but has evolved from Scripture itself: the Elohist, Yahwist, Priestly, and Deuteronomic traditions demonstrate successive generations of Israel claiming Torah as its own just as clearly as the communities of Mark, Matthew, Luke, and John recognized themselves in the Gospels they retold.

In a word, Christians have learned from their Jewish siblings how to tell time. The God of Israel and Jesus Christ intervenes in our history diachronically and synchronically, at one and the same time. The lectionary's curious structure replicates that curious fact of faith.

> The meaning of the Sabbath is to celebrate time rather than space. Six days a week we live under the tyranny of things of space; on the Sabbath we try to become attuned to holiness in time. It is a day on which we are called upon to share in what is eternal in time, to turn from the results of creation to the mystery of creation; from the world of creation to the creation of the world.[46]

Those words of Abraham Heschel teach, occasionally convict, the church of the irreducibly Jewish stamp on its own worship, including its lectionary, while reminding Christians of their own joyful responsibility to hallow the Sabbath as God's precious gift.

Wedded to the liturgical calendar, the lectionary can serve as midwife to the church's maturation in prayer, "until Christ is formed in us" (cf. Gal 4:19). In theory, and in Free Church practice, lectionaries can be compiled in hundreds of ways: thematically; as tightly "salvation-historicist," from Genesis to Revelation; in conjunction with national or other secular observances, like Indepen-

---

45. Henry Bettenson, ed. and trans., *The Early Christian Fathers: A Selection from the Writings of the Fathers from St. Clement of Rome to St. Athanasius* (London and Oxford: Oxford University Press, 1956), 63.

46. Abraham J. Heschel, *The Sabbath: Its Meaning for Modern Man* (New York: Farrar, Straus & Young, 1951), 10.

dence Day, New Year's Day, or harvest festivals. In conformation with the liturgical seasons, the Roman *Ordo* and its offspring deliberately bind themselves and their adherents to the life of Christ as confessed in the church's tradition, from Advent's turbulence to Pentecost's fiery tongues.

That decision continues to stir controversy. To the question, "Why must worship be so constrained?" the common lectionary rejoins: from and for what do Christian worshipers want to be freed? To the charge that lectionary preaching fosters historical obscurity in pursuit of vague "eternal truth," the lectionary replies: for Christians, the particular truth of the gospel illuminates history as nothing else can or ever will. To the rebuttal that Christocentric particularity prevents Christian engagement in a pluralistic age, the lectionary asks: where is the Christianity in worship that repudiates Christ?[47] If Christians do not acknowledge Christ's lordship over their own Scripture, worship, and lives, why on earth should anyone else take them seriously?

Let us consider a more positive prospect. Graced by the Holy Spirit, the lectionary may guide the church in prayer that, across time, draws Christians more intimately into Christ. Paul speaks for us all: "We don't know how to pray.... The heart's examiner knows the Spirit's way of thinking, for [the Spirit] pleads for the saints in accord with God" (Rom 8:26–27, AT). The same engine, I believe, drives the canticles in Luke's infancy narrative. When folk like Mary pray at the Spirit's behest, they do so *scripturally*, returning to God a biblical word:

My soul proclaims the greatness of the LORD, And my spirit has found gladness in God my Savior. (Luke 1:46b–47; cf. 1 Sam 2:1–2; Ps 35:9; Hab 3:18)[48]

> He has helped his servant Israel,
> in remembrance of his mercy,
> as he spoke unto our fathers,

---

47. For differently inflected considerations in this vein, see Paul W. Hoon, *The Integrity of Worship: Ecumenical and Pastoral Studies in Liturgical Theology* (Nashville and New York: Abingdon, 1971), esp. 79–148; Dietrich Bonhoeffer, *Christ the Center*, trans. John Bowden (New York: Harper & Row, 1978); Carl E. Braaten, "Scripture, Church, and Dogma: An Essay on Theological Method," *Int* 50 (1996): 142–55.

48. Unless otherwise indicated, all translations are the author's own.

to Abraham and his posterity forever. (Luke 1:54–55; cf. Ps 98:3; Isa 41:8–9).[49]

In the eighteenth century John and Charles Wesley hymned faith after the same kaleidoscopic fashion:

> Behold the servant of the Lord! (Luke 1:38)
> I wait thy guiding eye to feel, (Ps 32:8)
> To hear and keep thy every word, (Luke 11:28)
> To prove and do thy perfect will; (Rom 12:2)
> Joyful from my own works to cease, (Heb 4:10)
> Glad to fulfill all righteousness (Matt 3:15).[50]

And what of us? Can the lectionary serve the Spirit who would teach us, too, how to pray?

Drawn at random, the lections assigned for the Fifth Sunday after the Epiphany in Year A offer us a test case. Isaiah 58:1–12 is a clinical diagnosis of religious sin: the dis-integrity of a people who seek God while persisting in economic exploitation and social injustice. When deeds conform to righteous words, "Then shall your light burst through like the dawn/And your healing spring up quickly" (58:8ab NJPS). The reflective congregation that then sings Ps 112:1–10 may register uneasiness even in the face of its opening "Hallelujah!" Who is it, really, that fears the LORD, delights in his commandments, lends generously, frees the oppressed, and cares for the poor? If we automatically assume that the psalm is speaking of us, then we had better reread Isaiah 58. If, instead, we begin pondering points of discrepancy between our own confession and conduct, Ps 112:10 (skittishly parenthesized in the RCL) could sum up our cognitive dissonance: "The wicked will see it and be angry."

Just here, I believe, lies one of the strongest justifications for the church to take its Bible straight, without the lectionary's nervous watering down. For as long as we hide from ourselves the pettiness, anguish, injustice, folly, and murderousness of our forebears in faith, we shall continue to blind ourselves to the same pathologies that God is still laboring to heal within us. The harder we

---

49. Raymond E. Brown, *The Birth of the Messiah: A Commentary on the Infancy Narratives in Matthew and Luke*, rev. ed. (Garden City, NY: Doubleday, 1994), 358–59, thoroughly analyzes the background of the Magnificat.

50. Hymn 417 in *A Collection of Hymns for the Use of the People Called Methodists* (1780), quoted by Geoffrey Wainwright, "Towards an Ecumenical Hermeneutic: How Can All Christians Read the Scriptures Together?," *Greg* 76 (1995): 639–62; here, 660.

scour scripture of its offensiveness, the deafer it leaves us to our own offenses. No wonder that C. S. Lewis marveled at "the incessant whispering, tattling, lying, scolding, flattery" and gossiping throughout the Psalter. "No historical readjustments are here required, we are in the world we know. We even detect in that muttering and wheedling chorus voices which are familiar. One of them may be too familiar for recognition."[51]

Enter 1 Corinthians 2:1–16. One of Paul's points in this densely packed statement chimes with Trito-Isaiah's: God's deep purposes ("the fast I desire," 58:5a) are not what they seem to be—"otherwise, this world's authorities would never have crucified the Lord of glory" (1 Cor 2:8). How can one distinguish the "wisdom of this age" from the genuine article? Not by redoubled pursuit of this world's wisdom, which (as we may recall from the previous week's lection for the Fourth Sunday after the Epiphany) God has "moronized" (1 Cor 1:18–31, N.B. v. 20b). Only by the Spirit that comes from God—the Spirit that plumbs God's depths and discloses Christ's cross as God's power—can we grow in true discernment, acquiring "the mind of Christ" (1:18; 2:10–12, 16). Such a gift is received gratefully and humbly, lest we become insipid (Matt 5:13), craven (5:14–16), or lazy (5:19–20). Matthew 5:13–20 closes and reopens the circuit, returning us to Isaiah 58, which—by way of this Sunday's other lections—we may read with "maturing faith" (cf. 1 Cor 2:5–6). Our light and healing (Isa 58:8ab), our justice and steadfast heart (Ps 112:4, 7–8), the glory for which God has forever predestined us (1 Cor 2:7): all are embodied and disclosed in Christ (Matt 5:17–18; 1 Cor 2:2) to the end "that mortals may glorify [our] Father in heaven" (Matt 5:16).

Doxology properly concludes the exercise. To read scripture in this way is not to forsake disciplined exegesis. (How delightfully richer is the experience of reading in Hebrew Isaiah's reproof of those who "extend the finger" [*shelach 'etsba'*: 58:9cd]!) But critical exegesis itself needs discipline by prayer: the kind of ruminative, "prayed reading" in which our medieval ancestors were skilled, "believing in the real presence of God who speaks to us in the sacred text, while [themselves striving] to be present in a spirit of obedience and total surrender to the divine promises and demands."[52] Here we cannot read the text with scientific detachment. Nor can we hydroplane across the biblical surface, netting sermons on the fly. *Lectio divina* is not another technique for formulat-

---

51. C. S. Lewis, *Reflections on the Psalms* (New York: Harcourt, Brace & World, 1958), 75.
52. Louis Bouyer, quoted in Mariano Magrassi, *Praying the Bible: An Introduction to Lectio Divina*, trans. Edward Hagman (Collegeville, MN: Liturgical, 1998), 18. Magrassi's entire volume is highly recommended for its scholarship and devotion.

ing sermons. It is we who are formed by the Spirit to embody Scripture and, if it please God, to draw others out of themselves into its world of wonders.

So understood, Scripture is God's gift for the church: the bread of the word offered beside the bread of the sacrament. Our destination is Emmaus, where Christ reveals himself to his disciples "not solely in the eucharistic mystery, but also in the reading of Scripture"[53] (Rupert of Deutz, *Ad eccl.* 3:12, 13; cf. Luke 24:13–35). Too little noted in discussions of the common lectionary is its very commonality. Catholics and Protestants, laity and clergy, now sit at the same table to be fed by the Christ who died to draw all people to himself (John 6:35–51; 10:7–18; 12:32–33). Behold the mystery of God, once more hiding in plain sight (1 Cor 2:1–7).

Conclusion

The Revised Common Lectionary is an ornery conveyance. So was Balaam's ass (Num 22:21–35). Undefeated by our devices, God's Spirit blesses even blunt instruments to cultivate our sensibility for the Son, to order our disarray by the rhythm of his eternal life. No one need feel enslaved by the lectionary. It is merely a map, and Korzybski was correct: "A map is not the territory it represents."[54] For that matter, scripture itself is but an atlas—though indispensable, this side of paradise. The real estate for which we are created is life in God, into whom we are being relentlessly drawn until Christ is formed in us.[55]

---

53. *PL* 168 (1854): 1230–31 (AT), 72.

54. Alfred Korzybski, *Science and Sanity: An Introduction to Non-Aristotelian Systems and General Semantics* (Lancaster, PA: The International Non-Aristotelian Library Publishing Co., 1933), 58.

55. Dana Charry, MD,† Professor Roland E. Murphy, O. Carm.,† and the Reverend Mr. Patrick J. Willson generously read and commented on an earlier draft of this essay. For their assistance I remain grateful.

CHAPTER 20

The Kindness of Strangers

> We bear witness because this is how we build new narratives, because often this is the most beautiful task of an ally, which is to say of a human, to say, "I see what you see."
>
> —Hala Alyan

WHILE PREPARING THIS ADDRESS,[1] I have reviewed the names of this society's past presidents since 1912: a formidable roster indeed. It ought to inspire me. Instead it intimidates me. As Dirty Harry, Clint Eastwood said, "A man's got to know his limitations."[2] Nearing my seventh decade, I've drawn a clear bead on mine. I have no business delivering a presidential address to the American Theological Society. I know it. You know it. I am now going to prove it.

While scanning that list of past presidents and presentations, something else arrested my attention. In April, 1915, an entire program was dedicated to the topic, "Problems Suggested by the War." In 1960 the ATS took up Christian ethics, just war, limited war, and American policy. That makes sense, but these are surprising exceptions to the rule. During 1939 through 1945, 1950 through '54, and 1955 through '75, one can review the documentary evidence of our society scarcely knowing that a Second World War, the Korean War, and Vietnam War were occurring. In 2023 we again find ourselves in a world at war: a hot one of invasion in Ukraine, a cold civil one among the so-called United States. Throwing caution to the wind, I intend to address such circumstances from an angle so oblique that, as far as I know, it has never been investigated at length in an ATS session. Until now I certainly have never examined it. The subject I

---

1. Presidential Address to the 111th meeting of The American Theological Society (ATS) in Princeton, New Jersey, March 31, 2023. I have retained the character of personal address in my original delivery.

2. Ted Post, dir., *Magnum Force* (Burbank, CA: Malpaso/Warner Bros., 1973).

ask you to ponder with me this evening is kindness. My hypothesis is that, by sentimentalizing kindness or dismissing it outright, we have shrugged off its significance in biblical texts and diluted its import in Christianity and other religious traditions. Cruelty is our daily danse macabre. We have perfected a social media that brings all of us together that we might tear each other apart. It is not enough for us to suffer years of a novel coronavirus. We have augmented our debilitation and death tolls with novel expressions of bitter recrimination. How far can a society's fabric stretch when it numbers more guns than people, with six-score murders every day? Even if we and our loved ones dodge tomorrow's bullets, brutality of such magnitude is as exhausting as it is reprehensible. But hatred is not fated. We can choose to live otherwise. To do so requires an act of imagination and a sound theological basis for its superiority. If kindness be sneered at as too infantile for serious consideration, then a likely outcome is self-delusion that enables our evasion of mutual responsibility. Jesus did teach that the gates of God's kingdom are shut to all save those who become as children (Matt 18:3 // Mark 10:15 // Luke 18:17).

The Image of Mercy

Within a biblical frame of reference we begin, as always, with God. The most obvious starting point: the Priestly creation narrative in Genesis 1. On the sixth day of creation,

> God said, "Let us make 'adam [human creatures] in our *tselem* [image], after our *demuth* [likeness]. They shall rule the fish of the sea, the birds of the sky, the cattle, the whole earth, and all the creeping things that creep on the earth." And God created 'adam in his *tselem*, the *tselem* of God He created him; male and female He created them. (1:26–27 NJPS)

These familiar assertions invite analysis. Ancient Near Eastern potentates were reckoned the deity's "image" or "representation": agents with divine authorization.[3] Noteworthy in Genesis is that, by God's personal declaration, *all* humanity bears the divine stamp.[4] With wonder that belief is reiterated in Psalm 8:

---

3. Jon D. Levenson, *Creation and the Persistence of Evil: The Jewish Drama of Divine Omnipotence* (Princeton: Princeton University Press, 1988), 112–17.

4. The countercultural "democratization" of *imago Dei* in the world of ancient Israel

> What is man that you have been mindful of him,
> Mortal man that you have taken note of him,
> That you have made him little less than divine,
> And adorned him with glory and majesty? (vv. 5–6 NJPS)

The meaning of humanity's creation in God's image has been much disputed across the centuries.[5] Its correlation with God's likeness in Genesis 1:27 suggests, essentially, that "the pattern on which [human beings are] fashioned is to be sought *outside* the sphere of the created":[6] that is to say, in the most intimate communion with their Creator.

Humans, however, are not identical to God. Just as all teeming life made on the fifth and sixth days—birds of the sky, denizens of the deep, the earth's wild beasts, cattle and creepy crawlers (Gen 1:20-23)—*'adam* is mortal, contingent upon the Creator for its being. That which sets apart human creatures is their likeness to God by their derivative dominion (*radah*) over the animal kingdom, again hymned by the Psalmist:

> You have made him master over your handiwork,
>   Laying the world at his feet,
> Sheep and oxen, all of them,
>   And wild beasts, too;
> The birds of the heaven, the fish of the sea.
>   Whatever swims the paths of the seas. (Ps 8:7–9 JPS alt.;
>   cf. Wis 2:23; Sir 17:3)

Nowhere in Hebrew Scripture do such affirmations sanction ecological irresponsibility, let alone environmental devastation. Humanity does not *own* the rest

---

is underlined by J. Richard Middleton, *The Liberating Image: The Imago Dei in Genesis 1* (Grand Rapids: Brazos, 2005), N.B. 207.

5. Gunnlauger A. Jónsson, *The Image of God: Genesis 1:26-28 in a Century of Old Testament Research*, ConBOT 26 (Stockholm: Almquist & Wiksell, 1988); Douglas John Hall, *Professing the Faith: Christian Theology in a North American Context* (Minneapolis: Fortress, 1993), 213–18, 314–34; Dominic Robinson, *Understanding the* Imago Dei: *The Thought of Barth, von Balthasar and Moltmann* (Farnham and Burlington, VT: Ashgate, 2011); Claudia Welz, *Humanity in God's Image: An Interdisciplinary Exploration* (Oxford: Oxford University Press, 2016). Kari Elisabeth Børresen, ed., *The Image of God: Gender Models in Judaeo-Christian Tradition* (Minneapolis: Fortress, 1995), is an important collection of essays critiquing many patristic readings of *imago Dei* based on patriarchal presuppositions.

6. Gerhard von Rad, *Old Testament Theology*, vol. 1, trans. D. M. G. Stalker (New York: Harper & Row, 1962), 145, emphasis added.

of God's created world. As indicated in God's institutions of sabbatical and jubilee years (Exod 23:10–11; Lev 25:1–44), the sole Owner is the Creator, to whom human creatures are strictly accountable for beneficent stewardship (Lev 25:23–24). Human dominion is akin, not to force, but to caregiving and nurturance.[7]

"In the image of God He created humans; male and female He created them" (Gen 1:27).[8] Both sexes bear God's ineradicable mark (also 5:1–2). Their distinction assumes their congress in procreation: "Be fruitful and increase," a benevolent mandate by which God has just blessed swarms of fish and birds (1:21–22). Likeness with God is *inherently relational*, differentiation within similarity (cf. Gen 5:3).[9] "Let *us* make '*adam*," declares God, the CEO among a heavenly host (1:26; 1 Kgs 22:19–22; Isa 6:1–13; Job 1:6–2:7). "Be fertile and grow," proclaims the fecund God to creatures capable of offspring. Why is murder intrinsically heinous? It pours out the life of a fellow-creature made in God's *tselem*.

> Whoever sheds the blood of '*adam*,
> By '*adam* shall his blood be shed.
> For in his image
> Did God make '*adam*.
> Be fertile, then, and increase; abound on the earth and proliferate
>   on it. (9:6–7 NJPS alt.).[10]

Riffing on Genesis, Schleiermacher (1768–1834) wrote, "In the flesh of his flesh, and bone of his bone, [the first human] discovered humanity. In this first love he had a foretaste of all love's forms and tendencies—in humanity he found the world. From this moment on he was capable of . . . hearing the voice

---

7. A Rocha International, "a global family of conservation organizations working together to live out God's calling to care for creation," illustrates and activates this exegesis: https://arocha.org/en/?campaign_id=230&emc=edit_thw_20221218&instance_id=80452&nl=tish-harrison-warren&regi_id=13354003&segment_id=120218&te=1&user_id=ca5837c207685 3e744d619a0fc9cb685.

8. Unless otherwise indicated, this and subsequent translations are my own.

9. Likewise, Dietrich Bonhoeffer, *Creation and Fall: A Theological Exposition of Genesis 1–3*, trans. Martin Rütter and Ilse Tout, ed. John W. de Gruchy, DBW 3 (Minneapolis: Fortress, 1997), 65; Karl Barth, *Church Dogmatics: The Doctrine of Creation*, trans. G. T. Thomson, ed. Geoffrey W. Bromiley and Thomas F. Torrance (Edinburgh: T&T Clark, 1958, 1960), 3.1.228–30; 3.2.220–21, 323–24.

10. In *Jewish Ethics for the Twenty-First Century: Living in the Image of God* (Syracuse: Syracuse University Press, 2000), Byron L. Sherwin argues that particular offenses against human beings are unethical for the fundamental reason that they insult God's person and purpose.

of the Deity and answering it."[11] Tikva Frymer-Kensky (1943–2006) simplifies: "Social relationship is an indispensable part of both human nature and human purpose, and there can be no utterly single human being."[12]

At this point I want to open more widely the aperture through which we contemplate God's "image" in the HB. In so doing I shall draw some connections that seem to me of great importance. Simply put: without defining the *imago Dei* with much more precision than I have attempted, Jewish Scripture overflows with references to one of the Lord God's most salient characteristics: *hesed*.[13] Depending on context, this Hebrew term may be translated multifariously. In its most secular occurrences *hesed* normally refers, not to a disposition, but to positive acts that are social, mutual, and durative: specifically, that which promotes or preserves life and intervenes to relieve distress. Owing to its connotations of permanence and reliability, it is often associated with the covenant the Lord initiates with Israel (e.g., Deut 7:9, 12; 1 Kgs 8:23; Ps 106:45). Yet its fundamental origin appears to lie in the family and its bonds of compassion (e.g., Josh 2:12; Ruth 3:10; 2 Sam 10:2). *Hesed* assumes an unusual shape when, in fear of his life among foreigners, Abraham asks that Sarah present herself to Abimelech as sister, not as wife. When Gerar's king realizes the truth, upholding Sarah's honor with payment of damages incurred (Gen 20:3–10, 14–16), Abraham prays that fertility be restored to Abimelech's family (vv. 17–18) and defends the cover-up that is not reprimanded by God:

> Besides, [Sarah] is in fact my sister—my father's daughter though not my mother's; and she became my wife. So when God made me wander from my father's house, I said to her, "Let this be the *hesed* that you will do to me: to whatever place we come, say there of me, 'He is my brother.'" (20:12–13)[14]

While *hesed*—"goodness," "kindness," "mercy"—can be attributed to a human *hasid* (someone "kind" or "pious": e.g., 2 Sam 22:26; Pss 4:4; 12:3; 18:26), most frequently its agent is God, whose loving-kindness condescends to his

---

11. Friedrich Schleiermacher, *On Religion: Speeches to Its Cultured Despisers*, trans. John Oman; abridged, with an introduction by E. Graham Waring (New York: Ungar, 1955), 59.

12. Frymer-Kensky, *Studies in Bible and Feminist Criticism* (Philadelphia: Jewish Publication Society, 2006), 101. For pointing me in the directions of Schleiermacher and Frymer-Kensky, I am indebted to Janet Martin Soskice, *The Kindness of God: Metaphor, Gender, and Religious Language* (Oxford: Oxford University Press, 2007), 50–51.

13. A valuable study of this multifaceted term is Gordon R. Clark, *The Word* Hesed *in the Hebrew Bible*, JSOTSup 157 (Sheffield: Sheffield Academic, 1993).

14. Here and throughout all translations are my own unless otherwise indicated.

creatures' needs for maintenance of the covenant (Deut 7:9, 12; Mic 7:20; Ps 119:159), redemption from sin (Pss 25:7; 51:3), spiritual comfort (Ps 119:41, 76, 149), rescue from distress (Exod 15:13; Jer 31:3), and preservation of life from death (Ps 6:5; 86:13). God's *hesed* is abundant (Ps 69:17; Jonah 4:2), immeasurable (Num 14:19; Ps 145:8–9), and eternal (1 Chr 16:34, 41; 2 Chr 5:13; 7:3, 6; 20:21; Jer 33:11; Ezra 3:11). The familial bonds of *hesed*, kindness among those kindred, is asserted by Israel's God in prophetic metaphors most startling:

> In slight anger, for a moment,
> I hid my face from you.
> But with kindness everlasting
> I shall take you back into womblike love [*richamtik*].
>   —said the LORD your redeemer. (Isa 54:8)

> [O Israel] I shall betroth you to me forever;
> I shall betroth you to me in righteousness and in justice,
> In kindness and in mercy [*ubehesed uberachamim*]
> I shall betroth you to me in faithfulness;
> Then you shall be devoted to the LORD. (Hos 2:21–22)

Righteousness and justice, kindness and mercy, were hardly the experience of Canaan's indigenous peoples, who, according to the books of Joshua and Judges, were brutalized by violent Israelite conquest. The discordance is harsh. The land is the LORD's gift to those displaced, without safe residence, and a summons of fidelity to Israel's God (Josh 21:43–45). The land is also a lure to proprietary rapacity, a theater in which Torah's disobedience runs wild, the realm from which exile was constant as threat and as fact (Josh 10:16–12:24; Judg 2:2–3:7; Jer 6:13–15; 8:21–22). Parallels with European genocide of North America's native populations are gruesomely apt. From this clash of a territorial imperative and the agony of Israel's deportation emerged the notion of kindness to the *ger toshav*: the sojourner in Israel, its resident alien.

> For the LORD your God is the God of gods and the Lord of lords, the great, the mighty, and the awesome God, who is impartial and takes no bribe, but upholds the cause of the orphan and the widow, and befriends the stranger, giving him food and clothing. You also must befriend the stranger; for you were strangers in the land of Egypt. (Deut 10:17–19 JPS alt.)

> When a stranger sojourns in your land, you shall do him no wrong. The stranger who lives with you shall be to you as one of your own citizens; you

shall love him as yourself; for you were strangers in the land of Egypt: I the LORD am your God. (Lev 19:33–34 JPS alt.)

Of all peoples, Israel should recognize resident aliens as themselves. Hebrews repeatedly found themselves strangers in strange lands (Gen 23:4; 1 Chr 16:19; Ps 105:12).

COMPASSION CHRISTOLOGIZED

Turning to the NT, the picture is similar while acquiring christological definition. The Septuagint's usual translation of *hesed* into Greek, *eleos*, "mercy," is most often attributed to God (Matt 9:13; 12:7 [cf. Hos 6:6]; Luke 1:50, 54, 58, 72, 78; 6:36; 18: 13; Rom 9:23; 11:32; 12:1; 15:9; 2 Cor 1:3; 4:1; Eph 2:4; 1 Tim 1:2; 2 Tim 1:2; Titus 3:5; Heb 8:12; 2 John 3), as is God's "kindness" (*chrēstotēs*: Rom 2:4; 11:22; Eph 2:7), "loving-kindness" (*philanthrōpia*: Titus 3:4), or "tender familial mercy" (*oiktirmōn*: Luke 6:36; Jas 5:11). The NT correlates the Heavenly Father's kindness with that of his Son (*eleos*: 2 Tim 1:16, 18; Heb 2:17; Jude 21; *chrēstotēs*: Eph 2:7). No surprise there: in all the Gospels Jesus is consistently remembered for his mercy. Like Father, like Son.[15] The earliest Christians, most of whom were Gentiles, evidently reversed the adage: if this is the character of the Son, then so it is true of the Father. The image (*eikōn*) of God in the NT is Christ Jesus (1 Cor 11:7; 2 Cor 4:4; Col 1:15). In Paul's letters humanity is less expressly created in the *imago Dei*, more typically re-created in the *imago Christi*: believers are "conformed to the image of [God's] Son" (Rom 8:29), "being transformed into his likeness [or "the same image"] from one degree of glory to another [by action of] the Lord, the Spirit" (2 Cor 3:18). "As we have been born of the *eikōn* of the man of dust, we shall also bear the *eikōn* of the man from heaven" (1 Cor 15:49).[16] The reformatting of human-

---

15. In this regard Carly L. Crouch appeals to Adam's siring of Seth "in his own image" (Gen 5:3) as a guide for understanding "Genesis: 26–27 as a Statement of Humanity's Divine Parentage" (*JTS* 61 [2010]: 1–15). Fast-forwarding to contemporary dogmatics, Thomas A. Smail argues for a trinitarian anthropology: the Father's active communion with the Son and the Spirit empowers humans created in the divine image to exercise "their created exocentricity," to become "through the Spirit's perfecting creativity ... what they were made and meant to be" (Smail, *Like Father, Like Son: The Trinity Imaged in Our Humanity* [Grand Rapids: Eerdmans, 2005], 186–87).

16. The conceptual shift from *imago Dei* to *imago Christi* does not entail supersessionism. "[T]he *Leitmotif* that informs all themes Bonhoeffer takes up is God's becoming human in Christ to restore human beings to their full humanity" (Jens Zimmermann, *Dietrich Bonhoeffer's Christian Humanism* [Oxford: Oxford University Press, 2019], x).

ity's hard-drive is simultaneously ontological, pneumatological, soteriological, deontological, and eschatological.[17]

> Blessed be the God and Father of our Lord Jesus Christ! By his great mercy [*eleos*] we have been born anew to a living hope through the resurrection of Jesus Christ from the dead, into an inheritance that is imperishable, stainless, and unfading, kept in heaven for you, who by God's power are guarded through faith for a salvation ready to be revealed in the last time. (1 Pet 1:3–5)

> For we ourselves were once foolish, disobedient, led astray, enslaved by all sorts of passions and pleasures, passing our days in malice and envy, being hated and hating one another; but when the goodness [*chrēstotēs*] and loving-kindness [*philanthrōpia*] of God our Savior appeared, he saved us, not because of righteous deeds we had done, but because of his mercy [*eleos*], by the washing of rebirth and renewal by the Holy Spirit, which he plentifully poured out upon us richly through Jesus Christ. (Titus 3:3–6)

> But now you must be done with them all: wrath, anger, malice, slander, obscenity from your mouth. Stop lying to one another, seeing that you have taken off your old self with its practices and have put on your new self, which is being renewed in knowledge in the image of its creator [*kat' eikona tou ktisantos auton*]. Here there is no Greek and Jew, circumcised and uncircumcised, barbarian or Scythian, slave or freedman, but Christ is all, and is in all. (Col 3:8–11)

Within this heightened context, kindness is valued as equal in stature to knowledge, truthfulness, purity, forbearance, genuine love, the Holy Spirit, and even the power of God (2 Cor 6:6). *Chrēstotēs* is a fruit of Christ's spirit, alongside "love, joy, peace, patience, goodness, faithfulness, gentleness, and self-

---

17. Gabrielle Thomas makes a comparable argument for Gregory of Nazianzus's vision of the *imago Dei* in *The Image of God in the Theology of Gregory of Nazianzus* (Cambridge: Cambridge University Press, 2019). A précis of her monograph's argument may be found in "The Human Icon: Gregory of Nazianzus on Being an *Imago Dei*," *SJT* 72 (2019): 166–81. Divested of christological premises, Gregory's interpretation bears some remarkable resemblances with rabbinic interpretations of *tselem 'elohim*: as God's earthly representatives, human beings exhibit a divine structural form that extends God's presence in the created order. See Yair Lorberbaum, *In God's Image: Myth, Theology, and Law in Classical Judaism* (New York: Cambridge University Press, 2015).

control" (Gal 5:22). Colossians speaks of compassion and kindness (*splanchna oiktirmou // chrēstotēs*), not as natural dispositions, but as qualities in which God's holy ones are clothed alongside humility, gentleness, patience, tolerance, forgiveness, and "love that glues everything together in perfect harmony" (3:12–14). Especially is kindness to be extended to those strange to us (Heb 13:5; 3 John 5), for even Israel's ancestors were once "alien exiles on earth," let alone goyim who were once without hope, "strangers to the promised covenants" (Eph 2:12, 19). "Once you were no people but now you are God's people; once you had not received mercy but now you have received mercy" (1 Pet 2:10). Jesus warned his disciples that he will return as a stranger (*xenos*) whom they will either welcome or reject (Matt 25:35, 43).

Rabbinic, Patristic, and Medieval Amplifications

Beyond the biblical tradition, esteem of mercy persists in rabbinic and medieval Christian literature. Fearing transgressive anthropomorphism, many rabbis appear skittish about speaking of humanity in God's image.[18] Nevertheless, loving-kindness is the core of rabbinic ethics.[19]

> Simon the Just, one of the survivors of the Great Synagogue, used to say, "Upon three things does the world stand: upon Torah, upon worship, and upon deeds of lovingkindness." (m. 'Abot 1.2).

> The one who sustains God's creatures [acts] as though he had created them. (*Tanḥum. B. Noaḥ* 16a [eighth/ninth century CE])

> Though the people of the first temple practiced idolatry, among them there was *derek 'erets*. And what was this proper conduct? Almsgiving and deeds of lovingkindness. (*Tanḥum. Eliezer* 71)

---

18. Alexander Altmann, "'Homo Imago Dei' in Jewish and Christian Theology," *JR* 38 (1968): 235–59, N.B. 235–40. Similar reticence, for the same reason, may be evidenced in modern Islam: thus, Lisa Sowle Cahill, "Embodying God's Image: Created, Broken, and Redeemed," in *Humanity before God: Contemporary Faces of Jewish, Christian, and Islamic Ethics*, ed. William Schweiker, Michael A. Johnson, and Kevin Jung (Minneapolis: Fortress, 2006), 31–54.

19. Claude Goldsmid Montefiore and H. Loewe, eds., *A Rabbinic Anthology* (New York: Schocken, 1974), 412. From Montefiore and Loewe I have drawn the rabbinic excerpts that follow.

> In a city where there are both Jews and Gentiles, the alms-collectors collect both from Jews and from Gentiles; they feed the poor of both, bury both, comfort the mourners whether they be Jews or Gentiles, and they restore the lost goods of both—for the sake of peace. (j. Dem. 4 §6, f. 24a, l. 67)

> In the future world, man will be asked, "What was your occupation?" If he replies, "I fed the hungry," then they reply, "This is the gate of the Lord. He who feeds the hungry, let him enter." So with giving drink to the thirsty, clothing the naked, with those who look after orphans, and with those, generally, who do deeds of lovingkindness. All these are gates of the Lord, and those who do such deeds shall enter within them. (*Midrash on Ps* 118:19 [243b §17])

Food for the hungry, drink for the thirsty, welcome of the stranger, clothing of the naked, visitation of the sick and imprisoned; the rabbis admonished the mitzvah *gĕmîlût hăsādîm*, "the giving of loving-kindness." The parallels with Jesus's teaching in Matthew 25:31–46 are obvious and have long been so recognized by scholars both Jewish and Christian.[20]

Stunning declarations of God's kindness, to be replicated by Israel, were attached to the primordial story of God's salvation at the Red Sea (Exod 14–15). Thus, these midrashim:

> Why does Scripture give no [explicit] command to rejoice during Pesach? Because the Egyptians died during Pesach. . . . As Shemuel would quote: "Do not gloat at the fall of your enemy." (Prov 24:17; Pesiq. Rab Kah. 189a [fifth/sixth century CE])

> The Egyptians were drowning in the sea. At the same time, the angels wanted to sing before God, and the Lord God said to them: "My creations are drowning, and you are singing before me?" (b. Meg. 10b)

> The Holy One, Blessed be He, does not rejoice over the fall of the wicked. (b. Sanh. 39b)

---

20. Samiel Tobias Lachs, *A Rabbinic Commentary on the New Testament* (Hoboken, NJ, and New York: KTAV/Anti-Defamation League of B'nai B'rith, 1987), 394; W. D. Davies and Dale C. Allison Jr., *A Critical and Exegetical Commentary on the Gospel According to Saint Matthew*, vol. 3, ICC (Edinburgh: T&T Clark, 1997), 425–27.

What of the *imago Dei* and its claims of loving-kindness among later Christian thinkers? Here we can muse on only two.[21] In *De Trinitate* Augustine (354–430) writes, "There is such potency in this image of God in [the mind] that it is capable of cleaving to him whose image it is. . . . And then when it totally cleaves to him it will be one spirit" (*De Trin.* 14.4.20).[22] Augustine rejected heterodox claims that the female sex was defective, to be repaired by their makeover as men (*Gos. Thom.* 114).[23] Rather, "The woman, therefore, is just as much God's creation, as is the man. . . . Thus the one who established the two sexes will restore them both" (*De civ. Dei* 22.17). The world in its entirety—the faithful, sinners, and pagans—all are imbued with holy kindness: "[One wants to] be at peace with all men, so far as it is in his power, with that peace among men which is the properly ordered contact of man with man; and this concord's order is, first, to harm no one and, second, to help anyone that one can" (*De civ. Dei* 19.14).[24] As Janet Martin Soskice (1951-) paraphrases, "To be fully human, even to praise God, we need others who are different from ourselves."[25] Returning to Augustine: "The serene love with which we

---

21. Susan Wessel, *Passion and Compassion in Early Christianity* (Cambridge: Cambridge University Press, 2016), enlarges the scope through inspection of the works of Tertullian (155–240), Gregory of Nazianzus (ca. 320–90), John Chrysostom (347–407), Pope Leo I (ca. 400–461), Gregory the Great (ca. 540–604), and Maximus the Confessor (ca. 580–662).

22. Saint Augustine, *The Trinity*, trans. Edmund Hill, ed. John E. Rotelle, WSA 5 (Brooklyn, NY: New City Press, 1991), 386.

23. See also Jerome, *Comm. Eph.* 5:29.

24. This and the previous quotation from *De civitate Dei* are translations by William Babcock, Saint Augustine, *The City of God (De Civitate Dei, XI–XXII)*, ed. Boniface Ramsey, WSA 7 (Hyde Park, NY: New City Press, 2013), 2.527, 371.

25. Soskice, *Kindness of God*, 50. For an acute and academically courageous exegesis of Shakespeare's plays from this point of view, see Paula Marantz Cohen, *Of Human Kindness: What Shakespeare Teaches Us about Empathy* (New Haven and London: Yale University Press, 2021). "Empathy is not simply a matter of imagining what 'I' would feel in another's position. It is imagining what someone else feels who is not me—someone with a background, situation, and body different from my own. . . . [Shakespeare's] plays present the case for the Other without idealizing victimhood or forgetting the degree to which we all participate in the tragedy of the human condition: that we are all sentenced to death and ought to be humbled and compassionate in this awareness" (12). Beneath the execution of death itself, the tragic sin of war is its dehumanization of humanity, its evisceration of humankind. "While in the heat of combat, I didn't think of those 25 as people. You can't kill people if you think of them as people. They were chess pieces removed from the board, Bads taken away before they could kill Goods. I'd been trained to 'other-ize' them, trained well" (Prince Harry, The Duke of Sussex, and J. R. Moehringer, *Spare* [New York: Penguin Random House, 2023]). Soldiers who survive to return can never come home until their heart's distress is stilled in the heart of God (Augustine, *Conf.* 1.1.1).

love God and the neighbor comprises the entire greatness and breadth of the divine sayings. In what you understand of them, love is manifest; in what you do not understand, love is concealed" (*Serm.* 350.2).[26]

Imago Dei, God's *hesed*, the indissoluble union of divine and human, human with human, of the persons of the Godhead: all converge in the *Shewings* of the Augustinian anchoress Julian of Norwich (1343–c. 1416). Whereas Augustine was inclined to identify the human creature's *mens*, inner intellectuality, with the image of God (*De Trin.* 15.1.1),[27] Julian is more at home—and, in my view, more firmly footed in Scripture—with the *embodiment* of divine and human love. "Our true Mother Jesus," "by the takyng of oure kynd gave us life, and by his blessed dying on the Cross he bore us to endless life. And since then ... he feeds us and fosters us, just as the great supreme lovingness of motherhood wishes, and as the natural need of childhood asks" (*Revelations* §63).[28] By the incarnation of divine love, Christ is of our kind: he is our kin,[29] which rhymes

---

26. *Obras completes de San Agustín XXVI: Sermones* (6.0) 339–396, trans. Pio De Luis (alt.), BAC 461 (Madrid: Biblioteca de Autores Cristianios, 1985), 166–67.

27. Edmund Hill injects a cautionary reservation: "But to rid our minds of preconceptions about a dualist (body-soul) versus a unitary (living organism) concept of man, which are in fact strictly irrelevant to what Augustine is doing in this section of the *De Trinitate*, let me translate his word *mens*, which is properly rendered 'mind,' by 'self'" (Hill, *The Mystery of the Trinity*, ICT [London: Chapman, 1985]), 125.

28. Julian of Norwich, *Showings*, trans. Edmund Colledge and James Walsh (alt.), CWS (Mahwah, NJ: Paulist, 1978), 304. Cf. Middleton's compatible interpretation: "God in Genesis 1 is like no one as much as a mother, who gives life to her children, blesses them, enhances their power and agency, and then takes the parental risk of allowing her progeny to take their first steps, to attempt to use their power, to develop toward maturity" (Middleton, *Liberating Image*, 294–95).

29. Unable to better it, I quote in extenso Frederick Christian Bauerschmidt's etymological summary:

> In Middle English the word "kindness" has a very complex set of meanings that today are largely lost to us: it indicates the *benevolence* that we mean today when we speak of someone as "kind"; it also indicates the *nature* of a thing, what "kind" of thing it is, as when we speak of "humankind"; and somewhere between benevolence and nature, it indicates the *relationship* between those who share a common nature—thus the words "kin" and "kindred." In any particular instance, the word "kind" may well carry all of these meanings. To say that someone treated you "kindly" would be to say that she acted in a benevolent way (kindly), as if you were her relative (kindred), and in a way that is only natural to someone like her (her kind). Julian's use of this term encompasses all of these meanings. Thus, when she says that "God is kind in his being" [*Revelations* §62] she is making a claim not only about God's benevolence, but also about God's relationship to us, as well as naming God, not as a created nature (*natura naturata*) but as nature's creator (*natura naturans*), and thus making a claim about the nature of reality

with the assurances in Ephesians that, before the world's foundation, "[God] has adopted us as his children through Jesus Christ" (1:5) and in Romans that God has predestined, called, justified, and glorified "those conformed to the image of his Son, that he might be the firstborn within an expansive family" (8:29–30). In short, "at-one-being" (atonement) is grounded in God's kindness: that is to say, God's decision to become our kind, "know[ing] and lov[ing] us before time began" (*Revelations* §59). Julian's trinitarian attribution of maternalism to God and to Christ may be anchored—though I know of few theologians who have—in the prologue of the Fourth Gospel: "He was in the world, and the world was made through him, yet the world knew him not. He came to his own home, and his own people received him not." The *logos* dwelled among us as a stranger. "But whoever received him, those who trusted in his name, he empowered to become children of God: begotten, not by blood nor of the will of the flesh nor by the will of man, but by God" (John 1:9–13). "No one has ever seen God; it is God, the one-of-a-kind Son, ever in the Father's bosom, who has revealed him" (1:18). The child (the second person of the Trinity), suckled at the breast of the first person, has begotten believers not once but twice: at their first creation with the rest of the world, then by being "begotten again," or "from above" (*anōthen*), through the incarnate Word's Spirit (the third person: 3:5–8).

We have slogged a long way. Let's catch our breath. I have proposed that humanity's creation in God's image may best be understood as mortal communion with God's eternal loving-kindness, expanded by early Christians as transformation into the likeness of Jesus Christ. Classical interpretations of the *imago Dei*—functional, relational, and noetic[30]—effectively subdivided what Scripture consolidated, though the biblical stress usually falls on the relational, even familial, aspect: humanity's life from God, in Christ, with one another. For this reason *hesed* or *eleos* is mandated as the divine benchmark of faithful conduct among human beings, particularly those who seem to us strangers. We reciprocate to

---

as a whole. (Bauerschmidt, "Order, Freedom, and Kindness: Julian of Norwich on the Edge of Modernity," *ThTod* 60 [2003]: 63–81; quotation, 73)

30. Ian A. McFarland, "Theological Anthropology," in *The Cambridge Dictionary of Christian Theology*, ed. David S. Fergusson, Karen Kilby, Ian A. McFarland, and Iain R. Torrance (Cambridge: Cambridge University Press, 2011), 501–4, N.B. 502–3. To these alternatives Ryan S. Peterson has suggested the superiority of another: that of identity. Humanity's representation of God simply *is* human identity (*The Imago Dei as Human Identity: A Theological Interpretation* [Winona Lake, IN: Eisenbrauns, 2016]). For an appreciative yet critical appraisal of this proposal see Laura M. Lysen's review of *The Imago Dei as Human Identity*, by Ryan S. Peterson, *IJST* 19 (2017): 117–20.

one another the enduring mercy with which God has blessed us and which his Messiah, Jesus, incarnated. Following tracks laid down in their Scriptures, our Jewish and Christian ancestors maintained and dilated these convictions in their own distinctive ways. And Julian concluded, "All will be well, and you will see it yourself, that every kind of thing will be well" (*Revelations* §305).

The Eclipse of Kindness

Well, now. If all or at least much of this be accepted, why has kindness so faded away to a point now rarely taken seriously? That, my dear colleagues, is a question I put before you. I have only hunches, some of which I'll set up as signposts for your consideration.

The trivialization of kindness may be explored historically or theologically. I can appraise neither at length; you will be relieved to know that I shan't try. Historically regarded, kindness fell from favor as Western culture became increasingly secularized in its bellicosity.[31] Take Thomas Hobbes (1588–1679). Gone, in *Leviathan* (1651), is the belief in goodwill inherent in humanity. Instead the world is a battlefield, a relentless *bello omnium contra omnes*, "warre of alle against alle."[32] It is human nature to invade and to destroy. Absent a social contract of submission to an absolute sovereign, "The life of man [is] solitary, poor, nasty, brutish, and short" (*Leviathan* 13).[33] David Hume's (1711–76) moral sentimentalism acknowledged human resonance with others' pleasures and pains,[34] but nature, not God, produces fellow feeling.[35] Rousseau (1712–78) said, "When I was quite alone there was a void in my heart, which wanted nothing more than another heart to fill it up."[36] Yet for him, theoret-

---

31. For further discussion of these and other thinkers mentioned in this paragraph, consult Adam Phillips and Barbara Taylor, *On Kindness* (New York: Picador/Farrar, Straus & Giroux, 2009), 23–93.

32. Thomas Hobbes, *Leviathan*, 2 vols., ed. Noel Malcolm (Oxford: Clarendon, 2012), 2:196–97.

33. Hobbes, *Leviathan*, 2:192.

34. David Hume, *A Treatise of Human Nature* [1739–40]: *A Critical Edition*, ed. David Fate Norton and Mary J. Norton (Oxford Clarendon, 2007), 2.1.12–2.2.2 (211–24), 3.3.1–3.3.2 (377–78).

35. Hume, *Dialogues concerning Natural Religion* [1779] 6, 12, in *Dialogues concerning Natural Religion; The Posthumous Essays: Of the Immortality of the Soul; and Of Suicide; From an Enquiry concerning Human Understanding of Miracles*, ed. Richard H. Popkin, 2nd ed. (Indianapolis: Hackett, 1980), 39, 88–89.

36. Jean-Jacques Rousseau, *Confessions*, trans. Angela Scholar, OWC (Oxford: Oxford University Press, 2000), Book 7.

ically, the optimal stage in human development was primitive savagery, the *beatus medium* between animal brutality and social corruption.[37] A century later, Freud (1856–1939) deemed an instinct for kindness impossible unless perversely eroticized: from infant toward parent, as a form of incest; from one adult to another, as a form of seduction. Freud wrote *Three Essays on the Theory of Sexuality* (1905)[38] without once mentioning kindness, which surprises only when we forget his assumption that humans are naturally cruel creatures disposed to rape and exploit. God, of course, is only a wish-fulfilling illusion, whose future is at best socially equivocal.[39]

Conspicuously absent from this hit-or-miss survey is the God of Israel and of the church.[40] Fade out, theology; fade in, ideology, whatever its flavor: political, sociological, psychological. Wherever there is ideology, its exponent is an ideologue, often every whit as dogmatic as the religious adherent who must in every case be exposed as fraudulent. Theocentricity must be toppled by anthropocentricism. And when woman or man becomes the measure of all things, the overreach inevitably recurs: humans deny their creaturely being in God's image and make gods of themselves. As the apostle Paul perceived long ago (Rom 1:18–32), sin at its root is idolatry: humanity's urge to create gods on its own terms that patronize divided loyalties, authorize tribal prejudices, and are conveniently manipulable. The homage paid to such idols, called out by biblical prophets and sages, is recorded in every day's news. "When pride comes, then comes disgrace" (Prov 11:2). "You give your mouth free rein for evil, and your tongue frames deceit" (Ps 50:19). "Woe to those who decree wicked decrees, . . . [who] thwart the needy from justice and rob the poor of my people of their right, that widows may be their plunder, . . . that they may make the orphans their prey!" (Isa 10:1–2). "Woe to those who . . . rely on horses, who trust in chariots" (Isa 31:1; for which we may substitute handguns and missiles). "God, I thank thee that I am not like other people: extortioners, bigots, adulterers, and back-stabbers" (Luke 18:10). Idols promise freedom,

---

37. Rousseau, *A Discourse on the Origin of Inequality* [1755] 2 (*On the Origin of Inequality, on Political Economy, and the Social Contract*, trans. G. D. H. Cole, EL [London: Dent & Sons, 1920]).

38. Sigmund Freud, *Three Essays on the Theory of Sexuality*, trans. and ed. James Strachey (New York: Avon, 1962).

39. Sigmund Freud, *The Future of an Illusion*, trans. and ed. James Strachey (New York and London: Norton, 1971; German original, 1927); Freud, *Civilization and Its Discontents*, trans. and ed. James Strachey (New York and London: Norton, 2010; German original, 1930).

40. The exception, up to a point, is Rousseau: "Everything is good as it leaves the hands of the Author of things; everything degenerates in the hands of man" (Rousseau, *Émile: or, On Education*, trans. Allan Bloom [New York: Basic Books, 1979], 37). Consult Ronald Grimsley, ed., *Rousseau: Religious Writings* (Oxford: Clarendon, 1970).

facts, and power but deliver only bondage, deceit, and impotence. It cannot be otherwise, for they are nothing but the ventriloquism of their devotees' own ruthlessness. *Ruth*, the Hebrew cognate for "companionable pity" (*re'ut*), is a homeless stranger—invisible, unrecognizable, stripped of dignity—in a delusory world deaf to the voice of the living LORD, before whom there are no other gods (Deut 5:7; Isa 2:8–18; 43:10–11; Zeph 2:11), including the bogus god of the autonomous self.

In mouth and in heart, the word is very near us, and doable (Deut 30:14). "You shall love the LORD your God with all your heart, and with all your soul, and with all your mind, and with all your strength. . . . [and] you shall love your neighbor as yourself" (Mark 12:30–31; cf. Deut 6:5; Lev 19:18). Kierkegaard was correct: objections to Christianity spring, not from doubt, but from rebellious disobedience.[41]

KINDNESS UNDEFEATED

And yet. No matter how estranged we are from one another, even within ourselves, the God of Abraham and of Jesus Christ is not defeated, the God "who creates life out of death and calls into being that which is nonbeing" (Rom 4:17). If the testimony of both biblical testaments is reliable, then the image of God in human beings has been warped but is reparable; our self-built walls can be breached. Liberated from its Victorian fustiness, kindness can be re-viewed with eyes that discern resilience, not mush. Self-imposed quarantine by race, by gender, by class, is futile, because it diminishes and finally destroys us.[42] All women and men belong to one another. All, without exception, are

---

41. Kierkegaard, *The Journals of Søren Kierkegaard*, ed. and trans. Alexander Dru (London, New York, and Toronto: Oxford University Press, 1938), 193.

42. One need not be a theist to endorse this. Thus, Tenzin Gyatso, His Holiness the Dalai Lama:

> Compassion is not something childish or sentimental. . . . Whenever I meet people I always approach them from the standpoint of the most basic things we have in common. We each have a physical structure, a mind, emotions. We are all born in the same way, and we all die. All of us want happiness and do not want to suffer. Looking at others from this standpoint rather than emphasizing secondary differences such as the fact that I am Tibetan, or a different color, religion, or cultural background allows me to have a feeling that I am meeting someone just the same as me. I find that relating to others on that level makes it much easier to exchange and communicate with one another. . . . *We need to actively cultivate the antidotes to hatred: patience and tolerance.* . . . [Hatred, t]his internal enemy, this inner enemy has no other function than causing us harm. It is our true enemy, our ultimate enemy. It has no other function than simply destroying

of humankind, kindred in a single family of God. "If anyone says, 'I love God,' and hates his sister, he is a liar; [and] she who does not love her brother whom she has seen, cannot love God whom she has not seen" (1 John 4:20). Grasp the shovel, dig as far down as we can, strike bedrock, and find that our Creator has built us to love. "We love, because God first loved us" (4:19).

No theologian in my lifetime wrestled more profoundly with "'whole-making,' [an inner demand] for a completion in and of things, for inclusive consummation"[43] than Howard Thurman (1900–1981). He resolutely practiced what Reinhold Niebuhr dubbed "a spiritual discipline against resentment":[44] victims' resistance of the natural but self-defeating tendency to righteously trumpet their victimhood. Thurman refused membership in what he called "Self-Righteousness Anonymous"—"[whose] watchword is bigotry," "whose numbers are always right"[45]—while granting, without flinching, the agony of reconciliation:

> Every person stands in need of forgiveness. No one escapes, however blameless his life may seem to him to be. This fact must never be forgotten. . . . Forgiveness is possible between two persons only when the offender is able to stand *inside* of the harm he has done and look out at himself as if he were the other person. One must remember also that guilt, however devastating it may be, is shared in some sense by the person who is injured. Why this is true, I am not sure that I understand, but that it is true, I have no doubt.[46]

As stunning as are those remarks from a mentor of America's beleaguered civil rights activists in the mid-twentieth century, even more extraordinary is Thurman's analysis of kindness in its most irrefragable expression:

> Here is a mystery: If sweeping through the door of my heart there moves continually a genuine love for you, it by-passes all your hate and all your indifference and gets through to you at your center. You are powerless to do

---

us, both in the immediate term and in the long term. (*The Art of Happiness: A Handbook for Living*, ed. Howard C. Cutler [New York: Riverhead/ Penguin/Random House, 1998], 61, 82, 245, 247, emphasis original)

43. Howard Thurman, *The Search for Common Ground: An Inquiry into the Basis of Man's Experience of Community* (New York: Harper & Row, 1973), 76. Analogous veins are opened by the essays in Philip J. Ivanhoe et al., eds., *The Oneness Hypothesis: Beyond the Boundary of Self* (New York: Columbia University Press, 2018).

44. *Moral Man and Immoral Society: A Study in Ethics and Politics* (New York: Scribner's Sons, 1932), 248–49.

45. Howard Thurman, *Deep Is the Hunger: Meditations for Apostles of Sensitiveness* (New York: Harper & Row, 1951), 133–34.

46. Thurman, *Deep Is the Hunger*, 97–98.

anything about it. You may keep alive in devious ways the fires of your bitter heart, but they cannot get through to me. Underneath the surface of all the tension, something else is at work. *It is utterly impossible for you to keep another from loving you.* True, you may scorn his love, you may reject it in all ways within your power, you may try to close every opening in your heart—it will not matter. This is no easy sentimentality but it is the very essence of the vitality of all being. The word that love is stronger than hate and goes beyond death is the great disclosure to one who has found that when he keeps open the door to his heart, it matters not how many doors are closed to him.[47]

In moments of crisis our real selves are exposed, even to ourselves. On January 13, 1982, the doors to Arland D. Williams Jr.'s heart were revealed to the world as welded open. You remember his story. Williams was a passenger aboard Air Florida Flight 90, which, after takeoff from National Airport, crashed into Washington's 14th Street Bridge, then into the icy Potomac River. Seventy-three passengers perished almost immediately. Fighting a lifelong fear of water, clinging to twisted wreckage, Arland Williams handed over to five other survivors one lifeline after another. When all but Williams had been lifted ashore, the helicopter returned to the site to save him. He was gone.[48]

The kindness of strangers is no utopian fantasy. We may never know of it, but mark my words: it happens every day.

The kindness of strangers cannot be generated by leaders in houses of worship, by teachers in classrooms, by members of academic societies. Only a Power outside ourselves can free us from the bondage within, spiritually endowing those able to receive it.[49] The best we can do is to recognize it, honor it, and cultivate those conditions in which it may flourish. For God's sake, for the sake of all humankind created in God's image, we dare do no less.

---

47. Howard Thurman, *The Inward Journey* (New York: Harper & Row, 1961), 42–43, emphasis added.

48. Roger Rosenblatt, *The Man in the Water: Essays and Stories* (New York: Random House, 1994). Cf. Bonhoeffer, *Creation and Fall*, 63: "Being free means being 'free-for-the-other,' because I am bound to the other. Only by being in relation with the other am I free."

49. Hans Urs von Balthasar: "Man becomes whole [*heil*] only in God's salvation [*Heil*]. The sign of the God who empties himself into humanity, death, and abandonment by God, shows us why God came forth from himself, indeed descended below himself as creator of the world: it corresponds to his absolute being and essence to reveal himself in his unfathomable and absolutely uncompelled freedom as inexhaustible love" (*Love Alone Is Credible*, trans. D. C. Schindler [San Francisco: Ignatius, 2004], 145).

Part 3

FEUILLETONS

CHAPTER 21

A Tale of Two Pities

> "There *are* books of which the backs and covers are by far the best parts."
>
> —Charles Dickens

"We've got problems," said my companion at lunch, eyeing a breast of chicken covered in cornsilk gravy. "Too few clergy, too many churches."

"How bad is it?" I asked.

"In some areas, we're desperate. If somebody appeared before the Board of Ministry, had a pulse, and claimed they had so much as heard of Jesus, we'd probably let 'em in."

I was back home, attending an annual conference of clergy and laity assembled on a Winslow Homeresque lakeshore in the Great Smoky Mountains. It's a region whose deep Scotch-Irish roots still bear lush outcroppings of Presbyterians and Methodists. In late spring I return there as often as possible for comfort food, rejuvenation of my Piedmont North Carolina patois, to pick up a little of the native politics, and—most important—to catch up with friends from schooldays, if not even farther back.

An incurable biblioholic, I have always made a beeline to the conference's denominational bookshop. For convenience, let's call it the DBS. Of this particular store I have warm memories, baked over many years. I had practically grown up with it. The first book I can remember buying there—the first piece of serious theology I can recall purchasing, in fact—was a new, 95¢ copy of Bonhoeffer's *Letters and Papers from Prison*, its scarlet cover depicting a stylized white dove sailing through black bars. I must have been twelve or thirteen when I took it down from a long wall of books, shelved from floor to ceiling, labeled "Theology." Though knowing that lust was a sin, I lusted for my own library, so abundantly furnished. Bonhoeffer's *Letters* started mine.

When I walked into the DBS by the lake this year, tall, revolving racks of greeting cards stood sentinel on either side of the double doorway. Immediately to my right was the sales counter; to my left, two cabinets of books marked "Religious" (prominently featuring *Billy Graham: A Tribute from Friends*[1]). Beside them was another cabinet of "Devotional" publications, a jumble of everything from *The Prayer of Jabez*[2] to Kallistos Ware's *The Orthodox Way*[3] (which seemed at a loss to know what it was doing there). Beside that, two cabinets of "Spiritual Growth," followed by another of "Fiction" (*At Home in Mitford*[4]) and two of "Nonfiction" (Charles Colson's *Justice That Restores*[5]). "Self-Help" occupied the next two cabinets (*Get Healthy Now! With Gary Null*[6]), even though self-help is not a conspicuous topic in the Christian Bible.

So it went, aisle after aisle. "Theology and Church History" (combined) occupied four shelves near the front, alongside equal shelving for "Social Concerns." Predictably, for a Protestant store, "Preaching" outnumbered "Worship and Lectionary" two-to-one. "Bible Study" (books about Jesus, mostly) got as many shelves as "Worship and Lectionary," followed immediately by several racks of illustrated books, toys, videos, and other paraphernalia for children (from infants through teenagers). Anthropomorphic celery stalks grinned hallucinatorily from neckties, for those who accessorize with their

---

1. Ed. Vernon McMellan (New York: FaithWord, 2000). It's hard for an old coot like me to realize that post-millennial readers may not recognize the name of Billy Graham (1918–2018), the world's most famous Christian evangelist in the mid-twentieth through the early twenty-first century. For a fair-minded assessment of his career, consult Grant Wacker, *America's Pastor: Billy Graham and the Shaping of a Nation* (Cambridge, MA: Belknap, 2014).

2. Wilkinson, *The Prayer of Jabez* (New York: Multnomah Books, 2000). An allegedly inspirational book by Bruce Wilkinson (1940–), based (well, propped up) on 1 Chr 4:9–10 (New York: Multnomah Books, 2000), which topped international bestseller lists and was taken to heart in some sectors of fundamentalist Pentecostalism. Criticized as exemplary of the "prosperity gospel," the book and its merchandising spinoffs have indisputably enhanced its author's fortune: its 2005 edition claims more than ten million copies sold, netting his assets at about twelve million dollars.

3. Ware, *The Orthodox Way* (London: Mowbray, 1979). Ware (1934–2022), a metropolitan bishop (2007–22), was one of the most celebrated theologians of the Eastern Orthodox Church.

4. Karon, *At Home in Mitford* (New York: Doubleday, 1994). The first (1994) of nine popular novels by Jan Karon (1937–) about an Episcopal rector in a small North Carolina town.

5. Colson, *Justice That Restores* (Carol Stream, IL: Tyndale House, 2001). Colson (1931–2012), a hatchet-man for President Richard M. Nixon, was converted to Christianity in 1973, served a seven-month prison sentence in 1974 for obstruction of justice during the Watergate scandal, and founded Prison Fellowship Ministries in 1976.

6. Null, *Get Healthy Now! With Gary Null* (New York: Seven Stories Press, 1999). Null (1945–) is an American talk-show radio host, known for promoting "alternative medicine" and his hostility toward mainline medicine.

VeggieTales.[7] In the shop's back corner were series commentaries for laity and seminarians (including William Barclay's warhorse[8] and the fresher fillies it has sired), corralled by Bibles of various shapes, versions, and thresholds of annotation. Along the back of the DBS were liturgical stoles, pulpit gowns, and choir robes. Perpendicular to that colorful array was another rainbow of curriculum resources, taking up as much space as, opposite them, "Fiction," "Nonfiction," "Self-Help," and Bibles. At the center of the DBS were "Hispanic Studies," "African-American Studies," "Gender Studies" (with parity of shelving for both genders[9]), hymnals, CDs, and other music resources. The longest aisle, directly opposite the tills, held denominational resources and, on its flip side, were not fewer than sixty linear feet of shelved "Leadership" (*Carpe Mañana: An 8-Track Church in a CD-World*[10]).

The biggest departure from the DBS of my youth, however, was its fully stocked gift section. Exactly half of the store's floor area—I calculated roughly 28 feet by 42 feet from a fast count of carpet squares—was furnished not with books but with gewgaws: CDs, bookmarks, baseball caps, Beanie Babies, toys, tote bags, throw pillows, framed lithographs, crosses, T-shirts, personalized Swingline staplers (beats me—I couldn't figure that one, either), coffee cups, pens, jigsaw puzzles, plaques, clocks. Some of the bric-a-brac carried religious themes (mugs emblazoned with John 17:19), others not. Festooning entry to this section was a prominent display with patriotic colors: memorabilia of 9/11, trivets proclaiming "God Bless America," embroideries ("Tough Times Don't Last, Tough People Do").

Later that day, I drove a few miles south into a pleasant mountain town nearby. Erupting from the hills en route were the familiar pockmarks of Homogenized America: McDonald's, Wal-Mart, Pep Boys. I was heartened to see vestigial remnants of the region's distinctive character: motels whose signs thanked tourists for traveling; Granny's Chicken Palace, where the Rotary meets every Thursday at 12:30 p.m.; cinderblock churches with ground-level marquees,

---

7. A media franchise (1993–present), created by Phil Vischer (1966–) and Paul Nawrocki (1966–), specializing in children's Bible stories, humorously retold with animated, humanoid vegetables.

8. Barclay (1907–78) was a Church of Scotland pastor and professor (University of Glasgow, from 1947) whose 17-volume *Daily Study Bible* on the New Testament (Saint Andrew Press) has remained in print since the 1950s.

9. Although the term dates back to 1965, transgender studies for lay audiences were practically nonexistent at the turn of the twenty-first century.

10. I am unable to retrieve bibliographical information about this book, which appears to have gone the way of 8-track magnetic tape cartridges (c. 1965–c. 1988).

announcing next Sunday's sermons ("Sin Is the Greatest Detective—Be Sure Your Sins Will Find You Out"); Blue Ridge Pawn and Gun, whose own marquee offered tomatoes at 79¢ per pound. Parking my car in town, the second or third store that I noticed was The Christian Bible Bookstore (its very name, hereafter abbreviated CBB). Considering this a coincidence too choice, even providential, to ignore, I crossed Main Street and walked to its door. A small stall at the threshold presented slender books of Protestant saints, some of whose names I recognized (Charles Colson, Catherine Marshall[11]), most of whom I did not know.

Entering the CBB, which was somewhat smaller than the DBS, I first came upon the collected works of Billy Graham and Robert Schuller,[12] flanked by a lithographic display, "The Master Pearce Collection: Reclaiming the Arts for Christ." Cheek by jowl with Master Pearce was a "Self-Help" rack (*Your Roadmap for Savings*;[13] *The Prayer of Jabez for Teenagers*), shelves of "Christian Fiction" (most noticeably, Tim LaHaye's *Left Behind* saga[14]), shelves for "Christian Women" (*Coaching Your Kids in the Game of Life*[15]). Behind the sales counter and flanking it on both sides were Bibles, zippered Bible covers, concordances, and study helps. Strolling from the rear of the CBB, along its opposite side, I noticed a few choir robes, hymnbooks, audiocassettes and CDs (*Great Hymns, Vol. 2*, featuring "A Mighty Fortress," "What a Friend We Have in Jesus," "They'll Know We Are Christians by Our Love," "Holy, Holy, Holy," "Kum Ba Yah"). Reproductions of Thomas Kinkade's[16] oils (an oleaginous re-

---

11. Ms. Marshall (1914–83) was the bestselling author of *Christy* (New York: McGraw Hill, 1967) and *A Man Called Peter: The Story of Peter Marshall* (New York: McGraw Hill, 1951), the story of her famous Presbyterian minister-husband, Peter Marshall (1902–49). The latter book was adapted for cinema in 1955 as Henry Koster, dir., *A Man Called Peter* (Los Angeles: Twentieth-Century Fox, 1955).

12. Schuller (1926–2015) was a popular American televangelist, whose Crystal Cathedral (dedicated in California, 1980) was one of the earliest, most opulent megachurches in the United States.

13. Like *Carpe Mañana*, this volume seems to have vanished alongside 8-track tapes.

14. A series of thirteen novels (1995–2007), written by LaHaye (1926–2016) and Jerry B. Jenkins (1949–), which blends millenarianism with far-right-wing American politics. Its cinematic adaptation (Vic Armstrong, dir. [Los Angeles, CA: Entertainment One/Stoney Lake Entertainment, 2014]), starring Nicholas Cage, left critic Christy Lemire thinking "it's hard to imagine that this incarnation of the story will persuade anyone else to find the Lord unless they're sitting in the theater praying for the dialogue or special effects to improve" (October 3, 2014: https://www.rogerebert.com/reviews/left-behind-2014).

15. Coauthored by Ricky Byrdsong, Dave Jackson, and Neta Jackson (Grand Rapids: Bethany House, 2000): still in print, at this writing, and available on Amazon.

16. Criticized for his art and business practices, Kinkade (1958–2012) claimed to be "the most controversial artist in the world" (Susan Orlean, "Art for Everybody," *The New Yorker*,

ligious naturalism) draped a portal to the CBB's knickknack paddywhacks: among others, more goofy Veggie-stuff; bumper stickers; plastic frames for license plates, inscribed with cautions for motorists ("The Fellow Who Acts as Though There Were No God Had Better Be Right"; "Warning: In Case of the Rapture, This Vehicle Will Become Unattended"), postcards, greeting cards, boxes of greeting cards, candles, and coffee mugs.

A small plaque in one of these stores posed a question: "What Do I Know When I Know What I Know?" I'm still working on that one. I do know better than to judge the postal service from two pieces of mail, higher education from two of its graduates, the state of America's theological health from two clean, well-lit bookstores in the Mid-Atlantic South. Nevertheless, my visits to the latter were instructive up to a point, even if they should be heavily salted.

One lesson rang clear: my mainline colleagues may enter The Christian Bible Bookstore without fear, embarrassment, or stealth, as once they might have. The CBB's inventory is, overall, a virtual photocopy of its mainline, denominational counterpart. Walk into either and you can find Billy Graham, Robert Schuller, VeggieTales, "Kum Ba Yah," and this season's winner of Andy Warhol's fifteen minutes of fame, *The Prayer of Jabez*. America's iconic book—the Bible—continues to draw sales, though its placement and accessories may differ from store to store. The DBS carries more commentaries; its sister down the street, more concordances. In itself, that's an intriguing difference. Do CBB patrons prefer their own word studies, the DBSers more "expert opinion"? The denominational shop carries only a few protective coverings for its Bibles. Do their purchasers carry them less frequently than CBB shoppers? (I hesitate to infer that transport translates into perusal. In a simple quiz given the previous week in my daughter's mainline Sunday School, a visiting child from an evangelical home appeared to know less of the Bible's content than most of those in Caroline's class.) Most interesting to me—heaving read somewhere about the fantastic concessions that Kellogg's pays supermarkets for optimal shelving of its cornflakes—was where in these bookstores customers would find Bibles. True to its name, The Christian Bible Bookstore put them near the till, where in my grocer's you find candy bars, Altoids, tabloids, and *TV Guide*. The denominational emporium stocked Bibles deep in its rear corner, where you'd find facial tissue, toilet paper, and home canning supplies.

The sameness of stock was especially striking in the self-help section. Biblical or not, works of that genre show booming business. Their authors may

---

October 15, 2001, https://www.newyorker.com/magazine/2001/10/15/art-for-everybody-2). Who am I to argue?

reach into different religious and cultural traditions, but common to them all is an audience of selves seeking help: in dating, mating, rearing children, losing weight, fighting cancer, managing money, managing expectations of their gender or ethnic identity, managing their congregations. At the DBS managing the church is a very big deal, a considerable slice of the self-help pie that led me to wonder: can pastors or laity learn leadership from a book? Just how transferable are Jack Welch's lessons at General Electric[17] for The United Methodist Church? How many changes on Dale Carnegie (1888–1955), the button-down salesman of self-improvement[18] when I was a kid, can the internet generation ring?

In both stores I was struck by the extensive, nearly equal number of shelves groaning with leadership, self-help, and spiritual growth. Are there not merely correlations but perhaps deeper connections here? Are the leaders looking for means to grow spiritually? Are those led hungry for spiritual nourishment and, when not receiving it from their leaders, struggling to help themselves? Is the momentary popularity of *The Prayer of Jabez* symptomatic of a culture's inability to distinguish devotion from spiritual growth from self-help?

Are those who frequent the CBB more gregarious or less religiously self-conscious than customers at the DBS? It's the postal cards and greeting cards that got me wondering. The CBB stocks them by the yard, even by the box. Do mainline Christians favor Hallmark for their stationery? Do they write fewer letters than the CBB patrons? Most of my friends do not evangelize through their license plates, unless I count the college athletic teams they support.

Generally, and in spite of their comparably cordial personnel, I left both stores with a profound sense of loneliness: the solitary, quietly desperate search for guidance and direction, for connections and attachments. What, O Man, does the LORD require of you? What, O Woman, does this generation expect of you? What are congregations demanding of their pastors? In a dry season for mentors, will a flood of softcover leadership slake an anxious thirst? Does Billy Graham continue to sell, less for his theology than for his reassurance:

---

17. Welch (1935–2020) was Chairman and CEO of General Electric from 1981 to 2001. His contributions to American letters were *Straight from the Gut* (coauthored with John Byrne [New York: Warner Business, 2001]) and *Winning* (with Suzy Welch [New York: HarperCollins, 2005]). His royalties from these bestsellers were droplets in a bucket: at retirement, his severance payment from GE was $417,000,000.

18. Carnegie's most famous book, *How to Win Friends and Influence People* (New York: Simon & Schuster, 1936), remains in print some ninety years and thirty million copies later. It is generally regarded as the grandaddy of all self-help books.

an evangelical Sheriff Andy of Mayberry?[19] Why does the bookstore of any Christian flock, conservative or liberal, *need* self-help? And why are they getting it from American business moguls?

I don't have answers for these questions. I wouldn't bet even on whatever it is I think I know. But as surely as tomatoes went for 79¢ a pound last June at Blue Ridge Pawn and Gun, I know that I didn't see Bonhoeffer's *Letters and Papers from Prison*[20] at either the DBS or the CBB. I was searching for it in homes stripped of their own letters and family albums, which, after all, is what books in theology and church history are. Will the twelve-year-olds behind me, at the bookstores by their lakes, find reasons for their being, food for their vocational yearning, in baseball caps and personalized staplers? I doubt it. But if I'm wrong, then we may all be sure that we've got problems.[21]

---

19. *The Andy Griffith Show* (CBS, 1960–68) is still available on DVD (Sheldon Leonard and Danny Thomas, producers, *The Andy Griffth Show: The Complete Series* [1960–68; Los Angeles: Paramount Pictures Home Entertainment, 2020]) and through streaming services.

20. Thank God it remains in print: Bonhoeffer, *Letters from Prison*, trans. and ed. Isabel Best, John de Gruchy, Lisa E. Dahill, Reinhard Krauss, and Nancy Lukens, DBW 8 (Minneapolis: Fortress, 2010).

21. Two decades later (2023), both the DBS and CBB have been shuttered.

CHAPTER 22

Three

> "So attention must be paid."
>
> —Arthur Miller

TO BEGIN WITH THE SECOND-ODDEST COINCIDENCE: all three were at home with theater. When asked how he wanted to be remembered, Arthur Miller (b. 1915) answered, "I hope as a playwright. That would be all of it." In 2002 Spain awarded him its Premios Principe de Asturias for Literature as "the undisputed master of modern drama," but the fulfillment of Miller's hope will be renewed for as long as audiences behold the tragedies of Eddie Carbone and his niece Catherine,[1] John Proctor and his wife Elizabeth, Linda Loman and her husband Willy.

Though she will be best remembered for her essays and cultural criticism, Susan Sontag (b. 1933) wrote several plays (among them *Alice in Bed* [1993], concerning the invalid sister of Henry and William James), screenplays (including *Duett für Kannibaler* [*Duet for Cannibals*: 1969]), in addition to six novels (the best known, *The Volcano Lover* [1992][2] and *In America* [1999][3]). In the summer of 2003, Sontag staged Beckett's *Waiting for Godot* (1953) in Serb-besieged Sarajevo, the silence of M. Godot's nonappearance punctuated by thundering armored carriers and the crack of sniper fire.

As Nazi soldiers squeezed Poland and marched through Russia in August 1941, twenty-one-year-old Karol Jósef Wojtyla (b. 1920) and four other students of Jagiellonian University co-founded the Rhapsodic Theater. At nineteen he had written *David, Job, and Jeremiah*, a blank-verse biblical trilogy; *Our God's Brother* at twenty-three, while an underground seminarian; at forty, under the

---

1. Arthur Miller, *A View from the Bridge: A Play in Two Acts* (New York: Viking, 1955).
2. Sontag, *The Volcano Lover* (New York: Farrar, Straus & Giroux, 1992).
3. Sontag, *In America* (New York: Farrar, Straus & Giroux, 1999). It won the U.S. National Book Award Prize for Fiction.

pseudonym Andrzej Jawien, *The Jeweler's Shop* (1960).[4] Two years later saw the beginning of Vatican II and Wojtyla's appointment as Bishop of Krakow. By 1988, when *The Jeweler's Shop* was adapted as a motion picture starring Burt Lancaster (1913–94),[5] Wojtyla had served a decade in the role for which he would forever be known: as Pope John Paul II.

Strangest of all coincidences: These three twentieth-century figures all had fathers in the garment business. Wojtyla's father was a tailor; Sontag's, a Jewish fur trader. When the Great Crash of 1929 wiped out Isodore Miller's prosperous coat manufacture, fourteen-year-old Arthur found in his father a prototype for Willy Loman.

"Theater" has its etymology in an ancient Greek verb meaning "to gaze." No modern thinker pondered more intensely the act of gazing than Sontag. While her "Notes on 'Camp'" (1964)[6] and its proposition of "a good taste of bad taste" secured for her fame among America's avant-garde, her most enduring piece of aesthetic criticism may turn out to be *On Photography* (1973),[7] which probed questions of image and reality in the motley company of Plato, Nietzsche, Richard Avedon, and Madison Avenue come-ons. In 2003, Sontag sharpened the focus in her most harrowing essay, *Regarding the Pain of Others*: "Ever since cameras were invented in 1839, photography has kept company with death."[8] With that thesis in hand, Sontag conducts her readers on an intellectual tour that includes the iconography of suffering in Christian art, Titian's *The Flaying of Marsyas* (1575–76), Goya's *Disasters of War* (1810–20), Matthew Brady, Robert Capa's World War II photojournalism (circulated in *Life* magazine), and iconic photographs of the Vietnam War (shrieking, napalm-doused children; the Vietcong suspect executed on a Saigon street). "One can gaze at these faces for a long time and not come to the end of the mystery, and the indecency, of such co-spectatorship."[9] The true subject of *Regarding the Pain of Others* is war: its ruination, its hideous spectacle, our sick ambivalence about what we behold (or, if we occupy positions of power, what we forbid others from beholding), the deadening of feeling that comes with regarding the dead, the mind's reeling before images of war's dead:

4. Jawien, *The Jeweler's Shop* (San Francisco: Ignatius, 1992).

5. Michael Anderson, dir., *La bottega dell'orefice* [The jeweler's shop] (1988; Rome: Alliance Entertainment, 2010), DVD.

6. Sontag, "Notes on 'Camp,'" *Partisan Review* 31.4 (Fall, 1964): 515–30; repr. *Against Interpretation* (New York: Farrar, Straus & Giroux, 1966).

7. Sontag, *On Photography* (New York: Farrar, Straus & Giroux, 1973).

8. Sontag, *Regarding the Pain of Others* (New York: Farrar, Straus & Giroux, 2003), quotation, 24.

9. Sontag, *Pain of Others*, 60.

"We"—this "we" is everyone who has never experienced anything like what they went through—don't understand. We don't get it. We truly can't imagine what it was like. We can't imagine how dreadful, how terrifying war is; and how normal it becomes. Can't understand, can't imagine. That's what every soldier, and every journalist and aid worker and independent observer who has put in time under fire, and had the luck to elude the death that struck down others nearby, stubbornly feels. And they are right.[10]

For Sontag, our approach/revulsion to war, to all forms of brutality, is in part a function of our proximity to it. The more remote our experience of the reality, in time or space, the easier it is for us to romanticize it. This, she argues, is why, at the time she wrote, there was no Museum of the History of Slavery—the full story—anywhere in the United States.[11] To gaze upon photographs of white Americans grinning beneath mutilated bodies of black men and women, hanging from trees, would compromise Americans' belief in American exceptionalism and require that we begin coming to terms with the evil done *here*. "Americans prefer to picture the evil that was *there*, and from which the United States—a unique nation, one without any certifiably wicked leaders throughout its entire history—is exempt."[12] It's no surprise that, when the Abu Ghraib photographs were revealed to the world in 2003, pictures depicting Iraqi detainees tortured—Sontag insists on the word—by American soldiers, they reminded her of nothing so much as those lynching photographs shot in the American South between the 1890s and 1930s. Published in the *New York Times Magazine*,[13] Sontag's "Regarding the Torture of Others," is more than a blistering indictment of the George W. Bush administration (though it is certainly that). It is a journey into America's own heart of darkness in the early twenty-first century: not the cranky leftist's boilerplate Schadenfreude that Americans are morally worse than the rest of the world, but, rather, one self-reflective humanist's cry that, under particular pressures—timorous acquiescence to domestic and foreign policies that underwrite an endless "war on terror" which winks at, thereby sanctioning, an Abu Ghraib—we can no longer believe that we are *better* than the rest.

10. Sontag, *Pain of Others*, 125–26.
11. This ignominy was to some degree rectified in December 2003, with the Smithsonian's establishment of the National Museum of African American History and Culture. Its permanent home in Washington was dedicated on September 24, 2016.
12. Sontag, *Pain of Others*, 88.
13. May 23, 2004: 24–29; https://www.nytimes.com/2004/05/23/magazine/regarding-the-torture-of-others.html, §II.

Considered in this light, the photographs are us. . . . The lynching photographs were souvenirs of a collective action whose participants felt perfectly justified in what they had done. So are the pictures from Abu Ghraib.[14]

In *Mrs. McGinty's Dead* (1951),[15] from which Sontag quotes in *On Photography*, Agatha Christie has one of her characters observe that hate, like love, can motivate the keepsake of a photograph. "To keep a desire for revenge alive. Someone who has injured you—you might keep a photograph to remind you, might you not?"

Arthur Miller's special gift lay in dramatic snapshots of flawed characters ground down by corrupted societies. The fissure between good and evil that runs, not between nations, but within every human heart was exposed in Miller's first theatrical success, *All My Sons* (1947). Its central character is Joe Keller, a maker of aircraft parts, who allows a run of defective cylinder heads to be sold to the Army Air Force lest he risk losing his government contract and, ultimately, the business he hopes to bequeath to his sons. He knows full well that his factory's faulty products could result in catastrophic failure and the death of Allied airmen. Worse, in the subsequent court case, he perjures himself, disavowing responsibility and allowing an employee, his neighbor, to take the blame and go to prison. The chickens come home to roost on an August night in which that neighbor's daughter, Ann, produces a letter she received from her fiancé Larry—one of Keller's sons, a pilot who himself never returned from the war—that expresses awareness of the court trial and rage at his father. "How could he have done that?" asks the voice from beyond the grave. "Every day three or four men never come back and he sits back there doing business. . . . I'm going out on a mission in a few minutes. They'll probably report me missing."[16] In this light, Keller and his other son Chris, now engaged to Ann, have their inevitable showdown, in which the truth exposes all self-deceit:

KELLER: What should I want to do? Jail? You want me to go to jail? . . . Who worked for nothin' in that war? When they work for nothin,' I'll work for nothin.' Did they ship a gun or a truck outa Detroit before they got their price? Is that clean? It's dollars and cents, nickels and dimes; war and peace,

---

14. Sontag, "Regarding the Torture of Others," 26, 27.
15. Christie, *Mrs. McGinty's Dead* (London: Collins, 1951; repr. New York: HarperCollins, 2011), 207.
16. Arthur Miller, *All My Sons: A Drama in Three Acts* (New York: Penguin, 2000), 83.

it's nickels and dimes, what's clean? Half the Goddam country is gotta go if I go! . . . Then . . . why am *I* bad?

CHRIS: *I* know you're no worse than most men but I thought you were better. I never saw you as a man. I saw you as my father. . . .

KELLER [*later, looking at the letter in his hand*]: Then what is this if it isn't telling me? Sure, [Larry] was my son. But I think to him they were all my sons. And I guess they were, I guess they were. I'll be right down. [*Exits into house.*][17]

Joe Keller never returns. He kills himself. But Miller's judgment rests not on Keller alone. When he wrote the play, "everybody knew that a lot of hanky-panky was going on. . . . A lot of illicit fortunes were being made, a lot of junk was being sold to the armed services, we all knew that. The average person violated rationing. All the rules were being violated but you wanted not to mention it."[18] No less than all others, Tom Brokaw's "Greatest Generation"[19] was stained by greed and selfishness and deceit. And now, as Sontag reminds us, the rules of the Geneva conventions (1949) and other agreements to which the United States is signatory are being violated, and nobody wants to acknowledge it.[20] Our sons and daughters terrify captives with photographs of their being sodomized and threatened with electrocution for the cameras. Their victims are all our sons, as well.

The rending of the social fabric is complete in *The Crucible* (1952), a dramatization of the 1692 Salem witch trials that thinly veiled Miller's outrage over McCarthyism (c. 1947–62). Claiming never to have joined the Communist Party, Miller refused to name names before the House Un-American Activities Committee. (So also, in his moment of truth, John Proctor: "I speak my own sins; I cannot judge another. [*Crying out, with hatred:*] I have no tongue for it.")[21] In 1957 Miller was cited for contempt of Congress, a verdict overturned a year later in appellate court. (It was not until 1992—three centuries later—that the Massachusetts General Court acknowledged the state's full responsibility

---

17. Miller, *All My Sons*, 82, 83.
18. Arthur Miller, quoted by Christopher Bigsby, introduction to Miller, *All My Sons*, xii.
19. The title coined by the NBC news broadcaster for his bestselling book (Brokaw, *The Greatest Generation* [New York: Random House, 1998]).
20. Sontag, "Regarding the Torture of Others," 26.
21. Arthur Miller, *The Crucible: A Play in Four Acts* (New York: Penguin, 1993), 131.

for the hanging of nineteen women and men and two dogs.)[22] Transcending American society's hysteria in both the seventeenth and twentieth centuries, however, are *The Crucible*'s fundamental themes, which touch on all peoples at all times: the seduction of power, both sexual and political; the fragility of charitable bands that hold society together; imperfect men and women faced with the ultimate test of trading their integrity for their own lives and the lives of those they love. Perhaps for that reason *The Crucible* remains the most frequently produced, the world over, of all Miller's dramas. "I can almost tell what the political situation in a country is when the play is suddenly a hit there," the playwright observed in his autobiography *Timebends* (1987). "It is either a warning of tyranny on the way or a reminder of tyranny just past."[23]

Tested—scarred, some might say—in the crucible of fascism and communism, Karol Wojtyla had first-hand knowledge of tyranny and its pulverizing of the individual conscience. He escaped the Third Reich's deportation and imprisonment (first) as a stonecutter in a Krakow quarry, (later) by fleeing to the home of Krakow's archbishop, where he lived until the war's end. He was disillusioned by American-style capitalism, which he considered equally capable of chewing up and spitting out myriad Willy Lomans, "riding on a smile and a shoeshine."[24] ("Everything is for sale," says a character in Sontag's *In America*.[25]) For Wojtyla, only the church—its faith, discipline, and mystery—could fill the void of a modernity that was at worst oppressive, at best vacuous. Thus, the paradox of his pontificate: at once the most progressive in style—employing to the fullest modern technology, media savvy, and the papacy's capacity to intervene in international affairs—and among the most intransigent in matters of theology and ethics. John Paul II championed religious freedom for persecuted Christians, reaching out even to Jews and Muslims, while quashing dissent within his own ranks. When three hundred theologians signed the Cologne Declaration (1989) in protest of Rome's authoritarianism, the Vatican retaliated by imposing on all in ecclesial authority an oath of obedience to the teachings of the Pope and his College of Bishops.

Wojtyla's political legacy will be remembered for the push Poland gave in communism's collapse. Mikhail Gorbachev conceded that communism would never have ended so swiftly, and so peacefully, without John Paul II.[26] His theo-

---

22. In Salem, Miller unveiled the winning design for a memorial to those who had died.
23. Arthur Miller, *Timebends: A Life* (New York: Grove, 1987), 348.
24. Arthur Miller, *Death of a Salesman: Certain Private Conversations in Two Acts and a Requiem* (New York: Viking, 1949), 138.
25. Sontag, *In America*, 379.
26. Joseph Bottum, "John Paul the Great," *The Weekly Standard* (April 18, 2005): 1–2;

logical legacy lies chiefly in thirteen papal encyclicals (1979–2003). The press has given extraordinary attention to *Evangelium vitae* (1995), because there one finds John Paul II's hard line against abortion, euthanasia, and capital punishment. (It is this encyclical that excoriates modernity's "culture of death," which some have appropriated, selectively interpreted, as a slogan for attachment to political adversaries.) Less attention is paid to the pope's theological reasons, expressed in *Evangelium vitae* (19.2–24.2), for the dissipation of human dignity in our time:

- An untruthful account of human existence: the notion that human dignity resides in what we accomplish, rather than in our very being as creatures made in God's image;
- An untruthful account of human authority: the self construed as utterly autonomous, thus deriving absolute power over and against others, apart from human solidarity;
- An eclipse of the sense of God, which entails loss of a sense of the world's mystery and the corruption of humanity by materialism, utilitarianism, and individualism;
- The darkening of human conscience, both personal and societal.[27]

Following Romans 1:25, *Evangelium vitae* ascribes to sin the human being's exchange of the truth about God for a lie (36.1). In one of the few passages I know where Miller spoke theologically, he seemed to be on Wojtyla's wavelength:

> No one of my generation can be understood without reference to his relation to Marxism as "the God that failed," but I have come to think the phrase is wrong. It was an idol and no God. An idol tells people exactly what to believe, God presents them with choices they have to make for themselves. The difference is far from insignificant; before the idol men remain dependent children, before God they are burdened and at the same time liberated to participate in the decisions of endless creation.[28]

Coming from a self-styled fatalist—whose dramatic protagonists seem repeatedly crushed by an Aeschylean fate—that is an extraordinary statement. And

---

Anonymous, "Pope Stared Down Communism in His Homeland—and Won," *CBC News Online* (Religion News Service; April, 2005).

27. Pope John Paul II, *Evangelium vitae*, 1995; https://www.vatican.va/content/john-paul-ii/en/encyclicals/documents/hf_jp-ii_enc_25031995_evangelium-vitae.html.

28. Miller, *Timebends*, 259.

yet the diagnosis of modern self-delusion in *Evangelium vitae* fits the most famous of Miller's characters like a straitjacket. Near his nadir, Willy Loman bellows, "You can eat the orange and throw the peel away—a man is not a piece of fruit!"[29] His wife, Linda, explains to her sons that their father is exhausted and suicidal, dying on the altar of the Bitch-Goddess Success:

> I don't say he's a great man. Willy Loman never made a lot of money. His name was never in the paper. He's not the finest character that ever lived. But he's a human being, and a terrible thing is happening to him. So attention must be paid. He's not to be allowed to fall into his grave like an old dog. Attention, attention must finally be paid to such a person.[30]

All three were public intellectuals, all passionately concerned with what it means to be human at this time. Among them, Sontag may have possessed the finest mind: the largest capacity for thinking through subjects of her own choosing, constantly reversing field, shifting planes, correcting herself. (Clearly that was not Wojtyla's forte; absolutism resists reconsideration.) Yet Sontag's essays can frustrate, in part because there is no end to the rabbit-holes she tunnels. Where Sontag infuriates, Miller sears. For that I can vouch, lately having listened again to an audio presentation of *Death of a Salesman* (1949), surprised to find myself emotionally shattered on my own back porch. For Miller, as for Sontag, the problem of human existence must be grappled with, but solutions are few. There, Karol Wojtyla—the only one among them who would have felt comfortable with the project of exploring our life in God's light—is most forthcoming. That is so, not merely because he was pope and such was expected of him, but because he believed *himself* chosen by the One Subject who, in Jesus Christ, has revealed the truth about humanity in all its wretchedness and all its glory.

For all three, the morality of remembering was crucial. Sontag: "That memories are recovered—that is, that the suppressed truths do reemerge—is the basis for whatever hope one can have for justice and a modicum of sanity in the ongoing life of communities."[31] Some memories—those of a Joe Keller or a Willy Loman—are too unbearable to recover, if they expose little more than

---

29. Miller, *Death of a Salesman*, 82.
30. Miller, *Death of a Salesman*, 56.
31. Sontag, "The Wisdom Project," first published in *The New Republic* 24.12 (March 19, 2001): 29–34; repr., Sontag, *Where the Stress Falls* (New York: Farrar, Straus & Giroux, 2001); quotation, 55.

the futility on which one's life has been staked. Some memories redeem, as John Paul II demonstrated by publicly forgiving his would-be assassin, Mehmet Ali Agca, in 1999. "Forgive us our sins, for we ourselves forgive everyone indebted to us" (Luke 11:4). Attention must be paid.

The lives of all three were redoubts against fear. John Proctor, to his wife as he ascends the gallows: "Give them no tear. Tears pleasure them! Show honor now, show a stony heart, and sink them with it."[32] Sontag's books *Illness as Metaphor* (1977)[33] and *AIDS and Its Metaphors* (1988)[34] demystify cancer and demilitarize the metaphors applied to AIDS. Both are acts of raw intellectual courage. John Paul II opened his papacy in his homeland with simple words that began a regime's toppling: "Don't be afraid."[35]

A final coincidence: All three died within a period of just over three months. Susan Sontag succumbed to leukemia at the age of seventy-one on December 28, 2004. Arthur Miller's heart failed on February 10, 2005; he was eighty-nine. Karol Wojtyla's debilitated body came to rest on April 2, 2005. The pope was eighty-four.

---

32. Miller, *Crucible*, 133.
33. Sontag, *Illness as Metaphor* (New York: Farrar, Straus & Giroux, 1977).
34. Sontag, *AIDS and Its Metaphors* (New York: Farrar, Straus & Giroux, 1988).
35. "Homily of His Holiness John Paul II for the Inauguration of His Pontificate," October 22, 1978, https://www.vatican.va/content/john-paul-ii/en/homilies/1978/documents/hf_jp-ii_hom_19781022_inizio-pontificato.html.

CHAPTER 23

The Man in Black

> I wear the black for the poor and the beaten down
> Livin' in the hopeless, hungry side of town.
> I wear it for the prisoner who has long paid for his crime
> But is there because he's a victim of the times.
>
> —John R. Cash

JOHNNY CASH IS CONSIDERED A PIONEER of "outlaw music," yet even his secular compositions beat with a moral and religious core. Cash's childhood was stamped by country music and his mother's devotion to the Pentecostal Church of God. When J. R. was twelve, several months after accepting Christ, his older brother Jack—a preacher—was killed in a farming accident.[1] Thirty-five years later, Cash's instantly recognizable stage costume was not the sequin-spangled eye-poppers of his Grand Ole Opry colleagues, but the black frock coat of a 1920s circuit rider or undertaker.[2]

In 1954, after his discharge from the US Air Force, Cash signed with Sam Phillips (1923–2003), the legendary producer of Sun Records in Memphis who also mentored the fledgling career of Elvis Presley (1935–77).[3] Three years and

---

1. For Cash's own account of his brother's death and its aftermath, see *Cash: The Autobiography of Johnny Cash*, written with Patrick Carr (San Francisco: HarperSanFrancisco, 1997), 22–29.
2. "I wore black because I liked it. I still do, and wearing it still means something to me. It's still my symbol of rebellion—against a stagnant status quo, against our hypocritical houses of God, against people whose minds are closed to others' ideas" (Jordan Taylor Sloan, "Johnny Cash Did More for Today's Music Than You Probably Even Realize," *Mic*, December 9, 2014, https://www.mic.com/articles/105954/johnny-cash-did-more-for-today-s-music-than-you-probably-even-realize).
3. See Peter Guralnick, *Sam Phillips: The Man Who Invented Rock 'n' Roll* (New York: Little, Brown & Co., 2015).

forty hit singles later, Cash left Sun for a new contract with Columbia—never, he maintained, for better money but because he wanted to record spiritual songs that Phillips prohibited, claiming he didn't know how to market them. True to its word, Columbia released as the second LP by their new artist *Hymns by Johnny Cash* (1959), followed by *Hymns from the Heart* (1961). What's notable about all his religious recordings is their manifest genesis in Cash's own convictions, not in some agent's decision that the requisite Christmas album would burnish his image in mid-twentieth-century middle-class America.

The song that consolidated Cash's "outlaw" reputation is "Folsom Prison Blues" (1955), sung from the point of view of a jailed killer listening to a distant train-whistle. The climax comes in the second stanza:

> When I was just a baby, my momma told me, "Son,
> Always be a good boy; don't ever play with guns."
> But I shot a man in Reno just to watch him die.
> When I hear that whistle blowin', I hang my head and cry.

The convict weeps not merely because he's in prison, but because he's imprisoned to sin: the sheer meanness of gunning down someone in cold blood for no reason but the hell of it. A later stanza nails it down:

> But I know'd I had it comin',
> I know I can't be free.
> But those people keep on movin',
> And that's what tortures me.[4]

Music critic Neil Strauss puts his finger on a crucial difference between the sinners in Cash's songs and most of the protagonists in today's gangsta rap. The latter are often vicious, with no center but nihilism. Those locked away in Folsom are guilt-racked, famished for real redemption from real misery.[5]

Cash's musical persona had some basis in fact. During his thirties he seemed bent on destroying himself with painkillers, amphetamines, and barbiturates, which decimated his body and his first marriage. When out of control—which was far too often—Cash wrecked property, nearly killed himself in a borrowed

---

4. "Folsom Prison Blues," music and lyrics by John R. Cash, track 5 on disc 1 of *Johnny Cash at Folsom Prison*, 1955; New York: Legacy Edition, 2008, 2 compact discs and DVD.

5. Neil Strauss, "New Rebel for the 90's: Meet Johnny Cash, 62," *New York Times*, September 14, 1994, https://www.nytimes.com/1994/09/14/arts/new-rebel-for-the-90-s-meet-johnny-cash-62.html.

car, and was arrested seven times. After one arrest in Lafayette, Georgia, Sheriff Ralph Jones released him. "I'm going to give you your money and your dope back because you know better than most people that God gave you a free will to do with yourself whatever you want to do.... Now you can throw the pills away or you can take them and go ahead and kill yourself. Whichever you want to do, Mr. Cash, will be all right with me."[6] After a halfhearted suicide attempt, Cash quit drugs cold turkey—for a time, at any rate[7]—upheld by the Christian conviction of a woman who in 1968 would become his second wife: June Carter (1929-2003), of country music's legendary Carter Family.[8] They remained married until a heart attack claimed her life on May 15, 2003.

Three months after temporarily kicking his habit, he recorded *Johnny Cash at Folsom Prison* (1968),[9] regarded by many as his best and by some as the finest live concert by any popular performer on record.[10] By then he had done shows in many prisons, perfecting a repertoire peppered with his own hits ("I Walk the Line" [1956], "Ring of Fire" [1963][11]), rock, ballads, comic novelties and spirituals. Cash knew his listeners:

> Prisoners are the greatest audience that an entertainer can perform for. We bring them a ray of sunshine in their dungeon and they're not ashamed to respond, and show their appreciation.... The culture of a thousand years is shattered with the clanging of the cell door behind you.... You sit on your cold, steel mattressless bunk and watch a cockroach crawl out from under the filthy commode, and you don't kill it. You envy the roach as you watch

---

6. Quoted in Johnny Cash, *Man in Black* (Grand Rapids: Zondervan, 1975), 139.

7. With his family's encouragement, he entered the Betty Ford Center at Rancho Mirage, California, in December, 1983. Marshal Grant, his musical partner and road manager, claims that Cash struggled with addiction most of his life. "There's nothing funny about someone who's lost his soul to drugs, nothing at all" (Marshal Grant with Chris Zar, *I Was There When It Happened: My Life with Johnny Cash* [Nashville: Cumberland House, 2006], 297).

8. Born and raised in southwest Virginia, Sara (1898-1979), her husband A. P. (1891-1960), sister-in-law Maybelle (1909-78), and brother-in-law Ezra J. "Eck" (1898-1975) were the first vocal group to become country music stars. Their influence on Southern gospel, bluegrass, pop, and rock music is immeasurable. Maybelle and Ezra had three daughters: Helen (1927-98), Anita (1933-99), and June, all of whom enjoyed success as country musicians and frequently toured with Cash.

9. *Johnny Cash at Folsom Prison*, live album, produced by Bob Johnston; released by Columbia Records on May 6, 1968.

10. The definitive study of this album, its background and repercussions, is Michael Streissguth, *Johnny Cash at Folsom Prison: The Making of a Masterpiece* (Cambridge, MA: Da Capo/Perseus, 2004).

11. "Ring of Fire," written by June Carter and Merle Kilgore (1934-2005).

it crawl out under the cell door.... Your big accomplishment for the day is a mathematical deduction. You are positive of this, and only this: There are nine vertical, and sixteen horizontal bars on your door.[12]

At Folsom Prison still sounds fresh, even raw. It conveys the electricity of two thousand inmates, under tight guard, with intermittent announcements over a warden's loudspeaker and Cash chuckling obscenities to the delight of his listeners and the dismay of his producer. For all its up-tempo numbers, the concert is shot through with deep melancholy that seems to have clicked with a literally captive audience. Cash's humor is outright gallows ("25 Minutes to Go" [1962])[13]—before a noose snaps the narrator's neck) or brokenhearted goofy ("Flushed from the Bathroom of Your Heart" [1966][14]). The songs are filled with pitch-black mines, deadly walls, orphans, adulterous wives, scoundrels hanged for the one crime they didn't commit, even ghosts ("The Long Black Veil"):

> She walks these hills in a long black veil.
> She visits my grave when the night winds wail.
> Nobody knows; nobody sees;
> Nobody knows but me.[15]

---

12. Liner notes for *Johnny Cash at Folsom Prison*, copyright 2008 Sony BMG Music Entertainment, 9–10. When asked why Cash kept returning to prisons for concerts, his friend and colleague Merle Haggard (1927–2016) answered, "I think, 'For the grace of God there go I.' That was his feelings towards the convicts. He was about a quarter of an inch from there himself. Had he not had money he probably would have wound up there. He was Johnny Cash, and he got away with things that he knew he shouldn't have got away with. There's probably guys in prison for doing less than things he did every day. And he knew that. One time he told me, 'Haggard, you're everything that people think I am.' I said, 'Yeah, but not by choice.' He never really had been to jail. He spent like four hours one time in a jail. But he identified. He understood somehow, and the convicts knew it" (quoted by Michael Streissguth, "Merle Haggard's Lost Interview: Country Icon on Johnny Cash, Prison Life," *Rolling Stone*, January 4, 2017, https://www.rollingstone.com/music/music-country/merle-haggards-lost-interview-country-icon-on-johnny-cash-prison-life-193183/).

13. "25 Minutes to Go," music and lyrics by Shel Silverstein, track 10 on disc 1 of *Johnny Cash at Folsom Prison*, 1968; New York: Legacy Edition, 2008, 2 compact discs and DVD.

14. "Flushed from the Bathroom of Your Heart," lyrics by Jack Clement, track 17 on disc 1 of *Johnny Cash at Folsom Prison*, 1968; New York: Legacy Edition, 2008, 2 compact discs and DVD. Originally recorded by Archie Campbell (1914–87) on Campbell, *Have a Laugh on Me* (Nashville: RCA Victor, 1966).

15. "The Long Black Veil," lyrics and music by Marijohn Wilkin and Danny Dill, track 13 on disc 1 of *Johnny Cash at Folsom Prison*, 1959; New York: Legacy Edition, 2008, 2 compact

And yet, there's redemption. The last number, "Greystone Chapel," written by Glen Sherley (1936–78), an inmate in the audience, thanks God for the only place at the prison whose door was never locked:

> Now this Greystone Chapel here at Folsom—
> It has a touch of God's hand on every stone.
> It's a flower of light in a field of darkness,
> And it's given me the strength to carry on.
> Inside the walls of prison, my body may be,
> But my Lord has set my soul free.[16]

The concert ends as it began, with thousands in jail. But in-between eternity invades a prison cafeteria.[17]

If *Folsom* is plangent, *Johnny Cash at San Quentin* (1969)[18] is a hellraiser that morphs into camp meeting without a shred of camp. The concert was Cash's fourth at San Quentin. Among his back-up musicians were June Carter, her mother, and her sisters. Thirty-one years later she confessed how terrified she was: "San Quentin is a maximum security prison. Some men are here for armed robbery, rape, pedophilia, arson, murder. And there were a few innocent men. It felt like a dream. 'O Lord,' I cried."[19]

After some opening crowd-pleasers, Cash strums his guitar and addresses his audience in a no-nonsense tone that immediately gives them back some *freedom* of choice:

---

discs and DVD. Lefty Frizzell's version of the ballad was selected by the Library of Congress in 2019 for preservation in the National Recording Registry as "culturally, historically, or aesthetically significant."

16. John R. Cash, "Greystone Chapel," music and lyrics by Glen Sherley, track 24 on disc 1 of *Johnny Cash at Folsom Prison*, 1968; New York: Legacy Edition, 2008, 2 compact discs and DVD.

17. The Rev. Floyd Gressett (1903–95), who served as a liaison between Columbia Records and Folsom's authorities, remembered: "When Johnny sang 'Greystone Chapel,' two thousand men stood to their feet in honor of the poor cuss who wrote that song" (Christopher S. Wren, *Winners Got Scars Too: The Life and Legends of Johnny Cash* [New York: Dial, 1971], 199).

18. *Johnny Cash at San Quentin*, 1969; New York: Legacy Edition, 2006, 2 compact discs and DVD.

19. Liner notes, *Johnny Cash at San Quentin*, copyright 2008 Sony BMG Music Entertainment, 32.

> I tell you what: . . . [The producers] said, "You gotta do this song, you gotta do that song; you know, you gotta stand like this or act like this." And I just don't get it, man. You know, I'm here—I'm here to do what *you* want me to and what *I* want to do.

With that, a thunderous holler went up. From there on, Cash held his audience.

A good thing, too. When his agent asked if more guards were needed to protect the stage, the security chief replied that one hundred, even two hundred guards couldn't control a thousand, spring-loaded prisoners if things spun out of control. They didn't.

Midway through the concert, however, Cash took a chance that caused his producer and the guards to flinch. Talk about dangerous. He introduced a song he had written for the occasion: an angry, four-stanza damnation of the concert hall. In part:

> San Quentin, may you rot and burn in hell.
> May your walls fall, and may I live to tell.
> May all the world forget you ever stood,
> And may all the world regret you did no good.
> San Quentin, I hate every inch of you.[20]

Almost every line of "San Quentin" (1969) drew a roar of approval, and Cash the Badass immediately gratified the crowd's yell for an encore. He made no excuses for what men had done to land them in hell, but neither did he vindicate the hell others had made for them.

Later, having broken the tension with "A Boy Named Sue"[21] (the premiere of a feisty novelty that eventually sold in excess of a million copies), Cash and crew again reversed field by rendering Thomas A. Dorsey's (1899–1993) spiritual, "(There'll Be) Peace in the Valley" (1939). As it turned out, "Peace" was no pious aberration but, rather, the first in a series of four religious numbers, which Cash slyly introduced as "a serious note" in the concert. Of course, he

---

20. "San Quentin," music and lyrics by John R. Cash, tracks 1 and 2 on disc 2 of *Johnny Cash at San Quentin*, 1969; New York: Legacy Edition, 2006, 2 compact discs and DVD. Producer Bob Johnston: "God, I've never seen anything like it. . . . [The prisoners] were on the tables, yelling. . . . I'm backed up to the door with all these guards and guns, and I'm thinking, 'Man! I should have brought Tammy Wynette and George Jones—*anybody* but Johnny Cash!'" (liner notes, *Johnny Cash at San Quentin*, 12).

21. "A Boy Named Sue," music and lyrics by Shel Silverstein, track 5 on disc 2 of *Johnny Cash at San Quentin*, 1969; New York: Legacy Edition, 2006, 2 compact discs and DVD.

had been dead serious from the start. What he really intended was to inject some evangelical Christian spirituality, now that San Quentin's inmates were ready to hear it. And they were.

The least well known of this set is, musically speaking, no great shucks. But as Cash's own proclamation of the gospel in that volatile context, it is a masterly piece of indirection whose real subject is the nobility of a derelict life changed by Christ:

> He turned the water into wine.
> He turned the water into wine.
> In the little Cana-town,
> The word went all around that
> He turned the water into wine.[22]

It takes no stretch to get the point: If Jesus could do that with something as ordinary as water (John 2:1–12), then he can make something out of the vulgar, the lonely, the lost—all the sinners, caught or not.

Probably the most famous inmate to witness Cash's first concert at San Quentin (1958) was Merle Haggard, who, after receiving a full pardon from California's Governor Ronald Reagan (1911–2004), became an acclaimed country-western singer himself. Of Cash, Haggard has said, "He brought Jesus Christ into the picture [at San Quentin], and he introduced Him in a way that the tough, hardened, hard-core convict wasn't embarrassed to listen to. He didn't point no fingers; he just knew how to do it."[23]

Fast forward to 2005 and the release of *Walk the Line*,[24] the blockbuster biopic based on Cash's life. The film skates across his years from 1944 to 1968: from his childhood in the deep Depression of Dyess, Arkansas; through military service in Germany, where he began writing songs; to a failed appliance salesman's desperate pitch, back in Memphis, recording with Sam. From there, director James Mangold (1963–) gets down to the story he really wants to tell: Cash's tumultuous reckoning with fame, a first marriage crashing in divorce (though

---

22. John R. Cash, "He Turned the Water into Wine," music and lyrics by John R. Cash, track 11 on disc 2 of *Johnny Cash at San Quentin*, 1969; New York: Legacy Edition, 2006, 2 compact discs and DVD.

23. Merle Haggard, interview with Marty Stuart; liner notes, *Johnny Cash at San Quentin*, 27.

24. James Mangold, dir., *Walk the Line* (Century City, CA: 20th Century Fox, 2005).

a union that produced Rosanne Cash[25] [b. 1955] can hardly be characterized a failure), addiction to pills, and his courtship of June Carter.

Director Sidney Lumet lampooned the 1950s films in which he learned his craft as specimens of the "rubber-ducky" school of drama: "Someone once took his rubber ducky away from him, and that's why he's a deranged killer."[26] *Walk the Line*'s rubber ducky is Cash's volcanic, then smoldering father Ray. Robert Patrick is directed to play this troubled man as a walking grudge who irrationally blamed twelve-year-old J. R. for a sawmill accident that claimed the life of Jack, the beloved eldest son. From Cash's autobiographies,[27] on which screenwriters Mangold and Gill Dennis based their script, there's no question that Jack's horrible death haunted Cash in later years. Less clear from those memoirs—but an easier dramatic pitch for today's audiences—is that Cash's crazed drive for success was an oblique attempt to thaw a father's frostbitten heart. Certainly, throughout his life Cash spoke of his father with sympathy and respect, which the years mellowed the more. Equally certain: Ray Cash was both backstage and in the audience for his son's seminal concerts at Folsom Prison (January 13, 1968), which you would never guess from *Walk the Line*.

Another thing you'd never know from this film is that Cash's mother Carrie exerted on her son an influence as strong as that of his father. Mangold has Shelby Lynne play this woman as a mousy cipher, cowed by her husband's meanness. That rings false to Cash's chronicles[28] and, more tellingly, to his songs, which feature wise, protective mothers ("Folsom Prison Blues," "Don't Take Your

---

25. Ms. Cash found it painful to watch the movie, "because it had the three most damaging events of my childhood: my parents' divorce, my father's drug addiction, and something else bad that I can't remember now" (Monika L. S. Robbins, "Rosanne Cash Discusses 'Walk the Line' and Her Memoir," *The Harvard Crimson*, April 8, 2010), https://www.thecrimson.com/article/2010/4/8/cash-emerson-movie-kirkland/.

> It was like having a root canal without anesthetic.... The three of them [in the film: her father, mother, and stepmother] were not recognisable to me as my parents in any way. But the scenes were recognisable, and the storyline, so the whole thing was fraught with sadness because they all had just died, and I had this resistance to seeing the screen version of my childhood. I don't resent them making it—I thought it was an honorable approach.... [But i]t's a Hollywood movie—very complex lives reduced to two hours—so how can it possibly show the depths of truth?" (Simon Garfield, "Family Ties," *The Guardian*, February 5, 2006, https://www.theguardian.com/music/2006/feb/05/popandrock.johnnycash).

26. Sidney Lumet, *Making Movies* (New York: Vintage/Random House, 1995), 37.
27. See nn. 1 and 6, above.
28. For instance: "What still depresses me the most about Jack's death: the fact that his funeral took place on Sunday, May 21, 1944, and on the morning of Monday, May 22, our

Guns to Town" [1958]) whose twilight summons to children playing outside that it's "Suppertime" (1958) Cash transmuted into a spiritual about the Lord's heavenly banquet. Carrie's impact on her son persisted into 2004, with Rick Rubin's posthumous release of Cash's American album, *My Mother's Hymn Book*.[29]

So we come to the most disappointing aspect of *Walk the Line*: its inability to deal with the deep Christian piety of either John or June. The way this movie tells it, young Cash the hellraiser was never more than nominally religious until Carter straightened him out with tough love, a copy of Kahil Gibran's *The Prophet*,[30] and a thirty-second visit to the First Baptist Church. All the real-life principals—Cash included—agree that, at his nadir, he probably would have killed himself had it not been for June's devotion to him. Nevertheless, Cash's own Christianity was a lot more pervasively entwined in his career than *Walk the Line* suggests. The audience never learns, for instance, that

- Cash left Phillips's Sun Records in 1958 for Columbia, not merely for more money (which he certainly got), but also for the freedom to record long-playing albums of spirituals;
- throughout their tours during the 1950s and afterward, The Johnny Cash Show consistently performed gospel—including Jimmy Davis and Fern Jones's "I Was There When It Happened" (1955),[31] which in the movie nearly provokes Phillips to give Cash a swift boot back onto 706 Union Avenue;
- the 1968 Folsom concert, arranged by Cash's pastor, Floyd Gressett, concluded with Glen Sherley's stunning ode, "Greystone Chapel"; or
- Cash and the Tennessee Two (eventually, Three)[32] had given prison concerts—including gospel songs—for *a full decade before* that epochal concert. As *Walk the Line* tells it, Cash first set foot in Folsom only after he got religion in 1967.

No motion picture—not even Robert Caro's fattest biographies—can tell us everything about any public figure. The point, rather, is that by trivializing

---

whole family—everybody, including the mother who had just buried her son—was back in the fields chopping cotton, working their ten-hour day" (*Cash: The Autobiography*, 27).

29. *My Mother's Hymn Book*, Nashville: American Recordings, 2003, compact disc.

30. Kahil Gibran, *The Prophet*, A Borzoi Book (New York: Knopf, 1923).

31. "I Was There When It Happened," originally recorded on *Johnny Cash with His Hot and Blue Guitar*, 1957; Memphis, Sun Records, 2002, compact disc.

32. The band's other members: bassist Marshall Grant (1928–2011), guitarist Luther Perkins (1928–68), who was succeeded by Bob Wootton (1942–2017), and drummer W. S. "Fluke" Holland (1935–2020).

Cash's Southern Protestant spirituality,[33] *Walk the Line* simplifies its unfathomably complicated protagonist, whose bouncy rhythms, onstage courtesy, gravitas, and goofiness must go unexplained and are, therefore, largely omitted.

Consequently, the capable Joaquin Phoenix (1974–) has the impossible task of impersonating an original while playing boilerplate—the confused, guilt-ridden young addict. Reese Witherspoon (1976–) draws the equally unhappy assignment of playing a concept: Moral Center, vaguely religious with Appalachian sass. So charismatic is her screen presence that she not only pulls that off but also manages, with Mangold's help, to steer the audience's sympathy away from Cash's perpetually pregnant though otherwise neglected first wife, Vivian Liberto (played by Ginnifer Goodwin [1978–]). Weirdly, Viv emerges as "the other woman" in this triangle,[34] while Ms. Witherspoon walks away with the movie tucked in her Grand Ole Opry crinolines—to say nothing of four international awards, including an Oscar for Best Actress (2006).

Cash's son (by June), John Carter Cash (1970–), was an executive producer of *Walk the Line*; its associate producer was the late performer's agent, Lou Robin (1930–2021). That is formidable quality control. The result is a good night at the movies. The pity is that so much material was available to make of it a magnificent one. Early on, Phillips tells Cash that he won't touch gospel with a ten-foot pole. Neither will Hollywood, where devotion to God is the love that dare not speak its name. The line this movie walks is strewn with clichés: abused boy saved by the love of a good woman. I can't think of a single song in Cash's discography that corny.

---

33. "I'm still a Christian, as I have been all my life" (*Cash: The Autobiography*, 7).

34. "My dad and June wanted [the movie] to happen," Rosanne said, "but it was torture for my mother. The idea that her worst fucking nightmare—she's a strict Catholic girl who had to get divorced—and now the film version is out there . . . it was intolerable to her. I thought it was very interesting and ironic that she died a few months before it came out" (Garfield, "Family Ties"). Fortunately, before her death, Vivian Cash wrote her own memoir, with Ann Sharpsteen, *I Walked the Line: My Life with Johnny* (New York: Scribner, 2007), dedicated to her four daughters—Rosanne, Kathy, Cindy, and Tara, "so you may better understand just how much I loved your Daddy" (iii).

CHAPTER 24

A Laugh in the Dark

> We come to Iraq with respect for its citizens, for their great civilization and for the religious faiths they practice. We have no ambition in Iraq, except to remove a threat and restore control of that country to its own people.
>
> —President George W. Bush

THE QUESTION HAD BEEN BUBBLING beneath the crust; it took a three-part article in the *New York Times* to push it into my consciousness. The *Times* invited three American playwrights to comment on the place of the theater in times like these.[1] Kenneth Lonergan (b. 1982) averred that theater remains important, because it "serves as a public imagination, where imaginations can meet."[2] Similarly, Wendy Wasserstein (1950–2006) identified theater as "where you and I become us": the place where strangers momentarily experience catharsis and share a laugh in the dark.[3] Predictably, American theater's grand old man, Arthur Miller (1915–2005), went "looking for a conscience" but concluded that Broadway was largely irrelevant to the shift he ruefully perceived in American foreign policy from benign democracy to bullying imperium.[4] As intriguing as I found these disparate views, they nudged me

---

1. "Address to the Nation," Office of the Press Secretary, March 19, 2003, announcing the invasion of Iraq by the United States' armed forces. Those troops were withdrawn in 2011. The Bush administration spanned 2001–9.

2. Lonergan, "Spring Theater: In Times like These," *New York Times*, February 23, 2003, https://www.nytimes.com/2003/02/23/theater/spring-theater-in-times-like-these.html?searchResultPosition=54.

3. Wasserstein, "Spring Theater: Where You and I Become Us," *New York Times*, February 23, 2003, https://www.nytimes.com/2003/02/23/theater/spring-theater-where-you-and-i-become-us.html?searchResultPosition=174.

4. Miller, "Spring Theater: Looking for a Conscience," *New York Times*, February 23,

to formulate a question of greater importance in the neighborhood where I live: What purpose does theology serve in times like these—when the world is again at war with a divided heart and equivocal reasons?

At this writing, mood swings of such extremity have become so customary that the world now resembles a bipolar personality twirling among medications. Months of diplomatic slouching toward Iraq and unprecedented global protestations for peace came to an abrupt end on March 19, 2003, when American and British coalition forces finally pulled the trigger. Since then, we have undergone war's predictable yet no less buffeting waves of anxiety, jingoism, bravery, atrocity, bravado, recriminations, and—underlying them all—fear. The collapse of Saddam Hussein's regime will not end the story. The only certainty is that no one can certainly predict how the volatile geopolitical saga in the Middle East will unfold. Theology had better not wait for history to be written by the victors: many of us will not live to take an accurate measure of that victory's dimensions, which could be decades in the reckoning.

Unlike Miller's jaundiced view of Broadway, theology had already assumed an important place during the months before and after the battle for Baghdad. More accurately put: religious language has loomed large across the globe, with theological reflection playing an occasional, supporting role—considerably more so than economics, whose practitioners seem to have been largely dismissed from current debate. That the international media paid scant attention to this phenomenon is no surprise, only business as usual. By now, however, it should be clear to anyone even half-awake that large swatches of militant Islam regard the West in general, and the United States in particular, as the Great Satan that must someday be exterminated. For them, the attacks of 9/11[5] were but dramatic salvos in an ongoing battle between Good and Evil; the emboldening offered and rewards promised to the hijackers were conspicuously religious. Far from repudiating such language, America's politicos embraced it. We have been catapulted, they tell us, in "a war against terrorism," targeted on "an axis of evil." This way of framing the matter has been no more

---

2003, https://www.nytimes.com/2003/02/23/movies/spring-theater-looking-for-a-consci ence.html?searchResultPosition=268. See chapter 22 for more on Miller.

5. On Tuesday, September 11, 2001, members of Al-Qaeda hijacked four commercial airlines to launch coordinated suicide attacks on the eastern United States, which destroyed the Twin Towers of the World Trade Center in New York City, damaged the Pentagon in Arlington County, Virginia, and crashed in rural Pennsylvania after a passenger uprising. It was this event that set in motion the global "War on Terror" in the early decades of the twenty-first century. See Garrett M. Graff, *The Only Plane in the Sky: An Oral History of 9/11* (New York and London: Avid Reader, 2019).

universally accepted by Christians in the West than by Muslims in the East. Those who lament that a moderate Islamic intelligentsia has not been more forthright in challenging a dualistic religious zealotry had better beware the log in their own eye. (More on that in a moment.) What cannot be doubted is that such rhetoric—however problematic, even deluded—captures the minds of antagonists with power to capitalize on them. It is sincere, albeit sincerely Manichean. Terrorism, it seems, is to some degree in the eye of the beholder, but many of those observers are indisputably religious, adopting theological language usually without theological analysis.

Though muted, theological reflection has not gone utterly AWOL. As always, local churches do not hold still long enough for their temperatures to be accurately taken. Nevertheless, denominational bodies as diverse as The Shalom Center and the World Alliance of Reformed Churches, as well as parachurch organizations like Sojourners, weighed in with thoughtful considerations of both political and theological dimensions of a war with Iraq before hostilities erupted. Though it might never have found a central spot on *The Times*'s op-ed page without having been written by a past president and recent Nobel Peace Prizewinner (2002), Jimmy Carter's public application of just-war criteria to hostilities with Iraq (three days before their commencement) was another encouraging sign.[6] That such analyses proved inadequate to prevent war is no reflection on their integrity, any more than a sound diagnosis should be faulted for losing a patient on the operating table. When war with Iraq proved inescapable, a cogent Christian articulation of its rationale would at least have addressed the concerns of those who found the reasons given—evidence of weapons of mass destruction, substitution of Saddam Hussein[7] for Osama bin Laden,[8] extending freedom to the Iraqi people by force—unconvincing.

When nation rises up against nation, Jesus warned his little band to stay awake (Mark 13:37). Good advice. Whatever their plumage, hawkish or dovish, Christian theologians must remain vigilant just now. For as long as organizations like the Southern Baptist Convention buy into, and feed, apocalyptic imagery that issues from Washington, other Christian points of view demand a

---

6. Carter, "Just War—or a Just War?," *New York Times*, March 9, 2003, https://www.nytimes.com/2003/03/09/opinion/just-war-or-a-just-war.html. Carter, born in 1924, was President from 1977 to 1981. At this writing, he entered hospice care in February 2023 at age 98.

7. Born in 1937, Hussein was Iraq's fifth president. He died in 2006.

8. Osama bin Mohammed bin Awad bin Laden was a militant Saudi Arabian and founder of the violent pan-Islamic organization Al-Qaeda. On May 2, 2011, he was assassinated in Pakistan by an American special operations unit.

hearing. When the American President assures Iraq's tortured populace that the day of their liberation is at hand, only a politics attuned to Jesus's preaching at Nazareth—a conscience able to distinguish genuine liberation of the oppressed from their displacement under one worldly tyranny to another (Luke 4:16–30)—can follow through with a compassion as pervasive as the bombs showered on them. Only those acquainted with the horrors recounted in the book of Judges can stay the hand of conquerors from corrupting interim strategies in an occupied nation's reconstruction. When America's leaders wrap their policies not only in the flag but also in the Bible, few but theologians will remind us that, though the emperor should be honored, God alone must be feared (1 Pet 2:17). When push comes to shove, that which Caesar gets is trumped by what we are expected to render unto God (Matt 22:21 // Mark 12:17 // Luke 20:25).

Recent American political rhetoric has lacked theological subtlety, to say the least. No one expects the Bush administration to sound like St. Augustine; one wishes only that it sounded less like the Iraqi high command. There now seems little doubt that one reason we are at war with Iraq is President Bush's conviction that God wills it. Has none of his religious counselors warned him—as his sober military commanders surely have done—of a reserve appropriate to fallible executives, susceptible to overreaching? Couldn't the same advisers who persuaded him to ditch the metaphor of crusade—to which the President appealed in declaring war on terrorism—help him to realize that the literal meaning of *jihad* is "striving," particularly "striving in the path of God" (*fi sabil Allah*)? Down the angrier stretches of that road lie the lacerating petitions of Mark Twain's "War Prayer" (1905):

> O Lord, our God, help us to tear their soldiers to bloody shreds with our shells; help us to cover their smiling fields with the pale forms of their patriot dead; help us to drown the thunder of the guns with the shrieks of their wounded, writhing in pain; help us to lay waste their humble homes with a hurricane of fire; help us to wring the hearts of their unoffending widows with unavailing grief; help us to turn them out roofless with their little children to wander unfriended the wastes of their desolated land in rags and hunger and thirst.... —for our sakes who adore Thee, Lord, blast their hopes, blight their lives, protract their bitter pilgrimage, make heavy their steps, water their way with their tears, stain the white snow with the blood of their wounded feet! We ask it, in the spirit of love, of Him Who is the Source of Love.[9]

---

9. Mark Twain, *Collected Tales, Sketches, Speeches, & Essays 1891–1910*, ed. Louis J. Budd, LOA 61 (New York: Library of America, 1992), 654–55.

An evangelical Methodist, George W. Bush would never pray such a parodic travesty. Would that he demonstrated a modicum of alertness to the totalizing religiosity that enables some adherents—Muslim, Jewish, and Christian—to do just that.

A very good reason that it should be of last resort is that war drives everyone and everything to extremes. Pacifists discount the monstrosities inflicted by Saddam's so-called dirty dozen as tangential; conscionable dissent is shouted down as unpatriotic and spiritually enervating. A well-calibrated theology, anchored in wisdom accrued across the church's two millennia, should retard and may forestall our plunging headlong into a cold whirlpool of insolence toward both the enemy and ourselves. Until many Iraqi citizens failed to exhibit the appropriate reactions, journalists headlined a military strategy of "shock and awe"[10] while seemingly forgetful of America's own devastation by the events of 9/11. No matter how bloodless the sanitized video feed from the frontlines to the States, only children whose experience of war extends no farther than a multiplex cinema will believe that precision bombing leaves innocents untouched. We need the church's theologians to remind us that war, even when defensible, is abominable because it subverts that crowning glory for which God intends all creation. We also need reminding that our quotidian ambitions are as evanescent as the morning's dew; that awe is ultimately the sole prerogative of the LORD God of Israel and of Jesus Christ, whose most shocking attribute is a mercy deeper than our wildest dreams of benevolence. If indeed we are engaged in "a war against terror," against diabolical forces, then all the world's weapons of mass destruction will never topple them—though the nastiest demons of our nature could someday commandeer them. According to the church's creed, victory in *that* war belongs only to Jesus Christ, who claimed initial skirmishes in his own wilderness, broke sin's back at Golgotha, and will put paid to all that is yet unredeemed under the aegis of Death.

In a sermon preached in October 1939, C. S. Lewis (1898–1963) confronted war's spiritual enemies—feverish distractions, frustrated and incomplete lives, the fear of pain and death—and astutely commented that "war creates no absolutely new situation; it simply aggravates the permanent human situation so that we can no longer ignore it. Human life has always been lived on the edge of a precipice. Human culture has always had to exist under the shadow of something infinitely more important than itself."[11] Precisely what the per-

---

10. This colloquial phrase for the military strategy of rapid, overpowering dominance was used by United States military leaders on *CBS News* on January 24, 2003.

11. Lewis, "Learning in War-Time," in Lewis, *The Weight of Glory and Other Addresses*, ed. Walter Hooper (New York: Simon & Schuster, 1996), 42–43.

manent human circumstance is, that which is "something infinitely more important" than human life and culture, the world's sages have forever debated. Homer sang of rage, "murderous, doomed," held hostage to capricious fortune (*The Iliad* 24.525–28):

> Such is the way the gods spun life for unfortunate mortals,
> That we live in unhappiness, but the gods themselves have
>   no sorrow.
> There are two urns that stand on the door-sill of Zeus.
> They are unlike for the gifts they bestow:
> An urn of evils; an urn of blessings.[12]

In *Macbeth* (5.5.24–28), Shakespeare gazed into the abyss and saw there, in the words of G. Wilson Knight, "the murk and nightmare torment of a conscious, absolute hell":[13]

> Life's but a walking shadow, a poor player
> That struts and frets his hour upon the stage,
> And then is heard no more; it is a tale
> Told by an idiot, full of sound and fury,
> Signifying nothing.

Apocryphally, but no less truthfully, Martin Luther was asked what he would do if he learned that Christ would return tomorrow. He answered that he would plant a tree.

I place my bet on Luther's reply, on the Christian hope that theology articulates—and not merely because "the heart has its reasons of which reason knows nothing" (Pascal). The very grandeur of Shakespearean verse, especially when rendered with the mellifluousness of a John Gielgud,[14] puts the lie to its own claim for life as nothing but furious noise. Those seized by the Christian gospel can no longer acquiesce to Homer's vision of human wretchedness unanswered by divine whim, not when he who was in God's own form emptied

---

12. *The Iliad of Homer*, trans. Richmond Lattimore (Chicago: University of Chicago Press, 1951), 489.

13. Knight, *The Wheel of Fire: Interpretations of Shakespearean Tragedy* (London: Routledge, 2001), 160.

14. A British actor and director (1904–2000), Gielgud's one-man recitations from Shakespeare's works, *The Ages of Man*, were highly acclaimed in the UK and the US from 1957 until about 1966.

himself, took upon himself the rock bottom of human misery, and by doing so founded a new creation that still is growing—in fits and starts—into the fullness of divine beauty and love for which we are irreversibly destined (Eph 1:5, 11; 3:19; Phil 2:5–11). In the face of cataclysm, we plant our trees: not out of cynical resignation, but in theology's reassurance, illumined by Christ's Spirit, that God will be God and, because that is so, where there is death there is hope.

Though indispensable, theology is too frail to go it alone. Apart from the Body of Christ, every human endeavor—be it militancy or theology—is tempted at least to cultural solipsism, at best to heroic Stoicism, at worst to Nietzschean hubris. Theology and theologians cannot function apart from the church's liturgy, the preached word, the renewing sacrament. With this daily bread, the unnatural makes perfect sense; the impossible becomes an everyday occurrence. Grace abounds, amazing to behold. Congregations that have deteriorated into squabbling cliques come together on a late Wednesday night to ask God's blessing on both George Bush and Saddam Hussein. A Marine chaplain urges his platoon before combat to pray not only for themselves but for their enemies as well: the Iraqis, he reminds them, are only soldiers, just like them, obeying the orders they've been given. On the battlefield, an Iraqi staggers toward an American, waving a white cloth, and receives long drafts of water from an enemy canteen. In a light this benighted world cannot comprehend, God Almighty redeems every theater, whether of war or of art. In the power of the Holy Spirit, the church creates a space where human imaginations not only meet but also are sanctified by the mind of Christ. In the heightened sensibility that war stimulates, theology recognizes, as though for the first time, its true vocation and holiness of duty. Congregated as the church, theologians, like all Christians, recognize strangers as friends and foes as siblings—where you and I are and will remain us—experiencing not merely catharsis but love, sharing with God a last laugh in the dark.

CHAPTER 25

Elegy for a Border Collie

> Heaven goes by favor. If it went by merit, you would stay out and your dog would go in.
>
> —Mark Twain

ON FEBRUARY 23, 2011, LIBYA WAS CONVULSED in civil revolt against Colonel Qaddafi,[1] who threatened to shed his last drop of blood while tracking and killing the protesters. Similar turmoil throughout the Arab world triggered a spike in crude oil prices, a plummet in stock values, and free-floating fear that much of the world, tottering after two years of economic anguish, would plunge into a deeper recessionary tailspin. On the same date, in an animal hospital in Princeton Township, New Jersey, a dog was quietly euthanized around 9:00 a.m. God forgive me, but it is the last event that I'll remember.

At death Pinky's age was sixteen years and six months, which for a border collie is very old. (One British study identified that breed's median age of death as twelve years, three months.) Harriet and I had purchased the pup a few months after he was weaned from his dam, when our daughter was five years old. Caroline grew up with Pinky, and he grew up with us. Though the expression may turn some stomachs, the fact remains that this dog was a member of our family, so regarded not only by us but also by friends who knew us best and were greeted by him at our door. Deprived of livestock he had been bred to drive, he herded the Blacks. He had the goods to do it. The papers accompanying his bill of sale testified to his purebred lineage among trial and show dogs in Sussex, a pedigree far more distinguished than I can claim. In 2011 a border collie reportedly recognized 1,022 words, probably not much fewer than I use in a given day. Unlike myself, Pinky never bit a person or even growled at

---

1. Muammar Qaddafi (c. 1942–2011), revolutionary and politician, was President of Libya, 1969–2011, until his assassination by a rebel militia.

one. His policy toward rabbits, cats, and other dogs was an unruffled live and let live. Only a bicycle's spinning spokes agitated him. If he could, he would have run every Schwinn to earth, then licked each peddler into compliance.

Standing beside him as he was "put to sleep"—as euphemisms go, a fair description of what we witnessed—my wife and I found ourselves traumatized, "piercingly wounded." This took me by greater surprise than I had anticipated. It was far from our first brush with death. At that time Harriet and I had buried three of our parents. When one reaches the far side of middle age, funeral homes (a less palatable euphemism) are no novelty. It was, as they say, only a dog. What, then, prevented me from washing Pinky's preferred cushion when I smelled in it his odor? Why was Harriet heartbroken at the sight on our porch of his cable tie-out, reminded of Tiny Tim's empty stool and abandoned crutch? Neither of us wears maudlin comfortably. What could account for such grief?

The answer ready at hand is a quality of companionship lost. Pinky may or may not have been capable of love as we experience it. Who knows? Evolutionary biologists tell us that, recognizing humans as ambulatory meal tickets, dogs have learned how to play their owners for saps. There may be truth in that. Nevertheless, when our collie laid his paws on my chest and licked my face, this sap could not experience such actions as other than affectionate, nor was I ever disposed to try. While Harriet unwound in our study, which ended up the dog's den as much as our own, Pinky expressed an uncanny intuition of human happiness or frustration, reacting to her with what appeared to us as empathy. Ray Bradbury (1920–2012) titled one of his books *Dogs Think That Every Day Is Christmas*.[2] Every day for more than sixteen years Pinky gave us canine Christmas presents. Of how many members among *Homo sapiens* could we say something comparable? To lose that is reason to grieve.

Another reason is the inescapability of death. To own and care for a pet during an extended period is to witness, as in time-lapse photography, one's own deterioration. Across sixteen years a furry fireball grew grayer, slower, blinder, deafer, and more arthritic. So have I. Like others who traffic in theology, I have upbraided our society's denial of death, while denying mortality in my own house. In his last months I cleaned up Pinky's accidental excretions as fast as I displaced from consciousness their cause: the inexorable wasting away of his internal organs. When he could no longer stand, much less walk—as we carried him on his cushion into the examining room for a final visit—my imagination toyed with prospective injections that might stay the decay, thus deflecting images of myself someday that is now sooner than later. Harriet and

---

2. Bradbury, *Dogs Think That Every Day Is Christmas* (Kaysville, UT: Gibbs Smith, 1997).

I long hoped that we would discover Pinky had died in his sleep. We talked little of euthanasia until the morning we could no longer avoid it. To keep a suffering animal alive, propped up by medical artifice, seemed to us cruel and self-serving. To place a beloved friend beyond misery's reach required our consent to destroy him. "First, do no harm," insisted Hippocrates and John Wesley. For us there was no available option that did not harm. We cried because death remains that bastard on the throne, until all things are subjected under the Son and true King (1 Cor 15:20–28).

Darwinians say that over 15,000 years of selective domestication have culminated in dogs' adoption of human habits. I wonder if the process works also in reverse. Across sixteen years did my dog caninize me, helping me to become more dog-like and, in the process, more Christlike? According to Robert Benchley, "A dog teaches a boy fidelity, perseverance, and to turn around three times before lying down."[3] Pinky taught me more than that. From him I learned adaptability. It could not have been easy for a working dog, bred for nonstop physical activity, to settle into indoor domesticity. Over the years Pinky did it, reminding me there are things more important than the stubbornness of demanding my way (Mark 8:31–9:1). He depended on Harriet and me to feed and care for him in ways that, in his changed environment, he could not do for himself. What is our life if not a school for trusting God, as circumstances we cannot control graduate us from helpless infancy to infirm elderliness? A slow learner, I suspect the Almighty has been using a collie to heighten my compassion for other creatures. Perhaps Pinky's finest lesson for one inclined to depression and anxiety was a holy joie de vivre: the unadulterated delight of a brisk walk, a good meal, easy relaxation, and a loving touch right now, never minding an unfetchable past and an uncertain future (Matt 6:25–34; Luke 10:38–42). I mourn the loss of a gentle pedadog, grateful for his lessons. That he never intended them makes no difference. My most influential teachers were never aware of what I was learning from them.

Just after Pinky's death several friends sent us an anonymous consolation called "Rainbow Bridge": a fable about a place "this side of heaven" where dead pets, revivified from maiming and disease, can romp together until the day they are reunited, "never to be parted again," with humans who loved them in this life. "Then you cross Rainbow Bridge together."[4] Though steeped in Hall-

---

3. Robert Benchley, "Your Boy and His Dog," in Benchley, *Chips Off the Old Benchley* (New York: Harper & Brothers, 1949), 94–96.

4. The origin of this consolation is disputed. In an article in *National Geographic* ("The Rainbow Bridge Has Comforted Millions of Pet Parents: Who Wrote It?," February 22, 2023), Rachel Nuwer ascribes authorship to Edna Clyne-Rekhy, a Scottish artist.

mark sentimentality not to my taste, some things in this parable chime with Scripture. The Bible ventures little about the souls of the departed, human or bestial, but its poetry is fearless in summoning all creation—angels, sun and moon and stars, deep-sea monsters and winging birds, fire and frost, hills and forests, princes and peoples, young and old—to praise the LORD (Ps 148). Extolling Israel's God is not humanity's exclusive prerogative. Who's to say that the good Lord does not accept as praise the bark of a border collie?

"Rainbow Bridge" also envisions a cosmic restoration of all that has been ruptured (Gen 9:8–10; Isa 11:6–9; Hos 2:18; Col 1:11–15; Rev 21:1–4), a post-mortem reconciliation of all earthly creatures resonant with Paul's claim that God is *everything's* source, means, and destination (Rom 11:36). Crossing the Rainbow Bridge into eternity is a way of expressing the Canticle's conviction that "love is strong as death" (Song 8:6) and Easter's evangel that death is finally feebler than God's perfecting love (1 John 4:7–12). Death, thou shalt die.

Meanwhile, shamelessly and with a love that can come only from the heart of God, I weep for the loss of a companion constant until death.

Rest in peace, Pinky.[5]

Photograph by the author

---

5. Far and away I have received more appreciations for these 1,650 words than for anything else I've published in four decades. It goes to show, I suppose, that people admire the Bible but love their pets.

Part 4

Declarations

CHAPTER 26

Biblical Preaching: Ruminations of a Geezer

> If I say, "I will not mention him, or speak any more in his name," there is in my heart as it were a burning fire shut up in my bones, and I am weary with holding it in, and I cannot.
>
> —Jeremiah 20:9

SOME YEARS AGO, FROM SOMEONE I no longer recall, a faded Xerox photocopy was put into my hands. It was a list of precepts for preaching by Krister Stendahl (1921–2008), a superb biblical theologian whose work has been cited elsewhere in this volume. Beginning in 1954 an affiliation with Harvard Divinity School that endured over thirty years, he served as its Andrew W. Mellon Professor of Divinity, Dean (1968–79), and first chaplain (1988–91) before (and after) his election as Bishop of Stockholm (1984–88) in his native Lutheran Church of Sweden. Subsequently he was appointed as the first Myra and Robert Kraft and Jacob Hiatt Distinguished Professor of Christian Studies at Brandeis University (1991–93), where he championed among a new generation of students his lifelong dedication to ecumenical camaraderie.[1]

Over the years I have presented to my students Stendahl's "Ten Commandments for Biblical Preaching,"[2] which I've taken the liberty of elaborating.

---

1. As recalled by Barbara Brown Taylor (*Holy Envy: Finding God in the Faith of Others* [New York: HarperOne, 2019], 63), Stendahl asserted three fundamental rules for religious understanding. "1. When you are trying to understand another religion, you should ask the adherents of that religion and not its enemies. 2. Don't compare your best to their worst. 3. Leave room for 'holy envy.'" By the latter he meant the generous recognition of components of other religious traditions that one admires and wishes could be adapted to one's own faith. For a concise biography of Stendahl's life and meritorious achievements, consult Will Joyner's statement from the News Archive of Harvard Divinity School: Joyner, "Krister Stendahl, 1921–2008," *Harvard Divinity School News*, April 16, 2008, https://news-archive.hds.harvard.edu/news/2011/02/07/krister-stendahl-1921-2008.

2. Presented among the Kellogg Lectures at the Episcopal Divinity School, Cambridge, MA, February 13–14, 1980.

Here, set in italics, are Stendahl's halakah. In proper talmudic fashion, I append my gemara, or interpretive exposition.

1. *Let your preaching grow out of meditation—lest your soul be maimed by your profession.*
    Exposition: (a) Responsible preaching grows out of disciplined exegesis, which also should emerge from prayerful meditation.[3] (b) The profession of ministry, particularly its proclamation of the gospel, is under relentless assault by "a wisdom of this age [and] the rulers of this age, who are doomed to pass away" (1 Cor 2:6 alt.; cf. Gal 1:4). "Stay awake. Watch" (Mark 13:32 AT).
2. *Make not relevance—be quiet until you find it.*
    Exposition: (a) "Be quiet": that is to say, *Listen.* "If only My people would listen to Me, / If Israel would walk in My paths" (Ps 81:13 NJPS). "Go near, and hear all that the LORD our God will say" (Deut 5:27 RSV). "Blessed are those who hear and who keep what is written [in the words of prophecy]" (Rev 1:3 NRSV). (b) If Scripture is a place where God has promised to meet us, and if we listen carefully to what is written therein, then our responsibility is to discern and help others understand how *we* have become irrelevant to the gospel.
3. *If Matthew (or Mark, or Luke, or John, or James, or Paul, . . .) were good enough for the Holy Spirit, each is good enough for you.*
    Exposition: Expand your pneumatology; reduce the weight of your anthropology. "Who has learned your counsel, / unless you have given wisdom / and sent your holy spirit from on high?" (Wis 9:17 NRSV). "And we are witnesses to these things, and so is the Holy Spirit whom God has given to those who obey him" (Acts 5:32).
4. *"You shall not think you already know the message."*
    Exposition: Down that road you will inevitably end up preaching yourself, not Jesus Christ (2 Cor 4:5). The craft of exegesis is learned not to preen our knowledge from the pulpit but to forestall our narcissism.
5. *"You shall not spiritualize—lest you deny the incarnation."*
    Exposition: In the Bible God meets us in all our human disarray (see Ps 137:1–9). Hold up Scripture to the congregation as a mirror of ourselves: both as we are and as God would have us grow to be. "For [God] has made us, creating us through our union with Christ Jesus for the life of goodness which God has predestined us to live" (Eph 2:10 Smith-Goodspeed).

---

3. See chapter 4 of the present volume.

6. *"You need not defend Me or the Bible."*

    Exposition: Among the finest explanations of this principle I have encountered is that of David Steinmetz: "Christian ministers are not merely witnesses; they are also messengers. And that message is valid, whether or not Protestant ministers believe it, whether or not they profit from it, whether or not they enjoy it. The power and truth of the message are quite independent of the personal faith of the messenger who delivers it. It is God's counsel and promise that ministers declare, not their own, and God is truthful, though every human being be false."[4]

7. *"You shall not read from the cookbook—serve the food."*

    Exposition: Switching metaphors: When you visit the doctor, you're not there for a lecture in organic chemistry. You want to know if there's any chance you can get well.

8. *"None of your stories for openers."*

    Exposition: Your job in the pulpit is not to be clever, beguiling, or entertaining. Neither is your personal experience, particularly your religious experience, the criterion of the Word faithfully preached. Like the sacraments, that Word is *extra nos*—outside of us—drawing us into communion with God, irrespective of your story or mine and perhaps even in spite of it.

9. *"You shall not use the word LOVE unless it is in the text."*

    Exposition: Rabbi Krister seems uncharacteristically dogmatic on this point. I think he is striving to wean Christian preachers from bad habits and sloppy thinking. (a) Without express scriptural basis and careful interpretation, "love" becomes a banal cliché. (b) Many biblical texts, in both Testaments, present God as above us, outside us, distant from us, alien to us: in a word, "holy" (*qadash*: e.g., Exod 3:5; Lev 5:15–16; 1 Chr 16:29 // Pss 29:2; 99:3; *hagios*, Rev 6:10). "For the word of God is living and active, sharper than any two-edged sword, piercing to the division of soul and spirit, of joints and marrow, and discerning the thoughts and intentions of the heart" (Heb 4:12 RSV).

10. *"No moral lesson on high holy days."*

    Exposition: Don't try to solve God's mystery. You can't. *Proclaim* it.

    A True Story from the Classroom

    A certain NT professor directed the class's attention to the plain meaning of Mark 4:11–12: Jesus taught in parables, not to clarify, but to confuse.

---

4. David C. Steinmetz, *Memory and Mission: Theological Reflections on the Christian Past* (Nashville: Abingdon, 1988), 77 (cf. Rom 3:4).

A student slammed her hand down on the desk.

"I **HATE** that. It makes no sense that Jesus would do such a thing."

The professor replied, "Is your heart hardened to that possibility?"

"**YES!**"

"Congratulations! You have just demonstrated the power of Scripture twenty centuries after it was written."

Stendahl: *"Finally and always: You shall not bear false witness against your neighbors."*

Exposition: This, of course, is the Decalogue's ninth commandment (Exod 20:16 // Deut 5:20). It applies to the citizen of a nation not your own; the member of a tribe not your own; the adherent of a religion other than your own; the advocate of a party different from your own; and the congregants seated before you, cheek by jowl, who may or may not be blood kin. The pervasiveness of perjury among us is frightening.

I shall be bold to add a few exhortations of my own.

11. Learn to read Scripture stereophonically, with one ear on the claims of the text and the other on your congregation's needs. Marrying those auditions is a priestly act. Think back to the best sermons you've ever heard: the ones you remember, if any. I'd bet that in most of them the preacher wasn't telling you what to think. The preacher articulated for you, through Scripture, what you wish you could have said if only you had found the words.[5]

12. When standing in the pulpit, plant your feet, look people in the eye, and, to the best of your understanding, tell them the truth of the gospel.[6] In the cacophony of relentless jabber, misinformation, and flagrant lies, it may be impossible for gospel truth to penetrate some minds and hearts. But one thing is certain: if *you* don't believe the truth of what you're saying, that lack of confidence will bleed through your words and body language so profusely that nobody in the pews is going to believe you.

13. As you preach, pray that God will open your heart to love those in your congregation whom you can't stand. Remember how Paul opens most of his letters: with thanks *to God* for the very imperfect saints in the churches he is writing (Rom 1:7; 1 Cor 1:2; 2 Cor 1:1; Phil 1:1; cf. Eph 1:1). In the Bible "saints" are not pious or capable or noble. "Saints" (*hagioi*) are those who have been "set

---

5. See Fred B. Craddock, *Preaching* (Nashville: Abingdon, 1985), 26–27.

6. Here I pilfered James Cagney's (1889–1986) primary rule for actors: "Walk in, plant your feet, look the other fellow in the eye and . . . tell the truth."

apart," just as you have, to bear witness to Christ in spite of all their confusion, stupidity, and unlikability.

This I promise you: Among those with whom you work there will be a few who behave in ways that lead you to suspect that God put them on this earth to make your life an absolute hell. It's inevitable. By this the Holy Spirit teaches us some important things that, quite posibly, we couldn't learn as well by any other means. For instance:

- We learn patience, tolerance, composure, and humility. Remember the counsel of Eleanor Roosevelt: "You wouldn't worry so much about what others think of you if you realized how seldom they do."
- From the cantankerous we learn the necessity of maintaining collegial friendships with other ministers: not to gossip, but to receive pastoral care from others. If neither Jesus nor Paul could go it alone in ministry, neither can we.
- The irritants remind us that, no matter how good our intentions, we probably have the same effect on some of them—and are completely unaware of it. They can teach us to step back and learn a little self-transcendence.
- It's good for our theology, even better for our souls, to be reminded that Christ gave his life for the unrighteous and loves those lunatics every bit as much as he loves us.

14. Preachers are not selling something. Preaching is not a sales pitch. In his own day Paul already witnessed the same temptation. Second Corinthians 2:17: "Unlike many we are not hucksters of God's word. When we speak, it is out of sincerity, as those standing right before God, in Christ" (AT). In *God in the Wasteland* David F. Wells writes, "The fact is that, while we may be able to market the church"—and I would add, while we may be able to market the seminary—"we cannot market Christ, the gospel, Christian character, or meaning in life. . . . Neither Christ nor his truth can be marketed by appealing to consumer interest, because the premise of all marketing is that the customer's need is sovereign, that the customer is always right—and this is precisely what the gospel insists cannot be the case."[7]

15. Learn the difference between moral encouragement and moralizing. Moral invigoration opens our congregations to the Holy Spirit's resetting of our moral compass (see, e.g., Gal 5:16–6:10). Moralizing blames, shames,

---

7. Wells, *God in the Wasteland: The Reality of Truth in a World of Fading Dreams*, 2nd ed. (Grand Rapids: Eerdmans, 1995), 82.

scolds, and books people on manipulative guilt trips. We already have enough of that coming at us from all directions. We don't need the church to make us sicker. As another bishop, William H. Willimon, observes, "Most Methodists come to church expecting a to-do list. 'This week the church wants you to work on your sexism, your racism, your classism. Come back next Sunday, and I'll give you another list.' Sermons like that make me grateful that our Lord is nonviolent."[8]

16. Offer your listeners the gospel's reasons to trust, ground for their hope, and limitless compassion. Folks: people are starving from a relentless diet of fear, despair, meanness, and meaninglessness. Until someone offers them real nourishment, they will continue to stuff themselves with Cheetos, opioids, or something even worse.

17. Remember that God grants people freedom to respond but never forces them to yield. Offer your testimony, but don't expect everyone to accept it. In the Gospels Jesus drove away more people than he attracted. According to Luke (4:16–30) his homecoming sermon in Nazareth nearly got him killed.

18. From the pulpit and in all other spheres, remember that the opposite of ministry is magistry. You and I are called to be *ministers*, not magistrates. None of us is The Oracle of Absolute Truth. All of us cast ourselves as the heroes of our own life stories, but none of us is the paladin who will save others' souls. *We are not Christ.* The gospel is finally not about me. And it's not about you, either. It would be a good idea for us to tape onto our bathroom mirrors, where every morning we could see, what John the Baptist says in the Fourth Gospel: "I am not the Christ. . . . There—behold the Lamb of God, who takes away the world's sin. . . . *He* must increase, but I must *decrease*" (John 1:20, 29; 3:30 AT). Read the Epistle to the Hebrews. Be reminded that God calls us to do our part (13:1–19), but the only indispensable ministry is that of Jesus Christ (4:14–16; 9:11–14).

19. Whether in preaching or any other pastoral activity, what you most need to be an effective minister depends on spiritual gifts and a genuine vocation that you bring with you to seminary but no school can ever give you. If you are receptive, your teachers may be able to open you to some avenues of which you were unaware, train your minds to think a little more sharply and learn some basic skills. Finally, however, no divinity school can give you what you most need to be a minister. Happily, the converse also holds true: "The gifts

---

8. Quoted in C. Clifton Black, *A Three-Dimensional Jesus: An Introduction to the Synoptic Gospels* (Louisville: Westminster John Knox, 2023), 81.

and the call of God are irrevocable" (Rom 11:29). Because the faculty cannot give it to you, neither have they the power to take it away.

20. Like all Christian ministry, preaching is an exercise in delayed gratification. Seventy-five percent of the sower's sowing never takes root (Matt 13:3–8 // Mark 4:3–8 // Luke 8:5–8). Twenty-five percent takes, and blasts off beyond anyone's expectation—*and you may never be there to see it happen.* Probably you won't be. On those weary days when you are convinced that nothing you say or do matters, I promise you this: if you have been faithful to Christ, you *are* planting seeds in some people, of which neither you nor they may be aware, but someday will sprout and blossom and flourish, long after you are gone.

CHAPTER 27

Return of the Double-Minded

> They went on from there and passed through Galilee. And he would not have anyone know it; for he was teaching his disciples, saying to them, "The Son of man will be delivered into the hands of men, and they will kill him; and when he is killed, after three days he will rise." But they did not understand the saying, and they were afraid to ask him.
> And they came to Capernaum; and when he was in the house he asked them, "What were you discussing on the way?" But they were silent; for on the way they had discussed with one another who was the greatest. And he sat down and called the twelve; and he said to them, "If anyone would be first, he must be last of all and servant of all." And he took a child, and put him in the midst of them; and taking him in his arms, he said to them, "Whoever receives one such child in my name receives me; and whoever receives me, receives not me but him who sent me."
>
> —Mark 9:30–37 (RSV)

For where jealousy and selfish ambition exist, there will be disorder and every vile practice. But the wisdom from above is first pure, then peaceable, gentle, open to reason, full of mercy and good fruits, without uncertainty or insincerity. And the harvest of righteousness is sown in peace by those who make peace.

What causes wars, and what causes fightings among you? Is it not your passions that are at war in your members? You desire and do not have; so you kill. And you covet and cannot obtain; so you fight and wage war. You do not have, because you do not ask. You ask and do not receive, because you ask wrongly, to spend it on your passions. Unfaithful creatures! Do you not know that friendship with the world is enmity with God? Therefore whoever wishes to be a friend of the world makes himself an enemy of God. Or do you suppose it is in vain that the scripture says, "He yearns jealously over the spirit which he has made to dwell in us"? But he gives more grace; therefore it says, "God opposes the proud, but gives grace to the humble." Submit yourselves therefore to God. Resist the devil and he will flee from you. Draw near to God and he will draw near to you. Cleanse your hands, you sinners, and purify your hearts, you men of double mind. Be wretched and mourn and weep. Let your laughter be turned to mourning and your joy to dejection. Humble yourselves before the Lord and he will exalt you.

—James 3:16–4:10 (RSV)

WELL, HERE WE ARE.[1] And darned if the busy elves that cobble together the lectionary throw at us spitballs of scripture that are no help at all. In the Gospel of Mark those idiot disciples are at it again: dense, scared, whining over which of them earned the highest GPA. Thank God, that doesn't look anything like us. The Letter of James warns fledgling disciples of Christ away from backbiting and jealousy, selfish ambition and intramural warfare, clambering over each other on their greasy pole to the top. Let us heave a relieved sigh that we are beyond all that, too. Lord have mercy: we're Princeton.

Just now, in the peachy dawn of a fresh academic year, it may seem to us incredible that we could ever resemble our great-grandparents in those backward congregations. As this year unfolds, however, it is remotely possible—a slim chance—that we may someday hold the Bible to our face and recognize there ourselves. Should that day come, here are some things I hope you will consider.

To begin with: "Where do all these wars and battles among us come from? They come from your cravings that are at war within you." That's Saint James's

---

1. A sermon preached on September 20, 2000, Miller Chapel, Princeton Theological Seminary, Princeton, New Jersey. With deep appreciation I acknowledge the profound lectures on Genesis and the Psalms delivered by my colleague Professor W. J. A. Power at Perkins School of Theology, Southern Methodist University, 1989–99. In this sermon I picked his pockets until they were threadbare.

diagnosis, and he refers to the disease as *dipsychia*, double-mindedness. The Hebrews had another name for this condition, *se'eph*, the divided heart:[2] the *lev* at odds with the *lev*.[3]

Now you know what the *lev* is. The psalmist prayed: "Prove me, O LORD, and try me; test my [*lev*] and my mind."[4] The *lev* is the seat of the psyche, the receptacle of our secret thoughts. Your *lev* is the real you, who hides behind the many masks we display to the world. Now the real you may be the you that you wouldn't want anyone to know about: the you that might be embarrassed were someone else to discern, because it seems so shallow or silly, or perhaps even so lusty or grasping. Sometimes in the OT, something like that is what the LORD finds when he probes the *lev*. But in its deepest chamber the real you—the authentic creature made in God's own image—is crafted for love. "You must love the LORD your God with all your *lev* and with all your *nephesh*—your appetite—and with all your physical strength."[5] The deepest you within you is built for love: to love one another and, most especially, to love and to enjoy God forever. All else is only instrumental to that end. All of our work, study, knowledge, prayer, aspirations, theology: everything, every last bit of it, is a tool intended to help us love God and one another more deeply.

And yet, as Saint Augustine reminds us, we get so easily confused. What we ought to be using, perversely we love. And those whom we should be loving, we twist to our use.[6] Our hearts get split; our minds, doubled; our cravings, divided. When our *lev* becomes internally conflicted, what happens? Typically, we do business the same way the world does: we lash out and grind down one another. That's what James says, and he's right.

"It's not my fault. Someone else is to blame." That's a pattern you can trace back to Eden. The LORD God asked the man, "Who told you that you were naked? Did you eat from the tree from which I forbade you to eat?" And the man said, "It was that woman you put at my side. She gave it to me. It's her fault that I ate it." And the LORD God said to the woman, "What the hell have you done?" The woman replied, "It was that serpent you made. He conned me. It's his fault that I ate it."[7]

---

2. Psalm 119:113.

3. The Talmud picks up this idea: "'With all thy heart': let not your heart be divided—i.e., not wholly one—as regards your love for God" (b. Šabb. 88b), a faint echo of which may occur in Luke 16:13. In Christian theology it is memorably developed by Søren Kierkegaard, *Purity of the Heart Is to Will One Thing: Spiritual Preparation for the Feast of Confession*, trans. Douglas V. Steere (New York: Harper & Brothers, 1938).

4. Psalm 26:2 ESV.

5. Unless otherwise indicated, all translations are my own.

6. *Doct. chr.* 1.3–4, 20–23.

7. Genesis 3:11–13.

Wait till the clouds come rolling in around November, and we'll all be back in Eden. "Well, I got a C on the Bible exam, but it's not my fault. It's those teachers whose class they made me take—those professors who don't know or care how devoted I am, how hard I worked. I doubt those jokers are even Christian. They are the ones to blame."

If you manage to overcome your suspicion and look to the seminary faculty to bail you out, you may as well forget it. We're in *dipsychia* up to our eyeballs. "Well, I'd give better lectures, by now I'd have that book finished, my promotion would be buttoned up, that juicy grant would be mine—if only the president and dean weren't determined to assign me to every time-wasting, brain-numbing committee that they can concoct. It's their fault."

Or it's the fault of our supervisors. Or of the session. Or the bishop. Our ministries would be ten times more effective if only the church would stay out of our way. It's the seminary's Board of Trustees who are to blame. One of them is visiting with us on the faculty this year. Frank, we appreciate your being so conveniently close for us to kick around this year. And while we play this jolly game of scapegoat—passing the buck until it's so thin you could read Barth's *Dogmatics* through it; yanking out each other's shirttail and setting it on fire—Saint James will whisper in our ear: "You want something and don't have it; so you murder. And you are jealous for something and cannot obtain it; so you fight and wage war. You don't have, because you don't ask. You ask and you don't receive, because you ask badly." You think making the grade at Princeton Seminary is tough? That's a Twinkie, compared with learning to become single-minded disciples of Jesus Christ.

Listen: "You are a people consecrated to the LORD your God; of all the peoples on earth the LORD your God chose you to be his treasured people. It is not because you are the most numerous of peoples that the LORD set His heart on you and chose you—in fact, you are the smallest of peoples."[8] It is not—I would add—that you are the most attractive, most likely to succeed, the brightest and best of scholars and pastors and professors that the LORD set His love upon you and selected you. "No, it is because the LORD loves you and is keeping a promise made to [Israel and] your forebears that the LORD liberated you with a mighty hand and rescued you from the house of bondage."[9] Only the LORD can redeem us: whether from the hand of Pharaoh or the self-captivity of our own deluded messianism. Why does God do this? Because, and only because, the LORD loves us and the LORD keeps his promise.

That is why this table is spread before us. The firstborn of all creation, in whom all things hold together—the *eikōn* of God who did not reckon equality

---

8. Deuteronomy 7:6–7.
9. Deuteronomy 7:8.

with God a thing to be exploited, the one who was first of all—emptied himself, took the form of a slave, became last of all and servant of all to the point of death. My God: even death on a cross.[10] With each return to this table, with every stabilizing consecration of our heavenly Father's name, our hearts are healed with a more abundant graciousness; our minds are more serenely conformed to the mind of Christ; our knees can bend with easier suppleness at the name of Jesus, who loved me and gave himself for me,[11] and for you, and for this tortured world that God embraces in healing and is still putting right.

Come to this table, now and throughout the coming days. Pray and sing and laugh, not to celebrate our own faith, but to thank God for continuing to have faith in us. Fight the devil, and he will run away from you. Come closer to God and—you may rest in confident peace—God will draw near to you in the name of the Father, and of the Son, and of the Holy Ghost.

---

10. Colossians 1:18; Phil 2:5–11.
11. Galatians 2:20.

CHAPTER 28

A View from the Parapet

> At that time the disciples came to Jesus, saying, "Who is the greatest in the kingdom of heaven?" And calling to him a child, he put him in the midst of them, and said, "Truly, I say to you, unless you turn and become like children, you will never enter the kingdom of heaven. Whoever humbles himself like this child, he is the greatest in the kingdom of heaven."
>
> —Matthew 18:1–4 (RSV)

FOR A CHRISTIAN TRAIT ONCE CHARACTERIZED by St. John Chrysostom as the "mother, nurse, and . . . center of all other virtues,"[1] humility has fallen on tough times. Long ago in the medieval twilight, Christian asceticism took some terribly wrong turns, occasionally mistaking humility with self-degradation and piety with masochism. In our own day I fear that Christian women have been especially prey to such deformed and deforming religiosity. For a fact I know that it warped too many years of my own life. But I can also tell you that in Matthew's Gospel Jesus never plumps for such sick self-destruction. Lately Christians have been tempted to the opposite extreme of error's arc, to fling themselves into America's culture of narcissism. But the healing of the church will never come by our exchanging one pathology for another. Matthew insists that we reexamine our vocation to *mini*stry, not *magi*stry. "The rulers of the Gentiles lord it over them, and the Big Guys throw their weight around. But it's not that way among you."[2]

When you think of "humility," I invite you to stroll outside and reacquaint yourself with "humus": that loamy soil produced by the decomposition of

---

This sermon was originally preached in Miller Chapel, Princeton Theological Seminary, November 18, 1999.

1. John Chrysostom, *Homilies on the Acts of the Apostles*, homily 30.
2. Matthew 20:25–26a (my paraphrase).

leaves and other stuff. We are humus, mortal, weak: "We are dust, and to dust we shall return."[3] That, I think, is why Jesus counterculturally insisted on acknowledging children; why he referred to those who believe in him as "little ones" with "little faith"; why he upheld little kids as models for his disciples to emulate as we lurch into the kingdom of heaven. It's not that children are innocent or simple or sinless. If you're a parent, you know that's not true. You know how Little Miss Mischief smiles, staring straight at you while sticking peas in her ears. Matthew is no sentimental idiot.

The critical thing about little kids is their immaturity. They are so needy, so utterly dependent on a caregiver to survive. That is why, if we don't turn round and become as small as children, we quite literally shall never fit into our Abba's New Creation. Whenever we turn from our favorite idols—our grades, our salaries, our status, our yearnings for the tallest steeple or plumpest promotion—whenever we let *God* be God of our lives, we can lay aside the mask of hypocrisy, quit pretending that we are ultimately in control—over ourselves, other people, and other things—and can shoulder the gentle yoke of our Lord, whose highest claim for himself was his humbleness of heart.[4] The humility of Jesus does not batter our spirits. It releases them and shows us kids the way home.

Dame Maria Boulding[5] recalls dreaming that she was on the flat, spacious roof of a tall building with a low parapet around the roof's edge. She was walking about, to and fro, with some adult friends, discussing some grave matter. Near them was a little boy of about five or six: a strikingly beautiful, exuberant child. He darted ahead and back again, lagged behind and then caught up, trying to attract their attention and calling them to play with him. The adults were too engrossed in their grim Princetonian conversation to pay him any mind whatever. He then ran ahead and jumped up onto the parapet, standing with his back to the terrible abyss, laughing. Most of the adults gasped with terror and lunged forward to seize him. Dame Maria says that she remained still, by now beginning to understand. Before they could grab him he laughed, waved, and jumped off backward. The friends were horrified, but somehow she knew—as in dreams we do—that on the face of the building, beyond the adults' line of vision but visible to the boy on the parapet, was some scaffolding on which stood the boy's father. The child was safe, and she knew it.

---

3. Genesis 3:19.
4. Matthew 11:29–30.
5. Maria Boulding, ed., *A Touch of God: Eight Monastic Journeys* (London: SPCK; Still River, MA: St. Bede's Publications, 1982), 40–41.

Then, she says, the scene shifted. She was still on the roof, her friends were gone, but the boy was back. The two of them now were alone. The child thought it a marvelous game, this jumping off. Sometimes he jumped forward, sometimes backward; sometimes looking and sometimes not—but always joyfully, brimming over with life and love, wanting Maria to play with him. She never saw the child's father but could guess what he must be like from the boy's utter confidence of being safely caught. Eventually Maria decided to play too—but it was time to wake up.

No one has ever seen God. The one-of-a-kind Son, nestled in his Father's bosom, has made him known.[6] Christ fell into death; in so doing he committed himself to his Father's embrace and lives again. We could never make that leap, we could never commit ourselves into God's hands unless Christ had first done so and invited us to go with him. And there am I on the rooftop, alone with the boy. I watch him jump, over and again, from the parapet into unseen arms, laughing with delight. Eventually, encouraged by playmates who keep me from stumbling, I too may decide to leap in the name of the Father, and of the Son, and of the Holy Spirit.

---

6. John 1:18.

CHAPTER 29

Where Do You Want to Eat?

And he called to him the twelve, and began to send them out two by two, and gave them authority over the unclean spirits. He charged them to take nothing for their journey except a staff; no bread, no bag, no money in their belts; but to wear sandals and not put on two tunics. And he said to them, "Where you enter a house, stay there until you leave the place. And if any place will not receive you and they refuse to hear you, when you leave, shake off the dust that is on your feet for a testimony against them." So they went out and preached that men should repent. And they cast out many demons, and anointed with oil many that were sick and healed them.

King Herod heard of it; for Jesus' name had become known. Some said, "John the baptizer has been raised from the dead; that is why these powers are at work in him." But others said, "It is Elijah." And others said, "It is a prophet, like one of the prophets of old." But when Herod heard of it he said, "John, whom I beheaded, has been raised." For Herod had sent and seized John, and bound him in prison for the sake of Herodias, his brother Philip's wife; because he had married her. For John said to Herod, "It is not lawful for you to have your brother's wife." And Herodias had a grudge against him, and wanted to kill him. But she could not, for Herod feared John, knowing that he was a righteous and holy man, and kept him safe. When he heard him, he was much perplexed; and yet he heard him gladly. But an opportunity came when Herod on his birthday gave a banquet for his courtiers and officers and the leading men of Galilee. For when Herodias' daughter came in and danced, she pleased Herod and his guests; and the king said to the girl, "Ask me for whatever you wish, and I will grant it." And he vowed to her, "Whatever you ask me, I will give you, even half of my kingdom." And she went out, and said to her mother, "What shall I ask?" And she said, "The head of John the baptizer." And she came in immediately with haste to the king, and asked, saying, "I want you to give me at once the head of John the Baptist on a platter." And the king was exceedingly sorry; but because of his oaths and his guests he did not want to break his word to her. And immediately the king sent a soldier of the guard and gave orders to bring his head. He went and beheaded him in the prison, and brought his head on a platter, and gave it to the girl; and the girl gave it to her mother. When his disciples heard of it, they came and took his body, and laid it in a tomb.

The apostles returned to Jesus, and told him all that they had done and taught. And he said to them, "Come away by yourselves to a lonely place, and rest a while." For many were coming and going, and they had no leisure even to eat. And they went away in the boat to a lonely place by themselves. Now many saw them going, and knew them, and they ran there on foot from all the towns, and got there ahead of them. As he went ashore he saw a great throng, and he had compassion on them, because they were like sheep without a shepherd; and he began to teach them many things. And when it grew late, his disciples came to him and said, "This is a lonely place, and the hour is now late; send them away, to go into the country and villages round about and buy themselves something to eat." But he answered them, "You give them something to eat." And they said to him, "Shall we go and buy two hundred denarii worth of bread, and give it to them to eat?" And he said to them, "How many loaves have you? Go and see." And when they had found out, they said, "Five, and two fish." Then he commanded them all to sit down by companies upon the green grass. So they sat down in groups, by hundreds and by fifties. And taking the five loaves and the two fish he looked up to heaven, and blessed, and broke the loaves, and gave them to the disciples to set before the people; and he divided the two fish among them all. And they all ate and were satisfied. And they took up twelve baskets full of broken pieces and of the fish. And those who ate the loaves were five thousand men.

—Mark 6:7–44 (RSV)

DECLARATIONS

I DON'T RECALL EVER PREACHING on a text as long as this.[1] Who knows how long this sermon may run? Some of you are consulting your watches. You can leave whenever the Spirit moves you, with no hard feelings. I may be here, still jabbering on, when part 2 of the institute starts next week.

Until tonight, I don't recall ever hearing a sermon preached on the death of John the Baptist. I know I haven't preached on it before. Earlier this week, I asked my pulpit predecessor about you and what sort of thing you might be expecting. She told me that most of you are pastors; that this sermon would send you off from this week at Princeton, back to your churches, if you hadn't already left. Naturally, for an inspirational word, I gravitated to the only text in the NT that narrates a beheading.

There are two reasons I selected such a large chunk of Scripture on which to preach. First, I have a reasonably high doctrine of Scripture, and I do believe—as did Augustine and Luther and Calvin and Wesley and many others before me—that Scripture preaches just by being read, and that sermons are, at best, footnotes to the word that proclaims itself without our help. As a preacher, to me this is a great comfort. You also should take comfort in it. More Bible, less Black, is invariably a reliable yardstick.

A second reason for selecting a text so long is my conviction that Mark really intended the stories of Jesus's sending of the Twelve, the execution of John, and the feeding of five thousand to be held together and remembered alongside one another, cheek by jowl by cheek. Why did Mark tell his story of Jesus this way? Perhaps because he wanted us to consider two very different approaches to ministry, and which one befits servants of the gospel of Jesus Christ.

First, Jesus sends out the twelve to engage in ministry very much like the one he himself performed: casting out unclean spirits and healing some who were sick. Impressive in this commission is its simplicity. The resources he tells them to take are so minimal as to be nearly incredible:

> A staff.
> > The sandals they are wearing.
> > > Overalls and underwear.
> > > > No bread.
> > > > > No beggar's bag.
> > > > > > No money in their fanny packs.[2]

---

1. A sermon delivered at Miller Chapel, Princeton Theological Seminary, for the 62nd Annual Institute of Theology, June 24, 2005.
2. In sermon manuscripts I occasionally adopt the convention of chain indentations,

Travel light. Don't linger in one place. Preach, and if they don't get it, move on. Simple.

When they return, sixteen verses later, the Twelve are quick to report all they've accomplished. But that's not really the point. We know that's not the point, because Jesus now commissions them to feed his hungry sheep, all five thousand of them, with five loaves. I forgot the fish: and two sardines. "You give them something to eat." The disciples don't get it. Most days neither do I.

Like the Twelve in Mark, I tend to think ministry is about me. Even after all these years, that's the trap I still spring on myself. It's about *my* ability to pull it off—whatever *it* is. The feeding of the multitude by Jesus's disciples should forever have laid that bird to rest.

The disciples don't do a thing but deliver to others what Jesus has already blessed and broken and given to God.

All are fed and satisfied.
They even have leftovers.

All because the little they have is offered to God and blessed by Jesus. He is the chef, not us. We're the Domino's pizza couriers—no more, but certainly no less.

Sometimes, when a class is helping me puzzle my way through the parables in Mark 4, I'll ask them if they or anyone they know has ever experienced something like the sower in that chapter. You know:

A sower went out to sow.
Seed falls beside the path. Nothing.
Seed falls into the rocks. Zilch.
Seed falls among the thorns. Zip.
Seed falls into rich soil and—*look out!*

There's a 30, 60, 100 percent yield, way off the charts.

Have you ever been interviewed for a pastorate and had someone ask you, "How would you evaluate yourself as a preacher?" And you answer, "Well, three

---

which guides my eye and calibrates my pacing. In their typescripts Sir Winston Churchill and the Rev. Dr. Peter Marshall did the same. See Keith Houston, "Miscellany No. 73: Per Churchill et commata," *Shady Characters* (blog), May 9, 2016, https://shadycharacters.co.uk/2016/05/micellany-73-churchill/; Marshall, *John Doe, Disciple: Sermons for the Young in Spirit*, ed. Catherine Marshall (New York: McGraw-Hill, 1963). Were I a more talented and self-assured preacher, I'd dispense with manuscripts altogether.

Sundays out of four, my sermons fizzle out and go nowhere. From the pulpit straight to the floor: the thing never gains altitude, just drops in the chancel like a dead duck. But every now and then—one Sunday out of four, I'd say—I make the very same pitch, no changes, and that sermon takes off like a rocket, pulling me and everyone else along with it." And you and the search committee stand up, and everybody shakes hands, and they say to you—What?

> Maybe they say to you, "Feed us, please. We're hungry.
> We are starving for some gospel.
> The real thing, not the fake stuff.
> Not *The Da Vinci Purpose-Driven Prayer of Jabez*.
> We've tried Gospel Lite and it tastes thin and we're still famished for the kingdom of God.
> Can you feed us some of that? Please?"

As a teacher of mine once said, these are scenes of heartrending famine that never make the cover of *Time* Magazine.

If we do not serve them gospel, who will? When you come down to it, that's finally the only reason any of us have for being in ministry. Doctors may keep us alive a little longer than some of our grandparents, but they can't tell us *why* we should go on living. Captains of industry can show us how their bottom lines stand at 25 percent over last year this time, and 55 percent higher than five years ago. Will they account for how that profit will be used, or just what it took to make it? Politicians? Please. I am still naive enough to hope that, maybe, somewhere in Washington there still is a Jimmy Stewart or a Tom Hanks who is decent, really cares about the American people, and will do the right thing even if it costs him reelection. Most days, however, I know that such figures have gone the way of Santa Claus and the tooth fairy.

I read in *The Washington Post* a comment by one of the capital's thousands of lavishly paid lobbyists, an offhand remark whose cold candor arrested my eye. This fellow said, "There are only two engines that drive Washington: One is greed, and the other is fear."

In particular cases, that may be wrong. Overall, however, I suspect that's right. It surely matches what I read in the papers and hear on the news. Greed and Fear: As old as politics itself, older even than Machiavelli, though he put into words what everyone had always known. Greed and Fear: the unseen, most frequent visitors to Herod's dinner table.

There they all are, at the Antipas birthday party: the cabinet, the Joint Chiefs of Staff, Galilee's highest and mightiest. And after one drink too many,

Herod, that lecherous fool, blurts out to his stepdaughter, who happens to be one sexy entertainer, "Whatever you want is yours, even half my kingdom. Come here, honey; name your price." And his wife Herodias finessed that offer and her daughter into eliminating the person she most despised: her harshest critic, John the Baptist. Greed and Fear: together again.

Mark tells us that, when Herod sprang the trap he had laid for himself, he was truly sorry. Though arrested for political protest, the Baptist was placed in protective custody. Herod respected John as a man of integrity. But if you're the head of state, you can't be proved a liar in your own home, at a state dinner, before a roomful of politicians and generals lusting for your power and who must be controlled. At the head table, Greed and Fear sit on either side of Herod, whispering reminders in his ears.

Perhaps, when John the Baptist was escorted from his cell, he heard Herod's voice whispering in his ear: *"John, even though we haven't always seen eye-to-eye, you know how much I admire you. I think you're the last honest man in Galilee."*

Down the hallway, Dead Man Walking hears Live King Whisp'ring: *"John, you understand the way the world works. I've gone too far; I can't back down now. I made it a promise—I'll grant you, one I should never have made—but a promise I have to keep."*

Into the Executioner's Chamber John is led, as Herod's voice keeps murmuring: *"If I lose face, I lose control. I lose control; all hell breaks loose. You know I can't have that. We can't have that."*

Up the steps, to the platform, where the officer holding the great axe stands silent beside a stained chopping block with the basket receptacle. And as he kneels, still the voice drones in John's ear: *"Though I could never say this publicly, John, you know how much I love you. I mean really love you. You got guts, John. How I admire your guts. You know, you're the only person I've ever—"*

WHAM!

This is how prophets die. Not in a blaze of heroic glory, but for the pettiest pretexts in lonely places haunted by hatred and shame. And the jailers holding keys to the death chamber are Greed and Fear. This is true of Galilee and of Washington. It is also, sad to say, true for city hall, the corporate boardroom, and even, at its weakest and worst, the church. John's disciples at least gave their teacher's body a decent burial. By the time Fear had worked over his closest followers, Jesus's body wasn't accorded even that final respect.

Two scenes, two suppers, side by side. First, Herod's: national power, festooned in wealth, draped with betrayal and guilt, fueled by Greed and Fear. Every instrument is at Herod's disposal, save savvy enough to elude manipulation and a means to check his overweening pride. He opens his big mouth, utters words that can't be retracted, and an innocent man's head is severed from his shoulders.

Next, the banquet over which Jesus presides: a desert in the middle of nowhere, populated by thousands of nobodies, attended by twelve fairly dumb waiters. There's nothing at Jesus's disposal, save compassion for the multitudes, like shepherd-less sheep, and faith in God, to whom Jesus offers what little his disciples have. He opens his mouth, teaches and pronounces blessing, and five thousand leave more than satisfied, abundantly refreshed.

Which banquet is real? Both of them. Never have God's people gone without nourishment, as early as Moses in Sinai, as late as yesterday in Princeton. And never have we been without Herods, scheming and schemed against, beheading their threats.

Which banquet will prevail? Only one: That sponsored by God, hosted by his Messiah, Jesus. With the resurrection of that Christ, crucified by another of Herod's agents, God saw to that. We see it with the eyes of faith. With common vision we see that before long, Herod was toppled. Finally, all the Herods are toppled, Herods then and Herods now.

At which banquet will you take your seat? That's the question before you and me and everyone with whom we preach and teach. We cannot make up their minds for them. Only for ourselves can we decide, offer the choice to others, then leave the rest to God: who still owns the vineyard and still calls to life what is sown while we sleep and rise, night and day, faith sprouting and growing, we know not how.

This much I know: I may be a sheep—which are conspicuously stupid and unteachable animals—but I'm one sheep who knows the sound of his Shepherd's voice. That voice is unmistakable and sounds nothing like Herod and his pals, Greed and Fear. Greed and Fear: that's all I hear on the news, and this lamb is sickened to death by their voice, sick of being jerked around by Greed and Fear. I have a hunch that most of you and most of the people in your churches are, too. It's past time for the church in America's heartland and across the world to wake up and hear the Shepherd's voice, which sings with Isaiah, not about Fear, but about Faith:

> Surely it is God who will save me;
>   I will trust in God and not be afraid.
>   For the LORD is my refuge and my sure defense,
>   The LORD will be my Savior.[3]

---

3. Isaiah 12:2 (AT).

You're a pastor. You give them something to eat.
And God will bless your offering.
God will multiply it beyond your knowledge and calculation.
And your people will be fed, with leftovers.
And rest assured: the Lord of the Banquet will be one greater than you.

CHAPTER 30

Jesus Christ Is Lord

> Christ is either Lord of all, or he is not Lord at all.
>
> —James Hudson Taylor

THIS EVENING YOUR PASTORS HAVE ASSIGNED me a topic: "Jesus Christ Is Lord."[1] For you who are beginning a year's intensive study of the NT, that is a sensible subject. If there is one thing on which the many-voiced choir of the NT harmonizes, it is surely that basic Christian confession: "Jesus Christ is Lord." Embedded in this subject, however, is a twin problem. On the one hand, we've heard that claim so often and so repeatedly that I suspect for many "Jesus is Lord" has become a shopworn slogan: something suitable for a sticker you can slap on your bumper beside "Visit Pigeon Forge." On the other hand, if taken as seriously as the NT takes it, the confession of Jesus as Lord is so bizarre, so startling, so hot to the touch, it's liable to scorch us. You may not believe that, but I've come a long way from a foreign land called New Jersey to tell you: that's the truth.

Over a half century ago, growing up in a small town in North Carolina, I answered an altar call while at a Methodist retreat center where Harriet and I now own a retirement cottage. My life has come full circle. It was expected that I would walk to the altar, acknowledging Jesus Christ as my personal Lord and Savior. Maybe some of you did the same thing at some point in your lives. Answering that altar call was the southern Methodist equivalent of a bar or bat mitzvah, without the party. I'm not disparaging altar calls. I never have. But I'll tell you: had I known then what I have come to learn since, I might have lingered in the pew a bit longer.

---

1. A kickoff for "A Year with the New Testament" at First Presbyterian Church in Nashville, Tennessee, September 14, 2011. A single date has been adjusted, below, for the sake of currency and clarity. Unless otherwise specified, all biblical translations are my own.

Jesus Christ is *Lord*. Let that sink in. Jesus is not some ancient great, about whom you can tune into the History Channel to learn scraps or, more often, speculation. Nor is Jesus my patron. Jesus is not my buddy. Jesus is not "just alright with me."[2] Jesus is *Lord*. If I take that seriously, then it changes the way I look at everything. If you take that seriously, it will change the way you look at everything. That's the bottom line of what I'm here to say tonight. And I'm here to tell you: this confession is the most awesome,[3] the most liberating you will ever make in your life. If you intend to study the NT there's no escaping this claim, because it's all over the pages of every book you will read in the year to come. I'm not here to scare anyone away from hard, serious, engagement with Holy Scripture. Would that more churches did that. I'm only offering you a truthful warning: if you lower your riveted defenses and let these texts get hold of you and go to work on you, they will change your life and the way you reckon everything. Do you really want that? Are you prepared for its consequences? I'm talking about bedrock gospel of the church: not a channel you can flip on your remote, not a motto for the Kiwanis Club or the Junior League. Jesus Christ is *Lord*. What does the NT mean when it issues that challenge to us?

First, a word of context. Some of you may have just finished a year with the OT. If so, then you know that Israel committed itself to the worship of one God, and the name by which Israel addressed that God was "The LORD." The LORD is God, and that LORD is Lord, not merely of Israel, but of the heavens and of the whole earth.

Hear, O Israel: The LORD our God is one LORD:
and you shall love the LORD your God with all your heart, and with all your soul, and with all your strength.[4]

When asked in the Gospels which of the commandments was the first and greatest, Jesus, himself a faithful Jew, repeated this creed.[5] Twenty centuries ago, when a small band of Jews began to identify Jesus of Nazareth with the LORD God of Israel, that was a tremendous leap—and you will see it happen-

---

2. Quoting a gospel rock song by Arthur Reynolds, covered by many bands, including the Doobie Brothers (track B1 on *Toulouse Street*, Warner Bros. Records, 1972, LP album).
3. I select this adjective for its strict sense: that which inspires reverential fear and wonder. However delectable, no hamburger is "awesome."
4. Deuteronomy 6:4–5.
5. Matthew 22:37 // Mark 12:29 // Luke 10:27.

ing in the NT's earliest documents, the letters of Paul. Paul wrote to fledgling Gentile Christians in Corinth, Greece:

> For though there may be so-called "gods" in heaven or on earth—and indeed there are many "gods" and many "lords,"—yet *for us* there is one God, the Father, from whom are all things and for whom we exist, and one Lord, Jesus Christ, through whom are all things, and through whom we exist.[6]

How does Paul know this?

No one can say "Jesus is the Lord" except by the Holy Spirit.[7]

While in prison, Paul wrote to another church in northern Greece, Philippi. In this letter he quoted a hymn that only a few years after the first Easter Christians were already singing. It goes like this:

> Have this mind among yourselves, which you have in Christ Jesus:
>
>> Who, though he was in the form of God, did not count equality with God a thing to be exploited,
>> But emptied himself, and taking the form of a slave, being born in human likeness:
>> And being found in human form he humbled himself and became obedient unto death, even death on a cross.
>> Therefore, God has highly exalted him and bestowed on him the name which is above every name,
>> That at the name of Jesus every knee should bow, in heaven and on earth and under the earth;
>> And every tongue confess that Jesus Christ is Lord, to the glory of God the Father.[8]

Ponder the lyrics of this hymn. It is saying several things; all are important.

To begin with: it is making a claim about Jesus. During his brief ministry on this earth, Jesus engaged all the invisible, diabolical powers and overcame them. This he did because God empowered him as the Lord of life and health.

---

6. 1 Corinthians 8:5–6.
7. 1 Corinthians 12:3.
8. Philippians 2:5–11.

In Jesus, God entered this sick world to restore it. And the capstone of Jesus's ministry was the stone over which everyone stumbles: self-sacrifice for a tortured world by torturous death on a cross—the most hideous form of execution that the ancients could concoct. Essentially this restates the announcement by the risen Jesus to his disciples in Matthew, some of whom worshiped while some doubted: "All power in heaven and on earth has been given to me."[9] Christ is now seated at the right of God in heaven, exalted with authority bequeathed to him by the eternal God, whose power in our life is propelled by the Holy Spirit. Christ is Lord over the living and the dead, as Paul wrote to Christians in Rome: "If we live, we live to the Lord, and if we die, we die to the Lord: so then, whether we live or whether we die, we are the Lord's."[10] Jesus does not belong to us as our personal valet. We belong to *Jesus* as his servants.[11] Before him, now and later, we either stand or stumble. If you want to know what God looks like, look at Jesus. James Denney, the Scots Presbyterian preacher, pointed to a cross and said, "God loves like that."[12] By raising Jesus from death, God declared that Jesus is Lord even over death, the ultimate captivity of sinners. Unlike the lords of this world, Jesus took no captives. The risen Lord has taken *captivity* captive. By his resurrection *death itself* has begun to die. Ultimately, in the fullness of time, death must die and shall die, because God is the God of the living.[13] If you look at the cross and can see nothing but empty tragedy, then nothing I or anyone else can say will ever change your mind. If you look at the cross and can see God's final victory—eternal life with our Creator in love—then no words are necessary. The Holy Spirit has graced you with vision to see the truth clearly.

Page after page, the NT puts this claim to us: "Jesus Christ is Lord." Do you believe that?

Exactly what does Jesus's lordship mean for his disciples? That old hymn Paul sang with the Philippians suggests an answer. By their baptism, servants who kneel before Jesus as Lord are incorporated into Christ himself. We are taken into his life, into his death, and into his resurrection.[14] I want you to be clear on this, because the church gets terribly confused. Jesus is not a dead hero whom we occasionally assemble to venerate. I assure you, there was nothing heroic in crucifixion. And Jesus is not simply a wise teacher, like Confucius or Socrates or

---

9. Matthew 28:18.
10. Romans 14:8 ESV.
11. Luke 17:9–10.
12. Cited by Thomas A. Langford, "The Minister as Scholar," *DDSR* 39 (1974): 135–41.
13. Matthew 22:32 // Mark 12:27 // Luke 20:38.
14. Romans 6:3–11.

the Buddha, who merely offers a new way of looking at life. To the contrary: Jesus *is* God's wisdom.[15] Jesus *is* life.[16] *Designed by God, Jesus is a new way of being human.* The new life that God breathed into Jesus in Good Friday's tomb is now *our* life. In Genesis, you will remember, Adam disobeyed God in a catastrophic attempt to be like God.[17] When he did that, Adam drew a curse upon creation, and all humanity after him. The last name of everyone in this room is Adam. Why? Because we were sucked into Adam's sin. We have fallen short of the glory God intended for us, and we die.[18] Unlike Adam, Jesus showed himself to be the very form of God precisely by not exploiting it. Instead of grasping for Godhood, Jesus emptied himself of his inherent divinity and humbled himself to the point of obedience unto death on a cross. For his supreme obedience, God has exalted Jesus for eternal glory. The followers of that Lord grow into God's glory by being conformed to Christ's own obedient, self-giving life.[19] To use a clumsy metaphor to make my point: through the Lord Jesus, God has reformatted humanity's hard drive after our operating system had crashed.

That means we are no longer our own, to live as we please.[20] The fact is, we never were. That is a delusion, based on our blind sense of independence from God: our sinful determination to go it alone, as though we were our own creator. No. We are creatures: weak, vulnerable, enslaved to powers beyond our control. The difference Christ the Lord makes in our lives is that we are no longer imprisoned by sin. Christ has released us from sin to serve a different Lord: himself.[21]

This could not possibly be more personal, and in Philippians Paul gets personal to make the point. I'll paraphrase what he says:

> If anyone thinks he has reason to trust in himself and achievements, I have more reason than them all. I was circumcised the eighth day, of the people of Israel, of the tribe of Benjamin, a Hebrew born of Hebrews; as to the law, a pious Pharisee; as to my zeal, a persecutor of the church. In everything the law requires I've been blameless. I am a 4.0 Jew. Nobody can touch me. But get this: everything I used to think counted for something—my religiosity, my competence—all these things, by comparison with living in

---

15. 1 Corinthians 1:24, 30.
16. John 11:25.
17. Genesis 3:5–7.
18. Romans 5:12–19; 1 Cor 15:20–22.
19. 2 Corinthians 3:18.
20. 1 Corinthians 6:19.
21. Romans 6:16–18.

Christ, I now regard as nothing. In order to know Christ Jesus as my Lord, I have lost everything; and it doesn't matter, because now I see that it was all crap. This alone matters: that I may live in Christ Jesus and the power of his resurrection, and may share in his sufferings, which conform me to his death; because only so may I be raised from death like Christ himself. Don't get me wrong: I don't believe I have reached this perfection. But I'll tell you what: I strain for it. I want to grasp Christ—because Christ Jesus has already grasped me.[22]

Paul puts his finger on the fundamental paradox of the Christian life: "Make me a captive, Lord, and then I shall be free."[23]

To know and be known by the Lord Jesus, are you ready to reconsider everything that has defined your life as horse turds?

What does discipleship look like in the real world where we live, when viewed through the lens of the gospel? According to Matthew, Jesus told his disciples a parable on the eve of Palm Sunday. I'll retell it to you in Clarence Jordan's Cotton Patch Version:

> When the son of man starts his revolution with all his band around him, then he will assume authority. And all the nations will be assembled before him, and he will sort them out, like a farmer separating his cows from his hogs, penning the cows on the right and the hogs on the left. Then the Leader of [God's] Movement will say to those on his right, "Come, you pride of my Father, share in the Movement that was set up for you since creation; for I was hungry and you shared your food with me; I was thirsty and you shared your water with me; I was a stranger and you welcomed me, ragged and you clothed me, sick and you nursed me; I was in jail, and you stood by me." Then the people of justice will answer, "Sir, when did we see you hungry and share our food, or thirsty and share our water? When did we see you a stranger and welcome you, or ragged and clothe you? When did we see you sick or in jail, and stand by you?" And the Leader of the Movement will reply, "When you did it to one of these humblest brothers [or sisters] of mine, you did it to me."
>
> Then he will say to those on his left, "Get away from me, you fallen skunks, and into the flaming hell reserved for the Confuser and his crowd.

---

22. Philippians 3:4b–12.
23. The opening verse of the hymn (1890) by Scottish pastor George Matheson (1842–1906).

For I was hungry and you shared nothing with me; I was thirsty and you gave me no water; I was a stranger and you didn't welcome me, ragged and you didn't clothe me, sick and in jail, and you didn't stand by me." Then these too will ask, "Sir, when did we see you hungry or thirsty or ragged or sick or in jail, and do nothing about your needs?" Then he'll answer, "When you failed one of these humblest people, you failed me." These will take an awful beating, while the just ones will have the joy of living.[24]

Absence makes the heart grow fonder. That's what they say.[25] Sometimes that may be true. Other times, not so much. Absence can make the heart grow *forgetful*. While Jesus is away, before he comes again, it's very easy to forget what he looked like. Instead of remembering Jesus, over time we begin thinking about our *notion* of Jesus. Nowhere does this happen more often, with the consistency of a dreary November rain, than in theological schools like the one where I teach. Too rarely on our campus do we listen to God, or talk to God. We become obsessed with talking *about* God. Talk, talk, talk, talk, talk about God. After a while it becomes awfully tedious. We talk so much about God that we probably put God to sleep. And here's the trap we lay for ourselves—not just in Princeton but also in Nashville and everywhere else: we reduce our Lord to a set of ideas, vague abstractions behind which we can hide while carefully avoiding any confrontation with the Lord himself. We do the same thing with big ideas like "charity for the world," which is a lot safer and happier to deal with than a real human being sitting beside us who can be dirty and ornery and hard to live with. It's the same thing Linus said to his crabby sister Lucy: "I love mankind . . . It's people I can't stand."[26] Same with Jesus. The temptation is to shrink him into a syrupy cliché: "All you need is love."[27] Over time we forget what Jesus really looked and sounded like and substitute our fondest, Barcalounger beliefs about what Jesus ought to look like. Guess what? We convince ourselves that he looks remarkably like us. We

---

24. Matthew 25:31–46; Clarence Jordan, *The Cotton Patch Version of Matthew and John: Including the Gospel of Matthew (Except for the "Begat" Verses) and the First Eight Chapters of the Gospel of John* (New York: Association, 1970), 84–85.

25. Specifically, Sextus Propertius (c. 45–15 BCE): *Semper in absentes felicior aestus amantes* (*Elegies* 2; §33).

26. Charles M. Schulz, *Peanuts* (United Features Syndicate, November 12, 1959).

27. From the song by John Lennon and Paul McCartney, "All You Need Is Love," track 5 on side B of *Magical Mystery Tour*, Parlophone Records, 1967, LP album. A child of the '60s, I love The Beatles' music, but theologians they weren't.

assure ourselves that when Jesus comes back we will immediately recognize him, because he'll look and sound just like us.

A crucial aspect of this parable that's easy to overlook is that no one—not one cow, not a single hog—*no one* recognizes Jesus when he returns. Both Elsie and Porky say the very same thing: "Sir, when did we see you?" The implication couldn't be clearer. "Why, Lord, if we had known it was *you*, we would have bent over backwards to treat you splendidly. We would have measured our mercy to guarantee you would be certain to recognize and reward us." That's not how a disciple responds to the Lord Jesus. That's how a child acts in front of Santa Claus. It's basically self-centered. In this parable Jesus is saying that, when he returns, he will invade our little islands of self-absorption and remind us of what he really looks like, which is not how our fuzzy memories and self-preoccupations have remembered him.

What does Jesus really look like? In this parable he looks hungry. Thirsty. He looks like a stranger: not one of "our kind of people." He's naked, sick, in jail. Jesus is "one of the least." In all these descriptions the common denominator is desperate need, utter vulnerability, with a heap of shame. It's one thing to donate a basket at Christmas or, on a larger scale, to apportion a congregation's offering to a presbytery's committee on benevolences. These are laudable things; not for a moment would I put down any of them. But let's be honest: these are very safe, very respectable gestures. The church or the presbytery has screened the families and the agencies to weed out the unworthy cases. But what this world judges as *worthy* is not yet what Jesus considers the *least*.

A student studying for ministry was serving in a church that had what they called an Emergency Fund. There was about $100 in it. The committee's chairman told the student that she could dispense the money at her discretion subject to the conditions. She said, "What are the conditions?" He said, "You're not to give the money to anyone who is in need because of laziness, drug abuse, or poor management." She said, "What else is there?" So what happened to the money? She said, "Beats me. As far as I know, the church still has it."[28]

If we feed a real person, we have to let go of our prejudices about why that person is hungry when we are not. If we offer hospitality to a resident alien, we have to look ourselves in the mirror and realize that, before God, *we are all aliens*. In ancient Israel the sojourner, the resident alien, has a claim on Israel, because the Israelites remembered that they too were once exiles.[29] If we nurse

---

28. Paraphrased from Fred B. Craddock, *Craddock Stories*, ed. Mike Grave and Richard F. Ward (St. Louis: Chalice, 2001), 48.

29. Leviticus 19:33–34; Deut 10:17–19.

the sick, we risk catching whatever they are suffering. If we visit prisoners, we risk identification with them and what they did to end up there. There's no way around it. Jesus makes the reason clear: he identifies *himself* with the prisoner, the sick, the hungry, the stranger. "When you did it to one of these humblest brothers or sisters of mine, you were doing it to *me*." For them, as for us, he gave his life by suffering the greatest ostracism that he could: on a cross. "He had no beauty or comeliness that any should desire him. He was one from whom people turned their faces. A man of sorrows, acquainted with grief."[30] Jesus is the ultimate stranger. Easter is God's way of telling us: "This Jesus, this stranger, got me right. He alone understood what I'm up to in your tormented world. In the strangest way possible—raising him from death—I've made sure that he won't leave you alone. And he won't go away. This stranger will keep coming back to you in the strangers who surround you. When I finally ring down history's curtain, then you will see Jesus for who he really is. And your masks will fall from your faces, and you will finally see yourselves for who you really are."

We are so easily confused; it is truly pathetic. We have snookered ourselves into thinking that discipleship requires heroic measures: the flash and celebrity this world celebrates. Matthew's little church struggled with the same kind of misapprehension, which is why the evangelist reminded his parishioners of something else Jesus said:

> Not everyone who glibly calls me "Lord, Lord," shall enter the God Movement, but [the one] who does the will of my spiritual Father. The time will come when many people will gather around and say, "L–o–ord, oh Lo–o–ord, *we* sure did preach in your name, didn't we? And in your name *we* gave the devil a run for his money, didn't we?" Then I'll admit right in front of everybody, "I've never known you. Get away from me, you wicked religious racketeers."[31]

Like you, in these years of angry babble within our country, I've taken a hard look at America. Most of what I've seen breaks my heart. It's not principled differences of opinion that bother me. Informed, reasonable people will always disagree over the best means to a common good. What distresses me is that a sense of *common* good has gone AWOL, and into its place has

---

30. Isaiah 53:2–3.
31. Matthew 7:21–23, as paraphrased by Jordan, *Cotton Patch Version of Matthew and John*, 37.

slipped never-ending, narcissistic, anxious, murderous selfishness: on Capitol Hill, on Wall Street, on Main Street. "You leave *me* alone. Keep your filthy hands off *my* health insurance. Don't you raise *my* taxes. Don't you touch *my* gun." "*Me me me me me.*" Folks, we haven't funded our own Medicare with our own money. Our Medicare is a gift our parents and grandparents gave to us. And we would be spending a lot less on health care with a lot fewer guns. Where did Christians, of all people, get the idea that everything is reducible to *me*, based on what *I* want and *I've* done? Have we entirely forgotten that, at our baptism, God embraced us, promising never to let us go, out of a generous mercy when we couldn't do a thing for ourselves?[32] When Jesus gives himself to us at the Lord's Supper,[33] we are not playacting pious theater. We are being nourished to leave the table and feed other strangers. If the church is to reclaim its unique identity as the Body of Christ, then it will take Christ to heal our hearts' dis-ease: a heart that operates with both the diastolic and systolic, taking in the gospel's fresh oxygen, so that it can pump life back into the world around us.

Again I ask you: Do you want to study Holy Scripture that will start studying *you*?

Christ has been crucified, raised from death, and exalted by God to the highest level, not just for Christians, *but for the entire world*: "So that at the name of Jesus *every* knee should bow, in heaven and on earth and under the earth; and *every* tongue confess that Jesus Christ is Lord, to the glory of God the Father."[34] God has made Christ Lord of the cosmos—Lord over all people, all things, all of creation, without exception.[35] The Lord's victory will finally be total, and it will not be complete until the cosmos is judged and reconciled to God, and made subject to its Creator.[36] The power Jesus now enjoys in heaven is being exerted right now in this world, a world not yet fully redeemed, against all the spiritual and political authorities that rule in this present evil age.[37]

Jesus and Paul talked about Satan.[38] I don't know if you believe in Satan. But whether you do or don't, can you look, not just at our country, but at the world around us and tell me, truthfully, that you don't see hell?

---

32. Romans 5:6–8.
33. Matthew 26:26–28 // Mark 14:22–24 // Luke 22:19–20.
34. Philippians 2:10–11.
35. Ephesians 1:20–23; Rev 5:12; 12:10.
36. 1 Corinthians 15:23–28.
37. John 16:33; 1 Cor 2:6, 8; Gal 1:4.
38. Matthew 4:10; 12:26 // Mark 3:26 // Luke 11:18; Luke 10:18; 22:31; 1 Cor 5:4–5; 7:5; 2 Cor 2:11; 11:14; 12:7; 1 Thess 2:18.

What do you see?

I'll tell you what I see. I see a world blinded by mammon and Caesar: the invasive claims of wealth, privilege, and imperial power.[39] The source of that blindness runs deeper than any particular culture or country. I might as well ascribe the blindness to Satan; it's as good as any explanation and would make the devil squirm to be taken seriously. Satan twists political authority, vested in particular governments, to inflame nationalistic fervor, so that all citizens place their fancied hopes first in *their* nation. Satan whispers in our ears—no matter where we live—that our nation's virtues are superior to everyone else's. Our nation's sovereignty is absolute; and because every nation on earth feels the same, Satan has a heyday stirring up self-centeredness, prejudice against others, constant strife, and murderous bigotry. Our nation's prestige and security become the primary consideration by which every citizen's actions are justified or damned. Listen to what Paul Minear wrote right after World War II:

> The climate of political opinion is so rigged by propaganda machines that people nervously avoid any deviation from the lock step. Thoughts and feelings, as well as behavior, are policed by invisible censors. When any danger to the present fortunes of the political unit appears on the horizon, it is accepted and heralded as a major crisis. The crisis, in turn, justifies the overruling of our duties to God and to our neighbor by the interests of the nation. In the name of that nation promises are given to the populace that are too rosy ever to be kept, and threats of disaster too dire to be executed. Allegiance narrower or wider than allegiance to the nation is submerged by [that] allegiance. And what holds true for the nation holds true, also, for [all] other types of earthly authority. There is no form of communal organization from which Satan's activity is excluded.[40]

---

39. That's what I said in 2011. Over a dozen years later that diabolical invasion has spread even more deeply and turned more toxic. Again I must absorb the breadth of perspective of a fifteen-year-old Jewish girl, locked with her family in an Amsterdam attic, who wrote in the early 1940s: "In spite of everything I still believe that people are really good at heart. I simply can't build up my hopes on a foundation consisting of confusion, misery, and death. I see the world gradually being turned into a wilderness, I hear the ever approaching thunder, which will destroy us too, I can feel the sufferings of millions and yet, if I look up into the heavens, I think that it will all come right, that this cruelty too will end, and that peace and tranquility will return again" (Anne Frank, *The Diary of a Young Girl*, translated by Barbara Mooyart-Doubleday, introduction by Eleanor Roosevelt, The Modern Library [New York: Random House, 1952], 278).

40. Paul S. Minear, *The Kingdom and the Power: An Exposition of the New Testament Gospel* (Philadelphia: Westminster, 1950; repr. Louisville: Westminster John Knox, 2004), 96-97.

Jesus Christ Is Lord

In order for hell to thrive on earth, human beings have to cooperate with that bastard lord, Satan. Again, pay attention to Minear's diagnosis:

> [Human beings] must fear the penalties and hope for the rewards that the group has at its disposal. They must identify their own pride, virtue, and rights with those of the group. They must view their personal lives within the horizons common to the herd, without challenging those horizons by their abnormality. They must strive for personal superiority according to the rules of the game, content with the limits set to their ambition and proud of their progress from the bottom of the ladder. Thus they turn social conventions into chains, making them inviolable laws of an invisible authority, although they are presumably dealing only with [human beings].[41]

Mark my words: when you reach the book of Revelation, you will find that John's analysis matches exactly what Minear was saying in 1950 and can as easily be said this year: the displacement of God's sovereignty with that we have invested in our nations and, finally, in ourselves.[42]

It does not have to be so. Christ the Lord has broken those chains, and those disciples freed and propelled by his Holy Spirit find the courage to refuse bending their knees to devilish extortions of power. I'm not talking about Fantasyland. When push has come to shove, in its most faithful moments the church has remembered and claimed the gospel and has pushed back against humanity's self-arrogation of a power that belongs only to its Lord Jesus. If you want an example, let me take you back to Barmen, Germany, in 1934, where a small group of Reformed and Lutheran pastors and laity issued a full-throated indictment of Hitler's Third Reich. I quote from their declaration:

> The impregnable foundation of the German Evangelical Church is the Gospel of Jesus Christ, as it is revealed in Holy Scripture and came again to the light in the creeds of the Reformation. In this way the authorities, which the church needs for her mission, are defined and limited. . . .
>
> Jesus Christ, as he is identified to us in the Holy Scripture, is the one Word of God, whom we are to hear, with whom we are to trust and obey in this life and in death. We repudiate the false teaching that the church can and must recognize yet other happenings and powers, images and truths as

---

41. Minear, *Kingdom and the Power*, 97.
42. Revelation 2:13–29; 3:15–22; 13:1–18; 18:1–24.

divine revelation alongside the one Word of God, as a source of her preaching. . . . Just as Jesus Christ is the pledge of the forgiveness of all our sins, just so—and with the same earnestness—is he also God's mighty claim on our whole life; in him we encounter a joyous liberation from the godless claims of this world to free and thankful service to his creatures. We repudiate the false teaching that there are areas of our life in which we belong not to Jesus Christ but another lord, areas in which we do not need justification and sanctification through him. . . . The Christian church is the community of brethren in which Jesus Christ presently works in the world and sacraments through the Holy Spirit. . . . We repudiate the false teaching that the church can turn over the form of her message and ordinances at will or according to some dominant ideological political convictions.

Verbum Dei manet in aeternum. [The word of God endures throughout eternity.][43]

Ladies and gentlemen, place your bets. My bet is that's the truth. Jesus Christ *is* Lord. Burning away this world's fears and fury, *that* confession of faith is finally the one true thing.

What do you bet?

---

43. Quoted in John H. Leith, ed., *Creeds of the Church: A Reader in Christian Doctrine from the Bible to the Present* (Atlanta: John Knox, 1982), 518, 520–21, 522.

Acknowledgments

THE AUTHOR AND PUBLISHER ARE GRATEFUL to the following publishers and copyright holders.

Abingdon Press for kind permission to reprint chapter 1, originally published under the title "Theology, New Testament," in *The New Interpreter's Dictionary of the Bible*, ed. Katherine Doob Sakenfeld, vol. 5 (Nashville: Abingdon, 2009), 556–60, © 2009 by Abingdon Press; and chapter 12, originally published under the title "*Ave Maria, Gratia Plena*: An Exemplar of Grace in the New Testament," in *Grace upon Grace: Essays in Honor of Thomas A. Langford*, ed. Robert K. Johnston, L. Gregory Jones, and Jonathan R. Wilson (Nashville: Abingdon, 1999), 33–40, © 1999 by Abingdon Press. All rights reserved.

Bloomsbury Publishing PLC for kind permission to reprint chapter 8, originally published under the title "Sin in the Synoptics" in *The T&T Clark Companion to the Doctrine of Sin*, ed. Keith L. Johnson and David Lauber (London: T&T Clark/Continuum, 2016), 61–78, © 2016 by Bloomsbury Publishing PLC; and chapter 13, originally published under the title "The Synoptic Gospels and Acts" in *The T&T Clark Handbook of Ecclesiology*, ed. Kimlyn J. Bender and D. Stephen Long (London: T&T Clark/Continuum, 2020), 24–38, © 2020 by Bloomsbury Publishing PLC. All rights reserved.

Brill Publishing for kind permission to reprint earlier versions of chapter 6, "Whose Kingdom? Whose Power? Whose Glory?," originally published in *Horizons in Biblical Theology* 36 (2014): 1–20, © 2014 by Koninklijke Brill NV, Leiden, The Netherlands; and chapter 14, "The Johannine Epistles and the Question of Early Catholicism," originally published in *Novum Testamentum* 28 (1986): 131–58, © 1986 by Koninklijke Brill NV, Leiden, The Netherlands. All rights reserved.

Wm. B. Eerdmans Publishers for kind permission to reprint chapter 7, "God's Promise for Humanity in the New Testament," originally published in *God and Human Dignity*, ed. R. Kendall Soulen and Linda Woodhead (Grand Rapids: Eerdmans, 2006), 179–95, © 2006 by Wm. B. Eerdmans Publishers. All rights reserved.

ACKNOWLEDGMENTS

The editors of *The Christian Century* for kind permission to reprint chapter 23, "The Man in Black," revised from "The Man in Black: Johnny Cash (1932–2003)," *The Christian Century* 120, no. 20 (October 4, 2003): 8–9, © 2003 by The Christian Century Foundation; "Man in Black," review of the motion picture *Walk the Line*, directed by James Mangold (2005), *The Christian Century* 122, no. 26 (December 27, 2005): 36–37, © 2005 by The Christian Century Foundation; and chapter 25, under the title "Unexpected Grief: Elegy for a Border Collie," in *The Christian Century* 128, no. 15 (July 26, 2011): 12–13, © 2011 by The Christian Century Foundation. All rights reserved.

Princeton Theological Seminary for kind permission to reprint earlier versions of chapter 2, "Biblical Theology Revisited: An Internal Debate," originally published in *The Princeton Seminary Bulletin* n.s. 29 (2008): 107–29, © 2008 by Princeton Theological Seminary; chapter 3, "Remembering Otto Piper," originally published in *The Princeton Seminary Bulletin* n.s. 26 (2005): 310–27, © 2005 by Princeton Theological Seminary; chapter 4, "Exegesis as Prayer," originally published in *The Princeton Seminary Bulletin* n.s. 23 (2002): 131–45, © 2002 by Princeton Theological Seminary; chapter 27, "Return of the Double-Minded," originally published in *The Princeton Seminary Bulletin* n.s. 22 (2001): 85–87, © 2001 by Princeton Theological Seminary; and chapter 29, "Where Do You Want to Eat?," originally published in *The Princeton Seminary Bulletin* n.s. 26 (2005): 299–303, © 2005 by Princeton Theological Seminary. All rights reserved.

SAGE Publications for kind permission to reprint earlier versions of chapter 9, "Shouting at the Legally Deaf: Sin's Punishment in the Gospels," originally published in *Interpretation: A Journal of Bible and Theology* 68 (2015): 311–22, © 2015 by SAGE Publications, https://doi.org/10.1177/002096431557820; chapter 15, "Christian Ministry in Johannine Perspective," originally published in *Interpretation: A Journal of Bible and Theology* 44 (1990): 29–41, © 1990 by SAGE Publications, https://doi.org/10.1177/002096438904400104; and chapter 19, "Journeying through Scripture with the Lectionary's Map," originally published in *Interpretation: A Journal of Bible and Theology* 56 (2002): 59–72, © 2002 by SAGE Publications, https://doi.org/10.1177/002096430005600106. All rights reserved.

SAGE Publications for kind permission to reprint earlier versions of chapter 5, "Short Shrift Made Once More," originally published in *Theology Today* 57 (2000): 386–94, © 2000 by SAGE Publications, https://doi.org/10.1177/004057360005700307; chapter 16, originally published under the title "*For the Life of the World*: Toward an Appraisal of Its Use of Scripture" in *Theology Today* 78 (2022): 375–84, © 2022 by SAGE Publications, https://doi

.org/10.1177/00405736211048802; chapter 18, originally published under the title "Critic's Corner: Revisiting the King James Bible" in *Theology Today* 61 (2004): 347–54, © 2004 by SAGE Publications, https://doi.org/10.1177/004057360406100306; chapter 21, originally published under the title "Critic's Corner: A Tale of Two Pities" in *Theology Today* 61 (2004): 217–21, © 2004 by SAGE Publications, https://doi.org/10.1177/004057360406100207; chapter 22, originally published under the title "Editorial: Three" in *Theology Today* 62 (2005): 147–53, © 2005 by SAGE Publications, https://doi.org/10.1177/004057360506200201; and chapter 24, originally published under the title "Editorial: A Laugh in the Dark" in *Theology Today* 60 (2003): 149–53, © 2003 by SAGE Publications, https://doi.org/10.1177/004057360306000201. All rights reserved.

The Society of Biblical Literature for kind permission to reprint an earlier version of chapter 10, "Pauline Perspectives on Death in Romans 5–8," originally published in *Journal of Biblical Literature* 103 (1984): 413–33, © 1984 by the Society of Biblical Literature. All rights reserved.

Westminster John Knox Press for kind permission to reprint an earlier version of chapter 11, "The Persistence of the Wounds," originally published in *Lament: Recovering Practices of Lament in Pulpit, Pew, and Public Square*, ed. Sally A. Brown and Patrick D. Miller (Louisville: Westminster John Knox, 2005), 47–58, © 2005 by Westminster John Knox Press. All rights reserved.

Wipf & Stock Publishers for kind permission to reprint chapter 17, originally published under the title "An Open Letter on a Wide-Open Subject" in *Guide Me into Your Truth: Essays in Honor of Dennis T. Olson*, ed. Rolf A. Jacobson, Jacqueline E. Lapsley, and Kristen J. Wendland (Eugene, OR: Wipf & Stock, 2023), 167–74, © 2023 by Wipf & Stock Publishers. www.wipfandstock.com. All rights reserved.

The image of Otto A. Piper, photographed by Ann Meuer, digitized by Brian Shetler, and reproduced in chapter 3, is printed by kind permission of Special Collections, Wright Library, Princeton Theological Seminary. All rights reserved.

Bibliography

Abbott, Walter M., and Joseph Gallagher, eds. *The Documents of Vatican II*. Chicago: Association/Follett, 1966.
Ábel, František. "'Death as the Last Enemy': Interpretation of Death in the Context of Paul's Theology." *ComViat* 58 (2016): 19–54.
Abraham, William J. *Canon and Criterion in Christian Theology: From the Fathers to Feminism*. Oxford and New York: Clarendon/Oxford University Press, 1998.
Achtemeier, Elizabeth. *The Old Testament and the Proclamation of the Gospel*. Philadelphia: Westminster, 1973.
Adam, A. K. M. *Making Sense of New Testament Theology: "Modern" Problems and Prospects*. Macon, GA: Mercer University Press, 1995.
Allen, Fred. *"All the Sincerity in Hollywood . . .": Selections from the Writings of Radio's Legendary Comedian*. Edited by Stuart Hample. Golden, CO: Fulcrum, 2001.
Allen, Horace T., Jr. *A Handbook for the Lectionary*. Philadelphia: Geneva, 1980.
Allen, Woody. *Without Feathers*. New York: Random House, 1975.
Altmann, Alexander. "'Homo Imago Dei' in Jewish and Christian Theology." *JR* 38 (1968): 235–59.
Anderson, Michael, dir. *La bottega dell'orefice* [The jeweler's shop]. 1988; Rome: Alliance Entertainment, 2010. DVD.
Anonymous. "Otto Alfred Piper 1891–1982." *PSB* n.s. 4 (1983): 52–55.
Anonymous. *The Pilgrim's Tale*. Edited by Aleksei Pentkovsky. CWS. New York and Mahwah, NJ: Paulist, 1999.
Anonymous. "Pope Stared Down Communism in His Homeland—and Won." *CBC News Online*. Religion News Service; April, 2005.
Anonymous. "Triennial Cycle." *Encyclopedia Judaica* 15 (1972): 1386–89.
Armstrong, James F., and James H. Smylie, eds. *Catalogue of Doctoral Dissertations, Princeton Theological Seminary 1944–1960*. Princeton: Princeton Theological Seminary, 1962.

Armstrong, Vic, dir. *Left Behind.* Los Angeles, CA: Entertainment One/Stoney Lake Entertainment, 2014.

Augustine of Hippo. *The City of God (De Civitate Dei, XI–XXII).* Edited by Boniface Ramsey. Translated by William Babcock. WSA 7. Hyde Park, NY: New City Press, 2013.

———. *Obras completes de San Agustín XXVI: Sermones* (6.0) 339–96. Translated by Pio De Luis. BAC 461. Madrid: Biblioteca de Autores Cristianios, 1985.

———. *The Trinity.* Edited by John E. Rotelle. Translated by Edmund Hill. WSA 5. Brooklyn, NY: New City Press, 1991.

Bailey, Lloyd R., Sr. *Biblical Perspectives on Death.* OBT. Philadelphia: Fortress, 1979.

———. "The Lectionary in Critical Perspective." *Int* 31 (1977): 139–53.

———. "Lectionary Preaching." *DDSR* 41 (1976): 25–35.

Balentine, Samuel E. *Prayer in the Hebrew Bible: The Drama of Divine-Human Dialogue.* OBT. Minneapolis: Fortress, 1993.

Balthasar, Hans Urs von. *Love Alone Is Credible.* Translated by D. C. Schindler. San Francisco: Ignatius, 2004.

Bar-Alin, Yihiel Michael. "Her Pain Prevails and Her Judgment Respected—Abortion in Judaism." *JLR* 25 (2009): 97–186.

Barclay, William. *Daily Study Bible.* 17 vols. Edinburgh: Saint Andrew Press, 1953.

Barr, James. *The Semantics of Biblical Language.* Oxford: Oxford University Press, 1961.

Barrett, Charles Kingsley. "Christocentric or Theocentric? Observations on the Theological Method of the Fourth Gospel." Pages 1–18 in Barrett, *Essays on John.*

———. *Church, Ministry, and Sacraments in the New Testament.* Grand Rapids: Eerdmans, 1985.

———. *A Commentary on the Epistle to the Romans.* HNTC. New York: Harper & Row, 1957.

———. *Essays on John.* Philadelphia: Westminster, 1982.

———. "'The Father Is Greater Than I' John 14.28: Subordinationist Christology in the New Testament." Pages 19–36 in Barrett, *Essays on John.*

———. "John 21.15–25." Pages 159–67 in Barrett, *Essays on John.*

———, ed. *The New Testament Background: Writings from Ancient Greece and the Roman Empire That Illuminate Christian Origins.* Rev. ed. San Francisco: HarperCollins, 1989.

Barrosse, Thomas. "Death and Sin in Saint Paul's Epistle to the Romans." *CBQ* 15 (1953): 438–59.

Barth, Karl. *The Doctrine of Creation: Church Dogmatics* 3.1, 3.2. Edited by Geoffrey W. Bromiley and Thomas F. Torrance. Translated by G. T. Thomson. Edinburgh: T&T Clark, 1958, 1960.

———. *The Doctrine of Reconciliation: Church Dogmatics* 4.1. Translated by Geoffrey W. Bromiley. Edinburgh: T&T Clark, 1956.

———. *Evangelical Theology*. Translated by Grover Foley. New York: Holt, Rinehart and Winston, 1963.

———. *Die kirchliche Dogmatik*. 14 vols. Zollikon: Verlag der Evangelischen Buchhandlung, 1932–70. Translated by Geoffrey W. Bromiley and Thomas F. Torrance as *Church Dogmatics*. 14 vols. Edinburgh: T&T Clark, 1936–77.

———. "The Ministry of the Community." Pages 830–901 in Barth, *The Doctrine of Reconciliation: Church Dogmatics* 3/2. Edited by Geoffrey W. Bromiley and Thomas F. Torrance. Edinburgh: T&T Clark, 1962.

———. *Römerbrief*. Bern: Baschlin, 1919. Translated by E. C. Hoskyns as *The Epistle to the Romans*. 6th ed. London: Oxford University Press, 1933.

Barton, John. *The Nature of Biblical Criticism*. Louisville: Westminster John Knox, 2007.

Bauer, Georg Lorenz. *Biblische Moral des Neuen Testaments*. 3 vols. Leipzig: Beygandfeschen Buchhandlung, 1804–5.

———. *Theologie des Alten Testaments, oder, Abriss der religiösen Begriffe der alten Hebräer*. Leipzig: Waygand, 1796. Translated into English as *The Theology of the Old Testament, or, A Biblical Sketch of the Religious Opinions of the Ancient Hebrews from the Earliest Times to the Commencement of the Christian Era*. London: Fox, 1838.

Bauerschmidt, Frederick Christian. "Order, Freedom, and Kindness: Julian of Norwich on the Edge of Modernity." *ThTod* 60 (2003): 63–81.

Baumgarten, Otto. *Die Johannesbriefe*. SNT 4. Göttingen: Vandenhoeck & Ruprecht, 1918.

Baur, Ferdinand Christian. *Die Epochen der kirchlichen Geschichtsschreibung*. Tübingen: Fues, 1852. Repr. Hildesheim: Olms, 1962.

———. *Geschichte der christlichen Kirche*. Tübingen: Fues, 1863–77.

Bearsley, Patrick J. "Mary the Perfect Disciple: A Paradigm for Mariology." *TS* 41 (1980): 461–504.

Beattie, Tina. *Rediscovering Mary: Insights from the Gospels*. Ligouri, MO: Triumph Books, 1995.

Beerbohm, Max. "A Small Boy Seeing Giants." Pages 366–74 in *The Prince of Minor Writers: The Selected Essays of Max Beerbohm*. Edited by Phillip Lopate. New York: New York Review of Books, 2015.

Benchley, Robert. "Your Boy and His Dog." Pages 94–96 in Benchley, *Chips Off the Old Benchley*. New York: Harper & Brothers, 1949.

Bergmeier, Roland. "Zum Verfasserproblem des II. und III. Johannesbriefs." *ZNW* 57 (1966): 93–100.

Best, Ernest, and Robert McLachlan Wilson, eds. *Text and Interpretation: Studies* in the New Testament Presented to Matthew Black. Cambridge and London: Cambridge University Press, 1979.

Bettenson, Henry, ed. and trans. *The Early Christian Fathers: A Selection from the Writings of the Fathers from St. Clement of Rome to St. Athanasius*. London and Oxford: Oxford University Press, 1956.

Bigsby, Christopher. Introduction to *All My Sons: A Drama in Three Acts*, by Arthur Miller. New York: Penguin, 2000.

Black, C. Clifton. "The Education of Human Wanting." Pages 248–63 in *Character and Scripture: Moral Formation, Community, and Biblical Interpretation*. Edited by William P. Brown. Grand Rapids: Eerdmans, 2002.

———. "The First, Second, and Third Letters of John." Pages 321–31 in *The New Interpreter's Bible: New Testament Survey*. Nashville: Abingdon, 2006.

———. "1, 2, and 3 John: Introduction, Commentary, and Reflections." Pages 363–469 in *The New Interpreter's Bible*. Vol. 12. Nashville: Abingdon, 1998.

———. *The Lord's Prayer*. IRUSC. Louisville: Westminster John Knox, 2018.

———. *Mark*. ANTC. Nashville: Abingdon, 2011.

———. Review of *Interpreting Scripture with the Great Tradition: Recovering the Genius of Premodern Exegesis* by Craig A. Carter. *RBL* (July 22, 2022): https://www.sblcentral.org/API/Reviews/1000331_72132.pdf.

———. *A Three-Dimensional Jesus: An Introduction to the Synoptic Gospels*. Louisville: Westminster John Knox, 2023.

———. "Trinity and Exegesis." Pages 8–34 in Black, *Reading Scripture with the Saints*. CB. Eugene, OR: Wipf & Stock, 2014.

Blackwell, Ben C. "The *Greek Life of Adam and Eve* and Romans 8:14–39: (Re-)creation and Glory." Pages 108–14 in Blackwell, Goodrich, and Matson, *Reading Romans in Context*.

———. "Immortal Glory and the Problem of Death in Romans 3.23." *JSNT* 32 (2010): 285–308.

Blackwell, Ben C., John K. Goodrich, and Jason Matson, eds. *Reading Romans in Context: Paul and Second Temple Judaism*. Grand Rapids: Zondervan, 2015.

Blazen, Ivan Thomas. "Death and Sin according to Romans 6:1–14 and Related Texts: An Exegetical-Theological Study with a Critique of Views." PhD diss., Princeton Theological Seminary, 1979.

Bloom, Anthony. *School for Prayer*. London: Darton, Longman & Todd, 1970.

Blumenthal, David R. "The Place of Faith and Grace in Judaism." Pages 104–14 in *A Time to Speak: The Evangelical-Jewish Encounter*. Edited by A. James Rudin and Marvin R. Wilson. Grand Rapids: Eerdmans, 1987.

Boccaccini, Gabriele, and Carlos A. Segovia, eds. *Paul the Jew: Rereading the Apostle as a Figure of Second Temple Judaism*. Minneapolis: Augsburg Fortress, 2016.

Bogart, John. *Orthodox and Heretical Perfectionism in the Johannine Community as Evident in the First Epistle of John*. SBLDS 33. Missoula, MT: Scholars, 1977.

Boismard, Marie-Emile. "The First Epistle of John and the Writings of Qumran." Pages 156–65 in *John and Qumran*. Edited by James H. Charlesworth. London: Chapman, 1972.

Bonhoeffer, Dietrich. *Christ the Center*. Translated by John Bowden. New York: Harper & Row, 1978.

———. *Creation and Fall: A Theological Exposition of Genesis 1–3*. Edited by John W. de Gruchy. Translated by Martin Rütter and Ilse Tout. DBW 3. Minneapolis: Fortress, 1997.

———. *Creation and Fall: A Theological Interpretation of Genesis 1–3; Temptation*. Translated by John C. Fletcher. London and New York: SCM/Macmillan, 1959.

———. *Letters and Papers from Prison*. Edited and translated by Isabel Best, John de Gruchy, Lisa E. Dahill, Reinhard Krauss, and Nancy Lukens. DBW 8. Minneapolis: Fortress, 2010.

———. *Life Together*. DBW 5. Edited by Gerhard Ludwig Müller, Albrecht Schönherr, and Geffrey B. Kelly. Translated by Daniel W. Bloesch. Minneapolis: Fortress, 1996.

———. "Vergegenwärtigung neutestamentlicher Texte." Pages 303–24 in Bonhoeffer, *Gesammelte Schriften*. Vol. 3: *Theologie-Gemeinde: Vorlesungen, Briefe, Gespräche*. Edited by Eberhard Bethge. Munich: Kaiser, 1960.

———. *The Way to Freedom: Letters, Lectures and Notes 1935–1939 from the Collected Works of Dietrich Bonhoeffer*. Vol. 2. Edited and translated by Edwin H. Robertson and John Bowden. London: Collins, 1966.

Bonsirven, Joseph. *Théologie du Nouveau Testament*. Paris: Aubier, 1951. Translated by S. F. L. Tye as *Theology of the New Testament*. London: Burns & Oates, 1963.

The Book of Common Prayer according to the Use of the Episcopal Church. New York: Church Publishing, 2007.

The Book of Common Prayer and Administration of the Sacraments and Other Rites and Ceremonies of the Church. New York: Seabury, 1953.

The Book of Common Prayer and Administration of the Sacraments and Other Rites and Ceremonies of the Church. N.p.: Seabury, 1979.

Borchert, Gerald L. "This Man—Otto Piper of Princeton." *The Seminarian* 12. May 4, 1962: 3–4.

Boring, M. Eugene. "The Gospel of Matthew: Introduction, Commentary, and Reflections." *NIB* 8 (1995): 87–505.

Bornkamm, Günther. *Paul*. Translated by D. M. G. Stalker. London: Hodder and Stoughton, 1971.

Børresen, Kari Elisabeth, ed. *The Image of God: Gender Models in Judaeo-Christian Tradition*. Minneapolis: Fortress, 1995.

Bottum, Joseph. "John Paul the Great." *The Weekly Standard*. April 18, 2005: 1–2.

Boulding, Maria, ed. *A Touch of God: Eight Monastic Journeys*. London: SPCK; Still River, MA: St. Bede's Publications, 1982.

Bousset, Wilhelm. *Kyrios Christos: Geschichte des Christusglaubens von den Anfängen des Christentums bis Irenaeus*. Göttingen: Vandenhoeck & Ruprecht, 1913. Translated by John E. Steely as *Kyrios Christos: A History of the Belief in Christ from the Beginnings of Christianity to Irenaeus*. Nashville: Abingdon, 1970.

Bowen, C. A., ed. *The Cokesbury Worship Hymnal*. Baltimore: Methodist Publishing House, 1938.

Braaten, Carl E. "Scripture, Church, and Dogma: An Essay on Theological Method." *Int* 50 (1996): 142–55.

Braaten, Carl E., and Robert W. Jenson, eds. *Christian Dogmatics*. Philadelphia: Fortress, 1984.

Bradbury, Ray. *Dogs Think That Every Day Is Christmas*. Kaysville, UT: Gibbs Smith, 1997.

Brett, Mark G. "Canonical Criticism and Old Testament Theology." Pages 63–85 in *Text in Context: Essays by Members of the Society for Old Testament Study*. Edited by A. D. H. Mayes. Oxford: Oxford University Press, 2000.

Brokaw, Tom. *The Greatest Generation*. New York: Random House, 1998.

Brown, Charles E. "'The Last Enemy Is Death': Paul and the Pastoral Task." *Int* 43 (1989): 380–92.

Brown, David. *Trinity and Imagination: Revelation and Change*. Oxford: Oxford University Press, 1999.

Brown, Raymond E. *The Birth of the Messiah: A Commentary on the Infancy Narratives in the Gospels of Matthew and Luke*. New updated ed. ABRL. New York: Doubleday, 1993.

———. *The Churches the Apostles Left Behind*. New York: Paulist, 1984.

———. *The Community of the Beloved Disciple: The Life, Loves, and Hates of an Individual Church in New Testament Times*. New York: Paulist, 1979.

———. *The Death of the Messiah: From Gethsemane to the Grave*. 2 vols. ABRL. New York and London: Doubleday, 1994.

———. "*Episkopē* and *Episkopos*: The New Testament Evidence." *TS* 41 (1980): 322–38.

———. *The Epistles of John: Translated with Introduction, Notes, and Commentary*. AB 30. Garden City, NY: Doubleday, 1982.

———. *The Gospel according to John: Introduction, Translation and Notes*. AB 29. Garden City, NY: Doubleday, 1966.

———. *An Introduction to the New Testament.* ABRL. Garden City, NY: Doubleday, 1997.

———. "The Pater Noster as Eschatological Prayer." *TS* 22 (1961): 175–208.

———. "The Qumran Scrolls and the Johannine Gospel and Epistles." *CBQ* 17 (1955): 403–19, 559–74.

———. "The Relationship to the Fourth Gospel Shared by the Author of 1 John and by His Opponents." Pages 57–68 in *Text and Interpretation: Studies in the New Testament Presented to Matthew Black.* Edited by Ernest Best and Robert McLachlan Wilson. Cambridge and London: Cambridge University Press, 1979.

———. "The Roles of Women in the Fourth Gospel." *TS* 36 (1975): 688–99.

Brown, Raymond E., Karl Paul Donfried, Joseph A. Fitzmyer, and John Reumann, eds. *Mary in the New Testament.* Philadelphia: Fortress, 1978.

Brown, William P., ed. *Character and Scripture: Moral Formation, Community, and Biblical Interpretation.* Grand Rapids: Eerdmans, 2002.

Browne, Joanne Carlson, and Rebecca Parker. "For God So Loved the World?" Pages 1–30 in *Christianity, Patriarchy, and Abuse: A Feminist Critique.* Edited by Joanne Carlson Browne and Carole R. Bohn. New York: Pilgrim, 1989.

Bruce, Frederick Fyvie. "Paul on Immortality." *SJT* 24 (1971): 457–72.

Brueggemann, Walter. *Israel's Praise: Doxology against Idolatry and Ideology.* Philadelphia: Fortress, 1988.

Brueggemann, Walter, Charles B. Cousar, Beverly R. Gaventa, and James D. Newsome. *Texts for Preaching: A Lectionary Commentary Based on the NRSV.* Louisville: Westminster John Knox, 1993–95.

Brunner, Emil. *The Christian Doctrine of God.* Philadelphia: Westminster, 1950.

Bultmann, Rudolf. *Das Evangelium des Johannes.* Göttingen: Vandenhoeck & Ruprecht, 1950. Translated by G. R. Beasley-Murray, R. W. N. Hoare, and J. K. Riches as *The Gospel of John: A Commentary.* Edited by Beasley-Murray, Hoare, and Riches. Philadelphia: Westminster, 1971.

———. *Jesus.* Berlin: Deutsche Bibliothek, 1929. Translated by Louise Pettibone Smith and Erminie Huntress as *Jesus and the Word.* New York: Scribner's Sons, 1934.

———. *Jesus Christ and Mythology.* New York: Scribner's Sons, 1958.

———. *The Johannine Epistles.* Hermeneia. Philadelphia: Fortress, 1973.

———. *Primitive Christianity in Its Contemporary Setting.* New York: World, 1956.

———. "Prophecy and Fulfillment." Pages 50–75 in *Essays on Old Testament Hermeneutics.* Edited by Claus Westermann. Translated by James Luther Mays and James C. G. Greig. Richmond, VA: John Knox, 1964.

———. *Theologie des Neuen Testaments.* Tübingen: Mohr Siebeck, 1948. Translated by Kendrick Grobel as *Theology of the New Testament.* 2 vols. New York: Scribner's Sons, 1951, 1955.

Burke, David G., John F. Kutsko, and Philip H. Towner, eds. *The King James Version at 400: Assessing Its Genius as Bible Translation and Its Literary Influence*. BSNA. Atlanta: Society of Biblical Literature, 2013.

Burkert, Walter. *Ancient Mystery Cults*. Cambridge: Harvard University Press, 1987.

Bush, George W. "Address to the Nation." Office of the Press Secretary. March 19, 2003.

Byrdsong, Ricky, Dave Jackson, and Neta Jackson. *Coaching Your Kids in the Game of Life*. Grand Rapids: Bethany House, 2000.

Byrne, Robert. *The 2,548 Best Things Anybody Ever Said*. New York: Simon & Schuster, 2003.

Cahill, Lisa Sowle. "Embodying God's Image: Created, Broken, and Redeemed." Pages 55–77 in *Humanity before God: Contemporary Faces of Jewish, Christian, and Islamic Ethics*. Edited by William Schweiker, Michael A. Johnson, and Kevin Jung. Minneapolis: Fortress, 2006.

Caird, George Bradford. "John, Letters of." *IDB* 2:946–52.

———. *New Testament Theology*. Compiled and edited by L. D. Hurst. Oxford: Clarendon, 1994.

Campbell, Douglas A., ed. *The Call to Serve: Biblical and Theological Perspectives on Ministry in Honour of Bishop Penny Jamieson*. Sheffield: Sheffield Academic Press, 1996.

Campenhausen, Hans von. *Ecclesiastical Authority and Spiritual Power in the Church of the First Three Centuries*. Stanford: Stanford University Press, 1969.

Cardenal, Ernesto. *The Gospel in Solentiname*. Maryknoll, NY: Orbis, 1976.

Carnegie, Dale. *How to Win Friends and Influence People*. New York: Simon & Schuster, 1936.

Carter, Craig A. *Interpreting Scripture with the Great Tradition: Recovering the Genius of Premodern Exegesis*. Grand Rapids: Baker Academic, 2018.

Carter, Jimmy [James Earl, Jr.]. "Just War—or a Just War?" *New York Times*. March 9, 2003. https://www.nytimes.com/2003/03/09/opinion/just-war-or-a-just-war.html.

Cash, John R. (Johnny), vocalist. "A Boy Named Sue." Music and lyrics by Shel Silverstein. Track 5 on disc 2 of *Johnny Cash at San Quentin*. 1969; New York: Legacy Edition, 2006, 2 compact discs and DVD.

———, vocalist. "Flushed from the Bathroom of Your Heart." Lyrics by Jack Clement. Track 17 on disc 1 of *Johnny Cash at Folsom Prison*. 1968; New York: Legacy Edition, 2008, 2 compact discs and DVD.

———. "Folsom Prison Blues." Music and lyrics by John R. Cash. Track 5 on disc 1 of *Johnny Cash at Folsom Prison*. 1955; New York: Legacy Edition, 2008, 2 compact discs and DVD.

———, vocalist. "Greystone Chapel." Music and lyrics by Glen Sherley. Track 24 on disc 1 of *Johnny Cash at Folsom Prison*. 1968; New York: Legacy Edition, 2008, 2 compact discs and DVD.

———. "He Turned the Water into Wine." Music and lyrics by John R. Cash. Track 11 on disc 2 of *Johnny Cash at San Quentin*. 1969; New York: Legacy Edition, 2006, 2 compact discs and DVD.

———. *Johnny Cash at Folsom Prison*. 1968; New York: Legacy Edition, 2008, 2 compact discs and DVD.

———. *Johnny Cash at San Quentin*. 1969; New York: Legacy Edition, 2006, 2 compact discs and DVD.

———. *Johnny Cash with His Hot and Blue Guitar*. 1957; Memphis, Sun Records, 2002, compact disc.

———, vocalist. "The Long Black Veil." Lyrics and music by Marijohn Wilkin and Danny Dill. Track 13 on disc 1 of *Johnny Cash at Folsom Prison*. 1959; New York: Legacy Edition, 2008, 2 compact discs and DVD.

———. *Man in Black*. Grand Rapids: Zondervan 1975.

———. *My Mother's Hymn Book*. Nashville: American Recordings, 2003, compact disc.

———. "San Quentin." Music and lyrics by John R. Cash. Tracks 1 and 2 on disc 2 of *Johnny Cash at San Quentin*. 1969; New York: Legacy Edition, 2006, 2 compact discs and DVD.

———, vocalist. "25 Minutes to Go." Music and lyrics by Shel Silverstein. Track 10 on disc 1 of *Johnny Cash at Folsom Prison*. 1968; New York: Legacy Edition, 2008, 2 compact discs and DVD.

Cash, John R., with Patrick Carr. *Cash: The Autobiography of Johnny Cash*. San Francisco: HarperSanFrancisco, 1997.

Cash, Vivian, with Ann Sharpsteen. *I Walked the Line: My Life with Johnny*. New York: Scribner, 2007.

Cassidy, Ronald. "Paul's Attitude to Death in II Corinthians 5:1–10." *EvQ* 43 (1971): 210–17.

Cerfaux, Lucien. *The Christian in the Theology of St. Paul*. London: Chapman, 1967.

Chapman, Dom John. *The Spiritual Letters of Dom John Chapman*. Edited by Roger Hudleston. London: Sheed and Ward, 1935.

Charlesworth, James H. *Critical Reflections on the Odes of Solomon*. JSPSup 22. Sheffield: Sheffield Academic Press, 1998.

———, ed. *John and Qumran*. London: Chapman, 1972.

Chesterton, G. K. *Generally Speaking*. New York: Dodd, Mead & Co., 1928.

Childs, Brevard S. *Biblical Theology in Crisis*. Philadelphia: Westminster, 1970.

———. *Biblical Theology of the Old and New Testaments: Theological Reflection on the Christian Bible*. Minneapolis: Fortress, 1993.

---. *The New Testament as Canon: An Introduction.* Philadelphia: Fortress, 1984.
---. "Toward Recovering Theological Exegesis." *ProEcc* (1997): 16–26.
Chittister, Joan. *The Rule of Benedict: Insights for the Ages.* SLB. New York: Crossroad, 1992.
---. *Wisdom Distilled from the Daily: Living the Rule of Saint Benedict Today.* San Francisco: HarperSanFrancisco, 1990.
Christie, Agatha. *Mrs. McGinty's Dead.* London: Collins, 1951. Repr., New York: HarperCollins, 2011.
Clark, Gordon R. *The Word* Hesed *in the Hebrew Bible.* JSOTSup 157. Sheffield: Sheffield Academic Press, 1993.
Cohen, Paula Marantz. *Of Human Kindness: What Shakespeare Teaches Us about Empathy.* New Haven and London: Yale University Press, 2021.
Cohen, Shaye J. D. *The Beginnings of Jewishness: Boundaries, Varieties, Uncertainties.* Berkeley: University of California Press, 1999.
Colson, Charles. *Justice That Restores.* Carol Stream, IL: Tyndale House, 2001.
The Common Lectionary. New York: Church Hymnal Corporation, 1983.
Conzelmann, Hans. *An Outline of the Theology of the New Testament.* New York: Harper & Row, 1969.
---. *Theologie als Schriftauslegung: Aufsätze zum Neuen Testament.* BEvTh 65. Munich: Kaiser, 1974.
---. "'Was von Anfang war.'" Pages 194–201 in *Neutestamentliche Studien für Rudolf Bultmann zu seinem siebzigsten Geburtstag am 20. August 1954.* Edited by Walther Eltester. BZNW 21. Berlin: Töpelmann, 1954; 2nd ed., 1957.
The Council in Action: Theological Reflections on the Second Vatican Council. New York: Sheed and Ward, 1963.
Cousar, Charles B. "Paul and the Death of Jesus." *Int* 52 (1998): 38–52.
Craddock, Fred B. *Craddock Stories.* Edited by Mike Grave and Richard F. Ward. St. Louis: Chalice, 2001.
---. *Preaching.* Nashville: Abingdon, 1985.
Craddock, Fred B., John H. Hayes, Carl R. Holladay, and Gene M. Tucker, eds. *Preaching the New Common Lectionary.* Nashville: Abingdon, 1984–87.
Cranfield, C. E. B. *A Critical and Exegetical Commentary on the Epistle to the Romans.* ICC. Edinburgh: T&T Clark, 1975.
Cremer, Franz Gerhard. "Der 'Heilstod' Jesu im paulinischen Verständnis von Taufe und Eucharistie: Eine Zusammenschau von Röm 6,3f und 1 Kor 11,26." *BZ* 14 (1970): 227–39.
Crouch, Carly L. "Genesis: 26–27 as a Statement of Humanity's Divine Parentage." *JTS* 61 (2010): 1–15.
Cullmann, Oscar. *Christus und die Zeit: Die urchristliche Zeit- und Geschichtsauffassung.* Zollikon-Zürich: Evangelischer, 1946. Translated by Floyd V. Filson

as *Christ and Time: The Primitive Christian Conception of Time and History*. Philadelphia: Westminster, 1950.

———. *Heil als Geschichte: Heilsgeschichtliche Existenz im Neuen Testament*. Tübingen: Mohr, 1965. Translated by Sidney G. Sowers as *Salvation in History*. New York: Harper & Row, 1967.

———. *Immortality of the Soul or Resurrection of the Dead? The Witness of the New Testament*. London: Epworth, 1958.

Culpepper, R. Alan. *The Johannine School: An Evaluation of the Johannine-School Hypothesis Based on an Investigation of the Nature of Ancient Schools*. SBLDS 26. Missoula, MT: Scholars Press, 1975.

Culpepper, R. Alan, and C. Clifton Black, eds. *Exploring the Gospel of John in Honor of D. Moody Smith*. Louisville: Westminster John Knox, 1996.

Cumont, Franz. *After Life in Roman Paganism*. New Haven: Yale University Press, 1923.

Cunningham, Mary B., and Elizabeth Theokritoff, eds. *The Cambridge Companion to Orthodox Christian Theology*. Cambridge: Cambridge University Press, 2008.

Curtis, Edward M. "Image of God (OT)." *ABD* 3:389–91.

Dahl, Nils A. "The Neglected Factor in New Testament Theology." *Reflections* 75 (1975): 5–8. Repr. in Dahl, *Jesus the Christ: The Historical Origins of Christological Doctrine*. Edited by Donald H. Juel. Minneapolis: Fortress, 1999, 153–63.

[His Holiness] the Dalai Lama [Tenzin Gyatso]. *The Art of Happiness: A Handbook for Living*. Edited by Howard C. Cutler. New York: Riverhead/Penguin/Random House, 1998.

Daniell, David. *The Bible in English: Its History and Influence*. New Haven and London: Yale University Press, 2003.

———. *William Tyndale: A Biography*. London and New Haven: Yale University Press, 2001.

Davies, Donald McKay. "The Old Ethiopic Version of Second Kings." ThD dissertation, Princeton Theological Seminary, 1944.

Davies, William David. "Light on the Ministry from the New Testament." Pages 231–45 in Davies, *Christian Origins and Judaism*. London: Darton, Longman & Todd, 1962.

———. *Paul and Rabbinic Judaism: Some Rabbinic Elements in Pauline Theology*. 4th ed. Philadelphia: Fortress, 1980.

Davies, William David, and Dale C. Allison Jr. *A Critical and Exegetical Commentary on the Gospel according to Saint Matthew*. Vol. 3. ICC. Edinburgh: T&T Clark, 1997.

De Caussade, Jean Pierre. *Abandonment: or, Absolute Surrender to Divine Providence*. New York: Benziger Brothers, [1887] 1952.

De Jonge, Marinus, ed. *L'Évangile de Jean: Sources, redaction, théologie.* BETL 44. Leuven: Leuven University Press, 1977.
De Wet, Chris L. "The Practice of Everyday Death: Thanatology and Self-Fashioning in John Chrysostom's Thirteenth Homily on Romans." *HTSTS* 71 (2015): 1–6.
De Wette, Wilhelm Martin Leberecht. *Biblische Dogmatik: Alten und Neuen Testaments: oder, kritische Darstellung der Religionslehre des Hebraismus, des Judenthums und Urchristenthums: zum Gebrauch akademischer Vorlesungen.* 3rd ed. Berlin: Reimer, 1831.
The Dead Sea Scrolls in English. Translated by Géza Vermes. Harmondsworth, Middlesex: Penguin, 1962.
Derrida, Jacques. *De la grammatologie.* Paris: Les Éditions de Minuit, 1967.
Descamps, Albert, and André de Halleux, eds. *Mélanges bibliques en hommage au R. P. Béda Rigaux.* Gembloux: Duculot, 1970.
Dibelius, Martin. *Die Formgeschichte des Evangeliums.* Tübingen: Mohr, 1919. Translated by Bertram Lee Woolf as *From Tradition to Gospel.* New York: Scribner's Sons, 1965.
Di Cesare, Mario A., ed. *George Herbert and the Seventeenth-Century Religious Poets.* New York and London: Norton, 1978.
Diezinger, Walter. "Unter Toten freigeworden: Eine Untersuchung zu Röm. iii–viii." *NovT* 5 (1962): 268–98.
Documents on the Liturgy 1963–1979: Conciliar, Papal, and Curial Texts. Collegeville, MN: Liturgical, 1982.
Dodd, Charles Harold. *According to the Scriptures: The Sub-Structure of New Testament Theology.* London: Nisbet, 1952.
———. *The Epistle of Paul to the Romans.* MNTC. New York: Harper & Brothers, 1932.
———. "The First Epistle of John and the Fourth Gospel." *BJRL* 21 (1937): 129–56.
———. *The Interpretation of the Fourth Gospel.* Cambridge: Cambridge University Press, 1953.
———. *The Johannine Epistles.* MNTC. New York: Harper & Brothers, 1946.
Donahue, John R. "Tax Collectors and Sinners: An Attempt at Identification." *CBQ* 33 (1971): 39–61.
Donfried, Karl Paul. "Ecclesiastical Authority in 2–3 John." Pages 325–33 in *L'Évangile de Jean: Sources, redaction, théologie.* Edited by Marinus de Jonge. BETL 44. Leuven: Leuven University Press, 1977.
Donin, Hiyam Halevy. *To Be a Jew: A Guide to Jewish Observance in Contemporary Life.* New York: Basic Books, 1972.
Dunn, James D. G. *Unity and Diversity in the New Testament: An Inquiry into the Character of Earliest Christianity.* London and Philadelphia: SCM/Westminster, 1977.

Dunstan, Gordon Reginald. "Editorial." Review article of *Christian Ethics*, by Otto A. Piper. *Theol* 74 (1971): 497–99.

Eastman, Susan Groves. "Christian Experience and Paul's Logic of Solidarity: The Spiral Structure of Romans 5–8." *BibAnn* 12 (2022): 233–53.

Ebeling, Gerhard. *Wort und Glaube*. Tübingen: Mohr Siebeck, 1960. Translated by James W. Leitch as *Word and Faith*. London: SCM, 1963.

Edwards, Jonathan. *A Treatise Concerning the Religious Affections*. Edited by John E. Smith. New Haven: Yale University Press, 1959.

Edwards, Ruth B. "Ministry and Church Leadership in the Gospel of John." Pages 117–41 in *The Call to Serve: Biblical and Theological Perspectives on Ministry in Honour of Bishop Penny Jamieson*. Edited by Douglas A. Campbell. Sheffield: Sheffield Academic Press, 1996.

Eichrodt, Walter. *Theologie des Alten Testaments*. 3 vols. Berlin: Evangelische Verlagsanstalt, 1948. Translated by J. A. Baker as *Theology of the Old Testament*, 2 vols. Philadelphia: Westminster, 1961, 1967.

Elliott, John H. "A Catholic Gospel: Reflections on 'Early Catholicism' in the New Testament." *CBQ* 31 (1969): 213–23.

———. *A Home for the Homeless: A Social-Scientific Criticism of 1 Peter, Its Situation and Strategy, with a New Introduction*. Minneapolis: Fortress, 1990.

[His Eminence Archbishop] Elpidophorous of America. Letter of 2020, issued from the Greek Orthodox Archdiocese of America. www.goarch.org.

Elshtain, Jean Bethke. *Sovereignty: God, State, and Self (The Gifford Lectures)*. New York: Basic Books, 2008.

Emerson, Ralph Waldo. "The American Scholar: An Oration Delivered before the Phi Beta Kappa Society at Cambridge, August 31, 1837." Pages 51–71 in Emerson, *Essays & Lectures*. Edited by Joel Porte. LOA. New York: Library of America, 1983.

Englezakis, Benedict. "Rom. 5,12–15 and the Pauline Teaching on the Lord's Death: Some Observations." *Bib* 58 (1977): 231–36.

Erickson, Richard J. "Divine Injustice? Matthew's Narrative Strategy and the Slaughter of the Innocents (Matthew 2.13–23)." *JSNT* 64 (1996): 5–27.

Esler, Philip S. *New Testament Theology: Communion and Community*. Minneapolis: Fortress, 2005.

Evans, Craig A. "Jesus' Action in the Temple: Cleansing or Portent of Destruction?" *CBQ* 51 (1989): 237–70.

Farris, Stephen. *The Hymns of Luke's Infancy Narratives: Their Origin, Meaning and Significance*. JSNTSup 9. Sheffield: JSOT, 1985.

Faskekaš, L. "Taufe als Tod in Röm. 6,3ff." *TZ* 22 (1966): 305–18.

Faw, Chalmer E. "Death and Resurrection in Paul's Letters." *JBL* 27 (1959): 291–98.

Feldmeier, Reinhard, and Hermann Spieckermann. *Der lebendige Gott: Eine Ein-*

führung in die biblische Gotteslehre. Tübingen: Mohr Siebeck, 2011. Translated by Mark E. Biddle as *God of the Living: A Biblical Theology*. Waco, TX: Baylor University Press, 2011.

———. *Menschwerdung*. TBT 2. Tübingen: Mohr Siebeck, 2018. Translated by Brian McNeil as *God Becoming Human: Incarnation in the Christian Bible*. Waco, TX: Baylor University Press, 2021.

Fergusson, David S., Karen Kilby, Ian A. McFarland, and Iain R. Torrance, eds. *The Cambridge Dictionary of Christian Theology*. Cambridge: Cambridge University Press, 2011.

Feuillet, André. "Mort du Christ et mort du Chrétien d'après les épîtres pauliniennes." *RB* 66 (1959): 481–513.

———. "Le règne de la mort et le règne de la vie (*Rom*., v. 12–21): Quelques observations sur la structure de l'Epître aux Romans." *RB* 77 (1970): 481–521.

Filson, Floyd V. "Petition and Intercession: The Biblical Doctrine of Prayer (2)." *Int* 8 (1954): 21–34.

Finkel, Asher. "The Prayer of Jesus in Matthew." Pages 131–69 in *Standing before God: Studies on Prayer in Scriptures and in Tradition*. Edited by Asher Finkel and Lawrence Frizzell. New York: KTAV, 1981.

Fitzmyer, Joseph A. *The Gospel according to Luke (x–xxiv): Introduction, Translation, and Notes*. AB 28A. Garden City, NY: Doubleday, 1985.

———. *Pauline Theology: A Brief Sketch*. Englewood Cliffs, NJ: Prentice-Hall, 1967.

Florovsky, Georges. *Bible, Church, Tradition: An Eastern Orthodox View*. Belmont, MA: Nordland, 1972.

Flusser, David. "Mary and Israel." Pages 7–16 in *Mary: Images of the Mother of Jesus in Jewish and Christian Perspective*. Edited by David Flusser, Jaroslav Pelikan, and Justin Lang. Philadelphia: Fortress, 1986.

For the Life of the World: Toward a Social Ethos of the Orthodox Church. https://www.goarch.org/social-ethos.

Ford, David F. *Barth and God's Story: Biblical Narrative and the Theological Method of Karl Barth in the "Church Dogmatics."* SIGC 27. Frankfurt am Main: Lang, 1981. Repr. Eugene, OR: Wipf & Stock, 2008.

Fortna, Robert T. "Romans 8:10 and Paul's Doctrine of the Spirit." *ATR* 41 (1959): 77–84.

Frank, Anne. *The Diary of a Young Girl*. Translated by Barbara Mooyart-Doubleday. Introduction by Eleanor Roosevelt. The Modern Library. New York: Random House, 1952.

Fretheim, Terrence E. "The Old Testament in Christian Proclamation." *WW* 3 (1983): 223–30.

———. *The Suffering of God: An Old Testament Perspective*. OBT. Philadelphia: Fortress, 1984.

Freud, Sigmund. *Civilization and Its Discontents*. Edited and translated by James Strachey. New York and London: Norton, 2010.

———. *The Future of an Illusion*. Edited and translated by James Strachey. New York and London: Norton, 1971.

———. *Three Essays on the Theory of Sexuality*. Edited and translated by James Strachey. New York: Avon, 1962.

Frymer-Kensky, Tikva. *Studies in Bible and Feminist Criticism*. Philadelphia: Jewish Publication Society, 2006.

Fuller, Reginald H. *Preaching the Lectionary: The Word of God for the Church Today*. Rev. ed. Collegeville, MN: Liturgical, 1984.

Funk, Robert W., ed. *The Gospel of Jesus: According to the Jesus Seminar*. Santa Rosa, CA: Polebridge Macmillan, 1999.

Furnish, Victor Paul. *Theology and Ethics in Paul*. 2nd ed. NTL. Louisville: Westminster John Knox, 2009.

Gabler, Johann Philipp. "On the Proper Distinction between Biblical and Dogmatic Theology and the Specific Objectives of Each." In John Sandys-Wunsch and Laurence Eldredge, "J. P. Gabler and the Distinction between Biblical and Dogmatic Theology: Translation, Commentary, and Discussion of His Originality." *SJT* 33 (1980): 133–58.

Gadamer, Hans-Georg. *Wahrheit und Methode: Grundzüge einer philosophischen Hermeneutik*. Tübingen: Mohr, 1960. Translated by Joel Weinsheimer and Donald G. Marshall as *Truth and Method*. New York: Crossroad, 1989.

García Martínez, Florentino, ed. *The Dead Sea Scrolls*. Translated by Wilfred G. E. Watson. Leiden: Brill; Grand Rapids: Eerdmans, 1996.

Gardner, Helen, ed. *The New Oxford Book of English Verse, 1250–1950*. New York: Oxford University Press, 1972.

Garfield, Simon. "Family Ties." *The Guardian*. February 5, 2006. https://www.theguardian.com/music/2006/feb/05/popandrock.johnnycash.

Gaventa, Beverly Roberts. *Mary: Glimpses of the Mother of Jesus*. SPNT. Columbia: University of South Carolina Press, 1995.

———. "Neither Height nor Depth: Discerning the Cosmology of Romans." *SJT* 64 (2011): 265–78.

Geertz, Clifford. *The Interpretation of Cultures: Selected Essays*. New York: Basic Books, 1973.

Gerstenberger, Erhard. *Theologien im Alten Testament: Pluralität und Synkretismus alttestamentlichen Gottesglaubens*. Stuttgart: Kohlhammer, 2001.

Gibran, Kahil. *The Prophet*. A Borzoi Book. New York: Knopf, 1923.

Gnilka, Joachim. *Theologie des Neuen Testaments*. HThKNTSup 5. Freiburg im Breisgau and Basel: Herder, 1994.

Godsey, John, ed. *Karl Barth's Table Talk.* SJTOP 10. Edinburgh: Oliver and Boyd, 1963.

Goppelt, Leonhard. *Apostolic and Post-Apostolic Times.* HT. New York: Harper & Row, 1970.

———. "The Existence of the Church in History according to Apostolic and Early Catholic Thought." Pages 193–209 in *Current Issues in New Testament Interpretation: Essays in Honor of Otto Piper.* Edited by William Klassen and Graydon F. Snyder. New York: Harper & Brothers, 1962.

———. *Theologie des Neuen Testaments.* 2 vols. Edited by Jürgen Roloff. Göttingen: Vandenhoeck & Ruprecht, 1975–76. Translated by John E. Alsup as *Theology of the New Testament*, 2 vols. Edited by Jürgen Roloff. Grand Rapids: Eerdmans, 1981–92.

Graef, Hilda C. *Mary: A History of Doctrine and Devotion.* London: Sheed & Ward, 1985.

Graf, F. W. "Lutherischer Neurealismus: Otto Piper, ein früher Pazifist." *LM* 8 (1988): 357–61.

Graff, Garrett M. *The Only Plane in the Sky: An Oral History of 9/11.* New York and London: Avid Reader, 2019.

Graham, Elaine L. "The 'End' of the Human or the End of the 'Human'? Human Dignity in Technological Perspective." In Soulen and Woodhead, *God and Human Dignity*, 263–81.

Grant, Marshal, with Chris Zar. *I Was There When It Happened: My Life with Johnny Cash.* Nashville: Cumberland House, 2006.

Graubard, Baruch. "The *Kaddish* Prayer." Pages 59–72 in *The Lord's Prayer and Jewish Liturgy.* Edited by Jacob J. Petuchowski and Michael Brocke. New York: Seabury, 1978.

Green, Joel B. *The Gospel of Luke.* NICNT. Grand Rapids: Eerdmans, 1997.

Green, Joel B., Thomas G. Long, Luke A. Powery, Cynthia L. Rigby, and Carolyn J. Sharp, eds. *Connections: A Lectionary Commentary for Preaching and Worship; Year B, Volume 1: Advent through Epiphany.* Louisville: Westminster John Knox, 2020.

———. *Connections A Lectionary Commentary for Preaching and Worship; Year B, Volume 2: Lent through Pentecost.* Louisville: Westminster John Knox Press, 2020.

———. *Connections: A Lectionary Commentary for Preaching and Worship; Year B, Volume 3: Season after Pentecost.* Louisville: Westminster John Knox, 2020.

———. *Connections: A Lectionary Commentary for Preaching and Worship; Year C, Volume 1: Advent through Epiphany.* Louisville: Westminster John Knox, 2018.

Green, Joel B., and Max Turner. *Between Two Horizons: Spanning New Testament Studies and Systematic Theology.* Grand Rapids: Eerdmans, 2000.

Green, Jonathan, ed. *The Book of Political Quotes*. New York: McGraw Hill, 1982.

Grimsley, Ronald, ed. *Rousseau: Religious Writings*. Oxford: Clarendon, 1970.

Grundmann, Walter. "The Teacher of Righteousness at Qumran and the Question of Justification by Faith in the Theology of the Apostle Paul." Pages 85–114 in *Paul and Qumran: Studies in New Testament Exegesis*. Edited by Jerome Murphy-O'Connor. Chicago: Priory, 1968.

Guralnick, Peter. *Sam Phillips: The Man Who Invented Rock 'n' Roll*. New York: Little, Brown & Co., 2015.

Gustafson, James M. *Ethics from a Theocentric Perspective: Theology and Ethics*. Vol. 1. Chicago: University of Chicago Press, 1982.

Gyatso, Tenzin. *See* [His Holiness] the Dalai Lama.

Hahn, Ferdinand. *Theologie des Neuen Testaments*. 2 vols. Tübingen: Mohr Siebeck, 2002.

Haleem, Muhammad Abdel. *Understanding the Qur'an: Themes and Style*. London and New York: Tauris, 1999.

Hall, Douglas John. *Professing the Faith: Christian Theology in a North American Context*. Minneapolis: Fortress, 1993.

Hals, Ronald M. *Grace and Faith in the Old Testament*. Minneapolis: Augsburg, 1980.

Hand, Thomas A. *Augustine on Prayer*. New York: Catholic Book Publishing, 1986.

Hanson, Paul D. *The People Called: The Growth of Community in the Bible*. San Francisco: Harper & Row, 1986.

Hardy, Daniel W., and David F. Ford. *Praising and Knowing God*. Philadelphia: Westminster, 1985.

Haroutunian, Joseph. Review of *God in History* by Otto A. Piper. *JBR* 7 (1939): 205–7.

Harrisville, Roy A. "God's Mercy—Tested, Promised, Done! (An Exposition of Genesis 18:20–32; Luke 11:1–13; Colossians 2:6–15)." *Int* 31 (1977): 165–78.

[Prince] Harry, The Duke of Sussex, and J. R. Moehringer. *Spare*. New York: Penguin Random House, 2023.

Hays, Richard B. *Echoes of Scripture in the Gospels*. Waco, TX: Baylor University Press, 2016.

———. *Echoes of Scripture in the Letters of Paul*. New Haven: Yale University Press, 1993.

Hegel, Georg Wilhelm Friedrich. *Elements of the Philosophy of Right*. Translated by T. M. Knox. London: Oxford University Press, 1976.

Heidegger, Martin. *Sein und Zeit*. Halle: Niemeyer, 1927.

Heidemann, W. M. "'. . . immer Fühlung mit allen Teilen der Kirche': Der münsterische Theologieprofessor Otto A. Piper auf dem Weg in die Emigration 1933–1938." *JWK* 80 (1987): 105–51.

Heinemann, Joseph. *Prayer in the Talmud: Forms and Patterns*. SJ 9. Berlin and New York: de Gruyter, 1977.

Hengel, Martin. *Judaism and Hellenism: Studies in Their Encounter in Palestine during the Early Hellenistic Period*. 2 vols. Translated by John Bowden. Philadelphia: Fortress, 1974.

Heschel, Abraham Joshua. *Between God and Man: An Interpretation of Judaism*. Edited by Fritz A. Rothschild. New York: Free Press, 1959.

———. *The Insecurity of Freedom: Essays on Human Existence*. New York: Farrar, Straus & Giroux, 1966.

———. *The Sabbath: Its Meaning for Modern Man*. New York: Farrar, Straus & Young, 1951.

Hessel, Dieter T., ed. *Social Themes of the Christian Year: A Commentary on the Lectionary*. Philadelphia: Geneva, 1983.

Higgins, Angus John Brockhurst, ed. *New Testament Essays: Studies in Memory of Thomas Walter Manson*. Manchester: Manchester University Press, 1959.

Hill, Edmund. *The Mystery of the Trinity*. ICT. London: Chapman, 1985.

Hitchcock, Francis Ryan Montgomery. "St. Paul's Views of the Body and Death Contrasted with Plato's." *Churchman* 30 (1916): 558–65.

Hitchens, Christopher. "The Medals of His Defeats: Examining the Revisionist Version of Winston Churchill." *The Atlantic Monthly* 289 (April, 2002): 118–37.

Hobbes, Thomas. *Leviathan, or The Matter, Forme and Power of a Common Wealth Ecclesiastical and Civil*. New York: Penguin, 1983.

———. *Leviathan*. Edited by Noel Malcolm. Oxford: Clarendon, 2012.

Holden, D. T. *Death Shall Have No Dominion*. St. Louis: Bethany, 1971.

Holladay, William L. *The Psalms through Three Thousand Years: Prayerbook of a Cloud of Witnesses*. Minneapolis: Fortress, 1993.

Holtzmann, Heinrich Julius. *Hand-Commentar zum Neuen Testament*. Freiburg: Mohr, 1892.

The Holy Qur'an: Text, Translation and Commentary. Edited by Abdullah Yasuf Ali. Elmhurst, NY: Tahrike Tarsile Qur'an, 2011.

Hooker, Morna D. *The Gospel according to Saint Mark*. BNTC. Peabody: Hendrickson, 1991.

———. "'Who Died for Our Sins, and Was Raised for Our Acquittal': Paul's Understanding of the Death of Christ." *SEÅ* 68 (2003): 59–71.

Hoon, Paul W. *The Integrity of Worship: Ecumenical and Pastoral Studies in Liturgical Theology*. Nashville and New York: Abingdon, 1971.

Horst, William. *Morality, Not Mortality: Moral Psychology and the Language of Death in Romans 5–8*. Lanham: Lexington Books, 2022.

Horváth, Tibor. "3 Jn 11b: An Early Ecumenical Creed?" *ExpTim* 85 (1974): 339–40.

Hoskyns, E. C., and Noel Davey. *The Riddle of the New Testament*. London: Faber and Faber, 1931.
Houf, Horace Thomas. Review of *God in History* by Otto A. Piper. *RL* 8 (1939): 471.
Houlden, J. Leslie. *A Commentary on the Johannine Epistles*. BNTC. London: Adam & Charles Black, 1973.
Houston, Keith. "Miscellany No. 73: Per Churchill et commata." *Shady Characters* (blog). May 9, 2016. https://shadycharacters.co.uk/2016/05/micellany-73-churchill/.
Hübner, Hans. *Biblische Theologie des Neuen Testaments*. 3 vols. Göttingen: Vandenhoeck & Ruprecht, 1990–95.
Hume, David. *Dialogues concerning Natural Religion; The Posthumous Essays: Of the Immortality of the Soul; and Of Suicide; From an Enquiry concerning Human Understanding of Miracles*. Edited by Richard H. Popkin. 2nd ed. Indianapolis/Cambridge: Hackett, 1980.
———. *A Treatise of Human Nature: A Critical Edition*. Edited by David Fate Norton and Mary J. Norton. Oxford: Clarendon, 2007.
Hunter, Archibald M. *Paul and His Predecessors*. New rev. ed. Philadelphia: Westminster, 1961.
The Iliad of Homer. Translated by Richmond Lattimore. Chicago: University of Chicago Press, 1951.
IMDB. *The Mike Wallace Interview*. Season 1, episode 57. Adlai Stevenson. Aired June 1, 1958. See https://www.imdb.com/title/tt2123762/.
"The Iraq Body Count Project." https://www.iraqbodycount.org/database/.
"Iraq Coalition Casualty Count." https://www.iraqbodycount.org.
Ivanhoe, Philip J., Owen J. Flanagan, Victoria S. Harrison, Hagop Sarkissian, and Eric Schwitzgebel, eds. *The Oneness Hypothesis: Beyond the Boundary of Self*. New York: Columbia University Press, 2018.
Jackayya, B. H. "Ἀλήθεια in the Johannine Corpus." *CTM* 41 (1970): 171–75.
Jacob, Edmond. "Death." *IDB* 1:802–4.
Jaquette, James L. "Life and Death, Adiaphora, and Paul's Rhetorical Strategies." *NovT* 38 (1996): 30–54.
Jawien, Andrzej. [Karol Jósef Wojtyla]. *The Jeweler's Shop*. San Francisco: Ignatius, 1992. *See also* [Pope] John Paul II.
Jensen, Joseph. "Prediction-Fulfillment in Bible and Liturgy." *CBQ* 50 (1988): 646–62.
Jenson, Robert W. "Second Locus: The Triune God." Pages 102–5 in *Christian Dogmatics*. Edited by Carl E. Braaten and Robert W. Jenson. Philadelphia: Fortress, 1984.
Jeremias, Joachim. *Neutestamentliche Theologie*. Gütersloh: Mohn, 1971. Trans-

lated by John Bowden as *New Testament Theology*. New York: Scribner's Sons, 1971.

———. *The Parables of Jesus*. 2nd rev. ed. Translated by S. H. Hooke. London: SCM, 1972.

Jervell, Jacob, and Wayne A. Meeks, eds. *God's Christ and His People: Festschrift for N. A. Dahl*. Oslo: Universitetsforlaget, 1977.

Jesuit Supplement to the Roman Catholic Lectionary. 2002. https://catholic-resources.org/Lectionary/Supplement-Jesuit.htm.

Jewett, Robert. *Romans: A Commentary*. Hermeneia. Minneapolis: Fortress, 2006.

[Pope] John Paul II. [Karol Jósef Wojtyla.] *Evangelium vitae*. 1995. https://www.vatican.va/content/john-paul-ii/en/encyclicals/documents/hf_jp-ii_enc_25031995_evangelium-vitae.html.

———. "Homily of His Holiness John Paul II for the Inauguration of His Pontificate." October 22, 1978. https://www.vatican.va/content/john-paul-ii/en/homilies/1978/documents/hf_jp-ii_hom_19781022_inizio-pontificato.html. See also Jawien, Andrzej.

Johnson, Sherman E. *The Year of the Lord's Favor: Preaching the Three-Year Lectionary*. New York: Seabury, 1983.

Jónsson, Gunnlauger A. *The Image of God: Genesis 1:26–28 in a Century of Old Testament Research*. ConBOT series 26. Stockholm: Almqvist & Wiksell, 1988.

Jordan, Clarence. *The Cotton Patch Version of Matthew and John: Including the Gospel of Matthew (Except for the "Begat" Verses) and the First Eight Chapters of the Gospel of John*. New York: Association, 1970.

Joyner, Will. "Krister Stendahl, 1921–2008." *Harvard Divinity School News*. April 16, 2008. https://news-archive.hds.harvard.edu/news/2011/02/07/krister-stendahl-1921-2008.

Julian of Norwich. *Showings*. Translated by Edmund Colledge and James Walsh. CWS. Mahwah, NJ: Paulist, 1978.

Kant, Immanuel. *Critique of Pure Reason*. Translated by Norman Kemp Smith. New York: Modern Library, 1958.

Karon, Jan. *At Home in Mitford*. New York: Doubleday, 1994.

Käsemann, Ernst. "Amt und Gemeinde im Neuen Testament." Pages 109–34 in *Exegetische Versuche und Besinnungen*. Vol. 1. Göttingen: Vandenhoeck & Ruprecht, 1960.

———. "The Canon of the New Testament and the Unity of the Church." Pages 95–107 in Käsemann, *Essays on New Testament Themes*. Translated by W. J. Montague. SBT 41. London: SCM, 1964.

———. *Commentary on Romans*. Translated by Geoffrey W. Bromiley. Grand Rapids: Eerdmans, 1980.

———. *Essays on New Testament Themes*. Translated by W. J. Montague. SBT 41. London: SCM, 1964.

———. *Exegetische Versuche und Besinnungen*. 2 vols. Göttingen: Vandenhoeck & Ruprecht, 1960, 1965.

———. "Ketzer and Zeuge: Zum johanneischen Verfasser-problem." *ZTK* 48 (1951): 292–311. Repr. as pages 168–87 in Käsemann, *Exegetische Versuche und Besinnungen*. Vol. 1. Göttingen: Vandenhoeck & Ruprecht, 1960.

———. "Ministry and Community in the New Testament." In Käsemann, *Essays on New Testament Themes*, 63–94.

———. *New Testament Questions of Today*. Translated by W. J. Montague. Philadelphia: Fortress, 1969.

———. "On Paul's Anthropology." Pages 1–31 in Käsemann, *Perspectives on Paul*. Translated by Margaret Kohl. London: SCM, 1971.

———. "Paul and Early Catholicism." In Käsemann, *New Testament Questions of Today*, 236–51.

———. "The Problem of a New Testament Theology." *NTS* 19 (1972–73): 235–45.

———. *The Testament of Jesus: A Study of the Gospel of John in the Light of Chapter 17*. Translated by Gerhard Krodel. Philadelphia: Fortress, 1968.

Katz, David S. *God's Last Words: Reading the English Bible from the Reformation to Fundamentalism*. New Haven: Yale University Press, 2004.

Keck, Leander E. *The Bible in the Pulpit: The Renewal of Biblical Preaching*. Nashville: Abingdon, 1978.

———. "Derivation as Destiny: 'Of-Ness' in Johannine Christology, Anthropology and Soteriology." In Culpepper and Black, *Exploring the Gospel of John*, 274–88.

———. "Ethics in the Gospel according to Matthew." *IlRev* Winter, 1984: 39–56.

———. "New Testament Views of Death." Pages 33–98 in *Perspectives on Death*. Edited by Liston O. Mills. Nashville: Abingdon, 1969.

———. "Rethinking 'New Testament Ethics.'" *JBL* 115 (1996): 3–16.

———. *Who Is Jesus? History in Perfect Tense*. SPNT. Columbia: University of South Carolina Press, 2000; repr. Minneapolis: Fortress, 2001.

Kee, Howard Clark. "A Century of Quests for the Culturally Compatible Jesus." *ThTod* 52 (1995): 17–28.

Kelly, Walt. *Pogo: We Have Met the Enemy and He Is Us*. New York: Simon & Schuster, 1972.

Kelsey, David H. *The Uses of Scripture in Recent Theology*. Philadelphia: Fortress, 1975. Repr., *Proving Doctrine: The Uses of Scripture in Modern Theology*. Philadelphia: Trinity Press International, 1999.

Kermode, Frank. *The Classic: Literary Images of Permanence and Change*. Cambridge: Harvard University Press, 1983.

———. "John." Pages 440–66 in *The Literary Guide to the Bible*. Edited by Robert Alter and Frank Kermode. Cambridge: Harvard University Press, 1987.

Khalidi, Jarif. *The Muslim Jesus: Sayings and Stories in Islamic Literature*. Cambridge: Harvard University Press, 2001.

Kierkegaard, Søren. *The Journals of Søren Kierkegaard*. Translated by Alexander Dru. London: Oxford University Press, 1938.

———. *Purity of the Heart Is to Will One Thing: Spiritual Preparation for the Feast of Confession*. Translated by Douglas V. Steere. New York: Harper & Brothers, 1938.

Klassen, William, and Graydon F. Snyder, eds. *Current Issues in New Testament Interpretation: Essays in Honor of Otto A. Piper*. London: SCM, 1962.

Klein, Günter. "'Das wahre Licht scheint schon': Beobachtungen zur Zeit- und Geschichtserfahrung einer urchrislichen Schule." *ZTK* 68 (1971): 261–326.

Klotz, Leopold, ed. *Die Kirche und das dritte Reich: Fragen und Förderungen Deutscher Theologen*. Gotha: Klotz, 1932.

Knight, G. Wilson. *The Wheel of Fire: Interpretations of Shakespearean Tragedy*. London: Routledge, 2001.

Knowles, Michael. *Jeremiah in Matthew's Gospel: The Rejected Prophet Motif in Matthean Redaction*. JSNTSup 68. Sheffield: Sheffield Academic Press, 1993.

Korzybski, Alfred. *Science and Sanity: An Introduction to Non-Aristotelian Systems and General Semantics*. Lancaster, PA: The International Non-Aristotelian Library Publishing Co., 1933.

Koster, Henry, dir. *A Man Called Peter*. Los Angeles: Twentieth-Century Fox, 1955.

Kraft, Robert A. "The Multiform Jewish Heritage of Early Christianity." Pages 174–99 in *Christianity, Judaism and Other Greco-Roman Cults: Studies for Morton Smith at Sixty. Part 3: Judaism before 70*. Edited by Jacob Neusner. SJLA 12. Leiden: Brill, 1975.

Kraus, Hans-Joachim. *Theology of the Psalms*. Translated by Keith Crim. CC. Minneapolis: Fortress, 1992.

Kraynak, Robert P. "'Made in the Image of God': The Christian View of Human Dignity and the Political Orders." Pages 81–118 in *In Defense of Human Dignity: Essays for Our Times*. Edited by Robert P. Kraynak and Glenn Tinder. Notre Dame: University of Notre Dame Press, 2003.

Kümmel, Werner Georg. *Die Theologie des Neuen Testaments nach seinen Hauptzeugen: Jesus, Paulus, Johannes*. Göttingen: Vandenhoeck & Ruprecht, 1969. Translated by John E. Steely as *The Theology of the New Testament according to Its Major Witnesses: Jesus—Paul—John*. Nashville: Abingdon, 1973.

Küng, Hans. "'Early Catholicism' in the New Testament as a Problem in Controversial Theology." Pages 159–95 in *The Council in Action: Theological Reflections on the Second Vatican Council*. New York: Sheed and Ward, 1963.

Kyle, Donald G. *Spectacles of Death in Ancient Rome*. London: Routledge, 2000.

Kysar, Robert. *The Fourth Evangelist and His Gospel: An Examination of Contemporary Scholarship*. Minneapolis: Augsburg, 1975.

———. "The Fourth Gospel: A Report on Recent Research." *ANRW* 3/2 (1985): 2380–480.

———. *John*. ACNT. Minneapolis: Augsburg, 1986.

Lachs, Samiel Tobias. *A Rabbinic Commentary on the New Testament*. Hoboken, NJ: KTAV, 1987.

LaCocque, André. "The Great Cry of Jesus in Matthew 27:50." Pages 138–64 in *Putting Body & Soul Together: Essays in Honor of Robin Scroggs*. Edited by Virginia Wiles, Alexandra Brown, and Graydon F. Snyder. Valley Forge: Trinity Press International, 1997.

LaHaye, Tim, and Jerry B. Jenkins. *Left Behind*. 16 vols. Carol Stream: Tyndale House, 1995–2007.

Lammé, Nicholas. "Blasphemy against the Holy Spirit: The Unpardonable Sin in Matthew 12:22–32." *MAJT* 23 (2012): 19–51.

Lane, Anthony. "Scripture Rescripted." *The New Yorker*. October 2, 1995: 97–98.

Langford, Thomas A. "The Minister as Scholar." *DDSR* 39 (1974): 135–41.

LaPierre, Wayne. Press release by the National Rifle Association of America. December 21, 2012.

Lash, Archimandrite Ephrem. "Biblical Interpretation in Worship." Pages 35–48 in *The Cambridge Companion to Orthodox Christian Theology*. Edited by Mary B. Cunningham and Elizabeth Theokritoff. Cambridge: Cambridge University Press, 2008.

Lash, Nicholas. *Theology on the Way to Emmaus*. London: SCM, 1986.

Lattke, Michael. *The Odes of Solomon: A Commentary*. Hermeneia. Minneapolis: Augsburg Fortress, 2016.

Leclercq, Jean. *The Love of Learning and the Desire for God: A Study of Monastic Culture*. New York: Fordham University Press, 1961.

Lectionary for Mass Supplement. Collegeville, MN: Liturgical Press, 2017.

Legarreta-Castillo, Felipe de Jesus. *The Figure of Adam in Romans 5 and 1 Corinthians 15: The New Creation and Its Ethical and Social Reconfigurations*. Minneapolis: Augsburg Fortress, 2014.

Leith, John H., ed. *Creeds of the Church: A Reader in Christian Doctrine from the Bible to the Present*. Atlanta: John Knox, 1982.

Lemire, Christy. Review of *Left Behind*. RogerEbert.com. October 3, 2014. https://www.rogerebert.com/reviews/left-behind-2014.

Lennon, John, and Paul McCartney. "All You Need Is Love." Track 5 on side B of *Magical Mystery Tour*. Parlophone Records, 1967, LP album.

Leonard, Sheldon, and Danny Thomas, producers. *The Andy Griffith Show: The Complete Series*. 1960–68; Los Angeles: Paramount Pictures Home Entertainment, 2020. DVD.

Lessing, Gotthold Ephraim. *Lessing's Theological Writings: Selections in Translation with an Introductory Essay*. Edited and translated by Henry Chadwick. London: Adam & Charles Black, 1956.

Levenson, Jon D. *Creation and the Persistence of Evil: The Jewish Drama of Divine Omnipotence*. Princeton: Princeton University Press, 1988.

Levinas, Emmanuel. *Ethics and Infinity*. Pittsburgh: Duquesne University Press, 1985.

Levine, Lee I. *The Ancient Synagogue: The First Thousand Years*. New Haven: Yale University Press, 2000.

Lewis, C. S. "Learning in War-Time." In Lewis, *The Weight of Glory and Other Addresses*, 41–52.

———. *Letters to Malcolm: Chiefly on Prayer*. New York: Harcourt Brace Jovanovich, 1963.

———. *Reflections on the Psalms*. New York: Harcourt, Brace & World, 1958.

———. *The Weight of Glory and Other Addresses*. Edited by Walter Hooper. New York: Simon & Schuster, 1996.

Lieu, Judith M. "'Authority to Become Children of God': A Study of 1 John." *NovT* 23 (1981): 210–28.

———. *The Second and Third Epistles of John: History and Background*. SNTW. Edinburgh: T&T Clark, 1986.

———. *The Theology of the Johannine Epistles*. NTT. Cambridge: Cambridge University Press, 1991.

Lindars, Barnabas. *The Gospel of John*. NCBC. Grand Rapids: Eerdmans, 1972.

Locke, John. *The Works of John Locke in Nine Volumes*. 12th ed. London: Rivington, 1824.

Lockett, Darian R., ed. *The Catholic Epistles: Critical Readings*. CCRBS. London; New York: T&T Clark, 2021.

———. *Letters from the Pillar Apostles: The Formation of the Catholic Epistles as a Canonical Collection*. Cambridge: James Clarke & Co., 2017.

Loisy, Alfred. *The Gospel and the Church*. Edited by Bernard B. Scott. LJS. Philadelphia: Fortress, 1970.

Lonergan, Kenneth. "Spring Theater: In Times like These." *New York Times*. February 23, 2003. https://www.nytimes.com/2003/02/23/theater/spring-theater-in-times-like-these.html?searchResultPosition=54.

Longarino, Joseph. "Apocalyptic and the Passions: Overcoming a False Dichotomy in Pauline Studies." *NTS* 67 (2021): 582–97.

Longenecker, Richard N., ed. *Into God's Presence: Prayer in the New Testament.* Grand Rapids: Eerdmans, 2001.

Lorberbaum, Yair. *In God's Image: Myth, Theology, and Law in Classical Judaism.* New York: Cambridge University Press, 2015.

Louth, Andrew. *Discerning the Mystery: An Essay on the Nature of Theology.* Oxford: Clarendon, 1983.

Lumet, Sidney. *Making Movies.* New York: Vintage/Random House, 1995.

Luther, Martin. *Career of the Reformer IV.* Edited by Helmut T. Lehmann and Lewis W. Spitz. *LW* 34. St. Louis: Concordia, 1960.

———. *The Large Catechism of Martin Luther.* Translated by Robert H. Fischer. Philadelphia: Fortress, 1959.

———. "Preface to the Epistle to the Romans." Pages 104–18 in *Luther's Spirituality.* Edited and translated by Philip D. W. Krey and Peter D. Krey. CWS. New York and Mahwah, NJ: Paulist, 2007.

———. "Preface to the Revelation of St. John [I]." Pages 398–99 in *LW* 35: *Word and Sacrament* I. Edited by E. Theodore Bachmann. Philadelphia: Fortress, 1960.

Luz, Ulrich. *Matthew 8–20: A Commentary.* Hermeneia. Minneapolis: Fortress, 2001.

———. *Matthew 21–28: A Commentary.* Hermeneia. Minneapolis: Fortress, 2005.

Lysen, Laura M. Review of Lyle Peterson, *The* Imago Dei *as Human Identity*, in *IJST* 19 (2017): 117–20.

MacDonald, Neil B. *Karl Barth and the Strange New World within the Bible: Barth, Wittgenstein, and the Metadilemmas of the Enlightenment.* PBTM. Carlisle and Waynesboro, GA: Paternoster, 2000.

Machiavelli, Niccolo. *The Prince.* New York: Norton, 1977.

Macquarrie, John. *Mary for All Christians.* Grand Rapids: Eerdmans, 1990.

Magrassi, Mariano. *Bibbia e preghiera: La* lectio divina. Milan: Editrice Àngora, 1990. Translated by Edward Hagman as *Praying the Bible: An Introduction to* Lectio Divina. Collegeville, MN: Liturgical, 1998.

Malherbe, Abraham J. "The Inhospitality of Diotrephes." Pages 222–32 in *God's Christ and His People: Festschrift for N. A. Dahl.* Edited by Jacob Jervell and Wayne A. Meeks. Oslo: Universitetsforlaget, 1977.

Mangold, James, dir. *Walk the Line.* Century City, CA: 20th Century Fox, 2005.

Marcus, Joel. "Birkat Ha-Minim Revisited." *NTS* 55 (2009): 523–51.

———. *Mark 1–8: A New Translation with Introduction and Commentary.* AB 27. New York: Doubleday, 2000.

Marshall, Bruce D. *Trinity and Truth.* CSCD. Cambridge: Cambridge University Press, 2000.

Marshall, Catherine. *Christy.* New York: McGraw Hill, 1967.
———. *A Man Called Peter: The Story of Peter Marshall.* New York: McGraw Hill, 1951.
Marshall, Christopher D. *Beyond Retribution: A New Testament Vision for Justice, Crime, and Punishment.* Grand Rapids: Eerdmans, 2001.
Marshall, I. Howard. *New Testament Theology: Many Witnesses, One Gospel.* Downers Grove, IL: InterVarsity Press, 2004.
Marshall, Peter. *John Doe, Disciple: Sermons for the Young in Spirit.* Edited by Catherine Marshall. New York: McGraw-Hill, 1963.
Martyn, J. Louis. *Galatians: A New Translation with Introduction and Commentary.* AB 33A. New York and London: Doubleday, 1997.
———. *History and Theology in the Fourth Gospel.* 3rd ed. NTL. Louisville: Westminster John Knox, 2003.
Marx, Groucho. *The Groucho Letters: Letters from and to Groucho Marx.* New York: Simon & Schuster, 1967.
Matera, Frank. *New Testament Theology: Exploring Diversity and Unity.* Louisville: Westminster John Knox, 2007.
Mayes, Andrew David Hastings, ed. *Text in Context: Essays by Members of the Society for Old Testament Study.* Oxford: Oxford University Press, 2000.
Mays, James Luther. "Prayer and Christology: Psalm 22 as Perspective on the Passion." *ThTod* 42 (1985): 322–31.
———. "The Self in the Psalms and the Image of God." In Soulen and Woodhead, *God and Human Dignity,* 27–43.
McBrien, Richard P. *Catholicism: New Edition.* San Francisco: HarperCollins, 1994.
McCord, James I. "Otto Piper: An Appreciation." Pages xi–xiv in *Current Issues in New Testament Interpretation: Essays in Honor of Otto A. Piper.* Edited by William Klassen and Graydon F. Snyder. London: SCM, 1962.
McFarland, Ian A. "Theological Anthropology." Pages 501–4 in *The Cambridge Dictionary of Christian Theology.* Edited by David S. Fergusson, Karen Kilby, Ian A. McFarland, and Iain R. Torrance. Cambridge: Cambridge University Press, 2011.
McGrath, Alister. *In the Beginning: The Story of the King James Bible and How It Changed a Nation, a Language, and a Culture.* New York: Anchor Books, 2002.
McMellan, Vernon, ed. *Billy Graham: A Tribute from Friends.* New York: FaithWord, 2000.
Meeks, M. Douglas. "The Economy of Grace: Human Dignity in the Market System." In Soulen and Woodhead, *God and Human Dignity,* 196–214.
Meeks, Wayne A. *The First Urban Christians: The Social World of the Apostle Paul.* New Haven: Yale University Press, 1983.
———. "The Man from Heaven in Johannine Sectarianism." *JBL* 91 (1972): 44–72.

———. "Why Study the New Testament?" *NTS* 51 (2005): 155–70.
Meier, John P. *The Vision of Matthew: Christ, Church and Morality in the First Gospel.* TI. New York: Paulist, 1979.
Meyer, Paul W. "'The Father': The Presentation of God in the Fourth Gospel." In Culpepper and Black, *Exploring the Gospel of John*, 255–73.
———. "The Worm at the Core of the Apple: Exegetical Reflections on Romans 7." Pages 57–77 in Meyer, *The Word in This World: Essays in New Testament Exegesis and Theology.* Edited by John T. Carroll. NTL. Louisville: Westminster John Knox, 2004.
Middleton, J. Richard. *The Liberating Image: The Imago Dei in Genesis 1.* Grand Rapids: Brazos, 2005.
Milgrom, Jacob. *Leviticus 17–22: A New Translation with Introduction and Commentary.* AB 3A. New York: Doubleday, 2000.
Mill, John Stuart. *On Liberty.* New York: Penguin, 1983.
Miller, Arthur. *All My Sons: A Drama in Three Acts.* New York: Penguin, 2000.
———. *The Crucible: A Play in Four Acts.* New York: Penguin, 1993.
———. *Death of a Salesman: Certain Private Conversations in Two Acts and a Requiem.* New York: Viking, 1949.
———. "Spring Theater: Looking for a Conscience." *New York Times.* February 23, 2003. https://www.nytimes.com/2003/02/23/movies/spring-theater-looking-for-a-conscience.html?searchResultPosition=268.
———. *Timebends: A Life.* New York: Grove, 1987.
———. *A View from the Bridge: A Play in Two Acts.* New York: Viking, 1955.
Miller, Patrick D. "'Enthroned on the Praises of Israel': The Praise of God in Old Testament Theology." *Int* 39 (1985): 5–19.
———. *They Cried to the Lord: The Form and Theology of Biblical Prayer.* Minneapolis: Fortress, 1994.
Mills, Liston O., ed. *Perspectives on Death.* Nashville: Abingdon, 1969.
Minear, Paul Sevier. "The Audience of the Fourth Evangelist." *Int* 31 (1977): 339–54.
———. *Eyes of Faith: A Study in the Biblical Point of View.* Philadelphia: Westminster, 1946.
———. *Images of the Church in the New Testament.* NTL. Louisville: Westminster John Knox, 2004.
———. *The Kingdom and the Power: An Exposition of the Gospel.* Philadelphia: Westminster, 1950. Repr., Louisville: Westminster John Knox, 2004.
———. "The Messiah Forsaken . . . Why?" *HBT* 17 (1995): 62–83.
———. "Two Secrets, Two Disclosures." *HBT* 29 (2007): 75–85.
Mitton, C. Leslie. "Paul's Certainties: V. The Gift of the Spirit and Life Beyond Death in 2 Corinthians v. 1–5." *ExpTim* 69 (1958): 260–63.
———. "Romans—vii. Reconsidered." *ExpTim* 65 (1953/54): 78–81, 99–103, 132–35.

Moberly, R. W. L. *The Bible, Theology and Faith: A Study of Abraham and Jesus.* CSCD. Cambridge: Cambridge University Press, 2000.

———. "Biblical Criticism and Religious Belief." *JTI* 21 (2008): 71–100.

Moffatt, James. *Grace in the New Testament.* New York: Long & Smith, 1932.

Moloney, Francis J. *The Gospel of John.* SP 4. Collegeville, MN: Liturgical, 1998.

Montefiore, Claude Goldsmid. *Rabbinic Literature and Gospel Teachings.* New York: KTAV, 1970.

Montefiore, Claude Goldsmid, and H. Loewe, eds. *A Rabbinic Anthology.* New York: Schocken, 1974.

Moore, George Foot. *Judaism in the First Centuries of the Christian Era.* 2 vols. New York: Schocken Books, 1971.

Morgan, Florence A. "Romans 6:5a: United to a Death like Christ's." *ETL* 59 (1983): 267–302.

Morgan, Robert. "Can the Critical Study of Scripture Provide a Doctrinal Norm?" *JR* 76 (1996): 206–32.

———, trans. and ed. *The Nature of New Testament Theology: The Contribution of William Wrede and Adolf Schlatter.* SBT 2nd ser. London: SCM, 1973.

Moule, Charles Francis Digby. "Death 'to Sin,' 'to Law,' and 'to the World': A Note on Certain Datives." Pages 367–75 in *Mélanges bibliques en hommage au R. P. Béda Rigaux.* Edited by Albert Descamps and André de Halleux. Gembloux: Duculot, 1970.

———. "A Neglected Factor in the Interpretation of Johannine Eschatology." Pages 155–60 in *Studies in John Presented to Professor Dr. J. N. Sevenster on the Occasion of His Seventieth Birthday.* Edited by W. C. van Unnik. NovTSup 24. Leiden: Brill, 1970.

———. "Punishment and Retribution: An Attempt to Delimit Their Scope in New Testament Thought." Pages 235–49 in Moule, *Essays in New Testament Interpretation.* Cambridge: Cambridge University Press, 1982.

———. "St. Paul and Dualism: The Pauline Conception of Resurrection." *NTS* 13 (1966): 106–23.

Moxnes, Halvor. *The Economy of the Kingdom: Social Conflict and Economic Relations in Luke's Gospel.* OBT. Philadelphia: Fortress, 1988.

Moynahan, Brian. *God's Bestseller: William Tyndale, Thomas More, and the Writing of the English Bible—A Story of Martyrdom and Betrayal.* New York: St. Martin's, 2002.

Muddiman, John. "'Adam, the Type of the One to Come.'" *Theol* 87 (1984): 101–10.

Munck, Johannes. "Presbyters and Disciples of the Lord in Papias." *HTR* 52 (1959): 223–43.

Murdoch, Iris. The *Times* of London. April 15, 1983.

Murphy, Roland E. "Forum: A Note on the Biblical Character of the Lectionary." *Worship* 74 (2000): 547–50.

Murphy-O'Connor, Jerome, ed. *Paul and Qumran: Studies in New Testament Exegesis*. Chicago: Priory, 1968.

Myers, Jacob M. *Grace and Torah*. Philadelphia: Fortress, 1975.

[Name withheld.] Interview with William O. Harris. October 14, 1997. Archives of Princeton Theological Seminary.

[Name withheld.] Letter to George Irving, General Director of the Department of Faith and Life for the Board of Christian Education of The Presbyterian Church, USA. June 16, 1938. Archives of Princeton Theological Seminary.

[Name withheld.] Letter to George Irving. June 17, 1938. Archives of Princeton Theological Seminary.

[Name withheld.] Letter to John A. Mackay, Princeton Theological Seminary, April 21, 1940. Archives of Princeton Theological Seminary.

[Name withheld.] Letter to Otto A. Piper. January 9, 1946. Archives of Princeton Theological Seminary.

Nasr, Seyyed Hossein. *The Heart of Islam: Enduring Values for Humanity*. New York: HarperOne, 2002.

Navone, John. *Toward a Theology of Beauty*. Collegeville, MN: Liturgical, 1996.

Neill, Stephen. *The Interpretation of the New Testament, 1861–1961*. Oxford: Oxford University Press, 1964.

Nellas, Panayiotis. *Deification in Christ: Orthodox Perspectives on the Nature of the Human Person*. Crestwood, NY: St. Vladimir's Seminary Press, 1987.

Nelson, Richard. "Reading Lectionary Texts in Pairs." *Di* 2 (1982): 95–101.

Neusner, Jacob. *Christianity, Judaism and Other Greco-Roman Cults: Studies for Morton Smith at Sixty. Part 3: Judaism before 70*. SJLA 12. Leiden: Brill, 1975.

Neville, David J. "Toward a Teleology of Peace: Contesting Matthew's Violent Eschatology." *JSNT* 30.2 (2007): 131–61.

Nicholson, Adam. *God's Secretaries: The Making of the King James Bible*. New York: HarperCollins, 2003.

Nickelsburg, George W. E. *1 Enoch: A Commentary on the Book of 1 Enoch, Chapters 1–36, 81–108*. Edited by Klaus Baltzer. Hermeneia. Minneapolis: Fortress, 2012.

———. *Resurrection, Immortality, and Eternal Life in Intertestamental Judaism*. HTS 26. Cambridge: Harvard University Press, 1972.

Niebuhr, H. Richard. "The Doctrine of the Trinity and the Unity of the Church." *ThTod* (1946): 371–84.

———. *The Kingdom of God in America*. New York: Harper & Row, 1937.

———. *The Meaning of Revelation*. New York: Macmillan, 1941.

Niebuhr, Reinhold. *Moral Man and Immoral Society: A Study in Ethics and Politics*. New York: Scribner's Sons, 1932.

Nietzsche, Friedrich Wilhelm. *On the Genealogy of Morals*. Translated and edited by Walter Kaufmann. New York: Vintage, 1989.

———. *The Will to Power*. Translated and edited by Walter Kaufmann. New York: Vintage, 1968.

Nijf, Onno M. van. *The Civic World of Professional Associations in the Roman East*. DMAHA 17. Amsterdam: Gieben, 1997.

Nolland, John. "Grace as Power." *NovT* 28 (1986): 26–31.

Null, Gary. *Get Healthy Now! With Gary Null*. Seven Stories Press, 1999.

Nussbaum, Martha C. *The Therapy of Desire: Theory and Practice in Hellenistic Ethics*. Princeton: Princeton University Press, 1994.

Nuwer, Rachel. "The Rainbow Bridge Has Comforted Millions of Pet Parents: Who Wrote It?" *National Geographic*, February 22, 2023.

Obras completes de San Agustín XXVI: Sermones (6.0): 339–396. Translated by Pio De Luis. BAC 461. Madrid: Biblioteca de Autores Cristianios, 1985.

Ochs, Peter, ed. *The Return to Scripture in Judaism and Christianity: Essays in Postcritical Scriptural Interpretation*. TI. New York: Paulist, 1993.

O'Connor, Flannery. *Mystery and Manners: Occasional Prose*. Edited by Sally and Robert Fitzgerald. New York: Farrar, Straus & Giroux, 1961.

O'Day, Gail R. "Singing Woman's Song: A Hermeneutic of Liberation." *CurTM* 12 (1985): 203–10.

Ogden, Schubert M. *The Point of Christology*. San Francisco: Harper & Row, 1982.

Old, Hughes Oliphant. *The Patristic Roots of Reformed Worship*. Zurich: Theologischer, 1975.

Olson, Dennis T. "Seeking 'The Inexpressible Texture of Thy Word': A Practical Guide to Brevard Childs' Canonical Approach to Theological Exegesis." *PTR* 14 (2008): 53–68.

Opinion Research Business Survey. https://orb-international.com.

Ordo Lectionum Missae. Rome: Vatican Polyglot Press, 1969.

Orlean, Susan. "Art for Everybody." *The New Yorker*. October 15, 2001. https://www.newyorker.com/magazine/2001/10/15/art-for-everybody-2.

Osiek, Carolyn, and David L. Balch. *Families in the New Testament World: Households and House Churches*. Louisville: Westminster John Knox, 1997.

Paine, Gustavus Swift. *The Men Behind the King James Version*. Grand Rapids: Baker, 1977.

Painter, John, R. Alan Culpepper, and Fernando Segovia, eds. *Word, Theology, and Community in John*. St. Louis: Chalice, 2002.

Park, Jeongsoo. "Sündenvergebung im Matthäusevangelium: Ihre theologische und soziale Dimension." *EvT* 66 (2006): 210–27.

Parkes, James E. "The Bible in Public Worship: A Source of Antisemitism." *FF* 2 (1976): 3–6.

[Pope] Paul VI. *Dogmatic Constitution on Divine Revelation* (1965). Rome: Vatican Archives. https://www.vatican.va/archive/hist_councils/ii_vatican_council/documents/vat-ii_const_19651118_dei-verbum_en.html.

Pelikan, Jaroslav. *Mary through the Centuries: Her Place in the History of Culture*. New Haven: Yale University Press, 1996.

Perkins, Pheme. "*Koinōnia* in 1 John 1:3–7: The Social Context of Division in the Johannine Letters." *CBQ* 45 (1983): 631–41.

Perrin, Norman. *The New Testament: An Introduction*. New York: Harcourt Brace Jovanovich, 1974.

Petersen, Anders Klostergaard. "Paul the Jew Was Also Paul the Hellenist." Pages 273–99 in *Paul the Jew: Rereading the Apostle as a Figure of Second Temple Judaism*. Edited by Gabriele Boccaccini and Carlos A. Segovia. Minneapolis: Augsburg Fortress, 2016.

Peterson, Ryan S. *The* Imago Dei *as Human Identity: A Theological Interpretation*. Winona Lake, IN: Eisenbrauns, 2016.

Petuchowski, Jakob J., and Michael Brocke, eds. *The Lord's Prayer and Jewish Liturgy*. New York: Seabury, 1978.

Phillips, Adam, and Barbara Taylor. *On Kindness*. New York: Picador, 2009.

Piper, Otto A. "I John and the Didache of the Primitive Church." *JBL* 66 (1947): 437–51.

———. "The Apocalypse of John and the Liturgy of the Ancient Church." *CH* 2 (1951): 10–22.

———. "The Authority of the Bible." *ThTod* 6 (1949): 159–73.

———. *The Biblical View of Sex and Marriage*. New York: Scribner's Sons, 1960.

———. *Christian Ethics*. London: Nelson, 1970.

———. "Christian Hope and History." *EvQ* 26 (1954): 82–89, 154–66.

———. *The Christian Interpretation of Sex*. New York: Scribner's Sons, 1941.

———. *The Christian Meaning of Money*. Englewood Cliffs, NJ: Prentice-Hall, 1965.

———. "The Church in Soviet Germany." *ChrCent* 67 (1950): 1386–88.

———. Citation in "Current and Quotable." *These Times* (October, 1960): 9.

———. "The Depth of God." Review of *Honest to God*, by John A. T. Robinson. *PSB* 57 (1963): 42–48.

———. *God in History*. New York: Macmillan, 1939.

———. "The Gospel of Thomas." *PSB* 53 (1959): 18–24.

———. *Gottes Wahrheit und die Wahrheit der Kirche*. Tübingen: Mohr (Siebeck), 1933.

———. "Der 'Großinquisitor' von Dostojweski." *Die Furche* 17 (1931): 249–73.

———. *Die Grundlagen der evangelischen Ethik*. 2 vols. Gütersloh: Bertelsmann, 1928, 1930.

———. "Á Interpretacão Cristã da Historia." *Revista* 9 (1954): 17–32, 265–81; *Revista* 10 (1955): 23–36; *Revista* 11 (1955): 23–45; *Revista* 12 (1956): 27–47, 313–40.

———. "The Interpretation of History in Continental Theology." *USQR* 50 (1939): 211–24, 306–21.

———. "Jeanne d'Arc: Wes Geistes Kind war sie?" *HK* July 3, 1929, Morgen Ausgabe.

———. "Johannesapokalpyse." *RGG*. 3rd ed. (1958), cols. 822–34.

———. "Kerygma and Discipleship: The Basis of New Testament Ethics." *PSB* 56 (1962): 14–20.

———. Letter to John A. Mackay. November 15, 1945. Archives of Princeton Theological Seminary.

———. Letter to John A. Mackay. February 28, 1948. Archives of Princeton Theological Seminary.

———. Letter to students of the classes of 1938–1947. February 10, 1948. Archives of Princeton Theological Seminary.

———. Letter [to unknown addressee]. February 10, 1948. Archives of Princeton Theological Seminary.

———. Manuscript of a lecture delivered in Miller Chapel, November 21, 1972. Archives of Princeton Theological Seminary.

———. "Meister Eckharts Wirklichkeitslehre." *Theologische Blätter* 15 (December, 1936): 294–308.

———. "Modern Problems of New Testament Exegesis." *PSB* 36 (1942): 3–14.

———. "Piper Discusses Need for Thanksgiving in Worship." *The Seminarian* 11. Friday, April 14, 1961: 3.

———. "Praise of God and Thanksgiving: The Biblical Doctrine of Prayer." *Int* 8 (1954): 3–20. Repr., with Floyd V. Filson, *The Biblical Doctrine of Prayer*. Atlanta: Presbyterian Church of the USA, c. 1954.

———. "Principles of Graduate Study in Theology." *PSB* 38 (1944): 21–25.

———. "Principles of New Testament Interpretation." *ThTod* 3 (1946): 192–204.

———. "The Professor Was Dispensable, So . . ." *The Province*. Vancouver, British Columbia. July 9, 1960: 22.

———. *Protestantism in an Ecumenical Age: Its Root, Its Right, Its Task*. Philadelphia: Fortress, 1965.

———. *Recent Developments in German Protestantism*. London: SCM, 1934.

———. *Das religiöse Erlebnis: Eine kritische Analyse der Schleiermacherschen Reden über die Religion*. Göttingen: Vandenhoeck & Ruprecht, 1920.

———. "That Strange Thing Money." *ThTod* 16 (1959): 215–31.

———. [Unknown title.] *British Weekly*. January 14 and 21, 1954.

———. *Weltliches Christentum. Eine Untersuchung über Wesen und Bedeutung der außerkirchlichen Frömmigkeit der Gegenwart*. Tübingen: Mohr (Siebeck), 1924.

———. "What the Bible Means to Me: The Bible as 'Holy History.'" *ChrCent* 63 (March 20, 1946): 362–64.

———. "What the Bible Means to Me: Discovering the Bible." *ChrCent* 63 (February 27, 1946): 26–68.

———. "What the Bible Means to Me: How I Study My Bible." *ChrCent* 63 (March 6, 1946): 299–301.

———. "What the Bible Means to Me: The Theme of the Bible." *ChrCent* 63 (March 13, 1946): 334–36.

Piper, Otto A., J. Jocz, and Harold Floreen. *The Church Meets Judaism*. Minneapolis: Augsburg, 1961.

Placher, William C. *The Domestication of Transcendence: How Modern Thinking about God Went Wrong*. Louisville: Westminster John Knox, 1996.

Post, Ted, dir. *Magnum Force*. Burbank, CA; Malpaso/Warner Bros., 1973.

Price, James L. "Light from Qumran upon Some Aspects of Johannine Theology." Pages 9–37 in *John and Qumran*. Edited by James H. Charlesworth. London: Chapman, 1972.

Procter-Smith, Marjorie. "'Reorganizing Victimization': The Intersection between Liturgy and Domestic Violence." *PJ* 40 (1987): 17–27.

Pulleyn, Simon J. *Prayer in Greek Religion*. Oxford: Clarendon, 1997.

Rad, Gerhard von. *Genesis: A Commentary*. Rev. ed. OTL. Philadelphia: Westminster, 1972.

———. *Old Testament Theology*. Vol. 1. Translated by D. M. G. Stalker. New York: Harper & Row, 1962.

Radner, Ephraim, and R. R. Reno, eds. *Inhabiting Unity: Theological Perspectives on the Proposed Lutheran-Episcopal Concordat*. Grand Rapids: Eerdmans, 1995.

Räisänen, Heikki. *Beyond New Testament Theology: A Story and a Programme*. London: SCM, 1990.

Raitt, Thomas M. "Jeremiah in the Lectionary." *Int* 37 (1983): 160–73.

Reumann, John. "A History of Lectionaries: From the Synagogue at Nazareth to Post–Vatican II." *Int* 31.2 (1977): 116–30.

The Revised Common Lectionary: Consultation on Common Texts. Nashville: Abingdon, 1992.

Reynolds, Arthur Reid. "Jesus Is Just Alright." Recorded by the Doobie Brothers. Track B1 on *Toulouse Street*. Warner Bros. Records, 1972, LP album.

Ricouer, Paul. *Interpretation Theory: Discourse and the Surplus of Meaning*. Fort Worth: Texas Christian University Press, 1976.

Robbins, Monika L. S. "Rosanne Cash Discusses 'Walk the Line' and Her Memoir." *The Harvard Crimson*. April 8, 2010. https://www.thecrimson.com/article/2010/4/8/cash-emerson-movie-kirkland/.

Robinson, Dominic. *Understanding the Imago Dei: The Thought of Barth, von Balthasar and Moltmann*. Farnham: Ashgate, 2011.

Robinson, James M., and Helmut Koester. *Trajectories through Early Christianity*. Philadelphia: Fortress, 1971.

Robinson, John A. T. *Honest to God*. Philadelphia: Westminster, 1963.

Rohrbagh, Richard L. *The New Testament in Cross-Cultural Perspective*. CB. Eugene, OR: Wipf & Stock, 2006.

Rorty, Richard. *Objectivity, Relativism, and Truth*. Cambridge: Cambridge University Press, 1991.

Rose, Gillian. *Judaism and Modernité: Philosophical Essays*. Oxford: Blackwell, 1993.

Rosenblatt, Roger. *The Man in the Water: Essays and Stories*. New York: Random House, 1994.

Rousseau, Jean-Jacques. *Confessions*. Translated by Angela Scholar. OWC. Oxford: Oxford University Press, 2000.

———. *Émile: or, On Education*. Translated by Allan Bloom. New York: Basic Books, 1979.

———. *On the Origin of Inequality, on Political Economy, and the Social Contract*. Translated by G. D. H. Cole. EL. London: Dent & Sons, 1920.

———. *On the Social Contract [or, Principles of Political Right] with Geneva Manuscript and Political Economy*. Edited by Roger D. Masters. Translated by Judith R. Masters. New York: St. Martin's, 1978.

Rowe, C. Kavin. "New Testament Theology: The Revival of a Discipline." *JBL* 125 (2006): 393–410.

Ruby, Bertrand. *Mary, the Faithful Disciple*. New York: Paulist, 1985.

Rudin, A. James, and Marvin R. Wilson, eds. *A Time to Speak: The Evangelical-Jewish Encounter*. Grand Rapids: Eerdmans, 1987.

Rudolph, Kurt. *Gnosis: The Nature and History of Gnosticism*. Translated and edited by Robert McLachlan Wilson. San Francisco: Harper & Row, 1987.

Russell, Letty M., ed. *Feminist Interpretation of the Bible*. Philadelphia: Fortress, 1985.

Saint Benedict's Prayer Book for Beginners. York: Ampleforth Abbey, 1993.

Saldarini, Anthony J. *Pharisees, Scribes and Sadducees in Palestinian Society: A Sociological Approach*. Wilmington, DE: Glazier, 1988.

Saliers, Don E. *The Soul in Paraphrase: Prayer and the Religious Affections*. New York: Seabury, 1980.

Sanday, William, and Arthur C. Headlam. *A Critical and Exegetical Commentary on the Epistle to the Romans.* 5th ed. ICC. Edinburgh: T&T Clark, 1902.

Sanders, E. P. *Jesus and Judaism.* Philadelphia: Fortress, 1985.

———. *Judaism: Practice and Belief, 63 BCE–66 CE.* London: SCM, 1992.

———. *Paul and Palestinian Judaism: A Comparison of Patterns of Religion.* Philadelphia: Fortress, 1977.

Sandys-Wunsch, John, and Laurence Eldredge. "J. P. Gabler and the Distinction between Biblical and Dogmatic Theology: Translation, Commentary, and Discussion of His Originality." *SJT* 33 (1980): 133–58.

Sartre, Jean-Paul. *No Exit and Three Other Plays.* New York: Vintage, 1955.

The Sayings of the Desert Fathers: The Alphabetical Collection. Rev. ed. Translated and edited by Benedicta Ward. CSS 59. Kalamazoo, MI: Cistercian Publications, 1984.

Schillebeeckx, Edward. *Ministry: Leadership in the Community of Jesus Christ.* New York: Crossroad, 1986.

Schlatter, Adolf. *Die Theologie des Neuen Testaments.* 2 vols. Calw: Verlag der Vereinsbuchhandlung, 1909–10.

———. "The Theology of the New Testament and Dogmatics." Pages 117–66 in *The Nature of New Testament Theology: The Contribution of William Wrede and Adolf Schlatter.* Translated and edited by Robert Morgan. SBT 2nd ser. London: SCM, 1973.

Schleiermacher, Friedrich. *On Religion: Speeches to Its Cultured Despisers.* Translated by John Oman. Abridged, with an introduction by E. Graham Waring. New York: Ungar, 1955.

Schnackenburg, Rudolf. *The Church in the New Testament.* New York: Herder and Herder, 1965.

———. *The Gospel according to St. John.* Vol. 3. New York: Crossroad, 1987.

———. "Zum Begriff der 'Wahrheit' in den beiden kleinen Johannesbriefen." *BZ* 11 (1967): 253–58.

Schnelle, Udo. *Theologie des Neuen Testaments.* Stuttgart: Vandenhoeck & Ruprecht, 2007. Translated by M. Eugene Boring as *Theology of the New Testament.* Grand Rapids: Baker Academic, 2009.

Schrage, Wolfgang. *The Ethics of the New Testament.* Translated by David E. Green. Philadelphia: Fortress, 1988.

Schuller, David S., Merton P. Strommen, and Milo L. Breecke, eds. *Ministry in America: A Report and Analysis, Based on an In-Depth Survey of 47 Denominations in the United States and Canada, with Interpretation by 18 Experts.* San Francisco: Harper & Row, 1980.

Schuller, Eileen M. "The Bible in the Lectionary." Pages 440–51 in *The Catholic*

Study Bible: The New American Bible. Edited by Donald Senior et al. New York: Oxford University Press, 1990.

———. "Prayer in the Dead Sea Scrolls." Pages 66-88 in *Into God's Presence: Prayer in the New Testament*. Edited by Richard N. Longenecker. Grand Rapids: Eerdmans, 2001.

Schultz, Siegfried. *Die Mitte der Schrift: Der Frühkatholizismus im Neuen Testament als Herausforderung an den Protestantismus*. Stuttgart: Kreuz, 1976.

Schulz, Charles M. *Peanuts*. United Features Syndicate. November 12, 1959.

Schüssler Fiorenza, Elisabeth. "The Quest of the Johannine School: The Apocalypse and the Fourth Gospel." *NTS* 23 (1976-77): 402-27.

Schweiker, William, Michael A. Johnson, and Kevin Jung, eds. *Humanity before God: Contemporary Faces of Jewish, Christian, and Islamic Ethics*. Minneapolis: Fortress, 2006.

Schweitzer, Albert. *Geschichte der Leben-Jesu-Forschung*. Tübingen: Mohr/Siebeck, 1913. Translated by W. Montgomery, J. R. Coates, Susan Cupitt, and John Bowden as *The Quest of the Historical Jesus*. Minneapolis: Fortress, 2001.

———. *The Quest of the Historical Jesus: A Critical Study of Its Progress from Reimarus to Wrede*. Translated by W. Montgomery. New York: Macmillan, 1968.

Schweizer, Eduard. "The Concept of the Church in the Gospel and Epistles of St. John." Pages 230-45 in *New Testament Essays: Studies in Memory of Thomas Walter Manson*. Edited by A. J. B. Higgins. Manchester: Manchester University Press, 1959.

———. "Dying and Rising with Christ." *NTS* 14 (1967): 1-14.

———. *Jesus*. London: SCM, 1971.

———. *Lordship and Discipleship*. London: SCM, 1960.

Schwöbel, Christoph. "Recovering Human Dignity." In Soulen and Woodhead, *God and Human Dignity*, 44-58.

Scroggs, Robin. "Romans vi.7: Ο ΓΑΡ ΑΠΟΘΑΝΩΝ ΔΕΔΙΚΑΙΩΤΑΙ ΑΠΟ ΤΗΣ ΑΜΑΡΤΙΑΣ." *NTS* 10 (1963): 104-8.

Segovia, Fernando F. "Recent Research in the Johannine Letters." *RelSRev* 13 (1987): 132-39.

Seitz, Christopher. "The Lectionary as Theological Construction." Pages 173-91 in *Inhabiting Unity: Theological Perspectives on the Proposed Lutheran-Episcopal Concordat*. Edited by Ephraim Radner and R. R. Reno. Grand Rapids: Eerdmans, 1995.

Senior, Donald, et al., eds. *The Catholic Study Bible: The New American Bible*. New York: Oxford University Press, 1990.

The Service of the Small Paraklesis (Intercessory Prayer) to the Most Holy Theotokos. Brookline, MA: Holy Cross Orthodox Press, 1984.

Shakespeare, William. *Julius Caesar*. Edited by David Daniell. AS 3rd ser. New Delhi: Bloomsbury India, 2013.
Shelp, Earl E., and Ronald Sunderland, eds. *A Biblical Basis for Ministry*. Philadelphia: Westminster, 1981.
Sherwin, Byron L. *Jewish Ethics for the Twenty-First Century: Living in the Image of God*. Syracuse: Syracuse University Press, 2000.
Sinclair, Daniel. "The Legal Basis for the Prohibition of Abortion in Jewish Law." *ILR* 15 (1980): 109–30.
Sloan, Jordan Taylor. "Johnny Cash Did More for Today's Music Than You Probably Even Realize." *Mic*.com. December 9, 2014. https://www.mic.com/articles/105954/johnny-cash-did-more-for-today-s-music-than-you-probably-even-realize.
Sloyan, Gerard S. "The Jews and the New Roman Lectionary." *FF* 2 (1976): 5–8.
———. "The Lectionary as a Context for Interpretation." *Int* 31 (1977): 131–38.
———. "Some Suggestions for a Biblical Three-Year Lectionary." *Worship* 63 (1989): 521–35.
Smail, Thomas A. *Like Father, Like Son: The Trinity Imaged in Our Humanity*. Grand Rapids: Eerdmans, 2005.
Smalley, Beryl. *The Study of the Bible in the Middle Ages*. Notre Dame: University of Notre Dame Press, 1964.
Smith, D. Moody, Jr. *The Composition and Order of the Fourth Gospel*. YPR 10. New Haven: Yale University Press, 1960.
———. "Ethics and the Interpretation of the Fourth Gospel." Pages 109–22 in *Word, Theology, and Community in John*. Edited by John Painter, R. Alan Culpepper, and Fernando Segovia. St. Louis: Chalice, 2002.
———. "Johannine Christianity: Some Reflections on Its Character and Delineation." *NTS* 21 (1974–75): 222–48.
———. "John, Letters of." *IDBSup* (1976): 486–87.
———. "Theology and Ministry in John." Pages 186–228 in *A Biblical Basis for Ministry*. Edited by Earl E. Shelp and Ronald Sunderland. Philadelphia: Westminster, 1981.
———. *The Theology of the Gospel of John*. NTT. Cambridge: Cambridge University Press, 1995.
Smith, John E. "Jonathan Edwards: Piety and Its Fruits." Pages 277–91 in *The Return to Scripture in Judaism and Christianity: Essays in Postcritical Scriptural Interpretation*. Edited by Peter Ochs. New York and Mahwah, NJ: Paulist, 1993.
Soares-Prabhu, George M. *The Dharma of Jesus*. Edited by Francis X. D'Sa. Maryknoll, NY: Orbis, 2003.
Sontag, Susan. *AIDS and Its Metaphors*. New York: Farrar, Straus & Giroux, 1988.

———. *Illness as Metaphor*. New York: Farrar, Straus & Giroux, 1977.
———. *In America*. New York: Farrar, Straus & Giroux, 1999.
———. "Notes on 'Camp.'" *Partisan Review* 31.4 (Fall, 1964): 515–530. Repr. *Against Interpretation*. New York: Farrar, Straus & Giroux, 1966.
———. *On Photography*. New York: Farrar, Straus & Giroux, 1973.
———. *Regarding the Pain of Others*. Farrar, Straus & Giroux, 2003.
———. "Regarding the Torture of Others." *New York Times Magazine*. May 23, 2004. 24–29. https://www.nytimes.com/2004/05/23/magazine/regarding-the-torture-of-others.html.
———. *The Volcano Lover*. New York: Farrar, Straus & Giroux, 1992.
———. "The Wisdom Project." *The New Republic* 24:12 (March 19, 2001): 29–34. Repr. *Where the Stress Falls*. New York: Farrar, Straus & Giroux, 2001.
Sony BMG Music Entertainment. *Johnny Cash at Folsom Prison*. Album liner notes. 2008.
Sony BMG Music Entertainment. *Johnny Cash at San Quentin*. Album liner notes. 2008.
Soskice, Janet Martin. *The Kindness of God: Metaphor, Gender, and Religious Language*. Oxford: Oxford University Press, 2007.
Soulen, R. Kendall, and Linda Woodhead, eds. *God and Human Dignity*. Grand Rapids: Eerdmans, 2006.
Spicq, Ceslas. "La place ou le rôle des jeunes dans certaines communautés néotestamentaires." *RB* 76 (1969): 508–27.
Springsted, Eric O. *The Act of Faith: Christian Faith and the Moral Self*. Grand Rapids: Eerdmans, 2002.
Stanton, Graham. *A Gospel for a New People: Studies in Matthew*. Edinburgh: T&T Clark, 1992.
Stegemann, Ekkehard D., and Wolfgang Stegemann. *The Jesus Movement: A First Century of Its Social History*. Translated by O. C. Dean Jr. Minneapolis: Fortress, 2001.
Steinmetz, David C. *Memory and Mission: Theological Reflections on the Christian Past*. Nashville: Abingdon, 1988.
Stendahl, Krister. "Theology, Biblical." *IDB* 4:418–32.
Stevenson, James, ed. *Creeds, Councils and Controversies: Documents Illustrating the History of the Church AD 337–461*. Revised by W. H. C. Frend. London: SPCK, 1989.
Stookey, Lawrence H. "Marcion, Typology, and Lectionary Preaching." *Worship* 66 (1992): 251–62.
Strauss, David Friedrich. *Das Leben Jesu*. 4th ed. Tübingen: Oslander, 1835–36.

Translated by George Eliot as *The Life of Jesus Critically Examined*. Edited by Peter C. Hodgson. LJS. Philadelphia: Fortress, 1972.

Strauss, Neil. "New Rebel for the 90s: Meet Johnny Cash, 62." *New York Times*. September 14, 1994. https://www.nytimes.com/1994/09/14/arts/new-rebel-for-the-90-s-meet-johnny-cash-62.html.

Strecker, Georg. *The Johannine Letters: A Commentary on 1, 2, and 3 John*. Translated by Linda M. Moloney. Hermeneia. Minneapolis: Fortress, 1996.

———. *Theologie des Neuen Testaments*. Edited by Friedrich Wilhelm Horn. Berlin: de Gruyter, 1996. Translated by M. Eugene Boring as *Theology of the New Testament*. New York: de Gruyter, 2000.

Streissguth, Michael. *Johnny Cash at Folsom Prison: The Making of a Masterpiece*. Cambridge, MA: Da Capo/Perseus, 2004.

———. "Merle Haggard's Lost Interview: Country Icon on Johnny Cash, Prison Life." *Rolling Stone*. January 4, 2017. https://www.rollingstone.com/music/music-country/merle-haggards-lost-interview-country-icon-on-johnny-cash-prison-life-193183/.

Stuhlmacher, Peter. *Biblische Theologie des Neuen Testaments*. 2 vols. Göttingen: Vandenhoeck & Ruprecht, 1992–99. Translated by Daniel P. Bailey with Jostein Adna as *Biblical Theology of the New Testament*. Edited by Bailey and Adna. Grand Rapids: Eerdmans, 2018.

Stylianopoulos, Theodore G. *The New Testament: An Orthodox Perspective*. Brookline, MA: Holy Cross Orthodox Press, 1997.

———. "Scripture and Tradition in the Church." Pages 21–34 in *The Cambridge Companion to Orthodox Christian Theology*. Edited by Mary B. Cunningham and Elizabeth Theokritoff. Cambridge: Cambridge University Press, 2008.

Sundberg, Walter. "Limitations of the Lectionary." *WW* 10 (1990): 14–20.

Suskind, Ron. "Without a Doubt: Faith, Certainty, and the Presidency of George W. Bush." *New York Times Magazine*. October 17, 2004: 42–51, 64, 102, 106.

Talbert, Charles H. *Literary Patterns, Theological Themes, and the Genre of Luke-Acts*. SBLMS 20. Missoula, MT: Scholars, 1974.

Tannehill, Robert C. *Dying and Rising with Christ: A Study in Pauline Theology*. BZNW 32. Berlin: Töpelmann, 1967.

Taylor, Barbara Brown. *Holy Envy: Finding God in the Faith of Others*. New York: HarperOne, 2019.

Terrien, Samuel. *The Magnificat: Musicians as Biblical Interpreters*. New York: Paulist, 1995.

Theissen, Gerd. *Die Religion der ersten Christen: Eine Theorie des Urchristentums.* Gütersloh: Gütersloher, 2000.

———. *Lokalkolorit und Zeitgeschichte in den Evangelien: Ein Beitrag zur Geschichte der synoptischen Tradition.* NTOA 8. Göttingen: Vandenhoeck & Ruprecht, 1989. Translated by Linda M. Moloney as *The Gospels in Context: Social and Political History in the Synoptic Tradition.* Minneapolis: Fortress, 1991.

Theron, Daniel J. "Remembering Professor Otto Piper." *inSpire* 6 (Summer/Fall, 2001): 41.

Thistlethwaite, Susan Brooks. "Every Two Minutes: Battered Women and Feminist Interpretation." Pages 96–107 in *Feminist Interpretation of the Bible.* Edited by Letty M. Russell. Philadelphia: Fortress, 1985.

Thomas, Gabrielle. "The Human Icon: Gregory of Nazianzus on Being an *Imago Dei.*" *SJT* 72 (2019): 166–81.

———. *The Image of God in the Theology of Gregory of Nazianzus.* Cambridge: Cambridge University Press, 2019.

Thomas, R. W. "The Meaning of the Terms 'Life' and 'Death' in the Fourth Gospel and in Paul." *SJT* 21 (1968): 199–212.

Thompson, Marianne Meye. *The Humanity of Jesus in the Fourth Gospel.* Philadelphia: Fortress, 1988.

———. *The Promise of the Father: Jesus and God in the New Testament.* Louisville: Westminster John Knox, 2000.

Thornton, Lionel Spencer. *The Dominion of Christ.* London: Dacre, 1952.

Thurman, Howard. *Deep Is the Hunger: Meditations for Apostles of Sensitiveness.* New York: Harper & Row, 1951.

———. *The Inward Journey.* New York: Harper & Row, 1961.

———. *The Search for Common Ground: An Inquiry into the Basis of Man's Experience of Community.* New York: Harper & Row, 1973.

Travis, Stephen H. *Christ and the Judgement of God: The Limits of Divine Retribution in New Testament Thought.* 2nd ed. Peabody, MA: Hendrickson, 2008.

Trible, Phylis. *Texts of Terror: Literary-Feminist Readings of Biblical Narratives.* OBT. Philadelphia: Fortress, 1984.

"Triennial Cycle." *EncJud* 15: 1386–89.

Tsui, Teresa Kuo-Yu. "'Baptized into His Death' (Rom 6,3) and 'Clothed with Christ' (Gal 3,27): The Soteriological Meaning of Baptism in Light of Pauline Apocalyptic." *ETL* 88 (2012): 395–417.

Twain, Mark. *Pudd'nhead Wilson: A Tale.* Pages 913–1056 in Twain, *Mississippi Writings: The Adventures of Tom Sawyer, Life on the Mississippi, Adventures of Huckleberry Finn, Pudd'nhead Wilson.* Edited by Guy Cardwell. LOA. New York: Library of America, 1982.

———. "The War Prayer." Pages 652–55 in Twain, *Collected Tales, Sketches, Speeches, & Essays 1891–1910*. Edited by Louis J. Budd. LOA 61. New York: Library of America, 1992.

Tyndale, William. *Tyndale's New Testament*. Edited by David Daniell. London: Yale University Press, 1996.

———. *Tyndale's Old Testament*. Edited by David Daniell. London: Yale University Press, 1992.

Ulanov, Ann, and Barry Ulanov. *Primary Speech: A Psychology of Prayer*. Atlanta: John Knox, 1982.

Underhill, Evelyn. *Collected Papers of Evelyn Underhill*. Edited by Lucy Menzies. London: Longmans, Green and Co., 1946.

Unnik, W. C. van, ed. *Studies in John Presented to Professor Dr. J. N. Sevenster on the Occasion of His Seventieth Birthday*. NovTSup 24. Leiden: Brill, 1970.

Unnik, Willem C. van. "The Authority of the Presbyters in Irenaeus' Works." Pages 248–60 in *God's Christ and His People: Festschrift for N. A. Dahl*. Edited by Jacob Jervell and Wayne A. Meeks. Oslo: Universitetsforlaget, 1977.

Van Harn, Roger E., ed. *The Lectionary Commentary: Theological Exegesis for Sunday's Texts*. 3 vols. Grand Rapids: Eerdmans, 2001.

Vanhoozer, Kevin. *Is There a Meaning in This Text? The Bible, the Reader, and the Morality of Literary Knowledge*. Grand Rapids: Zondervan, 1998.

Via, Dan O., Jr. *Self-Deception and Wholeness in Paul and Matthew*. Minneapolis: Fortress, 1990.

Volf, Miroslav. *Exclusion and Embrace: A Theological Exploration of Identity, Otherness, and Reconciliation*. Nashville: Abingdon, 1996.

Vorster, Willem S. "Heterodoxy in 1 John." *Neot* 9 (1975): 87–97.

Vouga, François. *Une théologie du Nouveau Testament*. MB 43. Geneva: Labor et Fides, 2001.

Wacker, Grant. *America's Pastor: Billy Graham and the Shaping of a Nation*. Cambridge, MA: Belknap, 2014.

Wagner, Günther. *Pauline Baptism and the Pagan Mysteries*. Edinburgh: Oliver and Boyd, 1967.

Wainwright, Geoffrey. "Towards an Ecumenical Hermeneutic: How Can All Christians Read the Scriptures Together?" *Greg* 76 (1995): 639–62.

Ware, Kallistos. *The Orthodox Way*. London: Mowbray, 1979.

Wasserstein, Wendy. "Spring Theater: Where You and I Become Us." *New York Times*. February 23, 2003. https://www.nytimes.com/2003/02/23/theater/spring-theater-where-you-and-i-become-us.html?searchResultPosition=174.

Watson, Francis. *Text, Church and World: Biblical Interpretation in Theological Perspective*. Edinburgh: T&T Clark, 1994.

Waugh, Evelyn. *Brideshead Revisited*. EL 172. New York: Knopf, 1993.
Webster, John. *Holy Scripture: A Dogmatic Sketch*. CIT. Cambridge: Cambridge University Press, 2003.
Wedderburn, A. J. M. "The Theological Structure of Romans v. 12." *NTS* 19 (1973): 339–54.
Weems, Ann. *Psalms of Lament*. Louisville: Westminster John Knox, 1995.
Weil, Simone. "Reflections on the Right Use of School Studies with a View to the Love of God." Pages 105–16 in Weil, *Waiting for God*. New York: Harper & Row, 1951.
Weiss, Bernhard. *Biblical Theology of the New Testament*. 3rd rev. ed. Translated by David Eaton. Edinburgh: T&T Clark, 1882–83.
Welch, Claude. *In This Name: The Doctrine of the Trinity in Contemporary Theology*. New York: Scribner's Sons, 1952.
Welch, Jack, with John Byrne. *Straight from the Gut*. New York: Warner Business, 2001.
Welch, Jack, with Suzy Welch. *Winning*. New York: HarperCollins, 2005.
Wells, David F. *God in the Wasteland: The Reality of Truth in a World of Fading Dreams*. 2nd ed. Grand Rapids: Eerdmans, 1995.
Wells, Kyle B. "The Liberation of the Body of Creation: Towards a Pauline Environmental Ethic." *JTS* 73 (2022): 92–103.
Welz, Claudia. *Humanity in God's Image: An Interdisciplinary Exploration*. Oxford: Oxford University Press, 2016.
Werner, Eric. *The Sacred Bridge: The Interdependence of Liturgy and Music in Synagogue and Church during the First Millennium*. London: Dobson, 1959.
Wessel, Susan. *Passion and Compassion in Early Christianity*. Cambridge: Cambridge University Press, 2016.
Westcott, Brooke Foss. *The Epistles of St. John: The Greek Text with Notes*. London: Macmillan & Co., 1905.
Westermann, Claus. *Blessing in the Bible and the Life of the Church*. OBT. Philadelphia: Fortress, 1978.
———, ed. *Essays on Old Testament Hermeneutics*. Translated by James Luther Mays and James C. G. Greig. Richmond, VA: John Knox, 1964.
———. *Genesis: An Introduction*. Minneapolis: Fortress, 1992.
———. *Praise and Lament in the Psalms*. Atlanta: John Knox, 1981.
Wilckens, Ulrich. *Theologie des Neuen Testaments*. 3 vols. Neukirchen-Vluyn: Neukirchener, 2002.
Wilder, Amos N. "The First, Second, and Third Epistles of John: Introduction and Exegesis." *IB* 12 (1957): 207–313.

Wiles, Virginia, Alexandra Brown, and Graydon F. Snyder, eds. *Putting Body & Soul Together: Essays in Honor of Robin Scroggs.* Valley Forge: Trinity Press International, 1997.

Wilkinson, Bruce. *The Prayer of Jabez.* New York: Multnomah Books, 2000.

Williams, Rowan D. *On Christian Theology.* CCT. Oxford: Blackwell, 2000.

Windhorst, Christof. "Luther and the 'Enthusiasts': Theological Judgments in His Lecture on the First Epistle of John (1527)." *JRH* 9 (1977): 339–48.

Witten, Marsha. *All Is Forgiven: The Secular Message in American Protestantism.* Princeton: Princeton University Press, 1993.

Wojtyla, Karol Jósef. *See* [Pope] John Paul II.

Wolff, Hans Walter. *Anthropology of the Old Testament.* Philadelphia: Fortress, 1974.

Woll, D. Bruce. *Johannine Christianity in Conflict: Authority, Rank, and Succession in the First Farewell Discourse.* SBLDS 60. Chico, CA: Scholars, 1981.

Wolterstorff, Nicholas. *Lament for a Son.* Grand Rapids: Eerdmans, 1987.

Work, Telford. *Living and Active: Scripture in the Economy of Salvation.* SD. Grand Rapids: Eerdmans, 2002.

Worthington, Jonathan. "Philo of Alexandria and Romans 5:12–21: Adam, Death, and Grace." In Blackwell, Goodrich, and Matson, *Reading Romans in Context,* 80–86.

Wrede, William. *Das Messiasgeheimnis in den Evangelien.* Göttingen: Vandenhoeck & Ruprecht, 1901. Translated by J. C. G. Greig as *The Messianic Secret.* LTT. London: James Clarke, 1971.

———. "The Task and Methods of 'New Testament Theology.'" Pages 68–116 in *The Nature of New Testament Theology: The Contribution of William Wrede and Adolf Schlatter.* Translated and edited by Robert Morgan. SBT 2nd ser. London: SCM, 1973.

Wren, Christopher S. *Winners Got Scars Too: The Life and Legends of Johnny Cash.* New York: Dial, 1971.

Wright, G. Ernest. *The Book of the Acts of God: Christian Scholarship Interprets the Bible.* Garden City, NY: Doubleday, 1957.

Wright, G. Wilson. *The Wheel of Fire: Interpretations of Shakespearean Tragedy.* London: Routledge, 2001.

Wright, N. T. *Jesus and the Victory of God.* London: SPCK, 1996.

———. *The New Testament and the People of God.* London: SPCK, 1992.

Yeago, David S. "The New Testament and the Nicene Dogma: A Contribution to the Recovery of Theological Exegesis." *ProEcc* 3 (1994): 152–64.

Young, Frances M. *The Art of Performance: Towards a Theology of Holy Scripture.* London: Darton, Longman, and Todd, 1990.
Zaleski, Philip, and Carol Zaleski. *Prayer: A History.* Boston: Houghton Mifflin, 2005.
Ziesler, John A. "Anthropology of Hope." *ExpTim* 90 (1979): 4–9.
———. *The Meaning of Righteousness in Paul: A Linguistic and Theological Enquiry.* SNTSMS 20. Cambridge: Cambridge University Press, 1972.
Zimmermann, Jens. *Dietrich Bonhoeffer's Christian Humanism.* Oxford: Oxford University Press, 2019.

Index of Authors

Abbott, Walter M., 298n6
Abel, František, 179n54
Abraham, William J., 28n33
Achtemeier, Elizabeth, 306n40
Adam, A. K. M., 14–15
Adna, Jostein, 13n43
Ainsworth, Henry, 289
Ali, Abdullah Yasuf, 105n49
Allen, Fred, 25, 144
Allen, Horace T., Jr., 299n12, 303n36
Allen, Woody, 17, 18n1
Allison, Dale C., Jr., 124n29, 322n20
Alsup, John E., 14n51
Alter, Robert, 204n28
Altmann, Alexander, 321n18
Alyan, Hala, 313
Anderson, Michael, 341n5
Anonymous, 51n42, 72n42, 307n43, 345–46n26
Aquinas, Thomas, 4, 17, 32
Armstrong, James F., 55n56
Armstrong, Vic, 336n14
Augustine of Hippo, 3, 32, 61, 69, 70, 90, 119, 323–24, 382

Babcock, William, 323n24
Bacharach, Burt, 86n21
Bachmann, E. Theodore, 4n2
Bailey, Lloyd R., Sr., 13n43, 159n5, 171n35, 298n4, 299n11, 300n23, 301n25, 303n34
Baker, J. A., 35n51
Balch, David L., 215n8
Balentine, Samuel E., 63n9
Balthasar, Hans Urs von, 330n49

Baltzer, Klaus, 150n12
Bar-Alin, Yihiel Michael, 278n24
Barclay, William, 335
Barr, James, 158n2
Barrett, C. K., 88n26, 165n17, 184n8, 257n4, 261n12, 263n16
Barrosse, Thomas, 164–65n16
Barth, Karl, 9–11, 14, 24–25, 44, 76n53, 156n22, 261n11, 270–71, 316n9
Barton, John, 16n59
Bartsch, Hans-Werner, 270, 273–74
Bauer, Georg Lorenz, 5–6, 16n59, 17–18
Bauer, Walter, 43
Bauerschmidt, Frederick Christian, 324–25n29
Baumgarten, Otto, 81n8
Baur, Ferdinand Christian, 6, 230n2
Bearsley, Patrick J., 196n13, 207n34
Beasley-Murray, G. R., 11n31
Beattie, Tina, 207n35
Beerbohm, Max, x
Benchley, Robert, 368
Bergmeier, Roland, 245n37
Best, Ernest, 82–83n
Best, Isabel, 339n20
Bethge, Eberhard, 36n53
Betram, Georg, 125n2
Bettenson, Henry, 308n45
Biddle, Mark E., 13–14n50
Bigsby, Christopher, 344n18
Black, C. Clifton, ixn3, 73–74n46, 88n26, 96n18, 116n17, 202n26, 214n7, 231n4, 277n19, 281n2, 378n8
Blackwell, Ben C., 162n13, 172–73n39

INDEX OF AUTHORS

Blazen, Ivan Thomas, 167n22
Bloesch, Daniel W., 37n57
Bloom, Allan, 327n40
Bloom, Anthony, 74–75
Blumenthal, David R., 197n15
Boccaccini, Gabriele, 159n4
Bogart, John, 230n1, 247n44
Bohn, Carole R., 93n11
Boismard, Marie-Emile, 252n55
Bolt, Robert, 292
Bonhoeffer, Dietrich, 36–37, 102, 309n47, 316n9, 319n16, 330n48, 333, 339
Bonsirven, Joseph, 11
Borchert, Gerald L., 44n6, 56n59
Boring, M. Eugene, 3n1, 11n34, 27n29, 205n31
Bornkamm, Günther, 175–76n46, 236n16
Børresen, Kari Elisabeth, 315n5
Botterweck, G. Johannes, 19
Bottum, Joseph, 345n26
Boulding, Maria, 386–87
Bousset, Wilhelm, 7, 22
Bouyer, Louis, 311n52
Bowden, John, 9n22, 14n51, 36n54, 159n4, 309n47
Bowen, C. A., 265n22
Braaten, Carl E., 31n37, 309n47
Bradbury, Ray, 367
Breecke, Milo L., 268n27
Brett, Mark G., 304n37
Brocke, Michael, 94n13, 103n43, 104n45
Brokaw, Tom, 344
Bromiley, Geoffrey W., 9n20, 10n27, 25n24, 156n22, 261n11, 316n9
Brown, Alexandra, 186n11
Brown, Charles E., 179n55
Brown, David, 28n32
Brown, Raymond E., 73n45, 82–85, 86, 88n28, 91, 145n3, 195n8, 195n9, 200n21, 203n27, 205n30, 206n32, 230n1, 238n20, 239n25, 241n27, 243n32, 244n34, 246n41, 246n42, 247n44, 248n46, 250n51, 250n52, 250n53, 252n55, 252n56, 259n6, 259n7, 266n25, 310n49
Brown, William P., 73–74n46, 91n6
Browne, Joanne Carlson, 93n11
Bruce, F. F., 172–73n39

Brueggemann, Walter, 63n9, 304n38
Brunner, Emil, 156n20
Budd, Louis J., 362n9
Buechner, Frederick, 256
Bultmann, Rudolf, ix, 9–11, 14, 22, 24, 27, 32, 35, 44, 80, 161n10, 163n15, 177–78n48, 233n8, 238n21, 244n33, 247n45, 250n51, 251n54, 260n9, 270, 274, 281n6
Burke, David G., 287n1
Burkert, Walter, 210n3
Bush, George W., 359n1
Byrdson, Ricky, 336n15
Byrne, John, 338n17
Byrne, Robert, 33n46

Cahill, Lisa Sowle, 321n18
Caird, George Bradford, 13, 14, 242n30
Campbell, Douglas A., 259n6
Campenhausen, Hans von, 242n31
Cardenal, Ernesto, 184n7
Cardwell, Guy, 97n20
Carnegie, Dale, 338
Carr, Patrick, 349n1
Carroll, John T., 118n20
Carter, Craig A., 30–31n36
Carter, Jimmy, 361
Cash, John R. (Johnny), 349–58
Cash, Vivian, 358n34
Cassidy, Ronald, 179n55
Caussade, Jean Pierre de, 96n19
Cerfaux, Lucien, 179n55
Chadwick, Henry, 26n27
Chapman, Dom John, 69
Charlesworth, James H., 66n22, 252n55
Chesterton, G. K., 230
Childs, Brevard S., 13, 18, 28, 65n20, 84n15
Chittister, Joan, 79n1, 88n28
Christie, Agatha, 343
Churchill, Sir Winston, 158, 390–91n2
Clark, Gordon R., 317n13
Clyne-Rekhy, Edna, 368n4
Coates, J. R., 9n22
Cohen, Paula Marantz, 323n25
Cohen, Shaye J. D., 211n4
Cole, G. D. H., 327n37
Colledge, Edmund, 324n28
Colson, Charles, 334, 336

Index of Authors

Conzelmann, Hans, 80–85, 168n26, 195n10, 233n10, 246n39, 247n45
Cousar, Charles B., 178n50, 304n38
Craddock, Fred B., 304n38, 376n5, 403n28
Cranfield, C. E. B., 170n34
Cremer, Franz Gerhard, 167n21
Crim, Keith, 65n18
Crouch, Carly L., 319n15
Crouch, James E., 143n32, 222n11
Cullmann, Oscar, 9, 35, 172–73n39
Culpepper, R. Alan, 88n26, 116n16, 116n17, 210n3, 239n22
Cumont, Franz, 161n10
Cunningham, Mary B., 273n9, 275n16
Cupitt, Susan, 9n22
Curtis, Edward M., 109
Cutler, Howard C., 328–29n42

Dahill, Lisa A., 339n20
Dahl, Nils Alstrup, 12, 13n43, 87–88
Dakake, Maria Massi, 106n52
Dalai Lama, the (Tenzin Gyatso), 328–29n42
Daniell, David, 287n2, 288–90, 292, 295
Davey, Francis Noel, 9
David, Hal, 86n21
Davies, Donald McKay, 53n49
Davies, W. D., 159, 261n12, 322n20
Dean, O. C., Jr., 225n13
De Luis, Pio, 324n26
Denny, James, 262
Derrida, Jacques, 15, 25, 32
Descamps, Albert, 167–68n23
DeShannon, Jackie, 86n21
De Wet, Chris L., 178–79n53
Dibelius, Martin, 8
Di Cesare, Mario A., 76n55
Dickens, Charles, 333
Didion, Joan, ix
Diezinger, Walter, 168n24
Dodd, C. H., ix, 13, 27, 81, 86n20, 114, 163n14, 172n37, 243n31, 257, 281n3
Donahue, John R., 131n12
Donfried, Karl Paul, 195n8, 238n19, 241n26
Donin, Hiyam Halevy, 307n44
Dru, Alexander, 155n18, 328n41
D'Sa, Francis X., 103n42

Dunn, James D. G., 12, 230n2, 234n12
Dunstan, Gordon Reginald, 57n68
Dyke, Henry van, 190n16

Eastman, Susan Groves, 174n41
Eaton, David, 6n9
Ebeling, Gerhard, 29, 35n52
Edwards, Jonathan, 69
Edwards, Ruth B., 259n6
Ehrhardt, Marianne, 193n3
Eichrodt, Walter, 35
Eldredge, Laurence, 5n3, 18n4
Eliot, George, 6n8
Elliott, John H., 215n9, 231n6
Elpidophorous, Archbishop of America, 271
Elshtain, Jean Bethke, 100n28
Eltester, Walther, 80n4
Emerson, Ralph Waldo, 100–101n33
Englezakis, Benedict, 172–73n39
Erickson, Richard J., 184n6
Esler, Philip S., 11
Evans, Craig A., 142n29

Fabry, Heinz-Josef, 195n11
Farris, Stephen, 200n21
Faskekaš, L., 168n24
Faw, Chalmer E., 179n55
Feldmeier, Reinhard, 13–14n50
Fergusson, David S., 325n30
Feuerbach, Ludwig, 15
Feuillet, André, 166n19, 168n24
Filson, Floyd V., 9n23, 45–46n10, 66n25
Finkel, Asher, 94n14
Fischer, Robert H., 72n42
Fitzgerald, Robert, 155n17
Fitzgerald, Sally, 155n17
Fitzmyer, Joseph A., 130n10, 133n14, 160n6, 195n8
Fletcher, John C., 102n39
Floreen, Harold, 58n71
Florovsky, Georges, 273n9
Flusser, David, 207n36
Foley, Grover, 76n53
Ford, David F., 10n28, 68n30
Fortna, Robert T., 172–73n39
Frank, Anne, 406n39
Freedman, David Noel, 195n11
Frend, W. H. C., 198n17

INDEX OF AUTHORS

Fretheim, Terence E., 189n15, 305n39
Freud, Sigmund, 327
Friedrich, Gerhard, 8–9, 19
Frizzell, Lawrence, 94n14
Frymer-Kensky, Tikva, 317
Fuller, Reginald H., 9, 303n36, 304n38
Funk, Robert W., 73n45
Furnish, Victor Paul, 119n21

Gabler, Johann Philipp, 4–7, 8, 11, 18–22
Gadamer, Hans-Georg, 15, 32
Gallagher, Joseph, 298n6
García Martínez, Florentino, 150n13
Gardner, Helen, 100n29
Garfield, Simon, 356n25, 358n34
Gaventa, Beverly Roberts, 124n29, 174n42, 197n14, 304n38
Geertz, Clifford, 23n16
Gerstenberger, Erhard, 22
Gibran, Kahlil, 357
Gnilka, Joachim, 12, 14
Godsey, John, 15n57
Goodrich, John K., 162n13
Goppelt, Leonhard, 14, 242n28, 244n35
Graef, Hilda C., 194n5, 195n9
Graf, F. W., 43n3
Graff, Garrett M., 360n5
Graham, Billy, 334n1, 336, 337, 338–39
Graham, Elaine L., 123n27
Grant, Marshal, 351n7
Graubard, Baruch, 104–5
Grave, Mike, 403n28
Green, David E., 263n17
Green, Joel B., 15, 195n8, 304n38
Green, Jonathan, 101n37
Greig, James C. G., 24n22, 31n40
Grimsley, Ronald, 327n40
Grobel, Kendrick, 10, 24n18, 281n6
Gruchy, John W. de, 316n9, 339n20
Grundmann, Walter, 125n2, 161n7
Gunkel, Hermann, 22
Guralnick, Peter, 349n3
Gustafson, James M., 178n49

Haenchen, Ernst, 121n25
Hagman, Edward, 38n60, 69n35, 311n52
Hahn, Ferdinand, 12, 27n29

Haleem, Muhammad Abdel, 106n51, 106n53
Hall, Douglas John, 315n5
Halleuz, André de, 167–68n23
Hals, Ronald M., 208n38
Hample, Fred, 144n1
Hand, Thomas A., 69n35
Hanson, Paul, 18
Harder, Günther, 126n6
Hardwick, Elizabeth, ix
Hardy, Daniel W., 68n30
Haroutunian, Joseph, 58n72
Harrisville, Roy A., 299n13
Harry, Duke of Sussex, 323n25
Hayes, John H., 304n38
Hays, Richard B., 13
Headlam, Arthur C., 169n27
Hegel, Georg Wilhelm Friedrich, 14, 100
Heidegger, Martin, 14, 32, 48
Heidemann, W. M., 44n6
Heinemann, Joseph, 104n46
Heitmüller, Wilhelm, 230n2
Hengel, Martin, 159
Henley, William Ernest, 100n29
Herbert, George, 76n55
Heschel, Abraham Joshua, 66n24, 104, 308
Hessel, Dieter T., 299n12
Higgins, A. J. B., 233n9
Hill, Edmund, 323n22, 324n27
Hitchcock, Francis Ryan Montgomery, 162n12
Hitchens, Christopher, 75n50
Hoare, R. W. N., 11n31
Hobbes, Thomas, 100, 326
Hoffmann, J. C. K. von, 46
Holden, D. T., 161n9, 168n24
Holladay, Carl R., 304n38
Holladay, William L., 302n30
Holtzmann, Heinrich Julius, 6
Honderich, Holly, ixn2
Hooke, S. H., 121n25
Hooker, Morna D., 176n47, 202n26
Hoon, Paul W., 309n47
Horn, Friedrich Wilhelm, 11n34, 27n29
Horst, William, 178n52
Horváth, Tibor, 234n12
Hoskyns, E. C., 9, 25n23

Index of Authors

Houf, Horace T., 57n64
Houlden, J. Leslie, 235n14, 245n36
Houston, Keith, 390-91n2
Hübner, Hans, 13
Hudleston, Roger, 69n32
Hume, David, 294, 326
Hunter, A. M., 165n18
Huntress, Erminie, 14n53
Hurst, L. D., 13n43, 88n27

Ibn Hanbal, Ahmad, 105n50
Ivanhoe, Philip J., 329n43

Jackayya, B. H., 245n36
Jackson, Dave, 336n15
Jackson, Neta, 336n15
Jacob, Edmond, 179n55
Jaquette, James L., 179n55
Jawien, Andrzej (pseud. for Karol Jósef Wojtyla), 341
Jenkins, Jerry B., 336n14
Jensen, Joseph, 305n39
Jenson, Robert W., 31
Jepsen, Alfred, 285n16
Jeremias, Joachim, 14, 121
Jervell, Jacob, 237n17, 240-41n25
Jewett, Robert, 278n23
Jocz, J., 58n71
John Paul II, Pope (Karol Jósef Wojtyla), 340-48
Johnson, Michael A., 321n18
Johnson, Sherman E., 304n38
Jonge, Marinus de, 238n19
Jónsson, Gunnlauger A., 315n5
Jordan, Clarence, 401-2, 404n31
Joyner, Will, 373n1
Juel, Donald H., 13n43, 87n25
Julian of Norwich, 324-26
Jung, Kevin, 321n18

Kant, Immanuel, 14, 100
Karon, Jan, 334n4
Käsemann, Ernst, 12, 119n21, 171n36, 172n38, 174n43, 231n6, 242n29, 259n6, 265n21
Katz, David S., 287n2, 294-95
Kaufmann, Walter, 99n26

Keck, Leander E., xi, 79n2, 98n25, 110, 116n17, 153n15, 158n1, 174, 178n51, 284n10
Kee, Howard Clark, 73n45
Kelly, Geffrey B., 37n57
Kelly, Walt, 39
Kelsey, David H., 269-74
Kermode, Frank, 89, 204
Khalidi, Jarif, 105n50
Kierkegaard, Søren, 155n18, 328, 382n3
Kilby, Karen, 325n30
Kittel, Gerhard, 8-9, 19
Klassen, William, 57n63, 242n28
Klein, Günter, 234n11
Klotz, Leopold, 45-46n10
Knight, G. Wilson, 364
Knowles, Michael, 183n5
Knox, T. M., 100n33
Koester, Helmut, 255n61
Korzybski, Alfred, 296, 312
Koster, Henry, 336n11
Kraft, Robert A., 159n4
Kraus, Hans-Joachim, 65n18
Krauss, Reinhard, 339n20
Kraynak, Robert P., 108n1
Krey, Peter D., 286n17
Krey, Philip D. W., 286n17
Krodel, Gerhard, 259n6
Kümmel, Werner Georg, 14
Küng, Hans, 254n59
Kutsko, John F., 287n1
Kyle, Donald G., 161n10
Kysar, Robert, 261, 264n19

Lachs, Samiel Tobias, 322n20
LaCocque, André, 186
LaHaye, Tim, 73, 336
Lammé, Nicholas, 141n26
Lane, Anthony, 295
Lang, Justin, 207n36
Langford, Thomas A., 194n6, 262n15, 399n12
LaPierre, Wayne, 102
Lash, Ephrem, 275n16
Lash, Nicholas, 26n28
Lattimore, Richmond, 364n12
Lattke, Michael, 193n3
Leclerq, Jean, 71n41

INDEX OF AUTHORS

Legarreta-Castillo, Felipe de Jesus, 178n53
Lehmann, Helmut T., 4n2
Lehmann, Paul L., 55n56
Leitch, James W., 29n34
Leith, John H., 408n43
Lemire, Christy, 336n14
Lennon, John, 402n27
Leonard, Sheldon, 339n19
Lessing, G. E., 26n27
Levenson, Jon D., 314n3
Levinas, Emmanuel, 25, 109n7
Levine, Lee I., 211n4
Lewis, C. S., 75, 97, 311, 363–64
Lietzmann, Hans, 43
Lieu, Judith M., 84–88, 246n42
Lindars, Barnabas, 203n27
Locke, John, 100
Lockett, Darian R., 230–31n3
Loewe, H., 151n14, 321n19
Loisy, Alfred, 210
Lonergan, Kenneth, 359
Longarino, Joseph, 166n20
Longenecker, Richard N., 66n22
Lopate, Phillip, xn5
Lorberbaum, Yair, 320n17
Louth, Andrew, 34n49, 71n41
Lukens, Nancy, 339n20
Lumet, Sidney, 356
Lundbom, Jack R., 195n11
Luther, Martin, 4, 32, 72n42, 86, 125, 156n20, 286, 290, 291n12, 364, 390
Luz, Ulrich, 143n32, 222n11
Lysen, Laura M., 325n30

MacDonald, Neil B., 9n24
Machiavelli, Niccolo, 100
Mackay, John A., 44, 51n44, 52, 54n53
Macquarrie, John, 207–8n36
Magrassi, Mariano, 38n60, 69n35, 311n52
Malcolm, Noel, 326n32
Malherbe, A. J., 240–41n25
Mangold, James, 355n24
Marcus, Joel, 138n23, 265n20
Marshall, Bruce D., 32n45
Marshall, Catherine, 336, 390–91n2
Marshall, Christopher D., 149n11

Marshall, Donald G., 32n44
Marshall, I. Howard, 12, 14
Marshall, Peter, 390–91n2
Martyn, J. Louis, 39, 113n14, 205n29, 264n19, 265n20
Marx, Groucho, 25n25
Marx, Karl, 15
Masters, Judith R., 100n33
Masters, Roger D., 100n33
Matera, Frank, 13, 14
Matheson, George, 401n23
Matson, Jason, 162n13
Mayer, Günter, 64n14
Mayes, A. D. H., 304n37
Mays, James Luther, 24n22, 108, 189n15
McBrien, Richard P., 194n4, 208n37
McCartney, Paul, 402n27
McCord, James I., 57
McFarland, Ian A., 325n30
McGrath, Alister, 287n2, 289–90, 293, 295
McMellan, Vernon, 334n1
McNeil, Brian, 13–14n50
Meeks, M. Douglas, 123n27
Meeks, Wayne A., 8n19, 22–23, 237n17, 240–41n25, 248n47, 266n24
Meier, John P., 111, 222n10
Menzies, Lucy, 74n47
Merckling, Kaitlynn C., 147n6, 193n3
Metzger, Bruce M., 55n56
Meyer, Paul W., 88n26, 118n20
Middleton, J. Richard, 314–15n3, 324n28
Miles, C. Austin, 265n22
Milgrom, Jacob, 278n23
Mill, John Stuart, 100–101n33
Miller, Arthur, 340–48, 359
Miller, Patrick D., 62n3, 62n4, 63n6, 63n9, 66
Mills, Liston O., 158n1
Minear, Paul S., 12, 18, 187n12, 229n17, 258n5, 284n11, 406–7
Mitton, C. Leslie, 170n34, 179n55
Moberly, R. W. L., 16n59, 18
Moehringer, J. R., 323n25
Moffatt, James, 193n3
Moloney, Francis J., 203n27
Moloney, Linda M., 8n19, 81n8
Monod, Wilfred, 48

Montague, W. J., 12n38, 231n6
Montefiore, Claude G., 104n46, 151n14, 321n19
Montgomery, W., 9n22, 185n9
Moore, George Foot, 161n8
Mooyart-Doubleday, Barbara, 406n39
More, Sir Thomas, 290–92
Morgan, Florence A., 168n26
Morgan, Robert, 6n10, 7, 15, 18n3, 20n7
Moule, C. F. D., 154n16, 167n23, 179n55, 252n56
Moxnes, Halvor, 132n13, 226n15
Moynahan, Brian, 287n2, 290–92
Muddiman, John, 120n22
Müller, Gerhard Ludwig, 37n57
Munck, Johannes, 237n17
Murdoch, Iris, 280
Murphy, Roland E., 305n39
Murphy-O'Connor, Jerome, 161n7
Myers, Jacob M., 208n38

Nasr, Seyyed Hossein, 105n49
Navone, John, 209n39
Neill, Stephen, 230n2
Nellas, Panayiotis, 122n26
Nelson, Richard, 300n16, 301
Neusner, Jacob, 159n4
Neville, David J., 154n16
Newsome, James D., 304n38
Nicholson, Adam, 287n2, 292–94, 295
Nickelsburg, George W. E., 150n12, 159n5, 161n7, 172n39
Niebuhr, H. Richard, 264, 285n13, 300n21
Niebuhr, Reinhold, 329
Nietzsche, Friedrich, 15, 99
Nijf, Onno M. van, 210n3
Nolland, John, 195n10
Norton, David Fate, 326n34
Norton, Mary J., 326n34
Noth, Martin, 22
Null, Gary, 334n6
Nussbaum, Martha C., 123–24
Nuwer, Rachel, 368n4

Ochs, Peter, 69n34
O'Connor, Flannery, 154–55
O'Day, Gail R., 199n20

Ogden, Schubert M., 208n37
Old, Hughes Oliphant, 300n17
Olson, Dennis T., 28n31
Orlean, Susan, 336n16
Osiek, Carolyn, 215n8

Paine, Gustavus Swift, 287n1
Painter, John, 116n16
Park, Jeongsoo, 140n25
Parker, Rebecca, 93n11
Parkes, James E., 303n34
Pascal, Blaise, 89
Paul VI, Pope, 298n5
Pelikan, Jaroslav, 207n33, 207n36
Pentkovsky, Aleksei, 72n42
Perkins, Pheme, 238n21
Perrin, Norman, 249–51
Petersen, Anders Klostergaard, 159n4
Peterson, Ryan S., 325n30
Petuchowski, Jakob J., 94n13, 103n43, 104n45
Phillips, Adam, 326n31
Piper, Otto A., 9, 41–60, 61–68, 70, 71–75, 233
Placher, William C., 70n37
Popkin, Richard H., 326n35
Porte, Joel, 100–101n33
Post, Ted, 313n2
Price, James L., 179n56, 252n55
Procter-Smith, Marjorie, 302n31
Pulleyn, Simon J., 66

Quell, Gottfried, 125n2

Rad, Gerhard von, 159n5, 171n35, 315n6
Radner, Ephraim, 298n7
Räisänen, Heikki, 9, 11, 14
Raitt, Thomas M., 306n40
Ramsey, Boniface, 323n24
Reno, R. R., 298n7
Reumann, John, 195n8, 296n2
Riches, J. K., 11n31
Ricoeur, Paul, 15, 32
Ringgren, Helmer, 19
Robbins, Monika L. S., 356n25
Robertson, Edwin H., 36n54
Robinson, Dominic, 315n5

INDEX OF AUTHORS

Robinson, J. A. T., 48n28
Robinson, James M., 255n61
Rohrbagh, Richard L., 148n8
Roloff, J., 14n51
Roosevelt, Eleanor, 406n39
Rorty, Richard, 32
Rose, Gillian, 109n7
Rosenblatt, Roger, 330n48
Rotelle, John E., 323n22
Rothschild, Fritz A., 104n47
Rousseau, Jean-Jacques, 100, 326–27
Rowe, C. Kavin, 15n58
Ruby, Bertrand, 207n34
Rudin, A. James, 197n15
Rudolph, Kurt, 117n19
Russell, Letty M., 302n32
Russell, Mark, 25
Rütter, Martin, 316n9

Saldarini, Anthony J., 134–35n20
Saliers, Don E., 69n34
Salinger, Elizabeth, 44
Sanday, William, 169n27
Sanders, E. P., 134n18, 136n21, 161n8, 170n33
Sandys-Wunsch, John, 5n3, 18n4
Sartre, Jean-Paul, 101–2
Scharbert, Josef, 62n4
Schillebeeckx, Edward, 262n14
Schindler, D. C., 330n49
Schlatter, Adolf, 7–10, 12, 13, 20–24, 25, 31–32
Schleiermacher, Friedrich, 316–17
Schnackenburg, Rudolf, 203n27, 206n32, 245n36, 249n49, 266n24
Schnelle, Udo, 3n1
Schniewind, Julius, 232n7
Scholar, Angela, 326n36
Schönherr, Albrecht, 37n57
Schrage, Wolfgang, 263n17
Schrenk, Gottlob, 169n28
Schuller, David S., 268n27
Schuller, Eileen M., 66n22, 307n41
Schuller, Robert, 336, 337
Schultz, Siegfried, 230n2
Schulz, Charles M., 402n26
Schüssler Fiorenza, Elisabeth, 256n1

Schweiker, William, 321n18
Schweitzer, Albert, 9n22, 185
Schweizer, Eduard, 112n13, 167n21, 229, 233n9
Schwöbel, Christoph, 109n6
Scroggs, Robin, 169n29
Segovia, Carlos A., 159n4
Segovia, Fernando, 82, 116n16
Seitz, Christopher, 298n7, 300
Senior, Donald, 307n41
Shakespeare, William, 187n12, 288n4, 292, 323n25, 364
Sharpsteen, Ann, 358n34
Shaw, George Bernard, 287
Shelp, Earl E., 268n28
Sherwin, Byron L., 316n10
Silverstein, Shel, 352n13, 354n21
Sinclair, David, 278n24
Sloan, Jordan Taylor, 349n2
Sloyan, Gerard S., 299n14, 300, 301n25, 301n27, 303
Smail, Thomas A., 319n15
Smalley, Beryl, 70n38
Smith, D. Moody, Jr., 11n31, 116n16, 248n47, 252n57, 256n1, 266n24, 268n28, 282
Smith, John E., 69n34
Smith, Louise Pettibone, 14n53
Smith, Norman Kemp, 100n33
Smith, Stevie, 39
Smylie, James H., 55n56
Snyder, Graydon F., 57n63, 186n11, 242n28
Soares-Prabhu, George M., 103n42, 106n52
Sontag, Susan, 340–48
Soskice, Janet Martin, 317n12, 323
Soulen, R. Kendall, 108n2, 123n27
Sowers, Sidney G., 9n23, 35n51
Spicq, Ceslas, 240n23
Spieckermann, Hermann, 13–14n50
Spitz, Lewis W., 4n2
Springsted, Eric O., 124n28
Stählin, Gustav, 125n2
Stalker, D. M. G., 159n5, 175n46, 315n6
Stanton, Graham, 111n9
Steely, John E., 7n13, 14n51
Steere, Douglas V., 382n3
Stegemann, Ekkehard D., 225n13

464

Index of Authors

Stegemann, Wolfgang, 225n13
Steinmetz, David C., 68, 375
Stendahl, Krister, 5, 373–76
Stevenson, Adlai, 38, 101
Stevenson, James, 198n17
Stookey, Lawrence H., 299n15
Strachey, James, 327n38, 327n39
Strauss, David Friedrich, 6, 32
Strauss, Neil, 350
Strecker, Georg, 11–12, 27n29, 81n8
Streissguth, Michael, 351n10, 352n12
Strommen, Merton P., 268n27
Stuhlmacher, Peter, 12, 14
Stylianopoulos, Theodore G., 11, 273n9, 276n17
Sundberg, Walter, 298n8, 300
Sunderland, Ronald, 268n28
Suskind, Ron, 37n58, 101n34

Talbert, Charles H., 228n16
Tannehill, Robert C., 167n21, 168, 179n55
Taylor, Barbara, 326n31
Taylor, Barbara Brown, 373n1
Terrien, Samuel, 199n19
Tetzel, Johann, 291n12
Theissen, Gerd, 8n19, 22
Theokritoff, Elizabeth, 273n9, 275n16
Theron, Daniel J., 45n9, 56n60
Thistlethwaite, Susan Brooks, 302n32
Thomas, Danny, 339n19
Thomas, Gabrielle, 320n17
Thomas, R. W., 175n45
Thompson, Marianne Meye, 92n10, 124n29, 265n21
Thomson, G. T., 25n24, 316n9
Thornton, Lionel Spencer, 270–71, 274
Thurman, Howard, 329–30
Tillich, Paul, 44, 48, 270–71, 274
Tinder, Glenn, 108n1
Torrance, Iain R., 325n30
Torrance, Thomas F., 10n27, 25n24, 261n11, 316n9
Tout, Ilse, 316n9
Towner, Philip H., 287n1
Travis, Stephen H., 149n11
Trible, Phyllis, 147

Tsui, Teresa Kuo-Yu, 167n21
Tucker, Gene M., 304n38
Turner, Max, 15
Twain, Mark, 96, 97n20, 362, 366
Tye, S. F. L., 11n33
Tyndale, William, 288–95

Ulanov, Ann, 73n44, 90n5
Ulanov, Barry, 73n44, 90n5
Underhill, Evelyn, 74
Unnik, Willem C. van, 237n17

Van Harn, Roger E., 304n38
Vanhoozer, Kevin, 15
Vermes, Géza, 259–60n8
Via, Dan O., Jr., 111n10
Vicente, Raul, ixn1
Volf, Miroslav, 156n20
Vorster, Willem S., 245n36
Vouga, François, 12, 27n29

Wacker, Grant, 334n1
Wagner, Günther, 167n21
Wainwright, Geoffrey, 310n50
Walsh, James, 324n28
Ward, Benedicta, 76n54, 111n12
Ward, Richard F., 403n28
Ware, Kallistos, 334
Warfield, B. B., 270, 273–74
Waring, E. Graham, 317n11
Wasserstein, Wendy, 359
Watson, Francis, 15
Watson, Wilfred G. E., 150n13
Waugh, Evelyn, 292
Webster, John, 31n39, 58n73
Wedderburn, A. J. M., 166n20
Weems, Ann, 180, 187
Weil, Simone, 71, 90
Weinsheimer, Joel, 32n44
Weiss, Bernhard, 6
Welch, Claude, 116n18
Welch, Jack, 338
Welch, Suzy, 338n17
Wells, David F., 377
Wells, Kyle B., 174n41
Welz, Claudia, 315n5
Werner, Eric, 296n2, 307n43

465

INDEX OF AUTHORS

Wesley, Charles, 310
Wesley, John, 69, 310, 368
Wessel, Susan, 323n21
Westcott, Brooke Foss, 249, 251
Westermann, Claus, 24n22, 62n4, 66n23, 109n4
Wette, Wilhelm Martin Leberecht de, 6
Wilckens, Ulrich, 12, 14, 27n29
Wilder, Amos N., 241n26
Wiles, Virginia, 186n11
Wilkinson, Bruce, 334n2
Williams, Rowan, 34, 71n39
Wilson, Marvin R., 197n15
Wilson, Robert McLachlan, 82–83n13, 117n19
Windhorst, Christof, 86n22
Witten, Marsha, 144
Wojtyla, Karl Jósef. *See* John Paul II, Pope (Karol Jósef Wojtyla)
Wolff, Hans Walter, 99n27
Woll, D. Bruce, 239n22
Wolterstorff, Nicholas, 187n12, 192
Woodhead, Linda, 108n2, 123n27
Woolf, Bertram Lee, 8n18
Work, Telford, 58n73
Worthington, Jonathan, 162n13
Wrede, William, 6–9, 10, 14, 18–24, 27, 29, 31–32
Wren, Christopher S., 353n17
Wright, G. Ernest, 9, 270
Wright, N. T., 13, 14

Yeago, David S., 31
Young, Frances M., 15, 34–35

Zaleski, Carol, 90
Zaleski, Philip, 90
Zar, Chris, 351n7
Zemmar, Ajmal, ix
Ziesler, John A., 120n22, 169n30
Zimmermann, Jens, 319n16

Index of Subjects

Akiba, Rabbi, 103
All My Sons: A Drama in Three Acts (Miller), 343–44
American Theological Society (ATS), 45, 313
Aquinas, Thomas, 4, 17, 32
Arian controversy, 198n17
Aristotelianism, 32
Arnold, Matthew, 294
At Home in Mitford (Karon), 334
Augustine of Hippo, 3, 32, 61, 70, 119, 382; on loving-kindness and the *imago Dei*, 323–24; on the Pater Noster, 90; on prayer, 69, 90

Bancroft, Richard, 294
Barmen Declaration, 407–8
Bay Psalm Book, The (1640), 289
Bentley, Richard, 294
Bernard of Clairvaux, 70
biblical exegesis. *See* exegesis and prayer
biblical preaching, 373–79, 390–92; avoid moral lessons, 375–76; be a minister, not a magistrate, 378; be both witness and messenger, 375; divinity school can't make you a good minister, 378–79; don't bear false witness, 376; don't be a salesperson, 377; don't expect everyone to accept your testimony, 378; expand your pneumatology, 374; humility, 374; learn the difference between moral encouragement and moralizing, 377–78; learn to read Scripture stereophonically, 376; let preaching grow out of meditation, 374; listen, 374; offer listeners the gospel's reasons to trust and hope, 378; pray that God will open your heart to those you dislike, 376–77; remember that preaching is an exercise in delayed gratification, 379; Stendahl's "Ten Commandments for Biblical Preaching," 373–76; tell the truth of the gospel, 376, 392; using the word "love," 375. *See also* "Jesus Christ Is Lord" (sermon; Black); lectionary preaching
biblical theology, ix–x, 5, 9, 13, 16, 17–40, 65, 304; Barth, 9–11, 14, 24–25; Bultmann, ix, 9–11, 22, 24, 27, 32, 35; eighteenth-century, 29; Gabler, 4–7, 8, 11, 18–22; philosophy and, 14–15, 32; Piper and, 41–60, 61–68; postwar twentieth-century movement, 9, 13, 41–60, 61–68; Schlatter, 7–10, 12, 13, 20–24, 25, 31–32; six suggestions for remapping as Christian scriptural theology, 27–40; Wrede, 6–9, 10, 18–24, 27, 29, 31–32. *See also* New Testament theology; Piper, Otto A.; scriptural theology
biblical truth, 280–86; *alētheia* and cognates in the Gospels and 1 John, 245–46, 280–81; John's Gospel, 281–82, 284–85; the Old Testament, 285–86; Paul and, 282–84, 285, 286; and revelation, 281–86; the Synoptic Gospels, 280–86
Bishops' Bible (1568), 294
Bonhoeffer, Dietrich, 36–37, 102, 319n16, 330n48, 333, 339
Book of Common Prayer, 156, 285, 307n41
Book of Psalms (Ainsworth) (1612), 289
Boulding, Maria, 386–87
Bruce, Lenny, 33
Buddhism, 103n42, 106n52, 328–29n42
Bush, George W., 37, 342, 359, 362–63, 365

INDEX OF SUBJECTS

Calvin, John, 70
canon criticism, 13, 28
Carnegie, Dale, 338
Carter, Jimmy, 361
Carter, June, 351, 353, 356, 358, 359
Carter family, 351n8
Cash, John Carter, 358
Cash, Johnny, 349–58; early life, 349, 355–57; "Folsom Prison Blues," 350, 356; Folsom Prison concert and live album (1968), 351–53; "outlaw" reputation, 349, 350; religious recordings, 350, 354–55, 357; San Quentin concert and live album (1969), 353–55; *Walk the Line* (2005) based on life of, 355–58
Cash, Rosanne, 356, 358n34
Cash, Vivian, 358
Catholicism, early, 230–55; and eschatology in the Johannine community, 251–52, 253; and the image of the church in the Johannine epistles, 248–51, 253; and the issue of authority in the Johannine epistles, 232–43, 253; the question of "early Catholic" elements in the Johannine epistles, 230–55; and the understanding of faith in the Johannine epistles, 243–47, 253; whether the category of "early Catholicism" is adequate pursuit, 253–55
Christian bookstores, 333–39; Bibles in, 337; books in, 334–35, 336, 337–39; gift sections, 335, 336–37
church in the Synoptic Gospels and Acts, 210–29; attention to the impoverished, 225–26; bearing witness under persecution, 227–28; the commissioning of Simon Peter, 221–22, 262–63; and the enduring presence of the hidden Christ, 219–20; and existence of associations in Second Temple Judaism, 210–11; as family or household of God, 229; forgiveness and, 218–19; Gospels' views of the disciples and discipleship, 212–15, 217–22; the Holy Spirit and, 224–25; Jesus's inaugural sermon in Nazareth, 223–24; Jesus's preaching on the kingdom of God, 217; Luke-Acts (c. 85–95 CE), 222–28; Mark (c. 70 CE), 211–15; Matthew (c. 85 CE), 215–22; Matthew on *hē dikaiosynē*, 110, 118, 217–18; and parable of the judgment of nations, 220; the relationship between the church and Israel, 216, 217–18, 223, 224, 226–27, 228–29; the relations of Jews and Gentiles/Jewish Christians, 216, 226–27, 229
cognitivist model of religion, 22, 23
Cologne Declaration (1989), 345
Colson, Charles, 334, 336
common good, 404–5
"contextual theology," 26n26
Council of Ephesus (431), 198n17
creation myths, 109
Crucible, The (Miller), 344–45

Darwin, Charles, 294
death: in ancient Greek and Hellenistic thought, 161–62, 174; as completion/depletion, 164, 175n44, 177; death of a child, 180–81, 187, 192; death of a pet, 366–69; Gnostic perspectives, 162–64, 175, 176; in intertestamental literature, 160, 163, 166; Jewish and Greco-Roman views (the Pauline milieu), 159–64, 175–79; notions of a "good" or "bad" death, 162n11; in the Old Testament, 160; and the Qumran community, 160–61; in Semitic thought, 159–61; the tannaitic literature, 161; understood biologically, mythologically, metaphorically, 159–61, 164. *See also* death (Pauline perspectives on); lament
death (Pauline perspectives on), 158–79; analogy of marriage, 170; the Christian's new life in the Spirit, 172–73; as completion/depletion, 164, 175n44, 177; conception of *thanatos*, 158n2, 159n3, 170, 171–72, 173–74, 179; conclusions and further questions, 175–79; contrast between Adam and Christ, 166; cosmic sweep of Paul's thinking, 173–74; death and salvation, 174; and Jewish and Greco-Roman views (the Pauline milieu), 159–64, 175–79; motif of Christ's atoning death, 165–66, 176; motif of heroic death, 165–66; relationship between the law and sin, 170–72; relationship of sin and death

468

Index of Subjects

(mortality and morality), 166–73, 175–76, 178; Romans 5–8, 165–74; Romans 5:1–11, 165–66; Romans 5:12–21, 166–67; Romans 6:1–14, 167–69; Romans 6:15–7:6, 169–70; Romans 7:7–25, 170–72; Romans 8:1–11, 172–73; Romans 8:12–30, 173–74; Romans 8:13–39, 174; as tyrannical, cosmological power, 169, 172, 176; where death originated, 175–76. *See also* death
Death of a Salesman (Miller), 347
Denney, James, 399
divine judgment in the Synoptic Gospels, 144–57; and the conduct of the community of disciples, 153; a fearful symmetry of reward and punishment, 153–54; grace and judgment as dynamic actions, 153; justice rendered by God (not humanity), 151–52; parable of the unforgiving servant, 147–49, 219; parables of judgment in Matthew's Gospel, 145–51; proceeding from divine grace, 152; the quality of surprise, 154, 157; the separation of the sheep from the goats (eternal punishment), 149–51; the weeds among the chaff, 145–47
docetism, 82, 246n42
dogs, love of, 366–69
Dorsey, Thomas A., 354
double-mindedness (*dipsychia*), 380–84; the *lev*, 382
Driver, Sir Godfrey, 289

Eastern Orthodox Church, 269–79, 334n3. See also *For the Life of the World: Toward a Social Ethos of the Orthodox Church (FLW)*
ecclesiastical formulations. See *For the Life of the World: Toward a Social Ethos of the Orthodox Church (FLW)*
Edward VI, King, 289
Einstein, Albert, 55–56, 108
Enlightenment: belief in the sovereign self, 100–101; ideal of individual genius, 36; New Testament theology, 4–6; secularization and the eclipse of kindness, 326–27
Epicureanism, 162, 178, 184, 210
Erasmus, Desiderius, 288–89
Evangelium vitae (John Paul II), 346–47

exegesis and prayer, 61–76; biblical prayer and biblical exegesis, 68–76; a disposition for grateful praise, 74–76; a disposition for holiness, 70–71; a disposition for transfigured affection, 72–74; dispositions of prayer essential for proper exegesis, 69–76; Piper on the biblical doctrine of prayer, 61–68, 69, 70–72, 74–75; as spiritual gift, 72–73

form criticism (*Formgeschichte*), 8–9, 22, 233
For the Life of the World: Toward a Social Ethos of the Orthodox Church (FLW), 269–79; the application and warrants of particular scriptural texts, 275–79; on contraception and abortion, 278; the *discrimen*, 271, 272–73; on the equal dignity of men and women, 278–79; and Kelsey's framework for appropriating scripture for theological reflection, 269–71, 272–74; on marriage, 277; the mode of scriptural appeal (concrete actuality), 273–74; New Testament citations, 275–76; Old Testament citations, 275; scriptural authority, 270; scriptural warrants for ethical claims, 276–79; on sexual orientation and human sexuality, 277–78; the statement's purpose, 271; the statement's structure, 271–72; on suicide, 279; the use of scripture in, 272–74
Freud, Sigmund, 327

Geneva Bible (1560), 289, 290, 292, 294
Get Healthy Now! With Gary Null (Null), 334
Gielgud, John, 364
Gnosticism, 13, 83, 246n42, 259; and Hermeticism, 163n14; perspectives on death, 162–64, 175, 176; Piper and, 57
Good Friday, 143, 187, 191, 400
Gorbachev, Mikhail, 345
grace: and divine judgment in the Synoptic Gospels, 152, 153; Mary as paradigm of grace in the New Testament, 193–209. *See also* Mary (mother of Jesus)
Graham, Billy, 334n1, 336, 337, 338–39
"Great Church," 38, 83, 231, 248–49, 253
Great Commission, 113, 116

INDEX OF SUBJECTS

Greek New Testament (1516), 288–89
Gregory of Nazianzus, 278, 320n17
Gressett, Floyd, 353n17, 357

Haggard, Merle, 352n12, 355
Henry VIII, King, 289, 291–92
"hermeneutics of conviction," 15
"hermeneutics of suspicion," 15
Hermeticism, 163n14
Hinduism, 29, 103n42
historical criticism, 4–6, 10–11, 19–22, 24, 26–28, 31, 39–40, 49, 70
history-of-religion school, 10, 21, 24
Hobbes, Thomas, 100, 326
humanity, public intellectuals on: Miller, 340–48; Sontag, 340–48; Wojtyla, 340–48
humanity in the New Testament, 108–24; christological concentrations, 111–13, 122; eschatological visions, 113, 119, 121–22; the human being as inextricably related to God, 122–24; humankind's creation "in the image" (*tselem*) and "likeness" (*demut*) of God, 108–10, 120–21; the *imago Christi* and human kindness, 319–20; the Johannine vision, 113–17; and language of human dignity, 108, 109, 123–24; the Matthean vision, 110–13; Matthew on human "hypocrisy," 111; the Pauline vision, 117–21; Paul on humanity's restoration in accordance with the divine image (*hē eikōn*), 120; Paul's contrast between Adam and Christ, 119–20; points of commonality in Matthew, John, and Paul, 113–17, 121–24; the separation of Christians from Jews in John's Gospel, 113–15; sin and redemption, 117–18
Hume, David, 294, 326
humility, 385–87; and asceticism, 385; and biblical preaching, 374; children and, 386–87
Hutchinson, John, 294

Iraq. *See* US invasion of Iraq (2003–11)
Irenaeus of Lyons, 3, 35–36, 119, 120n23
Irving, George, 52–53
Islam, 29, 105–7, 255, 321n18, 345; militant, 360–61; the *Surat al-fāti'a* and the Qur'an's first chapter, 105–7

James VI of Scotland (James I of England), 293
"Jesus Christ Is Lord" (sermon; Black), 396–408; implications for discipleship in the real world, 401–5; Matthew on the risen Jesus's announcement to his disciples, 399; Paul's letters, 398, 399, 400–401; what Jesus's lordship meant for his disciples, 399–400
Jesus Seminar, 73
Jeweler's Shop, The (Jawien), 341
Johannine epistles, 79–88, 266–67; apocalyptic eschatology in the Johannine community, 251–52, 253; authorship of 1 John and relation to the Fourth Gospel, 79n3, 231n4; Brown on 1 John and the Johannine community, 82–84, 86; Conzelmann on 1 John and the Johannine community, 79–85; ecclesiocentricity and the Johannine community, 79–85; the image of the church, 248–51, 253; the issue of authority, 232–43, 253; Lieu on 1 John as polemical writing, 84, 86–87; perspectives on Christian ministry in the Johannine community, 266–67; references to Jesus as "Son" in 1 John, 87; the schism in the early Johannine community, 81–83, 84, 266–67; theocentricity and view of God in 1 John, 85–88; the understanding of faith, 243–47, 253. *See also* Johannine epistles and the question of early Catholicism
Johannine epistles and the question of early Catholicism, 230–55; *alētheia*, 245–46; the "Diotrephes affair" of 3 John, 240–43, 248n46, 253, 254, 267; eschatology and the Johannine community, 251–52, 253; and the "Great Church," 38, 83, 231, 248–49, 253; *homologein*, 244–46; the image of the church, 79–81, 248–51, 253; the issue of authority, 232–43, 253; official authority (the question of offices), 236–43, 253; *pistis* and *pisteuein*, 244; the role of the *presbyteros*, 236–38; a shift toward *fides quae creditur*, 244–46, 253; traditional authority (the role of tradition), 232–36, 253; the understanding of faith, 243–47, 253
Johannine perspectives on Christian minis-

try, 256–68; accents of the Johannine proclamation, 257–60; the calling to discipleship as loving service, expressed in faith, 259–60, 262–63; centrality of Jesus, 257–58, 261; context of sectarian conflict between Pharisaic Judaism and Jewish Christianity, 113–15, 264–66; living in the presence of eternity (realized eschatology), 260, 263; ministerial reflection, 260–64; ministry and the Epistles of John, 266–67; ministry in the Gospel of John, 256–64; personal bonding to Christ, 258–59, 262; and roles of women in the Gospel of John, 259, 279; theological liabilities, 264–66; witness within the "world," 260, 263–64

Johnny Cash at Folsom Prison (1968), 351–53

Johnny Cash at San Quentin (1969), 353–55

John Paul II, Pope, 341, 345–48. *See also* Wojtyla, Karol Jósef

John the Baptist, 129, 156, 196, 203, 214, 261, 278, 378; death of, 388–95

Judaism: John 8 on Christianity's origins and, 39–40; John's Gospel and the separation of Jews and Christians, 113–15, 264–66; Matthew's Gospel and, 113, 114; the Pater Noster and Jewish prayer, 94, 103–5, 107; Piper's comments on, 58; Sabbath observance, 307–8

judgment. *See* divine judgment in the Synoptic Gospels

Julian of Norwich, 324–26

Kelsey, David H., 269–71, 272–74

kindness of strangers, 313–30; Augustine on loving-kindness and the *imago Dei*, 323–24; the Dalai Lama on compassion, 328–29n42; the eclipse and trivialization of kindness, 326–28; Freud and, 327; God's *hesed* in Hebrew Scriptures, 317–19, 325–26; humanity's creation in God's image in the Hebrew Scriptures, 314–17; human stewardship of creation in the Hebrew Scriptures, 315–17; the image of mercy in Hebrew Scriptures, 314–19; Jesus as image of kindness and compassion in the New Testament, 319–21; Julian of Norwich on Jesus as the embodiment of the divine and human love, 324–26; Julian of Norwich on relationship between "kin" and "kindness," 324n29; rabbinic, patristic, and medieval amplifications (mercy and loving-kindness), 321–26; rabbinic literature on loving-kindness, 321–22; and secularization of Western culture, 326–27; Thurman on forgiveness and, 329–30

King James Bible, 287–95; and Daniell's *The Bible in English*, 288–90, 295; and Katz's *God's Last Words*, 294–95; and McGrath's *In the Beginning*, 289–90, 293, 295; and Moynahan's *God's Bestseller*, 290–92; and Nicholson's *God's Secretaries*, 292–94, 295; and Tyndale, 288–95

Kinkade, Thomas, 336–37

LaHaye, Tim, 73, 336

lament, 180–92; confusing grief with, 187; and the death of a child, 180–81, 187, 192; and hope, 188–89; Jeremiah on Rachel's weeping and lamentation, 180–81; Matthew on Golgotha and the crucified Jesus's cry of lament, 184–86; Matthew's infancy narrative and citation of Jeremiah on Rachel's weeping, 181–84; Paul and, 190, 192

LaPierre, Wayne, 102

lectio divina, 38, 311–12

lectionary preaching, 296–312; and anti-Judaism, 302–3; and the Consultation on Common Texts (CCT), 297–98, 302; critique of misogyny and violence against women, 302–3; critiques and objections to the lectionary, 297–303; description of the lectionary and cycles, 297; features of the common lectionary that enhance the journey into Scripture, 305–8; intertextuality, 305; and the intracanonical conversation, 305–6; justifications for a common lectionary, 303–12; the liturgical calendar's patterns inherited from the Torah and Judaism, 307–8; and the Psalter, 302, 309–11; readings that offer insight into salvation history, 305–6

Left Behind (film), 336n14

INDEX OF SUBJECTS

Left Behind series (LaHaye and Jenkins), 336
Leo X, Pope, 4
Letters and Papers from Prison (Bonhoeffer), 333, 339
Lewis, C. S., 75, 97, 311, 363–64
Locke, John, 100
Lonergan, Kenneth, 359
Lord's Prayer. See Pater Noster (Lord's Prayer or the "Our Father")
Lord's Supper (Eucharist), 95–96, 225n14, 405
love command, 71, 115–16, 232, 244, 266
Lumet, Sidney, 356
Luther, Martin, 4, 32, 86, 125, 286, 291n12, 364

Mackay, John A., 44, 51, 52, 54–55
Mangold, James, 355–56
Marcionites, 208n38
Marcion of Sinope, 13
Marshall, Catherine, 336
Mary (mother of Jesus), 193–209; the angel Gabriel's visitation (Luke), 194–96; the Annunciation (Luke), 196–98; biblical cameos of Mary as paradigm of grace, 193–209; as the concerned yet mistaken parent, 200–204; Jesus's attitude toward (Mark), 201–2; the Magnificat (Luke), 198–200, 225; and the miracle of the wine at the wedding in Cana (John), 202–4; revealing the truth about God/God's grace, 207–8; revealing the truth about ourselves, 208–9; role in Jesus's youth (Luke), 200–201; roles across the history of Christian doctrine, 206–7; Theotokos, 198n17; as the virgin who will conceive God's messiah (Luke), 194–200; visitation to Elizabeth (Luke), 198; as vulnerable woman and mother, 204–6
Matthew's Bible (1537), 292
McCarthyism, 344–45
Melanchthon, Philipp, 4
"method of doctrinal concepts," 6–7, 18, 27
Miller, Arthur, 340–48, 359–60
ministry. See Johannine perspectives on Christian ministry
More, Sir Thomas, 290–92
mystery cults, 163n15, 210

Nawrocki, Paul, 335n7
Nazi Germany, 44–45, 56, 75, 345, 407–8
neo-orthodoxy's "theology of the word," 9–10
Neoplatonism, 32, 33–34, 162
Nestorians, 198n17
New Age spirituality, 259
New English Bible (1961–70), 289, 294
New International Version (1978), 290
New Jerusalem Bible (1985), 290
New Revised Standard Version (1990), 290
New Testament theology, 3–16, 22; approaches to, 11–12; bearing on dogmatics, witness, and practice, 15; the early and medieval church, 3–4; from the Enlightenment through the twentieth century, 4–11; Gabler and his successors, 4–7, 8, 11, 18–22; historical trajectory of, 3–11; Luther and Reformation orthodoxy, 4; the nature of, 6–9, 18–24; from the patristic era through the Reformation, 3–4; philosophy and, 14–15, 32; question of whether Jesus's proclamation is intrinsic to, 14; question of whether the New Testament exhibits a unifying core, 12–13; recurring questions for continued study, 11–15; relation to Old Testament theology, 5–6, 13, 17–18, 24–25, 27–29; re-proclaiming the kerygma (Barth and Bultmann), 9–11, 24–25; Schlatter, 7–10, 12, 13, 20–24, 25, 31–32; Wrede, 6–9, 10, 18–24, 27, 29, 31–32. See also biblical theology; scriptural theology
Newton, Isaac, 294
Nicene-Chalcedonian Creed, 38, 206, 228
9/11 attacks, 360–63
Null, Gary, 334n6

Orthodox Way, The (Ware), 334

Pascal, Blaise, 89
Pater Noster (Lord's Prayer or the "Our Father"), 89–107; appeal to God as Father, 91–93, 106–7; applications to contemporary civil religion, 98–102; eschatological aspects, 91, 94–95, 97–98; exegetical aspects and essential features, 91–98; the "hallowing" of the name of God, 94–95;

472

Index of Subjects

as invitation to interreligious communion, 102–7; and Jewish prayer, 94, 103–5, 107; and Muslim prayer, 105–7; petition for daily bread, 95–96; petition for forgiveness of sins and debt-forgiveness, 96–97, 139–40, 149; petition not to fall into temptation, 97–98; theocentricity of, 99; undermining the belief in the sovereign self, 99–102
Pelagianism, 72
Pentecostalism, 334n2, 349
philosophy and biblical theology, 14–15, 32
Piper, Otto A., 9, 41–60, 61–68, 70–72, 74–75, 233; ambiguous legacy and lasting influence, 56–60; on biblical exegesis and prayer, 61–68, 69, 70–72, 74–75; on biblical interpretation as processes of exegesis and appropriation, 49–50; early life, 43; four hermeneutical axioms, 48–49; in Germany during and after World War II, 43–45, 56, 58, 75; pacifism, 43; and the postwar biblical theology movement, 41–60, 61–68; and Princeton Seminary, 50–56; and Princeton Seminary's doctoral program, 53–55; Princeton teaching load and courses, 50–52; principles, 48–50; scholarly publications, 45–48, 53, 56–57; theme of Christian ethics, 47–48, 57; theme of God's action in human history (revelation), 46–47, 57; World War I service, 43, 75
Pius XI, Pope, 292
postmodernism, 20, 32, 36, 37, 58, 99, 109, 122
prayer, 61–76; dispositions essential for proper exegesis, 69–76; exegesis as, 61–76; Jewish, 94, 103–5, 107; Muslim, 105–7; Piper and the biblical doctrine of, 61–68, 69, 70–72, 74–75; Qumran Essenes, 66; in secular society, 90. *See also* exegesis and prayer; Pater Noster (Lord's Prayer or the "Our Father")
Prayer of Jabez, The (Wilkinson), 334, 337, 338
preaching. *See* biblical preaching; lectionary preaching
Presbyterian Church (USA), 52–53, 144, 296n1
Princeton Theological Seminary, xi, 41–45,
48, 50–56, 381–84, 390n1; Piper and, 50–56; Piper and the doctoral program, 53–55; Piper's courses, 50–52
Prophet, The (Gibran), 357
"prosperity gospel," 334n2
Pythagoras, 210

Qumran community, 259–60n8; Community Rule, 151; perspectives on death, 160–61; prayer, 66

Reagan, Ronald, 355
redaction criticism, 31n40, 251n54, 303n36
Reformation, 4, 9, 28, 58, 288, 407
Regarding the Pain of Others (Sontag), 341–42
regula fidei ("rule of faith"), 3, 35–37, 243–45
Revised Common Lectionary (RCL). *See* lectionary preaching
Revised English Bible (1989), 289
Revised Standard Version (1952), 290, 294
Reynolds, John, 293
Rogers, John, 292
Rousseau, Jean-Jacques, 100, 326–27

Satan: hell and, 405–7; Jesus and, 129, 141–42, 213, 405–6; Luther on, 125; Piper and, 46–47, 56
Schuller, Robert, 336, 337
Scofield's Reference Bible, 294–95
scriptural theology, 27–40; the aim of, 36–37; as attitude/approach (not method), 33–35; interpretation of John 8:31–59, 38–40; interpreting the Christian Bible as Scripture, 29–30; the practice of, 30–32; reconsidering both Testaments, 27–29; and the rule of faith (*regula fidei*) of the church, 35–36; six suggestions for remapping biblical theology as, 27–40. *See also* biblical theology; New Testament theology
scripture and ecclesiastical formulations. See *For the Life of the World: Toward a Social Ethos of the Orthodox Church (FLW)*
scripture for theological reflection: a *discrimen*, 271, 272–73; Kelsey's framework,

473

269–71, 272–74; scriptural authority, 270; three modes of scriptural appeal, 270–71, 273–74. See also *For the Life of the World: Toward a Social Ethos of the Orthodox Church* (*FLW*)
self-help books, 334, 337–38, 339
Sermon on the Mount, 112, 217, 218
Sermon on the Plain, 133
Shakespeare, William, 187n12, 288n4, 292, 323n25, 364
Shalom Center, The, 361
Sherley, Glen, 353, 357
sin in the Synoptic Gospels, 125–43; aberrant (*adik-*), 127, 128; Christ's fraternization with sinners and welcoming into the kingdom, 135–36; concept of Jesus's self-sacrifice, 143; deviation from Old Testament thought, 128–29; and dynamics of salvation, 130–34; and forgiveness in the Lord's Prayer, 96–97, 139–40, 149; and Jesus's proclamation of the kingdom of God (*hē basileia tou theou*), 129–30; John on redemption and, 117–18; liability (*opheil-*), 126–27; Luke's story of the tax collector Zacchaeus, 130–34; Mark on blasphemy against the Holy Spirit, 140–42; Matthew on redemption and, 117–18; missing the mark (*hamart-*), 117, 125–26, 127; patterns of thought about sin, 128–36; as personified power, 136–37; and purity, 142; and self-righteousness, 134–35; sin, sickness, and calamity, 137–39; substandard, bad (*ponēr-*), 126, 127–28; vocabulary of sin, 125–28
Smith, Miles, 295
social-scientific criticism, 8–9, 22–23
Society for New Testament Studies, 23
Society of Biblical Literature, 45
Sojourners, 361
Son of Man: in Jewish apocalypticism, 133n15; in Synoptic traditions, 115, 122, 133n15, 137, 143, 146, 152, 154, 156, 185, 214–15, 220

Sontag, Susan, 340–48
Southern Baptist Convention, 144, 361–62
Stendahl, Krister, 5, 373–76
Stevenson, Adlai, 38, 101
Stoicism, 32, 123–24, 165, 365
Swedenborg, Emanuel, 294
systematic theology (or dogmatics), 5, 6, 7–8, 20–21, 26, 44–45

theater, 340–41, 359–60
theological anthropology, 6, 108. See also humanity in the New Testament
Theotokos, 198n17
Thurman, Howard, 329–30
Today's English Version (1976), 289
truth. See biblical truth
Twain, Mark, 96, 362, 366
Tyndale, William, 288–95

United Presbyterian Church, USA, 45
Uses of Scripture in Recent Theology, The (Kelsey), 269–71, 272–74
US invasion of Iraq (2003–11), 37, 101, 342, 360–65

VeggieTales, 334–35, 337
Vischer, Phil, 335n7
Vulgate, 290

Walk the Line (film), 355–58
war, 313–14, 341–44, 359–65, 380–82; theology and, 359–65; "war against terrorism," 342–43, 360–63
Ware, Kallistos, 334n3
"War Prayer" (Twain), 362
Wasserstein, Wendy, 359
Weil, Simone, 71, 90
Welch, Jack, 338n17
Williams, Arland D., 330
Willimon, William H., 378
Wojtyla, Karol Jósef, 340–48
World Alliance of Reformed Churches, 361
Wyclif, John, 288
Wycliffite Bible, 294

Index of Scripture

Old Testament

Genesis

Ref	Page
1	120n24
1–2	275n15, 302
1:1–2:4a	283, 302
1:2	197
1:20–23	315
1:21–22	316
1:22	61–62
1:24–31	275n15
1:26	275n15, 276n18, 316
1:26–27	108, 314
1:26–28	120
1:27	120n24, 121, 282, 315, 316
1:31	275n15
2	120n24
2–3	160, 172–73n39
2:7	71, 172–73n39
2:17	171
2:18–24	305
2:19	94
2:21–23	120n24
2:24	275n15, 277, 282
3	70, 173
3:1–21	128
3:5–7	400n17
3:11–13	382n7
3:14–19	171
3:19	386n3
4:7	136
4:8	232
5:1–2	316
5:1–3	108
5:3	316
6:5	142n30
8:21	142n30
9:6	108
9:6–7	316
9:8–10	369
9:9–11	275n15
12:3	275n15
15:6	286
15:15	162n11
17:4–6	216
17:6–8	199
18:1–8	133
18:9–15	196
18:11	196
18:14	197
18:18	199
20:3–10	317
20:12–13	317
20:14–16	317
20:17–18	317
21:1–7	196
21:10	92
22:17	199
23:4	319
25:8	162n11
25:21–26	196
27:1–41	61–62
30:1	196
30:22–24	196
32:11	286
32:23–32	76
32:28	94, 286
35:18	159
35:20	180
39:21	195
46:30	162n11
48:21	160
49:28	213

Exodus

Ref	Page
1:15–2:10	182
2:12	228
3:5	375
3:21	195
4:1	286
6:6	199
11:1–10	182
11:3	195
12:29–32	182
12:36	195
12:49	275n15
13:8	307
14–15	322
15:11	70
15:13	318
15:25b–26	137
16:4–25	95
20:1–20	283
20:2–17	99
20:11	307
20:12–16	215
20:13	282
20:13–14	218
20:14	282
20:16	376
21–22	275n15

INDEX OF SCRIPTURE

21:22–25	278	25:35–38	275n15	14	142
21:24	282	25:36–37	275n15	14:3–21	282
22	275n15			15:1–11	275n15
22:25	275n15	**Numbers**		17:12	142
23:9	275n15	6:27	227	19:15	219
23:10–11	316	9:1–14	143	19:21	282
23:21	129	14:19	318	21:22–23	186
24:4	213	15	128	23:19–20	275n15
24:8	143	15:30–31	142	23:21	282
24:15–18	197	16:26	136	24:1–4	282
28:21	213	22–24	186n10	26:8	199
31:17	307	22:21–35	312	27:19	275n15
33:12–13	284	30:2	282	28:15–68	137
34:6	195, 199			30:14	328
34:15–16	129	**Deuteronomy**		30:15	160
34:30	147n6	1:27	132	30:19	160
34:34	283	4:26	305	31:2–3	160
39:14	213	4:30–31	305	31:16	128
		4:35–39	39	32:7	41
Leviticus		5:6–21	99	32:46–47	284n12
1–7	142	5:7	328	34:10–12	284
4–5	128	5:15	307		
5:15–16	375	5:16–20	215	**Joshua**	
11	142	5:17	282	2:12	317
12:1–8	278	5:17–18	218	4:4	213
15:19–24	278	5:18	282	10:16–12:24	318
15:25–30	278	5:20	376	21:43–45	318
16	143	5:27	374	22:18–19	129
16:17	222	6:4	39	24:7	234n13
17:1–16	282	6:4–5	107n56, 142, 215,		
18:1–30	278		397n4	**Judges**	
18:19	278	6:5	328	2:2–3:7	318
19:9–10	275n15	6:25	217	2:7	199
19:12	282	7:6–7	383n8	4–5	279
19:15–18	219	7:7	228	5:24	198n16
19:18	142, 215, 282, 328	7:8	383n9	6:24	275n15
19:32	277n22	7:9	317, 318	9:50–54	279
19:33–34	319, 403n29	7:12	317, 318	11:12–40	74
19:34	275n15	9:4–6	217	13:2–25	196
20:18	278	9:10	222	19:1–30	74
23:22	275n15	10:12–11:32	283	21:1–25	74
24:20	282	10:17–19	275n15, 318,		
25:1–44	316		403n29	**Ruth**	
25:8–12	226	11:7	199	1:2–14	92
25:23–24	316	12:5–11	94	2:2	195

Index of Scripture

2:10	195	19:4	160	**Ezra**	
2:13	195	19:19	212	3:11	318
3:10	317	22:13–18	286		
		22:19–22	316	**Nehemiah**	
1 Samuel				5:5	148
1:1–28	196	**2 Kings**		9:17	195
2:1–2	309	2:3	160	9:31	195
2:1–10	199	4:1	148	11:1	223
2:9	136	4:42–44	129n8	11:18	223
2:26	201	5:1–15	226		
10:2	180	17:24–29	226	**Esther**	
12:14–15	129	19:4	141	2:15	195
15:22	142	19:6	141	2:17	195
15:23	128	19:22	141	5:2	195
16:13	197				
16:14–23	137	**1 Chronicles**		**Job**	
16:22	195	4:9–10	334n2	1:6–2:7	316
20:3	195	10:4–5	279	1:21	160
31:4–5	279	13:2	222	2:1–8	137
		15:28	198	5:26	162n11
2 Samuel		16:4	198	9:16–18	286
7:11–16	199	16:5	198	14:1	205
7:12–17	196	16:19	319	15:14	205
7:15	199	16:29	375	18:13	159
7:16	197	16:34	318	22:5–11	137
7:28	286	16:41	318	25:4	205
10:2	317	16:42	198	27:6	217
17:23	279	17:21	216, 227	29:14	217
18:14	301	25:8	212n6	30:26	189n14
18:32–33	162n11			31:32	275n15
22:26	317	**2 Chronicles**		34:5–9	137
		5:13	318	34:14–15	99–100, 159
1 Kings		6:3	222	36:13–14	162n11
3:6	217	6:12	222	42:2	197
3:15	223	7:3	318		
8:3–53	137	7:6	318	**Psalms**	
8:23	317	7:14	136	2:2–7	217
10:9	217	7:19	128	4:4	317
12:3	222	9:8	217	5:10	302
12:20	222	20:21	318	6:5	318
14:1–16	137	21:11–15	137	7:17	217
16:18	279	24:20–22	39	8:1[2]	91
17:1–16	226	30:9	195	8:5–6	314–15
18–21	129	30:13–27	223	8:5–9	108
18:40	301	33:7	128	8:7–9	315

477

8:9[10]	91	71:2	217	118	64
9:1–20	283	78:10	128	118:19	151n14, 220, 322
9:2	64n14	78:37	128	119:1	284n12
9:8–9	217	78:55	216	119:41	318
11:4	187	80:1	91	119:43	286
12:3	317	81:13	374	119:53	128
13:1–3a	189	84	64	119:76	318
13:3–4	160	84:11	195	119:97	68
13:5	189	85	64	119:105	108
15:5	275n15	86:13	318	119:113	382n2
18:1[2]	91	86:15	195, 286	119:142	284n12, 286
18:2[3]	91	87:5–6	168n24	119:149	318
18:26	317	89:10	199	119:151	286
19:7	284	89:13	199	119:155	136
22:1	184, 189, 306	89:15	286	119:159	318
22:7	306	89:26	91n8	119:160	286
22:8	306	90:3	159	122:3–9	223
22:18	306	90:12–14	160	128:5	223
22:22–31	184–85	93:1	91	128:6	275n15
23:1	91	98:3	310	131:2	76
23:1–4	294	99:1	91	132:11	286
23:3	217	99:3	375	133:1	275n15
24:1	38	102:6	289	135:6	95
24:5	199	103:1	62	136	64
25:7	318	103:2	64	136:1–9	197n15
26:2	382n4	103:8	195	137:1–9	374
29:2	375	103:13	91n8	137:3	289
31:1	217	104:24	63	137:5–6	223
31:6	286	105:12	319	138:1–6	284
32:8	310	106:3	217	139:19–22	302
33:6	197	106:6–47	129	145:1	91
34:1[2]	62	106:24–25	132	145:8	195
35:9	309	106:41	216	145:8–9	318
40:12	286	106:45	317	146:3	275n15
40:15–16	302	107:17–18	137	146:6	286
44:22	174	109:25	306	146:9	275n15
50:19	327	111	64	148	369
51:3	318	111:3	217		
51:6	284n12	111:4	195	**Proverbs**	
63:1–8	302n29	111:9	200	1:3	217
63:9–11	302, 302n29	112:1–10	310	1:8–7:27	277n22
68:5	91n8	112:4	311	2:9	217
69:17	318	112:7–8	311	3:5–8	142n30
69:21	306	112:10	310	4:11	284n12
69:22–28	302	116:5	195	4:19	129
69:30	200	116:17–19	223		

Index of Scripture

5:18–20	277n21	10:1–2	275n15, 327	55:8–9	99
8:20	217	11:1	182n4	56:3–5	160
8:22–31	121	11:1–9	283	58:1–12	310
10:7	160	11:6–9	369	58:5a	311
11:2	327	11:12	201	58:6–7	275n15
15:29	136	12:2	199, 394n3	58:7	151, 220
16:12	217	12:6	64n14	58:8ab	310, 311
16:22	284n12	24:5	128	58:9cd	311
18:22	277n21	25:6	132n13	59:14	217
19:14	277n21	25:6–8	159	61:1	224, 226
20:28	217	25:8	160	61:10	277
22:11	195	26:10	136	62:5	277
24:17	322	26:19	160, 186n10	65:17	277
31:10–31	277n21	28:1–29	156	66:3	141
		29:14	284	66:22	173
Ecclesiastes		29:24	132		
1:9–11	69n33	31:1	327	**Jeremiah**	
5:9–12	277n21	32:1	217	2:20–25	277
9:9	277n21	32:15	197	3:1–3	277
		38:1–3	162n11	5:1–6:30	283
Song of Solomon		38:10–12	162n11	5:1–9:26	110
4:10–11	277n21	38:19	286	5:5	284
5:1	277n21	40:2	96	5:27–28	275n15
8:6	156, 369	40:19	128	6:13–15	318
		40:21	64	8:21–22	318
Isaiah		40:27	63	9:24	217
1:20	129	40:31	63	11:10	128
1:21	129	41:8	199	18:15	128, 129
1:27	217	41:8–9	310	20:9	373
1:28	128	42:1–4	143	22:9	128
2:1–4	223	42:21	217	23:5	217
2:4	216	43:10–11	328	28:1–17	286
2:8–18	328	45:21–24	39	28:16	129
3:13–15	275n15	46:3–4	277n22	30:3	181
5:8	275n15	50:1	148	30:4–31:22	180
5:16	217	51:1–2	221	30:7	181
6:1–13	316	52:1	223	31:3	318
6:3	63	52:5	141	31:4	181
6:9–10	117	52:13–53:12	143	31:8	181
7:14	182n4, 220	53:1	286	31:11	181
8:8	182n4	53:2	182n4, 183	31:12	204n28
8:10	182n4	53:2–3	404n30	31:15	180–81, 182n4
9:2	183	53:7–8	283n9	31:15–17	183n5
9:6	91n8	54:8	318	31:16–17	181, 183
9:7	197, 217	55:6–7	96	31:18–20	181
		55:6–9	140n24		

31:31–34	140n24	2:18	369	2:11	328
31:34	96, 284	2:19	217	3:14	195n8
32:41	286	2:21–22	318	3:17	199
33:10–11	64n14	4:10–15	129		
33:11	318	6:6	219, 319	Zechariah	
48:8	129	7:14	129	8:1–8	223
52:12–13	215	8:1	128	8:6	197
		9:4	215	9:11	143
Lamentations		10:6	128	13:7	214
1:1	188	11:1	182n4		
3:16–17	188			Malachi	
3:21–22	188	Joel		1:6	91n8
		1:9	215	2:5–10	128
Ezekiel		2:10	186n10	2:8	129
3:27	147	2:13	195	2:10	39
12:21–14:23	110			2:14	277
16	277	Amos		3:5	275n15
16:32	129	1:3–3:2	137	4:5–6	196
17:18–19	128	2:10	234n13		
18:17	275n15	4:1	275n15	**New Testament**	
22:17–22	147	5:14–25	156		
23:49	128	5:24	218	Matthew	
33:8	136	9:9	216	1–2	205–6
34:1–31	258	9:13–14	204n28	1:1	182, 216
35:12	141			1:1–17	205, 207, 209, 306
36:22–23	94	Jonah		1:3	205, 216
36:22–32	140n24	2:8	128	1:5	216
36:25–27	95	3:1–4:11	286	1:5a	205
37:3–12	160	4:2	195, 318	1:5b	205
37:12	186n10			1:6	216
39:17–20	132n13	Micah		1:6b	205
47:13	213	5:2	182n4	1:11	207, 208
		6:6–8	156	1:16a	205
Daniel		7:20	318	1:17–18	216
3:1–30	137, 147			1:18	224
6:1–28	137	Nahum		1:18–19	208
7:14	197	1:5–6	186n10	1:18–20	205
8:16	196			1:18–2:23	181–84
9:21	196	Habakkuk		1:19	208, 218
11:1–12:13	137	2:4	121	1:19–20	205
12:1–3	146	3:18	309	1:20	208, 224
12:2	186n10			1:20–25	205
12:2–3	160	Zephaniah		1:21	126n4, 130, 182
		2:1	222	1:21–23	220
Hosea		2:9	216	1:22–23	111, 205, 207, 306
2–3	277			1:23	110, 113, 122, 156,

Index of Scripture

	182n4, 186, 198n17, 207	3:7–12	156	5:25–26	219
1:23bc	183	3:8	138	5:25–30	153
2:1	216	3:11	224	5:27	282
2:1–2	186n10, 205	3:13–15	218	5:27–32	218
2:1–3	182	3:13–17	111, 185	5:28–30	147
2:1–12	182	3:15	128, 310	5:31	282
2:2b	205	3:16	224	5:33	282
2:3–4	205, 207	3:16–17	218	5:37	126n7, 137, 153
2:4	216	3:17	92n9	5:38	282
2:5	207	4:1	98n24, 224	5:38–39	130
2:5–6	306	4:1–11	110, 128, 137, 153, 217	5:38–42	115, 219
2:5b–6	205	4:10	405n38	5:39	126n7
2:6	182n4	4:13–16	306	5:42	275n15
2:6b	183	4:16	183	5:43	282
2:7–8	182, 205	4:17	111, 121, 138, 217	5:43–44	130, 218
2:9–10	205	4:18	221	5:43–48	115, 132, 151, 220, 266, 275n15
2:9–12	205, 216	4:23	216		
2:10	132	5:1–12	152	5:44	115
2:10–11	205	5:1–7:28	217	5:44–47	219
2:12–14	208	5:1–7:29	110	5:45	127, 137
2:12–15	205	5:3	218, 224, 225	5:45–48	218
2:13	205, 207, 208	5:4	151, 275n15	5:45b	126
2:13–14	183	5:5	150, 219	5:46–47	131
2:13–17	112	5:6	128	5:47	216
2:13–23	182	5:7	150	5:48	110, 112, 123
2:14–15	306	5:9	275n15	6:1–4	116
2:15	111, 182n4, 183, 207	5:10	128, 218	6:1–18	218
2:15b–18	205	5:11	126n7	6:2	111
2:16	182, 205, 207	5:13	147, 311	6:3	275n15
2:16–17	206	5:13–20	311	6:5	111
2:16–18	208	5:14	146	6:7	216
2:17	111	5:14–16	311	6:9–10	140
2:17–18	182n4, 207, 306	5:16	146, 311	6:9–13	275n15
2:18	113, 182, 183	5:17	282	6:9b	93
2:19–23	183, 205	5:17–18	218, 311	6:9c–10a	95
2:20–22	208	5:17–19	128	6:9c–10ab	106n51
2:22	205, 207, 208	5:17–20	110, 111, 118	6:10bc	95
2:23	182n4, 207	5:19–20	218, 311	6:11	140
2:23b	205	5:20	114, 128, 282	6:11–13	92
2:25–32	206	5:21	282	6:12	126, 139, 140n24, 149
2:33–35	206	5:21–22	218		
3:1–5	128	5:21–48	112, 138, 218, 282	6:12–15	219
3:1–10	129	5:22–23	154	6:12a	140
3:2	138, 217	5:23–24	142n28	6:13	97n22, 126n7, 137, 140
3:6	117, 126	5:23–26	219	6:13b	97n22, 153
3:7–10	128, 134	5:23–34	219	6:14	127
		5:24	154	6:14–15	140, 149

481

INDEX OF SCRIPTURE

Reference	Pages	Reference	Pages	Reference	Pages
6:14–24	111	8:19	111	10:24	219
6:15	127	8:20	112, 133n15, 275n15	10:26–39	219
6:16	111	8:21–22	92, 93, 202n25	10:28	145
6:16–18	135	8:25	220	10:28–33	153
6:19–20	275n15	8:26	221	10:29	275n15
6:19–34	218	8:28–9:1	137	10:34–36	97n23
6:21	111	9:1–6	219	10:42	218
6:23	126n7	9:1–8	128, 134, 138	11:2–6	112, 129
6:24	132	9:2	126n4, 138, 149	11:5	225n12
6:25–34	131, 368	9:3	139	11:6	139, 152
6:30	221	9:4	126n7, 137	11:11	205, 218
6:32	216	9:5	126n4	11:12	130n10, 216
6:33	128, 151, 275n15	9:6	92n9, 126n4, 133n15, 149	11:15	147
6:34	127			11:17	131
7:1	152	9:8	92n9	11:19	112, 126n5, 156, 219
7:1–5	111, 135, 219	9:9	211	11:20–24	135, 152
7:2	140	9:10	126n5, 215, 219	11:25	64, 149, 153
7:2–5	152	9:10–11	132	11:25–26	284
7:7–12	218	9:10–13	131	11:25–27	113, 218, 284
7:9	95	9:11	126n5	11:25–30	122
7:9–11	113	9:11–13	135	11:27	92, 186, 222
7:9–12	93	9:12–13	123	11:28	275n15
7:11	118, 126n7, 136, 153	9:13	126n5, 219, 319	11:28–30	219
7:12	151	9:14	139	11:29–30	152, 219, 386n4
7:13–14	154	9:22	138	12:1–14	118
7:15	135	9:27	111	12:1–15	134
7:15–23	218	9:28	215	12:3–7	281
7:17	126n7	9:29	111, 138	12:7	219, 319
7:17–18	154	9:32–33	137	12:9	216
7:18	126n7	9:34	139	12:10	139
7:21	217	9:35	216	12:14	139
7:21–23	72, 92, 116, 135, 154, 404n31	9:36	150	12:18	92n9, 224
7:22–23	147	10:1–4	217	12:22–32	141, 202
7:23	127	10:1–6	216	12:24	139, 141
7:24–25	146	10:2	221	12:26	405n38
8:1–9:3	111	10:3	211, 219	12:28	129, 217, 224
8:1–9:34	152	10:5–14	152	12:31	117, 126n4, 141
8:4	142n28	10:5–42	217	12:31–32	141, 149, 224
8:5–13	132, 216	10:7	217	12:31–37	219
8:10	106n53	10:8	140	12:32	141, 144
8:10–12	134	10:12–14	216	12:33–37	153
8:11	95, 216	10:16–23	135, 219	12:34	126n7
8:12	145, 216	10:17	216	12:34–35	137
8:14	215	10:18	216	12:34–39	116
8:17	183	10:20	224	12:35	126n7
		10:21–22	215	12:36	147

12:38–42	135, 149	13:36–43	129, 137, 145–47, 149, 151	15:21–28	216, 219
12:39	126n7, 129, 217			15:21–39	152
12:40	133n15	13:37	146	15:22–28	137
12:41a	144	13:37–38	113, 152	15:28	138
12:42	150	13:37–39	153	15:32–39	95n17
12:45	126n7, 137	13:38	126n7, 146	15:34	184
12:46–50	202, 215	13:38–39	137	16:1–4	135
13:1	216	13:38–39a	146	16:2–4	147
13:1–3	152	13:39a	146	16:4	126n7, 129, 217
13:1–52	110, 145, 217	13:39b	146	16:8	221
13:3–8	379	13:39c	146	16:12	220
13:3–23	145	13:40–42a	153	16:13	133n15
13:3b	146	13:40–43	146	16:13–16	129
13:8	146	13:41	127, 146	16:16	117, 216, 221, 222
13:9	147	13:41–42	133n15, 156	16:17	117
13:11	121, 217	13:42	145, 146, 147	16:17–19	221, 222
13:14–15	117	13:42–43	153	16:17b	222
13:16	220	13:42b–43	153	16:18	110, 222
13:18–22	112	13:43	146, 147	16:19–31	154
13:18–23	129	13:43b	147	16:20	216
13:19	126n7, 137	13:44	132, 146, 217	16:21	133n15
13:21	98	13:44–46	218	16:21–28	306
13:23	146	13:45	146, 217	16:22–23	222
13:24	146, 152, 153, 217	13:47	217	16:27	133n15, 154
13:24–30	112, 129, 137, 145–47, 151	13:47–48	146, 217	17:1	221
		13:47–50	147	17:1–8	186, 218
13:25	146, 153, 217	13:49	126n7, 137	17:2	147
13:25–26	146	13:49–50	217	17:5	92n9
13:26–27	153	13:50	145	17:6–7	221
13:27	146, 153	13:51	220	17:12	133n15
13:27–28	217	13:51–52	146	17:13	220
13:27–29	146	13:52	218	17:14–18	137
13:27–30	154, 217	13:53–58	223	17:20	221
13:27b	146	13:54	216	17:22	133n15
13:28	217	14:13–21	95n17	17:22–23	306
13:28a	146	14:13–26	152	17:24–27	221
13:28b–29	146	14:15–21	129n8	18:1–4	152, 218, 385
13:28b–30	153	14:28	112, 221	18:1–10	129
13:29	146	14:28–33	221	18:1–35	145, 217
13:30	146	14:30	112	18:3	217, 314
13:30b	153	14:31	221	18:4	275n15, 276
13:31	146, 217	14:33	221, 280, 281	18:6	218, 275n15, 277
13:31–32	145	15:1–20	142	18:6–9	128
13:33	146, 217	15:14	134	18:7	146
13:34–35	116	15:15	222	18:7–10	153
13:36	216	15:19	126n7, 136	18:8	145

483

INDEX OF SCRIPTURE

18:8–9	147	19:23–24	217, 225n12	22:37–39	275n15, 276
18:10	153, 218	19:24	217	22:37–40	115
18:10–22	149	19:26	155, 277	22:41	275n15
18:14	218	19:27	222	22:43	224
18:15	117, 125n3	19:28	213	23:1–2	111
18:15–18	151	20:1	217	23:1–23	113
18:15–20	219	20:1–16	129, 154, 219	23:1–36	134, 143n32
18:15–22	149	20:11	132	23:1–39	111
18:15–35	219	20:13	127	23:2–3	143n32, 216
18:17	131, 216, 219, 222	20:15	126n7	23:4–32	216
18:17a	149	20:17–19	306	23:5–7	111
18:18–29	222	20:18	133n15	23:5–36	218
18:19	152	20:19	216	23:8–12	222
18:20	113, 152, 219	20:20–21	221	23:9	93
18:21	117, 221, 222	20:25	216	23:10	217, 218
18:21–22	148, 219	20:25–26a	385n2	23:13	111, 222
18:21–35	97n21, 140	20:28	133n15, 143, 156, 186	23:16	127, 134
18:21b	125n3	21:12	275n15	23:16–22	147
18:23	147, 217	21:12–13	142	23:18	127
18:23–25	153, 154, 219	21:18–22	142	23:23	111
18:23–35	92, 129, 134, 145, 147–49, 151, 155	21:21	218	23:24	134
		21:23	139	23:25–28	111
18:24	126, 147	21:23–23:29	142	23:27–36	135
18:25	148	21:31	217	23:28	111, 127
18:26	148	21:31–32	131, 219	23:29–39	39
18:27	148, 152	21:31b	136	23:37–39	152
18:27–30	153	21:32	128, 217	24:1–51	142
18:28	127, 148	21:33–41	113	24:1–25:30	149
18:28–30	153	21:33–44	112	24:1–25:46	145, 152, 217
18:29	148	21:33–46	134	24:11	135
18:30	127, 148	21:43	216, 217	24:12	127
18:31	148, 153	22:1–10	132n13	24:14	146, 216, 223
18:32	126, 126n7	22:1–14	216	24:24	135
18:32–33	148, 152, 153	22:2	217	24:26–44	122
18:32–34	153	22:10	126n7	24:30–31	146
18:34	127, 148, 156	22:13	145	24:31	217
18:34–35	153, 154n16	22:15–22	280	24:36	217
18:35	149, 155	22:15–40	130n11	24:36–44	154
19:5–6	275n15, 277	22:16	280	24:36–25:30	220
19:7	221	22:18	126	24:37–44	133n15
19:12	217	22:19–20	120	24:40–41	217
19:13	218	22:21	275n15, 362	24:45–51	134n17
19:14	275n15, 276	22:23–33	134, 281	24:51	145
19:16–22	134, 277	22:32	399n13	25:1	217
19:16–30	131, 275n15	22:35–40	130	25:14–30	135, 147
19:21	225n12	22:37	107n56, 397n5	25:20	220

Index of Scripture

25:21	132	26:36–45	220	28:8	132
25:23	132	26:36–46	222	28:8–10	221
25:26	126n7	26:37	185	28:11–15	216
25:30	145	26:40	185	28:16	221
25:31	150	26:40–45	185	28:16–17	191, 221
25:31–33	133n15, 153	26:41	98	28:16–20	110, 156, 306
25:31–36	135	26:45	126n5, 133n15, 185	28:18	92n9, 113, 221, 399n9
25:31–46	73, 145, 149–51, 154, 220, 275n15, 276, 322, 402n24	26:46–50	185	28:18–20	122, 146
		26:47–68	216	28:19	116, 216, 219, 223, 224, 225n14, 228
		26:51	224		
25:32	223	26:51–52	220		
25:32–33	150	26:56	185	28:19–20	115, 216
25:34	150	26:57–68	185	28:19–20a	221
25:34–36	275n15	26:58	221	28:20	113
25:35	321	26:59–68	134	28:20b	220
25:35–36	152	26:69–75	135, 185, 220, 222		
25:35–39	151, 155, 220	26:73	280	**Mark**	
25:37–39	151, 153, 220	27:3–10	185, 220, 279	1:1–6	128
25:40	153, 275n15	27:3–26	135	1:4	126n4
25:41	137, 155	27:4	117, 125n3	1:5	126n4
25:41–45	275n15	27:11–54	302n33	1:8	141, 224
25:41–46a	154n16	27:15	185	1:9–15	211
25:42–43	151, 152, 220	27:15–26	185	1:10	141, 224
25:42–44	155	27:19	218	1:12	224
25:43	321	27:21–23	185	1:13	98n24
25:44	151, 153, 220	27:24–25	302n33	1:15	129, 138, 217
25:44–45	275n15	27:25	185	1:16–20	211
25:45	153, 220	27:26–50	156	1:17	211
25:45–46	153	27:27–31	185	1:21–28	137
25:46	150, 151, 153, 156, 275n15	27:32–56	306	1:21–2:12	212
		27:37	185	1:22	92n9
26:1–5	149	27:38	185	1:29	215
26:2	133n15	27:39–43	185	1:30	211
26:6	216	27:40–44	135	1:44	142n28
26:13	146	27:41–43	216	2:1	215
26:14–16	185, 220	27:44	185	2:1–12	128, 138
26:14–27:66	302n33	27:45	185	2:1–3:6	152, 212
26:18	216	27:46	184, 185, 189	2:5	126n4, 138, 138n23, 152, 214
26:25	185, 220	27:47–49	185, 186		
26:26–28	405n33	27:50	186	2:5–10	141
26:26–29	186	27:51–53	186, 187	2:6–10	152
26:28	126n4, 143, 219	27:51–54	185, 186	2:6–12	138–39
26:31	185, 220	27:54	280, 281	2:7	126n4, 139
26:31–32	156	27:57	131	2:9	126n4
26:33–35	221	28:1–10	279	2:10	92n9, 126n4, 133n15
26:35	222	28:5–7	156		

485

2:11	215	3:31–32	208, 215	6:34–35	213
2:12	134	3:31–35	200n22, 201–2, 208	6:35	212
2:13–14	211			6:40–44	129n8
2:14	211	3:32	202	6:41	212
2:14–17	131	3:35	207, 214, 215	6:45	212
2:15	126n5, 152, 215	4:1–34	217	6:50	213
2:15–16	212	4:3–8	379	6:52	153, 213, 220
2:15–17	132	4:10	212	7:1–23	36, 142, 215
2:16	126n5	4:11–12	129, 202, 375	7:2	212
2:16–17	135, 152	4:12	220	7:5	212
2:17	141, 214	4:13–20	214	7:14–15	282
2:17b	126	4:17	98	7:17	212, 215
2:18	139, 152, 212	4:22	129	7:18	213
2:19–22	152	4:24	140	7:19b	282
2:23	152, 212	4:24–25	135	7:21	136
2:23–3:6	134	4:25	129	7:22	126, 126n7
2:25–26	281	4:26	217	7:23	126n7
2:25–28	152	4:30	217	7:24	215
3:1–3	152	4:34	212	7:24–30	137, 216
3:1–6	215	4:38	213, 220	7:29	214
3:1–12	212	4:40	213	7:30	215
3:2	139	5:1–17	215	8:1	212
3:4	152	5:1–20	137	8:1–10	95n17, 215
3:5	152	5:1–43	212	8:2–4	213
3:6	139	5:18–20	212	8:4	212
3:7	212	5:19	215	8:6	212
3:13–19a	211, 262	5:31	212	8:10	212
3:14–15	212	5:33	280	8:11	202
3:18	213	5:34	138, 214	8:11–13	135
3:19	215	5:35–43	215	8:12	202
3:19a	212, 213	5:36	214	8:16–17	213
3:19b–20	215	5:37	213	8:17	153, 220
3:19b–35	202n26	6:1	212	8:18	220
3:20	202	6:1–6a	202, 215, 223	8:21	213, 220
3:21	202, 208	6:4	202, 215	8:26	215
3:21–27	215	6:5	212	8:27	212
3:22	139, 141, 202	6:7	140, 212	8:27–29	129
3:22–30	141	6:7–11	212	8:29	213
3:23	141, 202	6:7–44	388–89	8:31	133n15, 213
3:23–26	202	6:8	95	8:31–33	202
3:26	405n38	6:10	215	8:31–9:1	214, 368
3:28	125, 141	6:12	138	8:32	213
3:28–29	140–41	6:12–13	212	8:32–33	213
3:29	144, 224	6:14–29	129	8:33	213
3:30	141, 202	6:29	214	8:33–34	212
3:31	202	6:30–44	95n17, 215	8:34–9:1	153, 213

Index of Scripture

8:35–37	213	10:18–19	215	12:27	399n13
8:38	126n5, 129	10:21	225n12	12:28–34	134
9:1	129, 217	10:23	212, 217	12:28–35	142
9:2	213	10:23–25	215, 225n12	12:29	397n5
9:5–6	221	10:23–27	129	12:29–30	107n56
9:7	92n9	10:27	155, 214	12:29–31	215
9:12	133n15	10:28	214, 215	12:30–31	328
9:14	212	10:29	215	12:32	280
9:14–29	137	10:29–30	214, 215	12:34	217
9:17–18	213	10:29–31	92	12:36	224
9:18	212	10:32	212	12:38–40	134
9:19	213	10:32–45	214	12:41	131
9:24	214	10:33–34	133n15, 213	12:41–44	225n12
9:28	212	10:35–37	221	12:43	212
9:28–29	213	10:35–41	213	13:1	212
9:30–31	213	10:35–42	213	13:1–2	215
9:30–37	380	10:35–45	202	13:1–37	142, 217
9:31	133n15, 212	10:39	229	13:3	213
9:31–50	214	10:42–45	153, 215	13:3–37	215
9:32	220	10:43–45	213	13:5–13	97n23
9:32–41	202	10:45	133n15, 143, 213	13:9–13	92, 135, 214
9:32–48	229	10:46	212	13:10	223
9:33	215	10:48	214	13:11	224
9:33–34	213	10:50	214	13:12–13a	215
9:35	212	10:52	138, 214	13:12b–13	214
9:35–37	213	10:52b	214	13:22	135, 252
9:38	213	11:1	212	13:26–27	214
9:38–39	214	11:12–14	142	13:32	374
9:40	214	11:14	212	13:33	213
9:42	275n15	11:15–19	142	13:37	213, 361
9:42–47	128	11:17	215, 223	14:1	202
9:42–50	129, 215	11:18	202	14:3	215
9:46	145	11:20–25	140, 142	14:3–9	214
9:47	217	11:22–26	215	14:10	212, 213
10:2–12	130	11:25	127	14:11	202
10:2–16	215, 305	11:27–12:44	142	14:12–14	212
10:7–8	275n15, 277	11:28	139	14:16	212
10:10	212	12:1–12	134	14:17	212
10:13	212	12:6	92n9	14:18b–21	213
10:13–14	213	12:12	202	14:20	212
10:14	217	12:13–14	130n11	14:22–24	405n33
10:14–15	129	12:13–17	215, 280	14:22–25	95
10:14–16	275n15	12:14	280	14:24	143, 213
10:15	314	12:15–16	120	14:27	214
10:17–22	134, 212	12:17	362	14:28	214
10:17–31	131, 275n15	12:18–27	134, 281	14:29	213

INDEX OF SCRIPTURE

14:32	212	1:19	196	1:49	199, 200, 208
14:33	213	1:24	196	1:50	199, 319
14:34	213	1:26	196, 207	1:51	199
14:36	93	1:26–27	196	1:51b	199
14:37	213	1:26–31	194–96	1:52	199
14:37–41a	213	1:26–56	194–200	1:52–53	133, 199
14:38	98, 224	1:26–2:40	200	1:53	132, 199, 225
14:40	213	1:27	196	1:54	199, 319
14:41	126n5, 133n15	1:28	182, 193n3, 194, 195, 195n12, 196, 207, 209	1:54–55	199, 207, 310
14:43	212, 213			1:56	194, 198
14:50–51	214	1:29	208	1:57	198
14:54	213	1:29–30a	196	1:57–80	196
14:55	202	1:30	193n3, 195–96, 195n12, 207, 209	1:58	319
14:55–65	134			1:59–64	200
14:61–64	213	1:31	196	1:64	226
14:66–72	135, 213	1:32	198, 207	1:64–67	209
14:68	213, 220	1:32–33	207	1:67	198, 224
14:70	280	1:32–38	194, 196–98, 208	1:68	182, 226
14:71	213	1:32a	197	1:68–79	64
14:72	214	1:33	130, 197	1:68–80	198
15:1–15	135	1:34	196, 197	1:72	319
15:29–32	135	1:34–35	207	1:75	217
15:33	185	1:35	197, 224	1:76	223
15:35–38	185	1:36	196, 207	1:76–77	130
15:39	280, 281	1:36–37	197	1:77	126n4, 128
15:40–41	214	1:37	197, 207	1:77–78a	223
16:1	214	1:37–38	201	1:78	319
16:6	214	1:38	197, 208, 310	1:80	201, 225
16:7	212, 214	1:39	198	2:10	132, 182, 195n8
16:7–8	214, 221	1:39–45	194, 198	2:11	226
16:8	154	1:41	198, 224, 275n15, 278	2:18	198
		1:41–42	209	2:19	201, 208
Luke		1:42	198	2:21–25	200
1–2	224, 279	1:42–48	182	2:22–24	223
1:1–4	223, 285	1:43	198	2:22–40	142n28
1:5–25	196	1:43–45	198, 207	2:25	223, 225
1:5–2:52	196	1:44	132, 196, 198, 275n15, 278	2:26	225
1:6	198, 200			2:27	209, 223, 224
1:7	196	1:45	207	2:28	182
1:8–23	142n28, 223	1:46	74, 200, 209	2:28–32	152
1:14	132, 195n8	1:46–53	208	2:29–32	227
1:14–17	198	1:46–55	64, 194, 198–200, 207, 208	2:32	275n15
1:15	224	1:46b–47	309	2:34	39, 224
1:16	226	1:47	197, 199, 207, 208	2:34–35	152, 208
1:17	196, 224	1:48	197, 199	2:35	182
				2:37–51	223

Index of Scripture

2:38	223	4:22	195n12	6:17–19	226
2:39	200	4:22–29	226	6:20	129, 133, 225
2:40	195n12	4:23–30	39, 139	6:20–23	226
2:41–42	200	4:25	280	6:22	126n7
2:41–52	200–201, 208	4:25–30	134	6:22–24	133
2:44	200	4:29	275n15	6:24	132, 225
2:45	200	4:30	227	6:24–25	275n15
2:46	200	4:31	224	6:26	135
2:46–49	207	4:31–37	137, 224	6:27–28	266
2:47	201	4:31–41	226	6:32	126n5, 195n12
2:47–48	201	4:33–38	224	6:32–34	131
2:48	202, 208	4:36–37	224	6:32–36	132, 266
2:49	201, 207	4:38–39	132	6:33	126n5, 195n12
2:49b	202	4:41b	226	6:34	126n5, 195n12
2:50	201	4:42–44	132	6:35	126n7
2:50–51	208	4:43	226	6:36	319
2:51a	201	5:1–11	132	6:37	128
2:51b	201	5:1–26	134	6:37–42	152
2:52	195n12, 201, 275n15	5:6	226	6:38	140
2:68	223	5:8	126n5, 135, 228	6:39	134
3:1–6	128	5:12–16	132	6:41–42	135
3:3	126n4, 128, 223	5:12–32	226	6:45	126n7, 137
3:3–14	129	5:14	142n28	6:46	135
3:7–9	128, 134	5:17–26	128, 132, 138	7:1–10	132
3:7–18	156	5:20	126n4, 128, 138	7:1–23	226
3:8	134n19, 138	5:21	126n4, 128, 139	7:3	279
3:12	131	5:23	126n4, 128	7:5	224
3:16–22	224	5:24	126n4, 128, 133n15	7:9	106n53
3:19	126n7	5:25	226	7:10	197n14
3:28	128	5:26	132	7:16	226
4:1	224, 225	5:27–29	225n14	7:18–23	129
4:1–13	128, 137	5:27–32	132	7:21	126n7, 137, 195n12
4:2	98n24	5:29–30	132	7:22	133, 225n12
4:13	98n24	5:29–32	131, 135	7:23	139
4:14	224	5:30	126n5	7:27	223
4:16–20a	224	5:32	126n5	7:28	205
4:16–30	223, 224, 362, 378	5:33	139	7:29	131
		6:1–9	224	7:34	126n5, 131
4:18	132, 133, 224	6:1–11	134	7:36–50	135, 225n14, 226
4:18–19	275n15	6:3–4	281	7:37	126n5, 228
4:18–21	275n15	6:6	224	7:39	126n5, 228
4:18a	224	6:6–11	132, 224, 226	7:40–43	140
4:18b	225	6:7	139	7:41	126
4:18c	226	6:11	139	7:42	195n12
4:19	226	6:13	227, 262n13	7:43	195n12
4:21	132, 198, 226	6:15	213	7:47	126n4, 128, 195n12

489

INDEX OF SCRIPTURE

7:48	126n4, 128	10:17	132, 195n8	12:10	128, 144, 202, 224
7:49	126n4	10:17–20	226	12:10a	141
7:50	138	10:18	405n38	12:12	225
7:59–60	202n25	10:19	127, 146	12:13–21	225
8:1–3	226	10:21	225	12:14	152
8:1b–2a	126n7	10:21–22	284	12:16–21	132
8:2	137	10:22	92	12:22–31	131
8:2–3	279	10:25–28	130n11, 134	12:32	129, 198, 207
8:5–8	379	10:25–42	153	12:33	275n15
8:12	137	10:27	107n56, 397n5	12:33–34	133
8:13	98, 195n8	10:30–37	226	12:41–48	226
8:19–21	200n22, 202	10:38–42	368	12:44	280
8:22–56	226	11:1–13	223	12:49–53	97n23, 224
8:26–33	224	11:2	140	12:58–59	275n15
8:26–39	137	11:2b–4	90	13	319
8:28	197	11:2bc	95, 106n51	13:1–5	138
8:39	226	11:3	140	13:2	126n5
8:40–42	279	11:3–4	92	13:4	126
8:41	224	11:4	126n4, 128, 139, 348	13:6–9	138
8:48	138	11:4a	140	13:10	224
8:49	131	11:4b	127, 140	13:10–17	224, 226
9:1–2	140	11:11–13	93	13:14	131, 224
9:1–6	226	11:13	126n7, 137, 225	13:20	223
9:5	228	11:14	137, 226	13:22	223
9:10	226, 262n13	11:14–23	202	13:27	127
9:10–17	95n17, 226	11:15	139	13:28	145
9:12–17	129n8	11:18	405n38	13:29	129
9:18–20	129	11:20	129, 217, 226	13:32–33	132, 226
9:20	226	11:24–26	224	13:33	223
9:22	133n15, 227	11:26	126n7, 137	13:33–34	227
9:26	133n15	11:27–28	226	14:1–5	224
9:27	280	11:28	310	14:1–6	226
9:34	197	11:29	126n7	14:1–24	132
9:35	197	11:29–32	135	14:7–24	129
9:37–43	226	11:30	133n15	14:12–13	225
9:37–43a	137, 224	11:32a	144	14:12–24	132, 132n13
9:43	226	11:34	126n7	14:13	133, 275n15
9:44	133n15	11:37–44	134	14:15	95
9:51–53	223	11:39	126	14:21	133, 225
9:51–56	134n19, 147	11:49	262n13	14:33	226, 275n15
9:58	133n15, 275n15	11:53–54	139	15:1	126n5
9:59–60	129	12:5	145	15:1–2	131, 132
9:60	129	12:7	275n15	15:2	132
10:1–12	226	12:8–9	133n15	15:6–10	227
10:13–15	135	12:8–10	141	15:7	126n5, 134, 195n8
10:16	226	12:8–12	141	15:10	126n5, 132, 195n8

15:11–32	140, 144, 154	18:9–14	131, 142n28	20:45–47	134
15:18	125n3	18:10	327	20:46–47	275n15
15:21	125n3	18:11	127	21:1	131
15:24	133	18:13	126n5	21:1–4	225n12
15:32	133	18:13–14	136	21:3	280
16:1–8	135	18:15–17	132	21:4	133
16:1–9	225	18:15–30	226	21:5–36	142
16:5	126	18:16–17	129	21:12–19	135
16:7	127	18:17	314	21:13	228
16:8	127	18:18–25	134	21:24	227
16:9	127, 275n15	18:18–30	131, 133, 275n15	22:3	154
16:10	127	18:22	133, 225n12	22:7–27	225n14
16:11	127, 280	18:24–25	225n12	22:14	262n13
16:13	132, 226, 382n3	18:26–27	155	22:19–20	405n33
16:14	225	18:28	92	22:20	143
16:15	134	18:31	223, 227	22:25	227
16:16	130	18:31–33	133n15	22:27	198
16:17	130	18:32	227	22:29	198
16:19–31	132, 225	18:35–43	132, 226	22:29–30	95
16:20	133	18:43	226	22:30	213
16:22–31	134	18:48	138	22:31	405n38
16:25	275n15	19:1–8	225	22:31–32	154, 228
17:1–2	128	19:1–10	130–31, 135	22:37	127
17:1–4	129, 226	19:5	132, 226	22:40	98
17:2	275n15	19:6	132	22:46	98
17:3	125, 128	19:7	126n5, 132	22:49–51	226
17:3–4	97n21, 138	19:8	133	22:54b–62	135
17:4	125n3, 128	19:9	133, 134n19, 225, 226	22:59	280
17:5	262n13	19:10	133	22:63–23:48	227
17:7–10	134n19, 140	19:11–27	135, 155	22:66–71	134
17:9	195n12	19:22	126n7	22:70–71	228
17:9–10	399n11	19:27	145	23:1–25	135
17:10	127, 153, 226	19:34	132	23:13–14	143
17:11	223	19:37	226	23:13–25	226
17:11–19	226	19:45–48	142	23:24	226
17:14	142n28	20–26	280	23:34	128, 185
17:15	226	20:1–2	139	23:35–38	135
17:18	226	20:1–21:4	142	23:43	132, 185
17:19	138	20:9–19	134	23:46	185, 286
17:20–21	91, 129	20:13	92n9	23:47	228
17:26–27	133n15	20:20–40	130n11	23:54–56	224
17:28–30	133n15	20:21	280	24:7	126n5, 133n15
18	319	20:24	120	24:10	262n13
18:1–14	223	20:25	362	24:13–35	312
18:6	127	20:27–40	134, 281	24:27	226, 282
18:6–17	275n15	20:38	399n13	24:35	225n14

INDEX OF SCRIPTURE

24:39	191	2:1–4	208	4:15	204
24:41	132, 195n8	2:1–10	277	4:18	281, 281n4
24:47	126n4, 128, 223	2:1–11	275n15	4:19	204
24:49b	223	2:1–12	200n22, 202–4, 206,	4:21	262
24:52	142n28, 195n8		207, 355	4:22	39, 114
24:52–53	223	2:3	203	4:23	262, 281n4
		2:4	203, 206, 207	4:24	281n4
John		2:5	203, 204, 208	4:25–26	264
1:1–3	38	2:6	204	4:28–30	259
1:1–5	206	2:6–8	203	4:29	204
1:1–13	123	2:9	203	4:37	281n4
1:1–18	257	2:9–10a	203	4:39–42	259
1:5	233	2:9b–10	203	4:42	281n4
1:6–8	203	2:11	208, 257	4:46–54	262
1:7	264	2:11a	203	4:47–50	203
1:7–8	261	2:11b–12	203	4:50–54	204
1:9	232, 258, 281, 281n4	2:12	204	4:54	257
1:9–13	325	2:13–17	258	5:1–9	40, 262, 302
1:9–14	206	2:13–22	142	5:7–8	302
1:10	114, 260	2:23–25	203	5:16	260
1:12	203, 206	2:43	10–11	5:16–18	114
1:13	116, 206	3:1–2	115	5:17	92, 263
1:14	87, 114, 203, 251, 281n4	3:1–17	38	5:18	107n55, 265
1:15	203	3:1–21	262	5:19	92, 204, 257, 265, 281
1:16	204	3:3	116	5:19–24	87n23, 116, 206
1:16–18	206	3:3–15	115	5:19–46	264
1:17	281	3:5–8	206, 325	5:19–47	265
1:18	115, 284, 325, 387n6	3:8	116	5:24	114, 260
1:19–28	203	3:13–15	206	5:26–27	92n9
1:20	378	3:14–16	115	5:28–29	145
1:29	206, 233, 378	3:16	206, 208, 260, 261	5:30	92n9, 265
1:29–34	203	3:16–17	114	5:30–38	152
1:35–39	203	3:17	275n15	5:30–47	114, 260
1:35–42	262	3:18	260	5:31	281n4
1:40–42	203	3:18–21	38	5:32	281n4
1:41	282	3:19	114, 121, 152, 232, 263	5:33	281n4
1:42	221	3:21	115, 251, 281n4	5:35	251
1:43–51	114, 262	3:26	206	5:37–47	263
1:43–5:29	122	3:28	261	5:39–40	118
1:45	204n28, 282	3:30	261, 378	5:45–47	282
1:45–49	203	3:31	38, 206	6:14	281n4
1:46	196	3:33	281n4	6:32	92, 281
1:47	281, 281n4	3:36	154, 260	6:35	281
1:51	87	4:1–42	262	6:35–51	312
2:1	202–3	4:10	204	6:35–55	264
		4:10–14	203	6:38	265

6:40	115	8:31–32	116	11:4	257
6:44	117	8:31–36	117	11:9–10	152, 251, 260
6:47	115, 260	8:31–47	153	11:13	259
6:51	96, 269	8:31–59	38–40	11:25	400n16
6:51–58	251	8:32	281n4	11:25–26	265
6:51b	233	8:34–36	114	11:27	259
6:53–58	96	8:37	39	11:40–42	257
6:54	251	8:39	281	11:41–42	92, 93
6:54–58	260	8:39b–40	39	11:45–53	260, 263, 264
6:55	281n4	8:40	39, 281n4	11:47–48	203
6:60	259	8:41	39	11:52	259
6:60–65	206	8:42	281	12:2–8	259
6:66	259	8:44	39, 114, 245, 258, 267, 281n4	12:16	259
6:68	221			12:20–22	259
6:69	259	8:45	281n4	12:23	63, 204, 206
6:70	154, 258	8:46	281n4	12:24	233
7:1–10	204	8:48	141	12:24–26	263
7:1–52	264	8:50	281	12:25	115
7:3–8:59	113	8:51–58	265	12:26a	153
7:14–44	114	8:54	63	12:27	204
7:16–18	265	8:58–59	107n55	12:27–33	93
7:18	281	9:1–41	262	12:28	63
7:20	141	9:3	257, 275n15	12:31	114–15, 260
7:26	281n4	9:5	251	12:32	258
7:28	281, 281n4	9:13–41	113	12:32–33	115–16, 206, 312
7:30	204	9:18–23	92	12:35–36	251
7:35b	259	9:22	113, 265	12:35–37	114–15
7:37–39	40, 302	9:34–35	242	12:40	117
7:39	117	9:35–41	121	12:41	203
7:40	281n4	10:1–18	115, 263	12:42	113, 265
7:53–8:11	130n11, 302	10:7–18	312	12:42–43	116
8:11	130	10:11	258	12:44	115, 261
8:12	251, 260	10:11–18	206	12:44–50	152
8:12–30	152	10:14	263	12:46	114, 251, 260
8:12–59	264	10:15–38	92	12:47	152
8:13	281n4	10:16	259	13:1	204, 206
8:14	281n4	10:18	258, 281	13:1–17:26	257
8:16	281	10:21	116	13:2	154
8:17	281n4	10:27–28	260	13:3	63
8:18	281	10:30	265	13:3–5	258
8:20	204	10:31–39	260	13:6–8	221
8:21–59	114, 263	10:33	114, 265	13:7	261
8:23	38, 116, 206, 260	10:35	282	13:16	238, 261, 262n13
8:24	267	10:36	265	13:18	258
8:26	281, 281n4	10:38	265	13:21–30	206
8:31	39, 260, 281, 281n4	10:41	281	13:23	221, 263

INDEX OF SCRIPTURE

Reference	Pages	Reference	Pages	Reference	Pages
13:24	221	15:12–17	115, 206, 247, 266	17:19	281n4, 335
13:25	221	15:13	263, 266, 275n15	17:20	260, 262
13:26	221	15:15	260, 263	17:20–26	123, 206
13:31	117	15:16	117, 258, 263	17:21	275n15, 276n18
13:34	71	15:16a	260	17:22	114
13:34–35	115, 206, 247, 259, 266	15:18–19	259	17:23	262, 276n18
13:35	263, 275n15	15:18–25	115	17:24	114
14:2–17:25	92	15:18–27	115, 260	18:1–20:31	257
14:6	281, 285	15:18–16:11	117	18:10	221
14:6–14	206	15:19	260, 266	18:15–16	221
14:8–9	92	15:20	219	18:15–25	221
14:8–11	38	15:22	114, 117	18:15–27	259
14:9	63	15:24	114	18:28–19:16	263
14:9–10	257	15:25–26	116	18:33–38	113
14:10–11	115	15:26	281n4	18:36	258, 275n15
14:13	63	15:26–27	258	18:36–37	116
14:14–17	38	15:27	235	18:37	245, 281
14:15	246, 260	16:1–11	260	18:38	281n4
14:15–17	262	16:2	113, 115, 260, 265	19:14	206
14:16	116	16:7	258, 281n4	19:17	258
14:16–17	258	16:7–11	38, 116	19:17–42	258
14:17	116, 260, 281n4	16:8–11	260	19:25	204
14:19	114	16:12–25	38	19:25b–27	206, 207, 208, 259
14:20–21	206	16:13	237, 281n4	19:26	263
14:21	246	16:13–14	258	19:26–27	221
14:24	260	16:16–19	203	19:27–28	209
14:25–31	38	16:20–21	263	19:28	185
14:26	237, 258	16:21–22	198n18	19:30	185
14:27	114, 275n15	16:21–33	115	19:31–37	191
14:27–28	260	16:22–33	260	19:34	250n53
14:28	257	16:33	263, 266, 405n37	19:34–35	250
14:30	114	17:1	204, 206	19:35	221, 281, 281n4, 285
15:1	281, 281n4	17:1–26	93, 264	20:1–10	206, 221
15:1–10	260	17:3	251, 258, 260, 281, 281n4	20:1–18	279
15:1–11	262	17:5	117	20:2	221
15:4–10	203	17:8	115, 281	20:11–18	259
15:5	258, 281	17:11	275n15	20:17	92
15:8	63	17:11–12	258	20:17–21	92
15:9	259	17:14	115, 116	20:19–23	238n21
15:10	246, 251	17:14–15	275n15	20:21	258
15:10–17	204	17:14–18	260	20:22	251, 258
15:11	260	17:14–19	260, 266	20:27	191
15:12	259	17:16	266	20:28	265
15:12–13	232	17:17	281n4	20:29–31	251
				20:30–31	204, 257

Index of Scripture

20:31	259, 285	2:47	195n12, 226	7:51–8:1	225
21:2–11	221	3:1–10	226	7:52	227
21:7	206, 221	3:1–6:7	223	7:54–8:3	227
21:15–19	262	3:8–9	226	7:55	224
21:15–21	221	3:11–16	226	8:1	228
21:20	263	3:14	195n12	8:1b	224
21:20–24	206, 221	3:19	134n16	8:2	228
21:24	263, 281n4, 285	4:1–18	227	8:2–25	226
25:45–46	152	4:5–22	226	8:3	224, 226
		4:8	224, 225	8:4	228
Acts		4:10	227	8:4–13	226
1:1–5	223	4:24–27	227	8:9–24	225
1:2	224	4:24–30	223	8:12–16	225n14
1:4	223	4:25	224	8:14–17	224
1:5	224, 225n14	4:25b–30	228	8:14–27	223
1:8	197, 224, 226	4:27	227	8:26–40	283n9
1:8b	223	4:29	197n14	8:27–30	283n9
1:14	201n23, 223	4:29–31	226	8:29	225
1:15	213	4:31	224, 225	8:31	283n9
1:15–16	227	4:32–37	275n15	8:35	283n9
1:15–20	227	4:33	195n12, 228	8:36–38	225n14
1:16	224	5:1–9	225	8:36–39	283n9
1:21–22	227	5:11	224	8:39	225
2:1–11	224	5:12–16	226	9:2	223, 227
2:1–42	223	5:17	246	9:10–19a	226
2:4	225	5:17–32	226	9:13	227
2:8–11	225	5:17–42	227	9:15	227
2:17	197	5:29	275n15	9:17	224
2:17–18	224	5:31	134n16, 225, 226	9:18	225n14
2:18	197n14, 198, 225	5:32	225, 374	9:21	227
2:22	226	5:32–37	225	9:26–30	223
2:23–24	228	5:38–39	228	9:31	224, 225
2:26	198	5:42	226	9:32–43	226
2:29	227	6:1–6	227	9:36–43	226
2:32–35	275n15	6:3	224, 225	10:1–8	227
2:33	224, 225	6:5	224, 225	10:1–16	223
2:36	227	6:8	195n12, 226	10:19	225
2:37–41	226	6:9–14	224	10:24–48	226
2:38	134n16, 225	6:10	225	10:30–33	227
2:38–41	225n14	6:11	141	10:31	225, 227
2:42	223, 225n14	7:2	227	10:36	226
2:42–46	275n15	7:9–16	226	10:38	224
2:44–45	275n15	7:10	195n12	10:39	227
2:44–47	225	7:45	216, 226	10:42	228
2:46	225n14	7:46	195n12	10:43	134n16, 228
		7:51–60	228	10:44–48	224

495

10:45	227	14:2	227	17:11	224
10:48	225n14	14:3	195n12, 228	17:16–31	226
11:1	227	14:3–4	226	17:23	275n15
11:2–22	223	14:8–18	226	17:26–28	92
11:11–17	224	14:11–18	226	18:4	224
11:12	225	14:16	226	18:5	224
11:16	225n14	14:16–17	228	18:6	227
11:18	227	14:19–20	224	18:7–10	226
11:19–21	228	14:23	224	18:8	225n14
11:22	224	14:26	195n12	18:12–17	227
11:23	195n12	14:27	224, 227	18:19–20	224
11:24	224, 225	15:1–7a	227	18:22	224
11:26	224	15:1–35	223	18:25	225
11:26c	224	15:3	224, 227	18:27	195n12
11:28	225	15:5–29	275n15	18:28	224
11:29	227	15:6–8	224	19:1–7	224
12:1	224	15:7	227	19:3	225n14
12:4–17	226	15:8	228	19:6	225
12:5	224	15:10	226, 284	19:8–9	224
12:20–24	228	15:11	195n12	19:9	223
12:25	223	15:12	227	19:11–20	225, 226
13:1	224	15:14	227	19:20	226
13:2	225	15:17	227	19:21	225
13:4	225	15:19	227	19:23	223
13:7	227	15:21	224	20:7	225n14
13:9	224	15:22	224	20:11	95
13:13	223	15:23	195n8, 227	20:13–22	223
13:14	224	15:28	225	20:17	224
13:15	227	15:40	195n12	20:22	225, 227
13:16	226	16:1–5	223	20:23	225
13:19–20a	226	16:6	225	20:24	195n12, 228
13:23	226	16:6–10	228	20:28	224, 225
13:26	227	16:7	225	20:32	195n12
13:26a	223	16:13	224	20:36	223
13:27	227	16:14–15	226	21:3–7	226
13:30–31	223	16:15	225n14	21:4	225
13:33	226	16:16–18	224, 226	21:11	225
13:33–43	226	16:17	197n14	21:11–12	227
13:38	134n16, 227	16:22–40	226	21:15–23:11	223
13:42–43	224	16:25–34	226	21:17–36	227
13:43	195n12	16:33	225n14	21:18–20a	227
13:44	224	16:40	226	21:20	227
13:46	227	17:1–9	227	21:27–36	227
13:48	227	17:2–4	224	22:5	227
13:52	224, 225	17:10	224	22:15	228
14:1–7	224, 227	17:10–16	224	22:16	134n16, 225n14

Index of Scripture

22:17–20	227	1:17	121, 285	6:1–4	168n24
22:18	228	1:18–32	216, 327	6:1–11	177
22:20	228	1:18–2:1	156	6:1–14	121, 165, 167–69, 176
22:21	227	1:18–3:20	117	6:1–23	118, 136
23:6	227	1:21	64	6:1–7:6	172
23:6–10	224	1:23	119, 120	6:2	167, 178
23:11	228	1:25	346	6:3	167n21, 168, 175, 177
23:26	195n8	1:32	158n2, 173, 175	6:3–11	399n14
23:26–30	227	2:4	319	6:4	168, 175
24:5	246n40	2:12	117	6:4–5	121
24:27	195n12	2:15	275n15	6:5	168, 175
25:1–7	227	3:4	95	6:5a	168n26
25:3	195n12	3:9	136	6:6	169, 173, 175
25:9	195n12	3:9b	118	6:6b	167, 178
25:11	195n12	3:20	118	6:7	168–69, 178
25:13–18	227	3:21	118	6:8	168, 178
25:16	195n12	3:24–25	267	6:9	168
25:24	227	3:25	233	6:9a	175
25:33–37	227	3:31	118	6:9b	169, 176
26:10	227	4:5	283	6:10	168, 175
26:16	228	4:17	176, 328	6:10–11	167, 169, 178
26:17	227	5–8	158–79	6:11	173, 175
26:18	134n16	5:1–2	119	6:12–13	166
26:20	227	5:1–5	165	6:12–14	169
26:23	227	5:1–11	165–66	6:13	169, 178
26:28	224	5:6–8	405n32	6:15–23	169, 171, 174
26:29	226	5:6–21	157	6:15–7:6	165, 169–70, 172
26:30–32	227	5:7	165, 176	6:16	170, 175, 176
27:13–44	228	5:8	165, 176	6:16–18	400n21
27:24	195n12	5:11	165	6:17–23	117
27:33–44	226	5:12	166, 175	6:18	170
27:35	225n14	5:12–19	400n18	6:19	178
28:7	226	5:12–21	122, 136, 165, 166–67, 169, 171	6:21	170, 175, 176
28:8–9	226			6:22	170
28:17–18	227	5:12c	166	6:23	170, 172, 175, 176
28:20	226	5:14	119, 128, 166, 175, 176	7:1	170–71n34, 178
28:22	246n40	5:16b–19	166	7:1–6	170
28:25–27	224	5:17	166, 176	7:1–8:8	118
28:28	227	5:18	175	7:2–3	170, 175
		5:18–19	166, 175, 176	7:4	167n23, 170, 173, 177, 178
Romans		5:19	166, 175	7:5	170, 171, 175
1–3	119	5:20	170	7:6	167n23, 170, 176, 178
1:1–8	207	5:20–21	119, 170	7:7	118
1:7	376	5:21	166	7:7–8	171
1:16–27	278	6:1–2	169	7:7–25	74, 117, 136, 165, 170–72
		6:1–3	168		

497

INDEX OF SCRIPTURE

7:9	171, 175	8:39	174, 175	2:1–7	312
7:9–11	171, 175	9–11	58, 229	2:1–16	32, 311
7:10	171, 282	9:1–5	94n14	2:2	177–78n48, 192, 311
7:12	118	9:23	319	2:5–6	311
7:13	118, 171, 175	10:9–10	244n34	2:6	374, 405n37
7:14–25	170n34	10:17	295	2:7	121, 311
7:24	171, 176	11:16–24	275n15	2:8	311, 405n37
8:1–11	165, 172–73	11:22	319	2:10	283
8:1–39	118	11:26	174	2:10–12	311
8:2	172, 176	11:29	379	2:16	283, 311
8:3	204	11:32	319	3:10–14	222
8:3–6	173	11:36	369	3:22	221
8:4	172, 175	12:1	319	4:1–21	255n60
8:6	172, 175	12:1–13:14	118	4:6–7	72
8:7	172, 175	12:2	121, 199, 310	4:8–13	255n60
8:10	173, 175	12:8	213	5:1–13	255n60
8:10–11	172, 178	12:11	213	5:4–5	405n38
8:11	172–73, 177–78n48	13:1–7	275n15	5:7b	308
8:12–30	165, 173–74	14:7	158n2, 175	5:13	136
8:13	173, 175, 178	14:7–8	167n23	6:1–6	255n60
8:14–17	173	14:8	158n2, 175, 399n10	6:2	22
8:15	93, 173, 176	14:9	158n2, 175	6:9	278
8:17	174	14:15	158n2, 176	6:14	283
8:18	67, 283	15:9	319	6:19	275n15, 400n20
8:18–19	188	16:1	279	7:1–40	255n60, 277n22
8:18–25	173, 198n18	16:3	279	7:5	98n24, 405n38
8:19	275n15	16:6	279	7:14	275n15, 277
8:20	173, 174, 176	16:12–13	279	8:1–13	70
8:20–21	173–74, 176	16:15	279	8:5–6	398n6
8:20–22	175	16:25–27	63	8:6	38
8:21	275n15	16:26	216	8:7–13	255n60
8:22	173, 275n15			8:12	117
8:22–24a	188	**1 Corinthians**		9:1–14	255n60
8:23	174, 176	1–2	192	9:5	211, 221
8:24–25	199	1:2	255n60, 376	9:24–27	275n15
8:26–27	72, 309	1:12	221	10:13b	98
8:28	275n15	1:13b–17a	255n60	10:16–17	255n60
8:28–39	64	1:18	118, 311	10:31	68
8:29	119, 120, 319	1:18–31	73, 311	10:32	255n60
8:29–30	325	1:18–2:16	120–21, 284	11:2–16	120n24
8:31–39	165, 174	1:20b	311	11:4–18	225n14
8:32	93	1:22–25	190	11:5–6	279
8:34b	174, 175	1:24	400n15	11:7	119, 120, 120n24, 319
8:35	174	1:30	400n15	11:22	255n60
8:36	174, 176	2:1	121	11:23	255n60
8:38	174, 175, 176			11:23–24	255n60

11:23–26	95, 225n14	4:5	374	4:4	204, 207, 208
11:24	165n18	4:6	63, 275n15	4:4–7	117, 207
11:25	143n31	4:7–12	179	4:6	93, 207, 209
12:3	255n60, 283, 398n7	4:8–12	189	4:6–7	92
12:4–30	258	4:11	174, 176	4:19	308
12:27–30	255n60	5:1–5	172–73n39	5:16–6:10	377
13:5	275n15	5:1–10	179	5:22	321
13:12	275n15, 276n18, 286	5:14b	167n23	6:10	92
14:33b–36	278	5:15	119, 167n23	6:14	167n23
15:1–11	255n60	5:16–19	122		
15:3	165n18	5:16–21	118	**Ephesians**	
15:3–4	118	5:17	275n15, 308	1:1	376
15:9	255n60	5:19	169	1:1–5:20	277
15:12–58	179	5:19–21	73	1:3	62, 64
15:20–22	400n18	6:6	320	1:3–14	63, 67
15:20–28	97, 119, 368	7:10	176	1:5	67, 325, 365
15:21–22	166	11:2	277	1:5–6	75
15:22	128, 174	11:14	405n38	1:11	365
15:23–28	405n36	12:7	405n38	1:13	62
15:25–26	166, 176			1:20–23	405n35
15:26–28	176	**Galatians**		1:22	222
15:28	58, 283	1:4	117, 374, 405n37	2:1–10	157
15:31	176	1:18	221	2:1–22	94n14
15:35–58	255n60	2:5	286	2:4	319
15:42–57	121	2:7–11	211	2:5–6	168
15:49	119, 120, 319	2:9	221	2:7	319
15:53–54	172–73n39	2:10	118	2:10	374
15:56	170	2:11–14	221	2:11–22	39, 308
		2:14	286	2:12	321
2 Corinthians		2:15	131	2:19	92, 321
1:1	376	2:16	118	2:19b–21	222
1:3	319	2:19	167n23	3:10	222
1:3–12	63	2:20	72, 305, 384n11	3:19	365
2:11	405n38	2:20–21	205, 285	3:23	222
2:14–16	64	2:21	118	4:12	275n15
2:17	377	3:1–29	118	5:21	275n15, 277n20
3:6	170	3:21	282	5:21–33	277, 302
3:12–4:6	123	3:22	136	5:22–24	278
3:14	283	3:23–26	118	5:27	222
3:16	283	3:27	167n21	5:29	222
3:17	283	3:28	275n15, 278	5:32	222
3:18	120, 275n15, 276n18, 319, 400n19	3:29	39	6:1–4	93
		4:1–7	204–5, 205n29, 208	6:10–20	97
4:1	319	4:1–9	207	6:18	93
4:4	120, 275n15, 319	4:3	207		

INDEX OF SCRIPTURE

Philippians
1:1	376
1:19–26	179
1:21	177
2:5–11	38, 121, 365, 384n10, 398n8
2:6–7	275n15
2:6–11	177
2:7	205
2:10–11	405n34
3:1	195n8
3:4b–12	401n22
3:6	213
3:7–8	64
3:20–21	123
4:2–3	279
4:4	195n8
4:8	275n15
4:19	119

Colossians
1:11–15	369
1:15	319
1:15–20	38, 63, 121
1:16	275n15
1:18	222, 384n10
1:22	159n3
1:24	222
1:24–29	187
2:9–15	157
2:11–12	121
2:12	168
2:12–13	121
2:13–15	97
2:20	159n3
3:1	121
3:3	72, 159n3, 190
3:3–4	121
3:8–11	320
3:10	121
3:12–14	321
3:15–17	121

1 Thessalonians
1:10	177–78n48
2:18	405n38
3:5	98n24
4:5	216
4:13	102
5:1–11	122
5:16–18a	62

2 Thessalonians
2:3	252
2:7	97n23, 252
2:9	252

1 Timothy
1:2	319
2:4	275n15
2:5–6	267
2:11–15	278
3:1–7	279
3:8–11	279
3:15	92
3:16	63
5:3–16	279
5:6	159n3
5:17–21	279
5:18	275n15
6:16	159n3

2 Timothy
1:2	319
1:10	159n3
1:16	319
1:18	319
2:11	159n3
2:19	222
3:6–7	278
3:13	136

Titus
1:5–9	279
1:12	216
1:13	285
2:5	141
2:10	285
3:3–6	320
3:4	319
3:5	319

Philemon
15–16	275n15

Hebrews
2:17	233, 319
4:1–13	284
4:10	310
4:11–13	71
4:12	375
4:14–16	378
5:7	156
5:7–8	93
8:12	319
9:11–14	378
11:1	199
11:13	275n15
13:1–19	378
13:2	133, 275n15
13:5	321
13:14	275n15, 276n18

James
1:1	195n8
1:13	98
2:6	275n15
3:16–4:10	380–81
5:9	132
5:11	319

1 Peter
1:3–5	320
1:3–9	63
1:17	92
2:9–10	39
2:10	321
2:17	362
2:21–25	157
2:24	167n23
3:15b	23

Index of Scripture

4:1	167n23	2:6	247n43		247n43, 249n48,
4:16	224	2:7	235–36n15, 240		252, 267
4:17	92	2:7–8	267	2:29	247
4:34	216	2:7–11	247	3:1	85n19, 235
		2:8	234, 252	3:1–2	238
2 Peter		2:8b–10	251	3:1a	87
1:4	276n18	2:9	240, 249n48	3:1b	248
2:1	246n40	2:9–11	246	3:2	85n19, 87, 240, 267,
3:9	275n15	2:10	240, 252		275n15, 276n18
		2:10–11	247	3:3	86
		2:11	240	3:4	247, 252
1 John		2:12	86, 236, 240, 249	3:4–10	247
1:1	235	2:12–14	239, 240, 249n48	3:5	83, 233
1:1–3	235–36n15, 267	2:13	85n19, 235	3:6	247
1:1–4	80, 234, 239n22	2:13–14	252	3:7	236, 240, 247, 249n48
1:1–5	238	2:14	85n19, 235, 236	3:8	85n19, 87n23, 252
1:2	85n19, 251	2:15	85n19	3:9	85n19, 247, 249, 250
1:3	85n17, 85n19, 87n23,	2:15–17	248, 252	3:10	85n19, 247, 252
	248	2:15–19	240	3:11	232, 233, 235–36n15,
1:3a	238	2:16	85n19		247
1:5	85n19, 233, 235–36n15	2:17	85n19	3:11–18	39
1:5–7	232, 258	2:18	233, 236, 249n48,	3:12	232
1:5–7b	86		252	3:13	240, 248
1:5–10	245	2:18–22	267	3:14	240, 251
1:5–2:2	251	2:18–27	240, 245	3:14–15	267
1:6	245	2:18–29	301	3:15	249n48
1:6–7	248	2:19	81–82, 238, 239n22,	3:16	85n19, 87, 240, 263
1:6–2:17	233n8		243, 246n38, 248,	3:16–18	267
1:7	85n17, 87n23, 233,		250, 266	3:17	85n19, 240
	247, 251, 252	2:20	234, 237, 238, 249,	3:18	236, 240, 245,
1:8	245, 247		250, 251, 267		249n48, 263
1:8–10	247n44	2:21	245	3:19	245
1:9	86, 245	2:22	81–82, 85n17, 85n19,	3:20	85n19, 233
1:12–13	250		87n23, 246n41, 252,	3:21	85n19, 240
2:1	85n17, 85n19, 236,		266–67	3:22	246
	240, 241, 247,	2:22–23	246	3:23	85n17, 87n23, 244,
	249n48	2:23	85n19, 87, 87n23,		250
2:1–2	249–50		244	3:24	233, 246, 247n43,
2:2	233, 267	2:24	85n19, 87n23,		251
2:3	247		235–36n15, 247n43	3:24b	251
2:3–4	246	2:26	248	4:1	85n19, 233, 234, 235,
2:3–6	247, 267	2:27	233, 234, 237, 238,		240, 244, 246, 252,
2:4	267		247n43, 249, 250,		267
2:4–5	260		251, 267	4:1–3	234, 237
2:5	85n19, 252	2:28	233, 236, 240,	4:1–6	240

501

INDEX OF SCRIPTURE

4:1–12	246	5:3	85n19, 244	4	236, 249n48
4:1b	246n38	5:4	85n19	5	248, 249n48, 321
4:1b–3	82	5:4–5	248	6	85n18, 248
4:2	80n7, 83, 85n17, 85n19, 244, 244n35, 267	5:4b	244	8	245, 248
		5:5	85n17, 87n23, 244, 250	9	85n18, 241, 248, 267
		5:5–8	234	9–10	236, 242
4:2–3	233, 246	5:6	85n17, 245, 249, 250	10	85n18, 238, 242–43, 248, 266
4:3	85n17, 85n19, 244, 248, 266–67	5:7–8	250n53		
		5:8	250	10a	243
4:4	85n19, 236, 240	5:9	85n19, 87n23	10b	248, 249n48
4:5	248, 252	5:10	85n19, 87n23, 244, 250	11	249n48
4:5–6	267			12	245, 248
4:6	85n19, 245	5:11	85n19, 87n23		
4:7	85n19, 86, 240	5:12	85n19, 87n23	**Jude**	
4:7–12	252, 259, 369	5:13	85n19, 87n23, 244, 250	21	319
4:7–5:5	247	5:16	240		
4:8	85n19, 247	5:16–17	141	**Revelation**	
4:9	85n19, 87n23	5:18	85n19	1:3	374
4:9–10	267	5:19	85n19, 248, 252	1:15	147
4:10	85n19, 87n23, 233, 267	5:20	85n17, 85n19, 86, 87n23, 233, 251	2:13–29	407n42
				3:10	97n23
4:11	85n19, 240	5:21	240, 249n48	3:15–22	407n42
4:12	85n19			4:8	63
4:13–15	247n43	**2 John**		5:5–10	190–91
4:13–21	259	1	245, 248–49, 251	5:12	190–91, 405n35
4:14	85n19, 87n23	3	245, 319	6:10	375
4:15	85n17, 85n19, 87n23, 244	4	245	7:9–17	97n23
		4–5	267	7:11	275n15
4:16	85n19, 244, 251	5	232, 235	7:13–17	95
4:16b	156	5–6	235	9:2	147
4:17	252, 267	6	235–36n15	11:17–18	64
4:17–21	267	7	244, 248, 252, 266	12:1–17	194n4
4:19	86, 329	7–9	239n22	12:10	405n35
4:20	85n19, 233, 240, 249n48, 267, 329	9	235, 245, 247, 251, 267	13:1–18	407n42
		10	246, 246n38	13:6	141
4:20–21	246, 247	10–11	243, 248	14:6	232n7
4:20–5:2	244	13	236, 249, 251	16:11	141
4:21	85n19, 240, 247			16:21	141
5:1	85n17, 85n19, 233, 244, 250	**3 John**		18:1–24	407n42
		1	249n48	19:6–10	277
5:1–5	250	2	249n48	21:1–4	369
5:1a	250	3	249n48	21:2–14	277
5:2	85n19	3–4	245	21:4	192
5:2–3	246				

Index of Other Ancient Sources

Deuterocanonical Books

Tobit
2:1–14	137
3:8	137
6:1–17	137
7:17	284

Judith
13:18	198n16
16:14	197

Wisdom of Solomon
1:4	136
1:10–11	132
1:13	160
2:1–10	160
2:17–24	187
2:18–20	306
2:21–22	160
2:23	315
2:23–24	160
3:4–5	160
3:9	150
3:10a	160
4:7–14	160
4:20	160
4:20a	150, 220
5:1–2	150, 220
5:15	150, 220
6:12–20	151
7:22b–10:21	150
9:17	374
10:5	150
10:13	136
12:12–22	151
14:3	91n8

Sirach
1:13	160
3:1–16	277n22
6:30	284
7:35	151, 220
11:21–28	160
17:3	315
21:2	136
23:1	91n8
23:4	91n8
24	121
24:1–29:28	140
25:24	160
27:10	136
28:2–6	139–40
38:9–10	137
40:17	195
40:22	195
43:31	200
44:1–2	160
44:12–13	160
46:7	132
51:26	284

2 Maccabees
6:18–7:42	143, 283
6:23–28	160
7:10–11	160
7:23	160
8:4	141
12:14	141
15:24	141

2 Esdras
3:7	160
7:[64]	160

4 Maccabees
5:1–18:23	283
6:1–7:10	143

Old Testament Pseudepigrapha

Apocalypse of Abraham
23	160

Apocalypse of Adam
5.76.9–28	164

Apocalypse of Moses
14	160
30	160
32	160n6

2 Baruch
21.4	197
48	160
51.3	147n6
54	160
54.15	160

1 Enoch
1.8	150

5.8	150	Prayer of Manasseh		4Q400–407	66
5.9	160	8	131		
10.16–18	151			4Q503	66
38.2	133n15	Psalms of Solomon			
39.5	150	17.1–32	129	4Q504	66
39.13	147n6				
42	284	Testament of Abraham		4Q548	
46.1	133n15	14	160	2.9–16	137n22
47.3	133n15				
48.10	133n15	**DEAD SEA SCROLLS**		**ANCIENT JEWISH WRITERS**	
50.3	150				
52.4	133n15	1QH (Hodayot or Thanksgiving Scroll)			
62.14	132n13			Josephus	
69.27–29	133n15	1.27	136		
84.4–6	160	4.29–30	136	Antiquitates judaicae	
90	192	6.29–34	161	1.49	160
90.20a	150, 220	11.3	161	1.51	160
90.26–27	150, 220	11.10–13	161	12–15	218
108.1	151	15.18–29	161	17.204	131
108.7	150			17.307	131
108.35	146n5			18.55	120
		1QS (Manual of Discipline, or Community Rule)			
2 Enoch				Bellum judaicum	
30.17	160	1.7.9–11	259–60n8	2.169	120
		1.9–10	137n22, 252		
4 Ezra		2.2–3	252	Philo	
7.28–29	133n15	2.24	151, 252	De agricultura	
7.31	146–47n5	3.8	150	98	162
7.36–38	284	3.17–22	161		
7.62–131	160	4.2–3	151	De confusione linguarum	
7.97	147n6	4.3	150	36–37	162
7.116–19	160	4.3–4	150	De fuga et inventione	
11.1–12.32	133n15	4.3–5	150	59	162
12.36–38	284	4.6b–8	150, 220		
		4.11b–14	150, 220	De somniis	
Jubilees		5.4	252	2.66	162
2.27	142n27	5.24–6.1	219	De specialibus legibus	
15.33–34	142n27	5.25	252	III.108–17	278
23.24	131	7.16–17	142n27	De vita Mosis	
		7.18–19	252	2.147	160
Odes of Solomon					
11.1	193n3	4Q177		Legum allegoriae	
11.1–2	193n3	13.7–11	137n22	1.105	162

Index of Other Ancient Sources

Rabbinic and Other Jewish Works

Babylonian Talmud

Baba Batra
115a	92

Bekhoroth
31a	131

Berakot
5a.2	142n30
16b	103n44
17a	103n44
28b	103n44
29a	103
29b	103–4n44
60b	98

Megillah
10b	322

Nedarim
41a	138n23

Pesachim
116b	234n13

Šabbat
24a	103–4n44
55a–b	161
88b	382n3
151b	161, 169

Sanhedrin
25b	131
39b	322
98a–99a	107

Ta'anit
25b	103

Bamidbar [Numbers] Rabbah
12.4	147n6
13.2	147n6

Genesis Rabbah
16.6	161

Jerusalem Talmud

Demai
4 §6, f: 24a, l: 67	322

Maimonides

Mishneh Torah: Hilchot Melachim
11–12	107

Midrash

Midrash on Psalms 118:19
243b §17	151n14, 322

Midrash Tanḥuma B: [Yelammedemu] on Eliezer
71	321

Midrash Tanḥuma B: [Yelammedemu] on Noah
16a	321

Mishnah

Baba Batra
10.8	148n9

Berakot
4.3	103
4.4	103

Kil'ayim
1.1	146n4

Pesachim
10.5	307

Terumot
2.6	146n4

Yoma
8.8	161

Pesiqta de-Rab Kahana
124a–b	142n30
189a	322

Pirke 'Abot
1	212
1.1	212n6
1.2	321
2.8	282
3.2	219
3.5	219

Seder Olam Rabbah
7.2	147n6

Shir Ha-Sharim Rabbah
1.2.1	147n6
3.10.1–4	147n6
4.12.2	147n6

Sifre Deuteronomy
333	161

Early Christian Writings

Apocryphon of John
2.20.29–21.14	163
2.27.5–12	164
2.31.4–23	163

Asclepius
6.76.7–20	164
21–29	163n14

Acts of Thomas
9.108–13	163–64

Ambrose

Expositio Evangelii secundum Lucam
7.142	119

505

INDEX OF OTHER ANCIENT SOURCES

Athanasius

De incarnatione
54.3 — 276n18

Orations against the Arians
3.29 — 198n17

Augustine of Hippo

Confessiones
1.1.1 — 323n25
2 — 61

De civitate Dei
14.10–11 — 119
14.26 — 119
19.14 — 323

De doctrina christiana
1.3–4 — 382n6
1.20–23 — 382n6
2.1–14 — 3
2.7.9–11 — 70

De Trinitate
14.4.20 — 323
15.1.1 — 324

Epistles
130.22 — 90

Sermon[es], Conversation[s]
9 — 69n35
350.2 — 324

Barnabas
19.5 — 278

Basil of Caesarea

De humana conditione
1.18 — 278

The Book of Thomas the Contender
2.143.11–27 — 163

Corpus Hermeticum
1.15 — 163, 175
1.28 — 163

Didache
2.2 — 278
5.1–2 — 278
8.2 — 97n22
10.7–13.1 — 240n24
11 — 243n32
11.3–6 — 240n24
11.10–11 — 240n24
13.1–2 — 240n24
15.2 — 240n24

Epistle of Peter to Philip
8.135.10–136.16 — 163
8.137.5–10 — 163

Eusebius

Historia ecclesiastica
3.39.3–4 — 237

The Gospel of Philip
2.75.2–15 — 163, 175
3.71–72 — 117n19

The Gospel of the Egyptians (Holy Book of the Great Invisible Spirit)
3.66.1–9 — 163n15

The Gospel of Thomas
114 — 323

The Gospel of Truth
1.22.2–16 — 164

Gregory Nazianzen

Discourses
37.6 — 278

The Hypostasis of the Archons
2.96.20–97.10 — 163

Ignatius of Antioch

To the Ephesians
2.2 — 236n16
4.1 — 236n16
5.3 — 242
20.2 — 251

To the Magnesians
2 — 236n16
7.1 — 242
11 — 82n10

To the Philadelphians
4.1 — 251
8.1 — 236n16

To Polycarp
4.1 — 242
5.2 — 242

To the Smyrnaeans
5.2 — 82n10, 244n35
7.1 — 82n10, 244n35
8.1 — 236n16, 242
9.1 — 242

To the Trallians
2.1–2 — 242
2.2 — 236n16
9.1 — 82n10
9.10 — 82n10
13.2 — 236n16

Irenaeus

Adversus haereses
1.10.1 — 3
1.14.1 — 163
3.18.1 — 119
4.20.1 — 36
4.38.1 — 119
4.38.1–3 — 119
5.16.2 — 120n23
5.19–21 — 119

Index of Other Ancient Sources

Jerome

Commentary on Ephesians
5.29   323n23

Epistulae
130.16   306

John Chrysostom

Homilies
1–55   385n1

Julian of Norwich

Revelations
§59   325
§63   324
§305   326

Justin Martyr

Apologia I
67   308

Origen

De oratione
27.7   96n18

The Paraphrase of Shem
7.7.18–31   163

Polycarp

To the Philippians
7   244n35

Rupert of Deutz

Ad ecclesiam
3.12   312
3.13   312

Thomas Aquinas

Summa theologiae
1a.1.10   34

The Treatise on the Resurrection
1.48.14–34   163

The Tripartite Tractate
1.106.15–26   163
1.129.7–15   163n15

Greco-Roman Sources

Aristotle

Ars rhetorica
2.7.1358a   195
2.23   161

Cicero

Tusculanae Disputationes
3.6   123

Epicurus

Letter to Menoeceus
19–30   162

Euripides

Alcestis
669   161

Iphigenia in Aulis
1252–53   161

Iphigenia in Tauris
321–33   162n11

Tröides
606–7   162
634   162

Hesiod

Theogony
758   161

Homer

Iliad
18.115–17   162
19.420–21   162
24.525–28   364

Odysseia
2.487–88   161

Marcus Aurelius Antoninus

Meditations
2.5   162
2.11   162
5.29   162
7.56   162

Plato

Cratylus
403b   161

Phaedrus
64a   162
67e   162
80e   162
114–15   162

Protagoras
315a–316b   212n6
349a   212n6

Plotinus

Enneads
1.6.6   162
1.7.3   162
4.8.3   162

Sextus Propertius

Elegies
2; §33   402n25

Sophocles

Aias Lokros
473   162n11

INDEX OF OTHER ANCIENT SOURCES

Tacitus

Agricola

45   234n13

Xenophon

Memorabilia

1.6.3   212n6

OTHER SOURCES

Mahāvagga

10.2.320   106n52

Qur'an

1.1–7   105n49

5.17   107n55

5.82   105n50

5.175.116   107n55

33.40   107n54

37.4   107n56

112.1–4   107